ENCYCLOPEDIA OF MICROCOMPUTERS

VOLUME 15

ENCYCLOPEDIA OF MICROCOMPUTERS

EXECUTIVE EDITORS

Allen Kent   *James G. Williams*

UNIVERSITY OF PITTSBURGH
PITTSBURGH, PENNSYLVANIA

ADMINISTRATIVE EDITORS

Carolyn M. Hall   *Rosalind Kent*

PITTSBURGH, PENNSYLVANIA

VOLUME 15
Reporting on Parallel
Software to SNOBOL

MARCEL DEKKER, INC.   NEW YORK • BASEL • HONG KONG

Library of Congress Cataloging in Publication Data

Encyclopedia of Microcomputers

1. Microcomputers - Dictionaries. I. Kent, Allen.
II. Williams, James G. III. Kent, Rosalind.
QA76.15.E52 1987   004.16'03'21   87-15428

ISBN: 0-8247-2713-4

Marcel Dekker, Inc
270 Madison Avenue, New York, New York 10016

Current printing (last digit)
10 9 8 7 6 5 4 3 2 1

Printed in the United States of America

CONTENTS OF VOLUME 15

CONTRIBUTORS TO VOLUME 15

STEVEN A. ARNDT Technical Advisor, U.S. Nuclear Regulatory Commission; and Assistant Professor, University of Tennessee, Chattanooga, Tennessee: *Simulations and Simulators--Their Role in Science and Society*

RICHARD S. BARR, Ph.D. Associate Professor, Department of Computer Science and Engineering, Southern Methodist University, Dallas, Texas: *Reporting on Parallel Software*

FRED J. CHARLWOOD Department of System Science, City University, London, England: *Risk Engineering: Analysis and Management*

YOGENDRA P. DUBEY, Ph.D. Professor, Computer Application, Department of Library and Information Science, Banaras Hindu University, Varanasi, India: *Simulation and Modeling*

ROGER R. FLYNN Associate Professor, Department of Information Science, University of Pittsburgh, Pittsburgh, Pennsylvania: *Search Methods; SNOBOL*

STEVEN E. FOLLIN Assistant Research Scientist, University Computing and Networking Services, The University of Georgia, Athens, Georgia: *Scientific Visualization*

HELEN M. GRINDLEY Academic Support Officer, Department of Information Studies, University of Sheffield, Sheffield, South Yorkshire, United Kingdom: *Similarity Searching in Databases of Three-Dimensional Molecules and Macromolecules*

TOR GUIMARAES, Ph.D. J. E. Owen Chairholder, Director, Institute for Technology Management, College of Business Administration, Tennessee Technological University, Cookeville, Tennessee: *Selecting Expert System Development Techniques*

BETTY L. HICKMAN, Ph.D. Assistant Professor of Computer Science, Department of Computer Science, University of Nebraska at Omaha, Omaha, Nebraska: *Reporting on Parallel Software*

LANCE A. LEVENTHAL, Ph.D.   Consultant, Emulative Systems, Co., Inc., Rancho Santa Fe, California: *Simulation Technology*

YANNIS MANOLOPOULOS   Assistant Professor, Department of Informatics, Aristotle University, Thessaloniki, Greece: *Seek Time Evaluation*

SOLOMON MARCUS, Ph.D.   Universite Laval, Faculte des Sciences Sociales, Departement d'anthropologie, Cite Universitaire, Quebec, Ontario, Canada: *Semiotics and Formal Artificial Languages*

MARC H. MEYER   Walsh Research Professor and Research Director, Center for Technology Management, The College of Business, Northeastern University, Boston, Massachusetts: *Risk Management in Financial Services: Current Applications of Technology and Business Reengineering*

JONATHAN D. MOFFETT, Ph.D.   Senior Research Fellow, Department of Computer Science, University of York, Heslington, York, United Kingdom: *Security and Distributed Systems*

ROCHIT RAJSUMAN   Assistant Professor, Computer Engineering and Science, Case Western Reserve University, Cleveland, Ohio: *Semiconductor Memory Testing*

SOLOMON E. SHIMONY, Ph.D.   Lecturer (Assistant Professor), Mathematics and Computer Science Department, Ben-Gurion University, Beer-Sheva, Israel: *The Role of Relevance in Abductive Reasoning*

MARK L. SWINSON, Ph.D., P.E.   Unmanned Ground Vehicle Joint Project Office, Redstone Arsenal, Alabama: *Robotics, Military*

JEAN-LUC VIDICK   Consultant, Medoc Media Documentaire; Professor, Universite Libre de Bruxelles, Brussels, Belgium: *Research and Development in Information Retrieval*

PETER WILLETT, Ph.D.   Professor, Department of Information Studies, University of Sheffield, Sheffield, South Yorkshire, United Kingdom: *Similarity Searching in Databases of Three-Dimensional Molecules and Macromolecules*

YOUNGOHC YOON, Ph.D.   Assistant Professor, Computer Information Systems, Southwest Missouri State University, Springfield, Missouri: *Selecting Expert System Development Techniques*

REPORTING ON PARALLEL SOFTWARE

Computational reporting has a wide range of purposes, depending on the needs of its consumer. Some applications include comparing parallel machines for marketing or purchasing decisions, identifying an efficient approach to solving a class of problems, and seeking insight into the performance of algorithms. The focus of this article is measuring the performance of algorithms and their implementations on parallel computer systems.

Algorithm development is at the heart of mathematical programming research, wherein more efficient algorithms are regarded as the goal. As an indicator of algorithmic performance, efficiency reflects the level of resources (central processor time, iterations, bytes of primary storage) required to obtain a solution of given quality (percent optimality and accuracy) (1,2). A variety of measures and summary statistics has been devised to reflect efficiency and compare algorithms.

Recall that an *algorithm* defines a set of steps and data to accomplish a particular task. For example, the simplex method is an algorithm definition which includes some of the data requirements (basis, basis inverse, original data) and operations to be performed on that data (initial solution construction, pivot selection, pivot, and termination steps). A *code* is a specific implementation of a specific algorithm. There are many simplex-based codes, each with different internal structure and efficiencies. In empirical testing, we analyze executions of codes as an indirect means of testing algorithms, as algorithms are abstractions.

The efficiency of an algorithm relative to others has traditionally been determined by (1) theoretical order analysis and (2) empirical testing of algorithmic implementations, or *codes*. Although both approaches have merit, computational testing is increasingly an imperative for publication. This is due, in part, to the occasional failure of order analysis to predict accurately the behavior of an algorithm's implementation on problems of practical interest. For example, although the simplex method has daunting worst-case behavior, its efficiency as an optimizer for a wide variety of industrial applications is well documented (3,4).

One technological advance that holds great promise for solving difficult problems is application-level parallel processing, whereby the power of multiple processing elements can be brought to bear on a single problem. If the work associated with an algorithm can be properly subdivided and scheduled to separate processors for simultaneous execution, opportunities for dramatic reductions in solution times arise. As with traditional single-processor (*serial*) machines, solution efficiencies are directly tied to how well the algorithmic steps match the architecture of the underlying machine. Therefore,

Originally appeared in slightly different form as "Reporting Computational Experiments with Parallel Algorithms: Issues, Measures, and Experts' Opinions," *ORSA Journal of Computing*, Vol. 5, No. 1 (Winter 1993), pp. 2–18.

with the evolution in computing machinery comes a corresponding evolution in algorithms and their implementations.

This article addresses complications that arise when reporting on implementations of parallel algorithms. Several common metrics of the efficiency of parallel implementations result in measurement and comparison difficulties stemming from limitations imposed by machine designs, differences in machine architectures, the stochastic nature of some parallel algorithms, and the inherent opportunities for the introduction of biases. Of particular concern is *speedup*, a widely used measure for describing the efficiency achieved over serial processing by the use of multiple processors. In addition to documenting problems of traditional reporting of parallel experimentation, we also present the results of a survey of leading mathematical programming researchers regarding their views on the topic, and close with proposed guidelines for conscientious reporting. We begin with an overview of parallel processing as it relates to mathematical programming research.

BACKGROUND

What is Parallel Processing?

Parallel processing is the simultaneous manipulation of data by multiple computing elements working to complete a common body of work. Although most computers have some degree of parallelism, as with overlapped input-output and calculation, only recently have systems become commercially available that allow an applications programmer to control several processing units. A parallel programmer might, for example, minimize a function $f(x)$ for $0 \leq x \leq 10$, by using one processor to examine the interval for $0 \leq x < 5$, a second to simultaneously evaluate $5 \leq x \leq 10$, with the final result determined (in serial) on completion of the previous tasks. The objective would be to complete the work in roughly half the time required by a single processor.

Why use parallel processing to perform a task or solve a given problem? The most prevalent reasons are:

- *Absolute speed*:   the reduction of real ("wall clock") time, considering all technological options. Although application dependent, parallel processing is generally acknowledged to provide this capability, as evidenced by the multiprocessor design of all state-of-the-art supercomputers.
- *Relative speed and cost*:   improvement in real time, subject to a practical constraint such as cost or limited computing options. The expectation is that an ensemble of relatively inexpensive slow processors can complete the work more quickly than a faster cost-equivalent serial machine, or in the same time at a lower cost. Such "cheap thrills" have been achieved by some applications, such as database transaction processing, but are not always attainable. Although some writers believe that the range of applicability is a narrow one (5,6), most commercial parallel systems are designed with this result in mind.
- *Scalable computing*:   having the ability to improve performance with additional processing elements. A flexible design permits a computing system to grow in terms of processing power, in the same manner that additional disk drives increase storage capacity. An application that exploits any number of parallel computing units can use incremental system upgrades to speed up processing.

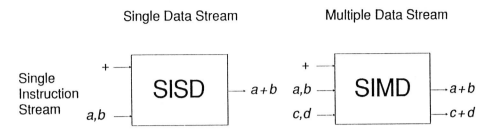

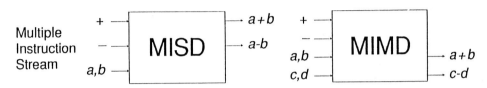

FIGURE 1   Flynn's machine classifications.

If real-time reduction is not important, traditional serial processing is usually easier and more cost-effective. Hence, the motivation for parallel machines springs from the need to solve existing problems faster or to make larger and more difficult ones tractable.

Types of Parallel Computers

Parallel processing computers are as varied in design as they are many; hence, classification schemes have proven useful in describing specific machines. One widely employed method of categorizing computer architectures was introduced by Flynn (7) and is based on the concepts of an instruction stream and a data stream. An instruction stream is a sequence of instructions carried out by a computer (i.e., program steps), whereas a data stream is the set of data on which an instruction stream is executed. This taxonomy delineates machine types by the number and type of simultaneously executing streams, as follows (see also Figure 1 from (8)).

- Single-instruction, single-data (SISD), the traditional serial, uniprocessor computer, that executes one series of instructions on a single set of data (for example, the IBM Personal Computer, Cray-1, Vax 780, and Sun IPC).
- Single-instruction, multiple-data (SIMD), a parallel machine design wherein all processors execute the same instruction in lockstep and apply it to different pieces of data (e.g., the Thinking Machines' CM-2 and CM-5, and DAP).
- Multiple-instruction, single-data (MISD), which applies multiple operations simultaneously to a single data stream (no general-purpose MISD computers are available today).
- Multiple-instruction, multiple-data (MIMD), the most widely employed parallel machine architecture; each such computing system contains multiple, independently executing processors which can operate on different datasets (including—but not limited to—the Cray Y-MP, IBM 3090 series, Vax 9000,

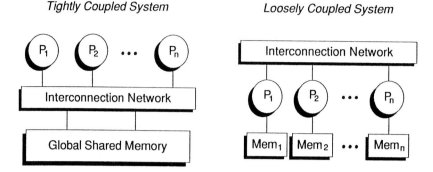

FIGURE 2   Tightly and loosely coupled parallel systems.

Sequent Symmetry 2000, BBN Butterfly, Encore 90, Convex C-2, CM-5, Intel iPSC and Paragon, Teradata DBC/1012, NCR System 3600, Pyramid, Alliant FX, Myrias, nCUBE/2, MasPar MP-1, and Silicon Graphics).

Processors in SIMD and MIMD parallel computers communicate either via a common shared memory accessed through a central switch, or by messages passed through an interconnection network in a *distributed* system. Shared-memory multiprocessors are called *tightly coupled* if the time required to access a particular memory location is the same for all processors, as opposed to being proximity dependent or *loosely coupled* (see Figure 2). Computer systems are termed *massively parallel* if they contain 1000 or more processors.

Each architecture has its own advantages and disadvantages. Shared-memory systems are simpler to program than distributed ones because processors can share code and data and can communicate via the globally accessible memory. Because distributed systems have no central switch, they can accommodate a larger number of processors, but at the expense of slower communication and more elaborate programming.

Of the many varieties of parallel machines, the dominant category appears to be tightly coupled MIMD. We estimate the installed base (number of commercial machines installed and operating at customer sites) for distributed SIMD and MIMD systems to be around 1000. This compares with the over 10,000 shared-memory multiprocessors installed by IBM and over 4000 by Sequent Computer Systems alone—although the proportion using the parallel capability is difficult to determine.

In addition to these advanced machine designs, software systems have emerged that permit parallel programming across independent computers connected by a local area network (9,10). Because of the widespread use of networked workstations in the engineering and scientific communities, coupled with their heavy computational needs and limited budgets, this truly distributed approach to parallel processing may prove to be a popular one.

Parallel Algorithm Research and Computational Testing

If increased speed in solving a given problem is the goal of parallelism, what are the sources of speed? The first source is the machine used, its architecture, and the speed of each of its operations, including integer and floating-point arithmetic, memory moves, and communications. Second, speed comes from the solution algorithm and its effectiveness for the problem. Third, speed depends on the algorithm's implementation, or code. A code is a program which maps the algorithm's steps and data requirements onto a given machine, and its speed depends on the compatibility of the mapping and the efficiency of the coding itself.

What is sought then, for a problem, is not only a fast machine but an efficient solution algorithm and an implementation whose steps and data needs match the machine's characteristics. Algorithm research is directed at the design and implementation of problem solution methods with these qualities. In a parallel setting, this means seeking efficient algorithms with steps that can be executed simultaneously. Hence, by designing algorithms to exploit the new machine architectures, researchers seek to answer the question: Can parallel computing lead to the solution of new problems and faster solutions to current problems?

Researchers need and want empirical evidence of an algorithm's efficiency, and performance of a code can be evidence for the effectiveness of the underlying algorithm. Order analysis is not always a good predictor of performance as it typically ignores the variety of machine operations involved in an implementation and is often concerned with worst-case behavior that may not be representative of behavior on problems of practical interest.

Computational experience summarizes all operations, in a given setting, on a specific problem set. Although the appropriateness of a test set may be questioned, computational testing gets to the heart of the matter. Is not the reason for building algorithms the solution of problems?

FOCUS: PARALLEL MATHEMATICAL PROGRAMMING ALGORITHMS AND CODES

The focus of this article is on the empirical testing of parallel optimization and mathematical programming algorithms. Traditional methods in this area tend to have different characteristics than those explored in the parallel processing literature. Examples of the "embarrassingly parallel" mathematical applications typically cited in this literature are wave mechanics, fluid dynamics, and finite-element applications; SIMD applications in the survey (12) included image processing, neural network training, and satellite orbit collision detection. In each case, the algorithm is highly parallelizeable (over 99.9% of the operations) and the problems easily decomposable, often linearly in terms of a single parameter.

In contrast, traditional mathematical programming optimization algorithms often have a strong serial component and the problems addressed are not decomposable in a simple manner. The problems attacked can have alternate optima, the ease or difficulty of their solution is not always predictable in terms of problem dimensions or other descriptive factors, and there are an enormous number of paths to an optimal solution. Hence, much creativity is required in parallelizing traditional methods, and new algorithms must be developed and previously rejected ones reexamined in light of these new computing paradigms.

Examples of Parallel Mathematical Programming Applications

To provide a flavor of the research on parallel optimization algorithms, research in two application areas (see (13) for an early survey) is summarized. Compare the characteristics of these algorithms with the typical parallel applications described previously.

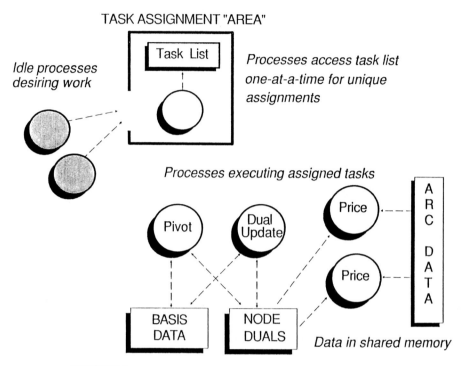

FIGURE 3   Example of a parallel network simplex code design.

Parallel Network Simplex

Numerous authors have built parallel implementations of the network simplex algorithm on shared-memory MIMD machines (14–17). Strategies employed in these codes included simultaneous pricing and pivoting, parallel pricing of different arc sets, and, in Refs. 14 and 15, decomposition of the pivot operation. Problems as large as 50,000 nodes and one million arcs have been solved in 12.2 min, and times were reduced to as little as one-sixteenth of serial methods using 19 processors (14).

In the implementation of Miller, Pekny, and Thompson (16), only the pricing operation is performed in parallel, so that the addition of processors results in a larger number of arcs considered for an incoming variable. Upon completion of the pricing step, all processors synchronize and perform the same pivot in local memory.

In contrast, the other codes assign simplex tasks to different processors. For example, in the authors' implementation (14), tasks are assigned on a self-scheduled, or "as available," basis. With all data in shared memory, some processors may be pricing variables, whereas others are performing different portions of the pivot operation (see Figure 3). When a processor completes its assignment, it selects another from a task list; when no tasks remain, the procedure terminates (18).

Although the self-scheduled approach is highly efficient in terms of machine utilization, it results in stochastic code performance. Because key decisions—such as choice of incoming variable—are timing dependent, microsecond timing differences from one run to the next can yield divergent results (i.e., number of pivots, solution time, alternate optimal solution). Hence, a program containing such timing-dependent logic—

known as a race condition—may have good load balancing among the processors, but it is often accompanied by significant variability in run-time behavior.

Parallel Branch-and-Bound

A branch-and-bound algorithm for (mixed) integer programming lends itself well to parallelism. Because hundreds or thousands of linear programming relaxations are typically solved to identify the optimal integer solution, an obvious parallelization approach is to assign different parts of the search tree to separate processors. Tightly coupled MIMD implementations (19–22) have been highly successful, but reporting difficulties arise for the same reasons described above: The codes exhibit significant stochastic behavior where race conditions and inherent system variability can result in differing numbers of subproblems examined from run to run.

As program decisions are made in real time and the discovery of a strong bound can eliminate from consideration a large number of subproblems, the *order* of discovery of ''good'' bounds can greatly affect the proportion of the search tree explored. This can result in ''anomalies'' where a parallel algorithm using p_2 processors can take more time than one using $p_1 < p_2$ processors, or can achieve speed improvements greater than p_2/p_1 (23). Our experience with shared-memory MIMD branch-and-bound codes is that significant variation in parallel execution times can result from the minute timing differences present even in dedicated machine environments.

Also of interest is the difficulty of identifying a reasonable one-processor base case for comparison purposes. Simply executing one processor's portion of a parallel code will yield a different order of tree traversal than the parallel case, potentially making the two results not comparable. On the other hand, simply directing a serial code to examine the tree in the same order as the parallel causes it to miss subproblem reoptimization opportunities, increasing its run time. (See the related discussion in the section Is superliner speedup possible?)

Distributed-Memory Network Algorithms

Some algorithms and problems are easily divisible, or *scalable*, and can more readily take advantage of distributed systems. On loosely coupled parallel systems, whether SIMD or MIMD, massive or non-massive, programmers must be concerned with the communication between processors and typically must contend with relatively small local processor memories (although the latter may change in future computer designs).

Different algorithmic approaches have been used to capitalize on this architecture. Notably, relaxation and row-action methods have been applied to nonlinear (12) and linear network models (24,25) and stochastic programming problems with network recourse (26,27). In the SIMD codes developed for those applications and implemented on massively parallel machines, each network node is assigned a processor to manage supply and demand, and each arc is represented by two processors, one at the arc's head and the other at its tail, to handle computation of the arc flows and duals. Efficient organization of data within the machine is crucial as information must be passed between processors via the interconnection network, and communication speed between adjacent processors is much faster than nonadjacent message passing and global broadcasting.

Unlike the previous applications, the synchronous nature of SIMD machines leads to uniform timing of events across different executions. Because of the extremely limited nature of individual processors and their memories in current systems, the impact of parallelism relative to a serial implementation has been difficult to determine. A linear problem with 50,000 nodes and 1 million arcs was solved in under 15 min on a 32,768-processor system (24).

Reporting of Computational Testing

Much work has been accomplished in constructing a set of guidelines for reporting on computational experimentation, particularly in the area of mathematical programming. Following a series of early articles (28,29) the classic work by Crowder, Dembo, and Mulvey (30) provides reporting guidelines for computational experiments that have been adopted by a number of scholarly journals. Unfortunately, these recommendations were written before parallel processing systems became generally available and, therefore, did not address multiprocessing issues. A recent follow-up report by Jackson et al. (2) extended the topics covered in (30). Relevant to this article are its sections on choosing performance measures and reporting of computational tests on machines with advanced architectures.

In its discussion of performance measures for evaluating mathematical programming software, Jackson et al. state that an efficiency measure should reflect computational effort and solution quality. ''(A)uthors [should] state clearly what is being tested, what performance criteria are being considered, and what performance measure is being used to draw inferences about these criteria. . . . (R)eferees should bear in mind that performance measures are summary statistics and, as much as possible, should conform to all of the accepted rules regarding the use thereof.''

In the sections that follow, we explore parallel performance measures and attempt to determine the accepted, or at least some acceptable rules for their use. Because of the differences in metrics used to describe shared-memory and distributed-memory applications, we devote a separate section to each category.

REPORTING EXPERIMENTS ON SHARED-MEMORY PARALLEL COMPUTERS

Of significant interest to researchers in mathematical programming and algorithm development are measures of the improvement over traditional serial computing achieved by the use of multiple processors. The measures are influenced by the type of machine studied because the architectures of parallel systems are quite varied. We will address metrics for the most prevalent class of commercial parallel design, tightly coupled MIMD.

What Is "Time?"

As the rationale for parallelism is time-based, it is reasonable that a performance or efficiency measure be temporal. With single-processor systems, a common performance measure is the *CPU time* to solve a problem; this is the time the processor spends executing instructions in the algorithmic portion of the program being tested, and typically excludes the time for input of problem data, output of results, and system overhead activities such as virtual memory paging and job swapping. CPU time for a job is maintained by the operating system software because many jobs may be sharing the same processor; the programmer uses this to compute that portion pertaining to the algorithm under study.

In the parallel case, time is not a sum of CPU times on each processor nor the largest across all. As the objective of parallelism is real-time reduction, time must include any processor waiting resulting from an unbalanced workload and any overhead activity time. Hence, the most prudent choice for measuring a parallel code's performance is the *real (wall clock) time* to solve a particular problem. Because this conservative measure includes all system paging, job swapping overhead, it is preferable that timings be made on a dedicated or lightly loaded machine.

What Is "Speedup?"

The most common measure of the performance of an MIMD parallel implementation is speedup. Based on a definition of time, speedup is the ratio of serial to parallel times to solve a particular problem on a given machine. However, using different assumptions, researchers have employed several definitions for speedup in their reporting.

Speedup Definitions

Definition 1.   Speedup. The *speedup*, $S(p)$, achieved by a parallel algorithm running on p processors is defined as

$$S(p) = \frac{\text{Time to solve a problem with the fastest serial code on a specific parallel computer}}{\text{Time to solve the same problem with the parallel code using } p \text{ processors on the same computer}}.$$

For example, assume the fastest serial time is 100 s for a specific problem on a parallel machine, and a parallel algorithm solves the same problem in 20 s on the same machine using six processors. The speedup from this experiment would be $S(6) = 100/20 = 5$. *Linear speedup*, with $S(p) = p$, is considered an ideal application of parallelism, although *superlinear* results, with $S(p) > p$, are possible in some instances (14) (see discussion below).

Definition 2.   Relative Speedup. Some researchers use *relative speedup* in their reporting, defined as

$$RS(p) = \frac{\text{Time to solve a problem with the parallel code on one processor}}{\text{Time to solve the same problem with the parallel code on } p \text{ processors}}.$$

This should be used in cases where the uniprocessor version of the parallel code dominates all other serial implementations. Unfortunately, some articles interpret relative speedup as speedup when the serial case is not dominant, leading to erroneous claims of efficiency.

Definition 3.   Absolute Speedup. The use of *absolute speedup* has also been proposed (32) to compare algorithms:

$$AS(p) = \frac{\text{Fastest serial time on any serial computer}}{\text{Time to execute the parallel code on } p \text{ processors of a parallel computer}}.$$

The rationale for $AS(p)$ reflects the primary objective of parallel processing: real-time reduction. Although this definition goes to the heart of the matter, it restricts research to those individuals with access to the fastest serial machine and cannot be determined until all relevant serial algorithms have been tested on all high-end systems because "fastest" may be dependent on a particular combination of algorithm and machine for each problem tested.

Related Metrics

Another measure of the performance of a parallel implementation is *efficiency*, the fraction of linear speedup attained:

$$E(p) = \frac{S}{p},$$

where $S = S(p)$, $RS(p)$, or $AS(p)$. This is speedup normalized by the number of processors, and $E(p) = 1$ for linear speedup. Note that because $E(p)$'s value is a function of the definitions used for speedup and time, this normalized speedup is susceptible to all of the same reporting concerns and difficulties as the other performance metrics detailed in this report.

Incremental efficiency has also been used in reporting, defined as

$$IE(p) = \frac{(p - 1)(\text{Time for the parallel code on } p - 1 \text{ processors})}{(p)\,(\text{Time for the parellel code on } p \text{ processors})},$$

where $p > 1$. This value shows the fraction of time improvement from adding another processor and will be 1 for linear speedup. This variant of relative speedup has been used where one-processor times are unavailable (17).

The section reporting on distributed systems testing describes additional speedup and efficiency measures used as performance metrics for distributed-memory systems.

Is Superlinear Speedup Possible?

Although superlinear speedup–with $S(p) > p$—has been reported (14,21), its existence is still debated. Those who say that it is not possible note that if a particular problem can be solved in time t on p processors, then simulating the parallel code on one processor will yield a serial time of pt. Hence, speedup is at most linear.

The other side of the argument is based on the belief that it is unfair to choose the "best" serial code, and tuning strategy, for each problem instance; that is, the best serial case should be chosen prior to particular problem instances. In this situation, superlinear speedup is possible. For example, with a parallel branch-and-bound code, one processor may find a good bound early in the solution process and communicate it to other processes for truncation of their search domain, possibly resulting in superlinear speedup.

It should also be noted that emulating a parallel environment on a serial machine is a difficult, and perhaps impossible, task. A naïve approach would be to execute the parallel code as a set of interacting processes on a single processor, letting the operating system allocate time and other system resources. Although such an arrangement would approximate a true parallel execution, it does not, for example, ensure the same ordering of events or replicate interprocess communication delays and resource contentions.

Issues in Reporting the Results of Parallel Testing

As with serial software, but even more so in parallel testing, performance measures abound, and a researcher must choose a small subset of measures to summarize succinctly the experimentation to draw conclusions about the underlying algorithm. The number of reported measures are limited by publication space restrictions and the potentially large number of values for p.

Hence, researchers must (1) select appropriate measures and (2) use the measures in an objective way to accurately reflect the behavior of the algorithm. Although easily stated, these are surprisingly complicated tasks, especially when studying the behavior of parallel codes.

Choosing a Measure for Parallel Implementations

Jackson et al. (2) recommend that ". . . when comparing a parallel algorithm with a scalar method, it is preferable to compare the parallel method not only with its scalar specialization, but also with the best scalar methods. In addition to reporting absolute speedups, times normalized by the number of processors are desirable." The authors clearly prefer $S(p)$ over $RS(p)$ and encourage the use of $E(p)$. (This would avoid instances such as (17) in which a parallel network code was compared with a slow serial code (33), yielding spectacular "results." Further analysis in (14)—this time using an efficient serial code—showed there was an average 3-processor speedup of only 1.4.

But "gray areas" in reporting may result from ambiguity in the definitions of time and speedup. What portion of the system overhead time (e.g., for process creation and termination) should be included in the serial and parallel results? If real time is used for the parallel algorithm, should this also be used for the serial, even though we have more accurate serial data available regarding the processor time spend executing algorithmic steps?

A more difficult question turns out to be: What constitutes the base, serial case? Because most implementations have "tuning" parameters, such as multipricing options, reinversion frequency, and tolerances—each of which influences a problem's solution time—how should these be set? It is widely known that, in many cases, experimentation to determine good values for the parameters can result in a significant reduction in execution times. If a researcher wishes to use the best possible serial time, how much testing with different *strategies* (parameter sets) should be performed? Further, does each code and strategy combination create a new algorithm to be considered separately?

Determining the parallel time involves the same question, but is further complicated by the fact that the value of individual strategies varies with p, the number of processors. A strategy that works well for a given p does not necessarily work well for a different number of processors. Should testing of numerous strategies be performed for each instance of p to be reported, and how extensive should such testing be? Or should a fixed strategy be used for all values of p? Should prescribed strategy formulas that vary with p be used instead?

Complicating matters further is the stochastic nature of some parallel algorithms. Many iterative procedures not only have multiple paths to a problem's solution, but the path chosen may be nondeterministic, due to timing-dependent decisions (race conditions) in the algorithm design. For example, multiple executions of our parallel network simplex codes (14,34,35) typically yield different solution times and number of pivots when applied to the same problem with the same strategy, under virtually identical operating conditions. In some cases, differences of thousands of pivots and 15% time variations were observed. This is due not only to alternate optima but also to slight differences in timings of events, resulting in different incoming variables, tie-breaking choices, and, therefore, a different sequence of extreme points traversed.

How should these results be tested and reported? Should multiple runs be performed for each combination of code, problem, strategy, and number of processors? Should all resultant timings be reported or summarized in statistics? If a researcher wishes to determine speedup, should the best, worst, or average times be used? (Averages would require a new definition of speedup.) Some researchers always use the best times, arguing that these show the actual capability of the code; is this reasonable? We attempt to answer these questions in the sections that follow.

Potential Sources of Bias in Reporting Parallel Results

As is evident from the previous discussion, many choices must be made in the design and reporting of experiments with parallel codes. Since this is a relatively new area of research, there are few generally accepted answers to the questions posed. Analysis of data variation is central to statistically designed experimentation (36–38), but in dealing with speedup there is variation in the components needed to compute this statistic, which is a different issue.

Also, because speedup is a ratio of serial to parallel time, we have the following observation:

Observation:The longer the serial time, the greater the parallel speedup, and vice versa.

Evidence: From inspection of the $S(p)$, $RS(p)$, and $AS(p)$ definitions.

Therefore, although fast single-processor times highlight the strength of the serial code, they can produce unimpressive parallel speedups. Conversely, a slow serial time can yield seemingly spectacular parallel results. Hence, it is a simple matter to influence (inadvertently or deliberately) the outcome of an experiment employing speedup as a performance measure through the choice of serial and parallel strategies. An advantageous set of strategies can, therefore, positively skew the research findings (of course, a disadvantageous set would have the opposite effect).

This has motivational implications for the level of effort expended in exploring alternate strategies. Nominal serial testing may be rewarded with strong parallel results, whereas a more thorough search for the best one-processor strategy could only downgrade the parallel findings.

An Example of Difficulties in Interpreting Reported Speedup

As noted previously, (16) reports on computational experimentation with a parallel network simplex code. The machine employed was a BBN Butterfly, a loosely coupled MIMD system, in which each of the 14 processors has its own "local" memory and can also access other processors' "remote" memories via a switching network.

In the code, only the pricing step was parallelized: each processor priced the arcs in its local memory and communicated the best candidate found to the others. All processors then executed the same pivot. To determine the serial times, one processor was used for computation, and the arc data were distributed across all processor memories. Hence, most data were accessed remotely in serial testing.

On the Butterfly, remote data access takes 20 times longer than local. Hence, on average, pricing an arc in the serial tests was much slower than in the parallel runs—as local memory was used only a fraction of the time.

The reporting difficulty is: What portion of the (relative) speedup comes from the application of parallelism, and what portion is due to the use of slower memory accesses in the serial case? Although (16) did not address this specific issue and simply reported speedups, the implementation was described in sufficient detail to permit identification of the ambiguity. Empirical testing would be required for a definitive answer.

How Should We Approach These Issues?

The preceding sections illustrate some of the difficulties that are encountered when attempting to objectively summarize experimentation with parallel codes. Although we made what we considered reasonable decisions for our research papers, we also sought the insight of others in the research community in hopes of finding clear-cut answers or, at least, a consensus on some of the issues.

SURVEY OF EXPERTS

To get a "sense of the community," we invited a group of computationally oriented mathematical programing researchers to participate in a survey. The design objectives for the survey were (1) to address definitional issues regarding the speedup of parallel algorithm implementations, (2) to help identify a consensus regarding the usefulness of speedup as a measure for reporting parallel performance, and (3) to elicit a high response rate.

To meet these objectives, we constructed a series of simple examples, accompanied by six short-answer questions. Each multiple-choice question included a user-definable response. Comments were welcomed on each question and on the survey as a whole, and respondents could remain anonymous. Commonly used speedup definitions were included for terminological consistency.

The survey was sent to 41 researchers, and 23 completed forms were returned, a strong 56% response rate. Our selections are not included in the totals, but in the accompanying discussion. The following sections explore each question and summarize and comment on the participants' responses; also included are selected, unattributed comments from consenting respondents.

Question 1: Effects of Tuning Parameters

The first survey question is shown in Figure 4. The issue involved is: How should times from different strategies be used in computing speedup? Code B represents a competing algorithm that is, for the most part, dominated by Code A.

Implicit in the choice to be made are several fundamental questions: Does a change in strategy form a different algorithm? Should the same strategy be used for both serial and parallel times? Should only the best times across all tested strategies be used? Should we average the speedups, or something else?

Survey Results

The distribution of answers is depicted in Figure 5. Of the "Other" responses, 58% wanted to include the entire table of times, 34% computed speedup for each code and strategy combination and included all values or the range, and 6% proposed a different calculation.

Question 1. Two optimization codes, A and B, are used to solve the same problem on the same parallel machine and identify the same optimal solution. Each code has a "tuning" parameter which is determined for each run using a "strategy" that fixes the parameter based on problem size and/or number of processors. Runs are made using four different strategies, giving the following results.

Code	A	A	A	B
Strategy	W	X	Y	Z
Serial Solution Time	100	90	200	150
Parallel Solution Time (with two processors)	60	70	50	100

The authors of code A wish to report speedups. What value for two-processor speedup should be reported? (Please mark your choice.)

☐ (a) $\dfrac{100}{60} = 1.67$ Strategy W (Both cases "good")

☐ (b) $\dfrac{90}{50} = 1.8$ Use the best individual times.

☐ (c) $\dfrac{90}{70} = 1.29$ Strategy X (Fixed strategy with best serial)

☐ (d) $\dfrac{200}{50} = 4.0$ Strategy Y (Best two-processor time)

☐ (e) $\dfrac{\dfrac{100}{60} + \dfrac{90}{70} + \dfrac{200}{50}}{3} = 2.32$ Average speedup across all A strategies tested.

☐ (f) Other: Rationale:

FIGURE 4   Question 1: The effect of tuning parameters.

Selected comments: (1) "The single number cannot capture all of the relevant information." (2) "The strategies perform differently enough to suggest three codes: AW, AX, and AY." (3) "There really isn't an appropriate summary of this data." (4) "[Use (e) and] report the standard deviation also." (5) "Reporting raw data as well as speedup is important."

Commentary

The leading selection was "Other," with a majority of those respondents wanting to include all data in reports. $S(2)$ was the dominant summary measure [choice (b)], comparing the best individual parallel and serial times across all codes and strategies, and the remaining responses varied widely.

Although we sympathize with the desire for all of the raw data, the sheer volume of such data generated by conscientious experimentation can become voluminous. For example, a small test bed might consist of 50 representative test problems, to be examined on 1 to 20 processors, with, say, 20 reasonable strategies in each case. This results in 20,000 combinations to test for a single code, ignoring the fact that multiple instances

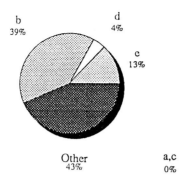

b
39%

d
4%

c
13%

Other
43%

a,c
0%

FIGURE 5   Question 1 responses.

of each combination may be required due to variations in timings or demands of a rigorous experimental design (36,37). Even with only 4 values for p, and an exploration of 10 strategies, 2000 problems must be run. And if the problems are substantial enough to demand the application of parallel processing, the total processing time (especially the search for the best serial case) makes the testing, much less the reporting, impractical.

From our viewpoint, an algorithm definition includes the strategy; the two notions should not be separated in reported results. Hence, we concur with comment (2) and believe that the times for a given code and strategy should be kept together. The strategy may be dynamic with the number of processors or problem characteristics but must be rule based and documented in the experimentation reports.

The difficulty then becomes: How to identify good code and strategy combinations? Conscientious researchers will work diligently to find a combination that has both strong serial and robust parallel performance across a wide range of problems. For all of these reasons, we would have picked responses (a) or (c) or, in the absence of other test problems, would have devised a hybrid stragegy from X and Y that would have yielded the experts' leading choice, (b).

Question 2: Definition of Speedup

Figure 6 depicts the survey's second question which concerns the proper definition and calculation of speedup. Serial code B, which only has a single strategy Z, has the fastest serial time on the problem from Question 1. Code A's parallel times vary with strategy. What is the speedup of code A?

Survey Results

The response percentages are given in Figure 7. Most of the "Other" responses had the same answer as in Question 1, and for the same reasons.

Selected comments: (1) "Present the table. The single number, speedup, cannot capture all of the relevant information. In this case it would be better to report the details. In the text of the paper, one could mention a range 90–200 of serial times and 50–70 of parallel times." (2) "More problems should be tested here."

Commentary

This question highlights the main objective of parallel processing, namely, reduction of the real time required to solve a given problem. Here, a serial code exists which runs

Question 2. Here we have the same scenario, but different results. In this instance, B is a serial code.

Code	A	A	B
Strategy	W	Y	Z
Serial Solution Time	100	90	80
Parallel Solution Time (with two processors)	60	70	N.A.

The authors of code A wish to report speedups. What value for two-processor speedup should be reported? (Please mark your choice.)

☐ (a) $\frac{100}{60} = 1.67$

☐ (b) $\frac{90}{70} = 1.29$

☐ (c) $\frac{90}{60} = 1.5$

☐ (d) $\frac{80}{60} = 1.33$

☐ (e) $\frac{80}{70} = 1.14$

☐ (f) Other: Rationale:

FIGURE 6   Question 2: Basic definition of speedup.

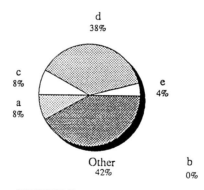

FIGURE 7   Question 2 responses.

faster than the one-processor parallel code; hence, better speedups could be reported by ignoring the existence of B. However, that would certainly be misleading because code B should be used for the serial time.

The majority of respondents selecting a speedup metric chose one based on serial code B [(d) or (e)], with which we concur. We also feel that, if at all possible, results

Question 3. The times for code A using strategy Z dominate all other code and strategy combinations. However, multiple executions of the same algorithm in the same circumstances gave different times. Differences in serial times are due to variability within the computer's timing mechanism, and the (larger) differences in parallel times are due to timing-dependent choices (race conditions) in the algorithm. The following results come from 14 runs of code A with strategy Z.

	Serial Runs	2-Processor Runs
Solution times	98,99,100,100,	50,50,60,60,
(7 observations each)	100,101,102	60,70,70
Mean time	100	60
Min, Max time	98, 102	50, 70

What value for two-processor speedup should be reported for code A? (Please mark your choice.)

☐ (a) $\dfrac{100}{60} = 1.67$ *Ratio of means*

☐ (b) $\dfrac{98}{60} = 1.63$ *Best individual serial over mean parallel*

☐ (c) $\dfrac{100}{50} = 2.0$ *Mean serial over best parallel*

☐ (d) $\dfrac{98}{50} = 1.96$ *Best serial over best parallel*

☐ (e) Mean of $\left(\dfrac{100}{50}, \dfrac{100}{50}, \dfrac{100}{60}, \dfrac{100}{60}, \dfrac{100}{60}, \dfrac{100}{70}, \dfrac{100}{70} \right) = 1.69$

    Mean of speedups with mean serial base case

☐ (f) Mean of $\left(\dfrac{98}{50}, \dfrac{98}{50}, \dfrac{98}{60}, \dfrac{98}{60}, \dfrac{98}{70}, \dfrac{98}{70} \right) = 1.66$

    Mean of speedups with best serial base case

☐ (g) Other: Rationale:

FIGURE 8   Question 3: Effect of timing variation.

from a well-known code, such as MINOS (39) or NETFLO (33), should be included in reports. Such reference codes give the reader an awareness of the overall efficiency of all software being tested and is of particular value on new, relatively unfamiliar technology.

Question 3: Effect of Timing Variations on Speedup

The third question, shown in Figure 8, focuses on a single problem, code, and strategy combination, illustrating the stochastic nature of both parallel and serial testing. Repeated executions of this combination under identical system conditions show variability in both the serial and parallel timings. Variation from the timing mechanism affects all

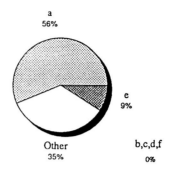

FIGURE 9   Question 3 responses.

values, and the larger parallel variability is due to time dependencies in the algorithm. How is speedup to be computed in this more realistic setting? (The italicized annotations in Figure 8 were not on the survey itself.)

Survey Results

Figure 9 shows the response percentages. Of the "Other" responses, 63% wanted some measures that reflected variability, 25% suggested the ratio of means or medians, and 12% wished to report the raw data.

Selected comments: (1) "The greater variance in the two-processor times is an important part of the data." (2) "Also, the standard deviation should be used [along with (e)]." (3) "For serial time, use the average—errors are due to timing anyway." (4) "Should provide variance measures since that is the purpose of the study."

Comments

This question yielded the clearest consensus thus far, with 57% of the respondents choosing (a), the ratio of mean times, and many indicated a desire for a supplementary indicator of variability. On this question we differ with the respondents. We feel that (e) is a similar, but slightly more correct, choice for the following reasons. The serial variation is due to random measurement error and, hence, should be averaged to form the base case, per responses (a), (c), and (e). With this base, speedup can be computed for each two-processor time and averaged to give the mean speedup ratio, instead of the ratio of mean times which does not follow any of the standard speedup definitions. This would also permit reporting speedup variability measures such as the standard deviation and range. We note that the harmonic—not the arithmetic—mean of the ratios should be taken (see (37), p. 188, for a full discussion), and is

$$\ddot{x} = \frac{7(100)}{50+50+60+60+60+70+70} = 1.667.$$

This situation underscores the difficulty in reporting all of the raw data and leads to the question: How many instances of each combination of problem, code, strategy, and number of processors should be run? The testing of 5 instances of 1 code on 50 problems, with 10 strategies, and 4 processor settings, involves 10,000 runs; practicalities will likely force compromises on such an experimental design.

Question 4. How much effort should be spent identifying the "best" serial time for a given problem? (For example, with a simplex-based algorithm, how much testing should be performed to identify the best pivot strategy?) Please express your answer on a scale from 1 to 10 where 1 = minimal testing and 10 = as exhaustive as possible.

Your answer: _____

FIGURE 10   Question 4: Effort for serial case.

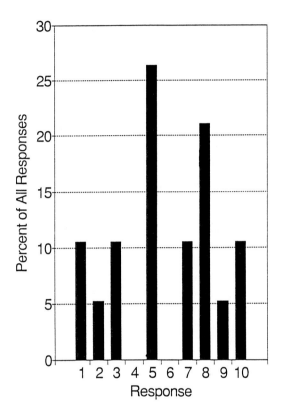

FIGURE 11   Distribution of responses to Question 4.

Question 4: Degree of Effort on Serial Case

Because of the crucial role of the serial time in computing speedup, the level of effort expended to identify a "best" value is a significant factor in reporting. Respondents expressed the importance of such experimentation on a scale of 1 to 10 (see Figure 10).

Survey Results

Of the 83% that gave a numerical answer, the "effort" statistics are as follows: mean, 5.8; median and mode, 5; standard deviation, 2.9; this distribution is shown in Figure 11. The 17% nonrespondents said that the answer depended on the purpose of the experimentation.

Question 5. The solution strategy used in a code can strongly affect execution times. When reporting results of testing a code on a given problem with different numbers of processors, the reported results should be based on a strategy which is:

☐ (a) Fixed, invariant of the number of processors
☐ (b) Rule-based, and can vary with the number of processors and problem parameters
☐ (c) The fastest of all tested for each number of processors
☐ (d) Other:

FIGURE 12   Question 5: Setting solution strategy.

Selected comments: (1) "[Expend] just as much effort as would be done for the parallel code." (2) "Use standard setting of parameters." (3) "Be reasonable. Give arguments as to why you made the choice. Realize that performance is highly problem-dependent and there may not be a 'best' serial version." (4) "In many cases it may be preferable to compare with a 'standard' algorithm (e.g., MINOS for simplex)." (5) "Difficult to answer, depends on reason for study."

Comments

With a full range of values, and slightly left-skewed distribution, the responses indicate that a reasonable amount of testing should be performed. We feel that our testing has been in the exhausting, but not exhaustive, 8 to 9 range. Comment (1) seemed appropriate, but we are reminded that the best code and strategy combination tends to vary from problem to problem and with number of processors used (i.e., the fastest for two processors is not necessarily fastest with six).

Question 5: Setting Strategies

The question posed in Figure 12 addresses the means by which strategies should be determined for reporting purposes. Implicit is the issue of whether researchers should be able to determine a unique strategy for each problem and processor combination and report the results of the best that was found empirically.

Survey Results

The response percentages are given in Figure 13. Of the "Other" respondents, 43% said "any," 29% "(a) and (b)," 14% "all", and 14% said that it depends on the research objective.

Selected comments: (1) "Report (a) and (b). The more the merrier." (2) "[Rule-based,] but part of the program." (3) "More important is to explicitly state which of the above was used."

Comments

Respondents are closer to a consensus on this issue, with a strong majority preferring a rule-based strategy, rather than individually tuned ones, and we agree. We note that re-

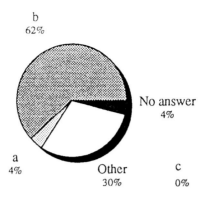

FIGURE 13   Question 5 responses.

Question 6. Should speedup be used as the primary measure of performance of a parallel algorithm?

☐ (a) Yes

☐ (b) No, we should use:

FIGURE 14   Question 6: Efficacy of speedup as metric.

sults can be easily biased if choice (a) is employed—simply choose a good multiprocessor strategy. In our experiments with the network simplex, a strategy that performed well in parallel typically worked poorly serially; hence, using such a fixed strategy could result in dramatic speedups. Choice (b) seems the most fair but leaves open the question of how to devise the rule.

Question 6: Validity of Speedup as a Metric

The last question, shown in Figure 14, allows participants to summarize their feelings about speedup's current role as the leading performance measure for reporting parallel testing.

Survey Results

The response percentages are shown in Figure 15. Suggested alternatives or additions included measures of cost-effectiveness, efficiency, robustness, quality of solution, and chance of catastrophic error.

Selected comments: (1) "I tend to be skeptical about one number measuring the goodness of an algorithm." (2) "No, but it is attractive to boil performance down to a single number, so it will likely continue as the dominant measure." (3) "[Use] a number of performance measures, just as we learned when dealing with serial algorithms." (4) "There must be a better method. But I do not know it."

Comments

A slight majority begrudgingly accepted speedup as the primary parallel performance measure but, as revealed in the comments, would prefer a better one. Several indicated the need for variation and cost-effectiveness to be represented in reportings.

FIGURE 15   Question 6 responses.

Overall Comments

The following quotations were selected from the general comments of consenting respondents regarding the questionnaire or the reporting of parallel experimentation.

"Rating the effectiveness of a parallel algorithm by a single measure, speedup, seems analogous to describing a probability distribution by reporting only its mean."

"As a rule, authors of a code will present the data so as to make their code appear best. That is human nature. More important is to explicitly state how they are reporting and how testing was performed, i.e. acknowledge their biases."

"The value of parallelism is an economic issue or real time speedup issue. . . . Without the cost of the parallel system the benefits of speedup are meaningless."

"Also we should report the actual times—not only speedups—and on problem sizes where speedup is of the essence."

"After the initial excitement of actual implementation of conventional or new algorithms on parallel machines, speedup factors are going to lose their allure. . . . However, if we show that what took an hour on a $10 million superframe now takes 15 minutes on a $500K multicomputer, it will have a significant impact whatever the speedup factor is."

"Rules to follow: (1) Avoid point samples, i.e., solve each problem instance several times and solve many problem instances. (2) Summarize data in more than one way. Be willing to report negative results."

"More people should think of these important details."

Survey Conclusions

The survey of leading researchers in computational mathematical programming in most cases did not yield a clear consensus. The large number of "Other" responses may be due in part to independent-thinking participants, ambiguities in the questions and answers, or simply the lack of obvious or appealing solutions to the situations posed. Even so, a general level of agreement was reached on the following.

- The use of speedup as a parallel performance measure is tolerable, but more than one measure of parallelism effect is desirable in reporting computational results.
- Measures of variation and cost-effectiveness are important also.
- Report as much of the raw data as possible.
- A rule-based strategy should be used when reporting results.

We also feel from the survey and our parallel testing experiences that:

- No strong consensus exists regarding the method for summarizing a large body of data.
- Although many survey participants wanted all raw data reported, this is clearly not feasible when there are many combinations of problem, code, strategy, numbers of processors, and numbers of repetitions. We must continue to work toward better numerical and graphical methods for summarizing the data.
- Reference values from well-known codes are needed, particularly in the serial case.
- Experimental design procedures should be used in reporting to accommodate the variability in timings and add rigor to the process.
- Even more complications will arise when using speedup as the response variable in a statistical experimental design.
- We should focus on the real time and cost required to solve difficult problems.

REPORTING ON DISTRIBUTED SYSTEMS TESTING

SIMD machines and distributed-memory MIMD machines are distinguished from shared-memory machines in that there is no main memory which is globally accessible by all processors. To date, massively parallel systems have tended to contain a large number of low-power processors; for example, the SIMD CM-2 uses thousands of 1-bit processors, with small local memories (40). These characteristics complicate the computation of speedup in a distributed-memory environment.

Because speedup is typically computed as the ratio of the single-processor to the multiprocessor times to solve the same problem, to compute speedup on such a distributed memory system the size of the problem must be restricted to one which will fit into the memory associated with a single processor. This clearly places severe limitations on the magnitude of problems on which speedup (in the traditional sense) may be reported. This restriction has led researchers to revert to earlier simpler metrics, to derive new ones, and to formulate alternative speedup models.

Performance Metrics Used with Distributed Optimization

One metric reported is the *MFLOPS* (*million floating-point operations per second*) rate. Typically the number of *megaflops* sustained by a program is given along with the peak MFLOPS possible on that machine. This measure is an indicator of how well a particular implementation of an algorithm exploits the architecture of the machine, but, as Bertsekas et al. (41) note, it ". . . does not necessarily indicate whether this is an efficient algorithm for solving problems. It is conceivable that an alternative algorithm can solve the same problem faster, even if it executes at a lower MFLOP rate." (Note that, as technology progresses, the measure is shifting to *gigaflops* and *teraflops*.)

Another common metric is the *real time* required to solve a given problem. It is valuable in that it provides a fairly unambiguous account of the efficiency of an implementation of an algorithm on a particular machine (assuming variability in timings is not an issue). Often only one set of times is reported; that is, each problem is solved for only one value of p, the number of processors. For example, (25) reports times required to solve network problems on a 16,384-processor CM-2 and (24) reports times required to solve similar problems on a 32,768-processor CM-2. This information is useful for comparative purposes to researchers who are using the same machine, and to those interested in absolute speed. However, with times for only one value of p, a researcher is unable to extrapolate regarding the value of additional processors.

To date, these have been the only performance measures used in reporting on SIMD implementations of parallel optimization algorithms, besides algorithm-specific statistics such as the number of major and minor iterations, and portion of time spent performing certain steps. Some loosely coupled MIMD applications report relative speedup (42,43).

In the next section, we describe a series of performance metrics which have been proposed for parallel testing. Some of these have been used for the comparison of computer systems and have been adopted for the comparison and testing of algorithms.

Additional Performance Measures for Distributed Algorithms

In some instances, times may be available for several different values of p but not for $p=1$. Consider, for example, a 1024-processor distributed-memory machine. Although a problem may be too large to run on one processor, it may be solvable on, say, 64 processors. It could then perhaps also be solved using 128 processors, then 256, 512, and 1,024. In (26), times are reported for solving linear stochastic programs on a 32,768-processor CM-2 using both 16,384 processors and 32,768 processors. In such cases, traditional speedup cannot be computed.

We propose an alternate model to quantify the value of additional processors, termed *generalized incremental efficiency*, computed as follows:

$$GIE(p, q) = \frac{(p)(\text{Time to execute parallel code on } p \text{ processors})}{(q)(\text{Time to execute parallel code on } q \text{ processors})}.$$

This value shows the fraction of linear speedup which was attained by increasing the number of processors from p to q. A value of 1 indicates linear speedup. For example, (26) reports that ". . . doubling the number of processors from 16K to 32K decreases the solution time by a factor of almost 2." In this case $GIE(16K,32K)$ would be close to 1.0, indicating near linear speedup. (The concept of incremental efficiency was reported by Peters (17), but was limited in that it only measured the value of adding one processor at a time. In terms of generalized incremental efficiency, this may be expressed as $IE(p) = GIE(p - 1, p)$.)

Although generalized incremental efficiency does indicate the value of additional processing elements, it does not allow one to fully utilize all memory available. (All processors would be required to solve a problem which required all available memory. Therefore, no comparisons could be made for different values of p.) One model which addresses this issue is *scaled speedup* (11,43,44). In this model, problem size increases with p. If we assume that the largest problem which may be stored in the memory associated with one processor is of size n and that storage is proportional to n, then p processors should be able to solve a problem of size np. Therefore, the scaled speedup is defined as

$$SS(p) = \frac{\text{Estimated time to solve problem of size } np \text{ on 1 processor}}{\text{Actual time to solve problem of size } np \text{ on } p \text{ processors}}.$$

This metric is attractive in that it allows for full utilization of the machine resources while quantifying the value of additional processors. Its major disadvantage is the uncertainty inherent in the numerator. Accurate estimation of the solution time based on one (or more) scaling factor(s) is impractical for many mathematical programming problems. For example, given only the time required to solve a linear program with m constraints, it is difficult to determine a precise estimate of the time to solve a linear program with $2m$ constraints because there are many influencing factors and $2m$ may be outside the observed experience range. Furthermore, many mathematical programming problems are not easily scalable.

Closely related to scaled speedup is *fixed time speedup* (45). The concept of fixed time speedup is more closely associated with measuring the performance of computers than algorithms but deserves notice in the present context. As with scaled speedup, the computation of fixed time speedup requires that the one-processor time be estimated. The difference between the two models lies in the size of the problem being solved. Scaled speedup is computed based on a problem size which is largest for the number of processors used. Fixed time speedup is computed based on a problem size which is the largest that can be solved in a particular amount of time. If we assume that the largest problem which may be stored in the memory associated with one processor is of size n, fixed time speedup is computed as follows:

$$FTS(p) = \frac{\text{Estimated time to solve problem of size } k \text{ on one processor}}{\text{Actual time to solve problem of size } k \text{ on } p \text{ processors}},$$

where k is the size of the largest problem which can be solved on p processors in no more time than one processor can solve a problem of size n. As with scaled speedup, fixed time speedup shares the disadvantage of estimating the one-processor solution time. Furthermore, the process of determining k is imprecise at best.

Also closely related to scaled speedup is an efficiency measure termed *scaleup*. According to (46), "(s)caleup is defined as the ability of an n-times larger system to perform an n-times larger job in the same elapsed time as the original system." Therefore, this measure allows for full utilization of system resources but, unlike scaled speedup, is not based on an estimated one-processor time. It is computed as follows:

$$Scaleup(p, n) = \frac{\text{Time to solve size } m \text{ problem on } p \text{ processors}}{\text{Time to solve size } nm \text{ problem on } np \text{ processors}}.$$

Linear scaleup occurs when $scaleup(p, n) = 1$. A form of scaleup is used in (26), which reports that ". . . the time to solve a 1024 scenario problem on a 16K machine is almost the same as that for solving a 2048 scenario problem on a 32K machine." In this instance, $scaleup(16K, 2)$ is close to 1, hence nearly linear.

To help explain their results, authors may wish to include statistics such as *fraction of time spent in communication* and *synchronization-related idle time*. Although indispensable for correct code operation, both communication and synchronization time are considered overhead items because no work, per se, is accomplished during that time. The inclusion of this type of measure can provide insight into the sources of inefficiency in the code and underlying algorithm.

Conclusions

Many of the newer performance metrics require an accurate model for estimating solution times for problems of a given "size" and number of processors. We feel that such a requirement is unrealistic within the domain of mathematical programming, where a large number of factors with undiscovered interrelationships determine problem solution difficulty and computational effort for a given problem.

Researchers testing massively parallel and distributed algorithms are struggling to find useful measures of the value of parallelism and the efficiency of their methods. For these settings, only the basic metrics have been reported in the optimization literature. This is probably due to the embryonic state of research in this area, the small number of standard test problems for comparative testing, and the lack of a generally accepted summary measure.

We encourage researchers in this domain to:

- Compare their results with standard codes, on other platforms if necessary, to provide a frame of reference for the timing data;
- Include system prices and address cost-effectiveness issues in solving problems of practical interest; and
- Explore the newer performance metrics, and hopefully devise better ones.

REPORTING ON PARALLEL EXPERIMENTS WITH HEURISTIC CODES

The objective of heuristic methods is the identification of "high-quality" feasible solutions to problems more quickly than can be done with provably optimizing approaches. This permits users to obtain solutions to problems that are known to be difficult (e.g., NP-hard) or not easily described by traditional mathematical formulations (as with some routing and scheduling problems). Key application areas for heuristics have been integer programming, combinatorial, and graph-theoretic models.

Many generalized approaches, or *meta-heuristics*, have emerged, including: *k*-exchange, simulated annealing, tabu search, genetic, neural network, GRASP, target analysis, ejection chain, and beam search algorithms. All of these methods are highly amenable to parallel exploitation.

Reporting on parallel implementations of heuristics has the same set of problems as with optimizing codes: stochastic results from race conditions, determination of the proper base case for speedup calculations, difficulty in summarizing a large body of data, and so on. In addition, heuristics have special reporting problems of their own:

- Because of the nature of some heuristic algorithms, including—but not limited to—those with a randomization component, serial and parallel executions are likely to return different solutions.
- Bounds on the optimal solution value can be weak or nonexistent; hence, the closeness to optimality cannot be determined accurately.
- Perhaps as a result, many procedures have no standard termination rule, other than: Stop when you run out of money or patience.
- Such arbitrariness permits the reporting of results using stopping rules based on preprocessing of the problems. For example, if a heuristic code is run for 10,000 iterations, but the last improving solution was found at repetition 890, then one could simply report timings based on the rule: Stop after 900 iterations.
- As with optimizing codes, heuristics often have a large number of control parameters to set. A given solution strategy may depend on a dozen or more decisions, such as candidate list lengths, descent rate, number of training

repetitions, tolerances, and thresholds, plus a stopping rule. Because execution times are often heavily influenced by tuning such values, researchers should document not only the parameter settings used in the testing but the robustness of those values.

Of primary interest in reporting on computational testing of heuristic-based codes are descriptive measures of the trade-off between time and solution quality. Does the code find a "good" solution quickly? Given enough time, does the code find a high-quality solution? For a benchmark problem, was the best known solution identified? Was a new best solution found?

Perhaps the best descriptor of heuristic performance on a problem is a graph of the best solution value found versus time. When variability results from parallelism, average and interval values can be graphed as well. Related statistics include time to first feasible solution, time to best solution, and time to n iterations.

Example metrics that have been used in parallel heuristic testing (47,48) are as follows: relative speedup; percent of cases examined where best known solution was found; minimum, average, and maximum times for n iterations and for various numbers of processors, p; and a graph of the cumulative number of problems in test set achieving a stated quality level, versus time, for various values of p.

SUMMARY AND GUIDELINES

In just the past few years, great strides have been made in harnessing the power of parallel computers to solve mathematical programming problems. To assist authors, referees, and editors, we offer the following guidelines for the reporting of computational experiments with parallel codes, based on our experiences and a survey of experts in the field. They are meant to augment previous reporting standards (29,30) and be considered a work-in-progress, to be refined and enhanced as experience, understanding, and insight grow.

Parallel Reporting Guidelines
  I. **Thoroughly document the process**
     A. Describe the code being tested. This includes the algorithm on which it is based, including any modifications; the overall design; the data structures used; and the available tuning parameters.
     B. Document the computing environment for the experimentation. Report all pertinent characteristics of the machine used, including the manufacturer, model, types and number of processors, interprocessor communication schemes, size of memories, and configuration.
     C. Describe the testing environment and methodology.
         1. State how times were measured.
         2. When reporting speedup, state how it was computed. In particular, indicate what was used for the base (serial) case.
         3. Report all values of tuning parameters.
 II. **Use a well-considered experimental design**
     A. Focus on the real time and cost required to solve difficult problems.

  B. Try to identify those factors that contribute to the results presented and their effects. This includes the impacts of problem characteristics, tuning-parameter strategy, and parallelism.
  C. Provide points of reference. If possible, use well-known codes and problems to determine reference values, particularly in the serial case, even if testing must be performed on different machines (as required with some distributed systems).
  D. Perform final, reported testing on a dedicated or lightly loaded system.
  E. Employ statistical experimental design techniques. This powerful, often neglected, methodology can highlight those factors that contributed to the results, as well as those that did not.

III. Provide a comprehensive report of the results
  A. For summary measures, use measures of center, variability, and cost-effectiveness.
  B. Use graphics where possible and when informative.
  C. Provide as much detail as possible. If a journal will not publish all pertinent data—perhaps due to space limitations—make them available in a research report.
  D. Describe the sensitivity of the code to changes in the tuning strategy.
  E. Be courageous and include your "failures," as they provide insight also.

Parallelism holds the promise of permitting operations researchers and computer scientists to reach the previously unattainable: the routine solution of problems and the support of models that were too large or complex for previous generations of computers and algorithms. By so doing, we bring the benefits of the "OR-approach" (49) to a wider audience, hopefully affecting and improving the lives of an increasingly larger portion of the world's populace. The accurate reporting of research is central to progress and the growing understanding of how to capitalize on these new opportunities so that we might realize the fruits of the promise.

ACKNOWLEDGMENTS

We wish to thank all of the survey participants for their time and thoughtful contributions. We are also grateful to the Editor of the *ORSA Journal on Computing* for the invitation to prepare this article. Finally, we note that some of the materials in this article appeared previously in (50).

REFERENCES

1. H. J. Greenberg, "Computational Testing: Why, How and How Much," *ORSA J. Computing*, *2*, 7–11 (1990).
2. R. H. F. Jackson, P. T. Boggs, S. G. Nash, and S. Powell, "Report of the Ad Hoc Committee to Revise the Guidelines for Reporting Computational Experiments in Mathematical Programming," *Math. Programming*, *49*, 413–425 (1990).
3. P. W. Purdom, Jr. and C. A. Brown, *The Analysis of Algorithms*, Holt, Rinehart and Winston, New York, 1985.
4. A. Schrijver, *Theory of Linear and Integer Programing*, John Wiley & Sons, Chichester, 1986.

5. M. L. Barton and G. R. Withers, "Computing Performance as a Function of the Speed, Quantity, and Cost of the Processors," *Proceedings of Supercomputing '89*, pp. 759–764.

6. P. Gregory, "Will MPP Always Be Specialized?" *Supercomputing Review*, 5(3) (1992).

7. M. J. Flynn, "Very High-Speed Computing Systems" *Proc. IEEE*, *54*, 1901–1909 (1966).

8. G. A. P. Kindervater and J. K. Lenstra. "Parallel Computing in Combinatorial Optimization," *Annals Oper. Res.*, *14*(1), 245–289 (1989).

9. N. Carriero and D. Gelernter, "How to Write Parallel Programs: A Guide to the Perplexed," *ACM Computing Surveys*, *21*, 323–357 (1989).

10. Parasoft, *EXPRESS: A Communication Environment for Parallel Computers*, Parasoft, Mission Viejo, CA, 1988.

11. J. L. Gustafson, G. R. Montry, and R. E. Benner, "Development of Parallel Methods for a 1024-Processor Hypercube," *SIAM J. Scientific Statis. Computing*, *9*, 609–638 (1988).

12. R. M. Hord, *Parallel Supercomputing in SIMD Architectures*, CRC Press, Boca Raton, FL, 1990.

13. S. A. Zenios, "Parallel Numerical Optimization: Current Status and an Annotated Bibliography," *ORSA J. Computing*, *1*(1), 20–39 (1989).

14. R. S. Barr and B. L. Hickman, "Parallel Simplex for Large Pure Network Problems: Computational Testing and Sources of Speedup," *Operations Research* 42(1), 65–80 (1994).

15. R. H. Clark, J. L. Kennington, R. R. Meyer, and M. Ramamurti, "Generalized Networks: Parallel Algorithms and an Empirical Analysis," *ORSA J. Computing*, *4*, 132–145 (1992).

16. D. L. Miller, J. F. Pekny, and G. L. Thompson, "Solution of Large Dense Transportation Problems Using a Parallel Primal Algorithm," *Oper. Res. Lett.* 9(5), 319–324 (1990).

17. J. Peters, "The Network Simplex Method on a Multiprocessor," *Networks*, *20*, 845–859 (1990).

18. E. L. Lusk and R. A. Overbeek, "Use of Monitors in FORTRAN: a Tutorial on the Barrier, Self-Scheduling Do-Loop, and Askfor Monitors," In *Parallel MIMD Computation: The HEP Supercomputer and its Applications*, J. S. Kowalik, (ed.), The MIT Press.

19. R. S. Barr and W. Stripling, "A Parallel Mixed-Strategy Branch-and-Bound Approach to the Fixed Charge Transportation Problem," Technical Report 92-CSE-19, Department of Computer Science and Engineering, Southern Methodist University, Dallas, 1992. (Presented at *Symposium on Parallel Optimization* 2, Madison, WI, 1990.)

20. R. L. Boehning, R. M. Butler, and B. E. Gillett, "A Parallel Integer Linear Programming Algorithm," *Eur. J. Oper. Res.*, *34*, 393–398 (1988).

21. D. L. Miller and J. F. Pekny, "Results from a Parallel Branch and Bound Algorithm for the Asymmetric Travelling Salesman Problem," *Oper. Res. Lett.*, *8*(3), 129–135 (1989).

22. M. K. Yang and C. R. Das, "A Parallel Branch-and-Bound Algorithm for MIN-Based Multiprocessors," *Perform. Eval. Rev.*, *14*(1), 222–223 (1991).

23. T. H. Lai and S. Sahni, "Anomalies in Parallel Branch-and-Bound Algorithms," *Commun. ACM*, *27*, 594–602 (1984).

24. X. Li and S. A. Zenios, "Data-level Parallel Solution of Min-cost Network Flow Problems Using ε-Relaxations," Report 91-05-04, Department of Decision Sciences, The Wharton School, University of Pennsylvania, Philadelphia, 1991.

25. S. S. Nielsen and S. A. Zenios, "Proximal Minimizations with D-Functions and the Massively Parallel Solution of Linear Network Programs," Report 91-06-05, Decision Sciences Department, The Wharton School, University of Pennsylvania, Philadelphia, 1991.

26. S. S. Nielsen and S. A. Zenios, "Solving Linear Stochastic Programs Using Massively Parallel Proximal Algorithms," Report 92-01-05, Decision Sciences Department, The Wharton School, University of Pennsylvania, Philadelphia, 1992.

27. H. Vladimirou and J. Mulvey, "Parallel and Distributed Computing for Stochastic Network Programming," Research Report SOR-90-11, Department of Civil Engineering and Operations Research, Princeton University, Princeton, NJ, 1990.

28. J. Gilsinn, K. Hoffman, R. H. F. Jackson, E. Leyendecker, P. Saunders, and D. Shier "Methodology and Analysis for Comparing Discrete Linear L1 Approximation Codes," *Commun. Statistics*, *136*, 399–413 (1977).

29. R. H. F. Jackson and J. M. Mulvey, "A Critical Review of Comparisons of Mathematical Programming Algorithms and Software (1953–1977)," *J. Res. Nat. Bur. Stand.*, *83*, 563–584 (1978).

30. H. P. Crowder, R. S. Dembo, and J. M. Mulvey, "On Reporting Computational Experiments with Mathematical Software," *ACM Trans. Math. Software*, *5*, 193–203 (1980).

31. R. S. Barr and M. Christiansen, "Parallel Auction Algorithm: A Case Study in the Use of Parallel Object-Oriented Programing," in *The Impact of Recent Computer Advances on Operations Research*, R. Sharda, B. L. Golden, E. Wasil, O. Balci, and W. Stewart (eds.), North-Holland, Amsterdam, 1989, pp. 23–32.

32. M. J. Quinn, *Designing Efficient Algorithms for Parallel Computers*, McGraw-Hill, New York, 1987.

33. J. L. Kennington and R. V. Helgason, *Algorithms for Network Programming*, John Wiley & Sons, New York, 1980.

34. R. S. Barr and B. L. Hickman, "A Parallel Approach to Large-Scale Network Models with Side Conditions," Technical Report 92-CSE-18, Department of Computer Science and Engineering, Southern Methodist University, Dallas, 1992.

35. B. L. Hickman, "Parallel Algorithms for Pure Network Problems and Related Applications," Doctoral dissertation, Southern Methodist University, Dallas, 1991.

36. M. M. Amini and R. S. Barr, "Network Reoptimization Algorithms: A Statistically Designed Comparison," Technical Report 90-CSE-4, Department of Computer Science and Engineering, Southern Methodist University, Dallas, 1990 (to appear in *ORSA Journal on Computing*).

37. R. Jain, *The Art of Computer Systems Performance Analysis*, John Wiley & Sons, New York, 1991.

38. R. L. Mason, R. F. Gunst, and J. L. Hess, *Statistical Design and Analysis of Experiments*, John Wiley & Sons, New York, 1989.

39. B. A. Murtagh and M. A. Saunders, "MINOS 5.1 Users Guide," Report SOL 83-20R, Stanford University, Stanford, CA, 1987.

40. W. D. Hillis, *The Connection Machine*, The MIT Press, Cambridge, MA, 1985.

41. D. Bertsekas, D. Castañon, J. Eckstein, and S. A. Zenios, "Parallel Computing in Network Optimization," Research Report 91-09-02, Department of Decision Sciences, The Wharton School, University of Pennsylvania, Philadelphia (to appear in *Handbook of Operations Research*).

42. C. Roucairol, "Parallel Branch and Bound Algorithms—An Overview," Rapports de Recherche N°962, Unitè de Recherche Intia-Rocquencourt, Domaine de Voluceau, Rocquencourt, Le Chesnay, France, 1989.

43. C. Seitz, "The Cosmic Cube," *Commun. ACM*, *28*, 22–23 (1985).

44. C. Moler, "Matrix Computation on Distributed Memory Multiprocessors," In *Hypercube Multiprocessors*, M. Heath (ed.), SIAM, Philadelphia, 1986, pp. 181–195.

45. J. L. Gustafson, "The Consequences of Fixed Time Performance Measurement," *Proceedings of the 25th Hawaii International Conference on Systems Sciences*, IEEE Computer Society Press, New York, 1992, pp. 113–124.

46. D. DeWitt and J. Gray, "Parallel Database Systems: The Future of High Performance Database Systems," *Commun. ACM*, *35*(6), 85–98 (1992).

47. T. A. Feo, M. G. C. Resende, and S. H. Smith, "A Greedy Randomized Adaptive Search Procedure for Maximum Independent Set." Technical Report, Operations Research Program, Department of Mechanical Engineering, University of Texas at Austin, Austin, TX, 1990.

48. P. M. Pardalos, A. A. Murthy, and Y. Li, "Computational Experience with Parallel Algorithms for Solving the Quadratic Assignment Problem," In *Computer Science and Operations*

Research: *New Advances in the Interfaces* O. Balci, R. Sharda, and S. A. Zenios (eds.), Pergamon Press, Oxford, 1992, pp. 267–278.

49. T. Cook, ''The Challenge of the 90's,'' Plenary speech at the TIMS/ORSA Joint National Meeting, Nashville, TN, 1991.

50. R. S. Barr and B. L. Hickman, ''On Reporting the Speedup of Parallel Algorithms: A Survey of Issues and Experts,'' In *Computer Science and Operations Research*: *New Advances in the Interfaces*, O. Balci, R. Sharda, and S. A. Zenios (eds.), Pergamon Press, Oxford, 1992, pp. 279–294.

RICHARD S. BARR
BETTY L. HICKMAN

RESEARCH AND DEVELOPMENT IN INFORMATION RETRIEVAL

INTRODUCTION

Uncertainty

The mechanization of information storage and retrieval using computer technology, best known as Information Retrieval, in short IR, has a history about as long as that of the modern computer. However, the roots of many of the ideas in Information Retrieval lie in the earlier traditional work of librarians.

Information retrieval has been traditionally described as the task of locating, in a textual database, those texts that are related to the information need of a person as expressed in a query. The state of the person engaged in active information seeking behavior such as submitting a query to an information retrieval system has been described as ''ASK'' (Anomalous State of Knowledge). This information need is fundamentally a conceptual need expressed by means of a natural language.

The query is a representation of the information need of the person. It must be expressed in a language understood by the system, traditionally a set of words. Some systems allow the user to directly express this need as natural language queries. Generally, however, those systems reduce the queries to their set of content words. Due to the inherent difficulty of representing an information need, the query in an information retrieval system is always considered as an approximation.

The meaning of the texts in the database must also be represented in such a form that it would be possible to make a comparison with the query. Usually, only the content words in the query and in the abstract of the document or in short documents are used in computing similarity. The words ignored are function words, that is, words belonging to closed syntactic categories such as articles, pronouns, or prepositions, which reflect nothing of the content of a particular document. The set of words chosen to represent the document in retrieval processing is called document-representative and the process of producing such representatives is called indexing.

Due to the linguistic nature of the texts, their representation is also considered as an approximation. Moreover, information need and texts can be considered as homogeneous because of the use of a natural language in order to express concepts. A concept can be described using whatever terms, sentences, or texts: This phenomenon is known as semiosis.

Because of the inherent error in representing the meaning of text and in capturing a person's information need, the retrieval module will, thus, retrieve texts that are not considered relevant by the user. That is the reason why the comparison of a query with texts, known as the matching function, leads to the selection of only possibly relevant items. The pertinence of the representation of both information need and text is uncertain; the relationship computed between them is also uncertain.

This intrinsic uncertainty of IR constitutes the major difference between information retrieval systems and other kinds of information systems. Although the matching function is strict in database models, it is not and cannot be strict in retrieval models. This is due to the intrinsic impossibility of comparing concepts. For database systems, an information need can always be mapped precisely into a query formulation, and there is a precise definition to which elements of the database constitute the answer. In information retrieval neither a query formulation can be assumed to represent an information need uniquely nor is there a clear procedure that decides whether a database object is or is not an answer.

Therefore, formal features (author, editor, etc.) have traditionally been added to the representation of texts. However, it remains that the textual nature of the objects manipulated by an information retrieval system is at the heart of Information Science and defines the main concepts of the field.

Evaluation

The intrinsic uncertainty of information retrieval also explains why evaluation is so important in this field. In fact, information retrieval has devoted considerable attention to the issue of evaluation.

Traditionally, evaluation is made in terms of effectiveness or relevance and efficiency. The distinction between efficiency and effectiveness of a retrieval system has occurred early and has stressed measuring effectiveness. A number of measures have been developed in order to measure effectiveness, the best known being recall and precision, which are typically presented as averages over sets of queries.

Precision is the proportion of relevant retrieved documents; recall is the proportion of relevant documents retrieved. From the two parameters, the first one can be calculated, the second one only estimated. Evaluation is not only important, it is also difficult.

Efficiency is also a major problem of information retrieval. Usually the database is very large: The index part of a database can take a huge amount of memory. Thus, a storage manager for storing and maintaining large collections of objects is necessary.

Evolution

Introduction

The evolving technology allows the evolution of the notion of a document. In the past, Information Retrieval systems were functioning with short textual documents, essentially abstracts.

The evolution of the notion of an electronic document has followed four paths:

- Documents have become full-text documents.
- Documents have become multimedia.
- Documents have become structured.
- Documents are integrated with factual databases.

Full-Text Documents

As already stated, retrieval was traditionally computed on short texts or abstracts. Nowadays, full-text document databases are established. The main question is whether or not the methods and results obtained with short texts are extensible to full-text documents.

One theoretical solution to this problem is to segment the text into smaller objects in order to retrieve text excerpts of varying size (1). This is now the direction of research taken in passage retrieval for full-text information systems. When text excerpts are available, the query similarity is often higher for the excerpt than for the full-text document. As a consequence, more relevant documents can be retrieved, both in terms of recall and precision.

Multimedia Documents

Evolving from unstructured textual information, documents now tend toward multimedia objects. One of the new questions arising with multimedia documents is the problem of the representation for the nontextual parts.

The research on indexing images is at an early stage and has to do with the fields of image processing and pattern recognition. For Information Retrieval, one of the questions arising is to know if those picture portions of a document must be indexed in a structured way or not.

Structured Documents

Evolving from unstructured textual information, documents now tend toward structured objects due to emerging standards such as SGML (Standard Generalized Markup Language) and ODA (Open Document Architecture), the existence of hypertext systems, and large, highly connected knowledge bases such as semantic nets.

A hypertext consists of a database of components links connecting text components. When the component are of a multimedia nature, one may speak about hypermedia systems. An Information Retrieval System should be able to take advantage of those structures.

Integration Between Information Retrieval Systems and Databases

The integration of text and fact retrieval is a major issue today (2). In the field of database, there is a growing interest in methods for coping with imprecision in databases. A first probabilistic model that can handle both vague queries and imprecise data exists. Probabilistic relational models combine probabilistic retrieval and relational algebra. This allows the user to ask for any kind of objects in the database, including documents.

Experimentation

Evaluation is tightly related to experimentation. As a consequence of the growing size of the texts and of the growing number of texts, databases are becoming larger; the problem of experimentation has become crucial. Experiments with real-sized corpus are necessary in order to evaluate and compare different information retrieval systems. It seems important to use test collections that are more representative for the intended applications, for example, collections with 10^5 and 10^6 documents with regard to large on-line databases.

Test collections have been developed in the past. Unfortunately, very few systems have been compared with the same collection, and there is a lack of test collection of realistic size. Evaluation using the small collections apparently existing may not reflect performance of systems in large databases. This is a major barrier to the transfer of laboratory systems into the commercial world.

It is the reason why, in the information retrieval community, conferences for the examination of full-text technologies (Text REtrieval Conference) are taking place. Their goal is to encourage research on text retrieval from large document collections by providing a large test collection and uniform evaluation procedures.

Experimentation with a large real-sized corpus is not only a problem of efficiency, it is also a problem of effectiveness. Both the sizes of texts and databases may affect the precision and recall levels of an Information Retrieval System.

THE NOTION OF RETRIEVAL MODEL

The notion of a retrieval model has the same fundamental importance as the notion of a data model in the field of databases: prior to implementation it sets out the intrinsic capabilities and limitations of any information retrieval system. Within the same class of systems, it becomes possible to compare the quality of distinct implementations. This combines programming aspects related to the completeness of the implementation and its efficiency.

Central to any effective information retrieval system is the identification and representation of document content, the acquisition and representation of the information need, and the specification of a matching function that selects relevant documents based on these representations. According to this, the basic architecture of all IR systems is the same: a query language for expressing the information need or problem, an indexing module for representing the content of the textual objects, and a retrieval module for comparing the query and object representation and deciding which to retrieve.

In this context, a retrieval model specifies the details of the document representation, the query representation, and the matching function, more specifically:

- A model for the documents that includes both the textual content and contextual attributes of the documents (author, editor, etc.)
- A model for the queries that includes the same two compounds within a query language that will be used to express the user's information needs
- A matching function that defines the way a query is matched against any modeled document. In other words, the matching function implements the notion of system relevance

Accordingly, research and development in information retrieval follows three avenues of interest:

- Acquisition of the query
- Document representation
- Matching

THE MODELS

Introduction

Three main classes of retrieval models are in current use (3): exact match models which form the basis of most commercial retrieval systems, vector space models which view documents and queries as vectors in a high-dimension vector space and use distance as a measure of similarity, and probabilistic models which view retrieval as a problem of estimating the probability that a document representation matches or satisfies a query.

Those three models are primarily focused on the comparison process and, thus, the matching function. They are based on word representations. As already stated, indexing a document or a query consists of lexical scanning to identify words, morphological analysis or masks tools to reduce different word forms to common stems, and counting occurrences of those stems. This approach, known as the key-word approach, is surprisingly effective as well as efficient and straightforward to implement.

The keyword approach postulates a rationalistic approach of semantics: A same concept is represented by the same words; in an Information Retrieval context, it would be very surprising that the same words would not be used in a query and in a text about the same subject (concept). This approach makes the economy of the meaning problem.

Boolean Model

The first one, the Boolean model, is based on the exact match principle; the other two are based on the concept of best match.

Boolean retrieval is based on the concept of an exact match of a query specification with one or more text surrogates (terms extracted from documents or formal features like dates, authors, manually assigned descriptors).

The result of the comparison operation in Boolean retrieval is a partition of the database into the set of retrieved documents and a set of nonretrieved documents.

The term Boolean is used because the query specifications are expressed as words combined using the standard operators of Boolean logic. It is important to distinguish between the use of Boolean operators in queries, which do not imply exact match model, and the use of Boolean logic as the interpretation of those operators. A Boolean query can be interpreted, for instance, using Boolean logic under an exact-match model using probability operators. Conversely, both of the best-match models can rank documents using Boolean queries. The distinction between the form of the query and the underlying retrieval model is, therefore, an important one.

The Boolean exact-match retrieval model is the standard model for current large-scale operational information retrieval systems. A major problem in this model is that it does not allow any form of relevant ranking of the retrieval document set. So, it is clear that some texts are more likely to be relevant (or are more relevant) to an information need than others. Presenting documents to the user in presumed order of relevance results in more effective and usable systems. Similarly, excluding documents that do not precisely match a query specification results in lower effectiveness.

Vector Space Model

Best-match retrieval models have been proposed in response to the problems of exact-match retrieval. The most widely known of these is the vector space model (4,5).

In the vector space model each document in the document collection is viewed as a set of words and is represented as a weighted-term vector. The document collection as a whole thus represents a vector space of dimension m, where m is the number of words in the collection. In this model, queries, like documents, are represented by weighted-term vectors.

The weight assigned to a particular term in a document vector is indicative of the contribution of the term in the meaning of the document. Although many vector-weighting schemes have been proposed, one of the most effective is *tf* − *idf* weighting, in which each term is represented by the product of its term frequency (the number of times the term occurs in the document) and a function of its inverse document frequency (the total number of documents in which the term appears). Thus *tf* − *idf* weighting reflects the importance of a term within the document itself and within the document collection as a whole.

In the vector space model, the similarity between a pair of items (e.g., a document–query pair or document–document pair) is represented by the mathematical similarity of their corresponding term vectors. One measure of the similarity of vectors is the cosine measure, the cosine of the angle between the two vectors: The smaller the angle between the corresponding vectors, the greater the similarity of the two vectors. Conceptually, the items are viewed as points in the vector space and the similarity of the items is inversely related to the distance between the two points.

Probabilistic Model

Probabilistic models have been developed, as the most successful approach for coping with uncertainty in information retrieval (6,7).

Probabilistic information retrieval models are based on the probability ranking principle. This states that the function of an information retrieval system is to rank the texts in the database in the order of their probability of relevance to the query. This principle takes into account that representation of both information need and text is uncertain and that the relevance relationship between them is also uncertain.

Probabilistic retrieval models compute the probability that a user's information need is satisfied given a particular text. Before it can be applied, any probabilistic model requires the estimation of certain parameters. Parameter estimation has been investigated for a long time. The probabilistic retrieval model generally estimates the probability of relevance of a text to a query on the basis of the statistical distribution of the terms in the database and in relevant and nonrelevant texts.

The binary independence model and the nonbinary independence models are two theoretical models that have been proposed in order to guarantee optimal retrieval. Optimality means that a document with higher probability of relevance to a query is assigned a higher similarity than a document with lower probability of relevance. The two models suppose a priori knowledge about some parameters used in the calculation of similarities. These two models make the same independence assumption: All terms are statistically independent within the relevant set and within the irrelevant document set. In the binary model, all document vectors are binary vectors. In the nonbinary model, the term frequency of each term in each document is taken into account. The models are strongly collection dependent: All the parameters of a model are only valid for the current collection. When a new collection is set up, the parameters from other collections cannot be transferred.

Information Retrieval as Inference

A new paradigm for information retrieval is emerging today; this paradigm views information retrieval fundamentally as an inferential process (8–10). This new paradigm generalizes the proof-theoretic model of database systems toward uncertain inference. This approach can be considered as a generalization of deductive databases, where queries and database contents can be viewed as logical formulas. Then, for answering a query, the query has to be proved from the database. For document retrieval, this means that a document is an answer to a query if the query can be proven from the document.

In order to cope with the intrinsic uncertainty of information retrieval, a logic for probabilistic inference must be introduced. As a probabilistic formalism for inference with uncertainty, Bayesian inference networks have been applied to document retrieval (11–13). These are directed, acyclic dependency graphs in which nodes represent propositional variables or constants and edges represent dependency relations between propositions. If a proposition represented by a node p ''causes'' or implies the proposition represented by a node q, a directed edge is drawn from p to q. The node q contains a matrix (a link matrix) that specifies $P(q/p)$ for all possible values of the two variables.

When a node has multiple parents, the matrix specifies the dependency of that node on the set of parents. It characterizes the dependency relationship between the node and all nodes representing its potential causes. Given a set of prior probabilities for the roots of the network, these networks can be used to compute the probability or degree of belief associated with all remaining nodes.

The network consists of a text network and a query network. The text network is built once for a collection. Its structure does not change during query processing. The query network consists of a single node representing the user's information need. A query network is built for each information need.

The text network consists of text nodes and so-called concept representation nodes. The assignment of a specific concept representation node to a text is represented by a directed arc to the representation node from each node representing a text to which the concept has been assigned. A representation node contains a specification of the conditional probability associated with the node, given its set of parent object nodes. Representation nodes (words) are generated through indexing. The estimation of the probabilities P(concept representation node/text node) is based on the occurrence frequencies of concepts in both individual texts and large collections of texts. In fact, the retrieval model based on the inference net model generally uses a form of $tf - idf$ weight for estimation of the P(concept representation node/text node).

The query network contains a single node corresponding to the event that an information need is met and multiple roots corresponding to the words that express the information need. A set of intermediate query nodes may be used to describe complex query networks, such as those formed with Boolean expressions.

For retrieval, a query network is built through interaction with the user attached to the object network. This allows the computation of the probability that the information need is met for any particular text and, consequently, to produce a ranked list of texts.

Comparison Among Models

The underlying theory is different for each of these model types and each has different performance characteristics, both in terms of retrieval effectiveness and computational requirements. At the same time, these models present a lot of similarities. The differences among these models can be viewed as differences in the way probabilities are estimated and combined in a probabilistic model. The estimation problems for the probabilistic and vector space models are essentially equivalent and exact-match models simply restrict the range of probability values to be considered (14).

The vector space and probabilistic models have been shown experimentally to offer significant improvements in retrieval performance over exact-match models. Some extensions to the Boolean model have also been proposed: The fuzzy set model and the extended Boolean model have been developed to overcome the fact that Boolean model does not support document ranking.

As most information retrieval models can be mapped onto an inference network, this formalism gives a unifying representation for the different models. It shows that the probabilistic approach is the current best theory for information retrieval.

In contrast to other models, the network approach does not require the derivation of a closed probabilistic formula so more complex interdependencies can be incorporated. Implementations of the model achieve high levels of recall and precision, relative to other systems.

Finally, there is a major problem today with the size of full-text retrieval collections. The difference in size with old ones is not only an efficiency problem. For instance, there is no certitude about the applicability of traditional methods, for instance, probabilistic, to those collections. So, the binary independence model seems inappropriate because it does not distinguish between a term that occurs once in a text and others that occur a lot of times and thus, represent an important concept of the document.

QUERY EXPANSION

Relevance Feedback

Introduction

It is well known that simple matching procedure between the terms contained in the queries and the terms describing the stored documents do not always produce acceptable retrieval output. For this reason, methods have been introduced in order to improve the retrieval of documents.

One of the most successful techniques developed in information retrieval is relevance feedback. Relevance feedback may be considered as an early form of learning and adaptation. Given the effectiveness of relevance feedback techniques, any information retrieval model should include this technique. In its simplest form, relevance feedback is used after an initial set of documents has been retrieved by comparing them to the query with a statistical ranking function. The person who generated the query then examines the top-ranked documents and identifies which of these documents are relevant. The words and word frequencies in these documents are then used to modify the initial query, and a new ranking of documents is formed.

Relevance feedback is the simplest method for acquiring more of the user's knowledge and using it to refine the query by adding related words and changing the relative importance of words in order to retrieve the relevant document and to discard the non-relevant ones. Retrieval experiments have shown that significant improvement in effectiveness can be obtained in this manner.

Drawbacks

Relevance feedback does, however, have some drawbacks. The principal ones are as follows:

- Identifying documents as relevant is a very crude way of identifying the information in the documents that is of particular interest. Many words from rele-

vant documents that are unrelated to the information need can be included in the query.
• Relevance feedback does not improve the initial search. If either no relevant documents or very few are found in the initial ranked list, users will be less likely to be satisfied with the system's performance.

Relevance Feedback and Inference Net Model
Relevance feedback was developed in the context of the vector space model. The development of an effective relevance feedback mechanism for inference nets is a potentially important area for further research. First results indicate that relevance feedback in inference networks is effective and that basic techniques of relevance feedback can be implemented in this retrieval model.

Relevance Feedback and Full-Text Collections
There have been results showing that the problem of choosing new terms from relevant documents to add to the queries becomes worse in full-text collections. Techniques that have been effective for terms selection in situations having small numbers of abstract-length documents do not appear to be sufficiently discriminating when used to select from thousands of possible terms.

Terms Clustering
A primary goal of IR research has been the development of effective methods for converting the original words of documents into a set of more effective content identifiers. Several of these representations make use of relationships between words in the original text. Term clustering attempts to group together terms with related meaning, so that if any one appears in a query, all can be matched with the documents.

Term clustering is a method that groups redundant terms, and this grouping reduces noise and increases frequency of assignment. If there are fewer clusters than there were original terms, then dimensionality is reduced as well. However, precision suffers because ambiguity can only be increased and meaning broadened.

Experiments using these techniques have not established their effectiveness, although a recent application of factor analysis shows some promise.

Encyclopedic Query Expansion
It is also possible to expand the terms of a query by using encyclopedic items considered as canonical texts about those terms. The texts produced are then confronted with the textual database using classical methods, for instance the vector space model (15).

DOCUMENTS CLUSTERING
Until now, it has been assumed that all the documents are independent from each other and that the retrieval of a document has nothing to do with other documents. Document clustering is used to group documents with related representations (16). In the case of

document clusters, representatives of the clusters are used for comparison with the query rather than the original text representations. The technique can be regarded, therefore, as transforming the original representations.

An advantage of the vector space model is that algorithms exist for structuring a collection of documents vectors in such a manner that similar documents are grouped together. A cluster hierarchy can be represented by a tree structure in which terminal nodes correspond to single documents and interior nodes (clusters) to groups of documents. Each cluster is represented by an artificial or typical element called the centroid. A search in a clustered file is more efficient than a normal retrieval process.

In a clustered search, the query is compared first to the centroids to determine those clusters most similar to the query and then to documents contained within the cluster(s) found most similar. One of the best-known algorithm for clustering is the complete-link clustering algorithm which produces tight clusters. The complete-link clustering algorithm is one of a class of agglomerative, hierarchical clustering algorithms. The theoretical properties of agglomerative, hierarchical algorithms are well known. These methods initially view the items to be clustered as singleton clusters.

The two most similar clusters are successively merged until only one cluster remains. In the complete-link method, the similarity between two clusters is defined as the minimum of the similarities between all pairs of documents, where one document on the pair is in one cluster and the other document is in the other cluster. As the criteria for joining two documents is very restrictive, the complete-link method tends to form small, tight clusters.

CONCEPTUAL INFORMATION RETRIEVAL

Introduction

Rather than using explicit inference rules, IR systems typically rely on implicit inferences in the form of key-word matching techniques. In the key-word approach, terms are chosen manually or automatically for the content identification of the various texts. It is widely believed that the key-word approach is not adequate for text content representation in information retrieval. Accordingly, attempts are made to refine the text indexing process by using more sophisticated linguistic and logical text analysis methods to obtain the needed text content representations.

Whatever philosophical approach of concept one can have, concepts are only investigatable through natural language. At a formal level, words and concepts are identical. It is, thus, possible to envisage procedures from words to concepts, and conversely.

Clustering of terms, for instance, may be considered as a kind of approach to conceptual information retrieval. In fact, a cluster of terms may be regarded as a concept representation. However, the automatic passage from terms to concepts implies the use of natural language techniques (17).

The first level of language traditionally used to represent meaning even in the keyword-based systems is morphology. The second one is syntax. Those two levels are considered as the most universal (formal) levels of languages.

Morphology

Morphology is a well-known level of language; it is used in information retrieval in order to reduce the inflected words to a canonical form because all word forms are meaning-preserving. This is of great interest especially for morphology-based languages (as opposed to syntax-based languages such as English).

Syntax

Syntactically based approaches to indexing have also been the subject of investigation. The domain independence of the language analysis is, indeed, an attractive feature for information retrieval applications.

Among the possibilities explored there is the use of syntactic analysis systems designed to identify multiword nominal constructs (noun phrases) for assignment to the texts replacing the standard single-term key words. The use of the phrase as part of a text representation or indexing language has been investigated since the beginning of information retrieval. It has always been felt that phrases, if used correctly, should improve the specificity of the indexing language and, consequently, the quality of the text representation. In fact, syntactic phrase indexing uses syntactic parsing to find groups of words in particular syntactic relationships and indexes a document on these groups. The underlying hypothesis is that syntactical analysis can reveal semantic relatedness or closeness. Each word in a phrase provides a context that removes ambiguity of the other and the meaning of a phrase is narrower than that of its component words.

The experimental results obtained with phrases do not, however, support this intuition. The results have been very mixed, ranging from small improvements in some collections to decrease in effectiveness in others. It has also been found that phrase index terms that have been automatically generated using statistical approaches yield about the same proportion of "acceptable indexing phrases" as the best-known methods which use language syntax, but the cost in computation time of using the statistical approaches is far less.

As a mean to overcome those limitations, there has been some research in order to use the structure of the resulting parse for indexing and representation. The dependency trees are used for searching through text in response to a query by generating a dependency structure from the analysis of the query input and by searching for tree structures and substructures in the stored database of dependency structures. The match also allows inferences of subphrases from larger ones to cater to syntactic variants. This can be used for a ranked match among phrases.

The results obtained suggest that the importance of representing structure in queries increases with document and collection size. However, the available experience with the use of automatic syntactic analysis indicates that such systems are not sufficiently powerful to generate large numbers of correct content identifiers in the absence of substantial semantic knowledge.

Conceptual Analysis

An ideal conceptual retrieval system requires semantic-level language processing. When natural language is processed at the semantic level, the process usually attempts to build up a representation of the meaning or actual content of the text and allows direct user queries on the content of the input texts. This usually requires a certain amount of world knowledge to be encoded and available to the language analysis process. Indeed, knowledge-based systems rely on having a detailed model of the applications domain. This domain knowledge can be quite complex, including arbitrary predicates on domain objects, causal relationships, and temporal relationships.

Knowledge-Based Systems

Knowledge-based systems analyze input texts into some knowledge representation formalism. Many formalisms have been proposed for the representation of knowledge, such as semantic nets, frames, scripts, or case-based reasoning.

Frame-based representation seems to be the most appropriate to represent knowledge in support of retrieval (18–20). A frame is a structured object, defined by a set of more general objects and a variety of restrictions on properties. Frames have an interpretation equivalent to noun phrases in natural language.

Network Structures

Network structures were devoted usually to knowledge representation, in which case the concepts of interest in a subject area are represented by network nodes, and the main relationships between concepts by network branches. The important issue is, of course, the network: how the search for plausible relationships between the concepts is conducted and how the overall credibility of those relationships is calculated.

In information retrieval, network structures are used with inference rules that specify how the representation must be used in attempting to relate the document representations to the query identifiers. Among the techniques used to derive query responses from the available document identifications are spreading activation methods and Bayesian inference techniques.

Bayesian inference techniques have already be described. The spreading activation techniques used in information retrieval are based on the existence of maps specifying the existence of particular relations between terms or concepts. The terms or concepts are represented by network nodes, and the relationships between terms or concepts are specified by labeled links between the nodes.

The node activation process used in the spreading models starts by placing a specified activation weight at some starting node representing a concept. The initial activation weight then spreads though the network, along the links originating at the starting node. The spreading action first affects those nodes located closest to the starting node, then spreads through the network along the links originating at the starting node. The spreading activation first affects those nodes located closest to the starting node and spreads through the network one link at a time. Normally, the activation weight of a node is computed as a function of the weighted sum of the inputs to that node from directly connected nodes.

Spreading activation systems differ from the earlier associative systems in several aspects.

- Each node is assigned a special activation weight, which depends on the starting activation weight and the link and nodes types traversed in the activation process.
- Distance constraints may be imposed in the activation process by stopping the activity at some specified distance from the original node.
- Nodes with a large branching ratio that are connected to many other nodes and, therefore, possibly representing ambiguous or general concepts may be bypassed in the activation process or may otherwise receive special treatment.

Obviously, the node activation process used in the spreading system is much more refined than the earlier node association procedures where all nodes and all links receive equal treatment. This implies that potentially, at least, much better retrieval results can be obtained by the spreading activation process than by the ordinary node association system.

The effectiveness of the process is, however, crucially dependent on the availability of a representative concept association map, and on the use of activation rules that can distinguish the useful from the extraneous nodes. It remains to be seen whether concept association maps can be designed for the subject areas covered by ordinary document collections and whether the refined spreading activation rules made possible by the system can actually be translated into workable node activation methods.

Frame and Networks

Until now, the work in inferential information retrieval has been based on quantitative inference. One of the problems associated with these quantitative approaches is that the user may not be able to or willing to provide a query represented by numbers, as humans frequently reason in qualitative rather than quantitative terms. In any case, one may have to make qualitative inference when the available information is not sufficient to provide a reliable estimation of the required numeric values.

It is possible to propose a framework for integrating different techniques and extending them to more interesting knowledge representations. For example, an information retrieval system can use case frame representations of query and document content produced by natural language processing techniques. So, the matching or inference component of the system would establish that the query case frame can plausibly be related to the document case frame by using relationships between concepts in a semantic network.

Evaluation

Substantial advantages have been claimed for the incorporation of knowledge representations and inference rules in information retrieval. It is likely that useful knowledge structures and reliable inference rules can be generated that may be valid in well-circumscribed situations within limited subject domains. However, doubt remains about the viability of techniques based on complex network representations when large text collections must be processed in unrestricted subject areas.

Any artificially constructed knowledge structure necessarily provides only partial and inadequate representation of meaning. As a result, it is not always clear what entities must be included in a knowledge base and what relationships between knowledge elements must be considered for particular applications. Attempts have been made to build very large knowledge bases covering unrestricted subject matter, but the applicability to large unrestricted document collections is unproven.

The main problem is, indeed, how to acquire the knowledge.

Knowledge Acquisition

Interactive Knowledge Acquisition

The use of knowledge-based and natural language processing techniques for document retrieval implies the ability to interactively acquire domain and linguistic knowledge from users. This is because in any real-time application, the knowledge that these techniques require will be incomplete or missing entirely. The determination of what type of knowledge can be acquired interactively and how it can be acquired is a fundamental issue.

In fact, this means that acquisition must be limited to types of knowledge that are both easily understood and directly applicable to retrieval such as "is-a," "instance-of," "part-of," "synonym-of," "related-to," all kinds of thesaurus like relations. The best way to do this is to suggest related concepts and ask the user to clarify and validate the relationship.

Relevance Feedback: Relevance feedback in information retrieval attempts to improve performance for a particular query by modifying the query, based on the user's reactions to the initial retrieved documents.

As already stated, classical relevance feedback has some drawbacks such as:

- Identifying documents as relevant is a very crude way of identifying the information in the documents that is of particular interest.
- Relevance feedback does not improve the initial search.

In order to overcome the drawbacks of relevance feedback, a lot of techniques have been used to acquire a detailed model of the information need. The relevance feedback process can be enhanced when the users not only specify the importance of retrieved documents but also the particular words and concepts that are important and their relationships to other concepts in the domain knowledge base. The dialogue between the system and the user must be designed to elicit as much as possible of the user's knowledge of the concepts mentioned in the query and in other domain concepts related to them.

Enhanced queries significantly improve the effectiveness of retrieval strategies. The users of an information retrieval system are able to provide a large amount of knowledge about the topic of their information needs and are able to make effective use of this knowledge.

Query Expansion: The typical use of knowledge in an information retrieval system is to expand the query terms with related concepts. In conceptual query expansion, in contrast to earlier method, queries are expanded by those terms that are most similar to the concept of the query, rather than selecting terms that are similar to the query terms (21). This can be done manually; it has been shown that user input about concepts related to those mentioned in an initial query, together with their relative importance, can significantly improve retrieval effectiveness. Conversely, other experiments have shown that expanding queries by having users select additional concepts from lists suggested by the system is often not effective. The reasons for these differences are not clear, although it appears that using only system suggestions is too restrictive and does not make full use of the user's domain knowledge.

An expert system can also provide on-line help for the reformulation of a query using knowledge-based processing techniques related to the domain of interest and eventually knowledge base of domain-independent search tactics.

Thesaurus

The missing semantic component might also be supplied by consulting thesauruses, and extracting from them the needed semantic specifications. Thesauruses of many kinds have been constructed, often tailored to particular topic areas, and designed to reveal a semantic relationship between thesaurus entries.

However, in practice, thesauruses are not easily incorporated into operational retrieval situations. The construction and use of vocabulary specification tools is an art, and there is no guarantee that thesauruses tailored to particular collections can be usefully adapted outside their original environment. In any case, it has not been possible to obtain reliable improvements in retrieval effectiveness by using preconstructed vocabulary schedules in heterogeneous text environments.

Lexicon

Another solution is to use lexical knowledge as provided by an electronical tool. At a lexical level, it appears that machine-readable dictionaries offer some interesting possibilities for indexing and representation of texts, but much experimental work must be done in order to determine how machine-readable dictionaries should be used effectively. Indexing by word senses using a machine-readable dictionary should lead to more effective text retrieval than indexing by word stems, and the huge amount of statistical information retrieval over recent decades could be used on representations consisting of word senses rather than word stems.

There is also a great deal of research in order not to use the lexicon for indexing or retrieval directly but to automatically deduce structured knowledge from text corpora. This is essentially concerned by the research on lexically and statistically based language processing.

The analysis determines the probability of word adjacencies based on the context and lexical knowledge. One has developed a procedure for building probabilistic grammars, which is being used to try to determine semantics from statistics. These kinds of development are promising for information retrieval because of the possibility of really integrating statistically based language analysis with the already developed methods of statistically based information retrieval. Progress can be expected in this area.

HYPERTEXT

Introduction

Hypertexts consist of a database of discrete component links connecting the text components and tools for creating and navigating through the combination of components and links (22). Hypertext allows easy linking, browsing, and navigation operations on pieces of texts. When combined with other media, (image, sound, etc.), one speaks of hypermedia.

The hypertext's flexible structure facilitates creation of multiple unique paths through a single corpus of texts. Hypertext links have three functions:

- Links denote associations between two highly related hypertext components.
- Links representing hierarchical structures allow for generalization and abstraction.
- Human computer interfaces can use links to facilitate vizualization of relationships denoted by the hypertext.

There has been a great interest in the information retrieval community about hypertext. Some researchers were convinced that hypertext was a new model of information retrieval (23,24). They made the assumption that the most elementary way of thinking and learning is by association.

Traditional hypertext link-based browsing is, indeed, a search process whose performance is deeply affected by the degree to which locally optimal choices result in a globally optimal hypertext path; performance deteriorates as a hypertext grows in size or becomes less formally structured. It is argued that in such circumstances browsing must be augmented with global search capabilities. These capabilities require the addition of an index structure "external" to the components and links constituting the hypertext database. The added index structure allows quicker access to individual components and allow access directly to two or more documents unconnected by links if the components share some string, keyword, or attribute. This structure is called the "hyperconcept database."

The hyperconcept database and the hypertext database can have different node and link types. Text nodes represent hypertext components in the hypertext database, and topic nodes represent indexing concepts in the hyperconcept database. Cross-reference links are used in the structuring of hypertext database components.

Semantic links made associations between topic nodes in the hyperconcept database (semantic association function). Connection links connect components in the hypertext database with topic nodes in the hyperconcept database (associative reading function).

The purpose of the semantic association function is to communicate the meaning the system assigns to the concepts with which the user expresses his information needs. Associative reading, instead, reduces the local disorientation of the user by providing a guide for browsing the structure of concepts and the hypertext of documents.

Automated Hypertext Generation

A major problem of hypertext is the determination of appropriate links between nodes. The more difficult task is in generating content-based links. Statistical methods have been used; they derive links that are available via a query that contains the text to the node. Strategy using knowledge-based methods for doing this is only usable in the limited subject domain of the knowledge base.

There exists, however, a model of knowledge-based text retrieval that transforms text representation structures into more abstract thematic descriptions of text content. This process attempts to discard irrelevant knowledge structures and to retain only salient concepts. The topical structure of the text is then represented in a hierarchical text graph which supports variable degrees of abstraction for conceptual retrieval. These text graphs provide a methodology for the automatic generation of hypertexts from text files. When applied to hierarchical hypertexts, these principles permit multiple levels of information granularity and abstraction features useful to design and use large-scale hypertext systems.

EFFICIENCY

Introduction

Because of the very large databases of texts used in information retrieval and the huge amount of auxiliary structures needed, efficiency is still a fundamental problem for information retrieval, despite the growth of the technology. It is constantly realized, for instance, that document collections grow faster than the sizes of the main memory that can be attached to computers. The effective implementation of information retrieval models depends crucially on an appropriate choice of information organization and on efficient file-access procedures (25,26). Due to the development of new storage technologies such as CD-ROM or WORM, research on access procedures on such devices also remains a fundamental issue.

Typically, during retrieval operations, words or phrases extracted from the query are presented to an index facility which maintains the text locations of all content words in the database. Depending on the application, the precision used to specify the location or address of a word may be extremely narrow (byte displacement in a text file) or very wide (the address of some text element, sentence, paragraph, or the text itself). Naturally, the precision of the address has an effect on the size of the index and on the nature of the queries that may be handled efficiently.

In response to a query, the retrieval system will access the index, extracting from it all required address lists, and it will then perform various manipulations on these lists in an attempt to determine the address of words that meet the constraints imposed by the query. The manipulations involve intersections, union, and sorting operations.

Numerous indexing techniques have been used for texts: the most classical ones are grounded on inverted lists. In most commercial systems, for instance, the Boolean retrieval model is still the underlying retrieval model. They generally make use of an inverted file, which associates with every term the documents and the locations where those terms occur.

One of the reason for the preponderance of Boolean retrieval is the amount of computing power needed for term-weighting retrieval. Term-weighting retrieval also make use of an inverted file, which associates with every term a list of postings. Such a posting is a pair, which means that the term in the consideration has a certain term weight in a particular document.

Inverted Files

Inverted lists can be implemented using a database dictionary and a posting file. A word from the query is found in the dictionary. The dictionary entry contains a pointer that selects a list of addresses specifying the text locations containing that word.

All such lists are stored in the posting file. Organization of the dictionary can be done using a variety of techniques such as b-trees or hashing. In most cases the technique will allow rapid updates to the dictionary when the database increases in size due to the appending of new documents. Accommodating list expansion in the posting file is a more challenging problem especially if one is concerned about space consumption of secondary storage.

Signature Files

A signature file is a more recent indexing technique. With a signature file, the contents of a record are encoded to form a bit string or signature for the record. During query processing, the signatures rather than the original data are searched to obtain the matching records.

For each record, each term is hashed onto a bit string of 512 bits, for instance. The hashed values of the terms are superimposed to form a single bit string for the record, which is called its signature. Because signatures are formed using superimposed coding, false matches may occur and must be identified. The bit strings for all the records are collected to form the signature file. The pointers to the data file are stored with the bit strings for fast access.

Index Compression

Text compression and image compression are problems that typically exceed information retrieval; the compression of the index is more typical problem for information retrieval. Information retrieval systems are great consumers of storage resources. This is due to the fact that in order to efficiently use the database, auxiliary structures must be created that themselves require a great amount of space.

The index of a full-text retrieval system is one of the largest components of a retrieval system: when uncompressed, it may be from 50% to 300% of the size of the uncompressed text. The index may become particularly large if it includes the positional information (e.g., section, paragraph, sentence, and word) needed to support a retrieval process that utilizes proximity information. Compression techniques for reducing index are, thus, very useful (27). For instance, an index may be stored as a bit matrix with rows corresponding to different words and columns to documents. Such a matrix is generally both very large and very sparse. It is possible to exploit possible correlations between rows and between columns by partitioning the matrix into small blocks and predicting the 1-bit distribution (presence of a word in a document) within a block. Each block is then encoded using traditional compression methods, that is, Huffman coding or arithmetic coding.

The drawback of compression in information retrieval is that fragments of the index must be decompressed at query time. In addition, in dynamic databases, the compression scheme must permit updates without excessive overhead. Parallel algorithms seem very useful in such context (28).

THE FUTURE OF INFORMATION RETRIEVAL

Introduction

Despite the progress that is made in mathematical formalism, it is widely believed that significant progress in information retrieval can only be made through the integration of conceptual retrieval tools and the embodiment of the retrieval models in new architectures taking the retrieval process as a whole, that is, including the context, the user in anomalous state of knowledge (ASK).

Traditionally, information retrieval models state what independent assumptions are being made but are less clear when it comes to defining relevance, that is, the aspects of the retrieval process related to the user. The vector space model, for instance, does not attempt to define anything to do with the external realities of users and information needs, and instead could be regarded as a mathematical description of one component of an information retrieval system rather than the information retrieval process as a whole. This situation has to be related to a state of the technique advocating a kind of division of labor division and a kind of rationalistic approach to the meaning problem.

First, the state of the technique: initially, mainframes with very complicated Boolean system led to a division of labor between the end user and the specialist, the information scientist. The interactive formulation of the query, that is, the context of the search, was out of the system. Today, the technical evolution allows systems dedicated directly to the end user.

This technical evolution goes along with a philosophical evolution in the information retrieval community. As in the artificial intelligence community, information retrieval has evolved from a so-called rationalistic to a dialogical and historical approach of meaning (29–31). This is essentially due to the influence of Wittgenstein and the ordinary language school with philosophers like Grice, Austin, or Searle in the computing science community.

The main hypothesis is that information retrieval is a language game in the sense of Wittgenstein; the structures used in information retrieval, essentially the structure of representation, must be able to support the way ordinary language is used. As most ordinary language is learned by demonstration rather than definition, and such demonstration requires immediate feedback, information retrieval systems must be built in order to facilitate the process of adaptive communication which typifies ordinary language usage.

Meaning is historical and dialogical, and information retrieval systems, as tools devoted to the construction of meaning in context, that is, the construction of the set of relevant documents, must be interactive systems. This approach to meaning implies that the interfaces have to be integrated as part of the information retrieval model.

The representation of information must be able to support a dialog between the user and the system, including research by association because a reasoning process of rational inference cannot explain all the aspects of meaning. This is due to the fact that documents not only have a content, but they have uses and these uses are not entirely deducible from the text of that document. The design of information retrieval systems cannot be separated from the activities in which they are embedded and must integrate knowledge about the procedural and application context where document are used (32).

Meaning is not only a rational process; meaning is also associative, and the system has to integrate tools able to support associative meaning construction process by browsing.

Consequently, the challenge of information retrieval research is to build into retrieval processes effective tools that the inquirer can use to challenge and assess the cooperativeness of the document retrieval process. This attitude has led to what is called intelligent information retrieval.

Intelligent Information Retrieval

Introduction

In the traditional architecture, information retrieval has considered the information retrieval process as a sequence of steps leading to a search statement or query, which is then put to the system. The system then responds to that statement, the user evaluates the response, and modification and iteration takes place as appropriate. In this view, interaction between the user and the other components of the system can take place at various steps, but its primary locus is at the search statement reformulation stage. The prototype model for this view of information retrieval is relevance feedback.

The above architecture dates from the late fifties, when the field of information science was emerging from the realm of library science. The automatic process of information retrieval was concentrated around the matching function. As already stated, the context of production of the query and the context of production of the texts were excluded. The integration of those contexts has led to new architectures called intelligent information retrieval. This architecture was founded on the recognition that information retrieval is inherently an interactive process. This alternative view is one of progressive development or refinement of a search formulation, to include search strategy, without necessarily establishing an explicit query formulation. In this view, the user's interaction with the database is construed as a process during which a search, and query, is gradually constructed through formulation and reformulation. Cognitive modeling of the user is of great interest in this context.

The main difference between this view of information retrieval and the more traditional one lies primarily in the status of the query, which in the traditional view is taken as an explicit statement of the user's information requirement but in the interactive view as a means to a possible desirable response. This is now the general approach taken by research in intelligent information retrieval. This approach lies at the basis of new design but applies equally to interfaces (33,34).

Because an interactive system allows more interactions than simply relevance feedback or query formulation, these interactions should be incorporated in new architectures, making the inference process explicit, allowing multiple formulation of queries, including conceptual information retrieval tools and browsing through hypertext links.

One advantage of the inferential net model is that it makes the plausible reasoning process explicit. Moreover, the inference net model allows the use of multiple sources of evidence including conceptual representations.

The new importance of interfaces, as being part of the information retrieval process, explains the importance of visualization. Visual representation can both provide a means for managing the complexity of large information structures and support an interface style well suited to interactive manipulation. It is convenient to use visually displayed graphic structures and a direct manipulation interface style to supply an integrated environment for retrieval. For instance, a common visually displayed network structure can be used for query, document content, and term relations. A query can be modified through direct manipulation of its visual form by incorporating terms from any other information structure the system displays. A thesaurus of terms and a document network provide information about a document collection that can complement other retrieval aids. Visualization of these large data structures makes use of fish-eye views and overview diagrams to help overcome some of the difficulties of orientation and navigation in large information structures.

Multiple Queries

Another way to enhance the process of information querying is to allow multiple queries. The inference net model offers a unified framework for the combination of different query formulations and types of query formulation in order to answer a single query: A Boolean and a probabilistic formulation can be used in parallel, where the network combines the results of both formulations. It is unlikely that any of these queries will correspond precisely to the information need, but some will better characterize the information need than others, and several query representations taken together may be a better representation and the information need than any of the individual queries.

Different search strategies and representations of document content retrieve different relevant documents for the same query. This fact is well known in information retrieval. Strategies that have similar average performance in terms of recall or precision can have different performance levels with particular queries, and the sets of retrieved documents tend to have low overlap.

Overlap measures quantify the uniqueness of sets of documents retrieved by different methods. Experiments using overlap measures have shown that different indexing methods result in the retrieval of different documents. These observations led to the investigation of techniques for choosing an optimal retrieval strategy for a particular query.

Browsing

In intelligent retrieval systems, the information need of the searcher is also satisfied by a process of navigation (browsing). Browsing implies that the information need is not only formulated into queries but formulation of the need is acknowledged as difficult and error-prone. Navigation is supported by advanced user interfaces, an aspect that is increasingly being recognized as influencing the effectiveness of the retrieval of information. It is the reason why the user interface should also be given consideration within the framework of the information retrieval model.

One way of merging information retrieval systems and hypertext is to use information retrieval techniques to generate hypertext links and then use browsing as the sole means of exploring the database. It is also possible to convert an SGML structure into hypertext links. The method consists in passing the text which is marked up in SGML to an SGML parser that validates the document by generating the SGML parse tree. The parse tree can then be used to produce nodes suitable for insertion to a database.

The inference net model can also easily be extended in order to include hypertexts links.

Conclusion

As a conclusion, the current interest, clearly stemming from the growth of computing power and the dialogical approach of meaning, is in integrated, customized information management systems. These are multifaceted information systems intended to bring together different types of information objects and to support different types of information use, from rational and inferential search to associative search, exploiting modern workstation technology, and most importantly, calling on artificial intelligence in manipulating the knowledge required to connect different objects and use conveniently transparent and personally oriented ways.

From a theoretical point of view, a well-defined paradigm is emerging. This paradigm is grounded on the fact that the process of information retrieval is essentially an inferential process. This paradigm leads to a much deeper understanding of the problem of information retrieval, opening up the prospect for a unified theory. A number of useful tools developed for probabilistic and belief inference networks, logic programming, and approximate reasoning can be applied directly to information retrieval.

Moreover, by interpreting information retrieval as a plausible inference or an approximate reasoning process, it becomes possible to take advantage of the semantics of the information items. This view overcomes some inherent limitations in conventional models that rely largely on statistical information. This constitutes one of the main advantage of the inference net framework: it allows multiple sources of evidence.

Finally, the inferential net model can be extended to traditional applications of information retrieval such as relevance feedback and new one such as hypertext.

Information retrieval has in the past received a lot of tools from related fields, such as natural language processing, artificial intelligence, human–computer interaction (HCI). In the future, models and tools developed in order to give an answer to the complexity of cooperative information retrieval will also be of great interest for those connected disciplines, especially through the integration of statistical and symbolic tools.

The homomorphism between the representations allowing expansion and reduction (indexing) of meaning in a dialogue process can be used as a tool for developing intelligent strategies, allowing better effectiveness of retrieval systems.

REFERENCES

1. G. Salton and C. Buckley, "Approaches to Passage Retrieval in Full Text Information Systems," *16th ACM–Sigir Conference*, Pittsburgh, 1993, pp. 49–58.
2. J. S. Deogun and V. V. Raghavan, "Integration of Information Retrieval and Database Management Systems," *Inform. Processing Management 24*(3) 303–313 (1988).
3. N. J. Belkin and W. B. Croft, "Retrieval Techniques, in *Annual Review of Information Science and Technology*, M. E. Williams (ed.), Elsevier, New York, 1987.
4. G. Salton and M. J. McGill, *Introduction to Modern Information Retrieval*, McGraw-Hill, New York, 1983.
5. G. Salton, *Automatic Text Processing*, Addison Wesley, New York, 1989.
6. N. Fuhr, "Probabilistic Models in Information Retrieval," *Comput Jl*, 243–255 (1992).
7. N. Fuhr and C. Buckley, "Probabilistic Document Indexing from Relevance Feedback Data," *13th ACM–Sigir Conference*, Brussels, 1990, pp. 45–61.
8. C. J. Van Rijsbergen, "A Nonclassical Logic for Information Retrieval, *Comput. J.* (1986).
9. C. J. van Rijsbergen, "A New Theoretical Framework for Information Retrieval," *9th ACM–Sigir Conference*, Pisa, September, 1986, pp. 194–200.
10. C. J. Van Rijsbergen, "Towards an Information Logic," *12th ACM–Sigir Conference*, Boston, 1989, pp. 77–86.
11. W. B. Croft and R. Das, "Experiments with Query Acquisition and Use in Document Retrieval Systems, *13th ACM–Sigir Conference*, Brussels, 1990, pp 349–368.
12. W. B. Croft, H. R. Turtle, and D. D. Lewis, "The Use of Phrases and Structured Queries in Information Retrieval," *14th ACM–Sigir Conference*, Chicago, 1991, pp. 32–45.
13. H. Turtle and W.B. Croft, "Efficient Probabilistic Inference for Text Retrieval," *Proceedings of RIAO*, Barcelona, 1991, pp. 644–661.
14. H. R. Turtle and W. B. Croft, "A Comparison of Text Retrieval Models," *Comput J.* 279–289.
15. G. Salton and C. Buckley, "Automatic Text Structuring and Retrieval Experiments in Automatic Encyclopaedia Searching," *14th ACM–Sigir Conference*, Chicago, 1991, pp. 21–29.
16. D. D. Lewis, "An Evaluation of Phrasal and Clustered Representations on a Text Categorization Task," *15th ACM–Sigir Conference*, Copenhagen, 1992, pp. 37–50.
17. A. Smeaton, "Progress in the Application of Natural Language Processing to Information Retrieval Tasks," *Comput. Jl*, 268–278.
18. K. Dahlgren, *Naive Semantics for Natural Language Analysis*, Kluwer Academic Publishers, Amsterdam, 1988.
19. E. A. Fox, "A Design for Intelligent Retrieval: The CODER System, *Second Conference on Computer Interfaces and Intermediaries for Information Retrieval*, May 1986, pp. 135–154.
20. E. A. Fox, "Development of the CODER System: A Test-Bed for Artificial Intelligence Methods in Information Retrieval," *Inform. Processing Management, 23*(4), 341–366 (1987).
21. D. Harman, "Towards Interactive Query Expansion," *11th ACM–Sigir Conference*, Grenoble, 1988, pp. 321–331.
22. M. E. Frisse, "Searching for Information in a Hypertext Medical Handbook," *Commun. ACM, 31*, 880–886 (1988).
23. M. Agosti, "Is Hypertext a New Model of Information Retrieval," *Proceedings of Online Information 88, 12th International Online Meeting Information*, London, 1988, pp. 57–62.
24. M. Agosti and P. G. Marchetti, "User Navigation in the IRS Conceptual Structure Through a Semantic Association Function," *Comput. J.*, 194–199, (1992).

25. F. J. Burkowski, "Surrogate Subsets: A Free Space Management Strategy for the Index of a Text Retrieval System," *13th ACM–Sigir Conference*, Brussels, 1990, pp. 211–226.

26. W. B. Frakes and R. Baeza-Yates, *Information Retrieval Data Structures and Algorithms*, Prentice-Hall, Englewoods Cliffs, NJ, 1992.

27. A. Bookstein and S. Klein, "Generative Models for Bitmap Sets with Compression Applications," *14th ACM–Sigir Conference*, Chicago, 1991, pp. 63–71.

28. C. Stanfill, "Partitioned Posting Files: A Parallel Inverted File Structure for Information Retrieval," *13th ACM–Sigir Conference*, Brussels, 1990, pp. 413–428.

29. D. C. Blair, *Language and Representation in Information Retrieval*, Elsevier, New York, 1990.

30. D. C. Blair, "Information Retrieval and the Philosophy of Language," *Comput. J.* 200–207, (1992).

31. T. Winograd and F. Flores, "Understanding Computers and Cognition," *A New Foundation for Design*, Addison-Wesley, Reading, MA, 1987.

32. A. Celentano, M. G. Fugini, and S. Pozzi, "Querying Office Systems About Document Roles," *14th ACM–Sigir Conference*, Chicago, 199, 183–190.

33. N. J. Belkin and P. G. Marchetti, "Determining the Functionality and Features of an Intelligent Interface to an Information Retrieval System," *13th ACM–Sigir Conference*, Brussels, 1990.

34. P. D. Bruza and T. P. van der Weide, "Stratified Hypermedia Structure for Information Disclosure," *Comput. J.* 208–220, (1992).

Y. Chiaramella and J. P. Chevallet, "About Retrieval Models and Logic," *Comput J.* 233–242 (1992).

C. Faloutsos and S. Christodoulakis, "Signature Files: An Access Method for Documents and its Analytical Performance Evaluation," *ACM Trans. Office Imform. Systm.*, 2(4), 267–288 (1984).

F. Rabitti and P. Zezula, "A Dynamic Signature Technique for Multimedia Databases," *13th ACM–Sigir Conference*, Brussels, 1990, pp. 193–10.

K. Sparck Jones, *Information Retrieval Experiment*, Butterworths, Needham, 1981.

T. Tzeras and S. Hartmann, "Automatic Indexing Based on Bayesian Inference Networks," *16th ACM–Sigir Conference*, Pittsburgh, 1993, pp. 22–34.

C. J. Van Rijsbergen, *Information Retrieval*, Butterworths, Needham, MA, 1979.

JEAN-LUC VIDICK

RISK ENGINEERING: ANALYSIS AND MANAGEMENT

MICROCOMPUTERS AND RISK

Microcomputers today are being employed in increasing numbers in commerce, industry, services, and research. In many applications, a malfunction of the computer or associated equipment for whatever reason may have serious financial, environmental, social, or life-threatening consequences. Clear examples are the control, monitoring, and shutdown systems of chemical or nuclear plant and cash-transfer systems. In this article a review of the methods available for identifying and quantifying risks are presented, although it must be stressed that a methodology for designing a risk-free computer system does not exist.

Risk can be defined as

Exposure to a situation which involves the possibility of loss or an unfavorable outcome.

The analysis of risk is essentially concerned with the likelihood of an event occurring and the consequence should that event occur. In most cases, a number of possible undesired events must be considered.

In examining risks associated with microcomputers it is important to consider the complete system and not just the computer itself. It is often possible to design systems where the computer can respond in a safe manner to failures in connected equipment and vice versa.

A hazardous situation may arise in a microcomputer system as a result of the following:

- A fault, failure, or malfunction of the computer or connected equipment
- An error in the design, manufacture, assembly, or operation of the system
- Human action which may be error or intentional actions such as hacking, fraud, malice, or the introduction of a virus.

The fault, error, or action may originate in the system hardware or software.

The mechanism by which a hazardous situation arises is usually one of the following:

- An incorrect action is taken: Shares are bought instead of sold; signal lights are set to green instead of red.
- An action is taken when it should not be or no action is taken when one should be: Reverse thrust on a jet engine is deployed in flight, or fire extinguishers are not activated in the event of a fire.

The underlying cause of such actions or inactions may be as follows:

- A failure event: The failure of a computer controlling a chemical plant may initiate actions leading to fire/explosion.
- The unavailability of the system: An air traffic control system is disabled by a computer being inoperative.

Risk engineering is a combination of risk analysis and risk management. Risk analysis forms the major part of the remainder of this article, but as it falls within the activities of risk management, the latter is briefly discussed first.

RISK MANAGEMENT

The principles of risk management can be summarized as a three stage process:

- **Risk Identification**. The assessment of potential physical damage and direct or consequential losses and liabilities.
- **Risk Reduction**. Corrective measures through changes in design, procedures, or organization taken if the first stage indicates an unacceptable level of risk. Organizational measures may involve risk transfer by legal or contractual provisions, the extent to which this is possible may be restricted by the national law of the country where the operation is based.
- **Risk Financing**. The establishment of financial backup through insurance or contingency funds which will be adequate to cover liabilities.

In practice, this is not a one-time process. The reassessment of potential damage will take place as corrective measures are taken and a balance will be struck between risk reduction and risk financing. Risk assessment is essentially contained within the risk identification stage.

The boundary of the analysis must be established as part of the risk management process. Generating electricity in the United Kingdom using coal-fired stations is low risk if the coal is mined in Poland and the effects of the pollution are in Scandinavia.

OVERVIEW OF RISK ANALYSIS

When considering the risks involved in employing a microcomputer-based system it is important to recognize that malfunctions during operations may originate at a much earlier stage in the life cycle of the system. Figure 1 illustrates, in outline only, the stages of the life cycle of a computer system.

The first stages of the life cycle, the requirements analysis and system specification, are human activities often requiring individual or group decisions and judgment. Errors at these stages can result in eventual malfunction or failure of the system. Such errors are particularly difficult to identify for the following reasons:

- They are not amenable to formal methods of analysis and quantification.
- Both the system design and the test and diagnostic procedures are based on the requirements analysis and specification. Hence, the tests will not reveal errors initiating from these stages.

The following stages follow normal hardware and software engineering practice, much abbreviated for the purpose of the diagram. From a risk point of view, the questions of testing, diagnosis, and maintenance deserve further comment.

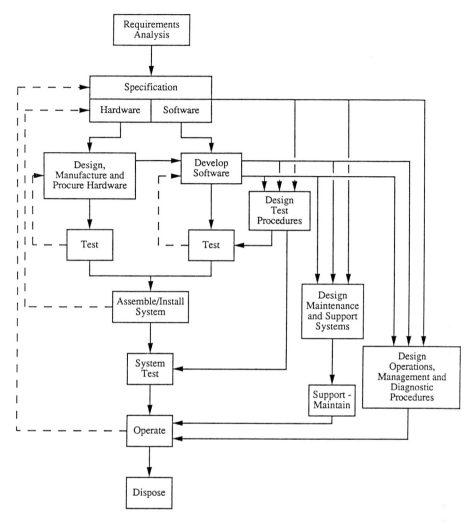

FIGURE 1   Typical stages in the life cycle of a microcomputer system.

- Testing can, in principle, be employed to demonstrate that a system is functioning as required by the specification. In practice, two factors prevent this. First, a complete end-to-end test is often not possible; one would not initiate a fuel melt in a nuclear reactor to test a shutdown system designed to deal with such an event. Second, some malfunctions may only occur following a specific sequence of input conditions, as there are effectively an infinite number of such sequences; exhaustive testing of the complete system is impossible. The second point is particularly pertinent to software testing.
- Diagnostic procedures may be off-line or on-line. Off-line diagnostics may be performed at regular intervals to reveal faults as a part of the maintenance process or after a malfunction of the system has been observed. On-line diagnostics monitor the system continually while it is operating; following the detection of

a fault, the operator may be alerted or some action may be taken automatically, for instance, to render the system safe if a fail-safe mode exists. It is important to recognize that on-line diagnosis increases the complexity of the system and, hence, the *total* number of system failures. What it does is reduce the number of high-consequence failures. There are many examples of automatic diagnosis (test) equipment generating more failures than the basic system itself. Both forms of diagnosis can contribute to risk reduction.

- Maintenance clearly influences the risk attributable to a computer system, particularly where the risk is related to the unavailability of a system rather than to a particular failure event.

It is during the operation stage that any risk associated with a computer system can lead to undesirable consequences. During operation, the system may have unrevealed within it faults resulting from errors in specification, design, manufacture, procurement, or assembly, or such faults may be created during periodic upgrades of hardware and software.

These faults may lead to failure of the system only under certain operating conditions. In addition, the system will be liable to component failures and human error (maintenance and operation) from time to time. Risk during system disposal is important in some systems but is unlikely to be a problem with microcomputers.

Throughout the design process it is important to recognize that microcomputers involve interaction between humans and machines. The following should always be in the designer's mind:

- Will the machine allow a human error?
- Can human intervention control a machine error?

Following from these we have:

- How can a human/machine detect an error in the other?

A framework within which risks may be analyzed is shown in Figure 2; this is general rather than specific to computer systems. There are three fundamental areas to be considered in the analysis of risks: the likelihood, the consequence, and the risk acceptance level. These three together form the basis on which decisions are made. The sections which follow discuss the three areas and the decision-making processes.

RISK LIKELIHOOD

Observed Risk

There are many cases where events occur with sufficient frequency for reliable estimates of risk to be determined from observation or measurement. The risk of fatalities at work or in transport are examples.

Some care may be needed in analyzing or interpreting the data as presented. For example, in comparing the risks involved in various modes of transport, the data could be presented in a number of ways:

Fatalities per passenger mile
Fatalities per passenger hour
Fatalities per journey
Fatal accidents per journey

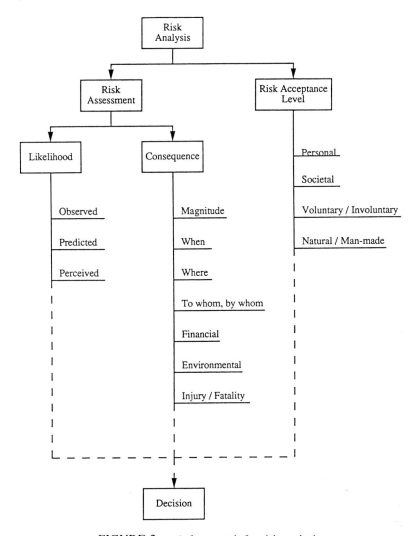

FIGURE 2   A framework for risk analysis.

The first favors air transport because each aircraft carries many people over long distances. For an individual, it could be argued that fatal accidents per journey is more meaningful, as air accidents are usually associated with take-off and landing and not particularly related to length of journey. Comparing the risk of travel by air or car needs consideration beyond the raw figures which are often quoted, as the risk of an accident on the road is related to the hours or miles driven.

In the case of microcomputers, data are readily available (although manufacturers are often reluctant to release it) for failure rates of processors and small systems, for example, flight control computers or electronic point of sale tills. These data in itself are usually insufficient for risk analysis purposes (it may be for some very simple systems). Systems, in which failure would lead to a significant loss, financial or otherwise, are designed to fail extremely rarely in such modes. Observations of common failures are helpful in that it provides data for prediction of critical mode failure rates.

Predicted Risk

System Structures

The techniques of Reliability Engineering may be employed or adapted to predict risk likelihood in many cases. The method requires a knowledge of how the component parts of a system are assembled (its structure) and the failure rates of these components.

Most basic engineering systems, including microcomputer systems, are, in reliability terms, in-series systems. The characteristic of such systems is that the whole system fails if any of its component parts fail. Figure 3 shows a simple microcomputer system as a series system.

The overall failure rate of in-series systems (typically expressed as failures per 1000 h) is the sum of the failure rates of the components. (Note at this stage we are referring only to the gross failure rate; we are not considering what happens when the system fails.) For systems in which the consequence of failure is small, such configurations are satisfactory, for example, personal computers used as word processors. The support, maintenance, and operational procedures are also related to the consequence of the system being unavailable; for example, frequency of data backup or availability of a spare processor or hard risk.

When a simple series system results in a failure rate which is too great, a number of alternative configurations may be employed:

- Parallel systems
- Standby systems
- *K* out of *N* systems (parallel)
- *K* out of *N* standby systems

It should be noted that the terms "series" and "parallel" refer to the effect on system reliability and not necessarily to the physical layout. Figure 4 shows fluid control values in parallel configuration for the cases where flow must stop and flow must start on receipt of a control signal.

The choice of configuration or structure depends on a number of considerations, with reference to microcomputer systems:

- Is the consequence a result of the failure event (e.g. false signal engaging reverse thrust of a jet engine in flight) or of the amount of time that the system is unavailable (many commercial applications). Parallel structures generally ensure no interruptions, whereas standby systems require time for failure-sensing and switch-over to take place.
- Benefits of standby systems are that components are generally less liable to fail in standby mode; they are not consuming energy while on standby, and it is often possible to switch over only a small part of the whole system after failure.

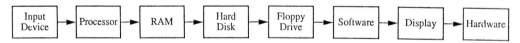

FIGURE 3   In terms of reliability, a microcomputer system consists of a number of items connected in series, that is, the system fails if any component fails. Downgraded operation as a result of partial failure is not addressed in this simple analysis.

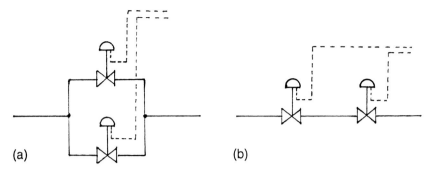

FIGURE 4   (a) Parallel system where it is essential that valves open on receipt of signal (b) Parallel system where it is essential that valves close on receipt of signal.

- A problem with computer systems is that if parallel units are used and one is faulty, it is not always obvious which one is faulty. They are giving different outputs but which is correct? In such cases, a two out of three configuration with majority voting is often employed.

It should again be noted that the use of parallel or standby units will *increase* the total number of failures while reducing the number of high consequence failures. See Refs. 1 and 2 for an extended discussion of structural methods.

Markov and State Transition Models

There are limitations to the methods of reliability analysis indicated earlier arising from assumptions:

- Failure rates are assumed to be independent of operating conditions; in practice, failure rates may depend on workload or whether an item is in operational or standby mode.
- Basic theory deals with components and systems that are either working or failed; in practice, systems may operate in a number of states between these extremes and risk may be a function of the current state.

Markov or state transition models can overcome these limitations in many cases. A set of operating states is defined:

$$X_i \qquad i = 1, M.$$

For each state, we can define the probability of the system existing in that state at some time t:

$$x_i(t) \qquad \text{(state probabilities)}$$

and some measure of system performance in that state

$$C_i \qquad \text{(capability)}$$

In the current context, C_i will be a measure of risk. State transition probabilities p_{ij} define the probability of the system when in state X_i making the transition to state X_j in some time interval. These p_{ij} are related to the failure and repair characteristics of the system

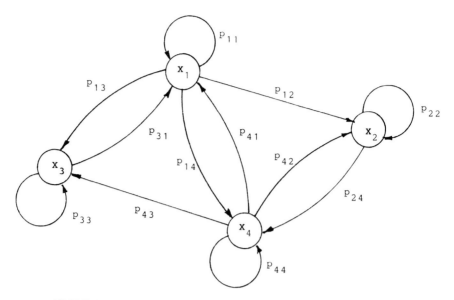

FIGURE 5   State transition, or Markov, model in diagrammatic form.

components and may be time and condition dependent. A state transition diagram of the form shown in Figure 5 can be constructed. (Many p_{ij} will be zero and such links are not shown.)

A state transition matrix corresponds to the diagram, and from this, the state probabilities can be calculated either transiently or in equilibrium if p_{ij} are not time variable. For a complete description of the methods, see Ref. 3. State transition methods are not without their difficulties; chiefly, the size and complexity of the models that can arise from only moderately large systems.

Event Tree Method

Event trees are a bottom-up approach to the analysis or prediction of risk where an undesired result may occur after a series of sequential events. A typical diagram is shown in Fig 6. Probabilities assigned to each event can be compounded through the tree to estimate the probability of the consequences at the right.

Related to event trees are failure mode and effect analysis (FMEA) and failure mode and effect and criticality analysis (FMECA). Here the results of the event tree are presented in tabular form (Table 1), although in many cases the tables are produced without formally going through the tree diagram process.

Once again, the problem of complexity arises because tree diagrams and FMEA tables can quickly become very large and the effort involved in creating and analyzing them can be considerable.

See Refs. 4 for a fuller description of event tree methods and Ref. 5 for FMEA and FMECA methods.

Fault-Tree Methods

Event-tree methods have the disadvantage that many branches can lead to consequences which are of little interest, for example, safe conditions. Fault-tree methods approach the

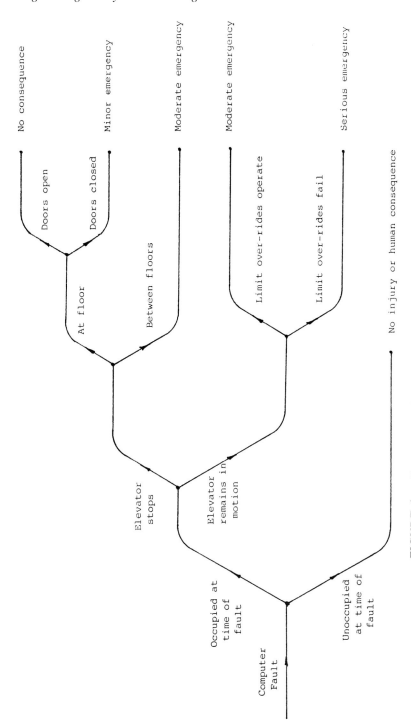

FIGURE 6 Event tree for failure of a microcomputer-controlled elevator.

TABLE 1   Examples of a Failure Mode and Effect Analysis; Based on a Computer Control System

Item	Failure mode	Operation phase	Probability per Year	Failure effect-criticality code[a]		Comment
Micro-processor	All output high	On-line	20×10^{-6}	Loss of Control	4	Emergency system should shut down plant.
	All output low	On-line	15×10^{-6}	Loss of control	4	Emergency system should shut down plant.
	Persistant random error	On-line	5×10^{-6}	Disturbance to plant operation	3	Operator should detect erratic plant behavior and report fault.
	Occasional random error	On-line	10×10^{-6}	Temporary disturbance to plant operation	2	May go unnoticed or may cause a transient that disturbs production.

[a]Criticality code: 1—minor consequence; 5—potentially catastrophic.

problem-from the top by considering a particular consequence (the top event) and then describing logically the events which would lead to its occurrence. The diagram consists of series-linked AND and OR functions with details added to make visual interpretation easier. An example is shown in Figure 7.

Once the diagram is created, which is essentially a manual task, computer analysis can be used to determine the combinations of events that will lead to the top event and the associated probabilities. The most likely causes of the top event are, thus, determined, which is helpful at the design stage if the likelihood has to be reduced or for diagnostic purposes if the event occurs during operation.

As with event trees, the size of fault trees can be a problem. The technique is used extensively for safety analysis in the nuclear industry in which trees containing hundreds of AND and OR gates have been generated. Reference 5 gives a detailed description of the method.

Both event-tree and -fault tree methods rely on manual construction of the basic trees that are produced by people with a knowledge of the system and its operation, and of how it may behave under various fault conditions. There is a potential weakness here in that all possible conditions may not be envisaged (possible cannot!) and that expected behavior under certain conditions may be mistaken on the part of the analyst.

Perceived Risk

In many cases, a designer or analyst must design a system that the customer or public judges to have an acceptable risk level. This judgment will often be based on a perception of risk rather than real knowledge of (or belief in) the available observed or predicted figures. The safety of nuclear power or an individual's fear of flying are obvious cases where risk perception is important.

Most people are not well informed about risk levels, either likelihood or consequence, and are influenced by reports in the media which are biased toward the unusual and dramatic and by psychological factors such as fear of the unknown. What general conclusions can be drawn indicate that people tend to underestimate high risks and over-

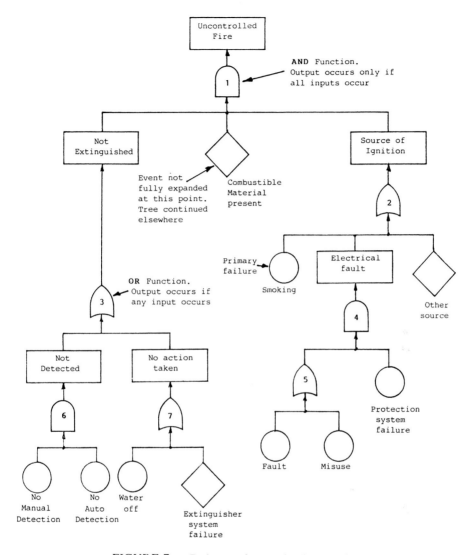

FIGURE 7   Fault tree of events leading to a fire.

estimate low risks, the latter posing a particular problem for those trying to design low-risk systems (6).

An anomaly is that following a major incident, actual risk decreases as a result of measures taken to prevent a repeat, but perceived risk increases due to media coverage.

Another aspect of perceived risk is the tendency of people to trust other people more than machines. Driverless trains are technically feasible, but their introduction has been slow because the traveling public has to be convinced of their safety.

RISK CONSEQUENCE

In parallel with the likelihood of an event, the consequence should that event occur must be considered. The consequence is usually expressed in one of the following ways:

- Financial loss
- Fatalities to people
- Injuries to people
- Damage to the environment
- Degradation of quality of life

In many cases, the consequence will be a combination of these in either an additive or trade-off sense; a flood defense scheme may save people but damage the environment.

Of the variables listed, financial loss and fatalities are quantifiable, although the actual level may be uncertain before an event occurs. Other variables are less easy to quantify and compare because they are not precisely defined, as the effects of an event are not sufficiently predictable.

Except in the case of a simple financial loss, moral and ethical issues may create problems in assessing consequences. Lives lost in an accident is one measure of consequence. An alternative is life-years lost, implying that the death of an older person is more acceptable than that of a young person whose life expectancy is longer; the actual variable is still quite precise. It has been suggested that quality-adjusted life-years (QALYS) lost could be a measure of consequence. This poses the question of quality of life (not a precisely defined variable), and if we assume that standard of living contributes partly to qualify of life, this implies that the death of a rich person is more serious than that of a poor person. Problems of this type may not cause difficulties in consequence evaluation, but they will when it comes to making decisions about which system to implement.

RISK ACCEPTANCE LEVELS

Most people go about their everyday activities without giving thought to risks which underlie the activities they are undertaking. Some people will avoid certain activities because they perceive the risk to be high (travel by underground railway perhaps); others will decline certain activities if an opportunity arises for the same reason (parachuting, for example). Others will campaign relentlessly to have a particular risk reduced, whereas other accept it without a thought.

In a financial sense, risk acceptance levels are related to the amount (consequence) that an individual or organization can withstand without significant effect to their normal behavior or operations. A consequence beyond that limit will lead to measures to avoid the risk or to ensure against it.

When the consequence involves injury or fatality, the establishment of acceptable risk levels is less easy and often less rational. There are a number of ways of presenting risk data; Tables 2 and 3 and Figure 8 illustrate some of these; to repeat what was stated earlier, most people are unaware of these figures.

One must be careful in interpreting or using these data. High-consequence events are relatively rare, and changes in real risk are probably taking place at a rate which is too fast for historical data to give a reliable indication. The data also vary considerably from country to country. Figure 8 illustrates the distortion that can occur through media coverage of events, with frequent low-consequence events contributing most to the fatality count and receiving the least attention.

TABLE 2   Expected Loss of Life Expectancy
Due to Various Causes (Days), U.S. Data

Cigarette smoking	2,250
Being 30% overweight	1,300
Low standard of education	850
Low socioeconomic status	700
Occupational accident	
High risk	300
Medium Risk	74
Low risk	30
Accident in the home	95

Note: Effects are often indirect and not necessarily independent. The reduced life expectancy for people of low
socioeconomic status reflects factors such as diet, health
care, and their propensity to smoke more.
Source: B. Cohen and I. J. Lee, Adapted from "A Cata-
log of Risks," *Health Phys.*, *36* (1979).

TABLE 3   Activities Estimated to Increase the Probability of Death in Any Year by
One Part in a Million

Smoking 1.4 cigarettes
Drinking 0.5 liters of wine
Working 1 h in a coal mine
Traveling 10 miles by bicycle
150 miles by car
1000 miles by jet
One chest X-ray
Living 2 months with a cigarette smoker

Note: For average males in the United Kingdom, the chance of death in 1 year at age 25 is 0.001,
and at age 70 is 0.056. For females, the figures are slightly lower.
Source: Adapted from R. Wilson, "Analyzing the Daily Risks of Life," *Technol. Rev.*, *81* (4) (1979).

Generally speaking, the level of "background" risk in developed countries reduces
with time as a consequence of improved technology, greater awareness, greater concern,
and social change.

For an individual, the level of risk acceptance is greatly altered if the risk is entered
into voluntarily; certain sporting activities are clear examples of this. The distinction between voluntary and involuntary is not always clear. If one can travel to work by car,
train, or bicycle, how much of the decision is voluntary?

DECISION PROCESSES

There are no universally recognized methodologies for making decisions in circumstances where risk is involved. What follows is a review of some of the procedures
adopted.

Where the risk involves only the loss of money, the principle for making decisions
is usually uncontroversial; an expected loss resulting from a risk situation can be offset

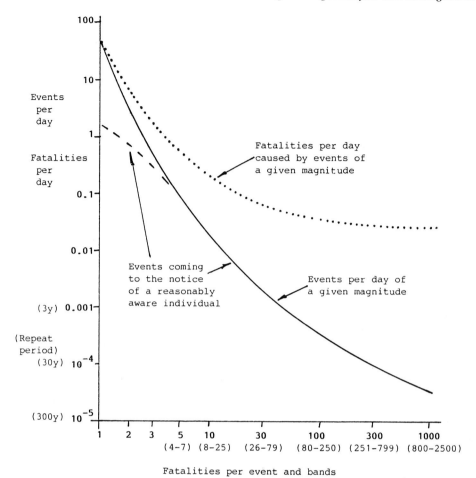

FIGURE 8   Everyday risk in the United Kingdom based on reported accidents. There are not sufficient observations for the above curves to be precise except at the low-consequence end.

against the benefit of installing the system. Insurance can often be used to offset small-likelihood–high-consequence risks. There may still be problems in that the likelihood or magnitude of the consequence may not be known precisely.

In many other cases, decisions are based on accepted national or international standards, and no direct calculation of risk is undertaken. Standards are updated as new technologies are introduced and often after events have shown them to be inadequate.

Where risks are concerned with fatality or injury decision strategies become much less precise, those adopted include:

- New better than old; machine better than man. This means that when a new device is installed to replace an existing device or a manual operation, the overall risk should be lower. This is very relevant to computer control in many areas from process plant to air-traffic control.
- Insignificant additional risk. Where new technology offers improved performance, this should be seen as introducing an insignificant additional risk. Flight-control computers which reduce fuel consumption are an example.

- Absolute minimum risk. In some cases a strategy of risk minimization is possible; medical diagnosis is an example where the hazard from X-ray examinations on a regular basis has to be offset against the benefit of detecting and successfully treating a disease.
- Statutory limits. In a few cases, authorities set limits for certain events in terms of likelihood. The Nuclear Regulatory Commission in the United States sets such limits for various reactor malfunctions.
- Cost–benefit approach. A financial consequence is placed on risks of all types. In the case of injury or fatality, the figure used often reflects litigation awards in similar cases. This approach has been used in some transport studies in the United Kingdom. A variation of this approach is to use utility rather than cost as a common variable to assess all factors.

A number of other factors affect the decision process:

- Is the decision-maker affected by the decision? Some decisions are personal in that the individual decides to take a risk, for example, taking a job at a chemical plant. In other cases, the decision-makers are not affected, sanctioning the building of a chemical plant near a town where they do not live.
- Risk-exposure relationships. In some cases, it is preferable (from a society point of view) that a few people are exposed to a high risk, the learning effect reducing the marginal risk as their exposure increases (deep divers on oil production platforms). In other cases where a risk threshold exists, exposing many people for a short time is preferable (exposure to chemical or nuclear hazard).

To conclude the discussion in decision processes, it is worth mentioning that decision are not "logical" across various risk areas affecting society. There are many examples, but one which illustrates the point is

According to some calculations, US society spends about $140,000 in highway construction to save one life and $15 million to save a person from death due to radiation exposure (7).

EXAMPLES OF A MICROCOMPUTER SYSTEM INVOLVING RISK

Figure 9 shows the essential features of a microcomputer-based protection system which is designed to monitor the operation of a chemical plant and shut it down safely if abnormal conditions arise. The system itself may be the cause of a hazard if due to faults in design, manufacture, or in operation, it fails to shut the plant down (a trip) or shuts it down for no reason (spurious trip).

An analysis of the system was carried out to examine the effects of hardware failures in service. Faults in design, manufacture, or software were not considered. The effects of hardware-component failures on the operation of the system could be classified as follows:

- Revealed faults

  - Faults with no functional effect that allow the continued operation of the system. Printout of daily records may not be possible, for example.
  - Faults detected by continuous on-line monitoring that lead to remedial action or shutdown if safety is threatened.

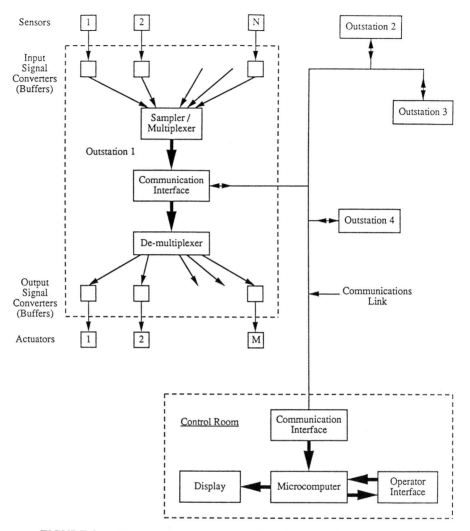

FIGURE 9   Structure of a computer-based monitoring and shutdown system.

- Faults detected by regular periodic tests, for example, by injecting false input signals with outputs inhibited. May lead to remedial action or shutdown if safety is threatened.
- Faults resulting in spurious action; a partial or total plant trip. Potential hazard.
- Unrevealed faults

  - Faults that have no noticeable effect on operation. An open-circuit failure of a noise-suppression capacitor may have no effect at all.
  - Faults that are dormant until some input or output condition occurs. May result in failure to trip the plant. Potential hazard.

Some results of the analysis are shown in Tables 4 and 5. One point to note is that more than two-thirds of the failures are of equipment attached to the computers and not of the computers themselves.

TABLE 4   Overall Failure Rate of a Computer-Based Protection System with 50 Sensors and 80 Actuators located in 3 outstations. Estimated from Component Count and Failure Rates

Component	Number in System	Failure Rate per 10^6 h	Total Failure Rate per 10^6 h
Microcomputer, memories (outstation)	3	50	150
Input buffers	50	2	100
Output buffers	80	3	240
Communications	1	60	60
Operator terminal	1	200	200
Input sensors	50	2	100
Actuators	80	4	320
		TOTAL	1170

Note: The total failure figure corresponds to about 10 failures per year.

TABLE 5   Source and Effect of Failures in 1 Year for Some Components of the Computer-Based Protection System

Source	Revealed Tolerable Faults	Spurious Trip	Trip Failure
Microprocessor, memories	0.13	1.05	0.0004
Input Buffers	0.43	0.43	0.00008
Output Buffers	1.05	1.05	0.01

Notes: The low figure for trip failures is due in part to the low proportion of time that the plant is in a condition where a trip is warranted (assumed to be 1 h per year).

The spurious trip resulting from a microcomputer fault is a planned and controlled fail-safe function in most cases.

A spurious trip or trip failure originating from an output buffer is likely to be partial; those originating from input buffers or computers are likely to be total.

The sensors and actuators are likely to be a more serious source of trip failure because on-line testing is often difficult or impossible.

REFERENCES

1.   E. E. Lewis, *Introduction to Reliability Engineering*, Wiley, New York, 1987.
2.   P. D. T. O'Connor, *Practical Reliability Engineering*. Hayden, Carmel, IN, 1985.
3.   J. G. Rau, *Optimization and Probability in systems Engineering*, Van Nostrand Reinhold, New York, 1970.
4.   J. R. Thomson, *Engineering Safety Assessment—An Introduction*, Longman, White Plains, NY, 1987.
5.   Society of Automotive Engineers, *Fault/Failure Analysis Procedure, SAE Aerospace Recommended Practice 1979*, ARP926A, Society of Automative Engineers, 1979.
6.   V. T. Covello et al. (ed.), *The Analysis of Actual Versus Perceived Risk*, Plenum Press, New York, 1983.
7.   R. A. Howard et al., "The Value of Life and Nuclear Design," in *Proceedings of the Tropical Meeting on Probabilistic Analysis of Nuclear Safety*, 1978.

BIBLIOGRAPHY

Dhillon, B. S., *Reliability in Computer System Design*, Ablex, Norwood, NJ, 1987.

Handmer, J., and E. Penning-Rowsell, *Hazards and the Communication of Risk*, Gower, Brookfield, VT, 1990.

Henley, E. J., and H. Kumamoto, *Reliability Engineering and Risk Assessment*, Prentice-Hall, Englewood, NJ, 19.

J. C. Consultancy, *Risk Assessment for Hazardous Installations*, Pergamon, Elmsford, NY, 1986.

Longbottom, R., *Computer System Reliability*, Wiley, New York, 1980.

Myers, G. J., *Reliable Software through Composite Design*, Van Nostrand Reinhold, New York, 1975.

Pradhan, D. K. (ed.), *Fault Tolerant Computing*, Prentice-Hall, Englewood Cliffs, NJ, 1986.

Rosenthal, L. S., *Guidance on Planning and Implementing Computer System Reliability*, National Bureau of Standards Special Publication 500-121, U.S. GPO, Washington, DC.

Withers, J., *Major Industrial Hazards*, Gower, Brookfield, VT, 1988.

Wong, K. K., *Computer Security—Risk Analysis and Control*, Hayden, Carmel, IN, 1977.

FRED J. CHARLWOOD

RISK MANAGEMENT IN FINANCIAL SERVICES: CURRENT APPLICATIONS OF TECHNOLOGY AND BUSINESS REENGINEERING

INTRODUCTION

Our purpose is to describe the application of computer technology to automate and provide decision assistance for risk management processes in financial services.

As a starting point, the industry's accumulated experience has clearly shown that the better a firm's understanding of a decision domain and the processes in that domain, the more likely will be its success in applying computer technologies to it. Second, risk management lies at the core of a company's effectiveness. Applying computers to it has strategic consequence. Those risk management system initiatives that we have observed in industry to be most successful have been intense, long-term efforts undertaken with the guidance and support of senior management. In other words, they tend to be "big ticket" projects targeting substantial returns in the areas of better decision making, reduced labor costs, and faster responsiveness for new and existing customers.

In banking, risk management involves many areas. These include credit authorization for both consumer and industrial loans, foreign currency risk, and various types of risk associated with changing interest rates. Investment banks and venture capital firms must constantly manage risk in their financing activities on behalf or in partnership with clients. In insurance, risk management encompasses many dimensions: the risk of death, of poor health, of injury and disability, and of damage or destruction to property.

To describe the decision-making processes for all these sectors is beyond the reach of a single article. Therefore, we will focus on one particular industry, insurance, and apologize to those readers wishing for cases in banking and other financial services arenas. However, we have found that the processes and technologies employed to improve risk management in insurance serve as a useful model for other financial service applications.

RISK MANAGEMENT IN INSURANCE

What does managing risk mean for insurance?

First, it is a very complex domain. For individuals and businesses, risk is the possibility of loss or injury and is an element of everyday life that cannot be avoided, be it the loss of life, health, or property (1). Insurance is the most common way that individuals and organizations protect themselves from certain well-defined potential financial losses. For a risk to be insurable, however, the element of chance must be present wherein the loss is caused by an uncertain future event. The ability to effectively manage risk lies at the heart of insurance companies. It directly translates into the margin between net premiums taken into a firm and claims paid out. Understanding the riskiness of new potential business for given insurance products also allows a company to fine-tune its pricing. Thus, improving the management of risk can enhance an insurer's competitiveness and profitability.

Insurers have developed substantial expertise in the management of risk. The insurer must make complex decisions about the selection, pricing, and claims adjudication of insured risks. At the core of these processes is underwriting. Underwriting operationalizes a company's various approaches to managing risk (2). Up until recent years, these decisions could only be made by individuals with considerable skill and experience. Today, however, these decision processes can be programmed, automating a certain percentage of underwriting decisions and providing underwriting assistance to human decision-makers for others. Herein lies the great opportunity for expert systems.

Underwriting is an information-intensive process in which decisions on individual risks are made in the context of actuarial and business principles. At the most general level, underwriting involves the examination of a specific risk, classifying it into a larger group of similar risks, and then calculating the financial impact of the potential loss. For life insurance, these risks take many forms: health problems (known as medical impairments), financial problems, and both occupational and vocational hazards. Risk assessment decisions must be made in the context of a competitive market environment, balancing the expected loss with the expected investment income from the use of the pooled funds. Often, the underwriting decision is based on incomplete and uncertain information. In life insurance, this could be observed physical symptoms that might be indicators of a range of potentially fatal medical conditions.

The quality and, more specifically, the correctness of individual decisions and the consistency of decisions for groups of similar cases have a direct, long-term impact on the insurer's profitability because, within the industry, the proportion of premiums paid for death claims is greater than that paid out to cover the insurer's administrative costs. Consistently good underwriting makes a company competitive; consistently poor underwriting will lead to a level of claims that, in a period of consolidation within the industry, will cause severe business damage.

Figure 1 shows the typical information flow through an insurance company. This insurance model applies broadly to life, health, and property insurers.

The first step in the information flow is that agents, known in the industry as "producers," sell insurance policies and complete with the applicant the standard form of the insurance company. This information passes into "Preliminary Processing," where routine details about the risk from insurance application forms are entered into a computer system. Screening may then occur (often called "Jet Screening"), where applications are checked for completeness, and a certain percentage "accepted" or "declined" based on simple company rules concerning acceptable and uninsurable risks.

The Data Entry and Preliminary Processing areas can collectively be referred to as the "front end" of the insurers' new business processing. A current trend in many sectors of the insurance industry is to allow Data Entry and Preliminary Processing to occur at agent's offices, reducing the insurer's home office clerical requirements and improving response time to the customer. Additionally, insurers working with expert system technology perform automatic underwriting on "simple" cases, that for some firms, can be a substantial portion of their business.

Applications still needing further information for decision making enter the "back-end" of the process. This is called "Underwriting" in Figure 1. Specific "problems" of

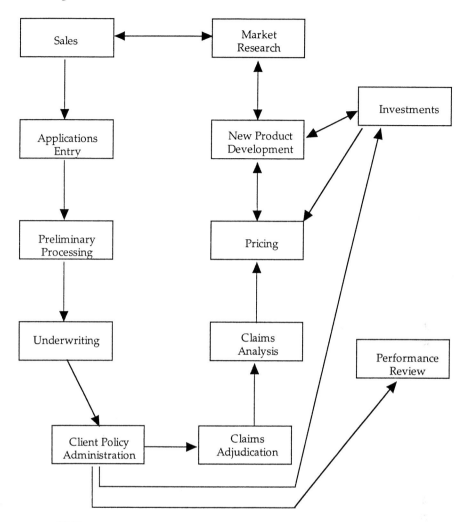

FIGURE 1   Insurance information flow and expert system opportunities.

a case are identified. This itself can be difficult for complex cases. The information needed in part or in whole to resolve these problems is then ordered, either by computer, telephone, or mail. Ordering and receipt of "requirements" can become a bottleneck; managing this process becomes an essential part of any comprehensive risk management system. One might call this phase of the process "Initial Underwriting." It should be noted that within "Initial Underwriting" a company can include highly complex heuristics for decision making. In life and health insurance, for example, these include analysis of occupations, hobbies, certain medical conditions, family history, and personal health.

Cases not resolved pass into the stage of underwriting that focuses on the investigation of medical problems for life insurers, and other types of very complex financial problem areas for property insurers. This stage of the process incorporates the most complex heuristics in terms of procedural and theoretical underwriting knowledge. Life insurers do medical impairment underwriting: medical examinations, including tests such as EKGs, are often studied by underwriters to resolve "problems." In health insurance, similar and more extensive types of medical information may be "ordered" by underwriters from health providers and assessed for risk. Effective underwriting may also require the assessment of interactions between individual problems. For example, in life insurance, the mortality probabilities increase with a combined situation of moderate diabetes and a history of coronary heart disease. Many diseases have levels of severity, which, once resolved, translate directly into different levels of risk and, hence, insurance premiums for those cases not rejected.

At any stage of the underwriting process, problem resolution (rejection of the case or acceptance) leads to a determination of applying either "standard" rates or a surcharge over standard based on a mapping of the level of nonstandard risk to increased premium rates. This mapping is insurer-specific, reflecting its philosophy in terms of risk management and product pricing. Underwriters must, therefore, consider the specific insurance product requested by the applicant.

Finally, just as the underwriting process is linked to many information sources both within and external to an insurance company, a comprehensive underwriting expert system must maintain linkages with many other distinct information systems. The major information linkages, using life underwriting as an example, are shown in Figure 2. At the front end of the process is the integration of the underwriting expert system with the company's Data Entry system. In the future, it is expected that the entry of new applications information will be increasingly distributed to producers in the field, making the systems integration task all the more complex. Then, during Preliminary Processing, the expert system must access the insurer's Alpha indices (to see the proposed insured's his-

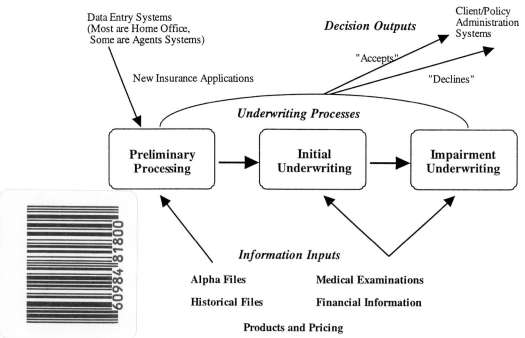

FIGURE 2   Information linkages in the new business processing.

tory with the company) and other specific historical databases. In the more extensive underwriting stages, interfaces are maintained with providers of medical examinations. At the back end of the underwriting process, including both Initial Underwriting and Impairment Underwriting, the expert system must also be integrated with the company's product pricing databases and, ultimately, with policy issue and administration systems. Therefore, computerized risk management in insurance, if taken to its logical conclusion, entails high degrees of systems integration and database administration.

To complete the workflow in Figure 1, accepted applications are then sent onto the company's administrative systems, "Client/Policy Issue and Administration," which deal with customer billing and agent commissions. "Claims" comes into effect upon a policy-holder's death. Claims are adjudicated, and then studied in statistical fashion to examine the effectiveness of product pricing and underwriting. Information from Claims is employed by an insurer's actuaries for research and insurance product development or pricing changes. The three workflow boxes in Figure 1 that represent these activities are "Claims Analysis," "Pricing," and "New Product Development." "Market Research," "Investments," and "Performance Review" comprise the remaining aspects of the insurance work flow. All of these areas are candidates for applying expert system technology to improve decision making.

To summarize, therefore, underwriting is part of what is generally known as the "New Business Process" in insurance companies. Great changes are afoot. The new business process is illustrated in the most general way in Figure 3. The left-hand side of the figure shows where most insurance companies stand today, and where they wish to be in the not too distant future.

There is a clear strategic consequence to expert systems in the insurance industry. Faced with increasing competitive pressures, insurance company managers, be it in life, property and casualty, or health businesses, know that their companies need to become more efficient and effective in keys areas. These include selling the products, providing services to customers, and administering current business. It is recognized that a significant part of meeting this challenge lies in the combination of applying new technologies such as expert systems and using organizational and job redesign techniques to achieve organizational flattening. Operating expenses tend to be higher in the two middle layers, Data Entry and Preliminary Processing, as compared to Sales and Underwriting. Technology may, therefore, provide a way to not only substantially reduce expenses but also to greatly improve service to the customer. However, this potential cannot be realized without immense effort in the areas of work-flow reengineering and large-scale organizational change.

BUILDING A RISK MANAGEMENT SYSTEM: JOHN HANCOCK

What technologies have insurers applied to risk management decision processes? What have been the tangible benefits providing by these computer applications?

Many insurers have applied knowledge-based system technology to underwriting. These have often been called underwriting "expert systems." Expert systems in insurance is a topic that has been explored by a number of authors in fairly recent publications. Davenport (3), Jones (4), and Conversano (5) all presented case study descriptions of expert system applications for insurance underwriting. Similarly, Meyer and Curley (6) use a case study of an life insurance underwriting system to illustrate a conceptual frame-

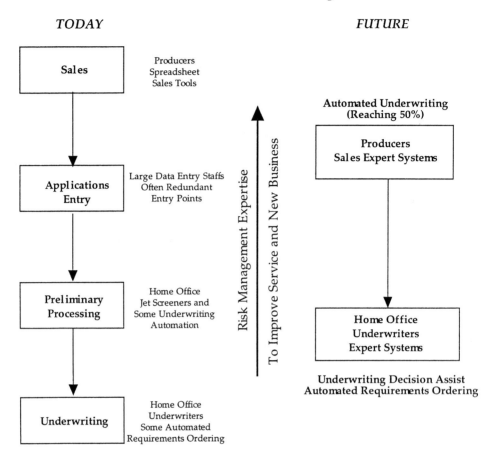

FIGURE 3   The potential of expert systems to change workflow, enhance productivity, and improve service; new business processing as an example.

work for managing expert system development by assessing embodied knowledge and technological complexity. DeTore (7) described the suitability of expert systems for the theoretical and procedural decision processes in insurance. May (8), Coopers and Lybrand (9), and Baker (10) provide more general descriptions of major trends in the application of new information technologies to insurance. Additionally, industry members now meet annually at the expert Systems in Insurance Conference to discuss expert system issues (11).

Just as a company must be focused in its business strategy, focus must be defined for technology applications. The ability to direct a company's energies to the most appropriate technological efforts is an essential part of "the art" of productive innovation. Whether it is the result of the intuitive insight of a powerful "champion", or of an effective strategic planning process, the ability to focus a firm's resources on new technological endeavors that "matter most" can have a powerful competitive impact. A large number of articles have reported the use of information technologies as a competitive weapon (12–15). In the domain of expert system technology, project selection has been considered from several basic perspectives. Davis (16), Prerau (17), and Leonard-Barton and Sviokla (18) have all observed the linkage between existing competitiveness in decision making and the need for and subsequent application of expert system technology. Feigenbaum et al. (19) showed how a number of large corporations leveraged key human decision-making assets through expert systems to become more responsive and productive as companies. Meyer and Curley (6) described how the accumulated industry insight of senior management makes its participation in the initial systems planning of major strategic expert system applications important. The general thrust of all these works is that major expert system applications are a direct outgrowth of business strategy, enhancing existing business processes, and potentially creating new business value by utilizing the firm's core "knowledge" assets.

A good example the application of knowledge-based system technology to risk management is John Hancock Mutual Life Insurance Company (20). John Hancock processes a very large volume of new insurance applications, in excess of several hundred thousand cases each year. New life insurance applications come from over 300 field offices maintained by John Hancock across the country. Underwriting had always been performed at corporate headquarters.

In 1986, an internal technology consultant in Corporate DP who was scanning a variety of new technologies as they might be applied to insurance, generated a game plan for applying expert systems. The concept was appealing to senior management, and the Underwriting Department agreed to both fund and contribute its domain expertise to the effort. Four years later, with the participation of five experienced underwriters and about a dozen computer programmers from Corporate DP, the expert system is now being distributed to the field. The applications from over 300 field offices are processed through the expert system.

The very nature of the John Hancock's business dictated a "front-end" focus for initial expert system development efforts, i.e., to automatically approve as many new cases as possible without human intervention. The nature of John Hancock's "retail" life insurance business, i.e., the large volumes of new applications, was highly amenable to a production-oriented underwriting system. In fact, it was a greater priority to provide broader underwriting knowledge to more cases than deeper underwriting knowledge to fewer, more complex cases.

The initial version of the system targeted Intelligent Data Entry and Preliminary Processing (the middle two boxes on the left-hand side of Fig. 1). The systems works in two parts. First, a data entry and preliminary processing system functions on PCs in agent offices to scan, validate, and otherwise review applications information "at the source." These data are then electronically communicated to the home office in Boston, where a "batch" automated expert system on a mainframe uses a specific set of heuristics or decision-making rules to actually make decisions on cases. The system approves a large percentage of new cases by examining applicant's occupations, financial issues, and certain medical conditions. To do this, it must check a number of other databases, some of which are external to the company: history of prior insurance and medical records. The percentage of automatically approved applications is approximately 33% and it occurs within 24 hours.

In a subsequent stage of development, the system has evolved toward the back end of underwriting by computerizing more complex aspects of decision making. The knowledge bases in John Hancock's "Automated Underwriting" modules define underwriting problems. Checks are made for additional information requirements depending on policy amount. The applicant's "insurable interest" is assessed, as are the ability to pay premiums, the riskiness of his avocations and vocations, family history, and certain medical conditions. New information requirements can also be ordered automatically at this point. The collective functionality of these two modules target the Initial Underwriting shown earlier in Figure 1.

Cases that are not approved by the expert system are available to human underwriters through an "Electronic Worksheet" the next day. Underwriters can then approve these cases, or order additional information requirements through the Worksheet. An additional percentage of new cases can be approved for issue at this point, still within the following day after initial data entry. Currently, that percentage is approximately 10%. For example, if a proposed insured admits to a minor illness 2 years ago, the system might automatically approve the case. A serious illness would mean that the case would be passed onto the Underwriting Department for human decision making. Speed is an important benefit: All new cases are reviewed by the expert system within 24 hours, wherein 43% of these cases are approved either automatically by the expert system or with underwriter assistance in the Electronic Worksheet.

Standing between the field office PCs and the home office mainframes are a series of modules for exchanging information from Intelligent Data Entry to the Expert Underwriting and Electronic Worksheet modules, as well as programs for ordering information requirements, and for sending completed applications to John Hancock's Issue and Policy Administration systems. These data communications modules are complex, and given the number of field offices involved as well as the high reliability required for transmissions, the development effort entailed substantial levels of systems integration and other "non-AI" programming. This was the role of approximately a dozen DP programmers assigned to the project.

A number of both specific and broader benefits are being derived from John Hancock's expert system. A 43% approval rate for new applications within 24 hours of initial data entry provides substantial expense reduction over noncomputerized new business processing.[*] The ability of field offices to issue new policies so quickly for a large number of new applications also increases the attractiveness of John Hancock's insurance offerings, leading to new business at the retail level that might have otherwise not been realized. "Next day" notification on the status of new cases is provided to field offices. Finally, the productivity of human underwriters is enhanced because they are now able to concentrate on complex cases filtered through Automated Underwriting. In short, this expert system exhibits a direct linkage to the firm's competitive advantage.

MANAGING THE DEVELOPMENT OF RISK MANAGEMENT SYSTEMS

John Hancock's underwriting system is but one example of the application of expert system technology to the risk management and the new business process in insurance. Can this example be generalized to other insurers?

To present what other insurers have achieved in this area, we turn to a new research framework developed over the past several years by myself and other colleagues at the Center for Technology Management at the College of Business at Northeastern University (21). The Center has conducted a worldwide study of expert systems in a variety of in-

---

*For another insurer, we once computed an estimate of approximately $200 spent in direct labor and materials for processing a single life insurance application. A small insurer processes about 50,000 applications a year. For a large insurer, volumes exceed several hundred thousand applications per year. The reader can see that ongoing savings of expert systems that automatically approve or reject 50% of new cases is, indeed, substantial.

dustries. The principle investigators on that project have been both surprised and delighted to find the extent to which industry had applied artificial intelligence and expert system approaches to solve real problems to competitive advantage.

We developed a general method of classifying systems based on two underlying dimensions: the complexity and depth of decision making in a system, and the complexity of the computer technology that it employs. There are three basic components at the core of decision making: the decision maker's knowledge of the paradigms and heuristics of a given field(s), the ''raw'' information used by the decision-maker, and the interpretation and synthesis of that information by applying domain-specific logic to resolve uncertainty and come to partial or complete decisions. A set of variables were identified to assess these components of decision making. Similarly, variables were developed to assess technology complexity: the diversity of technologies and tools used in development, the degree of networking and database intensity in applications, and the extent of the systems integration effort.

The purpose of the classification process was to observe differences in development cost, development time, organizational strategies, and staffing as knowledge and technological complexity both separately, and jointly, increased. The method to 108 major expert system efforts in different industries from around the world. About a quarter of these systems are from financial services organizations. The classification process yields the four industry-independent groups of expert systems shown in Figure 4. We can use this framework to describe the general types of expert systems developed by financial services companies around the world.

- Personal Productivity Systems. These systems are stand-alone systems that run on PCs. Their primary purpose is validate information or perform simple decision making. Four examples of this type of expert system are shown in Figure 4. BUILDSAFE is an expert system developed by a Japanese property insurer for disaster prevention. When structures are newly built, this system uses data such as construction conditions, structure details, and purpose of use in order to propose the most appropriate equipment for use by the company seeking construction insurance. It is used by a single professional inside the insurance company. MEDCLAIMS is an initial screening application for medical claims. The goal of these two systems is to facilitate a professional's decision making and work. They use PC or workstation platforms that were developed with expert system shells and have small databases.
- Knowledge Intensive Systems. These are highly complex decision-assistance systems that help professionals work through cases or problems. CARS is a property and casualty insurer's expert system for underwriting automobile insurance that works through an individual's driving history to help assess risk and set insurance premiums. PENSION is a pension planning and consultation system. Such systems are *groupware*, made for a single group of professionals and their managers. They tend to run on PC LANs or workstation client–server networks. Addressing core decision processes of a company, Knowledge Intensive systems require extensive logic modeling and knowledge-base development.
- Technology Intensive Systems. These systems are simple in decision making but highly complex in terms of computer technology. DEATH, for example, screens information obtained from death claim forms and notifies agents of pending activity. Running on a mainframe, it is networked to hundreds of local office across the United States. DISABILITY estimates the long-term loss of

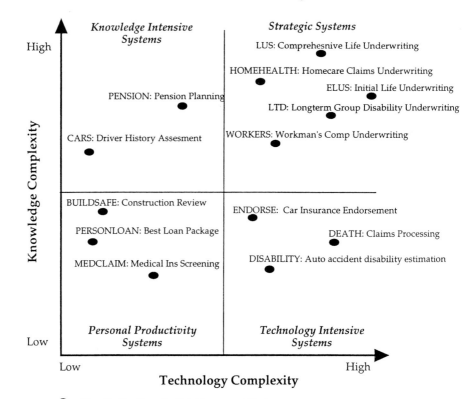

FIGURE 4   The classification framework: four generic types of software applications.

income for persons involved in serious automobile accidents. Although the knowledge based is relatively small, the systems integration efforts was large: DISABILITY is used by many people inside the company across many departments. ENDORSE automatically provides endorsement on car insurance policies. It accesses enormous databases and is networked to numerous agent offices around the country. All these systems run on mainframes and require substantial integration with other systems maintained by the company. They are the factory applications of a firm designed to reduce unit costs and achieve greater volumes in shorter time cycles.

• Strategic Systems.   These expert systems are complex in both decision making and computer technology. HOMEHEALTH, for example, is an expert system developed by a health insurer to automatically adjudicate nearly all claims for home health care services. It processes an enormous volume of cases and has allowed the firm to eliminate all backlogs and reduce staff from dozens of persons to only two. LTD is an expert consultation system for underwriting long-term group disability insurance for medium-sized groups. It is now central to the companies underwriting processes. Similarly, LUS is a comprehensive life insurance underwriting system that provides automated underwriting for simpler cases and extensive back-end decision assistance tools for more difficult cases. John Hancock's system is also shown in Figure 4, labeled as ELUS. Aimed at both better decision making and lower costs, such systems address core business processes.

The research showed that knowledge and technology complexity were associated with significantly different management approaches for development, ranging from who might best control projects to the time, money, and staffing needed to create working systems. These findings are summarized in Figure 5.

These findings also apply to risk management systems. For those risk management systems with high levels of knowledge complexity, one will typically find that initiatives were started in decision making (i.e., business) departments and continued to have strong business unit control and input into the development effort. The underwriting systems were by in large conceived and largely controlled by underwriting or medical research staffs (albeit with strong input from data processing departments). The complexity of the domain knowledge and the commensurate need to access domain experts mandated this type of control. On the other hand, for those systems with relatively simple decision mak-

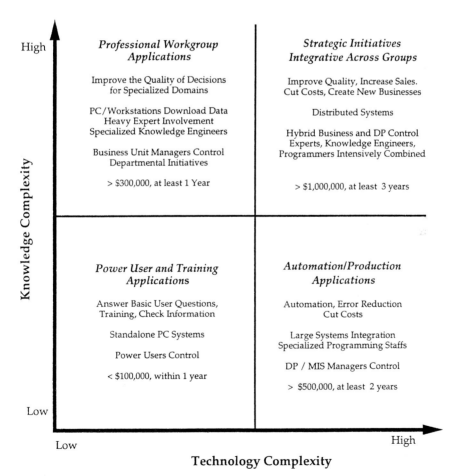

FIGURE 5 Contingent approaches for planning and implementation.

ing but that required extensive systems integration and distribution across the firm, control by data processing departments is more typical. The insurance endorsement and claims processing systems, linking the home office to agents, are examples.

Proof of concept prototypes for all these risk management systems could be developed with small teams working over the course of about a year. The expert system shells and database management systems available across multiple computer platforms facilitate this experimentation. However, to make production-version systems from prototypes, divergence in time and cost was found to be contingent on the embodied knowledge and technology complexity. Highly knowledgeable complex systems required more time to complete than technologically complex systems, the reason being that modeling complex decision making cannot be rushed. Technologically complex systems, however, consumed significantly larger budgets and had much larger teams. The systems integration entailed in these systems is the reason for this. As one might expect, those systems that had high levels of complexity in both dimensions had, by far, the longest durations, the largest budgets, and the biggest staffs.

THE ORGANIZATIONAL SIDE OF RISK MANAGEMENT SYSTEMS

The techniques and skills for turning human expertise into working systems are robust and make good business sense. However, to consider the system as only computer technology is limiting. The people, work processes, and organization, together with computers, comprise the full risk management system. How can firms reengineer their work processes and organizations to take the fullest advantage of risk management computer systems?

Computer integration can be difficult. In the case of John Hancock's system, programmers developed links between different computer systems running on different hardware and networks to share data. The typical insurer has many distinct applications for new business processing and administration that rarely share a common data model or architecture. Companies have either done this work themselves or outsourced the activity to firms that specialize in systems integration. Systems integration between expert systems and administration systems remains costly, but it should become simpler because firms are moving to common data models and open-system technologies.

Organizational integration of expert systems may prove even more challenging than systems integration. To achieve maximum benefit, a company cannot simply incorporate risk management computer applications into existing processing and workflow. Rather, management must revisit the way a company works: How can decision-making systems that address a core decision process be made a fully integrated solution that streamlines workflows and improve the interactions between entities both internal and external to the firm?

The starting point in business redesign is strategic: Management must set business focus. This guides systems development, organization change, and business positioning. Quinn (22) has studied the services industries extensively and has concluded that competitive pressures to reduce costs and to reduce applications processing time will lead firms to focus on core activities that lead to competitive dominance in their market niches and to eliminate or outsource others.

Insurance is no exception. Insurers must focus resources on areas of competence that are the basis of future competitive advantage. In the insurance model presented at the beginning of the article, a number of potential competencies were identified: Sales, Underwriting or Risk Management, Product Development and Pricing, and Investments. Accordingly, new systems development cannot ignore these areas of potential competence and business advantage. Nor do we believe that a firm tackle all areas at once. One period of time can be the "Year(s) of Risk Management." The knowledge, skills, and technology development in that effort can then serve as a platform for addressing other key areas of the business.

Once areas of focus are identified, reengineering may proceed. Hammer (23) has expressed basic reengineering principles that can be translated into the risk management and new business context:

- *Use new organization and technology to radically streamline workflows and improve responsiveness to prospective and existing customers*. This translates into automating or merging labor-intensive support functions into Sales and Underwriting.
- *Organize around outcomes, not tasks*. Using the insurance model presented in Figure 1, management should not necessarily place data entry, initial underwriting, requirements ordering, and facultative underwriting in separate organizational departments. These tasks are all part of a single core process.
- *Capture data at its source*. Agents can enter applications information on lap-top computers that is then either automatically underwritten through embedded expert systems or transferred to the home office for review.
- *Use information technologies to better manage a geographically dispersed business and reach new markets*. Computers can link agents more directly with underwriters, as seen in the insurance examples cited earlier, i.e., ENDORSE, ELUS, and DEATH.
- *Use technology to improve interactions with suppliers of information and services*. Several of the expert systems described earlier automatically order underwriting requirements from external suppliers. We think of this as the creation of "Information Alliances."
- *Empower decision-makers and push accountability and control down in the organization*. For the insurer, the computer will embody high levels of risk management expertise that will automatically underwrite simpler cases and provide decision assistance for harder ones. This will allow the insurer and its underwriters to have greater confidence in their decision making.

Now, to take these general ideas down to specific application, let us review another case in somewhat greater detail. The case involves the computerization of the more complex elements of the life underwriting process and the reengineering efforts accompanying systems implementation. The innovation started in 1986 within Lincoln National Life Company and continues to develop to this day in 40 other insurance companies in that these other firms have licensed Lincoln National's system. In Figure 4, this system is labeled "LUS." The reader can see that it contains the highest degree of knowledge complexity in the insurance sample as well as high levels of technology complexity. It is a comprehensive, complex risk management system. It stands in this author's opinion as one of the major innovations in insurance computer technology in the present decade.

The development history behind LUS is both interesting and instructive. The best domain experts in risk management in the company worked on the project. Senior management has strongly supported the initiative for the duration. As alluded to earlier, the effort has served as a basis for selling new knowledge and technology to other insurance companies.

Lincoln National's system started out in 1986 with a medical director in the Reinsurance Division prototyping the underwriting process for the asthma medical impairment using a simple PC expert system shell. Like all medical directors, his job had been to advise underwriters on risk parameters for a multitude of medical impairments, synthesizing existing medical research with a firm's mortality experience. Senior management soon believed that his prototype was the beginning of something much grander in scale, a technology that could have benefits not only for the reinsurance underwriting department but also for the industry as a whole. In a decisive and rapid manner, the company's best underwriting and computer experts were asked to participate in extending the prototype into a set of formal products and services to be marketed to the industry.

Understanding the complex aspects of risk management in life–health insurance had been one of the company's recognized strengths. In fact, compared to direct insurers, the quality and consistency of underwriting has an even heavier impact on a reinsurer's competitiveness. Reinsurers assume larger at-risk amounts, and the proportion of premiums received that are paid out in death benefits (i.e., mortality costs) are much higher than in a direct insurance operation. Thus, a successful reinsurer needs strong underwriting skills and stands to gain if it can leverage these skills with its customers. Lincoln National, for example, has maintained an underwriting research and development department generally considered to be one of the most advanced in the industry. The company's in-house medical department also offers a substantial information bank of medical knowledge. In a market that is extremely price competitive due to overcapacity, Lincoln National has been able to differentiate itself on the basis of value-added services to its reinsurance clients. The underwriting research and development department has published an underwriting impairment guide manual, containing information for hundreds of specific medical impairments and guidelines for assessing financial and nonmedical risks. Lincoln National's expert system was destined to be the ''next generation'' of these collective services.

Top management was heavily involved in both the higher-level system's objective setting and organization planning for the expert system project. A steering committee convened regularly to map out ''the future'' of life insurance workflows and how technology could enable the placement of information, responsibility, and decision making at key ''points of events,'' be they the selling of insurance products or the underwriting of new business.

Given the nature of Lincoln National's business and its existing underwriting resources, it was, therefore, consistent that Lincoln National started by focusing on the back end of the underwriting process, i.e., developing knowledge bases for medical impairments. This was the type of underwriting in which the reinsurance underwriters had always excelled. To acquire their expertise, a formalized knowledge engineering process was created early in the project. The process relies heavily on group meetings attended by medical directors, reinsurance underwriters, underwriters from Lincoln National's ''direct'' life business division, and systems personnel. This process facilitated a synthesis of the descriptive and procedural knowledge of the company's senior underwriters with prescriptive and theoretical knowledge of its medical directors and actuaries (24). Great care was also taken to make the deductive reasoning in the system emulate an underwriter's cognitive processes, i.e., to be consistent with the underwriter's ''approach'' to resolving problems. Over time, an increasing number of medical impairments were computerized as well as other expert modules that assess interaction effects between impairments.

The decision was made to employ expert system development tools that provided portability between PC and mainframe environments. The expert system evolved into earlier parts of the underwriting chain, targeting Initial Underwriting processes. Lincoln National's Initial Underwriting module incorporates basic underwriting heuristics for assessing occupations, hobbies, certain medical conditions, family history, and personal "build." Over time, however, Lincoln National has been able to move certain aspects of complex medical underwriting earlier into the workflow. If there is a history of a serious life-threatening disease, the system will not try to approve the case but pass it along to the Impairment Underwriting module. Prior to this exchange, the system determines any additional information needed by the underwriter, such as blood tests.

Subsequent development saw the creation of the various modules surrounding the core underwriting processes. In 1989, the Workflow Management module was enhanced for the individual underwriter to manage his or her own personal case load. For example, the front end of this module keeps track of cases, the status of requirements that have been ordered, and the status of specific underwriting problems. Each underwriter has an "in tray," where cases electronically assigned to the underwriter are presented for evaluation. For each case, the underwriter then works on a Problem Processing screen to manipulate, track, change, or resolve specific underwriting problems. Electronic notepads are also provided for the underwriter, so that, through electronic mail, he or she might have a new form of communications with agents in the field. Also during 1989, Lincoln National finished the Management Information and Administration module. In addition to providing a series of reports on both individual and department performance, underwriting managers can also adjust certain systems tables to modify the processing of the entire system in order to reflect the company's specific underwriting requirements and ideas. Examples might include the company's aggressiveness with respect to nonstandard ratings for particular medical impairments, or the policy amount ceiling below which automatic case approval can occur.

It should be noted that this expert system has an architecture that rigorously separates data from logic, i.e., databases from knowledge bases. Thus, the series of expert system modules consists of knowledge bases that read information from, and write information back to, a set of underlying tables through C programs that utilize a library of database procedures. The database is, therefore, an important foundation of the system: The data are shared between expert system modules, and the database manager provides a straightforward interface to external environments such as other mainframe applications or information services external to the user company. This architecture has allowed the expert system to evolve in a more modular and efficient fashion. Further, the database backbone has facilitated systems integration with a user company's existing client policy administration systems.

Lincoln National Risk Management was formed and funded by the reinsurance parent. The president of the new company was and continues to serve as the vice president of underwriting for the reinsurance company. In an organizational move reflecting the reinsurance parent's long-term commitment to the venture, underwriting research and development personnel were shifted to support the "R&D" of the new company. Leading these activities is the medical director who pioneered the underwriting system, and working with him are a half dozen senior underwriters and research staff formally from the reinsurance parent. In terms of programming, approximately 30 persons perform knowledge encoding, database programming, and various types of systems integration. They are managed by the former head of the reinsurance's division's own DP department. Marketing staff has also been hired into the new company as well.

Management knew that successful implementation of the expert system would demand business reeingineering. It is approached with several basic concepts: "point of event processing" and "workstation encapsulation." Point-of-event processing is enabling the decision making and processing required at any given point in a process to occur at that point rather than be pushed further down the process chain. Thus, data are captured once at the source, i.e., as it is entered by agents. Similarly, medical and financial information requirements are ordered automatically by the computer as soon as those requirements are determined (by the computer) for a given case. Workstation encapsulation is an enabling extension of point-of-event processing. Core tasks in the new business process are consolidated around powerful, intelligent workstations that match the needs of and support key professionals.

These concepts can be illustrated with an reengineering example taken from one of the firms that has implemented LUS. The first step in the redesign process is to accurately portray current workflow. A standard approach for paper-based processes is to attach logs on reasonable samples of cases running through the organization. These logs are then aggregated to show the steps, individuals and departments, time, and problems encountered in the process.

The business process can then be visualized in a number of ways. One such way is shown in Figure 6. This figure shows the before-LUS workflow of a medium-size life insurer. The central benefit of this representation format is that it maps specific events and decision points of a process to organizational entities. It also looks both within a company and at steps involving external entities. The organizational entities shown in Figure 6 are summary "mega entities." Specific departments or work groups unfold in more detailed workflow maps nested below the summary entities. For example, within New Business Clerical Departments might be separate data entry and jet screening departments. For the insurance company described here, the turnaround time for new applications ranged from 3 weeks to several months, depending on the complexity of the underwriting requirements.

A multidisciplinary team must be formed to redesign the existing workflow. It should include management, process analysts, systems analysts, and key professional decision-makers (such as underwriters, actuaries, or medical researchers). A new workflow may then be designed and tested either "on paper" or using powerful new systems dynamics packages on PCs. Metrics should be developed to carefully assess productivity and cycle times.

The new workflow developed for the insurance company is shown in Figure 7. The reader can note the simplicity and directness of the new workflow, particularly within the New Business Clerical Departments. Many of the steps previously performed with direct labor are now automated. The number of transfers of paper between different hands has been dramatically reduced, if not eliminated, through electronic media. Then, over the course of several years, systems integration, job redesign and retraining, and improved electronic communications with external suppliers were performed across the new process to make it a working reality. With that reality came vastly improved turnaround times and great opportunities for improving productivity in terms of direct labor per unit of case work.

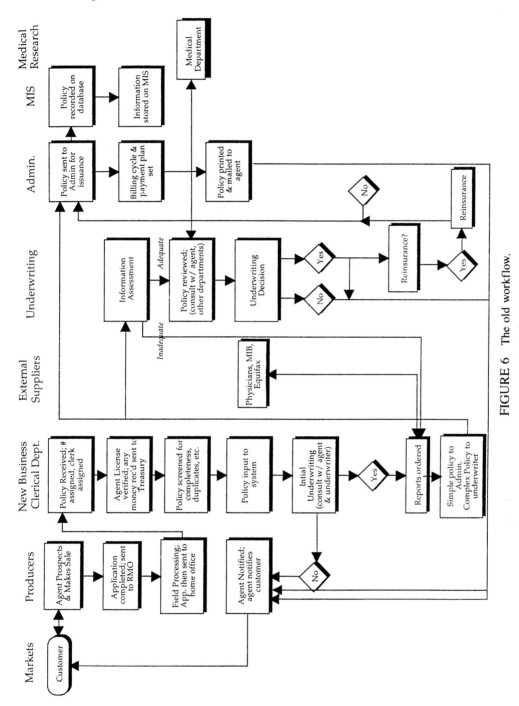

FIGURE 6 The old workflow.

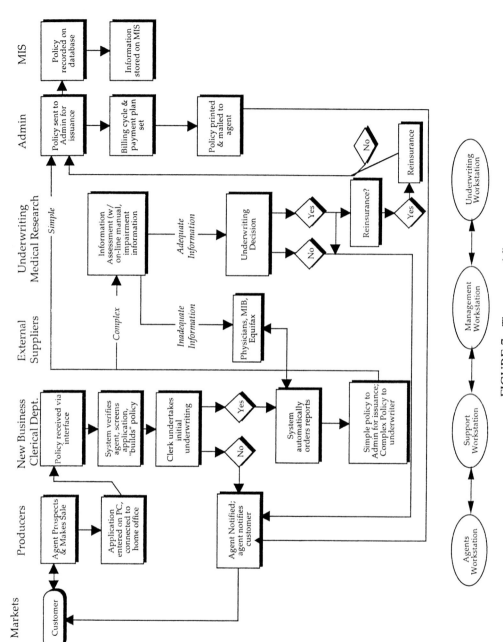

FIGURE 7   The new workflow.

As the company came to consensus on its new workflow, Lincoln began packaging its LUS modules in a way that suited the new process. Appropriate modules were placed on specific classes off workstations: one for producers, another for support clerks, another for underwriters, and another for underwriting managers. This is the "workflow encapsulation" mentioned earlier and is indicated at the bottom of Figure 6.

Many firms using LUS are pushing initial data entry of applications information out to agents' offices and, by consequence, onto lap-top computers. Simple modem-based communications send and receive these data between other computers in the home office that will perform the risk assessment. Additionally, some firms employing LUS are planning to physically combine New Business Clerical Departments with their respective Underwriting Departments. The key to this redesign is to create Underwriter–Support Personnel teams responsible for specific market segments or customer populations. Such department and job redesign forces accountability down to those directly responsible for providing service and making decisions.

A BROAD FOCUS TO RISK MANAGEMENT SOLUTIONS: INFORMATION ALLIANCES

Financial services industries such as insurance rely on gathering and using information to gain competitive advantage. Many of these data are gathered from outside the firm and its direct assigns, often by another company that maintains databases containing historical data on individuals and businesses. Therefore, in designing a decision-making or assistance system, a company must look beyond its own boundaries to identify external suppliers and to improve the flow of information itself and other companies. The analysis provides a risk management systems development group with a clear focus. It also identifies necessary external linkages and forces the group to consider how it can make its own systems architecture compatible, integratable, and easy to work with for other groups in the total solution set.

Figure 8 shows an alliances framework that we have found useful for understanding a firm's position in a industry where gathering and using information is a key aspect of competitiveness. As we have been focusing on life insurance, the framework contains life insurance examples.

The framework differentiates between products and service on the vertical axis and posits a value chain from physical components to intangible knowledge on the horizontal axis. At the left side of the value chain are companies that specialize in the base technology components used in a total solution. In the insurance context, for example, product providers include manufacturers of various types of computers, peripherals, and networks. The amount of processing power and storage capacity needed at the desktop or through networks makes technology choices at this level critical.

Service providers at this level are comprised primary of telecommunications companies. The reliability and cost requirements of distributed systems linking geographically dispersed sales forces with home offices makes partner selection critical. It is also likely to affect the overall design of the risk management application.

The next step along the value chain consists of tools: firms that either create software development tools or provide a "tool service" by integrating applications and their underlying technologies. Good choices in each dimension are essential to the overall success of a solution. In risk management systems, for example, tool products tend to in-

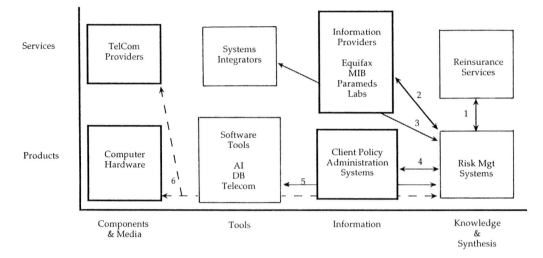

FIGURE 8   Alliances, technology, information, and services.

1. Medical and Underwriting Research, Automatic Reinsurance

2. Automated Ordering, Information Clearinghouses

3. Financial and Support Relationships with Major Integrators

4. Integration Modules for Leading Systems

5. Vendor Relations and New Tool Investigation

6. Work on Major Platforms, Explore New Solutions for Remote Processing by Agents

clude an knowledge-based development shell or language, a database management system, and other programming environments to create user interfaces and build distributed file access capability. As experience has shown that no single tool can meet all development requirements, firms must deal with multiple tool providers and insure that each vendor's tool has an "open architecture" so that it can be easily integrated with other tools used in developing the application. The use of relatively newer tool technologies (such as expert system shells) can be particularly hazardous because the firms providing them are often small, technically brilliant ventures experiencing the ebbs and flows of entrepreneurship. Both John Hancock and Lincoln National Life Company, for example, have contended with software vendor issues.

At the "tool services" region of the framework are the systems integrators. A risk management system is not a risk management solution until it is fully integrated within an organization's work and computing environment. Many large companies tend to have their own data processing departments perform the integration of a risk management system with other administration systems in the company. However, many if not most insurers turn to companies that specialize in this activity: Arthur Anderson, Electronic Data Systems, and American Management Systems are but a few examples. The choice of partner in this area is obviously critical. One firm that spent a million dollars to develop an underwriting expert found itself spending close to $5 million on systems integration and workflow reengineering. Our field research confirms that this experience is not atypical.

The next level of the Information Alliances value chain contains entities that either manage data within a firm or provide information needed in decision making to it. Information management products in insurance are the "client policy administration systems." These are typically mainframe systems that issue and administer insurance policies, perform client billing, and handle claims administration. Most insurers have developed their own administration systems, using older computing technologies. There are instances, however, of software companies that have successful developed new generation administration systems based on relational database technology, particularly in the property and casualty business.

Information services companies in insurance are the data services companies. When an individual applies for personal insurance, a series of medical, criminal, and financial databases must be checked. Under traditional schemes, these queries were ordered by a clerical assistant, received through the mail, and attached to the case folder for the underwriter to examine at a later point. Systems such as LUS can automatically determine what external data are needed for each specific case, order them automatically, and receive data in computerized form. This reduces processing time and cost dramatically. To achieve this level of automation, management had to systematically identify its "information partners" and initiate both technical and business efforts with them.

The last level on the value chain is comprised of organizations which apply their particular knowledge to information to reach the business decision. The knowledge products in our industry example are risk management expert systems. Here again, a firm must decide whether it wishes to build its own risk management system or license one from a vendor such as Lincoln National's LNRM. General-purpose risk management systems that can be easily configured to a company's specific markets and products, underwriting rules, and pricing are, indeed, rare. Thus, firms are inclined to build their own systems.

Knowledge services entities are comprised of a firm's own underwriting departments and reinsurers operating within its industry. Reinsurers apply their own risk management expertise to assume a portion of the risk given pieces of business. Computer linkages between a company and its reinsurers to exchange both case information and risk management expertise are clearly part of the future.

Thus, risk management systems are but part of a larger "virtual organization" that spans many entities both within and external to the firm. Managing this virtual organization is essential to achieving success with any risk management application. This management has two key aspects: internal focus and external partnering.

Internal focus itself has two parts. The first of these is whether the development initiative is targeted to build a "product" or provide a "service." Product-generating firms are structured differently, operate differently, have different types of employees, and make money and achieve leverage through different business models. The second part of focus is to select the point along the value chain where the firm has accumulated decision-making and technical capabilities. For example, we have observed that successful risk management systems development groups have focused on knowledge modeling and applications development. They have not ventured into building next generation client policy administration systems, nor created their own expert system development shells, nor invented new networking technology—however great the temptation.

External partnering also has two parts. The first is to identify necessary partners. Figure 8 identified six general types of relationships that risk management systems developers must invariably construct with external vendors to be a sustained success. The second key part of external partnering is to tailor the respective development or service activities of each partner to achieve compatibility of technologies, applications, and services. Corporate technologists must be encouraged to work closely with selected partners to build understanding and share knowledge far beyond the traditional notion of vendor and procurement management.

CONCLUDING IDEAS

Building risk management systems is a complex undertaking. We have proposed four central ideas:

- Effective systems development first requires competitively distinctive understanding and capabilities in the risk management decision domain.
- A system's embodied knowledge and technology complexity are directly associated with the time, cost staffing, and organizational control points required to build a working application.
- Risk management systems cannot be considered "stand-alone" technology: systems integration and workflow reengineering are equally important parts of a complete solution.
- In a similar sense, any group within a firm building a risk management system cannot consider its work in isolation from key product and service providers in an industry. The "virtual organization" is a very concrete and important concept for risk management systems.

The benefits of building risk management systems have proved significant for many companies. In the case of insurance, there is the cost savings made possible by automatically underwriting the "simple," more standard insurance cases. The magnitude of those savings were suggested in the John Hancock situation. Second, improved risk assessment can dramatically improve a firm's claims experience over time. Lincoln National Life Company, for example, estimates that just a 1% or 2% improvement in experienced morality in back-end underwriting can improve claims experience at a level comparable to the benefits of automated front-end underwriting. Third, there is the overall cost savings and improved responsiveness associated with wide-scale workflow redesign. The type of workflow redesign described earlier in this article can produce a company that is knowledge intensive, service responsive, and far leaner than today's norm. Our studies in other financial industries such as banking show similar types of benefits when decision making has been enhanced and workflows streamlined with computers.

The momentum for risk management systems in financial services is such that in order to compete, firms will have to undertake such initiatives. Insurance is an interesting case because most firms continue to focus the bulk of their new systems development efforts toward improving the administration of existing business through large projects to redesign client policy administration systems. This is true of life, health, and property insurers. Many, if not the majority, are consumed with multimillion dollar administration system overhauls.

They may be fighting yesterday's battle. There are limits to the returns afforded by mainframe-based, administration systems-oriented initiatives. For example, in life insurance, a recent American Council of Life Insurance (ACLI) study shows on average only 12% of insurers' budgets going to administrative expenses, whereas benefits and reserves consume 85%.

These numbers make a compelling case for intensifying efforts in improving risk management decision making. It is a key to future competitiveness. The approach to systems development must be holistic, incorporating decision-makers, workflows, and a form of computing that is desktop, knowledge based, and distributed.

REFERENCES

A. M. Best Company, *Best's Insurance Reports: Life Health 1990*, 85th Annual Edition, Oldwick, NJ, 1990.

R. Bailey, A. M Best, *Underwriting in Life and Health Insurance Companies*, Life Office Management Association, Atlanta, GA, 1985.

T. M. Davenport, "The Case of the Soft Software Proposal," *Harvard Business Rev.*, May/June, 1989.

D. Jones, "Insurer's Underwriting Staff Gets Expert Help," *National Underwriter*, 3 (5 October 1987).

J. Conversano, "Expert System Lightens Underwriters' Work Load," *Resource*, May/June, 1988.

M. H. Meyer, and K. Curley, "Putting Expert Systems Technology to Work," *Sloan Management Rev.*, 32(2)21–31 (1991).

A. D. DeTore, "An Introduction to Expert Systems," *J. Insurance Med.*, 21, 233–236 (1989).

K. May, "Knowledge-based Systems in the Insurance Industry," *Systems AI*, March 15, 1990.

Coopers and Lybrand, *Expert Systems in the Insurance Industry: 1987 Survey Report Update*, Boston, MA, 1987.

A. H. Baker, *Information Technologies: Strategic Opportunities for the Life Insurance Industry*, American Council of Life Insurance, 1988.

IBC, *The 2nd Annual Expert Systems in Insurance Conference Proceedings*, IBC USA Conferences, Natick, MA, 1990.

R. Benjamin, J. Rockart, M. Scott Morton, and J. Wyman, "Information Technology: A Strategic Opportunity," *Sloan Management Rev.*, 25(3), 3–10 (1984).

B. Ives, and G. Learmonth, "The Information System as a Competitive Weapon," *Commun. ACM*, 2(17–12), 1193–1201 (1984).

Y. Barkos, and M. Treacy, "Information Technology and Corporate Strategy: A Research Perspective," *MIS Quart.* 10(2), 107–119 (1986).

H. Johnston, and M. Vitale, "Creating Competitive Advantage with Interorganizational Information Systems," *MIS Quart.*, 12(2), 153–166 (1988).

R. Davis, "Amplifying Expertise with Expert Systems," *The AI Business*, P. Winston and K. Prendergast (eds.), MIT Press Cambridge, MA, 1984, pp. 17–40.

D. Prerau, "Selection of an Appropriate Domain for an Expert System," *AI Mag.*, 6(2), 26–30 (1985).

D. Leonard-Barton, and J. Sviokla, "Putting Expert Systems to Work," *Harvard Business Rev.*, 66(2), 91–98 (1988).

E. Feigenbaum, P. McCordick, and H. Nii, *The Rise of the Expert Company*, Times Books, New York, 1988.

M. H. Meyer, A. DeTore, A. Siegel, and K. Curley, "The Strategic Use of Expert Systems for Risk Management in the Insurance Industry," *Expert Syst. Appli.*, 5, 15–24 (1992).

M. H. Meyer and K. F. Curley, "An Applied Framework for Classifying the Complexity of Knowledge-Based Systems, *MIS Quart.*, 15(4), 455–475 (1991).

J. B. Quinn, with T. L. Doorley and P. C. Paquette, "Technology in Services: Rethinking Strategic Focus," *Sloan Management Rev.*, 31, 79–87 (1990).

M. Hammer, "Reengineering Work: Don't Automate, Obliterate," *Harvard Business Rev.*, July/ August, 1990.

P. E. Slatter, "Decision Making Research at the Interface Between Descriptive and Prescriptive Studies," *Med. Decision Making*, 8 (1988).

P. Shephard, and A. C. Webster, *Selection of Risks*, Society of Actuaries, Chicago, 1957.

MARC H. MEYER

ROBOT KINEMATICS–see Motion of Robot Mechanisms: Robots Kinematics

ROBOT VISION–see Machine Vision: Robots

ROBOTICS, MILITARY

Although "military robotics" has long been the stuff of science fiction, recent advances in computer processing capabilities have brought this dream to the early stages of realization. The family of military unmanned vehicles currently in various stages of development, whether Unmanned Aerial Vehicles (UAVs), Unmanned Underwater Vehicles (UUVs), or Unmanned Ground Vehicles (UGVs), offer the very real possibility of taking airmen, sailors, soldiers, and marines "out of harms way." Because we humans are creatures of the land, arguably the greatest potential (and, hence, the main focus of this article) will be on the Unmanned Ground Vehicle (UGV).

HISTORICAL PERSPECTIVE

> WHAT ONE MAN CAN IMAGINE, ANOTHER MAN CAN DO.
>
> *Jules Verne*

Automata (from the Greek "automatos," acting of itself) have fascinated people since time immemorial. The bronze sentinel, Talos, created and animated by Daedelus, and set to guard the sacred island of Thera, was described by Homer in The Argosy. In the second century B.C., Hero of Alexander constructed automata that were animated by water, air, and steam pressure. Among these were steam-powered statues that moved, doors that opened, and birds that sang. The eighteenth century saw the advent of elaborate mechanical dolls which could write short phrases, play musical instruments, and perform other simple, lifelike acts (1). In 1921, the Czech playwright, Karel Capek, captured the public's imagination with his play R.U.R. (*Rossem's Universal Robots*), coining the word "robot" from the Czech word "robota," which means serf or forced labor (2). (In the play, Rossem's anthropomorphic robots rebel and eliminate humanity. Then in the end, they become human themselves.) R.U.R. delineated a potential hazard which certainly has yet to be realized, but which popular films such as *Terminator* suggest may conceivably represent a serious threat in the future.

Evolving from clockwork, gear-filled devices to robots having sensors, effectors, and processors with artificial intelligence, automata are no longer simply items of amusement. They have become lethal instruments of war. This was vividly demonstrated to the world during the 1991 liberation of Kuwait from the hands of Iraq, via satellite television coverage.

A review of what has been done in the field of unmanned vehicles reveals the fact that most work has concentrated on the development of either unmanned aerial or underwater vehicles, rather than unmanned ground vehicles. There is a very logical reason for this emphasis on other than ground vehicles. Man is a ground-based animal.

Consequently, the ground is inherently a relatively benign environment for man, whereas the air and sea are inherently hostile environments to humankind. Any manned vehicle designed to support and allow man to effectively operate in either the air or under the water (including commercial vehicles) carries with it a large price tag in support and protection of the human operator/crew. The incredible lethality and precision of modern weapons, however, have "raised the ante" for military ground vehicles. Even when facing an inept opponent, losses due to fratricide alone can be staggering. Consequently, Desert Storm has elevated the need for unmanned ground vehicles to a more equal level with UAVs and UUVs.

Unmanned Aerial Vehicles

One of the first U.S. military attempts at unmanned aerial reconnaissance occurred during World War I when carrier pigeons were conscripted to carry timer-activated cameras "over the top" to photograph German trenches (3). Both the United States and Britain attempted to develop flying bombs during World War I. Perhaps the most notable results of these efforts were their contributions to the development and perfection of auto pilots by Dr. Elmer A. Sperry and his son.

The major UAVs of World War II (apart from the barrage balloons which protected London) were the German V-1 "buzz bombs" and the V-2 rockets. On the allied side, kamikaze missions with damaged, remotely controlled bombers were conducted, but were relatively unsuccessful.

Following World War II, target drones, intercontinental ballistic missiles, and cruise missiles were developed. However, cruise missiles were deemphasized for a number of years in favor of manned bombers and ICBMs, until technical improvements and a changing threat brought them back into favor.

Following the very public loss of a manned U-2 reconnaissance aircraft over the Soviet Union in 1960, the United States began purchasing Teledyne Ryan AGM-34 UAVs for aerial reconnaissance missions. With their small radar signatures, these UAVs proved to be very effective at conducting photo-reconnaissance missions over North Vietnam during the Vietnam War.

In 1973, the Israeli Air Force, after suffering heavy losses of manned aircraft while trying to storm Egypt's air defense systems, sent over Teledyne Ryan AQM-91 and Northrop Chukar remotely piloted vehicles (RPVs) to draw Egyptian fire. Manned Israeli bombers then hit the Egyptian air defense installations while they were reloading. After this initial success, the Israelis began carrying and firing Maverick missiles from their RPVs.

Following the Israeli-Egyptian war, the Israelis developed two remote-controlled model airplanes, the Scout and the Mastiff, which carried television cameras. In 1982, the Israeli Air Force used Scout and Mastiff RPVs to identify and spoof Syrian air defense radar sites so that manned Israeli aircraft could then knock them out with anti-radiation missiles. The Israeli RPVs also performed reconnaissance missions during these engagements.

The success of the Israelis and the heavy attrition of manned U.S. aircraft in Lebanon and Granada, as well as of British and Argentinean aircraft in the Falklands, has led to worldwide interest and efforts to develop UAVs, including fixed wing, short-takeoff-and-landing vehicles, as well as rotary wing and tilt wing, vertical-takeoff-and-landing aircraft. In the United States, the principal UAV developed during the 1980s was the AAI

Pioneer manufactured by AAI Corporation, in collaboration with the Israeli Mazlat Corporation (a joint effort between Israel Aircraft Industries and Tadiran). The Pioneer weighs 400 pounds, has a wingspan of 17 feet, carries a 100-pound payload, provides a maximum flight endurance time of 7 hours, and is currently in service with the U.S. Navy (4). Another UAV currently deployed by the U.S. Marine Corps is Aeroenvironment Corporation's electrically powered Pointer. The Pointer is hand launched, weighs 6.8 pounds, carries a 2.2-pound payload, has a 9-foot wingspan, and can remain aloft for 1 hour. (These interim UAVs are to be replaced by Joint Services-developed UAVs when these become available in the mid-1990s.)

Two other UAVs which came and went in the 1980s were the Lockheed-developed Aquila and the Developmental Sciences-produced Skyeye. The Aquila was a very ambitious UAV. It fell a victim to what is known as "requirements creep" and ultimately became too expensive to field. (Aquila was overly ambitious in that a single program attempted to satisfy requirements currently addressed by a family of UAVs. Several of the lessons learned from Aquila are applicable to all unmanned vehicle development efforts. The Skyeye was a relatively large UAV, used in Central America during the 1980s. It has been superseded by the Sky Owl vehicle created as a candidate for the U.S. Joint Services Short Range UAV (see discussion of UAV in Current Projects).

Unmanned Underwater Vehicles

Early experiments with remotely controlled boats date back to 1885 when an operator on board the British torpedo ship *Vernon* attempted to electrically control an unmanned boat via a cable. Remotely controlled torpedoes received British and German attention around the turn of the century. During World War I, Germany developed and fielded cable-controlled "kamikaze" boats for the defense of the German coastline. By the end of the war, Germany had developed radio-controlled boats with ranges up to 200 miles.

After World War I, little follow-up work occurred until 1957, when the U.S. Navy began development of a series of cable-controlled underwater recovery vehicles (CURVs) These CURVs were quite successful, carrying out a number of dramatic rescues. They inspired a family of remotely operated vehicles (ROVs) which have performed many useful underwater tasks for the U.S. Navy. One of these follow-on projects included the ANTHRO (anthropomorphic) program, in which the use of a head-coupled display was explored to control a small ROV. This program was succeeded by the Submersible Cable-Activated Teleoperator (SCAT) program, which also investigated head-coupled control systems incorporating three-dimensional vision. During the 1970s, a French company, Société ECA, built a mine destruction ROV called the PAP 104. Over 250 of these ROVs have been sold to 10 different navies. They were used by the British during the war in the Falklands. Another ROV, the Swedish-built Sea Owl, was used for mine-clearing in the Red Sea in 1984.

Unmanned Ground Vehicles

The first robotic military ground vehicle was probably the battery-powered, cable-operated Land Torpedo developed in 1918 by the Caterpillar Tractor Company. It was soon followed by the tricycle-based Electric Dog developed by the U.S. Naval Research Laboratory. Neither of these devices were pursued by the military.

During World War II, Germany developed and utilized the remotely controlled Borgward B1V and Goliath mine-clearing and demolition UGVs. After the war, the world's nuclear energy agencies became key customers for UGVs and teleoperated arms, which they employed to handle radioactive materials.

Another application has been that of teleoperated bomb-disposal UGVs such as the British Wheelbarrow, Hunter, and Hadrian. The Wheelbarrow typically carries a video camera, a shotgun, and a selection of modular mechanisms which may be installed to tailor it to a particular mission. The Hunter may be outfitted with one or two teleoperated arms. Hundreds of Wheelbarrows have been sold to military and police organizations around the world.

Other applications involve mobile surveillance platforms and the handling and delivery of ordnance. Among these were the Tactical Reconnaissance Vehicle (TRV) program (designed to develop a family of vehicles), the U.S. Army Military Police School's Robotic Observation Security Sensor System (ROS3), the U.S. Army Infantry School's Robotic Anti-Armor System (RAS), the U.S. Army Artillery School's Future Artillery Systems Technology (FAST) program, and the U.S. Marine Corp's Ground–Air Telerobotics Systems (GATERS) programs. None of these systems was ever fielded.

TECHNICAL ISSUES

Definition of a Military Robot

Attempts to define the term ''robot'' have probably consumed more time and trouble than any benefit likely to be derived from the effort. My personal favorite is that a robot is any device that can surprisingly (unexpectedly?) perform a task previously performed directly by humans; that is, today's robot may be tomorrow's smart appliance. At one time, a car wash might have been deemed a robot, although it is no longer so considered. A future automobile which can accept voice commands and can maneuver itself along specially instrumented roadways might well be considered a robot, at least for a time. Indeed, a highly computerized 1993 Mercedes might well be considered a robot by the standards of the 1970s, though probably no longer. A modern cruise missile is probably a robot, as will be future generations of ''brilliant'' munitions. The key point is that much future military equipment will be more and more highly automated and, yet, will probably not be considered robots by the standards of their day, or at least not after they become familiar. Fortunately, there should be little, if any, capability degradation associated with this inevitable nomenclature modification.

Machine Intelligence

From their moment of introduction in the 1940s, computers were orders of magnitude faster and more accurate at performing arithmetic than humans, and it was felt that it would only be a short time before robots began to displace human workers. The terms *automation*, *cybernetics*, *technological unemployment*, *artificial intelligence*, and *The Second Industrial Revolution* were coined to describe this anticipated shift toward robotic factories. Building on seminal work by leading mathematicians such as John von Neumann and Norbert Wiener, mathematicians began to attempt to implement reasoning and logical programs on computers. This proved to be more difficult than it had first appeared, with computers proving theorems and winning checker games through brute-force computational power rather than by synthesizing winning strategies. In the early 1970s, video cameras and manipulators were integrated with computers to allow them to "see" and manipulate objects in the real world. It was at this point that the magnitude of the problems of emulating the central nervous systems of living creatures became evident. The PDP 11/45s of that era were orders of magnitude too slow for machine vision systems. (This problem may also have been exacerbated by the relatively primitive state of machine vision algorithms at that time.) Computers were too slow to host the kinds of digital algorithms that would be needed to emulate human hand–eye coordination for fast, precise, digital control systems. Furthermore, machine-based thinking was rigid, uncreative, and totally lacking the real-world contextual understanding that characterizes human behavior.

In the meantime, robotics funding became a popular source of sponsorship for many in the research community. Mathematicians, for example, often expanded the early mathematical formalism developed for robotics into an art form, which today has distanced itself from any applied robotics research—a situation reminiscent of the nineteenth century when inventing was detached from "formal" science and engineering. One might even say that, in general, the research community probably owes more to robotics than robotics owes to the research community.

Machine intelligence research during the latter 1960s and early 1970s focused on *formal logic*, "*heuristic programming*", and the *trimming of decision trees*. In the 1980s, the term *expert systems* was created, together with the ideas of *rule-based logic* and *inference engines*. Expert, or rule-based, systems require that a large number of "If— then"-type rules reflecting the decisions which an expert would make in a particular area of expertise be programmed into a computer, which then simulates what the expert would be expected to decide. Expert systems can be very useful to the extent that their designers can anticipate all the situations to which they may be applied. However, the computer's lack of collateral knowledge or a "world model" limits their usefulness in situations which demand contextual reference or "common sense."

In the mid-1980s, the Japanese Ministry of International Trade and Industry (MITI) funded a $500 million 5-year cooperative program directed toward developing intelligent machines, the so-called fifth-generation computers. At the conclusion of the program in 1990, it was pronounced a failure because it failed to meet its goals of working effectively with ambiguous and incomplete information, adapting to changing conditions, and generalizing from experience. However, during the course of the program, two new approaches to machine intelligence were explored: neural networks and genetic learning. MITI announced that it intended to sponsor a $714 million 10-year, sixth-generation computer program aimed at developing intelligent machines ("neurocomputers") (5).

Computer Control

Revolutionary improvements in digital electronic circuit speeds and capacities in the commercial and military marketplaces promise to continue for at least another decade before physical and manufacturing limitations may slow the rate of progress. Note that progress in unmanned military vehicle control may well have profound implications for civilian manufacturing, environmental restoration, and transportation robotics.

Architectures

Serial Processors: Estimates of the computing speeds required to allow machine vision systems to rival the human eye range from a billion to a hundred billion operations per second,* whereas guesses concerning the computational speeds needed to mimic the human brain vary from 10 trillion (6) to 10,000 trillion operations per second (7). Present-day computers are, perhaps, billions of times faster than humans at performing arithmetic and rote-mechanical functions. Using brute-force computational strategies, they are perhaps equal to humans at logical inference and game playing. However, in tackling real-world problems, they are vastly inferior to most of the animal kingdom. Although this inferiority stems partially from inadequately adaptive algorithms, it has also partially been constrained by the limited computer speeds and memories of affordable latter-twentieth-century computers. During the next few years, as individual microprocessors accelerate from executing millions of instructions per second today to processing billions of instructions per second by the year 2000, and as supercomputers transition from their current gigops benchmarks to terops performance levels by 1995, military robotics systems may be expected to become more sophisticated than they are today. (Although such projected limitations have proved to be too conservative in the past, current projections place an upper limit of several billion operations per second on the speed of an individual microprocessor because of limitations imposed by the laws of physics as they apply to contemporary design techniques.)

Current onboard computers for unmanned ground vehicles use computers operating in, at most, the million-operations-per-second speed range. For example, the ALV discussed later employed an onboard VAX 11/785, whereas more recent UGVs have used Motorola 68020-class computers, and more recently yet, four onboard Sun workstations. Consequently, the introduction of billion-operation-per-second class serial computers might reasonably be expected to have major consequences for semiautonomous and autonomous vehicles.

Parallel Processors: The advent of ever-denser microprocessor chips at steadily declining prices permits the implementation of reliable, massively parallel computers in which parallel data streams and, in some cases, parallel instruction streams allow a number of microprocessors to work on the same problem at the same time. Several development efforts have recently been announced which promise massively parallel supercomputers capable of performing as many as 10 trillion floating-point operations per second by the year 2000 (8). Although such machines may be too large and expensive for use in unmanned ground vehicles, the shift to parallel processing which is now taking place may be expected to influence the designs of onboard computers for future military robots. For example, the Defense Advanced Research Projects Agency (DARPA) has recently taken delivery of a 64-unit parallel processor called Aladdin, which executes instructions at a maximum rate of about 1 billion operations per second. This coffee-can-sized onboard computer may significantly improve the capabilities of military robotic vehicles. A similar computer using 64 of the PowerPC 500-SPECmark, RISC-based, personal computer chips projected for delivery by IBM, Apple, and Motorola in 1995 might operate at a maximum speed of 32 billion operations per second. Here again, limitations imposed by the laws of physics as applied to current production techniques may eventually curtail further advances, but major improvements in capability will become available before this might happen.

Neural Networks: Neural networks endeavor to simulate animal nervous systems. They are well suited to tasks involving pattern recognition, but must be trained using a

---

*We note that recognition is an integral part of total cognition, involving learning as well as strictly mechanical functions, and is difficult to consider independently of the brain that does the seeing.

number of examples. Also, they are not automatically adaptable to new situations, but must be retrained when new patterns are introduced or the environment changes. They can be simulated on conventional computers, but special-purpose neural network hardware is becoming available. Neural network hardware may be the technology of choice for well-defined functions such as the front ends of machine vision and automatic target-recognition subsystems for unmanned military vehicles.

Genetic Learning: Genetic learning shares with neural networks the trait of optimization through learning, but adds a factor of random selection from a "gene pool." This implies that the performance of a genetic learning system may not always be quite optimal, but the system will be able to adapt to the unexpected, given sufficient time and tolerance for trial-and-error.

Levels of Control

Remote Control: The term "remote control" is used here to refer to the simplest (and least expensive) way to achieve a remote capability. Remote control refers only to the ability to remotely actuate those mechanisms necessary for the vehicle to perform some limited task (usually drive) under direct supervision. Radio-controlled toys demonstrate this level of control, whereby the operator always keeps the remotely controlled vehicle under direct observation. A remotely controlled battle tank, equipped with suitable plows or rakes, and with an operator safely located in another nearby tank, can be used to breach barriers or mine fields while keeping the operator out of harm's way. This type of control is only suitable for very limited, short-distance, "brute-force" types of applications. However, for those tasks, it is the simplest, cheapest, and most robust of the levels of control available.

Teleoperated Control: As with remote control, teleoperated UGVs depend on the operator's reflexes to control the vehicle. However, teleoperated vehicles may go beyond direct observation. Hence, the remote human operator must be given a sense of telepresence (usually a video display) as though he or she were actually on board the vehicle. Night vision may be required as well as the ability to see through fog and battlefield smoke. Because the operator needs a reasonably high-resolution video system to see the terrain ahead of and around the vehicle, high data-link bandwidths have been mandatory. The data link must also be non-line-of-sight (NLOS) because the UGV may have to navigate around obstructions. If analog video signals are transmitted, bandwidths of the order of 5–6 MHz per channel are required (10–12 MHz for nonfield sequential stereo). A radio-frequency (RF) link initially appears to be operationally ideal for this application. Unfortunately, the multimegahertz bandwidths required for real-time video in the NLOS region of the RF spectrum are not available in most locales, whereas higher frequencies at which such bandwidths are permissible do not exhibit the propagation characteristics necessary for NLOS operations. (Before a proposed weapons system can be approved for production, it must be granted a worldwide frequency allocation.) For this reason, reinforced fiber-optic (FO) cable is currently under evaluation as a candidate data link for controlling teleoperated UGVs. The disadvantages of FO cable reside in its logistical burden on the battlefield and in the cost of replacement. The advantages of FO cable lie in its wide bandwidth capacity and in the difficulty of detecting or intercepting cable-transmitted signals.

As television systems convert from analog to digital, the bandwidths required for video transmission become less easily estimated. Without image compression, full-motion, full-color, 525-line digital video requires a bandwidth of 198.45 MHz—much greater than the bandwidth required for a conventional analog TV picture. However, by making use of intraframe redundancies and interframe predictabilities, digital image compression techniques can currently provide video compression ratios of 100 : 1 to 200 : 1 without a major loss of perceived picture quality. This still requires bandwidths of 1–2 MHz, but reductions in picture resolution, color range, and frame update rate can permit the transmission of small-picture color video over voice grade (25 kHz) telephone lines. This imagery is not yet adequate for fully teleoperated UGV driving purposes, but as further major improvements are made in digital video compression technology, voice communications systems such as tactical radios might be able to support real-time remote driving, particularly if more than one channel could be made available for UGV control.

It should be noted that the introduction of high-definition TV during the 1990s should make 800-pixel × 1400-pixel digital video equipment available for military applications, although it will require a 6-MHz bandwidth.

Computer-Assisted Teleoperation: One approach to lowering the video bandwidth requirements for a UGV is that of giving the vehicle sufficient local autonomy to permit it to drive from waypoint to waypoint without directly articulating the actuators, such as steering and throttle. Then the driver's function becomes that of merely selecting the path, thus permitting a slower frame rate lying within the 16-kHz transmission speed of a voice-grade tactical radio channel. The Unmanned Ground Vehicle Joint Project Office (UGV JPO) recently demonstrated such a system known as FELICS (Feedback Limited Control System). Using FELICS, a six-wheeled all-terrain vehicle can be remotely maneuvered quite nicely with video frame rates as low as one frame every 3 seconds.

In addition to facilitating non-line-of-sight operations without a fiber-optic tether, Computer-Assisted Teleoperation (CAT) also dramatically reduces operator workload. Concerns related to workload are not simply humanitarian. Quite the contrary, high operator workload means rapid degradation in system performance because the operator soon becomes the "weak link." Reductions in operator burden pay immediate dividends in increased operational effectiveness of unmanned systems.

NASA's Jet Propulsion Laboratory is also pursuing research into computer-aided remote driving in conjunction with lunar and Mars roving vehicles, where frame rates may be on the order of one every several minutes. Within the U.S. Department of Defense, on the other hand, the Defense Advanced Research Projects Agency has sponsored extensive research supporting autonomous vehicles.

Autonomous: Because of the dramatically lower control bandwidth required for aerial and underwater vehicles (due to their compliant, fluid environments), "brilliant" autonomous aerial vehicles already exist in the form of the latest generation of cruise missiles and the "brilliant" weapons currently under development. Because the cognitive powers of fully-autonomous UGVs must be greater than those of semiautomated UGVs, fully-autonomous UGVs may be expected to appear at a later date (probably after the year 2000). Their first roles will likely come in semistructured environments, such as the guarding of ammunition dumps or airfields. The appearance of autonomous vacuum cleaners and floor scrubbers, if and when they arrive on the commercial scene, would probably exert a stimulative effect on military robots and vice versa.

During the 1980s, DARPA and the U.S. Army Engineer Topographic Laboratories sponsored trailblazing work on an autonomous land vehicle (ALV). By 1992, the DARPA-sponsored Autonomous Land Vehicle In a Neural Network (ALLVIN) was able to drive autonomously down Interstate 79 for 21 miles at a speed in excess of 55 miles an hour, using a mechanical vision system developed at Carnegie Mellon University to monitor road edge location.

Several military efforts have been mounted to develop autonomous sentry robots. Among these are the DARPA-sponsored PROWLER, which could detect nuclear–biological–chemical contaminants, a U.S. Navy-sponsored surveillance robot (ROBART), a Naval Ocean Systems Center Ground Surveillance Robot (GSR), and a U.S. Air Force Wright-Patterson Air Force Base robot called Marvin. One civilian sentry robot called the ScoutAbout is allegedly being brought to market in 1992 by Samsung Corporation.

Bystander safety will probably be perceived as an important issue in regions where humans and robots must share the same local environment. For this reason, the first autonomous robot may well take the form of small, nonharmful devices until they have demonstrated their safety in the field. However, the acceptance of antilock brakes and autonomous transit systems may help to mitigate these concerns.

Data Communication Alternatives

Considerable attention has been devoted to alternative communications schemes. Geosynchronous-satellite communications are unattractive because of electromagnetic propagation delays (1/2 second or longer), because of susceptibility to jamming, and because of the relative scarcity (or high cost) of available bandwidth. Low-orbit satellites could afford acceptable propagation delays, but a number of satellites would be required to ensure that at least one of them were in view at all times. Tracking could also become a problem. Airborne relays such as UAVs or balloons are possible, but mission complexity, antenna pointing, and time on station can become problematic. Micrometeorite communication systems are intermittent and expensive, but might be suitable for autonomous or semiautonomous UGVs requiring only intermittent communications. Ultraviolet communication is very dependent on atmospheric conditions (e.g., ozone concentrations), is visible to the enemy, and can be hazardous to personnel (9).

Current plans call for a redundant communications system for the initial Tactical Unmanned Ground Vehicle (TUGV). This system would probably consist of a narrow-band (tactical) RF link, a wide-band RF link, and a fiber-optic link. The wide-band RF, with commercially available data compression equipment, can provide near-real-time video as long as the line-of-sight can be maintained between transmitter and receiver. Real-time video is particularly desirable for remote surveillance tasks. Narrow-band RF (also known as tactical RF) provides good propagation characteristics for non-line-of-sight communications, but has very limited bandwidth (data capacity). Using Computer-Assisted Teleoperation and available data compression systems, the TUGV can be satisfactorily maneuvered using the single frame every 1–3 seconds that tactical RF systems can provide. (Note that as data compression techniques improve, so too will the available frame rates using narrow-band RF.) Single-use, fiber-optic packs, known as "battle packs," can be used for those operations where covert operations are more important than tactical flexibility, such as long-duration, stationary surveillance missions. (Note that fiber-optic cable, because it engenders a physical tether, tends to limit operational flexibility, particularly in a highly mobile environment.) These battle packs would permit real-time surveillance (audio and video) during "radio silence," thus virtually eliminating any possibility of detection or jamming. Single-use packs largely ameliorate the operational and logistical burden normally associated with reusable fiber-optic communication systems.

Human Factors Engineering

Because UAVs have now become semiautonomous vehicles with manual override and because changes occur relatively slowly in a three-dimensional medium, human factors is perhaps less of an issue in their design. A similar situation exists with respect to UUVs. However, human factors have proven to be a serious concern for teleoperated UGVs bouncing over rough terrain in the neighborhood of vulnerable bystanders. Unlike a UAV or a UUV, a remotely driven (as opposed to remotely controlled) UGV requires the undivided attention and split-second responses of its driver. The problems which have surfaced in conjunction with the direct teleoperation of UGVs lie in the difficulties of providing a driver with adequately realistic simulations of cab conditions in the vehicle being driven. Wide-angle displays are desirable not only when making a right-angle turn or spotting something approaching from the side, but also to keep the driver oriented. However, wide-angle displays require extra video bandwidth and wide screen displays. Sound is another desirable feedback clue, and stereo sound has been provided both to and from the UGVs which are currently under evaluation. A sizeable fraction of UGV ''drivers'' become nauseated, perhaps because of the disparity between what the driver sees and what the driver feels. (The full kinesthetic feedback used in some flight simulators may be desirable, but would be difficult to simulate in a mobile operator control unit.*) Fatigue has been another common companion of UGV drivers, perhaps because of the high levels of concentration necessary to offset the lack of realism they experience. Two common problems with experimental UGVs have been the dangers of unwittingly tilting the vehicles until they rolled over and of failing to see curbs, gullies, and dropoffs. Presumably, these problems arose because some of the early experimental UGVs lacked vehicle attitude feedback and high-resolution stereo video.

Both head-mounted and flat-screen displays have been explored for UGV control. Full color, high-resolution, head-mounted displays are difficult to implement and are fatiguing to their operators. They isolate the operators from what is going on around them. Flat-screen displays are bulkier than head-mounted displays and do not lend themselves as well to stereo presentations, but are the displays of choice for the current military UGVs.

One remaining issue is that of driving-camera stabilization. Lens stabilization systems are available which will steady the video image for the driver. Alternatively, the image can be electronically stabilized even though the camera may be bouncing around. For UGV driving purposes, an image stabilization system which filters out high-frequency and high-amplitude vibration would be ideal, leaving only the low-amplitude, low-frequency vibrations as visual cues for the driver as to road conditions.

As high-definition TV equipment becomes available, it may well be substituted for existing displays, perhaps affording the realism which has been missing from teleoperated driving controllers, albeit at the cost of extra bandwidth. However, as semiautonomous UGVs continue to rapidly evolve, they may indeed obviate much of the need for high-definition, wideband video, at least for the ''driving'' function.

It should be noted that with the dramatically reduced operator workload associated with Computer-Assisted Teleoperation, many of these Human Factors Engineering (HFE) issues may become less critical. Nonetheless, sound human factors engineering will remain an essential design consideration of any future military system, including UVs.

---

*One Soviet UUV program called ''Manta'' utilized a servo-controlled, hydraulically driven operator's chair. Results of the study are not known.

Other Technological Issues

Propulsion

Key propulsion issues with underwater propulsion systems are those of low-drag hulls and battery performance. Silver/zinc batteries with an energy capacity of 325 kWh are currently used to power DARPA UUVs. However, research is underway to triple this energy density to 1000 kWh or more by the mid-1990s, and to 10-fold it by the latter 1990s by switching to fuel cells or semicells.

Because they do not have to be man-rated, UAV designers have been able to gamble on and to profit from the high power-to-weight ratios of rotary engines. Three efforts are currently underway to adapt UAV engines to heavy fuel operation because gasoline-powered engines may no longer be fielded. Southwest Research Institute was funded to develop a 50-hp, two-stroke, Direct Injection Stratified Charge engine which will weigh only a little more than 1 pound per horsepower. Defense Group Incorporated is modifying an existing Wankel engine, the LCR400SD, to operate on heavy fuels. AAI Corporation is also exploring a Wankel design, using the Norton NR-631 rotary engine as a point of departure.

UGV propulsion has been the subject of several studies, including an in-depth study by the U.S. Army Tank and Automotive Command, summarized in the U.S. Army/Marine Corps Trade-Off Determination (TOD) (10). This study concluded that a six-wheeled vehicle with certain design parameters specified in the study offered great promise for UGVs, and these concepts have been incorporated into a Surrogate Teleoperated Vehicle (STV). However, many UGV experiments have utilized tracked or four-wheeled vehicles because of their availability in the armed services inventory.

Because tracked and wheeled vehicles can bog down in rough terrain, there has been long-term interest in developing multilegged propulsion systems which step over obstacles and climb the steepest grades. Two walking robots were developed in the 1950s and 1960s: the GE Quadroped "walking truck" and the Ohio State University Adaptive Suspension Vehicle (ASV). The four-legged Quadroped proved to be exhausting to control, but the six-legged ASV, with the innate stability which derives from keeping three legs on the ground at all times, was a qualified success. Because of this inherent stability, current ambulatory robots are generally hexapodal. One drawback to walking robots has been the fact that their power requirements are generally far greater than those required for wheeled vehicles. This led Carnegie Mellon University researchers to devise a multilegged vehicle with wheels for feet. The vehicle can roll over terrain which is not too rough, while stepping over or around larger obstacles.

Sensors

Onboard sensors for an unmanned ground vehicle must generally be solid-state devices to withstand the shock and vibration loads which may be imposed on them. FLIRS are desirable for night vision and for driving through obscurants, but the need to cool them can limit mission endurance. For reconnaissance purposes, the battery drain imposed by continuous-duty video cameras and their associated data links has impelled the use of low-drain acoustic sensors to cue the reconnaissance cameras, which remain in standby mode until alerted by the sonic sensors. Other desirable onboard sensors include inclinometers, stereo microphones, and shock and vibration transducers.

Navigation

Positions and routes of UGVs must be known within meters, and preferably, within 1 m. Current systems utilize Global Positioning System (GPS) satellite receivers as a coarse navigation aid, and dead reckoning or inertial systems for redundancy. Navigation beacons have also been used, although these imply a structured environment. Map-matching affords another potential approach, given sufficient computer power and detailed, a priori map data.

Navigation is a particularly demanding problem of UUVs because of the difficulty of transmitting GPS signals underwater. Dead-reckoning systems utilizing magnetic compass readings and acoustic ground velocity sensors are being explored as low-cost navigation systems for UUVs.

CURRENT PROJECTS

UAV

Unmanned drones have been widely used for target practice before, and particularly since World War II.

A number of companies in several countries now market unmanned aerial vehicles, including Canada's rotary-wing CL-227 Sentinel (nicknamed "the flying peanut"), the United Kingdom's fixed-wing GEC Phoenix and rotary-wing M.L. Sprite (nicknamed "the flying basketball"), Italy's Mirach-20 Pelican RPV, and the Israeli Mastiff and Scout, described earlier.

Currently, within the United States, the U.S. Navy is using the Pioneer as a ship-launched UAV and the Marine Corps is using the Pointer as an expendable drone until a Joint Services' family of unmanned aerial vehicles can be acquired and deployed. This family of interoperable UAVs will consist of a Close Range UAV, operating within 30 km of its ground station, a Short Range UAV, operating at distances up to 150 km (350 km with a relay), and a jet-engine-powered, Mid Range UAV, which is able to operate at ranges up to 650 km. These UAVs are expected to be equipped with at least video cameras and FLIRs.

UAV—Close Range (CR)

The Close Range (CR) UAV is currently undergoing a risk-reduction series of technical demonstrations. It must afford at least a 30-km range, with a 50-km range desired. Its gross takeoff weight must not exceed 200 pounds, and it must be able to take off and land in a small clearing among trees. It must have a mission duration of 3 hours, with a 4-hour duration desired. Support equipment must consist of no more than one High Mobility Multi-Wheeled Vehicle (HMMWV) and a trailer. It must satisfy the same target recognition and altitude ceiling requirements as those imposed on the Short Range UAV.

UAV—Short Range (SR)

Two companies competed for the role of supplying the U.S. armed forces with a Short Range (SR) UAV. The Sky Owl, created jointly by the McDonnell Douglas Corporation and Developmental Sciences, is essentially an upgrade to the Skyeye UAV currently in production (11). It has a wingspan of 24 feet, a launch weight of 1200 pounds, a 90-hp rotary engine which provides a top speed of 120 knots, and a maximum rate of climb of 750 feet per minute. It is launched using a hydraulic catapult and landed using either a parafoil or a skid landing gear. Its planned payloads consist of a CCD TV camera with a 10 : 1 zoom lens or a FLIR. The Sky Owl can perform its missions in an autonomous, preprogrammed mode using waypoint navigation, with optional manual override.

The Hunter, produced jointly by Israel Aircraft Industries and Thompson Ramo Wooldridge Corporation, is a twin-boomed, pusher-puller aircraft with a wingspan of 29 feet, a maximum gross takeoff weight of 1400 pounds, and a flight time of up to 12 hours. It is ruggedly designed, with redundant components where feasible, to increase its survivability and recoverability. Its fuselage cross sections, tail booms, and vertical tail surfaces are fabricated of materials which minimize detection. It utilizes sensor packages similar to those of the Sky Owl and, like the Sky Owl, can serve as a data relay. Launch and recovery may take place from unimproved airfields. Launch may also be provided from a zero-length launcher with a solid rocket booster system, and recovery may be effected utilizing an installed parachute retrieval system.

The UAV-SR contract was awarded to IAI for the Hunter System in July 1992. The delivery date for the initial systems is 1996.

UAV—Mid-Range (MR)

The Advanced Tactical Air Reconnaissance System (ATARS) Midrange (MR) UAV, created by Teledyne Ryan and Control Data Corporations, is a 2000 pound, jet-engine-powered, medium to high subsonic speed UAV with a maximum range of 650 km and a 300-pound payload (12). It can be ground or air launched and will be dry or wet recovered by parachute. ATARS will likely carry an interchangeable sensor module which will probably be called the common sensor suite (CSS). The basic members of this sensor module consist of the 152° field-of-view (FOV) Low Altitude Electro-Optic and Medium Altitude Electro-Optic sensors and a 140° FOV infrared line scanner (IRLS), with a synthetic aperture radar and a selection of FLIRs available when needed.

UAV—Maritime

A Maritime UAV which can "provide aerial coverage to small combatants, amphibious forces, and other naval forces outside the umbrella of carrier or shore based air (13). It will be a VTOL or tilt rotor craft and must be compatible with existing collateral hardware and command and control systems (14). It will be used for over-the-horizon targeting, battle damage assessment, communications relay, and ship defense and will be deployed between 1996 and 2000.

In addition to these formal developmental projects, the UAV Joint Project Office will continue experimentation with the CL-227 as a vertical takeoff and landing craft, the EXDRONE expendable drone, and tilt rotor/tilt wing vehicles.

Unmanned Underwater Vehicles

Experimental Autonomous Vehicle (EAVE)

Low-level functions such as initial data processing and vehicle control are performed by a set of three 68000-based computers. These processors are serially linked to a 12-slot VME-based system containing multiple 68020 single-board computers which handle the higher-level knowledge-based processing for this vehicle (15).

The Autonomous Benthic Explorer

Primary application of the Autonomous Benthic Explorer (ABE) will be repeated surveys of hydrothermal vent areas at depths of 4000 m (16). The computer system is distributed with low-powered single-chip microcomputers (68HC11) communicating serially. Several of the nodes have additional computing power implemented with transputers (T800).

EUREKA

Two concept vehicles are under development under the aegis of the EUREKA project: the Work and Inspection Robot (WIR) and the Autonomous Robot for Underwater Survey (ARUS). Among the technologies under study are AI for Autonomous Underwater Vehicles (AUVs), high-resolution obstacle avoidance and recognition sonar, automatic image recognition, precision guidance, underwater power generation, and long-range acoustic communications for AUVs.

AUTOSUB

The United Kingdom is mounting a UUV development effort centered around two vehicles: the Deep Ocean Long Path Hydrographic Instrument (DOLPHIN) and the Deep Ocean Geological and Geophysical Instrumented Explorer (DOGGIE). Key technological research areas are pressure hull design, low-drag, energy systems, sensors, control systems, and precise navigation.

Japanese Efforts

Japan has produced 1 autonomous and 12 tethered ROVs and is utilizing them to investigate fiber-optic gyros, acoustic telemetry of video information, acoustic imaging, pattern recognition, and laser ranging and propulsion system technologies.

UGV

Surrogate Teleoperated Vehicles

The U.S. Armed Forces are currently evaluating a small fleet of surrogate teleoperated UGVs to assess their battlefield utility. The platform vehicle is a six-wheeled "Polaris" all-terrain vehicle, powered either by a 25-hp diesel or a 3-hp electric motor. This UGV, called the Surrogate Teleoperated Vehicle (STV), is equipped with a 460-line, stereo day driving camera, a 500-line image-intensified, night driving camera, day and night monoscopic cameras (with the same respective resolutions as the driving cameras) for performing reconnaissance, surveillance, and target acquisition (RSTA), and a forward-looking infrared radiometer (FLIR). It also has a laser ranger/designator and acoustic sensors to alert the operator to the presence of potential objects of interest. The cameras are mounted on a 10-foot extendable mast. Remote stereo microphones and speakers are also provided to allow two-way conversations between the STV driver and personnel in the vicinity of the remote vehicle. The vehicle is equipped with remotely actuated steering, accelerator, brake and transmission controls. Video data and control signals between the vehicle and the operator traverse a fiber-optic-cable primary link or an RF secondary link. The fiber-optic cable is dispensed from and retrieved to a drum mounted on the back of the STV. The RF link is used for training and may be used as an emergency backup for the fiber-optic cable if the cable is severed, or during operations where fiber-optic cable is inappropriate. Navigation is provided by a GPS system with (10-m accuracy), and with a dead-reckoning backup system. The vehicle may also be driven by an onboard human operator by disengaging the remotely actuated controls. This test version of a STV has a top speed of 35 miles per hour. The operator control unit features two color video displays for driving/RSTA and navigation. The OCU has provision for displaying global, local, and driving maps (17).

This STV will be used to acquaint users with some of the possibilities and limitations of current tactical UGVs (TUGVs), and to obtain user feedback regarding desirable, affordable product improvements prior to production of the initial TUGV system.

Another promising possibility is the development of retrofit kits for existing military vehicles. One such kit is the Pele telerobotic control system for battle tanks developed by the Ramta Division of Israel Aircraft Industries. Universal remote kits, consisting of an OCU, data link, and actuator package (as well as appropriate sensors), can provide new options to the tactical field commander.

Rapid Runway Repair

One major wartime challenge is that of rapid repair of bomb-damaged runways after enemy attack, including the potential for contamination with unexploded ordnance as well as nuclear, biological, or chemical agents. To expedite runway repair, the U.S. Air Force contracted with John Deer and Company to build a telerobotic UGV. This was initially attempted using a commercial John Deere 690D excavator. A custom-designed vehicle is currently under development for this mission. The timetable calls for a demonstration of autonomous path-planning using inertial and GPS navigation in August 1993. A live demonstration of a complete system will be conducted in 1994, including multiple vehicle command, control, and communications.

Remote Ordnance Neutralization Device

A Joint Services Operational Requirement for a Remote Ordnance Neutralization Device (ROND) was released on 26 February 1990 and is currently scheduled for acquisition in 1997. The ROND consists of a six-wheeled mobile platform mounting a single television camera capable of normal or low-light-level operation, a fiber-optic link, an RF link, and a seven-function manipulator. It will be powered by a hybrid, lightweight diesel/electric battery system. The manipulator will be able to reach from 6 feet above ground to 2 feet below ground at 3 feet, from all the edges of the mobile platform. It will possess a quick tool change capability which can be performed telerobotically. Among the various tools which can be attached are a 0.50 caliber dearmer, a socket wrench, a mechanical impact wrench, and various common hand tools. The two efforts currently underway consist of a design/development contract and a nondevelopmental item approach to identify commercially available devices that most nearly meet the ROND requirements.

THE FUTURE

Unmanned vehicles are one of the potential few bright spots for the future of the U.S. defense industry. But more importantly, they may represent an important and fundamental shift in some of that industry's basic operating paradigms.

Unmanned systems, like any new military system, must contribute to war fighting capabilities. Furthermore, unmanned vehicles should help to minimize friendly casualties, including fratricide. But they may also represent a class of military systems whereby industry primarily exploits available technology to satisfy a military need, rather than using a military need to create a technology base for a unique subset of the defense industry.

Consider that most military commodities are sufficiently unique that they engender entire industries to support them. The building of war ships, war planes, and battle tanks are industries unto themselves, with apparently only limited spin-off potential for commercial or dual-use applications. Unmanned vehicles, on the other hand, primarily exploit vehicle, control, sensor, and display technologies that already exist or are already being developed for other uses. Furthermore, the ability to remotely maneuver a vehicle, be it under water, in the air, or on the ground, into a hazardous area and perform useful tasks has tremendous possibilities for both military and civil applications.

Hence, unmanned vehicles may well represent a new paradigm whereby America can retain sufficient military capabilities for an uncertain world while simultaneously managing scarce resources to address the many pressing social issues at home. Let us hope so.

REFERENCES

1. Steven M. Shaker and Alan R. Wise, *War Without Men: Robots on the Future Battlefield*, Future Warfare Series, Vol. II, Pergamon–Brassey's International Defense Publishers, Inc., New York, 1988.
2. Karel Capek, *Rossem's Universal Robots*, P. Selver (transl.), Washington Press, New York, 1973). Originally published in 1921.
3. George Fichtl, "The Army and UAVs: 'A History; The Future'," presentation given at Redstone Arsenal, August 24, 1988.
4. Gerald Green, "Washington Perspective," *Unmanned Systems: The Magazine of the Association for Unmanned Vehicle Systems*, 9 (1) 6 (1991).
5. "Japan Aims at Smarter Computers Again," *Popular Science*, 240 (3) 55, 1992.
6. Hans P. Moravec, *Mind Children: The Future of Human and Robot Intelligence*, Harvard University Press, Cambridge, MA, 1988.
7. "Danny Hillis Philosophizes on the Brain," *Electronic Engineering Times*, January 28, 1991.
8. George Miel, "Supercomputers and CFD," *Aerospace America*, 30 (1), 33 (1991).
9. Jeffrey A. Randorf and Robert N. Seitz, "NLOS Communications for Teleoperated Ground Vehicles: Overview '91," *Proceedings of the AUVS 91 Annual Symposium*, Washington, D.C., August 1991.
10. U.S. Army Tank and Automotive Command, *Trade-Off Determination: United States Tactical Unmanned Ground Vehicle (Caleb) and United States Marine Corps Unmanned Ground Vehicle (UGV)*, U.S. Army Tank and Automotive Command, Detroit, MI, September 1990 (2 vols.). This study was sponsored by the UGV JPO at Redstone Arsenal, AL.
11. Jim Bledsoe and Jim Schneider, "Sky Owl: A Total System for the 90s," *Unmanned Systems: The Magazine of the Association for Unmanned Vehicle Systems*, 9 (1), 38 (1991).
12. Michael S. Gaydeski, "Unmanned Air Reconnaissance System," *Unmanned Systems: The Magazine of the Association for Unmanned Vehicle Systems*, 9 (2), 41 (1991).
13. Rear Admiral George F. A. Wagner, USN, "UAV Program Overview," *Unmanned Systems*, 9(3) (Summer 1991) 10.
14. Edward E. Davis, "Maritime UAV: Challenge Ahead," *Unmanned Systems: The Magazine of the Association for Unmanned Vehicle Systems*, 9 (1), 22 (1991).
15. D. Richard Blidberg, "Autonomous Underwater Vehicles: A Tool for the Ocean," *Unmanned Systems: The Magazine of the Association for Unmanned Vehicle Systems*, 9 (2), 10 (1991).
16. Dana R. Yoerger, Albert M. Bradley, and Barrie B. Walden, "The Autonomous Benthic Explorer," *Unmanned Systems: The Magazine of the Association for Unmanned Vehicle Systems*, 9 (2) 17 (1991).
17. Robert Finkelstein, "Cyberforce: Troika Revisited," *Unmanned Systems: The Magazine of the Association for Unmanned Vehicle Systems*, 9 (2), 5 (1991).

BIBLIOGRAPHY

"AAI Corp. Will Deliver Initial Pioneer I to Navy in May," *Aviation Week & Space Technology*, April 28, 1986, p. 109.

Abronson, R., "Robots Go To War," *Machine Design*, December 6, 1984, pp. 72–79.

Adams, R., L. Lehman, and M. Herskovitz, "A Ship-Based High Altitude RPV Study," *Unmanned Systems*, 25–29, 4 (Winter 1985).

Alterman, S., and S. Stolfo, "The Application of Parallel Processor Technology to Future Unmanned Vehicles Systems," *Unmanned Systems*, 10–19 (Fall 1985).

"Architectures for Real-Time Intelligent Control of Unmanned Vehicles Systems," *Minutes of Workshop #1 on Concept of Operations and System Requirements, Joint Technology Panel for Robotics*, August 21–22 1990.

Arditi, J., "Design Procedure for a UAV Data Link," *Unmanned Systems*, pp. 33–37 (Spring 1989).

Asimov, I., "The Perfect Machine," *Science Journal*, 115–118 (October 1968).

Asimov, I., and K. Frenkel, *Robots: Machines in Man's Image*, Harmony Books, New York, 1985.

"The Autonomous Remotely Controlled Submersible (ARCS)," *Sub Notes*, 14–15 (June 1985).

Barradale, A., "U. K. Military Applications for Unmanned Vehicles," *Unmanned Systems*, 37–41 (Summer 1989).

Barrett, F., "The Robot Revolution," *The Futurist*, pp. 37–40 (October 1985).

Bartholet, T., "Odetics Pioneering Development of Advanced Intelligent Machines," *Unmanned Systems*, 13–15, 30 (Spring 1986).

Bledsoe, Jim, and Jim Shneider, "Sky Owl: A Total System for the 90s," *Unmanned Systems*, 38 (Winter 1991).

Blidberg, D. Richard, "Autonomous Underwater Vehicles: A Tool for the Ocean," *Unmanned Systems*, 10 (Spring 1991).

Bode, B., "Modifications of A Commercial Excavator for Rapid Runway Repair," paper presented at the *Government/Industry & Exposition* (*SAE Technical Paper Series*), Washington, DC, May 1984.

Bond, N., "Japanese Progress in Robotics: Tokyo Conference and Exhibition", *Scientific Bulletin Department of the Navy Office of Naval Research Far East*, 77–110 (October–December 1983).

"British Army Selects Real-Time Remote Artillery Direction System," *Aviation Week & Space Technology*, April 28, 1986, p. 61.

"British Companies Develop Range of Surveillance, Target Systems," *Aviation Week & Space Technology*, April 28, 1986, pp. 91–97.

"British RPV With Infrared Sensor Will Produce Real-Time Data," *Aviation Week & Space Technology*, April 8, 1985, p 42.

Britton, P., "Engineering The New Breed of Walking Machine," *Popular Science*, 66–69 (September 1984).

Broad, W., "Submersible Joins in Search for Challenger Debris," *New York Times*, February 16, 1986, p. 1.

Busby, F., "ROVs: Uncertain Times," *Sea Technology*, 41 (March 1985).

Byrne, Raymond H., and Klarer, Paul R., "Military Robotics Technologies at Sandia National Laboratories," *Unmanned Systems*, 42 (Springer 1992).

"Cable-Controlled Underwater Recovery Vehicle (CURV III)," *Seahorse*, 10 (Spring 1982).

Capek, K., *Rossum's Universal Robots*, P. Selver (transl.), Washington Press, New York, 1973 (original work published 1921).

Cerny, J., "Land Robot Revolution," *Unmanned Systems*, 12–13, 30 (Spring 1986).

Culver, W., and R. Smith, "Optical Links for Unmanned Vehicles," *Unmanned Systems*, 24–30 (Winter 1991).

Cushman, J., "Undersea Robots For Mines," *Navy News & Undersea Technology*, March 29, 1985, p. 5.

"Danny Hillis Philosophizes on the Brain," *Electronic Engineering Times*, January 28, 1991.

"DARPA Seeks Mobile Battlefield Robot Capable of Thinking for Itself," *Military Space Electronics Design*, 10–11 (December 1984).

Davis, Edward E., "Maritime UAV: Challenge Ahead," *Unmanned Systems*, 22 (Winter 1991).

DePauk, P., and J. Wullert, "Navy Technology Requirements for Unmanned Airborne Vehicles," *Unmanned Systems*, 38–40 (Fall 1985).

"Dornier Developing Argus 2 Battlefield Surveillance System," *Aviation Week & Space Technology*, June 10, 1985, p. 73.

"ECA Develops Epaulard Unmanned Submersible," *Jane's Defense Weekly*, April 20, 1985, p. 68.

Eisenstadt, S., "Lear Siegler and Egypt Near Agreement on Skyeye RPVs," *Defense News*, February 3, 1986, p. 1.

Everett, H., "Shipboard Applications—Are The Robots Really Coming?," paper presented at the *22nd Annual Technical Symposium, Association of Scientists and Engineers of the Naval Sea Systems Command*, Washington, DC, 1985.

Finkelstein, R. "Terrorism, Ants and Unmanned Vehicles," *Unmanned Systems*, 40, 45 (Summer 1985).

Finkelstein, R., "TROIKA: A Concept for a Robotic Weapon System," *Unmanned Systems*, 6–7 (Fall 1983).

Finkelstein, R., "Cyberforce: Troika Revisited," *Unmanned Systems*, 5 (Spring 1991).

Flynn, A., "Redundant Sensors for Mobile Robot Navigation," Master of Science thesis, Massachusetts Institute of Technology, 1985.

Fulsang, E., "AI and Autonomous Military Robots," *Unmanned Systems*, 8–16 (Spring 1985).

Fulsang, E., "Robots On The Battlefield," *Defense Electronics*, 77–82 (October 1985).

Gaydeski, Michael S., "Unmanned Air Reconnaissance System," *Unmanned Systems*, 41 (Spring 1991).

Gleason, T., "Mini-UAV Data Links," *Unmanned Systems*, 24–31 (xxx, 1988).

Green, Gerald, "Washington Perspective," *Unmanned Systems*, 6 (Winter 1991).

Hall, Jerry, "Unmanned Ground Vehicles—An Update," *Unmanned Systems*, 16 (Spring 1992).

Hambley, C., "Remote Possibilities," *Sea Power*, 24–35 (January 1987).

Hennebeck, L. M., "Lessons for Tomorrow's Battlefield," *Unmanned Systems*, 31 (Spring 1992).

Herman, M., and J. Albus, "Overview of MAUV: Multiple Autonomous Undersea Vehicles," *Unmanned Systems*, 36–52 (Winter 1988/89).

Hirose, S., "A Study of Design and Control of a Quadruped Walking Vehicle," *Int. J. Robotics Res.* 113–133 (Summer 1984).

Hirose, S., and Y. Umetari, "Some Considerations On A Feasible Walking Mechanism As A Terrain Vehicle," paper presented at the *Third CISM-IFYoMM International Symposium On Theory and Practice of Robots and Manipulators*, Udine, Italy, September 1978, pp. 357–375.

Isler, W., "Developments With DARPA's ALV," *Unmanned Systems*, 22–23 (Spring 1986).

"Japan Aims at Smarter Computers Again," *Popular Science*, 55 (March 1992).

Klass, P., "DARPA Envisions New Generation of Machine Intelligence Technology," *Aviation Week & Space Technology*, April 22, 1985, pp. 46–54.

Klemow, M., "Israel Aircraft Industries/TRW HUNTER Short Range UAV Program," *Unmanned Systems*, 42, 44–46 (Summer 1991).

Kozlov. N., and Ye Balanin, "Military Robots," *Soviet Military Rev.*, 26–27 (April 1983).

Lee, W., and M. Vuk, "A Mobile Military/Security System: Tactical Application of the PROWLER Robot," *Unmanned Systems*, 28–31 (Spring 1984).

Lindauer, B., J. Fini, and J. Hill, "Military Robotics: An Overview," *Robotics Age*, 16–21 (November 1985).

Liston, R., and Mosher, R., "A Versatile Walking Truck," paper presented at the *1968 Transportation Engineering Conference (ASME–NYAS)*, Washington, DC, 1968.

Lovece, J., "Military Robotics: 1990 And Beyond," *Unmanned Systems*, 11–15 (Winter 1990).

Manners, G., "Scicon's Intelligent Underwater Robot," *Jane's Defense Weekly*, September 21, 1985.

"Manufacturers Tailor Basic Engines For RPV Missions," *Aviation Week & Space Technology*, April 28, 1986, p. 111.

McDonnell, J., M. Solorzano, S. Martin, and A. Umeda," A Head Coupled Sensor Platform For Teleoperated Ground Vehicles," *Unmanned Systems*, 33–38 (Fall 1990).

McGhee, R., and K. Waldron, "The Adaptive Suspension Vehicle Project," *Unmanned Systems*, 34–43 (Summer 1989).

Meieran, H., "World Research Activities for Practical Mobile Robots," *Unmanned Systems*, 17–23 (Summer 1989).

Mettala, Erik B., "DEMO-II Supervised Autonomy for UGVs," *Unmanned Systems*, 39 (Spring 1992).

Metz, C., "Use of Fiber Optic Data Links in Marine Corps Unmanned Vehicles," *Proceedings of AUVS '88*, 12–17, 46–53 (1988).

Miel, George, "Supercomputers and CFD," *Aerospace America*, *30*(1), 33 (1991).

Minutes of *NATO DRUG Seminar on Battlefield Robotics*, Paris-ENSTA, 6–8 March 1991.

Mirick, C., "A Wild-Goose Chase: Early Navy Work on Pilotless Aircraft and Ships," *Proceedings*, 947–951 (July 1946).

"Mobile Robot for Perimeter Patrol," *Defense Electronics*, 188 (September 1984).

Moravec, Hans P., *Mind Children: The Future of Human and Robot Intelligence*, Harvard University Press, Cambridge, MA, 1988.

"NATO Strategies, Limited Resources Increase Uses for Unmanned Systems," *Aviation Week & Space Technology*, April 28, 1986, pp. 51–56.

Piper, R., "The Unmanned Air Reconnaissance System (UARS)," *Unmanned Systems*, 26, 28, 30 (Winter 1988/89).

Robinson, R., "Unmanned Untethered Submersibles for National Defense," *Unmanned Systems*, 32–37 (Fall 1985).

Schaphorst, R., and A. Deutermann, "Video Compression for Unmanned Airborne/Ground Vehicles," *Unmanned Systems*, 17–23 (Winter 1991).

"Sea Eagle and Pluto: Mine-Disposal Submersibles from Sweden and Italy," *Int. Defense Rev.* 500 (April 1984).

Seemann, G., "Unmanned Vehicle Systems Use Ranges from Pure Science to Military Tactics," *Defense Systems Rev.* 44–45 (July 1983).

Shaker, S., and A. Wise, "Research Progress in Unmanned Vehicles," *Armor*, 33–36 (July/August 1985).

Shaker, S., and R. Wise, "Walking to War: Research Efforts in Legged Vehicles," *National Defense*, 59–62 (March 1986).

Shaker, S., and A. Wise, *War without Men*, Pergamon-Brassey's International Defense Publishers, Inc., Mclean, VA, 1988.

Shoemaker, C., and J. Stephens, "Robotics on the Battlefield," *The Ordnance Magazine*, 3–4 (Winter 1986).

Shoemaker, Charles, "Robotics Vehicles: Technology and Research Testbeds Within the Department of Defense," *Unmanned Systems*, 35 (Springer 1992).

Simpkon, R., *Race to the Swift: Thoughts on Twenty-First Century Warfare*, Brassey's Defense Publishers, London, 1985.

Skutch, L., "Robotics-Only the Beginning," *Military Logistics Forum*, 71–73 (May 1985).

Sokol, A., "German Experiment With Remote Control During the Last War," *Naval Institute Proceedings*, 187–189 (February 1944).

Swinson, Mark L., "Go-GATORS (Ground Air Tele-Operated Robotic System), *Unmanned Systems*, 20 (Spring 1992).

Swinson, Mark L., and Hennebeck, L. M., "U.S. Tactical Unmanned Ground Vehicle Project," *Proceedings of the 3rd Conference On Military Robotic Applications*, Alberta Research Council, September 1991, pp. 12–18.

Tortolano, F. W. (ed.), "When Robots Go To War," *Design News*, April 22, 1991, pp. 74–76, 78.

Toscano, Michael, "Department of Defense Ground Vehicle Robotics Program," *Unmanned Systems*, 14 (Spring 1992).

"Walking Machine," *United States Army Tank—Automotive Command Historical Summary*, *Fiscal Year 1967 (Vol I)*, U.S. Government Printing Office, Washington, DC, 1967, pp. 307–308.

Williams, D., "Artificial Intelligence Emerges from Laboratory," *Defense News*, May 12, 1986, p. 15.

Yoerger, Dana R., Albert M. Bradley, and Barrie B. Walden, "The Autonomous Benthic Explorer," *Unmanned Systems*, 17 (Spring 1992).

MARK L. SWINSON

THE ROLE OF RELEVANCE IN ABDUCTIVE REASONING

INTRODUCTION

Explanation, finding causes for observed facts (or evidence), is frequently encountered in real life. For example, suppose that waking up in the morning, we observe that the road next to our house is wet. We may know about one or more events that, had they occurred, would cause the road to be wet. These events are the "possible causes" for the road being wet. One possible cause in this example is "rainfall during the night." If we actually conclude that it did rain last night (presumably, that is the cause of the observed state of the road), we have just made an abductive inference. It is a defeasible inference, because if we see later on that a main water pipe has burst, we might want to retract our "rain" explanation in favor of the "burst water pipe" explanation.

This form of explanation (or abductive reasoning) also occurs in medical diagnosis: Doctors try to find the disease that caused the observed symptoms. Abduction is also commonly used in solving crimes (the legendary Sherlock Holmes used to erroneously refer to this form of reasoning as "deduction"). These commonsense aspects of reasoning led to the interest in abductive reasoning within artificial intelligence (AI) and related fields.

Mechanized abductive reasoning probably started with automated medical diagnosis, using systems such as MYCIN (1). Much research, both theoretical and practical, has been done since (for example, (2–5)). In general, these systems use "diagnostic reasoning": They attempt to find the disease or set of diseases that explain the observed symptoms. Expressed in this form, diagnostic reasoning is abductive reasoning.

In natural language understanding, several researchers (see (6–8)) view understanding of natural language text as finding the facts (in an internal representation) that would explain the existence of the given text. In image processing and computer vision, problems are sometimes formulated in terms of finding some set of objects that would "explain" the given image. See, for example, Ref. 9 on image reconstruction, Ref. 10 on finding the most probable model describing a picture, and region analysis work in Ref. 11. Scientific theories are models that attempt to fit (or "predict") the given observations. Attempts were made to formalize the formation of scientific theories in terms of a theory of explanation, using a maximum likelihood approach (12).

Finding an explanation is characterized as follows: given world knowledge in the form of (usually causal) rules and observed facts (a formula), determine what needs to be assumed in order to *predict* the evidence. Additionally, one would like to select an explanation that is "optimal" in some sense.

Viewed in this way, many recognition problems can be naturally reformulated as explanation problems. This may be one reason for the prevalence of explanation within AI. But even though many domain-dependent solutions to the problem have been explored in the literature, there is relatively little work on a comprehensive theory of explanation that is sufficiently general. It may be argued that pure abductive reasoning does not exist but depends on a task to be performed by an intelligent system (the agent). Yet there seem to be cases where it is not clear how such tasks might affect abduction, such as in natural language understanding. Thus, a theory of pure abduction still seems to be worthwhile research.

In order to talk about an optimal explanation, we need a metric for comparing candidate explanations. Consider again the wet road example earlier. If we know of two possible causes for the road being wet, say rain or a street cleaning vehicle, either "event" could be an explanation for our wet road, but it is not obvious which of them would be the "better" explanation. Nevertheless, humans are rarely at a loss as to which explanation is better, even if they do frequently reach false conclusions.

Various criteria and metrics have been suggested in the literature, both for evaluating the goodness of an explanation and for evaluating an explanation system (or computer program) as a whole. A partial compilation of desiderata for a good explanation follows. As a rule, an explanation scheme should attempt to provide explanations that have these properties.

1. Plausibility, or likelihood: How plausible is the explanation in the world, or how likely (in a probabilistic setting)?
2. Simplicity: In essence, apply "Occam's razor."
3. Predictiveness: The explanation should predict the evidence.
4. Relevance: Facts not necessary to predict the evidence should not be a part of the explanation.
5. Consistency: The explanation should be internally consistent.
6. Degree of cover: As much of the evidence as possible should be explained by facts that are *distinct* from the observations.
7. Appropriate specificity: The explanation should be appropriately specific. Usually, the most specific explanation is to be preferred (for example, when we have a choice of actions in a taxonomic hierarchy to explain some state of the world), but this is not always the case. The correct specificity depends on the domain, and on how facts in the world are represented.
8. Completeness: The explanation should be as detailed as possible.

This list of desirables is not fully achievable because some of the requirements may be mutually contradictory, but ideally, an explanation scheme should have all of these features, at least to some extent. Several obvious trade-offs a system may have to make are between completeness versus relevance and simplicity, because if the explanation is very detailed, then it is complicated, and some parts of it may even be irrelevant. Consistency seems to be a special case of plausibility. However, there exist systems that try to evaluate plausibility in such a way that parts of the explanation may be plausible, but, overall, an inconsistent explanation may result.

One way of balancing the trade-offs would be to assign numbers indicating "goodness" along each of the dimensions (the desirables). Then one might ask: How do we combine the numbers? This issue is ignored here for the most part, in favor of looking at the issues of relevance, plausibility, predictiveness, and whether consistency is maintained. Of these, relevance, in particular, is an elusive concept. We think that we know (intuitively) what relevance means, but if we try to define it, we need to use concepts that are themselves not well defined. For now, we just state that relevant entities are things that have a bearing on the task at hand. In the following sections, we look at formal definitions of relevance (or irrelevance) suggested by various researchers.

After examining criteria for weighing explanations in various systems, and observing how they handle relevance, a short survey of algorithms for performing abductive inference is presented. Several such algorithms exist for each abductive scheme. Several abductive reasoning algorithms employ relevance, not just in evaluating candidate explanations but in generating them in the first place. Although, in general, computing abductive explanations over a propositional set of axioms and evidence is NP-hard, many algorithms execute in reasonable time in practice for problems ranging up to medium size. It is unknown whether this is true for large problems, but one may hope that by using independence or irrelevance to help prune the search trees, execution time will still be reasonable.

This article focuses on relevance in abductive reasoning, especially in a probabilistic uncertainty context. Hence, the next section deals with probabilities and with techniques used to represent Bayesian probabilistic knowledge. The section on Abductive reasoning schemes is a look at various abductive reasoning systems. However, on the whole, neither the treatment of abduction nor the presentation of probabilistic reasoning is intended as a comprehensive survey. For this information, refer to the annotated bibliography at the end. The section on Irrelevance-based explanation deals with formal definitions of relevance and abductive schemes that try to address primarily the relevance issue.

PROBABILISTIC WORLD MODELS

In real-world situations, uncertainty is omnipresent. It may be uncertainty about future events that are truly random, or may arise out of a lack of knowledge about the world. In order to reason in the presence of uncertainty, we need some way to formulate it. Various uncertainty formalisms exist in the literature, among them fuzzy logic (possibilistic logic), probabilistic logic, various forms of nonmonotonic logic, Dempster–Shafer probabilities, and Bayesian probabilities. Among these formalisms, the latter is best understood and is the formalism where most of the work on abduction centers. This section is a review of probability theory and of structuring methods used in AI and related fields to represent probability distributions.

Probability and Evidential Reasoning

In classical probability theory, we have a set of random variables V, each with its own domain ω_v of events,* where $v \in V$. All the values in ω_v are assumed to be *disjoint* events, and they span all the possible outcomes of v. If that holds, then ω_v is a sample space (or probability space). We say that for each v, the domain ω_v is the set of *outcomes* of any set of *trials* for the variable v.

For each variable, we can define a distribution over its sample space, i.e., a function $P : \omega_v \rightarrow [0, 1]$, called the *probability*. If $d \in \omega_v$, $P(d)$ is the probability of d, the

---

*Actually, random variables are functions defined over the probability space, but we choose to ignore that and just assume that it is always the identity function, thus that the sample space (the domain for each random variable v), is also the range of this function.

fraction of trials for v that comes out d, as the number of trials approaches infinity. The sum of all the probabilities over a sample space is 1.

Likewise, define a *joint sample space* over the set of variables V, as the Cartesian product of all the sample spaces:

$$\Omega_V = \prod_{v \in V} \omega_v \tag{1}$$

and a joint probability distribution $\mathscr{D}$ over that space. Again, the sum of probabilities over Ω_V is 1. We can also talk about the probability of any subset of the sample space. We write the probability of any such subspace A (also called an event) as $P_{\mathscr{D}}(A)$. If there is no danger of ambiguity, i.e., there is only one distribution $\mathscr{D}$ being considered, the subscript and also the reference to Ω_V are omitted.

For convenience, the axioms of of probability theory (converted into a form that makes the simplifying assumption that the joint sample space is finite) are

$$P(A) \geq 0, \quad \forall A \in 2^{\Omega_V}, \tag{2}$$

$$\sum_{A \in \Omega_V} P(A) = 1, \tag{3}$$

$$A \cap B = \emptyset \rightarrow P(A \cup B) = P(A) + P(B), \quad \forall A,B \in 2^{\Omega_V}. \tag{4}$$

The above axioms state that the probability of an event is greater than or equal to 0, that the sum of probabilities over the entire sample space is 1, and that the probability of the union of two disjoint events is the sum of probabilities of the individual events.

Let us use an example from the domain of simple commonsense explanation: Let the set of variables be {road-wet, rain}, each with the domain {T, F} (standing for true and false, respectively). Assume that the variables are ordered, for convenience, i.e., we actually have the pair of variables (road-wet, rain). Our sample space is {(F, F), (F, T), (T, F), (T, T)}. We can also use an assignment notation to refer to events, e.g., the event (T, T) can be written (road wet = T, rain = T). Assignments and events are used interchangeably throughout. One valid distribution for our sample space is

$$P(\text{F, F}) = 0.3, \quad P(\text{F, T}) = 0.1, \quad P(\text{T, F}) = 0.2, \quad P(\text{T, T}) = 0.4.$$

These numbers (together with the axioms of probability) are sufficient to allow us to determine the probability of any event. For example, the event rain = T is the union of the events {(rain = T, road-wet = F)} and {(rain = T, road-wet = T)}, and, thus, $P(\text{rain} = \text{T}) = 0.5$. The latter is known as a *marginal* probability, where we have just "marginalized" over all the possible values of road-wet.

Sometimes, only a subset of the sample space is used, by introducing a *conditioning event*, and the probabilities used w.r.t. the new sample space are called *conditional probabilities*. Conditional probabilities are denoted $P(A \backslash B)$ (probability of A given B), where B is the conditioning event, and are defined (whenever the probability of the conditioning event B is not 0) as

$$P(A|B) = \frac{P(A \cap B)}{P(B)}. \tag{5}$$

For example, the probability of Road-wet,* given Rain, is

$$P(\text{Road-wet|Rain}) = \frac{P(\text{Road-wet} \cap \text{Rain})}{P(\text{Rain})} = \frac{0.4}{0.5} = 0.8$$

Suppose that we want to find the probability of Rain, given Road-wet, and that we do not know the probability of Road-wet. In that case, we might wish to use Bayes' formula

$$P(A|B) = \frac{P(A)P(B|A)}{P(A)P(B|A) + P(\neg A)P(B|\neg A)} \qquad (6)$$

or its generalization, where we use the sum of any partition of the values of A in the denominator, instead of just adding two variables. In our example, in order to use Bayes' formula, we need to know the probability of Road-wet given no Rain (which we calculate out to be 0.4). Now we can write

$$P(\text{Rain|Road-wet}) =$$

$$= \frac{P(\text{Rain})P(\text{Road-wet|Rain})}{P(\text{Rain})P(\text{Road-wet|Rain}) + P(\neg \text{Rain})P(\text{Road-wet|}\!-\!\text{Rain})}$$

$$= \frac{0.5 \times 0.8}{0.5 \times 0.8 + 0.5 \times 0.4} = \frac{2}{3}.$$

Using Bayes' rule in such a manner is a simple instance of *evidential reasoning*, where we get evidence (Road-wet) and need to find the probability of a cause (Rain) given the evidence. Evidential reasoning is frequently used within probabilistic systems of explanation.

The problem of using an explicit distribution, as in this section, is twofold:

1. The size of the sample space is exponential in the number of random variables, which makes it hard to process and gather the statistics required for reasoning from the real world.
2. Human experts used for supplying the distributions directly (out of experience) usually find it much easier to supply conditional probabilities rather than joint probabilities.

For these reasons, models where the number of probabilities used is smaller and where mostly conditional probabilities are to be specified are preferred. Two such models are (Bayesian) Belief Networks and Markov Networks.

Conceptual and Statistical Independence

In the previous subsection, we reviewed probability and discussed the problem caused by the size of the sample space. We now define independence and show how it can be used to alleviate the representation size problem.

Many events in the real world are considered to be independent, for example, a pair of dice tossed in your office coming up double sixes is (usually) independent of the price

---

*When a random variable has only the states true and false, we sometimes use the capitalized name of the variable to denote the event that the variable is true. Likewise, we use the capitalized name of the variable with a preceding negation symbol to denote that the variable is false.

of tea in China. These events are conceptually independent. The somewhat similar *statistical independence* has a formal definition: Events *A* and *B* are statistically independent if and only if $P(A \cap B) = P(A)P(B)$. An alternate way to say it is that $P(A) = P(A|B)$, i.e., that the probability of *A* stays the same even if conditioned on *B*.

Statistical independence (and its generalization to many variables, joint independence) is very useful, because if in a set of random variables *V* of size *n* (each with *d* possible values) all variables are jointly independent, then it is sufficient to specify *nd* probability values, instead of an unwieldy d^n probability values. Having *all* the variables jointly independent is just wishful thinking. However, it is reasonable to expect that there are a great many independencies in the system that allows us to reduce the number of probabilities specified. We also need models that take advantage of the independencies, which is where probabilistic networks help.

Finally, note that there is an intuitive correspondence between conceptually independent events and statistically independent events. In AI, we want to be able to specify certain things in isolation whenever possible, essentially for the same reasons outlined previously with respect to specifying probability distributions. We can do that when whatever we are specifying is conceptually independent of everything else. That is why the AI community is interested in independence (or sometimes in the closely related *irrelevance*). This is also why formalisms that handle independencies are useful throughout AI, and not just for probabilistic reasoning.

Bayesian Belief Networks

Probabilistic models that handle independencies, and in which simple conditional probabilities may be specified instead of full joint probabilities, are extremely important. A very useful model is *(Bayesian) belief networks*.

Belief networks are directed acyclic graphs (DAGs) where each node stands for a random variable, and each arc stands for a direct statistical dependency. An arc frequently implies direct causal relationship, where the tail of the arrow is the cause and its head the effect. For each node, the conditional probabilities of (each value of) the node given all possible assignments to its parents are specified. These conditional probabilities fully determine the entire joint distribution of the network. For a node *v* that has no parents (called a *root* node), prior probabilities are specified, i.e., for each value in the domain of *v*, the probability of that *v* getting that value must be provided.

Formally, let $\mathcal{A}$ be an assignment to the network (i.e., an arbitrary function that for each variable, *v* gives a value in its domain, ω_v). Let $\mathcal{A}_S$ stand for the restriction of $\mathcal{A}$ to variable set *S*, i.e., $\mathcal{A}_S \in \mathcal{A}$, but the node set of $\mathcal{A}_S$ is *S*, and not all of *V*. The joint distribution of the network is

$$P(\mathcal{A}) = \prod_{v \in V} P(\mathcal{A}_{\{v\}} | \mathcal{A}_{\text{parents}(v)}). \tag{7}$$

This equation is equivalent to the assumption that once the assignment to the parents of a node *v* is known, *v* is independent of any of its other ancestors.*

---

*The terms *nodes* and *variables* are used interchangeably throughout. Lowercase names and letters stand for variable names, and their respective capitalized words and letters refer to either a particular state of the variable, or, as a shorthand, for a particular assignment event to the variable. In addition, a variable name appearing in an equation without explicit assignment stands for a set of equations, one for each possible

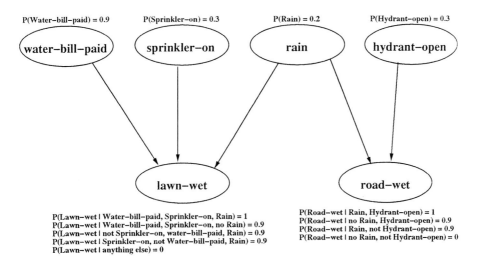

P(Lawn–wet I Water–bill–paid, Sprinkler–on, Rain) = 1
P(Lawn–wet I Water–bill–paid, Sprinkler–on, no Rain) = 0.9
P(Lawn–wet I not Sprinkler–on, water–bill–paid, Rain) = 0.9
P(Lawn–wet I Sprinkler–on, not Water–bill–paid, Rain) = 0.9
P(Lawn–wet I anything else) = 0

P(Road–wet I Rain, Hydrant–open) = 1
P(Road–wet I no Rain, Hydrant–open) = 0.9
P(Road–wet I Rain, not Hydrant–open) = 0.9
P(Road–wet I no Rain, not Hydrant–open) = 0

FIGURE 1   Belief network for example.

Let us extend our example slightly, now that we have the tool of belief networks and can easily specify a network with more variables. Our set of variables is {rain, sprinkler-on, water-bill-paid, hydrant-open, road-wet, lawn-wet}. Suppose that we know that the first four variables are independent and that the latter two variables are somehow caused by them (or, rather, by the events to which these variables refer). Suppose that we also know that the hydrant cannot affect the lawn and that the state of the sprinkler (or our water bill) cannot affect the road. Using arcs to represent the direct dependencies, we get the graph of Figure 1.

What we have now is the DAG underlying the belief network. We still need to specify the conditional probabilities for all nodes given their parents, as well as the prior probabilities of the root nodes (rain, sprinkler-on, water-bill-paid, hydrant-open). These probabilities are listed next to the nodes in Figure 1. As the nodes are all binary valued, we need to specify only one prior probability for each root node. That is because the axioms of probability theory dictate that, for example, $P(\neg\text{Rain}) = 1 - P(\text{Rain})$, and likewise for the other root nodes. For nonroot nodes (road-wet, lawn-wet), it is sufficient to supply the conditional probabilities for the positive assignment (Road-wet), and the probabilities for the negative assignment can be calculated using the axioms of probability theory. When a variable name appears in a probability equation, the meaning is that the equation holds for every possible state of the variable. Thus, the equation (from Fig. 1)

$P(\text{Lawn-wet}|\neg\text{Sprinkler-on, water-bill-paid, Rain}) = 0.9$

actually stands for the following two equations:

$P(\text{Lawn-wet}|\neg\text{Sprinkler-on, Water-bill-paid, Rain}) = 0.9,$

$P(\text{Lawn-wet}|\neg\text{Sprinkler-on, }\neg\text{Water-bill-paid, Rain}) = 0.9$

---

assignment to the variable. For example, $P(x) = P(y)$ where x and y are Boolean-valued nodes stands for $P(x = T) = P(y = T) \land P(x = F) = P(y = T) \land P(x = T) = P(y = F) \land P(x = F) = P(y = F).$

The joint distribution of the entire network is given by the product of all the conditional distributions, as in Eq. (7):

P(water-bill-paid, sprinkler-on, rain, hydrant-open, road-wet, lawn-wet) =

= P(hydrant-open)P(rain)P(sprinkler-on)P(water-bill-paid)

    P(road-wet|hydrant-open, rain)

    P(lawn-wet|rain, sprinkler-on, water-bill-paid).

We are now ready to perform evidential reasoning on our belief network. Conjunctive evidence is allowed, i.e., events that are assignments of values to a subset of the nodes in the network. Suppose that our evidence is {Road-wet, Lawn-wet}. We now wish to calculate the probability of each of the variables given our evidence. A well-known scheme for doing that is *evidence propagation*, proposed in Ref. 13. That method works (in time linear in the size of the network) when the DAG is a polytree, i.e., a DAG such that the underlying undirected graph is a tree. In the case of our simple example, this condition holds, so we use the algorithm to find the probabilities given the evidence (also called *posterior probabilities*). Results of applying the algorithm on the example problem are shown in Figure 2.

Sometimes, what we are after is an *explanation* of the evidence, i.e., the answer to the question, "Why are the road and lawn wet?" As stated in the Introduction, there is no agreed-upon, domain independent procedure for finding the answer. Two commonly used methods are discussed in this section:

1. Threshold on posterior probabilities
2. A maximum a-posteriori assignment (MAP)

To find the explanation for (Road-wet, Lawn-wet) using the first scheme, find the posterior probabilities as above. Do that by running an evidence propagation algorithm (such as that used by IDEAL (14)) on that network, with evidence {Road-wet, Lawn-wet}. The resulting posterior probabilities are shown in Figure 2. Then, use a threshold value of probability (say 0.5) to decide whether the event is a part of the explanation. In our example, P(Rain) = 0.766 and P(Water-bill-paid) = 0.926; thus, you can say that Rain and Water-bill-paid is the explanation of observed evidence.

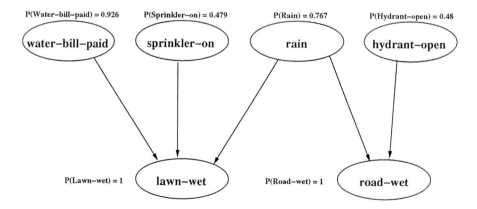

FIGURE 2   Posterior probabilities.

Using the MAP scheme, find the assignment to all the variables that has maximum probability given the evidence, and call that assignment the explanation for the observed evidence. Actually, it is sufficient to maximize the prior probability of the assignment, with the extra constraint that the evidence nodes are assigned consistently with the evidence. Here, the maximum probability assignment is

{Rain, Road-wet, Lawn-wet, Water-bill-paid, ¬Sprinkler-on, ¬Hydrant-open}

with a prior probability of approximately 0.0714 and a posterior probability of approximately 0.317.

Nodes are dependent if there is an arc between them. In order to find whether nodes are *independent*, however, a different criterion, called d-separation, should be used. In a belief network, d-separation implies independence. Reference 15 uses the notation $I(X, Z, Y)$ to mean that node set X is independent of node set Y given node set Z. $I(X, Z, Y)$ holds whenever X and Y are d-separated given Z. If nodes are d-separated (given some evidence, or even no evidence), then they are independent. Two (disjoint) nonempty sets of nodes X and Y are d-separated given node set Z (where Z may be empty and is disjoint from X and Y) if and only if the following conditions hold:

1. Every directed path from X to Y or vice versa passes through Z.
2. If v is a node such that there is a path from X to v and a path from Y to v, then $v \notin Z$ and there is no path from v to Z.

The first condition is obvious. The second condition appears a bit odd, but it is based on the following (see Fig. 1): We can see that rain is independent of hydrant-open with no evidence. But once we know that the road is wet, they become dependent. For example, if the road is wet, and we know that the hydrant is not open, the probability of rain goes up to 1.

Further discussion of probabilistic reasoning and explanation, as well as a discussion of the pros and cons of these schemes of explanation, appears in the section on Abductive reasoning schemes.

Markov Networks

Markov networks are undirected graphs, where the nodes are random variables, as in belief networks. Arcs stand for direct dependence of variables. A node v is independent of all the other nodes, given all its neighbors. The set of immediate neighbors of v forms a *Markov blanket* for v. This property is equivalent to stating that the Markov property holds w.r.t. v and its neighbors.

Specifying the distribution of the network is not as simple as for belief networks. You cannot just give conditional probabilities, as undirected cycles may lead to contradictions. Instead, one must specify a compatibility function for all the cliques of the graph, and from these the distribution can be computed. Because the graph is undirected, we have no way of enforcing the direction of causality. As abductive reasoning depends on that direction, it seems that Markov networks are not useful for abduction. However, there are several noncausal interactions that are best represented in an undirected manner. Additionally, the undirected networks are an intermediate computation step in several probabilistic reasoning algorithms (16) for Bayesian belief networks.

ABDUCTIVE REASONING SCHEMES

Schemes of explanation can be partitioned into numerical and nonnumerical approaches. Nonnumerical approaches are based on proof theory and set-theoretic criteria. Numerical methods are based either on a proof-theoretic approach plus a metric, or on systems that allow uncertainty.

In the following sections, these approaches are examined by looking at various systems and presenting their relative strengths and weaknesses. Particular attention is paid to probabilistic schemes of explanation. The section concludes with a survey of algorithms that are used to compute explanations in the various schemes. Note that an attempt is made here to separate out the criterion for evaluating candidate explanations, from the algorithm used to find candidates to evaluate. Such a separation is a useful notion, as more than one algorithm can be used to arrive at certain results once the desired results are specified in an unambiguous manner.

Nonnumeric Approaches

To form an explanation for a set of observed facts we use abductive reasoning. If we know that A causes B, which we write as the implication* $A \rightarrow B$, and are given B, inferring A is known as abduction. This is not valid inference in general, but if we are asked to explain B, then it makes some sense to conclude A. That is because we know of no other reason for B being true. Abduction is, naturally, a defeasible form of reasoning.

The nomological theory of explanation (see Ref. 17) states that an explanation is a set of facts from which the observed facts (the evidence) can be proved, in conjunction with some world knowledge in logical form. This is a form of abduction.

A problem with abduction is that there may be multiple causes for the observed evidence and, thus, many sets of facts that could be used to prove it. We need some method for preferring one explanation over the others, and that is not available in simple abductive reasoning. For example, Table 1 presents a set of rules that embody some world knowledge.

If we are now asked to explain the evidence lawn-wet $\wedge$ road-wet, we have three possible (positive literal) conjunctive explanations:

1. rain
2. sprinkler-on $\wedge$ bill-paid $\wedge$ hydrant-open
3. sprinkler-on $\wedge$ bill-paid $\wedge$ hydrant-open$\wedge$rain

Using classical logic, we may try to find the weakest condition for proving the evidence. That, however, may lead to an unwieldy result that is essentially meaningless (in the example case, we could just get the disjunction of explanations 1 and 2, but that is not

TABLE 1   Rules for Abduction Example

R_1:	hydrant-open $\rightarrow$ road-wet
R_2:	rain $\rightarrow$ road-wet
R_3:	rain $\rightarrow$ lawn-wet
R_4:	sprinkler-on $\wedge$ bill-paid $\rightarrow$ lawn-wet

---

*Conflation of causality and implication is frequently done in the literature.

very useful). Another weakness is that the answer may be of exponential length. The alternative is to select a conjunction of base facts (or an "assumption set") as the explanation. The result is compact, but the problem is that there are many possible sets of assumptions, that together with our knowledge of the world would serve to explain (prove) the desired facts. Somehow, a choice between the sets must be made. In the example case, we get the three conjunctive explanations presented and do not know how to choose between them.

Several researchers (18, 19) have used the latter technique and graded assumption sets by (a) only allowing some formulas to be assumed and (b) preferring a minimal number (or, alternately, minimal sets) of assumptions. Such a technique provides explanations that are relevant in the sense that the assumed facts are all necessary to prove the evidence (see also the section on Irrelevance-based explanation). This helps in many cases, but there is still no way to choose among the incomparable minimal sets, as shown by our example: Using set minimality considerations, explanation 3 is ruled out, but we still cannot choose between explanations 1 and 2. In fact, either a numerical approach or some other metric, such as preference default logic, is needed to be able to handle this problem.

Numeric Approaches Without Uncertainty

An obvious generalization of the theorem-proving techniques used earlier is to add a metric and to select an explanation that is extremal in this metric.

Weighted Abduction

Weighted abduction was proposed by Hobbs et al. (6) for use in the TACITUS natural language understanding program. This scheme takes a *least-cost proof* to be the best explanation. Weighted abduction allows any formula to be assumed, if necessary, in order to prove the evidence. Rules in the system are of the following form:

$$p_1^w \wedge p_2^{w_2} \wedge \cdots \wedge p_k^{w_k} \rightarrow q. \tag{8}$$

The cost of assuming a conjunct p_i is w_i times the cost of the consequent q. If we are assuming a conjunct that appears in more than one rule, the smaller cost is used. The best explanation is then the proof with the minimum total cost.

Hobbs et al. point out that $C = \sum_{i=1}^{n} w_i$ does not have to equal 1. If $C < 1$ (*most-specific abduction*), then the system will prefer to assume $p_1, \ldots, p_n$, as that will be less expensive than assuming q. On the other hand, if $C > 1$, then, everything else being equal, the system will tend to just assume q (*least-specific abduction*). However, even with least-specific abduction, cost sharing on common assumptions can make a more specific scenario cost less. Hobbs et al. believe that least-specific abduction (with cost sharing) is the way to go, at least for the abductive problems with which they are concerned (natural language comprehension).

As an example, suppose that we attach assumption weights to literals in the rules, as in Table 2.

If each of the evidence literals cost 1 to assume, the only resulting least-cost assumption set will be rain, for the cost of 0.5. The alternate solutions would cost at least 0.7. Explanations computed in weighted abduction are also relevant in the sense that the assumptions are (weakly) required to prove the evidence. We can see that weighted abduction works well with the current example and is sufficiently discriminating. In this

TABLE 2   Rules with Assumption Weights

R_1:	hydrant-open$^{0.3}$ $\rightarrow$ road-wet
R_2:	rain$^{0.5}$ $\rightarrow$ road-wet
R_3:	rain$^{0.6}$ $\rightarrow$ lawn-wet
R_4:	sprinkler-on$^{0.3}$ $\wedge$ bill-paid$^{0.1}$ $\rightarrow$ lawn-wet

system, the numbers are ad hoc, i.e., they are chosen so that the system will get the correct interpretation of sentences, rather than based on some well-understood semantic criterion. This is not disastrous, as a very similar scheme called "cost-based abduction" gives the weights a probabilistic semantics (20).

In cost-based abduction, any formula may be assumed, and all assumed formulas have a non-negative real number cost. A weight (or cost) C means that the probability of the event occurring in the real world is $-\log C$. Thus, in principle, statistical experiments might be conducted to determine these numbers. The best explanation is the proof with the minimum cost. In the example of Table 1, we might attach assumption costs to literals, as in Table 3. The resulting least-cost assumption set will be rain, for the cost of 5.

Coherence-Based Explanations

Another metric (21) proposed maximizing "coherence" as a way of evaluating explanations. The coherence measure takes cost sharing into account, in the sense that it would prefer explanations with a smaller number of primary causes.

The coherence metric is the (normalized) number of nodes in the proof graph that are on a path between evidence nodes. A node is counted multiple times, once for each pair of evidence nodes it connects. The normalization factor is the number that would result if the proof graph were a clique. Formally, if l is the number of evidence nodes (called *observations*, in the paper), N the number of nodes in the proof graph, and $N_{i,j}$ the number of distinct nodes in the proof graph that are on a path from evidence node i to evidence node j, then the coherence metric $\mathscr{C}$ is

$$\mathscr{C} = \frac{\left(\sum_{1 \leq i \leq j \leq l} N_{i,j} \right)}{N \binom{l}{2}} \tag{9}$$

With our example, the coherence of the "rain" explanation would be 1 (one node and only one possible path), whereas the coherence of the "sprinkler-on, bill-paid, hydrant-open" explanation is 0. Hence, the rain explanation is preferred, as desired.

TABLE 3   Costs for Cost-Based Abduction Example

Literal	Cost
rain	5
sprinkler-on	3
bill-paid	1
hydrant-open	3

The coherence method suffers from some anomalies, as shown in Ref. 22. Specifically, in the context of natural language, neighboring sentences may belong to a different discourse segment. In that case, coherence will attempt to find the same explanation for both sentences, which may be inappropriate. The metric also fails to deal with uncertainty, or with cases where rules or predicates have priorities, as in the Hobbs et al. least-cost proofs.

Explanation and Uncertainty

An alternate view is that the best explanation is the most likely one. That depends on some uncertainty calculus to make the decision as to which candidate explanation is the most likely. The issue of relevance is more complicated in systems with uncertainty. That is because in a proof-theoretic framework, if some proposition must appear in a proof for the evidence, then it is usually relevant. In a probabilistic scheme, things that are statistically independent from the evidence are irrelevant. However, many events that are statistically *dependent* may still be irrelevant. Thus, there seems to be no simple criterion for relevance when we deal with uncertainty.

Common Probabilistic Approaches and the Role of Relevance

In the probabilistic schemes, a common technique is to compute the posterior probability model (given the evidence $\mathscr{E}$) of all random variables in the model's distribution. Some explanation systems work in this manner. For example, Charniak and Goldman's WIMP (7), a story-understanding program, computes posterior probabilities, and then chooses to believe statements with probability higher than a certain threshold.

Pearl (15) argues, however, that explanations need to be *internally consistent* and that just taking sets of facts likely to be true given the evidence (say, above some threshold of probability) may not produce reasonable results. The lottery paradox is a case in point. Suppose that in a particular lottery, exactly one ticket is a winner. The probability of a certain lottery ticket is not a winner is almost 1. Using thresholding, however, the system would believe that no ticket is winner, which is false.

Pearl's solution is to find the most probable model given the evidence, i.e., find the assignment to all the variables of highest probability given the evidence. Pearl calls this model the *most probable explanation* (MPE), and others in the literature call the best model the maximum a posteriori (MAP) model. Formally, the MAP is the assignment $\mathscr{A}$ to all the variables that maximizes $P(\mathscr{A}|\mathscr{E})$.

The advantage of the MAP explanation scheme is that it maximizes both internal consistency of the explanation and its "predictiveness" of the evidence. Another plus is that there are effective algorithms for computing MAPs. By an *effective* algorithm we mean a well-defined, computable algorithm, which for some interesting class of problems executes in reasonable time in practice. We do not mean to imply that the algorithm is *efficient*; it could be potentially an exponential-time algorithm and might behave unacceptably for other problems (see review of algorithms in the next section).

A propagation algorithm (introduced in Ref. 13) runs on belief networks that are polytrees, and running time is linear in the size of the network. Unfortunately, the algorithm can only work on general belief networks by using clustering or conditioning, and both methods introduce exponential factors. In fact, it can be easily shown that computing MAPs is NP-hard. But an even worse disadvantage is that MAPs are not necessarily what we want to compute. Pearl ((15), Chap. 5) demonstrates at least one problem that emerges from the MAP treatment of explanation and occurs because values are assigned to all variables. This problem is called the *overspecification* problem (23). One of its instances is the following example, which is adapted from a similar problem instance in Ref. 15.

Example (the vacation-plan problem): My neighbor, Mr. Smith, is an elderly man whose enthusiasm for going on strenuous hiking trips is unsurpassed. Such trips are potentially hazardous for people with ill health. He told me that because of his age, he decided to have a physical checkup before making his vacation plans this year. Suppose that at his age, the prior probability of getting a clean bill of health (random variable "healthy") is 0.8. Having gone on leave (before learning anything else about Mr. Smith's adventures), I return a year later, to see·him standing in his back yard, very much alive. Being curious, but having no time to question Mr. Smith at the moment, I wish to find out why he is still alive (i.e., the evidence $\mathscr{E} = \{$alive $=$ T$\}$). There are several possibilities, with respect to whether he is in good health and whether he went on his hiking trip vacation. One representation for my knowledge of health, vacation, and living is as binary random variables, in the belief network of Figure 3. The network has three nodes: alive, healthy, and vacation location. The conditional probabilities come from my background knowledge, as to the possible danger in taking strenuous hiking trips, as well as my judgment of how likely is Mr. Smith to take such a trip given what he finds out about his state of health. As is evident, the MAP explanation for Alive is {Healthy, Went-on-trip}, with a prior probability of approximately 0.71, which is clearly reasonable.

Suppose, however, that I know that there are 100 possible locations for Mr. Smith to go hiking. For simplicity, let all vacation locations be equally likely given that he is healthy, and likewise for the case that he is of ill health. In addition, let all 100 locations be equally dangerous, as we have no other information. The representation of this modified scenario uses a belief network as before, except that the vacation location is now a 101-valued node, with 100 values corresponding Mr. Smith's going to the respective vacation location, and 1 corresponding to his staying at home. In the resulting network, however, as 100 vacation spots are possible, the probability of any scenario where Mr.

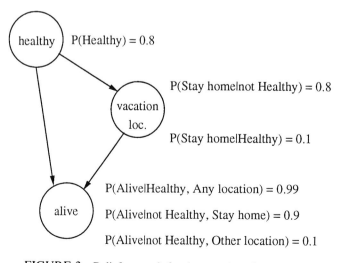

FIGURE 3   Belief network for the vacation-plan problem.

Smith is alive, healthy, and went on vacation (to a particular place) is approximately 0.007, and the scenario where he is of ill health and stayed at home is the MAP (probability approximately 0.15). This is an undesirable property of most-probable explanations because it is not reasonable to have the explanation change just because the model is refined in this manner (a change would be justified, however, if the conditional probabilities were modified, or other explanations for Mr. Smith being alive became known, such as the possibility of him dying and then being resurrected).

To alleviate the overspecification problem, Pearl proposes "circumscribing explanations." He suggests not deciding about variables with no evidence coming from below (the "evidential support" criterion). Evidential support seems like a good idea, as the consensus is that causality flows in the direction of the arrows in the belief network and that explanations are in terms of things causally prior. Therefore, an explanation of evidence need not include anything lower in the network. On its own, the use of evidential support is insufficient, however, because in the case of Figure 3, there is evidence coming from the alive node and that would mean assigning a value to the vacation spot node, whereas we would rather leave the node unassigned. That is because our intuition would suggest that the vacation location is *irrelevant* to being alive in the context of being healthy.

Evidently, not assigning values to some nodes may provide a solution to the problem. Another way to state the above is to say that the best (most probable) *partial* model is the explanation. The question is what criterion to use for leaving nodes unassigned in the models. Pearl's suggestion of not assigning values to nodes below the evidence is one such criterion. Other researchers essentially divide nodes into those that may be assigned (the primary causes), evidence nodes, and other nodes. For example, Cooper (see Ref. 2, or Ref. 24) finds most probable sets of diseases (causes) for a given set of symptoms (evidence) by using a best-first algorithm. The models are partial in the sense that nonroot nodes that are not in the evidence set are never assigned. Cooper's system does not handle the general case, as he assumes mutual independence of all causes (i.e., they all have to be root nodes). This implies that spontaneous occurrences of events at nonroot nodes cannot be explanations of the evidence, which means that nonroot nodes can never be causes. The latter is a deficiency of the theory if it were to be used for general case explanations. For example, look at the case of story understanding. We have the taking-a-bus action, which can explain a sentence, and the going-to(x) actions (with x all the possible locations to which one may take a bus), which are possible causes for taking-a-bus. Using Cooper's scheme, if we want the going-to(x) to be in our system at all, then we may not have taking-a-bus as a cause. That, in turn, means that we will always have to make up our minds about the location, even when it is undesirable (such as when there are thousands of locations, with no evidence for preferring any of them over the others).

Peng and Reggia (5) have defined a diagnostic problem which they solve by proposing a theory of parsimonious cover sets. The idea is that the set of symptoms should be *covered* by the hypothesized set of diseases; i.e., each symptom should have at least one causing disease in the hypothesis. They propose a probabilistic generalization of the cover set idea, based on a 2-level belief network, with symptoms at the bottom and diseases at the top. Their probabilistic scheme is more flexible than the pure cover set, in that they can now use prior probability of diseases to arrive at the most likely hypothesis, rather than just the smallest set of diseases. They also designed a best-first algorithm that finds hypotheses in decreasing order of probability given the set of observed symptoms.

It is not clear how their methods would generalize to an arbitrary belief network, given that one of their assumption is that all symptoms have causes (and, thus, root nodes cannot be evidence).

Despite its shortcomings, the MAP scheme is domain independent and sufficiently general and does not suffer from potential inconsistencies like posterior probabilities and cost-based abduction. Thus, MAP explanations can be used as a starting point, together with the argument that by using a *partial* MAP model as an explanation, the overspecification problem can be alleviated. The intuition is that some facts are *irrelevant* to the observed facts, and, thus, only models (explanations) where irrelevant variables remain *unassigned* are candidate explanations. For "pure" explanation, relevance is a sufficient and necessary criterion for including a node in an explanation. Issues such as the possible a priori *importance* of a node, which are task dependent, are not considered here. In these cases, the problem is no longer pure explanation and might be handled in a decision-theoretic framework.

Other Probabilistic Approaches

One other possible approach is trying to use the more general decision-theoretic methods to define explanation. Indeed, Poole (25) has claimed that talking of explanations without an "end use" clause (i.e., what do we need the explanation for) may be insufficiently determined. He pointed out six different ways of performing diagnosis:

1.   Most likely single-fault hypothesis
2.   Most likely posterior hypothesis
3.   Most likely interpretation (same as MAP)
4.   Probability of provability
5.   Covering explanation (as per Peng and Reggia)
6.   Utility-based explanations

Poole notes that all these methods produce different answers that may be greatly incompatible and have serious deficiencies. He argues that only the utility (or decision-theoretic) approach can be applied in an optimal way. The decision-theoretic approach is, by definition, domain dependent (at least as far as the utility function part is concerned), where the first five schemes are domain independent.

One might argue that pure explanation is essentially independent of utility. A likely explanation for the evidence may be useful, without having to consider for what the explanation will be used. This has the added advantage that such pure explanation schemes can be made domain independent, which is a desirable goal. After a likely explanation is found, we may still want to consider utility, but that is beyond the scope of this article.

Early diagnostic programs, such as MYCIN, should perhaps be classified under probabilistic schemes, because they use certainty factors which are functions of subjective probability. However, the semantics of probabilities there was initially ad hoc, and not the Bayesian semantics. In addition, the reasoning was not abductive per se but was applied in a forward manner; i.e., production rules were applied in order to find diseases from the symptoms, rather than requiring that the diseases be shown to cause the symptoms either proof-theoretically or by evidential reasoning.

Evaluating Probabilistic Schemes

When looking at abduction in a probabilistic context, several of the desiderata discussed earlier can be further specified.

1. Plausibility, or likelihood: How plausible is the explanation in the world, or how likely (in a probabilistic setting)? If explanations are assignments, this will be the probability of the conjunctive explanation $\mathscr{A}$, $P(\mathscr{A})$.
2. Simplicity: in essence "Occam's razor". One might use the number of assigned nodes as a measure of explanation complexity. Thus, a minimization of the number of assigned nodes is desired.
3. Predictiveness: The explanation should predict the evidence; i.e., maximize $P(\mathscr{E}|\mathscr{A})$.
4. Relevance: This term is still vague, as it is not a well-understood concept. It means both *not* assigning nodes irrelevant to the evidence and making sure that all relevant nodes are assigned. A definition in terms of statistical independence seems reasonable.
5. Consistency: When using probabilities, this becomes a value between 0 and 1, rather than just a Boolean value. Using probabilities, internal consistency is the same as the probability of the explanation.

Finding high-probability nodes given the evidence works well as far as likelihood of the explanation and completeness are concerned. However, this scheme may be bad on relevance (because nodes that have high prior probability, but are independent of the evidence, will be assigned a value). It may perform badly on internal consistency, if, for example, 10 different node assignments, each with probability 0.9, have 0 joint probability (where the acceptance threshold is 0.9). It does a moderately good job on simplicity, predictiveness, and degree of cover. Overall, this system is unacceptable, except in certain special cases. In the case of WIMP, for example, many of the disadvantages of the scheme do not occur because of domain-specific reasons: Bad relevance is avoided because nodes have very low prior probability of being true, and the inconsistency problem was not yet encountered in practice.

Finding complete model MAPs is good on likelihood (we are finding a maximum probability model). Its predictiveness is good because maximizing $P(\mathscr{A}|\mathscr{E})$ means maximizing $P(\mathscr{A})P(\mathscr{E}|\mathscr{A})$ [because $P(\mathscr{E})$ is a constant here], and in this term the prior of $\mathscr{A}$ is one term, and the predictiveness is another. Degree of cover and completeness is good because we get a complete model. Internal consistency is good, as it is measured by some of the terms in $P(\mathscr{A})$, which is a term in the maximized product (we are measuring overall posterior probability, which has the internal consistency as a factor). However, MAP explanations do poorly with respect to relevance (even irrelevant variables are assigned) and simplicity (having all the model's values assigned does not provide a simple explanation).

Algorithms for Computing Explanations

There are numerous algorithms for finding least-cost proofs, posterior probabilities in probabilistic networks (both Bayesian networks and Markov networks), and most-probable model selection. In general, all these problems are NP-hard, but in several special cases polynomial time algorithms exist.

Least-Cost Proof Algorithms

These algorithms are usually some form of heuristic best-first search and are mostly of the same basic structure. For particular cases, see Refs. 8 and 26, and a best-first heuristic based on cost sharing proposed in Ref. 27. Recently, algorithms based on other principles have emerged.

In Refs. 28 and 29, a least-cost complete model is found using linear programming methods. A set of simultaneous inequalities, of size linear in the system size, is created. An objective function to be optimized (signifying the cost of the proof) is also added. The system is then solved, using, say, the simplex method. If the resulting solution has only 0 and 1 values, which happens in a surprisingly large proportion of the problems, this provides the least-cost model. If there are other values assigned in the optimal linear-system solution, further branch and bound work has to be done (which may then be exponential time). In practice, as was shown in Refs. 28 and 29, the number of branches is typically very small, and, thus, the (empirically determined) multiplier in exponential term of the average runtime equation is very small.

Posterior Probability Algorithms

There are three basic classes of algorithms for evaluating posterior node probabilities. The computational complexity of these algorithms is the essentially independent of whether one needs to evaluate the posterior probability of one node or the posterior probability of all the nodes in the network.

1. Pearl's probability propagation algorithm (see Ref. 15, Chap. 4, or Ref. 13) which works on polytrees
2. Shachter's arc reversal algorithm (3)
3. Stochastic simulation algorithms

Unfortunately, all these algorithms are potentially exponential time algorithms for general belief networks. This is not surprising, because Bayesian inference is known to be NP-hard (see Ref. 30). For Pearl's algorithm, there are two basic methods of extending the algorithm to nonpolytree graphs: clustering and conditioning. The former method clusters sets of nodes into macronodes, on which Pearl's propagation algorithm can be used. The complexity of this method is exponential in the size of the maximum clique (see Ref. 16). Using the conditioning method, the graph is partitioned into polytrees by a cutset of nodes N. The probability of each state in $\mathscr{S}$ (the set of possible assignments to the nodes in N) is evaluated. The probabilities are then combined by weighting. The complexity in this case is obviously exponential in N. An approximation algorithm, called *bounded conditioning*, is based on conditioning and was proposed in Ref. 31. The idea is to evaluate only a small subset of $\mathscr{S}$, consisting of states of high probability given the evidence. If this sum of probabilities (given the evidence) over the high-probability states is close to 1, we get a good approximation.

The arc reversal algorithm is actually designed to operate on influence diagrams, which are more general than belief networks. The algorithm operates by reversing arcs that point to evidence nodes in such a way that the distribution of the network is preserved. Evidence absorption is performed, and the result is a simple, degenerate network where only direct conditional probabilities have to be evaluated. The complexity of the algorithm stems from the fact that the number of states to be considered when a certain arc is reversed may be exponential in the size of the DAG.

In the basic simulation algorithm, one attempts to randomly assign nodes, such that each state V of a node v has a probability of occurring equal to the conditional probability of v given its parents. Making sure that this constraint holds and counting only assignments where the evidence nodes are assigned the correct values, we can find an approximation for the posterior probability of $v = V$. We do that by dividing the number of assignments where $v = V$ by the total number of assignments. This quotient approaches $P(v = V)$ as the number of trials goes to infinity. Several variants of this basic simulation algorithm exist, for example, the one presented in Ref. 32.

Most-Probable Model Selection

Most-probable model selection is closely related to complete model least-cost proof computation, as shown in Ref. 23. Several algorithms exist for Markov networks, such as simulation and belief propagation. The accepted method for belief networks is belief revision, as described in Ref. 15, Chap. 5. The algorithm is good for polytrees but can be adapted to general belief networks using clustering. Using the relation between least-cost proofs and MAPs, a host of other algorithms becomes available, including heuristic search and the linear programming techniques discussed above.

The linear inequality method for finding MAPs is a variant of the method used for finding least-cost proofs. It is also possible to convert the linear programming solutions to work for various classes of partial models (33).

IRRELEVANCE-BASED EXPLANATION

The overspecification problem cannot be solved in MAP explanation purely by the method of "evidential support." Cost-based abduction handles relevance reasonably but may mishandle negation (thereby preferring an inconsistent explanation in certain cases) by failing to assign certain variables, due to unreasonable independence assumptions (23). An explanation scheme that treats relevance explicitly and does not provide inconsistent explanations is irrelevance-based explanation. In the vacation-plan example, this scheme would leave the "vacation spot" variable unassigned, agreeing with our intuition, which would suggest that "vacation spot" is "irrelevant" to "Alive" in the context of being healthy.

This section begins with the definition of irrelevance-based assignments and explanation, and then proceeds to define an instance of these, independence-based assignments and explanations. Independence-based assignments have interesting properties that facilitate design of an effective algorithm for computing them. A best-first algorithm for computing independence-based explanations is outlined. Shortcomings of this scheme are discussed at the end.

Irrelevance-Based Explanation—Definition

In irrelevance-based explanation, the best probabilistic explanation for the observed facts is defined as the most probable partial assignment (model) that ignores irrelevant variables. The criteria for deciding which variables are irrelevant can be defined in various ways, one of which is *independence-based assignments*, defined later.

For a set of variables V, an assignment* $\mathcal{A}_S$ (where $S \subseteq V$), is an *irrelevance-based assignment* if all the nodes $V - S$ are irrelevant to the assignment. In the vacation-plan

---

*Script letters denote assignments. The subscript denotes the set of assigned nodes. Thus, $\mathcal{A}_S$ denotes an assignment that is *complete* w.r.t. S, i.e., assigns values to *all* the nodes in S.

example, we would say that the vacation-location is irrelevant to the assignment {Alive, Healthy}; thus, {Alive, Healthy} is an irrelevance-based assignment.

For a distribution over the set of variables V with evidence $\mathscr{E}$, an assignment $\mathscr{A}_S$ is an *irrelevance-based MAP* w.r.t evidence $\mathscr{E}$ if it is the most probable irrelevance-based assignment that is complete with respect to the evidence nodes (i.e., all the evidence nodes are assigned by $\mathscr{A}_S$), such that $\mathscr{A}_S$ is consistent with $\mathscr{E}$. Using the "intuitive" definition, in the vacation-plan example, the irrelevance-based MAP is {Alive, Healthy}, which is the desired scenario.

The irrelevance-based MAP with respect to the evidence $\mathscr{E}$ is called the best explanation for $\mathscr{E}$. Note that the definition above is *not restricted* to belief networks. However, the formal definitions of irrelevance *are* restricted to belief networks and rely on the directionality of the networks, the "cause and effect" directionality. In belief networks, an arc from u to v states that u is a possible cause for v. The only possible causes of a node v are its ancestors, and, thus (as in Pearl's evidential support), all nodes that are not ancestors of evidence nodes are unassigned. Additionally, nodes that are irrelevant to the evidence given the causes (i.e., are not "interesting") are not assigned values. The ancestors are only *potentially* relevant, because some other criterion may determine these nodes to be *still* irrelevant, as shown in the next subsection.

Independence-Based MAPs

Probabilistic irrelevance is traditionally viewed as statistical independence, or even independence given that we know the value of certain variables. In Ref. 15, a notion of independence of one set of variables from a second set of variables, given a third set of variables (all disjoint), is used. The notation used there is $I(X, Y, Z)$ to mean that variable set X is independent of variable set Z given variable set Y. If the relation I obeys a certain set of axioms (called the "semigraphoid" axioms), then there exists a probability distribution that obeys any set of independencies implied by I. A belief network is one way to represent the distribution in an efficient form. In the belief network representation, a path-based criterion called d-separation is used to decide independence. Neither d-separation nor independence as defined by the I notation suffice as a criterion for deciding which nodes are irrelevant. In the vacation-plan example, the "vacation spot" and "alive" nodes are clearly not d-separated by the "healthy" node, nor are they independent given that the value of the "healthy" node is known, as would be required.

As a starting point for the notion of probabilistic irrelevance, Subramanian's strong irrelevance (34) might be used. There, $SI(f, g, M)$ is used to signify that f is irrelevant to g in theory M if f is not necessary to prove g in M and vice versa (see Ref. 34 for the precise definition). Probabilistic irrelevance borrows the syntax of that form of irrelevance, but uses a different semantics because we might be interested in irrelevance of f to g even if g is not true. Probabilistic irrelevance is defined w.r.t. to sets of models, rather than theories (as in Ref. 34). This is necessary because the general probabilistic representation does not have implications, just conditional probabilities.*

Partial assignments induce a set of models. For example, for the set of variables {x, y, z}, each with a binary domain, the assignment {$x = $ T, $y = $ F} with z unassigned in-

---

*Belief networks can be represented in terms of implications with weighted assumption costs, but the number of implications may be exponential in the number of nodes, in the general case.

duces the set of models $\{(x = T, y = F, z = F), (x = T, y = F, z = T)\}$. Potential explanations are limited to the sets of models induced by partial assignments, and, thus, the terms "models" and "assignments" are used interchangeably. The notation $In(f, g|\mathcal{A})$ denotes that f is independent of g given $\mathcal{A}$ (where $\mathcal{A}$ is a partial assignment), i.e., if $P(f|g, \mathcal{A}) = P(f|\mathcal{A})$. f and g may be either sets of variables or assignments (either partial or complete) to sets of variables. If the distribution is not strictly positive, it is possible for $P(f|g, \mathcal{A})$ to be undefined, because it is possible that $P(g, \mathcal{A}) = 0$. In such cases, assume that independence does, in fact, hold. Note that $I(X, Y, Z)$ does not require a certain assignment to Y, just that the assignment be known; whereas $In(f, g|\mathcal{A})$ does require it. For any disjoint sets of variables X, Y, Z, we have that $I(X, Y, Z)$ implies $In(X, Z|\mathcal{A}_Y)$ but *not* vice-versa.

Assignments are treated as sets of pairs (v, V) where v is a node and V is the value assigned to it. The function *span* gives the set of nodes mentioned in an assignment. Thus, span($\mathcal{A}$) is the set of nodes that are assigned in $\mathcal{A}$. By definition, if $S \subseteq$ span($\mathcal{A}$), i.e., assignment $\mathcal{A}$ is *complete* with respect to node set S, then span($\mathcal{A}_S$) = S.

An instance of irrelevance-based assignments, called *independence-based (IB) assignments*, is defined as follows: an assignment is IB if a certain condition, called the *IB condition*, holds at every node in the assignment. The IB condition holds at a node v w.r.t. an assignment $\mathcal{A}_S$ just when $\mathcal{A}_{\{v\}}$ is independent of the set of all the ancestors of v that are *not* in S, given the assignment made in $\mathcal{A}_S$ to the parents of v. The idea behind this definition is that the unassigned ancestors of each assigned node v should remain unassigned if they cannot affect v (and, thus, cannot be used to explain v). Nodes that are not ancestors of v are never used as an explanation of v anyway, because they are not potential causes of v.

Independence-based MAPs are defined as irrelevance-based MAPs where independence-based assignments are substituted for irrelevance-based assignments. Thus, an assignment $\mathcal{A}$ is an IB-MAP for evidence $\mathcal{E}$ if it is the maximum probability IB assignment that agrees with (and includes all of) the evidence. Because $\mathcal{A}$ assigns all the nodes assigned by $\mathcal{E}$ and is consistent with $\mathcal{E}$, then $P(\mathcal{E}|\mathcal{A}) = 1$ whenever $P(\mathcal{A}) \neq 0$.

In the vacation-plan example, using independence-based MAPs, the best scenario is {Alive, Healthy, vacation location undetermined} with a probability of 0.71 as desired. Assigning a value to vacation location can be avoided, because the only node u with unassigned ancestors is $u = $ alive, and the conditional independence In(Alive, vacation spot|Healthy) holds.

Several more definitions are needed in order to talk about properties of IB assignments and an algorithm for computing IB-MAPs. An assignment $\mathcal{A}$ *subsumes* assignment $\mathcal{B}$ iff $\mathcal{A} \subseteq \mathcal{B}$. This is equivalent to saying that the set of complete models satisfying $\mathcal{A}$ is a (not necessarily strict) superset of the set of complete models satisfying $\mathcal{B}$. Together with the axioms of probability theory, this implies that over any probability distribution, $P(\mathcal{A}) \geq P(\mathcal{B})$. Assignment $\mathcal{A}$ *strictly subsumes* assignment $\mathcal{B}$ iff $\mathcal{A}$ subsumes $\mathcal{B}$ and $P(\mathcal{A}) > P(\mathcal{B})$. Assignment $\mathcal{A}$ *properly subsumes* assignment $\mathcal{B}$ iff $\mathcal{A}$ subsumes $\mathcal{B}$ and $\mathcal{A} \neq \mathcal{B}$. When looking for most probable IB assignments, assignments that are maximal w.r.t. subsumption are preferred. If the distribution is strictly positive, proper subsumption implies strict subsumption, and only a maximal IB assignment can be an IB-MAP. The IB-MAP algorithm finds IB assignments that are maximal w.r.t. subsumption. Such assignments are also evidentially supported, i.e., all the nodes in such an assignment are above some evidence node.

Properties of Independence-Based Assignments

The independence constraints in the definition of independence-based assignments lead to several interesting properties that are desirable from a computational point of view. One property shown in Ref. 23 is the *locality property*: If, for each assigned variable v, v is independent of all of its unassigned *parents* given the assignment to the rest of its parents, then the independence-based condition holds at v, i.e., v is independent of *all* its unassigned *indirect ancestors* as well as its unassigned parents.

Thus, to test whether an assignment is independence based, one need only test the relation between each node and its parents and can ignore all the other ancestors. This property allows for testing whether an assignment in independence based in time linear in the size of the assignment and is, thus, an important theorem to use when considering the development of an algorithm to compute independence-based MAPs. The following equation allows for efficient computation of $P(\mathcal{A}_S)$:

$$P(\mathcal{A}_{\mathcal{G}}) = \prod_{v \in \mathcal{G}} P(\mathcal{A}_{\{v\}} | \mathcal{A}_{S \cap \text{parents}(v)}). \tag{10}$$

This equation can be used to compute $P(\mathcal{A}_S)$ in linear time for independence-based assignments, as the terms of the product are simply conditional probabilities that can be read off from the conditional distribution array (or other representation) of nodes given their parents.

Another property relates cost-based abduction to IB-MAPs. For AND/OR DAGs where conditional probabilities are restricted to be either 0 or 1 (except, perhaps, at root nodes), IB-MAPs are equivalent to partial model cost-based abduction (23) if only root nodes may be assumed. This holds because in cost-based abduction, if a node is assigned true, then it is independent of all of its unassigned parents, i.e., the IB condition holds at that node (actually, at the belief-network image of the node). This equivalence holds even if negation is allowed.

Independence-Based MAP Algorithm

The independence-based MAP algorithm presented here is based on a variant of the complete MAP algorithm, which was outlined in Ref. 35. Several modifications must be made to convert the algorithm to an IB-MAP computation algorithm.

Review of MAP Algorithm

An agenda of states is kept, sorted by the evaluation function P_a (estimated current probability), which is a product of all conditional probabilities seen in the current state. A state is essentially an assignment of values to some set of nodes, S. A flowchart of the algorithm is shown in Figure 4.

Expansion consists of selecting a fringe node of S (i.e., a node that has neighbors not in S) and creating a new agenda item for each of the possible assignments to neighboring nodes.

The heuristic evaluation function P_a for an agenda item, which is an assignment $\mathcal{A}_S$ to the set of nodes S, is the following product:

$$P_a = \prod_{v \in G(S)} P(\mathcal{A}_{\{v\}} | \mathcal{A}_{\text{parents}(v)}), \tag{11}$$

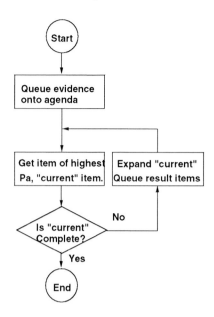

FIGURE 4   Top level of algorithm for finding MAPs.

where $G(S) = \{v|v \in S \wedge \forall w \in \text{parents}(v),\ w \in S\}$, i.e., the product is over all as-signed nodes that have all their parents assigned as well. The evaluation function is op-timistic and is precise for complete assignments, as the product reduces to exactly the joint distribution of the network in that case. Thus, P_a is an *admissible* heuristic evalu-ation function w.r.t. a best-first search algorithm.

The advantage of this best-first algorithm is that it can be easily modified to pro-duce the next-best complete assignments in order of decreasing probability. This is done in the following manner (refer to Fig. 4): Instead of ending with the first complete as-signment, output it and simply continue to loop (getting the next agenda item).

Algorithm Modifications
The algorithm modifications needed to compute the independence-based partial MAP are in checking whether an agenda item is complete, and in the expansion of an agenda item. The former holds for an agenda item iff it is an independence-based (partial) assignment. The other conditions are guaranteed because the evidence nodes are assigned initially. Checking whether an assignment is independence based is easy, due to the locality property.

The second modification is required because, when extending a node, some of the parents may not be assigned, as shown presently. In addition, only nodes with unassigned *parents* are considered fringe nodes, as assigning values to nodes with no evidence nodes below them is unnecessary. Completeness in the modified algorithm is different in that an agenda item may be complete even if not all variables are assigned.

To take advantage of the locality property, the following is precomputed: for each node v a set of all the cases where conditional independence occurs. These cases are called *independence-based hypercubes* and are actually subspaces of the conditional dis-tribution array (of v given its parents) with equal conditional probability entries. For ex-

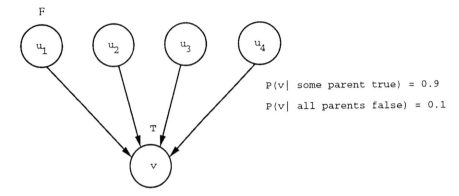

FIGURE 5   Expanding a node.

ample, in the case of the "dirty" OR node of Figure 5, $P(v = T|u_i = T) = 0.9$ (for $1 \leq i \leq 4$) is independent of u_j, $j \neq i$. This defines four 3-dimensional equiprobability hypercubes. We also have the 0-dimensional hypercube where all the $u_i = F$. When the algorithm expands v, it only assigns values to parents of which v is not independent (given the assignment to its other parents), i.e., it generates one agenda item for each such hypercube.

Naturally, because a belief network is not always a tree, some parent nodes may already be assigned. Consider, for example, Figure 5. We are at the noisy OR node v, with parents u_1, u_2, u_3, and u_4, where v has the value T, and u_1 has already been assigned F. We now have to expand all the (maximal w.r.t. subsumption) states of the parents of v, i.e., the states of the nodes u_i.

In the complete MAP case, we add the following eight assignments for the nodes (u_2, u_3, u_4):

$$\{(F,F,F),(F,F,T),(F,T,F),(F,T,T),$$
$$(T,F,F),(T,F,T),(T,T,F),(T,T,T)\};$$

that is, all possible complete assignments to these three variables. When we need to find the partial MAP, however, only the following four assignments are added:

$$\{(T,U,U),(U,T,U,),(U,U,T),(F,F,F)\},$$

where U stands for "unassigned." If a hypercube is ruled out by a prior assignment to a parent node (as is the case with the hypercube $u_1 = T$ here), it is ignored. Otherwise, the hypercubes are unified with the prior assignment, as in this case, the 3-dimensional hypercubes are reduced to 2-dimensional hypercubes by the prior assignment of $u_1 = F$. All the other assignments are ignored, because they would assign values to variables that cannot change the probability of v, i.e., they are subsumed by at least one of the four assignments listed above.

Finally, to compute next-best partial assignments in decreasing order, perform the same simple modification as for the complete MAP algorithm: simply continue to run, producing independence based partial assignments. A useful termination condition is now a probability threshold, i.e., stop producing assignments once the probability of an assignment is below some fraction of that of the first partial MAP produced.

Evaluating Independence-Based Explanation

In terms of the wish list, irrelevance-based explanation does well on likelihood, predictiveness, consistency, degree of cover, and completeness. That is because likelihood, predictiveness, and consistency are maximized directly, and every relevant node that is an ancestor of an evidence node is assigned. It does only moderately well on relevance, because slightly changing conditional probabilities may cause assignment to variables that are still intuitively irrelevant, which may, in turn, cause the wrong explanation to be preferred. The latter problem manifests if we slightly modify our vacation-planning problem, as shown in Figure 6 and described in the following paragraph.

Change the probability of being alive given the location so that staying at home (when healthy) still gives a probability of 1 of being alive, but going anywhere else only gives a probability of 0.99 of being alive (say, an accident is possible during travel). We no longer have independence and, thus, are forced into the counterintuitive case of finding the "not healthy" scenario as the best explanation.

The instability problem shown earlier becomes particularly acute if the belief network is constructed using probabilities calculated from real statistical experiments. That can be done either by first constructing the topology of the network and experimenting to fill in the conditional probabilities, or by using a method such as in Ref. 36 or 37 to get the topology as well as the conditional probabilities directly from the experiments. In either case, even if exact independence exists in the real world, the conditional probabilities computed based on experiments are very unlikely to be *exactly* equal. Definitions of irrelevance based on approximate independence are encountered in Ref. 23, as well as abduction schemes and algorithms that employ these definitions. Alternate algorithms for computing irrelevance-based MAPs can be found in Ref. 23, as well as experiments on the run-time of the algorithm on toy problems and on medium-sized randomly generated belief networks. However, even in the improved schemes suggested there, sometimes irrelevant variables are assigned, which leaves the issue of relevance an open problem.

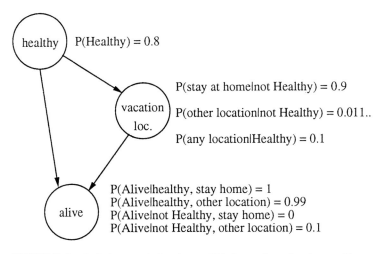

FIGURE 6   Belief network for the modified vacation-planning problem.

SUMMARY

Abductive reasoning (explanation) appears in various walks of life and, thus, several areas of artificial intelligence. In performing abductive reasoning, that is, finding the causes that explain a set of observed events, one must select one of a host of possible candidates. Several principles apply, among them the *relevance* of the abductive conclusion to the observed evidence.

The world being an uncertain place, representation using probabilities becomes necessary. By using Bayesian belief networks, structuring of the sample space is achieved, to reduce the size of the representation from exponential to something more manageable. Evidential reasoning can be used for explanation, in various ways, such as computing posterior probabilities, finding a maximum likelihood hypothesis or finding a maximum a posteriori probability (MAP) assignment to all the variables.

A great number of theoretical schemes and actual programs exist for performing abductive reasoning. Several were reviewed in previous sections. Most schemes attempt to address the issue of relevance, either implicitly (by letting the algorithm suggest only things that can be relevant) or explicitly (by having a formal definition of relevance or irrelevance, and using it to enumerate and evaluate explanations).

Several open research problems exist, both in finding better formal definitions of relevance and in finding new algorithms for computing relevant explanations. In particular, the following open problems are of interest:

1. Refining the issue of statistical independence as irrelevance.
2. Improved heuristics for the best-first search MAP algorithms. It remains to be seen whether the heuristic proposed in Ref. 27 can be made admissible for MAPs and partial MAPs while remaining a useful heuristic.
3. How well does the reduction of computation of partial MAPs to linear systems of inequalities work in practice? Either a theoretical analysis (probably impossible) or an empirical comparison of timing results between the best-first IB MAP algorithm and the performance of the linear systems method would be interesting.

REFERENCES

1. Edward H. Shortliffe, *Computer-Based Medical Consultation: MYCIN*. American Elsevier, New York, 1976.
2. Gregory Floyd Cooper, "NESTOR: A Computer-Based Medical Diagnosis Aid that Integrates Causal and Probabilistic Knowledge," Ph.D. thesis, Stanford University, 1984.
3. R. D. Shachter, "Evaluating Influence Diagrams," *Oper. Res.*, 34(6), 871–882 (1986).
4. Harry Pople, "The Formation of Composite Hypotheses in Diagnostic Problem Solving: An Exercise in Synthetic Reasoning," in *Proceedings of IJCAI* 1977, Vol. 5, pp. 1030–1037.
5. Y. Peng and J. A. Reggia, "A Probabilistic Causal Model for Diagnostic Problem Solving (Parts 1 and 2)," *IEEE Trans. Systems, Man Cybernetics*, 146–162, 395–406 (1987).
6. Jerry R. Hobbs, Mark Stickel, Paul Martin, and Douglas Edwards, "Interpretation as Abduction," in *Proceedings of the 26th Conference of the ACL*, 1988.
7. Eugene Charniak and Robert Goldman, "A Logic for Semantic Interpretation," in *Proceedings of the 26th Conference of the ACL*, 1988.
8. Mark E. Stickel, "A Prolog-like Inference System for Computing Minimum-Cost Abductive Explanations in Natural-Language Interpretation," Technical Report 451, Artificial Intelligence Center, SRI International (September 1988).

9. Stuart Geeman and Donald Geeman, ''Stochastic Relaxation, Gibbs Distributions and the Bayesian Restoration of Images,'' *IEEE Trans. Pattern Anal. Machine Intell.*, 6, 721–741 (1984).

10. J. W. Modestino and J. Zhang, ''A Markov Field Model-Based Approach to Image Interpretation,'' *Proceedings IEEE Computer Vision Pattern Recognition*, 1989.

11. Jerome A. Feldman and Yoram Yakimovsky, ''Decision Theory and Artificial Intelligence: I. A Semantics-Based Region Analyzer,'' *Artificial Intelligence*, 5, 349–371 (1974).

12. David B. Sher, ''Towards a Normative Theory of Scientific Evidence—A Maximum Likelihood Solution,'' in *Proceedings of the 6th Conference on Uncertainty in AI*, 1990, pp. 509–515.

13. Jin H. Kim and Judea Pearl, ''A Computation Model for Causal and Diagnostic Reasoning in Inference Systems,'' in *Proceedings of the 6th International Joint Conference on AI*, 1983.

14. Sampath Srinivas and Jack Breese, *IDEAL: Influence Diagram Evaluation and Analysis in LISP, Documentation and Users Guide*, Rockwell International Science Center, 1989.

15. Judea Pearl, *Probabilistic Reasoning in Intelligent Systems: Networks of Plausible Inference*, Morgan Kaufmann, San Mateo, CA, 1988.

16. S. L. Lauritzen and David J. Speigelhalter, ''Local Computations with Probabilities on Graphical Structures and Their Applications to Expert Systems, *J. Roy. Statist. Soc.*, 50, 157–224 (1988).

17. Drew V. McDermott, ''Critique of Pure Reason,'' *Comput. Intell.*, 3, 151–60 (1987).

18. Henry A. Kautz and James F. Allen, ''Generalized Plan Recognition,'' in *Proceedings of the Fifth Conference of AAAI*, August 1986.

19. Michael R. Genesereth, ''The Use of Design Descriptions in Automated Diagnosis,'' *Artificial Intelligence*, 411–436 (1984).

20. Eugene Charniak and Solomon E. Shimony, ''Probabilistic Semantics for Cost-Based Abduction,'' in *Proceedings of the 8th National Conference on AI*, August 1990, pp. 106–111.

21. Hwee Tou Ng and Raymong J. Mooney, ''On the Role of Coherence in Abductive Explanation,'' in *Proceedings of the 8th National Conference on AI*, August 1990, pp. 337–342.

22. Peter Norvig, Personal communication, January 1991.

23. Solomon E. Shimony, ''A Probabilistic Framework for Explanation,'' Ph.D. thesis, Brown University, 1991. Technical report CS-91-57.

24. Richard E. Neapolitan, *Probabilistic Reasoning in Expert Systems*, John Wiley and Sons, New York 1990, Chap. 8.

25. David Poole and Gregory M. Provan, ''What Is an Optimal Diagnosis?'' in *Proceedings of the 6th Conference on Uncertainty in AI*, 1990, pp. 46–53.

26. Eugene Charniak and Solomon E. Shimony, ''Probabilistic Semantics for Rule Based Systems,'' Technical Report CS-90-02, Computer Science Department, Brown University (February 1990).

27. Eugene Charniak and Saadia Husain, ''A New Admissible Heuristic for Minimal-Cost Proofs,'' in *Proceedings of AAI Conference*, 1991, pp. 446–451.

28. Eugene Santos Jr., ''Cost-Based Abduction and Linear Constraint Satisfaction,'' Technical Report CS-91-13, Computer Science Department Brown University (1991).

29. Eugene Santos Jr., ''On the Generation of Alternative Explanations with Implications for Belief Revision,'' in *Proceedings of the 7th Conference on Uncertainty in AI*, 1991, pp. 339–347.

30. Gregory F. Cooper, ''The Computational Complexity of Probabilistic Inference Using Bayesian Belief Networks,'' *Artificial Intelligence*, 42 (2–3), 393–405 (1990).

31. Gregory F. Cooper, Eric J. Horvitz, and H. Jacques Suermondt, ''Bounded Conditioning: Flexible Inference for Decisions under Scarce Resources,'' in *5th Workshop on Uncertainty in AI*, August 1989.

32. Max Henrion, ''Propagating Uncertainty by Logic Sampling in Bayes' Networks,'' Technical report, Department of Engineering and Public Policy, Carnegie Mellon University (1986).

33.   Solomon E. Shimony, "The Role of Relevance in Explanation I: Irrelevance as Statistical Independence," *Int. J. Approximate Reasoning* Vol. 8 num. 4 pp. 281–324 (1993).
34.   Devika Subramanian, "A Theory of Justified Reformulations," Ph.D. thesis, Stanford University, 1989. Technical report STAN-CS-89-1260.
35.   Solomon E. Shimony, "On Irrelevance and Partial Assignments to Belief Networks," Technical Report CS-90-14, Computer Science Department, Brown University (1990).
36.   Gregory F. Cooper and Edward Herskovits, "A Bayesian Method for the Induction of Probabilistic Networks from Data," Technical Report SMI-91-1, University of Pittsburgh (January 1991).
37.   Judea Pearl and T. S. Verma, "A Theory of Inferred Causation," in *Knowledge Representation and Reasoning: Proceedings of the Second International Conference*, April 1991, pp. 441–452.

BIBLIOGRAPHY

Charniak, Eugene, "Bayesian Networks Without Tears," *AI Magazine*, Winter 1991, AAAI. *An easily readable introduction to Bayesian belief networks and evidential reasoning.*

Charniak, Eugene, and Drew McDermott, *Introduction to Artificial Intelligence*, Addison Wesley, Reading, MA. 1986. *Chapter 8 is about abductive reasoning, mainly in the medical domain.*

International Journal of Approximate Reasoning. North-Holland. *Publishes work on probabilistic, possibilistic and other uncertain reasoning issues.*

Neapolitan, Richard E., *Probabilistic Reasoning in Expert Systems*, John Wiley and Sons, New York, 1988. *Presents probabilistic abductive reasoning, in medical diagnosis and other fields; Also discusses Bayesian networks and evidence propagation algorithms, as well as best-first algorithms for finding the most-probable hypothesis.*

Pearl, Judea, *Probabilistic Reasoning in Intelligent Systems: Networks of Plausible Inference*, Morgan Kaufmann, San Mateo, CA, 1988. *This is a comprehensive source-book on Bayesian belief networks and Markov networks. It also discusses diagnostic reasoning, decision theory, and influence diagrams.*

Srivinas, Sampath, and Jack Breese, *IDEAL: Influence Diagram Evaluation and Analysis in LISP, Documentation and Users Guide*, Rockwell International Science Center, 1989. *Documentation for a Common-LISP software package that includes influence diagram, Bayesian network, and Markov network creation and handling, message passing algorithms, arc-reversal algorithms, clustering, conditioning, and stochastic simulation algorithms, etc. Write the authors to get a copy of the software and manual through Internet.*

SOLOMON E. SHIMONY

SCIENTIFIC VISUALIZATION

INTRODUCTION

The field of scientific visualization encompasses many disciplines and technologies. In the very broadest sense, it spans all applications that use graphics to communicate scientific or engineering information. Using this broad definition, the field of scientific visualization even includes hand illustrations of data, such as hand-drawn graphs and medical illustrations. We shall focus on one segment of this field: using computer graphics to visualize scientific or engineering data. These data may come from a variety of sources, e.g., experiments, predictions, models, or computer simulations.

Throughout this article, we shall restrict the meaning of the term scientific visualization to be "the use of computer graphics to display and interpret scientific or engineering data." Dramatic price reductions and performance improvements in computer graphics technology have created tremendous activity and progress in this field over the last 10 years. Computer-generated animations and images have demonstrated that visual representations can often provide additional insight into data and more effectively communicate research results. Visualizations have been especially effective in making abstract, complex, or voluminous data more readily comprehensible.

Three-Dimensional Visualizations

In this article, we will focus on three-dimensional (3D) visualization: the use of computer graphics to produce visual representations of data, where these data have three or more dimensions of information associated with them. The two primary computer graphics requirements for 3D visualizations are

- Being able to create three-dimensional computer models (scenes)
- The ability to generate images (pictures) of that computer model as viewed from cameras placed somewhere in that scene

For example, a biologist may want to investigate three-dimensional data obtained from a computer program that calculates the positions of two complex molecules during an interaction. The biologist can use computer graphics to create an image showing the molecules interacting. Figure 1 shows such a visualization: an enzyme molecule interacting with a molecule of DNA, which the enzyme will eventually "snip."

In a 3D visualization, colored objects (points, lines, surfaces, solids, or fog) located in a three-dimensional space represent scientific or engineering data. The colors used often convey additional information about the three-dimensional data, such as the value of an additional component associated with the data (e.g., pressure, temperature). To view these "data objects," the user specifies the position of a hypothetical camera and the computer graphics system computes the view of the data objects from this camera.

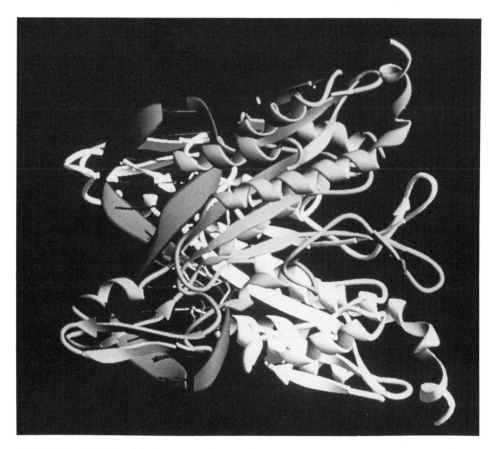

FIGURE 1   Biologist John Rosenberg of the University of Pittsburgh uses a ribbon model to visualize the interaction of the enzyme RI endonuclease and DNA. His calculations, done at the Pittsburgh Supercomputing Center (PSC), show how the endonuclease eventually "snips" the DNA molecule. The DNA is the medium-gray pair of wide ribbons at the left, which together resemble a figure "8." Image used with the permission of PSC and Dr. John Rosenberg.

The resulting image, similar to a television image of a real scene, may be displayed on a computer graphics monitor (which is similar to a television monitor but has higher resolution) or stored as a data file on the computer. Alternatively, if the graphics system includes the necessary output devices, the image can be output to paper, film, or videotape.

Three-dimensional data that depends on time (or some other additional parameter) can be visualized by creating an animation, which is a sequence of images of the data at different times. When stored on videotape or film and played back, the objects representing the data will appear to move, effectively showing how the data changes over time.

Some visualizations, especially in engineering, can be considerably more effective if the user can be "immersed" in the visualization; i.e., if the user's body and eye movements result in changes to the displayed image, the user may perceive himself or herself to be in the environment created by the visualization. This immersive technology, popularly called Virtual Reality (VR), has been successfully used for applications such as visualization of computed fluid flows, exploring computer-generated molecular force fields, and evaluating proposed designs for vehicle interiors.

Examples of 3D Data Visualization

We shall briefly discuss two examples of scientific visualization in order to demonstrate how it gets used by engineers and scientists. In both cases, each "data point" has three or more dimensions (its location in 3D space plus possibly additional data, such as pressure or temperature).

Figure 2 shows a visualization created to help understand a technique for testing "composite" materials used in the aerospace industry. Composite materials consist of layers of fibers, such as fiberglass or graphite, coated with an epoxy polymer. Composites offer high strength combined with low weight, which explains why fuselages and other components of high-performance aircraft utilize these materials. Examples of graphite–epoxy consumer goods include graphite tennis racquet frames and graphite golf club shafts.

In aerospace applications, material uniformity is extremely important. So, nondestructive techniques for testing the strength and stiffness of graphite–epoxy composites have become important. One testing method involves inducing stress waves into the composite material using an acoustic transducer (1). The transducer will cause two "stress" waves to be generated, a longitudinal one (called the QL wave) and a transverse one (QT

FIGURE 2   Dr. Ron Kriz at Virginia Polytechnic Institute visualized QL and QT stress waves propagating through a graphite/epoxy composite using software from the national Center for Supercomputing Applications (NCSA). The QL wave is on the left. Image used with the permission of NCSA and Dr. Ron Kriz.

wave). It turns out that QT and QL waves do not travel in the same direction. Moreover, the angle of propagation of the QT wave indicates the uniformity of the material. Figure 2 shows a representation of QT and QL waves traveling through a graphite–epoxy composite. These visualizations, along with accompanying animations, have proven to be valuable both for improving researchers' understanding of composites and for communicating the results obtained.

Figures 3 and 4 demonstrate changes in molecular structure that can be readily identified by using computer graphics to display the results of theoretical calculations. This example shows the results of two simulations, reported in (2), focusing on the behavior of long-chain molecules. Long-chain molecules play a critical role in certain applications involving metallic surfaces, such as lubricant design and medical implants.

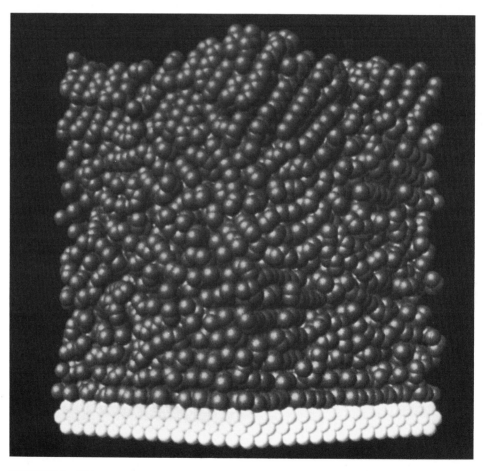

FIGURE 3   This computer-generated image shows a layer of gold (light gray) beneath long-chain (*n*-heptadecane) molecules (dark gray). The *n*-heptadecane is in a liquid state because the simulated temperature is 2° above its freezing point. At this temperature, only the bottom-most layer of *n*-heptadecane exhibits molecular ordering. The simulation was performed by Dr. Uzi Landman of the Georgia Institute of Technology on a Cray C90 at the Pittsburgh Supercomputing Center (PSC). Image used with the permission of PSC and Dr. Uzi Landman.

FIGURE 4   This 3D visualization shows a simulation of long-chain molecules (*n*-hexadecane) above a layer of gold at the freezing point of the *n*-hexadecane. The molecular ordering throughout the *n*-hexadecane shows that total crystallization has occurred. Studying animations of how molecules reach this ordered state from an unordered one, as in Figure 3, helps researchers understand which specific molecular components affect the properties of a liquid, such as a lubricant. This simulation was performed by Dr. Uzi Landman of the Georgia Institute of Technology on a Cray C90 at the Pittsburgh Supercomputing Center (PSC). Image used with the permission of PSC and Dr. Uzi Landman.

Scientists want to learn more about the behavior of long-chain molecules near surfaces so they can determine the best molecular structures to use in each situation.

In order to better understand these molecular liquids, scientists have developed computer simulation programs based on the physics governing long-chain molecule behavior. These simulations model the packing of these molecules as temperature, pressure, and other environmental variables change. Computer graphics visualizations have proven essential for understanding these computed results. Figure 3 shows how certain long-chain molecules orient themselves in an "unordered" way above a layer of gold when the temperature is just above freezing. In Figure 4, we can see the highly structured molecular configuration that occurs when a similar molecular liquid has crystallized at its freezing point. By studying computer-generated animations showing the transition from the "unordered" to "crystallized" state, investigators have learned how these transitions occur and which molecular features play an important role.

Other Scientific Applications Utilizing Computer Graphics

Before we discuss 3D scientific visualization in more detail, we must add that many other scientific and engineering applications utilize computer graphics, such as image processing and "device simulators." Image processing consists of using computers to modify existing images. For example, the National Aeronautics and Space Administration (NASA) uses image processing to modify images received from spacecraft; computer graphics systems remove spurious data (e.g., "noise") and create color images from special collections of black-and-white images.

Device simulators, such as airplane flight simulators, also use computer graphics. Simulation systems couple computer graphics with simulators in order to create a system that provides users with visual displays closely resembling those seen by someone operating the actual device or machine (e.g., an airplane).

Image processing and real-time simulation are only two of many scientific or engineering applications that utilize computer graphics. In *Visualization* (3), a book intended for nonspecialists and beautifully illustrated with computer-generated images, Friedhoff and Benton provide a wonderful survey of scientific, engineering, and artistic applications of computer graphics. We have chosen not to discuss many of these applications, such as image processing and device simulation, as they do not focus primarily on using computer graphics to provide insight into complex numerical data.

Goals and Organization

Three-dimensional visualization involves a multitude of technologies and knowledge of techniques in computing, computer graphics, video production, human visual perception, photography, and many other fields. In this article, we offer an overview of 3D visualization: its hardware and software requirements, basic computational techniques, commonly encountered data formats, data management issues, and human perception considerations.

Our coverage provides an understanding of the steps involved in creating a 3D visualization, frequently-encountered problems, and important visual considerations. We have chosen to discuss applications of Virtual Reality (VR) technology for scientific visualization as a separate topic in the section Use of Virtual Reality for 3D Visualization. This organizational scheme allows easy identification of the special resource and design considerations required for VR while emphasizing that the basic computational and input/output requirements remain the same as for any visualization.

The References and Bibliography at the end of this article contain more sources of information on the topics discussed. Naturally, we will use a number of technical computer graphics terms in our discussions. Rather than explain these when they first occur, we have collected these in the Glossary.

VISUALIZATION SYSTEMS

The improvements in computer graphics technology over the last 10 years border on revolutionary. Current graphics technology allows nonspecialists to compute, in minutes, photorealistic images that were not even possible 10 years ago. Although quite powerful, current visualization technology suffers from immaturity. As a result, highly reliable, turn-key solutions do not exist for data visualization applications as they do for well-established computer applications, such as business accounting or engineering structural analysis. These problems present a formidable barrier for scientists and other potential users.

One of the goals of 3D visualization is to produce realistic images. Computed images should show data as illuminated objects, located at specified locations and viewed from the camera position determined by the user. Adequate realism is essential so that the viewer will perceive the spatial relationships among the objects. Computer graphics technology makes it possible to create such images from input data.

The basic elements of a computer graphics system are a computer with mass storage (e.g., disk and tape drives), output device(s) for displaying images, and software for graphics processing. We briefly discuss each of these components.

Computer Systems for Graphics

Computer systems used for graphics can be classified into three categories: personal computer, workstation, and centralized computer. The latter classification includes machines accessed remotely; these systems are usually minicomputers, mainframes, or supercomputers.

Designing, creating, and previewing graphics output are highly interactive tasks. They are CPU intensive and require a high bandwidth between the processor and the graphics display device (e.g., monitor). For these reasons, personal computers or workstations are best suited for these activities.

Workstations generally have custom RISC (Reduced Instruction Set Computer) processors and provide higher performance than personal computer systems, which are based on industry-standard chips. The most common personal computers are PC-compatibles and Macintosh computers from Apple Computer. The PC-compatibles use CPU chips designed by Intel Corporation, such as the 80386, 80486, and Pentium processors. The machines from Apple utilize processors from Motorola, such as the 68020, 68030, 68040, and the PowerPC chips. As far as pricing, personal computers generally cost less than workstations, so a trade-off between price and performance exists.

Several vendors manufacture workstations designed especially for 3D graphics applications. These workstations contain special graphics processing chips that do many of the computations normally done in software (by application programs), but the chips do them considerably faster. Similarly, several companies sell 3D graphics processing boards that can be installed in personal computers or workstations.

Three-dimensional graphics requires both a powerful CPU and a large amount of machine memory. Computer system capabilities and capacities are, therefore, critical in determining graphics performance. In particular, inadequate memory (random access memory, commonly referred to as RAM) or disk capacity makes graphics processing undesirably slow and inefficient.

Table 1 below lists minimal 3D graphics hardware system configurations for personal computers and workstations.

Using the "minimum disk size" will require careful disk management: Continual archiving of images to disk or tape probably will be necessary. Larger disks (1 GB for

TABLE 1   Three-Dimensional Graphics Hardware System Configurations

System type	Minimum CPU	Minimum RAM	Recommended CPU and RAM	Minimum disk size
Workstation	30 MHz (RISC)	8 MB	100 MHz (RISC) 32MB	400 MB
PC-compatible	80386 w/ 80387 co-processor	4 MB	80486 16 MB	100 MB
Apple Macintosh	IIci (68030)	8 MB	Quadra (68040) 24 MB	200 MB

workstations, 500 MB for PCs and Macs) permit archiving to be done at regular intervals rather than continuously.

Both budget and processing requirements determine the computer graphics system to select. As of February 1994, PC-compatible systems with sufficient power for 3D graphics can be purchased for under $3000, minimally configured Macintoshes cost around $5000, and suitably configured graphics workstations cost $10,000 and up. All these prices are for the basic system (CPU, disk, graphics monitor, and keyboard); they do not include special graphics boards or peripherals. These prices should be considered only an indication of system cost, as prices drop daily and merchants regularly offer discounts.

Like most computer products, graphics processing capability becomes less expensive over time. We can expect the cost of computer graphics systems for 3D visualization to remain constant or to drop over the next 5 years. Be aware that this does not mean that graphics processing requirements will remain constant. Commercial computer graphics software continually becomes more complex, which means that users need faster CPU, more memory (RAM), and larger-capacity disks. To date, dropping prices have more than offset increasing processing requirements, resulting in overall lower costs for producing 3D graphics. For example, a graphics workstation system costing $75,000 in 1987 can be replaced in 1994 for under $15,000. Moreover, the new system will be five times faster and have five times the memory (RAM) and data storage capacity (disk) of the old one.

Graphics performance is determined by the power of the CPU, the amount of memory (RAM), the size and speed of the disk, and the input/output capabilities of the system. The performance required by the user is determined by the number of images to be computed, the image resolution (number of pixels in the horizontal direction times the number of pixels in the vertical direction), the image complexity (number of objects in the scene), and the complexity of the calculations (lighting, rendering method, etc.).

The computation times in Table 2 *very roughly* estimate the rendering capabilities of 3D graphics systems. This performance characterization pertains only to computing images (i.e., "rendering") once the scene has been created and the desired rendering options (lighting, etc.) have been specified by the user. Rendering is the most computationally intensive aspect of computer graphics. It does not require a high degree of interactivity with the user.

The primary value of the above estimates is that they indicate unreasonable expectations for each system class. For example, we can see that a user requiring hundreds of 1280 × 1024 images per month should probably not use a PC or a Macintosh. Similarly, we should not expect to produce hundreds of 4000 × 8000 images per month on a single CPU workstation.

TABLE 2 Typical Rendering Times per Image Using Commercially Available 3D Graphics Packages

Image resolution	PC (80486) or or Macintosh	Workstation (30 MHZ, 1 CPU)	Mainframe
640 × 480	5–30 min	3–15 min	1–10 min
1280 × 1024	20 min–2 h	10 min–1 h	5–45 min
2000 × 4000	2–13 h	1 h–6 h	30 min–5 h
4000 × 8000	8–50 h	4–25 h	2–20 h

Commonly Used Peripherals

The previous subsection discussed computer systems used for graphics and scientific visualization. The primary components of these systems are the CPU, memory (RAM), and disk. In this section, we will discuss peripheral devices that are commonly used in computer graphics. The integration of these peripherals transforms an ordinary computer system into a system suitable for computer graphics.

Table 3 lists commonly purchased graphics peripherals. Many more graphics peripherals are available, including extremely specialized and high-performance devices. Software for the host computer system (and often the peripheral) must be acquired in order for these devices to function.

The peripherals in Table 3 share a common trait: Each one provides either an input or an output capability for graphics. Thus, we see that graphics peripherals allow a computer system to either input or output graphics. Appendix 1 provides additional details about the peripherals in Table 3. Observe that input and output devices for all popular permanent media exist:

Medium	Computer graphics input device	Computer graphics output device
Paper, mylar	Flat-bed scanner	Hard copy device (e.g., color printer)
Photographic film	Slide scanner	Film recorder
Video	Video converter	Video converter or video animation system (for single-frame animation)

TABLE 3   Summary of Computer Graphics Peripherals

Device	Price range (1994)	Function
Graphics monitor	$300–$4,000	Interactive display of computer image
Graphics adaptor board	$40–$4,000	Allows computer CPU to drive graphics monitor on PCs or Macintoshes
GPIB board (general purpose interface bus)	$600–$1,000	Interfaces graphics peripherals (e.g., film recorder) to computer using IEEE 488 standard
Hardcopy device	$300–$50,000	Put computer graphics image on print media (paper, mylar, etc.)
Film recorder	$500–$70,000	Put computer graphics image on photographic film (35mm, etc.)
Flat-bed scanner	$500–$20,000	Input (digitize) graphics images from paper, prints, etc.
Slide scanner	$700–$10,000	Input (digitize) graphics images from 35mm slides
Video converter	$1,500–$10,000	Convert computer graphics (RGB) images to video (e.g., NTSC, PAL) images. Some also do the reverse transformation
Video animation system	$5,000–$100,000	Output computer graphics to video media. Capable of storing an image to a single video frame

Computer Graphics Software

Computer graphics software permits a user to create and modify graphics objects. These objects can be geometric models, data describing the behavior of a function in a 3D region, or computed images. Graphics packages minimally support the display of color images on a graphics monitor. Many packages also support image output to peripherals such as hardcopy devices, plotters, film recorders, and video systems.

The features and performance of graphics packages vary greatly. Some packages have a wide range of tools for creating, modifying, and rendering 3D models (or data), whereas others have only minimal capabilities. User interfaces range from poor to excellent.

Graphics software performance is determined by both the efficiency of the software and the speed with which the computer system can execute the functions specified by the graphics software. The speed of data communications between the user and the system significantly affects graphics performance because large amounts of data (e.g., images) must be transmitted.

Table 4 presents a summary of graphics software capabilities. Graphics software is divided into three categories: mainframe, workstation, and personal computer. This distinction reflects the very different performance obtained from these three types of sys-

TABLE 4   Graphics Software Characteristics

Mainframe Graphics Software

General Characteristics
    Limited interactivity
    Can do batch graphics processing using graphics routines
Pro: Convenient for quick wireframes of data on mainframe
    Excellent for high quality renderings (batch mode)
Con: Interactive features generally limited
    Raster image display often very slow

Workstation Graphics Software

General Characteristics
    Fast and highly interactive
    High image resolution and color capabilities
    Complete suite of graphics tools
Pro: Excellent for design or data exploration
    Good user interfaces, many tools
Con: CPU intensive
    Memory and disk intensive

Personal Computer Graphics Software

General Characteristics
    Highly interactive
    Moderate image resolution and color
    Complete suite of tools
Pro: Excellent for design or data exploration of moderate-sized data sets
    Excellent user interfaces; many tools
Con: Many operations are slow
    Limited resolution and color

tems. Mainframe graphics software performance is generally constrained by the relatively slow communication between the user's remote terminal and the CPU. Workstations and personal computers are differentiated because workstations usually process data significantly faster than PCs or Macintoshes.

The entries in Table 4 are self-explanatory. The primary differences to recognize are the following:

- Mainframe graphics software is not particularly desirable for highly interactive work as a result of the data communication constraints.
- Workstation graphics software generally has more features and is more responsive than PC software because workstation hardware is better suited to handle computer graphics' more intensive computing requirements.

Ideally, all three types of systems would be employed for graphics production. A powerful graphics workstation would be used for creating, modifying, or previewing the graphics output. If an animation consisting of hundreds or thousands of frames was to be produced, a central computer would be used to render the images: A batch (or background) job would generate and store the images. Finally, personal computers would be used to offload tasks from the workstation: drive a film recorder or video animation system, perform image compositing, etc. Compatible graphics software must exist on all three systems for this ideal situation to occur.

Although each category of computer system and associated graphics software has weaknesses, it is entirely feasible to use any one of these systems for all graphics processing. In particular, the rapid improvement in personal computer performance has made them very capable systems for 3D visualization provided the scene complexity is modest. Previous generations of personal computers, based on the Intel 80286 or Motorola 68020, simply did not have enough processing power to make 3D visualization practical.

Performance Measurements for Computer Graphics Systems

Performance of computer graphics systems can be characterized in several different ways. The most common performance measures, which manufacturers generally quote for each of their systems, indicate how rapidly a system can draw lines and produce shaded color objects (such as a colored sphere lit from above).

The measurement for line-drawing capability is given by the "vectors per second" rating, as a vector is simply a (colored) line drawn from one position on the screen to another. Some manufacturers refer to this measurement as "2D vectors per second" to distinguish this capability from taking a 3D vector (a colored line from one point in a 3D scene to another point in that 3D scene), *projecting* it onto the screen, shading the vector according to its closeness (near portions brighter, far portions fainter), and drawing it. The latter vector-drawing operation requires considerably more computation and the measurement associated with it is "3D depth-cued vectors per second." As of 1994, higher-end graphics systems achieve rates of at least 600,000 2D vectors per second and 450,000 3D depth-cued vectors per second.

The most common performance measurement for shaded object display capability is "shaded quadrilaterals per second." Many systems use quadrilaterals when representing object surfaces (e.g., the surface of a sphere is constructed from many small quadrilaterals), so speed in rendering and displaying quadrilaterals indicates how fast objects can be displayed and moved. The latter is of particular importance for users wishing to view animations on the monitor screen. Because different shading algorithms exist, manufacturers often specify the specific algorithm used, such as Gouraud Shading (see Ref. 4 for a good discussion of shading algorithms.) High-end systems in 1994 typical can process over 100,000 Gouraud-shaded quadrilaterals per second.

A sometimes useful variant of the quadrilateral measurement uses "3D triangular meshes (Tmesh) per second." This measurement pertains to situations arising in engineering where surfaces can be decomposed into triangles and the triangles can be ordered in a manner particularly well-suited for graphics processing. This ordering results in significantly higher graphics performance: Many 1994 graphics systems achieve 500,000 3D Tmesh per second.

Both vector and shaded object graphics processing speeds depend on the actual objects displayed: the length of the vectors and the size of the quadrilaterals, in particular. Thus, the performance measurements supplied by manufacturers lack uniformity, as no "standard" set of input data exists. These measurements provide only an indication of absolute graphics performance. More importantly, the variation in performance caused by different data means that users wishing to evaluate systems for a specific application should test candidate systems using *their* input data, not examples supplied by vendors.

Within the last several years, some efforts to develop standardized benchmarks for graphics systems have been successful. Suites of programs and data, such as the GPC Test Suite from the National Computer Graphics Association's Graphics Performance Committee, have been developed to test vector and shaded polygon performance. These tests do provide uniform results because they include the data to be displayed. Unfortunately, not all vendors publish the performance of their systems on benchmarks such as these.

INPUT DATA FOR VISUALIZATION SYSTEMS

Scientific visualizations give users insight into data and information that may otherwise be difficult to interpret. It follows that reading, sorting, and manipulating the data to be investigated is a key task in creating a visualization, 3D or otherwise. These input data can come from a variety of sources, such as computer models, experiments, simulations, calculations, and images. For 3D visualizations, input data have any number of dimensions (components) because they may represent three-dimensional objects that have many physical attributes associated with them, e.g., points in three space having temperature values (a total of four dimensions: three for location and one for temperature).

Commercial software packages for 3D visualizations generally provide capabilities for handling three types of input data: scalar (1D), images (2D), and 3D objects. Higher-dimensional objects (e.g., 3D objects with associated temperatures) often can be handled using the facilities provided for 1D, 2D, and 3D data. In the following subsections, we discuss common data formats for each of these three classes of data. Following that, in the subsection Management of input data, we provide an overview of the formats, structures, and techniques developed for managing and manipulating large or complex sets of input data.

One-Dimensional (Scalar) Data

Scalar input data, which consists merely of a list of numbers or characters, usually corresponds to some physical or theoretical structure: points on a line, numbers in a sequence, etc. Many data visualization programs, 2D and 3D, have commands, modules, or options that allow users to specify the formats (integer, floating point, character) of the elements in the list. These data can then be read into the program, stored in an array, and accessed as needed by the graphics software. Data format "standards" do not exist for scalars because arbitrary formats can be accommodated easily. Only application-specific conventions arise; visualization programs in many applications expect certain data formats, e.g., all floating-point scalars for a list of air temperatures.

Two-Dimensional Data

Image data comprises the most commonly encountered form of 2D data in graphics applications. These images may originate from film scanners, flat-bed scanners, photographs, laboratory equipment, computer simulations, or computer graphics applications, among other possibilities.

A multitude of file formats exist for image data. This condition will persist for the foreseeable future in spite of the graphics community's attempts to develop data standards. Below, we list a small sample of the image formats currently used in computer graphics:

> CGM, GIF, IFF, HDL, PCL, PBM, PICT, PostScript, TIFF, JPEG, Photoshop, PCX, Targa (TGA).

This diversity of incompatible formats, many of which were created by developers of graphics programs, complicates the processing of image data. Situations regularly arise in which a program does not support the data format of an image that needs to be input. Fortunately, most visualization programs do support a number of image formats and, in addition, many format conversion tools exist for PCs, Macintoshes, and workstations. These tools allow users to convert an image from one file format to another. A number of these programs can be obtained for free from public-access repositories on the Internet.

In regard to image formats, we need to add that "standards are not standards." Unfortunately, many of the format listed above have variants. For example, a TIFF file may specify colors using 8, 16, or 24 bits, the file can be compressed or uncompressed, and the byte-order can be Macintosh or PC-compatible. Thus, we regularly encounter situations where a program cannot input an image stored in a format, such as TIFF, that the program supposedly supports.

Another commonly encountered type of 2D input data represents function values associated with a surface. Usually, these data correspond to some scalar quantity (e.g., temperature, pressure) at grid points placed on a surface. Just as for scalar data, many 2D and 3D visualization programs provide the user with tools for specifying the format of these 2D data. In contrast to image data, where well-defined formats exist, only application-specific conventions govern the formats employed.

Three-Dimensional Data

Three-dimensional data generally take one of two forms: They describe a 3D object or they represent scalar function values (e.g., temperature) associated with a 3D grid of points. We will refer to the latter type of 3D data as 3D volume data; we present a common 3D data format and discuss volume visualization methods in the subsection Volume

Visualization. Most 3D data visualization programs allow the user to specify the format of the 3D data.

Data representing a 3D object, such as an airfoil or a car body, usually has been created by some graphics program or device, such as a 3D scanner. Normally, these programs store the data in a "standard" format, such as DES, DXF, IGES, MOVIE.BYU, or VDA. These formats store information about the location of the nodes defined on the object's surface and how one constructs the polygons (or other geometric surfaces) representing the object from these nodes. Some formats, such as MOVIE.BYU' only allow surfaces to be constructed from polygons. Others, such as IGES, support curvilinear surface elements.

Object data files tend to be quite complex, which has created file transportability problems for users. Standard formats, such as IGES, often get implemented somewhat differently by competing software manufacturers. These differences sometimes cause files created by one program to be unreadable by another program, even though both packages claim to support that standard. IGES and DXF are two of the more popular 3D object data formats. DXF tends to be favored in PC and Macintosh applications because Autocad, a very popular computer-aided design (CAD) program, stores 3D data in DXF format. IGES's popularity resides more in mainframe and workstation environments, because many high-end CAD programs utilize that format.

Many graphics applications support more than one 3D object data format, but very few of these programs can successfully read files in these formats that were created by other, unrelated programs. The complexity of the formats and the many options within each format cause this data transportability problem. Vendors of 3D graphics programs, especially CAD packages, have become aware of this problem and it appears that they will be working to reduce transportability problems.

Management of Input Data

Scientific and engineering data often consist of several scalar or vector quantities (e.g., temperature, pressure, velocity) associated with points in three-dimensional space. Interactive 3D visualizations can be used to explore these data by seeing how their values vary in 3D. In the case of computational fluid dynamics (CFD), which computes fluid flows around 3D objects, six or more variables become associated with each location in 3D space. Because an interactive visualization can normally display only four or five dimensions of data at a time, CFD visualization software must extract and display only the portions of the data that the viewer specifies. Thus, CFD visualizations often require sophisticated data management capabilities. This requirement becomes especially critical for Virtual Reality 3D visualizations because users expect real-time responses to their movements.

Several other fields have large, higher-dimensional input data sets. These include seismic sounding, medical imaging, computational chemistry, census analysis, genetic sequence mapping, and cartography. Due to the number of fields and their importance, researchers have begun developing data formats and management techniques especially for visualization input data. Treinish (5) discusses how visualization data management systems must reflect both the dimensionality of the input data and the geometric representations to be used. The article also discusses several of the data formats developed to date: CDF (NASA Goddard), netCDF (Unidata Program Center), HDF (National Center for Supercomputing Applications at the University of Illinois at Urbana-Champaign), and FITS (National Radio Astronomy Observatory).

BASIC VISUALIZATION TECHNIQUES

We use graphics software to create and modify computer graphics objects, compute (render) images from computer graphics data, and output images to monitors and peripheral devices. For 3D visualization, the data visualized will either be geometric objects (solids, surfaces, lines, points) in three-dimensional space or a collection of values (e.g., temperature, pressure) associated with points in three-dimensional space. We will refer to the former as geometric data (or scene geometry) and call the latter volume data.

The subsections below provide examples of these two data types and briefly describe the steps in visualizing them. *Computer Graphics: Principles and Practice* (4), which is an excellent source of information about all aspects of computer graphics, contains more information about these and other computer graphics techniques.

Geometric Modeling and Rendering

Two possible sources of geometric data for scientific visualizations exist: (1) geometric objects may be inherent in the scientific study itself or (2) geometric objects may be created to visualize computed quantities.

As an example of (1), geometric data is inherent in a computer simulation of airflow past an aircraft. The aircraft is a geometric object made up of surfaces. Visualizing the results of the airflow study involves obtaining data that describes the aircraft's surface and visualizing (rendering) that surface.

As an example of (2), consider the quantities (air pressure, velocity, etc.) computed in the airflow study mentioned in the previous paragraph. Aerodynamicists are particularly concerned with the flow around the aircraft. The computed air velocities quantitatively describe the nature of this flow. These data can be visualized by creating "particle traces": the paths that particles would follow if they were released at specified points.

Thus, we visualize air flow by choosing appropriate locations (nose of the aircraft, edges of wings, etc.) and creating particle traces starting there. These traces are geometric objects (lines) that we display to show the results of the simulation. Figure 5 shows such a visualization; these particle traces are generally called "streaklines" or "streamlines." Similarly, we often create surfaces by "contouring" three-dimensional data: we create and display the surface where a particular function always has a specified, constant value, e.g., air pressure equals 100 psi everywhere on this surface.

The diagram below shows the component operations and work flow for geometric modeling and rendering. These steps comprise the "traditional" method for generating images of 3D data. The paragraphs below provide additional information about each step in the diagram.

Rendering Information \
                    Renderer → Output Image \
                                          Image Compositing (Optional) \
     Scene Geometry /
                              Other Images or /
                              Text (Optional)

Scene Geometry: Geometric objects are either created or imported into the visualization program. These objects will either be specified as surfaces (collections of 2D polygons or curvilinear surfaces) or solids (unions and intersections of 3D solid primi-

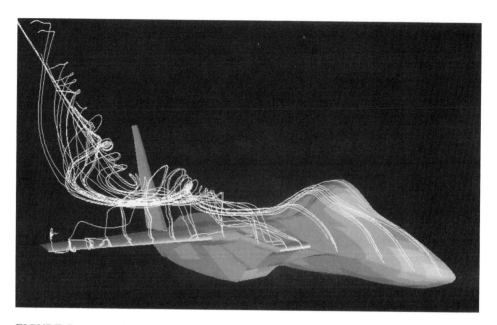

FIGURE 5   Aerodynamic properties of an F-15 aircraft are displayed in this image. Streaklines show the airflow by showing the path that a particle would follow. Dr. William Ribarsky of The Georgia Institute of Technology computed this visualization using the PLOT3D software package from NASA AMES Research Center. Image used with the permission of Dr. William Ribarsky.

tives such as spheres and cubes). Graphics packages normally provide for interactive creation and modification of these geometric objects.

Rendering Information: In addition to specifying the geometry of the objects to be visualized, we must "set the scene." All the considerations that apply to directing a film production apply. We specify the position of the camera, objects, and lights as well as the colors and surface textures of the objects. Most packages allow this to be done interactively.

Renderer: The rendering component of a computer graphics package uses the scene geometry and rendering information to create a 2D image of the scene. It produces a "snapshot" of the scene based on the input data. Many different rendering techniques exist and various levels of realism (e.g., with or without shadows being cast by objects) can be selected. Scene rendering can take anywhere from seconds to days, depending on the complexity of the scene and the rendering options chosen. Workstation graphics software usually has a "quick and dirty" renderer that can be used to preview scenes and a high-quality renderer for the final rendering. The former is used interactively while the latter is used in batch (or background) mode.

Output: Graphics packages allow us to display a rendered image and save it as a file (of digital data) on disk. Packages often support the display or transfer of images to peripherals such as film recorders and video systems.

Image Compositing: It is often useful to composite one or several images. Compositing software allows 2D images to be merged, cut, pasted, and modified. Compositing can be quite valuable for scientific visualization. For example, 2D titles, text, and legends can be "pasted" onto images generated by the renderer.

Volume Visualization

In contrast to geometric data, volume data does not have geometric characteristics associated with it. Volume data is often encountered when actual physical measurements are the source of the data. Medical applications are a prime example: CT (computed tomography) scans of animals provide X-ray data at a collection of points in three-dimensional space. The X-ray value at a point is associated with a property of the animal (tissue density), but no geometry is inherent in the data itself.

Although we could create geometry from the data (e.g., create a geometric surface where all the tissue densities have a given value), it is often desirable to visualize such data without imposing geometric structures. The computer graphics technology for accomplishing this is called volume rendering.

We use volume rendering to visualize the values of a function (technically, a scalar field) in a 3D region. We begin by specifying colors and opacities to be associated with each value of the function in the region. The volume rendering program then displays the 3D region using those assignments. By judiciously choosing the colors and opacities, we can make structures within the data very apparent.

For the CT data mentioned above, specifying the high tissue density values (e.g., bone) to be opaque and low tissue densities (e.g., soft tissue) to be transparent will result in an image that shows only the bone structure in the CT data. Specifying that a certain tissue density be opaque and all others be transparent will create an image showing the tissue of the specified density. Note that although geometric structure is visible (i.e., bone or tissue), no geometric model (solids, surfaces, lines) exists from which the image is generated. Volume visualization contrasts with geometric modeling and rendering techniques, described above, which require creating geometric objects and rendering them.

Volume rendering is a relatively expensive visualization technique. Results will only be acceptable if the data provide a good description of the region (i.e., sampling was sufficiently frequent). However, when successfully applied, volume rendering provides a powerful method for discovering and exploring the structures inherent in a set of 3D data.

The diagram below shows the component operations and work flow for volume visualization. The image compositing and output components are exactly the same as for geometric modeling and rendering. The subsequent paragraphs provide information about the other components.

Visualization Information ⟍

            Renderer →   Output Image ⟍

        3D Data ⟋   Image Compositing (Optional)

                       Other Images or ⟋

                       Text (Optional)

3D Data: Data associated with a region of three-dimensional space are input into the volume visualization program. Each data "point" in the data set assigns a single numerical value to a 3D point, e.g., (x, y, z) in the region. Frequently, the required data format is a sequence of 2D cross sections. For example, the X-ray data from a $64 \times 64 \times 64$ unit region would be 64 files, each of which is a 64×64 array of X-ray intensities. Each array corresponds to a cross section (e.g., fixed z-value, $z = z_0$). The content of each array is the X-ray intensities associated with a 2D grid, e.g., X-ray values at x–y grid locations.

Data format specifications vary between volume visualization programs but most support data input in a format similar to the one described above. In some cases, the function (e.g., X-ray) values must be integers, whereas in other cases, floating-point data can be used.

Visualization Information: Volume visualization programs require the users to assign color and opacity values to the function values input. In the case of the X-ray data, for example, if the X-ray intensities are integers in the range 0–100, the user might choose to have the locations with intensities above 90 be opaque and all others transparent. This choice would cause only the locations with high values (which might correspond to tissue with high density, such as bone) to be visible. Similarly, associating colors with function values permits the viewer to distinguish regions with different function values.

As for geometric modeling and rendering, the camera position and scene lighting must be specified. Unlike geometric models, surface texture information is not necessary because geometric objects, such as surfaces, do not exist. Perceived "objects" in a volume visualization arise from the visual properties (color, opacity and, possibly, luminance) associated with each volume element (called a voxel) in the 3D region.

Most volume visualization programs provide interactive control of visualization variables such as opacity, colors, lighting, and camera location. This interactivity provides an environment in which the user can experiment with different visualizations. If a region of interest is obscured, a change in the opacity assignments can quickly make it visible. Specific features, relationships, and details can be visualized by adjusting the opacities, colors, lighting, and viewpoint.

Renderer: The rendering component of a volume visualization program creates a 2D image of the scene as viewed from the camera location specified. The user selects the desired rendering options, which include the resolution of the final image. Volume visualization programs normally provide the capability to interactively visualize planar cross sections (slices) of the input data as well as the entire volume.

ELEMENTARY DESIGN AND PRESENTATION CONSIDERATIONS FOR 3D VISUALIZATIONS

This section examines issues that arise once the mechanics of production have been resolved. Content (what to visualize) and presentation (how best to display data or results) constitute the primary questions. Scientific significance and meaning determines which data, or which components of the data, should be displayed in a 3D visualization. Four factors affect the design of the visualization: its goal, the expectations of the intended audience, system output capabilities, and human perception factors. We discuss these in the following subsections.

The Interaction of Visualization Design and Objectives

The objectives of a 3D visualization largely determine the format and design of the eventual visual (and, possibly, audio) production. Is it intended to help researchers gain insight into some new data? Or, should it inform the audience about new results and their significance? Or, does it provide the audience with a deep understanding of a particular phenomenon? Different goals require entirely different presentation techniques. The basic design considerations comprise which media to use, the degree of interactivity with the user, and the image quality to employ. Visualizations to explore new data need high interactivity but can be relatively unpolished. On the other hand, visualizations designed for nonspecialists, and especially "lay" audiences," must be very polished. Ineffective visualizations abound because their authors either failed to clearly define the purpose of the work or they never identified the visualization needs of their audience.

Audience Expectations: Color and Format Conventions

Once an appropriate level of quality and interactivity has been determined for a visualization, the expectations and knowledge level of the target audience must be determined. Developers often overlook this critical step. The background and expectations of the intended audience often preclude the use of certain visual tools. Some audiences, radiologists for example, are accustomed to black-and-white images and will not be receptive to color images.

Technical specialists (physicists, economists, sociologists, etc.) often see data displayed using certain color conventions. For example, blue has come to be affiliated with "cool" and red with "hot" in certain fields. Similarly, many disciplines often use specific types of graphs or charts to interpret data, e.g., economists' use of pie charts to show how tax dollars are spent. An effective 3D visualization should incorporate the audience's expected color conventions and either make use of data format conventions or briefly show how the 3D data looks in one or more of the standard formats. Using familiar colors and formats helps the audience comprehend complex data and promotes their acceptance of any nonstandard display techniques employed.

A great deal has been written about effective and ineffective methods for presentation of technical data. The works of Tufte (6,7) and Tukey (8,9), are particularly notable. These authors include techniques for displaying data and discussions of how human perception capabilities interact with the various display methods.

Computer Graphics Output Capabilities and Limitations

Regardless of how a 3D visualization has been constructed and computed, some means must be used to communicate the results to viewers. A wide range of options for creating output exists for computer graphic systems. These options can be divided into three categories: image files, technologies that create images, and technologies that create objects. Image files consist of computer data files containing information describing one or more images. We covered these earlier when we discussed input data in the subsection Two-Dimensional Data. The subsections below examine the other two computer graphics output options.

Conventional Visual Graphics Output

The most common means for communicating the results of a 3D visualization is to create images or an animation (sequences of images). The images created may be conventional flat prints or they may use stereoscopic or holographic techniques that give the viewer the perception of depth when viewing the image. For single images, visual output options include photographic media (slides, prints), print media (paper, fabrics, mylar, plastics, etc.), visual displays (monitors, screens, projectors), head-mounted devices (helmets, goggles, glasses), holograms, and stereo image devices (stereo image pairs printed on paper, stereo image pairs displayed on the screen and viewed with special glasses.)

For animations, video has become the output medium of choice, followed by film (usually 35mm "CINE" format). Video allows easy, low-cost production of animations with the added advantage that video playback devices, such as video cassette recorders (VCRs), are ubiquitous. Image quality remains the primary drawback to video: resolution and color quality are considerably lower than for film-based media. As for single images, depth effects can be produced by creating and displaying stereo pairs of images. In regard to video, developers need to consider the geographic locations of their viewers, as several different, incompatible formats exist. NTSC (United States, Japan), PAL (Europe), and SECAM (France) constitute the primary ones.

Very important restrictions on the visual effects that can be created arise from the limitations inherent in the output medium chosen. For example, video media cannot accurately store and reproduce highly saturated colors, such as bright red: Saturated colors look smeared ("bleed"). Additionally, NTSC video cannot encode nearly as much color information in color as it can in black and white, so fine details can be better displayed using black and white. The color and resolution restrictions of video media are not unique. Color and resolution limitations exist for all output options because each technology has inherent physical limits to resolution and a set of colors (called the device's color gamut) that it can display. More information on device-related color problems and a brief overview of color gamuts is presented in Ref. 10.

A factor further complicating the production of color output arises from the *different* color gamuts that color output devices possess. The net effect is that no "device-independent" color standard currently exists; i.e., a computer graphics color specified digitally (e.g., Red = 10, Green = 20, Blue = 70, where Red, Green, and Blue range from 0 to 255) will not have an identical appearance when output using different devices. For example, a pink object on a monitor might appear light brown when output to 35mm film by a film recorder. Research, such as Ref. 11, has begun to devise methods to calibrate color output devices. In general, the lack of device-independent color poses a prominent problem that the computer graphics industry is currently attempting to resolve.

Solid Model Output

In addition to producing single images and animations, computer graphics systems can also be used to generate an actual three-dimensional object. If an object has been designed using a computer graphics system, the data describing that object often can be transferred to a milling, machining, or "solid imaging" system that uses the data to control the apparatus that actually builds or sculpts the object.

Solid imaging systems, which companies use to rapidly create prototypes, can be any of about a dozen different technologies. These include Laminated Object Manufacturing, Solid Ground Curing, Fused Deposition Modeling, Selective Laser Sintering, and Stereolithography. Stereolithography, the most common of these, employs a laser to cure a liquid, photosensitive polymer (in a tank) at locations where the surface of the object is to exist. It has the advantage that it can build seamlessly some 3D objects that would otherwise have seams, e.g., a sphere within a sphere. Currently (1994), object size limitations of 24 in. × 24 in. × 24 in. remain a primary disadvantage of stereolithography.

Human Perception

Designing and producing an effective scientific visualization not only requires knowledge of the color and resolution of output devices, as discussed in the subsection on Conventional Visual Graphics Output but also consideration of attributes of human visual perception. These arise both from properties of the human eye and how the human brain processes information from the eye. The examples below illustrate a few of these phenomena and their implication for visualization design.

1. Nonuniform sensitivity to red, green, and blue: The eye detects green best, then red, then blue. Because it processes blue least efficiently, highly saturated (i.e., strong) blue colors should not be used for fine details or fast-moving objects.

2. Spatial discrimination of black and white versus color: The eye's receptors for black and white have higher spatial discrimination than its color receptors. Thus, closely spaced, fine lines should be in black and white, if possible.

3. Red–green color blindness: A nontrivial portion of the human population cannot distinguish shades of red and green, so visualizations should not rely on the viewer being able to discern differences in these colors.

4. Edge sharpening: The human visual system attempts to increase the sharpness of edges. This visual system trait sometimes causes "bands," called Mach bands, to appear in regions with smoothly varying color intensity. It also can result in the appearance of lines along the borders of polygons, even though the colors have been nicely interpolated. More sophisticated shading algorithms often can be employed to overcome these problems.

There have been and continue to be many investigations into perceptual issues that arise specifically in computer graphics. Bailey (10) gives a nice overview of issues related to the use of color for scientific visualization; Refs. 12 and 13 provide more details about using color in computer graphics applications. Neuroscientists, such as Livingston (14), have developed recommendations for color maps (assignments of colors to numerical values) based on attributes of human visual perception.

USE OF VIRTUAL REALITY FOR 3D VISUALIZATION

Since about 1990, Virtual Reality (VR) technologies have become increasingly available and affordable. Scientists and engineers have begun employing these tools to help them more easily interpret complex 3D visualizations of data and engineering designs. We may characterize the application of VR to 3D visualization as follows: A VR 3D visualization provides a computer-generated environment that imbues the user with a sense of participation and immersion.

We need two computer system properties in order to create participatory and immersive sensations: (1) interactivity and (2) response to natural motions by the user. Typically, motions that create system response include moving the head, eyes, hands, or limbs.

To effect a feeling of total immersivity, the 3D visualization must respond quickly to head or eye movements; the image seen by the user must change according to changes in his or her line of sight. A head-mounted liquid crystal display (LCD) or a boom-mounted display system are among the devices that can be used for achieving this immersivity. The helmet has sensors to track the viewer's head position and an LCD panel, in front of the viewer's eyes, upon which the computer graphics system generates an image. The input from the sensors causes the system to change the image in response the user's head motion. Figure 6 shows such a helmet in use.

A boom-mounted system comprises a configuration of rods, connected by joints and gimbals, from which a small computer monitor (cathode ray tube, CRT) is sus-

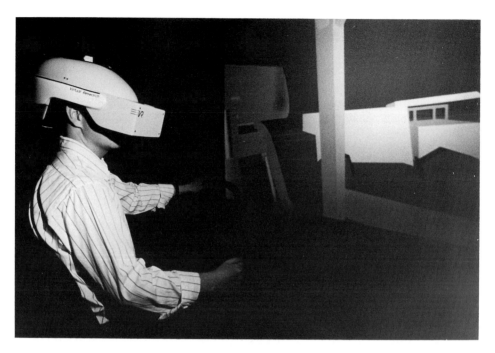

FIGURE 6   Caterpillar Inc. uses a virtual reality 3D simulator to evaluate designs for the cabs of its wheel loaders and backhoe loaders. This simulator, developed in cooperation with the National Center for Supercomputing Applications (NCSA), provides realistic views from the cab by using a special helmet, which displays images based on the motion of the operator's head. By using simulators, Caterpillar has reduced its need to build full-scale prototypes and considerably shortened its cab design cycle. Image used with the permission of the NCSA and Caterpillar Inc.

pended. The user holds handles on the CRT while viewing the image and moving around. The boom system senses the user's position, causing the computer graphics system to change the image based on the line of sight of the viewer. To create an illusion of depth, a pair of monitors can be substituted for the single monitor and stereo pairs of images displayed on these CRTs.

A user's sense of participation corresponds to the naturalness of interaction with the virtual environment. The visual changes generated by head and eye movements provide a portion of this sensation. Additional interactivity can be created by outfitting the user with a glove (''data glove'') or even a body suit containing sensors that track the positions of the user's hands and limbs. Some specialized applications, such as molecular force field modeling, even use devices that transmit forces to the viewer's hands as he or she steers through the virtual environment. Currently, data gloves have enjoyed the greatest popularity among VR system developers. Typically, the computer graphics system displays the data glove as part of the 3D visualization, allowing the user to interact with objects in the scene.

A considerable amount of the VR technology, and its use in 3D visualization, has been driven by aerospace applications. The Virtual Windtunnel, reported in Ref. 15, exemplifies this. This VR implementation attempts to create an immersive environment that allows the viewer to better understand a precomputed flowfield for an aircraft. The aircraft and the flows are visualized exactly as in Figure 5: streaklines going past the fuselage and wings. The Virtual Windtunnel uses a stereo, boom-mounted display (having two monochrome CRTs) and a data glove to allow the user to "walk around" in the windtunnel and release "seeds," which create streaklines. The viewer also can zoom-in on the simulation so that he or she is surrounded by a small portion of the flow (e.g., a vortex) or zoom-out so that the whole flowfield fits in the viewer's hand.

We have seen that applying VR to 3D visualization requires integrating specialized input and output devices, such as data gloves, body suites, and head-mounted displays. Employing this technology also has implications for graphics processing. The requirement for interaction with the user plus the need for rapidly updated, realistic displays currently (1994) exceeds the graphics processing capabilities of single or multiprocessor workstations. Only specially constructed simulators costing millions of dollars, such as a airplane flight simulators, can deliver realistic interactivity and visual displays.

Most VR scientific visualizations use high-end computer graphics workstations; developers generally compromise visual realism in order to maintain acceptable interactivity. In spite of using lower-resolution images, many complex applications still provide noticeably slow response to viewer actions. VR applications often use multiple processor workstation systems because these systems can readily employ parallel processing. Some of the processors can handle input–output tasks, whereas others perform graphics computations. We expect that as workstation processor, disk, and communication performance continue to improve, VR technology will become increasingly interactive and image realism will improve dramatically.

TRENDS IN SCIENTIFIC VISUALIZATION

The past decade has produced remarkable advances in computer graphics technologies. Equipment prices have plummeted, computing system performance has increased by two orders of magnitude, affordable software for 2D graphics has appeared, and sophisticated packages for creating 3D graphics have been developed. Scientific visualization, once an activity confined to the select few who had access to advanced computing systems, has become an integral part of scientific and engineering investigations. Many researchers use 2D and 3D visualizations to understand and communicate results of their experiments and computations.

The next 10 years promises more of the same: Computer graphics equipment prices will continue dropping, and more powerful, more economical visualization software will appear. These changes will make 3D graphics, such as 3D visualizations, more affordable. We will be able to produce color 3D visualizations of complex data on desktop systems costing under $3000. Good-quality color printers probably will cost under $1000 and 3D graphics packages will abound.

Although technology will make 3D visualization easier and more pervasive, we do not anticipate that scientific visualization will become a truly automated procedure. No one software program will be adequate for all disciplines; specialized programs and visualization tools will continue to be required. In spite of users' and industry's attempts to develop "standard" image and object formats, we will probably end up with a handful of formats that most software can handle reliably. Our production bottleneck probably will continue to be less-than-perfectly-reliable software that cannot fully utilize the power of the hardware on which it executes.

The next decade will be an exciting one for scientific visualization, and especially for 3D visualization. The arrival of faster hardware and better software will allow scientists, engineers, and visualization experts to concentrate more on effectively displaying data and less on the mechanics of production. It is safe to predict that we will not only gain fundamental insights into complex sets of data but also a better understanding of how humans process visual information.

APPENDIX: COMPUTER GRAPHICS PERIPHERALS

Graphics Monitor

A color graphics monitor is an essential component of a computer graphics system. Monitors interactively display raster and wireframe color images. Although a monochrome graphics monitor costs less than a color monitor, scientific visualization applications usually require a color monitor in order to be effective.

Many companies market color graphics monitors for PC-compatibles and Macintoshes. For workstations, the color monitors offered by the manufacturers are almost always capable of displaying graphics.

For remote hosts, a wide variety of monochrome and color graphics terminals exist. One category, the "X-terminal" deserves special mention. X-terminals derive their name from a communication protocol, called X11, that they support. X11 is a language that allows a computer (called the server) running the X11 "windowing system" to communicate with another system (called the client). X11, as opposed to previous protocols, contains many directives for creating and controlling windows on the screen of both the server and the client. In particular, if a terminal supports X11 (i.e., the terminal can process X11 directives), a graphics program on a remote computer can use X11 directives to open a window on the terminal and display color graphics in that window. X-terminals have become a popular choice for applications where color graphics must be generated by a host and displayed on a remote terminal.

In all cases, graphics monitors allow one of many colors to be assigned to each pixel (picture element) of the screen. Thus, the controlling software is not limited to displaying only predetermined forms (such as text characters) on the screen. Monitor prices reflect the number of colors supported (16 colors to 16.7 million colors), screen resolution (640×480 up to 1280×1040), and the "sharpness" (precision) of the monitor.

High-end workstation graphics monitors usually have a 19-in. diagonal screen, a resolution of 1280×1024, and can display 16.7 million colors (2^{24} colors). PC and Macintosh graphics monitors normally have a 14-in. diagonal screen and support up to 1024×768 resolution, and 256 colors. However, manufacturers do offer X-terminals, graphics adaptor boards, and monitors for PCs and Macintoshes that provide the resolution and color of a workstation monitor.

Graphics Adaptor Board

For PCs and Macintoshes, an interface board (often called an interface card) must be purchased so that the CPU can communicate with the monitor. For PCs, many different graphics cards are available and several standards are supported.

A common graphics board standard for PC-compatibles, as of early 1994, is VGA (Video Graphics Adaptor), which provides 640×480 resolution and 256 colors. An enhanced VGA, called SuperVGA, has become equally or more popular, due to its higher performance. Depending on the particular board and the memory installed on it, Super VGA can support up to 1024 × 768 resolution and 256 colors. Although Super VGA is slightly more expensive, its superior resolution justifies using it in applications requiring images to be displayed.

Video Converter

A video converter transforms the (analog) signal driving a computer graphics monitor from the standard expected by the monitor (RGB) to the television standard expected by a video device, such as a VCR or television monitor. The two most common television standards are NTSC (United States, Japan) and PAL (Europe).

Most video converters can also transform video input (e.g., signals from a VCR) into a computer graphics image. This capability is referred to as "video capture." The video signal (encoding a video image) is converted (digitized) into RGB (red, green, blue) values, stored in the memory of the video converter and displayed on the graphics monitor. The RGB values can subsequently be stored in a disk file, so the image can retained as digital data.

Video converters can either be external units or boards that are installed in the CPU cabinet. Converters are readily available for PCs, Macintoshes, workstations, and most minicomputers. Prices reflect the screen resolution that the converter can support and how fast the conversion can be done. High-end converters can transform 1280 × 1024 RGB images into NTSC or PAL images in real time.

GPIB Board

A GPIB (General Purpose Interface Bus) is not an actual peripheral; it merely permits peripherals that use a certain hardware interface standard (IEEE 488) to be connected to the computer system. Purchase of a GPIB interface will often be required in order to connect the devices listed below to PCs, Macintoshes, workstations, and minicomputers.

Hardcopy Device

Hardcopy devices allow graphic images to be put on paper, mylar, transparencies and other print media. The most common graphics hardcopy device in use is the "office" laser printer, which supports graphics but not color. Laser printers generally are unsuitable for scientific visualization because color is an essential visualization tool.

Recent price reductions have begun to make color hardcopy devices more affordable. As of early 1994, color printers providing reasonably good resolution and color could be purchased for under $8000. Photographic-quality printers using thermal dye sublimation or laser print technology cost $8000 or more.

Film Recorder

Film recorders put a computer graphics image on photographic film. The primary film format is 35mm. More expensive film recorders allow 4 in. × 5 in. and other camera backs to be attached.

Two types of film recorders exist: digital and analog. Digital film recorders require digital data for input. These data, supplied by the host computer in a format recognized by the film recorder, specify the color at each pixel of the image. Analog film recorders require analog input; they use the (analog) signals that drive the computer's monitor.

Digital film recorders are more expensive than analog ones, but they usually provide better imaging. In particular, they produce more consistent results because they do not depend on the signals generated to drive the monitor. These signals can vary greatly between computer systems and often change over time.

Flat-bed Scanner

Flat-bed scanners digitize existing images that are on paper, mylar, or other print media. They transform images into sets of numbers, which can be stored as (disk) files on the computer system and subsequently used (displayed, modified, etc.) by graphics programs. Low-end scanners have lower resolution, usually 300 dots per inch (dpi), and produce gray scale (i.e., black and white) digitized images. High-end scanners support color and have higher resolution, up to 1200×800 dpi. Flat-bed scanners are especially appropriate for inputting graphs, graphic designs, and photographs for use in computer graphics.

Slide Scanner

Slide scanners perform the same function as flat-bed scanners, except that they use 35mm slides for input; i.e., they digitize the image on a 35mm slide so it can be stored as a disk file. Slide scanner resolution varies from 1800 dpi to 5000 dpi, depending on price.

Video Animation System

A video animation system converts an image on a computer graphics monitor to a standard video image and stores it on a video medium, such as videotape. The primary feature of a video animation system is that it can store a graphics image on a *single* video frame. Thus, smooth animations (composed of thousands of computer graphic images, each of which could have taken minutes to compute) can be created by storing images one at a time on video tape.

A video animation system is designed to operate automatically. By having the proper graphics software on the host computer, hundreds or thousands of images can be rendered and automatically stored on a videotape.

An animation system has four parts: video storage device (e.g., video tape recorders), video converter (described above), animation controller and cables to connect these components together (and to the host computer).

The video storage device records the image on its storage medium, such as videotape. Professional-quality "editing" videotape recorders are often used for this purpose. These cost $7000 and up; they use $\frac{3}{4}$-in. or 1-in. videotape. Most consumer VCRs cannot be used for this purpose because they are not "single-frame addressable"; i.e., they cannot accurately position the tape to a specified frame.

The animation controller coordinates the activity of the video storage device, video converter, and the host computer. When the image to be stored is displayed on the screen, the computer signals the animation controller. The controller first triggers the video converter, causing it to generate an NTSC (or PAL) version of the image. The controller then activates the video storage device, causing it to store the image in the desired frame (or frames) on the video medium.

GLOSSARY

animation: An animation is a motion picture (usually made on videotape or film) consisting of a sequence of images. The sequence creates the illusion that figures or objects are in motion when it is viewed. A computer animation is an animation where each image is created using computer graphics (as opposed to having been drawn by hand or having been produced by a camera).

compositing: See image compositing.

digitize: Digitize means to convert to numbers. For example, flat bed scanners convert images (colors on paper) to files containing numbers, where the numbers represent the colors at various positions on the image.

dpi: The abbreviation dpi stands for dots per inch. This unit of measurement is commonly used for specifying the resolution of scanners and printers. The more dots per inch, the higher the resolution and performance of the device. Higher dpi means that the device can scan or print finer image details. A resolution of 300 dpi is typical, whereas a resolution of 800 dpi is quite high.

image compositing: Compositing is the creation of an image from two or more previously existing images. It is frequently used to create an image with the background of one image behind an object from another image. The object is electronically or photographically removed from the rest of its scene and placed on top of (i.e., made to cover a portion of) the image containing the background.

NTSC: NTSC is a standard for receiving and transmitting color video signals. This standard is used for most color video devices in the United States, Japan, and some other countries. The National Television Standards Committee (NTSC) proposed it in 1947.

orthogonal projection: A view of a 3D scene in which the objects or elements are projected onto one of the coordinate planes, e.g., x-y plane. The projection is done along the direction of the normal to the plane, e.g., along the direction of the z-axis onto the x-y plane.

PAL: PAL is a standard for receiving and transmitting color video signals. PAL is the primary video color standard used in Europe (except France, which uses a standard called SECAM). The corresponding U.S. standard is called NTSC.

pixel: Pixel is short for picture element. Most computer monitors (and all television monitors) display images or text by controlling the color of many tiny, rectangular regions. Each of these is called a pixel. A pixel is the smallest portion of the screen that can be controlled; each pixel can have only one color at a given time. Common monitor resolutions are (640 × 480) pixels and (1280 × 1024) pixels.

raster display: A raster display device is a device that displays images by controlling the color of small rectangular areas, called pixels (see definition above). A raster display differs fundamentally from a vector display device, which can only create lines.

raster image: A raster image is an image displayed on a raster display, or a file containing data that can be used to produce a raster image. In either case, there must be data specifying the color of each pixel on the raster display. A raster image is fundamentally different from a vector image, which is made up only of lines.

real time: Real time refers to the amount of actual time consumed by an operation rather than just the amount of CPU time. Computer programs are said to work in real time if they can process input sufficiently fast to keep up with the input stream. For example, a real-time NTSC image converter can convert incoming RGB images to NTSC video images as quickly as they appear; no incoming images are lost and no delays occur.

render: Render means to compute an image from input data. Computer graphics packages render images from geometric or volume data.

RGB: RGB is a standard for transmitting and receiving color data. RGB is the primary standard used for computer workstation color monitors. Three separate signals (Red, Green, Blue) are used to control the display screen. This RGB standard is not used for video devices (see NTSC and PAL). However, there is an NTSC video interface standard called RGB. This is not the same (or compatible with) the computer graphics RGB standard.

single-frame animation: An animation created by creating (e.g., using computer graphics) images individually and then storing them on videotape or film one at a time. Single-frame animation is required when image creation is so slow (e.g., seconds or minutes) that a smooth animation would not result if image storage was continuous.

Super VGA (SVGA): A enhanced version of the VGA graphics adaptor that provides higher resolution and more available colors. Resolution of 1024 × 768 and 256 colors is commonly available using Super VGA.

vector display device: A vector display device displays images by drawing lines. This contrasts with a raster device, which colors subregions (pixels) to display an image. A vector image is created by drawing lines specified by the vector image data. Images on vector devices are normally line drawings (i.e., not solid images like a television image).

vector image: A vector image is an image displayed on a vector device or a file containing data that can be used to generate a vector image. A vector image file contains instructions specifying where the lines comprising the image are to be drawn on the screen. A vector image differs fundamentally from a raster image; significantly less data is required for a vector image.

VGA: VGA (Video Graphics Adaptor) is a standard interface for personal computer (PC) monitors. A VGA graphics board allows a computer to display text and images on a computer monitor. VGA provides a resolution of 640 × 480 pixels and either 16 or 256 colors, depending on the amount of memory on the board.

wireframe: A wireframe image is an image composed only of lines (no solid surfaces). Additionally, all lines defining objects are visible; no "hidden" lines (e.g., the back edges of a cube) are removed.

ACKNOWLEDGMENTS

Portions of the text and tables in this article appeared previously in Refs. 16 and 17. We thank Duke University Press for its permission to include that material in this article. We express our gratitude to Dr. David Payne of the University of Georgia, who provided valuable editorial assistance. We also thank the National Center for Supercomputing Applications (NCSA), the Pittsburgh Supercomputing Center (PSC), and Dr. William Ribarsky of The Georgia Institute of Technology for providing images used in this article.

REFERENCES

1. Ronald D. Kriz, "Computer Simulation and Visualization of Stress Wave Propagation," *Sci. Computing & Automation*, 19–24 (April 1990).
2. T. Xia and U. Landman, "Surface and Dynamics of Surface Crystallization of Liquid *n*-Alkanes," *Phys. Rev. B*, *48*, 48 (1993).
3. R. M. Friedhoff and W. Benton, *Visualization*, Harry Abrams, Inc., New York, 1989.
4. J. Foley, A. van Dam, S. Feiner, and J. Hughes, *Computer Graphics: Principles and Practice*, Addison-Wesley, Reading, MA, 1990.
5. L. A. Treinish, "Unifying Principles of Data Management for Scientific Visualization," in *Introduction to Scientific Visualization Tools and Techniques*, SIGGRAPH 93 Course Notes 02, ACM SIGGRAPH, New York, 1993.
6. E. R. Tufte, *The Visual Display of Quantitative Information*, Graphics Press, Cheshire, CT, 1983.
7. E. R. Tufte, *Envisioning Information*, Graphics Press, Cheshire, CT, 1990.
8. J. W. Tukey, *Exploratory Data Analysis*, Addison-Wesley, Reading, MA, 1977.
9. *The Collected Works of John W. Tukey: Volume V, Graphical Methods*, Wadsworth, Inc., Pacific Grove, CA, 1988.
10. Mike Bailey, "Guidelines for the Use of Color in Scientific Visualization," in *Introduction to Scientific Visualization Tools and Techniques*, SIGGRAPH 93 Course Notes 02, ACM SIGGRAPH, New York, 1993.
11. M. B. Lamming and W. L. Rhodes, "A Simple Method for Improved Color Printing of Monitor Images", *ACM Trans. Graphics*, *9* (4), 345–375 (1990).
12. L. G. Thorell and W. J. Smith, *Using Computer Color Effectively*, Prentice-Hall, Englewood Cliffs, NJ, 1990.
13. *Understanding Visual Perception and its Impact on Computer Graphics*, SIGGRAPH 91 Course Notes 9, ACM SIGGRAPH, New York, 1991.
14. M. S. Livingston and D. H. Hubel, "Anatomy and Physiology of a Color System in the Primate Visual Cortex," *J. Neurosci.*, *4*, 309–356 (1984).
15. Steve Bryson and Creon Levit, "The Virtual Windtunnel: An Environment for the Exploration of Three-Dimensional Unsteady Flows," in *Introduction to Scientific Visualization Tools and Techniques*, SIGGRAPH 93 Course Notes 02, ACM SIGGRAPH, New York, 1993.
16. S. Follin, "The Essentials of Scientific Visualization: Basic Tools and an Example," *Social Sci. Computer Rev.*, *10*, 3 (1992).
17. S. Follin, "The Essentials of Scientific Visualization: Basic Techniques and Common Problems," *Social Sci. Computer Rev.*, *10*, 4 (1992).
18. *Computer Graphics*, ACM SIGGRAPH, New York, 1991, Vol. 25., No. 4.
19. *Visualization '90, First IEEE Conference on Visualization*, IEEE Computer Society Press, Los Alamitos, CA, 1990.

BIBLIOGRAPHY

Many books about computer graphics have been published in the last 10 years, so ample coverage of the scope and technical aspects of this field exists. Two books of particular note are by Friedhoff

(3) and Foley (4). The former is directed toward the layman. It discusses the entire range of computer graphics applications and is beautifully illustrated with computer-generated images. The latter book covers graphics terminology, algorithms, hardware, and applications. It is an excellent source of technical information and it contains many images demonstrating technical effects.

Computer graphics technology changes rapidly, so many of the techniques in common use have not yet been documented in textbooks. Among the journals that publish articles on graphics hardware and software developments are *Transactions on Graphics*, *Computer Graphics*, *Communications of the ACM*, and *IEEE Computer Graphics and Applications*.

The major annual graphics conference in the United States is the ACM SIGGRAPH Conference (Association for Computing Machinery Special Interest Group on Computer Graphics) Conference. It provides an excellent opportunity to see the graphics hardware and software commercially available, to learn about the current research on graphics algorithms and architectures, and to view the images and films produced by leading computer graphics organizations and individuals. The proceedings of each SIGGRAPH meeting, such as Ref. 18, contain the technical papers presented. These can be quite useful, as many state-of-the-art techniques are first presented at SIGGRAPH meetings.

A number of conferences that focus specifically on scientific visualization also exist. Some of these, such as the IEEE Conference on Visualization, have become annual conferences with published proceedings, e.g., Ref. 19. Conferences concentrating on visualization techniques for specific disciplines, such as aerodynamics or chemistry, are also becoming more prevalent.

Computer Graphics Systems: Performance and Peripheral Devices

Durbeck, R., and S. Sherr (eds.), *Output Hardcopy Devices*, Academic Press, New York, 1988.

Sherr, S. (ed.), *Input Devices*, Academic Press, New York, 1988.

Zyda, Michael, Mark Fichten and David H. Jennings, "Meaningful Graphics Workstation Performance Measurements," *Computers & Graphics*, *14*(3), 519–526 (1990).

Input Data Structure and Formats

Bancroft, G. V., F. J. Merritt, T. C. Plessel, P. G. Kelaita, R. K. McCabe, and A. Globus, "FAST: A Multi-Processed Environment for Visualization of Computational Fluid Dynamics," *Proceedings of IEEE Visualization '90*, 1990, pp. 14–27.

Brittain, D. L., J. Aller, M. Wilson, and S.-L. C. Wang, "Design of an End-User Data Visualization System," *Proceedings of IEEE Visualization '90*, 1990, pp. 323–328.

Brown, W., and S. Reynolds, *Computer Graphics File Formats*, Jones and Bartlett Publishers, Boston, 1992.

Butler, D. M., and C. Hansen (ed.), "Scientific Visualization Environments: A Report on a Workshop at Visualization '91," *Computer Graphics*, *26*(3), 213–216 (1992).

Campbell, W., N. Short, and L. Treinish, "Adding Intelligence to Scientific Data Management," *Computers Phys.*, *3*(3) (1989) pp. 26–32.

Dyer, D. S., "A Dataflow Toolkit for Visualization," *IEEE Computer Graphics Appl.*, CGA-*10*(4), 60–69 (1990).

French, J. C., A. K. Jones, and J. L. Pfaltz, "A Summary of the NSF Scientific Database Workshop," *Quart. Bull. IEEE Computer Soc. Techn. Committee Data Eng.*, *13*(3) (1990).

Lucas, B., G. D. Abram, N. S. Collins, D. A. Epstein, D. L. Gresh, and K. P. McAuliffe, "An Architecture for a Scientific Visualization System," *Proceedings of IEEE Visualization '92*, 1992, pp. 107–113.

Mackey, R., "NPSNET: Hierarchical Data Structures for Real-Time Three-Dimensional Visual Simulation," M.S. thesis, Naval Postgraduate School, Monterey, CA, 1991.

National Center for Supercomputing Applications, "Hierarchical Data Format (HDF) Version 3.0 Calling Interfaces and Utilities," University of Illinois at Urbana-Champaign (November 1990).

Rew, R. K., and G. P. Davis, "NetCDF: An Interface for Scientific Data Access," *IEEE Computer Graphics Appl.*, *CGA-10*(4), 76–82 (1990).

Volume Visualization

Bajura, M., H. Fuchs, and R. Ohbuchi, "Merging Virtual Objects with the Real World—Seeing Ultrasound Imagery within the Patient," *Computer Graphics*, *26*(2), 203–210 (1992).

Collins, B. M., "Data Visualization," in *Directions in Geometric Computing*, Information Geometers Ltd., Winchester, U.K., 1992.

Kaufman, A., "Introduction to Volume Visualization," *Volume Visualization*, IEEE Computer Society Press, Los Alamitos, CA, 1991.

Levoy, M., "A Taxonomy of Volume Visualization Algorithms," *Volume Visualization Algorithms and Architectures*, ACM SIGGRAPH '90 Course Notes, Course Number 11, ACM SIGGRAPH, 1990, pp. 6–12.

Ma, K. L., and J. S. Painter, "Parallel Volume Visualization on Workstations," *Computers & Graphics*, *17*(1), 31–37 (1993).

Nelson, T. R., and D. H. Pretorius, "Three-dimensional Ultrasound of Fetal Surface Features," *Ultrasound Obstet. Gynecol.*, 166–174 (1992).

Ney, D. R., and E. K. Fishman, "Editing Tools for 3D Medical Imaging," *IEEE Computer Graphics Appl.*, *CGA-11*(6), 63–71 (1991).

Ning, P., and L. Hesselink, "Vector Quantization for Volume Rendering, in *"Boston Workshop on Volume Visualization, Conference Proceedings* (special issue of *Computer Graphics*), 1992.

Santek, A., and W. Hibbard, "Interactivity is the Key," *Chapel Hill Workshop on Volume Visualization, Conference Proceedings*, ACM Press, New York 1992.

Color and Human Perception

Blinn, J., "NTSC: Nice Technology, Super Color," *Computer Graphics Appl.*, *CGA-13*, 17–23 (1993).

Cleavland, W. S., and R. A. McGill, "A Color-Caused Optical Illusion on a Statistical Graph," *Am. Statist.*, *37*(2), 101–105 (1983).

Commission Internationale de L'Eclairage (CIE), "Recommendations on Uniform Color Spaces. Supplement 2 to CIE Publication 15," Paris (E-1.3.1), 1971.

Cowan, W. B., "An Inexpensive Scheme for Calibration of a Colour Monitor in Terms of CIE Standard Coordinates," *Computer Graphics* (Proc. SIGGRAPH), *17*(3), 315–321 (1983).

Hall, R., *Illumination and Color in Computer Generated Imagery*, Springer-Verlag, New York, 1989.

Hurvich, L. M., *Color Vision*, Sinauer Associates, Sunderland, MA, 1981.

Kingdom, F., and G. Moulden, "Digitized Images: What Type of Gray Scale Should One Use?" *Perception*, *15*(1), 17–25 (1986).

Levkowitz, H., and G. Herman, "Color Scales for Image Data," *IEEE Computer Graphics Appl.*, *CGA-12*, 72–80 (1992).

Mullen, K. Y., "The Contrast Sensitivity of Human Color Vision to Red–Green and Blue–Yellow Chromatic Gratings," *J. Physiol.*, *359*, 381–400 (1985).

Robertson, P. K., and J. F. O'Callaghan, "The Generation of Color Sequences for Univariate and Bivariate Mapping," *IEEE Computer Graphics Appl.*, *CGA-6*(2), 24–32 (1986).

Stone, M., W. Cowan, and J. Beatty, "Color Gamut Mapping and the Printing of Digital Color Images," *ACM Trans. Graphics*, *7*(4), 249–292 (1988).

Thorell, L. G., and W. J. Smith, *Using Computer Color Effectively*, Prentice-Hall, Englewood Cliffs, NJ, 1990.

Travis, D., *Effective Color Displays*, Academic Press, New York, 1991.

Ware, C., "Choosing a Colour Sequence for Univariate Maps." *Proc. IEEE Conf. on Systems, Man and Cybernetics*, IEEE Press New York, 1986, Vol. 1, pp. 41–45.

Wyszecki, G., and W. S. Stiles, *Color Science: Concepts and Methods, Quantitative Data and Formulae*, John Wiley & Sons, New York, 1982.

Virtual Reality and 3D Data Visualization

Gibbs, W., "Body English: Controlling Computers with Twitch and Glance," *Scientific American* Vol. 269, No. 2 (August 1993) pp. 112–114.

Fisher, S., E. M. Wenzel, C. Coler, and M. W. McGreevy, "Virtual Environment Interface Workstations," *Proceedings of the Human Factors Society 32nd Annual Meeting*, Anaheim, CA, 1988.

Haimes, R. and M. Giles, "VIUSAL3: Interactive Unsteady Unstructured 3D Visualization," American Institute of Aeronautics 29th Annual Aerospace Sciences Meeting, Reno, 1991, paper AIAA-91-0794.

Helmick, R., "Virtual Reality: A Design Simulation Technique that Overpowers Design Content," *J. Interior Design*, *1*, 19 (1993).

McDowall, I. E., M. Bolas, S. Pieper, S. S. Fisher, and J. Humphries, "Implementation and Integration of a Counterbalanced CRT-Based Stereoscopic Display for Interactive Viewpoint Control in Virtual Environment Application," in *Proc. SPIE Conf. on Stereoscopic Displays and Applications*, 1990.

Smith, M. H., W. R. Van Dalsem, F. C. Dougherty, P. G. Buning, "Analysis and Visualization of Complex Unsteady Three-Dimensional Flows," *American Institute of Aeronautics 27th Annual Aerospace Sciences Meeting*, Reno, 1989, paper AIAA-89-0139.

Zyda, Michael, Robert McGhee, Ron Ross, Doug Smith, and Dale Streyle, "Flight Simulators for Under $100,000," *IEEE Computer Graphics Appl.*, *8*(1), 19–27 (1988).

STEVEN E. FOLLIN

SEARCH METHODS

INTRODUCTION

Search methods are methods of accessing a file. There are four primary operations with a file: insertion, deletion, search (find), and update (change). These are implemented when records are added to, deleted from, reviewed (retrieved), or changed (in the file).

The search methods are organized around the primary field (key) or the secondary fields. The methods used in accessing the file on the primary field include sequential, unordered and ordered, random (or direct), indexed sequential, and B-trees. The methods of accessing the secondary fields include various forms of index and linked lists. Some of these (indices) are referred to as inverted files. The linked list is used to access the records through pointers. The indices pregroup on given fields.

ACCESS ON THE PRIMARY FIELD

Sequential files are accessed in record order. Random access or direct files are accessed in random order, by directing the read/write mechanism (program) to the desired record. Indexed sequential files are accessed in order by key value. B-trees are a variation on indexed sequential files that employ the characteristics of a binary tree with a fixed but larger number of children.

Sequential files are discussed first, followed by the other data organizations and the introduction of database techniques. A database is a set of related data files.

SEQUENTIAL FILES

Sequential files are accessed in order, from the first record to the last, or appended to the end of the file. Ordered sequential files require the use of an auxiliary mechanism, like a sort, to maintain the order. They may also use linked lists (pointers) to maintain the order logically but not physically, thus allowing insertion of data records at the end of the file without sacrificing the order and deletion throughout (with some garbage collection).

Sequential files are of two types, unordered and ordered. These are discussed with respect to the primary field or identifying key.

UNORDERED SEQUENTIAL FILES

Unordered sequential files are unordered with respect to the key. The key is the field that identifies the record (logically), an item in the file. This is shown in Figure 1 which is an

```
1.  B
2.  A
3.  C
4.  D
5.  R
6.  M
```

FIGURE 1

```
1.  B
2.  A*
3.  C
4.  D*
5.  R
6.  M
```

FIGURE 2

```
1.  B
2.  C
3.  R
4.  M
```

FIGURE 3

abstract representation of a sequential file. It indicates the keys (B, A, C, · · ·) in "random" order (the order of insertion). This is accessed sequentially in making insertions (to the end of the file; one may keep track of the end of the file), deletions (at any point in the file), searches (for a particular record), and updates, as well as sequentially accessing the file (to process all records, a high "activity" file application, such as the payroll or the processing of grade reports).

Unordered sequential files are accessed at the end to insert records. This requires one access of the file (to insert the record). This is because the records are kept unordered. Records are deleted by finding the record (on the order of $n/2$) and marking it or moving the records up. If the record is marked, an extra field is maintained to indicate if the record is valid or not. This is shown in Figure 2.

Records 2 and 4 are deleted. They can be undeleted by unmarking the record. The file can be reorganized at times to actually delete the records. This saves processing time at the expense of storage.

If records are moved, this requires processing as the deletions occur. This is shown in Figure 3 for the data of Figure 2.

The records for A and D have been deleted. This requires approximately $n/2$ accesses for the find (location of the record) and approximately $n/2$ moves for the update (of the file). This is shown in Figure 4.

Figure 4 indicates the best, worst and average cases for the Find condition and the moves. The best case (in searching) is 1 (find or delete B); the worst case is n (find M), and the average is approximately $n/2$. This is $(n+1)/2$. This is shown in Figure 5.

The total number of accesses is the sum of the integers from 1 to n. This assumes equiprobable access (in finds and deletions). This is derived from the fact that the first

	Best	Average	Worst
Find	1	$\sim n/2$	n
Move	0	$\sim n/2$	$n-1$

FIGURE 4

$$\text{Sum}(i), i = 1, \cdots, n = (n+1)/2$$
(a)

$$
\begin{array}{ccccccc}
1 & + & 2 & + & \cdots & + & n \\
n & + & (n-1) & + & \cdots & + & 1 \\
\end{array}
$$
$$(n+1) + (n+1) + \cdots + (n+1)$$
$$n \text{ terms of } (n+1)$$
$$n(n+1)$$
$$n(n+1)/2$$
(b)

Total accesses: $n(n+1)/2$
Average number of accesses: $n[(n+1)/2](1/n)$
$$= (n+1)/2$$
(c)

FIGURE 5

1	B	.20
2	A	.05
3	C	.30
4	D	.20
5	R	.25

FIGURE 6

item is accessed in one access, the second in two accesses, and so on. The sum of the integers from 1 to n is $n(n+1)/2$. This can be derived by writing the integers 1 to n in left to right and right to left order and adding the two. This is shown in Figure 5b. The sums are uniformly $(n+1)$ and there are n terms. This is $n* (n+1)$. Dividing this by 2 gives the correct result.

The derivation was made by a number of mathematicians (1–4). The total number of accesses is $n(n+1)/2$. This, divided by n, gives the average number of accesses (assuming equiprobable access). This is shown in Figure 5c. The average number of accesses is $(n+1)/2$ (in the search, find condition).

Nonequiprobable Access

If the items are accessed with nonequiproble distribution, the calculation is the expected value. This is shown in Figure 6.

The items are accessed with probability (relative frequency) 0.2, 0.05, 0.3, 0.2, and 0.25. This results in the calculation $0.2(1) + 0.05(2) + 0.30(3) + 0.2(4) + 0.25(5)$ for the average number of accesses, where $p(0.2, \ldots)$ is the probability of ac-

		Probability (p) of access	Value (v) of access (number of accesses)	p*v
1	B	0.20	1	0.20
2	A	0.05	2	0.10
3	C	0.30	3	0.90
4	D	0.20	4	0.80
5	R	0.25	5	1.25
				3.25

FIGURE 7

		Probability (p)	Value (v)	p*v
1	C	0.30	1	0.30
2	R	0.25	2	0.50
3	B	0.20	3	0.60
4	D	0.20	4	0.80
5	A	0.05	5	0.25
				2.45

FIGURE 8

cess and the second value (1, 2, . . .) is the number of accesses for each item (in order). This is shown in Figure 7.

The calculation is the expected value

Sum (i), $i=1, . . .,n,$ $p(i)[v(i)]$,

the sum of the integers 1 to n weighted by the probability of access of each item. The values are the number of accesses to access a particular item. The probability is the relative frequency of access. This is summed over the whole distribution $(p(i)[v(i)])$, $i = 1$, . . . ,n. This results in the average number of accesses of 3.25. The total number of accesses depends on the total number of searches. This is 3.25 accesses/search. This can be improved by ordering the items in order of access distribution. This is shown in Figure 8.

The items are ordered by frequency of access (decreasing frequency of access). This results in an average (expected value, Sum(i), $i=1, . . . , n,$ $(p(i)[v(i)])$ of 2.45. This improvement over the first distribution is due to the optimized access distribution. The cost is in maintaining the distribution (if access probabilities vary).

If the items are ordered on number (relative frequency) of accesses, the average "length of search" (ALOS) is minimized. This is shown by considering that the number of accesses (value) is increasing in order and the probability decreasing (the smallest number of accesses is weighted most heavily). This ensures that the lowest frequency of access (relative frequency) is associated with the largest number (value or number of accesses). The intuitive proof is shown in Figure 9.

$p_1 + 2p_2 = 2p_1 + p_2$

if

$p_2 = p_1$ (subtracting p_1 and p_2 from each side).

$$
\begin{array}{ll}
1. & \text{assume } p_2 > p_1 \\
2. & p_1 + 2p_2 \quad > 2p_1 + p_2 \\
  & p_1 + 2p_2 \quad > 2p_1 + p_2 \\
  & p_2 > p_1
\end{array}
$$

FIGURE 9

$$
\begin{array}{l}
1. \text{ assume } p_j > p_i \quad (j > i, \text{ i.e., } v_j > v_i) \\
2. \quad v_j p_j + v_i p_i > v_i p_j + v_j p_i \\
\qquad (v_j - v_i) p_j > (v_j - v_i) p_i \\
\qquad\qquad p_j > p_i
\end{array}
$$

FIGURE 10

If

$$p_2 > p_1,$$

then

$$2p_2 + p_1 > 2p_1 + p_2$$
$$p_2 > p_1 \quad \text{(subtracting } p_1 \text{ and } p_2 \text{ from each side);}$$

that is, the larger value will be associated with the larger probability being given the larger access (5).

One can try it with individual numbers, say, 0.51 (p_2) and 0.49.

$$0.49 + 2(0.51) > 2(0.49) + 0.51,$$
$$2(0.51) > 2(.49) + 0.02,$$
$$0.51 > 0.49 + 0.01$$

The procedure generalizes to

$$p_2 = p_1 + e,$$
$$p_1 + 2p_2 > 2p_1 + p_2,$$
$$p_1 + 2(p_1 + e) > 2p_1 + p_1 + e,$$
$$p_1 + 2p_1 + 2e > 2p_1 + p_1 + e,$$
$$3p_1 + 2e > 3p_1 + e,$$
$$3p_1 + e > 3p_1,$$
$$2e > e,$$
$$e > (1/2)e.$$

The difference (in probability, e) is associated with a larger value (2) in the second access position. Hence, by exchanging the values, the difference will be minimized (in the average number of accesses per search). This is shown more formally in Figure 10.

Assume $p_2 > p_1$, where p_1 is the probability associated with value (access position) 1. Then $1p_1 + 2p_2 > 2p_1 + 1p_2$. This is shown by working the proof in Figure 9 backward. The smaller value can then be had by switching the values (places) of p_2 and p_1.

In the more generalized procedure, assume $p_j > p_i$, where p_j is associated with the higher value, v_j. This leads to the result that $v_j p_j + v_i p_i > v_j p_i + v_i p_j$. The smaller result can then be gained by exchanging the items (values) associated with p_j and p_i; that is, $v_j p_i + v_i p_j < v_j p_j + v_i p_i$.

Message	p (message)	Code	L(i)	P(i)	L(i)[P(i)]
A	0.50	0	1	0.50	0.50
B	0.25	10	2	0.25	0.50
C	0.125	110	3	0.125	0.375
D	0.125	111	3	0.125	0.375
					1.750

FIGURE 11

The actual proof is in the calculation:

$$p_j > p_i,$$
$$v_j p_j + v_i p_i > v_j p_i + v_i p_j,$$
$$v_j p_j - v_i p_j > v_j p_i - v_i p_i,$$
$$(v_j - v_i)p_j > (v_j - v_i)p_i,$$
$$p_j > p_i,$$

where $v_j > v_i$ ensures that $(v_j - v_i)$ $(j - i)$ is a positive number $(j > i)$.

The maintenance of the probability (of access) adds overhead to the maintainence of the file. Statistics must be maintained or the file can be ordered "on the fly" (as the items are accessed). If the statistics are static, the overhead is a one-time cost.

The computation of the expected value [average length of search (ALOS)] is the same as that of the average length of an optimum code (5). The number of accesses (length of the search for a given search) is analogous to the length (number of bits) of the code. The ALOS is analogous to the average length of the code (ALOC) or transmission.

The method was developed by Huffman (5–7). This is shown in Figure 11.

The messages are arranged in decreasing order of probability (frequency). The codes (variable length) are assigned with the shortest code (0, 1 bit) assigned to the most frequent message (A). The average length of the code (average number of bits sent per message) is calculated by the expected length (of the code). This is shown in the final column.

The expected length is the minimum (in this case). The method by which the code is developed is shown in Figure 12.

The messages are grouped by probability. This is shown in Figure 12a. These are then combined into subgroups, with the two least frequent messages forming the first subgroup (C, D, 0.125 + 0.125 = 0.25). This group ({C, D}) is then combined with B

```
A   0.50 _____ 1.0 {A, {B, {C,D}}}
B   0.25 _____|0.5 {B, {C,D}}
C   0.125 _____|0.25 {C,D}
D   0.125 ___|
              (a)

A   0.50 _____ 0 __1.0 {A, {B, {C,D}}}
B   0.25 _____ 0 _____|1  0.5 {B, {C,D}}
C   0.125 __0 ___|1  0.25 {C,D}
D   0.125 __1|
              (b)
```

FIGURE 12

(the next least frequent code). This group ({B,{C, D}}, probability (0.5) is then combined with A (1.0).

The groups are then assigned the digits (bits) 0 and 1; Figure 12b. The method is to place the 0 on the top group and the 1 on the bottom, although this can vary (6,7). The codes are read backward (from 1.0).

The average length of the code in the example is 1.75 bits per message (code value) sent. This is the optimal code in terms of information theory (the amount of information in the message, on average) (5–9). The Huffman code can be shown to be optimal in certain cases [the frequencies are powers (fractions) of 2] and to approach optimality in others (7,8).

The number of elements in the first subgroup can vary in multidigit (more than two code values, 0 and 1) codes (e.g., trivalued codes), depending on the number of messages (N) and the number of digits (D) in the code (5).

The optimum length of code and the optimum (average) length of search is obtained in a similar way, by the probabilities being arranged in decreasing order and the distribution of the lengths or the number of accesses being in increasing order. The codes (or access positions) are assigned (10,11).

The probabilities are arranged in decreasing order:

$$p(1) \geq p(2) \geq \cdots \geq p(N-1) \geq p(N)$$

or

$$p(N) \leq p(N-1) \leq \cdots \leq p(2) \leq p(1);$$

the lengths are arranged in increasing order:

$$L(1) \leq L(2) \leq \cdots \leq L(N-1) \leq L(N)$$

or

$$L(N) \geq L(N-1) \geq \cdots \geq L(2) \geq L(1).$$

The average length of the code is Sum(i), $i = 1, \cdots, n$, $(P(i) [L(i)])$, where $L(i)$ is the value (length) of the code, the number of digits (bits) sent for that particular message. The basic requirement is that the length of a given message code can never be less than the length of a more probable (message) code. If this requirement is not met, then a reduction in average message length can be obtained by interchanging the codes.

In an optimum code, $L(N) = L(N-1)$, though this need not hold in the development of the probabilities of access in the search method. This is indicated in the distribution as

$$L(1) \leq L(2) \leq \cdots \leq L(N-1) = L(N).$$

The two least probable codes (messages) have codes of equal lengths.

Insertion

Insertion of items into an unordered sequential file (or other data structure, e.g., an array) is relatively straightforward: insert at the end of the file (12,13).

Deletion is more difficult. The items must be moved ($\sim n/2$, $(n-1)/2$) or "marked." Unordered sequential files are easy to insert into but no easier to delete from than ordered sequential files. Ordered sequential files also experience difficulty with respect to insertion if they are physically adjacent in order. Files ordered by pointers (linked lists) are easier to insert into or delete from. This is due to the links, although it leads to the problem of garbage collection (on deletion) or the maintenance of used and available lists.

Deletions

The deleted items may be marked or moved. If they are moved, the least number of moves is zero (delete M in Fig. 1 or Fig. 2). The most is $(n-1)$ (delete B). The average is $(n-1)/2$. This is

$$\text{Sum}(i), \ i = 1, \ . \ . \ . \ , (n-1) = (n-1) \ (n/2)$$

for the total number of moves, and

$$(n-1) \ (n/2) \ (1/n) = (n-1)/2$$

for the average (assuming equiprobable deletions).

Update

Update (or change) is similar to Find or Deletion, with the exception that there is an additional write (to memory, in an assignment statement, or to the disk). If the write is to secondary storage, the write may be performed after the read (and change) if the medium allows, e.g., a disk. If the medium does not allow writing after reading (e.g., a tape), the entire file may have to be rewritten (depending on the access point).

Summary of Unordered Sequential Files

Unordered sequential files offer a search time of $n/2$ (approximately) in the Find condition and n in the "no-find" condition, relatively straightforward insertion and difficult (as ordered sequential) deletion if the file is kept physically contiguous. It allows more flexibility if the file is not kept contiguous, but there is little to be gained from this in unordered sequential files. They involve similar numbers in deletion ($\sim n/2$ moves) and update (treated as search).

ORDERED FILES

Ordered sequential files are ordered on the key. This is illustrated in Figure 13. The key is assumed to be the name (or social security number) or some other identifying field. This is A, B, C, . . . in the figure. The file is ordered (sorted or otherwise) on the key

```
1.  A
2.  B
3.  C
4.  D
5.  M
6.  R
```

FIGURE 13

```
                              1.  A
                              2.  B
                              3.  C
              Insert:  E      4.  D
                              5.  M
                              6.  R
```

FIGURE 14

```
              1.  A
              2.  B
              3.  C     Query:  E
              4.  D
              5.  M
              6.  R
```

FIGURE 15

value. The sort adds an overhead to the file (maintenance). The sort is of "order" (time required) n-squared (n^2) in the simpler ("crude") sorts, e.g., bubble or exchange sort, 1.65 $n^{5/4}$ or similar numbers in the sorts of more efficiency (Shell, quicksort, etc.) (14–18).

The sort contributes an overhead to the process of ordering (and maintaining) the file. This is illustrated in Figure 14 which depicts an insertion into a file organized by key contiguously (in arrays or on the disk). The insertion will require items to be moved (down). This will be 0 (insert Z) and n (insert before the first item, A here, but not necessarily the smallest possible item, i.e., key value), with an average of approximately $n/2$ if the insertions are equiprobable (by position) throughout the file [$(n-1)/2)$]. (This may not be the case with items like names, although it is more likely to be the case with numbers, such as the social security number, which exhibit less redundancy, i.e., more variability.)

Deletions are similar in analysis to unordered sequential files. The differences are in the search, whether this be sequential (due to the file or medium being sequential) or other, e.g., binary search (in a random access or direct access medium or array) (19,20).

The file may be searched sequentially or otherwise. If it is searched sequentially, the analysis is the same as for unordered sequential in the find case (the information in the "order" is not used). It is, however, different in the no find case. This is because the search can end early.

If the query is less than the item in the file (currently being accessed in the file), the search can terminate. This is illustrated in Figure 15.

When the query (E) is executed, the search can terminate after D (query < $A(i)$, $i=1, \ldots, n$, $i=5$, $A[5] = $ 'M'). This is 1 in the best case (before A), n in the worst case (query Z), and approximately $n/2$ in the average case [$(n+1)/2$] (the sum of the integers from 1 to n times $1/n$) (assuming equiprobable access).

The use of ordered sequential files increases the difficulty of insertion if the items are maintained contiguously, and it adds to the overhead of the sort (or other mechanism for maintaining the file). It does, however, improve performance in the search in the no find condition, even if a sequential, i.e., linear search is used (unordered sequential is uniformly n in the no find condition because the entire file must be searched). It can, however, be searched by other mechanisms, e.g., the binary search, if the file is organized as direct or random access. This is shown in Figure 16.

The file is divided into two parts, the "top" and the "bottom." This is done computationally in a computer program, but it can be done visually or physically by a human. The query is then formulated as, "Is it in the top?" (or "Is it in the bottom?"); the response, yes or no, is noted. This is done by comparing the query to the middle item in a program. This is shown in Figure 17.

Figure 17 is the algorithm for binary search from Cherry (15,21). It indicates the dividing of the list by the computation mid := (f + 1) div 2 [(first + last) div 2, integer division)]. This gives the "middle" element.

The list is divided. The query is then formulated as, "Is it in the top?"; the response, yes or no, is noted. If the response is yes (to the top), the top is searched next; if not, the bottom is searched. This is illustrated in Figure 18.

The query, F, is less than A[mid] (= A[4] = 'H'). The top is searched next. This is by setting l (last) to mid − 1. This is shown in Figure 19.

The query, F, is less than A[mid] (A[4], 'H'). Hence, the top is searched next. This is done by setting l to mid − 1. If the bottom were to be searched next, f = mid + 1. The calculation (of mid, $(f + l)/2$) is then reperformed. This is shown in Figure 20.

The new mid is A[2] (D)l. This is less than the query (F); hence, the bottom is searched next. This is done by setting f = mid + 1 = 3. At this point, $f=l=3$ and the new A[mid] is A[3] (F).

```
1. B
2. D
3. F   Top
4. H   Query: F
-----------------
5. K
6. M   Bottom
7. P
8. R
```

FIGURE 16

```
f := 1
l := n
repeat
   mid := (f + l) div 2;
   if query < A[mid] then
        l := mid - 1
   else
        f := mid + 1
until (A[mid] = query) or (f > l);
if A[mid] = query then
   writeln ('Found at', mid)
else
   write ('not found')
```

FIGURE 17

```
1. B
2. D
3. F    Top
4. H              Query: F
- - - -           A[mid] = A[4] = 'H'
5. K
6. M    Bottom
7. P
8. R
```

FIGURE 18

```
f=1      B
         D
         F    Top l=mid-1
mid=4    H
- - - -
         K
         M    Bottom
         P
l=n      R
```

FIGURE 19

```
f=1    B
       D    Top A[mid] = 2
- - - - -
l=3    F    Bottom
- - - - -
       H
       K
       M
       P
       R
```

FIGURE 20

In the no find condition, f will eventually exceed l. This is shown in Figure 21 with G replacing F in the query. The queries will proceed as before, eventually reaching the point where $f=l=3$, A[mid] = 3 (F). This will, however, not result in a match. G is greater than F, so the "bottom" will be searched next (f = mid+1 = 4). This results in $f=4$ is greater than $l=3$, which is the no find condition. This is shown in Figure 22.

The binary search is of order $\lg_2 n$. This indicates that an individual query of 1 million items will take about 20 accesses. The exact number depends on how the data (tree, contiguous array) is stored. A search of 32 items requires 5 ($\lg_2 32$) accesses.

Computed Addresses

The binary search can be bettered by computing the address of the "cell" (record, data item) wanted ("accessed"). This is shown in Figure 23 for a 2-dimensional array (2-D to 1-D transformation).

```
1. B
2. D
3. F   Top
4. H                Query: G
- - - - - -         A[mid] = A[4] = 'H'
5. K
6. M   Bottom
7. P
8. R
```

FIGURE 21

```
          B
          D
- - - - - - - -                    Query: G
f=1=3    F    Top=Bottom=mid        A[mid] = A[3] = 'F'
- - - - - - - -
          H                         f=mid+1=4
- - - - - - - -
          K
          M
          P
          R
```

FIGURE 22

```
Dim A(R,C)      A(5,3)        1-D array
  _ _ _ _ _ _ _ _
 |   |   |   |   |        1 |  _ _  |
  _ _ _ _ _ _ _ _         2 |  _ _  |
 |   |   |   |   |          : |  _ _  |
  _ _ _ _ _ _ _ _          . |  _ _  |
 |   |   |   |   |        8 |  _ _  |
  _ _ _ _ _ _ _ _          . |  _ _  |
 |   |   |   |   |          . |  _ _  |
  _ _ _ _ _ _ _ _
 |   |   |   |   |

Reference:       A (i,j)
                 A (3,2)
1-D cell     =   C* (i-1)+j    n |_ _ _|     n = R*C
             =   3* (3-1)+2
             =   3*2+2 = 8
```

FIGURE 23

The data is stored in the 1-D array. It is dimensioned as a 2-D ($R \times C$) array. This is A(R,C) = A(5,3) in the example, a total of RC=n "cells" (in the 1-D array). The transformation [2-D to 1-D] is the calculation C($i-1$)+j. This is the number of cells (per row) (in the dimension) times the reference (i, $i-1$) + the column reference (j). This is for 1-based arrays (in the dimension, 1-5 (R), 1-3 (C), 1-15 in the 1-D array). The calculation is C(i)+J for zero-based arrays [3(3)+2 = 9+2 = 11, the 12th cell, row 3 (the 4th physical row), column 2 (the 3rd physical column) for zero-based arrays] (The 1-D array is also zero-based, 0 to $n-1$, cell 11 is the 12th physical cell.).

The computation can be extended to 3-D. This is shown in Figure 24.

The dimension is extended to "pages" (P). These are the perpendicular (to the page) "pages." The calculation is extended to the "right" page (RC($k-1$), "skip over"

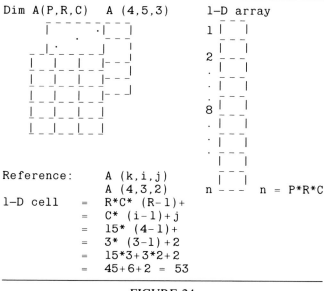

FIGURE 24

FIGURE 25

$k - 1$) (pages), and the Row and Column calculation added in. This results in cell 53 (cell 8 on page 4). The calculation is infinitely (nondefinitely) extendable (keep adding dimensions to the left).

The calculation results in a number of multiplications and additions (subtractions). It results, however, in 1 access per "query" (or assignment). This is better than a binary (or sequential, of order n) search.

The use of computed addresses is facilitated by regular data structures (rectangular arrays, triangular arrays). It is not always possible (variable-length data records). In that case, an index may be used.

A particularly fortuitous use of computed addresses occurs when the address matches the record number. This is illustrated in Figure 25.

The data record (information) is stored in the location matching the "id" (number). This is 1 for the first record, 2 for the second, · · ·, n for the last. This is not always possible but results in a direct "hash" (identity transformation) when it is.

Hash-Coding

Hash-coding was developed for situations in which direct transformation (by computation or identity) is not possible. This is illustrated in Figure 26.

```
ID #                    1-D array
321-40-6060
                            1 [ ¯ ]
         2                  2 [ ¯ ]
     29/60                  3 [ ¯ ]
        58                  : [ _ ]
        ___                   [ ¯ ]
         2                  : [ ¯ ]
     2+1 → 3                n [ _ ]
```

FIGURE 26

The identification number (or other, e.g., a name) is "hashed" (a computation is performed "on") into the storage address. This is by division/remainder (mod) in Figure 26.

The entire "id" or certain selected digits (60, the last two) are used in the computation. In this case, the computation is by 29 (29 is the divisor). This results in a set of remainders from 0 through 28. These are used as is or after adding 1 (1–29). This is location 3 in the example.

The divisor is selected with respect to the number of records ($1\frac{1}{2}$ n, $1\frac{1}{2}$ times the number of records). This is 29 in the example ($\sim 1\frac{1}{2}$ (20)). The divisor is usually prime; though this is not necessary; it results in a better distribution of remainders.

The remainders are the record addresses (as is or +1). This can result in "collisions." This is shown in Figure 27.

The "id" is 6031 (31). This results in a remainder of 2 (2+3→3). This results in a "collision" (physical location 3 is already occupied by . . . 60).

There are several methods of handling collisions. One is to place the data (record) in the next available location ("linear probing"). This is shown in Figure 28.

The record is placed in the next available location. This results in "primary clustering" (a higher probability of collisions in this area).

The use of a linear probe can be avoided by having an "overflow" area (separate data file or portion of the disk). In either case, however, the search of the area is linear (sequential). This results in a longer search (access) time for these ("collided") records (long chains, in some cases).

The average access time in hashed files is usually greater than 1. This is due to the collisions (chains).

```
321-40-6031    1-D array
                            1 |  _ _ _  |
          1                 2 |  _ _ _  |
      29/31                 3 |  ._._ 60|
         29                 . |    ˙˙   |
         ___                : |  _ _ _  |
          2                 n |  _ _ _  |
      2+1 → 3
```

FIGURE 27

```
321–40–6031    1–D array
                      - - - -
               1  |  - - - - |
         1     2  |  - - - - |
       29/31    3  |  . . .60|
         29    4  |  . . .31|
         ___    .  |  - - - - |
          2     :  |  - - - - |
                      - - - -
       2+1 → 3   n  |  - - - - |
```

FIGURE 28

```
321–40–6060    1–D array
                      - - - -
               1  |  - - e |
         2     2  |  - - e |
       29/60    .  |  - - - - |
         58    :  |  - - - - |
         ___    n  |  - - e |
          2        - - - -

       2+1 → 3
```

FIGURE 29

```
321–40–6060    1–D array
                      - - - -
               1  |  - - e |
         2     2  |  - - e |
       29/60    3  |  . . .60|
         58    .  |  - - - - |
         ___    :  |  - - - - |
          2     n  |  - - e |
       2+1 → 3     - - - -
```

FIGURE 30

The no find condition in hashed files requires an initialization of the file. This is shown in Figure 29.

The file is initialized to "empty." The data records are then hashed to this, as shown in Figure 30.

If the data record (location) is empty, the data is stored. If not, there is a collision. On retrieval, the chains are followed until e occurs. This is shown in Figure 31.

The query is for . . . 31 (321-40-6031). This results in a "hash" of 3 (R+1). This position is occupied by . . . 60 (321-40-6060). This is not yet a find. The "probe" (access) is continued (in the next location); this results in a match.

A no find is shown in Figure 32.

The query is for 321-40-6032 (R+1 = 4). This results in a "probe" of location 4 (. . . 31), a "no match." The probe is continued (in 5). This results in e; The diagnosis is no find.

The hashes may be to any location (3, 4, . . .) in the "clustered" area. The no find is denoted by e. Deletions are denoted by d (or some other symbol). This is shown in Figures 33 and 34.

```
Query: 321-40-6031   1-D array
                          1 | ¯ ¯ ¯e¯|
         1                2 |    _ e |
      29/31               3 |  ...60|
        29                4 |  ...31|
        ___               . |    _ e |
         2                . |        |
                          . |        |
      2+1 → 3             n | ¯ ¯ ¯e¯|
```

FIGURE 31

```
Query: 321-40-6032   1-D array
                          1 | ¯ ¯ ¯e¯|
         1                2 |    _ e |
      29/32               3 |  ...60|
        29                4 |  ...31|
        ___               . |    _ e |
         3                . |        |
                          . |        |
      3+1 -> 4            n | ¯ ¯ ¯e¯|
```

FIGURE 32

```
Insert: 321-40-6032   1-D array
                          1 | ¯ ¯ ¯e¯|
         1                2 |    _ e |
      29/32               3 |  ...60|
        29                4 |  ...31|
        ___               5 |  ...32|
         3                . |    _ e |
                          . |        |
      3+1 → 4             n | ¯ ¯ ¯e¯|
```

FIGURE 33

In Figure 33, . . . 32 (321-40-6032) has been inserted (in 5, the next available location). Record . . . 31 is then deleted. This is shown in Figure 34.

The query is for . . . 32. This results in a "hash" of 4 (R+1 = 4). This is a "not yet found" (as opposed to "no find"). The probe (access) is continued and a match found.

If *e* had been used for the deletion, an erroneous no find (for . . . 32) would have occurred. One must distinguish between the "empty" locations (deleted or empty) and the truly "empty" (never deleted) in a hashed-file organization. This is the only complication with the data structure (besides the collisions).

INDEXED SEQUENTIAL FILES

Indexed sequential files are files ordered on the key (value) and with an index (or set of indices). This is illustrated in Figure 35.

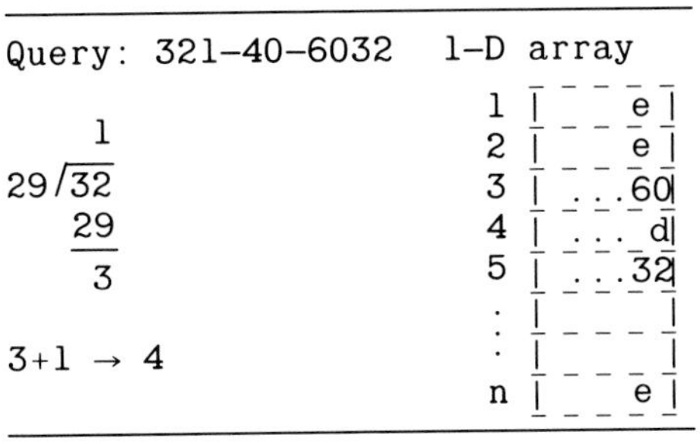

```
Query: 321-40-6032   1-D array
                            1 | _ _ e |
        1                   2 | _ _ e |
     ____                   3 | ...60|
   29/32                    4 | ... d|
     29                     5 | ...32|
     ___                    . | _ _ _ |
      3                     . |       |
                            . | _ _ _ |
   3+1 → 4                  n | _ _ e |
```

FIGURE 34

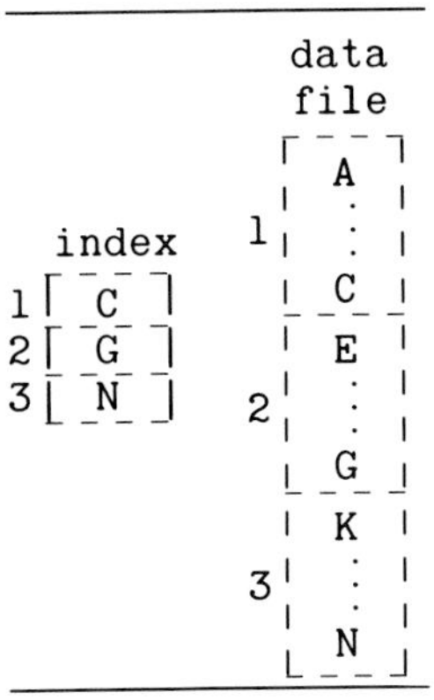

FIGURE 35

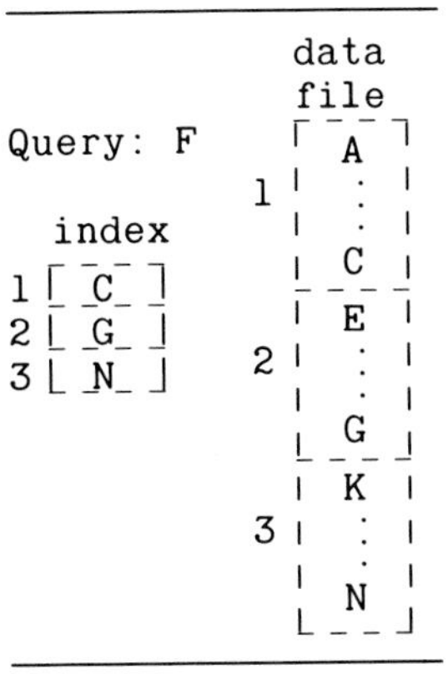

FIGURE 36

The file organization consists of two (or more) files. The index contains the last entry (key) of each block. There are several (*n*) blocks to the file. In this case, *n* is 3. A query is performed as shown in Figure 36.

The query is F. F is larger than C (searching the index). Keep going. F < G. If F is in the file, it is in Block 2 (between E and G). The block is searched sequentially or other (e.g., binary search if the medium is suitable).

n_1 = # of blocks
n_2 = block size (# of records in a block)
$n_1 + n_2$ = N (the access time in the search, worst case)
$n_1 n_2$ = the total number of records in the file

$$\frac{(n_1 + 1)}{2} + \frac{(n_2 + 1)}{2} = \frac{n_1 + n_2 + 2}{2} = [(n_1 + n_2)/2] + 1$$

= ALOS (average length of search)
BLOS = 2 (or the number of files, indices plus data file)

FIGURE 37

The file is searched through the index; the index and the file are kept "in order." This is to facilitate the search [to tell when the index point (of interest) has been reached (query < index[i], $i = 1, \ldots, n, n$ = the number of blocks or entries in the index)].

This results in only the block (of data) of interest being searched, which results in a faster access, at the expense of the overhead of keeping the files in order.

Indexed sequential files were developed as a compromise between random access files ("hashed" or otherwise) and ordered sequential files. They facilitate the search by breaking the ordered sequential file into pieces (blocks) by the index.

Hashed files do not (usually) preserve the order in the data; ordered sequential files do. The indexed sequential file is a combination of ordered files. It has a performance intermediate between ordered sequential and hashed organizations. This is shown in Figure 37.

The index is searched first. This results in $(n_1 + 1)/2$ accesses (on average). The selected block (only one) is searched next, $(n_2 + 1)/2$. This is $[(n_1 + n_2)/2] + 1$ accesses on average. The best case (BLOS) is 2 (or $i + 1$, the number of indices (i) plus 1). The worst is $n_1 + n_2$ [if sequential searching is used; a binary search or other may be used; in that case, the analysis is similar, $(\lg 2) n_1 + (\lg 2) n_2$].

Indexed sequential files incur an the overhead of keeping the file in order. This led to alternative data structures to keep the order dynamically.

B-TREES

B-trees were developed by Bayer and McCreight (22). An example is shown in Figure 38.

B-trees are ordered on the key. There are, however, several keys per node (block in Fig. 38). This is f, j; a, b, d; g, h; and k, m in Figure 38. The example is adapted from Kruse (18). It shows the keys, ordered left to right, as in a binary tree. A binary tree has ordered children. However, each node contains a single data record (and key). This is shown in Figure 39.

The binary tree is built with the algorithm "less goes left." It is searched with the same algorithm. The first data element becomes the root (15). The rest of the input is compared to the root. If it is less, it "goes left" (9 left of 15, left "child" of 15). If it is greater (18), it goes right. The comparisons are done recursively (compare 3 to 15, 3 to 9). The binary tree has only a left and a right child. This enables the algorithm "less goes left." The B-tree is a generalization of the binary tree (with more children).

The binary tree is "traversed" in LNR (left subtree, root, right subtree) (in-order) order. This is shown in Figure 40. The traversal is difficult to explain on paper. It is better illustrated "dynamically." However, it is good to remember that the traversal is "recur-

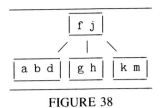

FIGURE 38

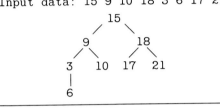

FIGURE 39

Input data: 15 9 10 18 3 6 17 21

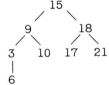

Traversal: 3, 6, 9, 10, 15, 17, 18, 21

FIGURE 40

Input data: 15 9 10 18 3 6 17 21

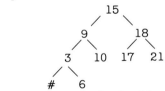

Traversal: 3, 6, 9, 10, 15, 17, 18, 21

FIGURE 41

sive." This indicates that a "node" (root of a subtree) is not visited until its left subtree (child) has been visited. This is 3 (left of 15, left of 9, left of 3, no child left of 3, visit 3) for the first element. This is illustrated in Figure 41 which shows the left child of 3 as the null pointer (child). This indicates that the "node" (root, 3) can be visited. The right subtree (6) is visited next. This is 3, 6 for the first two elements. This is the left subtree of 9 (visit 9). Then visit its right subtree (10). This is the "order" built into the tree (by the algorithm and the traversal, LNR).

The tree is kept in order "dynamically." This can be seen by inserting 2 (or 11). 2 is inserted to the left of 3. This is shown in Figure 42.

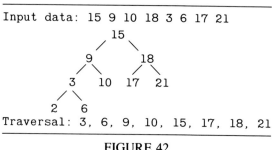

Input data: 15 9 10 18 3 6 17 21

Traversal: 3, 6, 9, 10, 15, 17, 18, 21

FIGURE 42

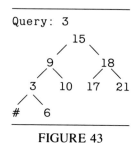

Query: 3

FIGURE 43

The new traversal is 2, 3, 6, 9, 10, 15, 17, 18, 21. The tree is kept in order "dynamically" (as items are inserted). This avoids the overhead of the sorts (at the expense of the pointers and the algorithm).

The tree is searched by the binary search as illustrated in Figure 43. The search is for 3 (record 3, "id" 3). This is found by the algorithm "less goes left" (in three accesses). A search for 2 (in Fig. 43) would result in a no find.

The binary tree implements the sort "dynamically," and the search is in the fashion of a binary search [($\lg_2$) n]. This is optimal for a tree with two children. The B-tree is an extension of the binary tree.

A B-tree of "order" m is a tree with m children. A B-tree has some maximum number of children. In the example of Figure 38, this is 5. This is illustrated in Figure 44. Figure 44a is the tree (node) befor j is inserted. The record (j, key) is inserted (Fig. 44b). The key is inserted in its proper place; then the middle element (key, f) is "elevated." The tree grows "up." This is in contrast to the binary tree, which grown downward. This enables the tree to remain balanced and fixed with respect to size (depth) within given (calculated) limits.

The B-tree grows "up." It does so by virtue of the maximum record (node) size. This is one less (key) than the number of children. This is m (5) for the number of children, $k = m - 1 = 4$, for the number of keys in Figure 38. There is also a minimum number of keys (and children). It is $m/2$ ("floor," i.e., truncated) or 2 for the tree of Figure 38 (or Fig. 44).

The B-tree gives a guaranteed search time for a given number of records (keys) and children (or keys) per tree (node). It also allows for dynamic insertion ("and ordering") of the keys (hence, the records).

The B-tree also grows downward (on deletions). This is shown in Figure 45. Before m is deleted, the tree is as in Figure 45. After m is deleted, the tree is as shown in Figure 46a. It is then coalesced, as in Figure 46b.

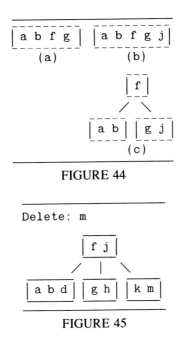

FIGURE 44

Delete: m

FIGURE 45

Delete: m

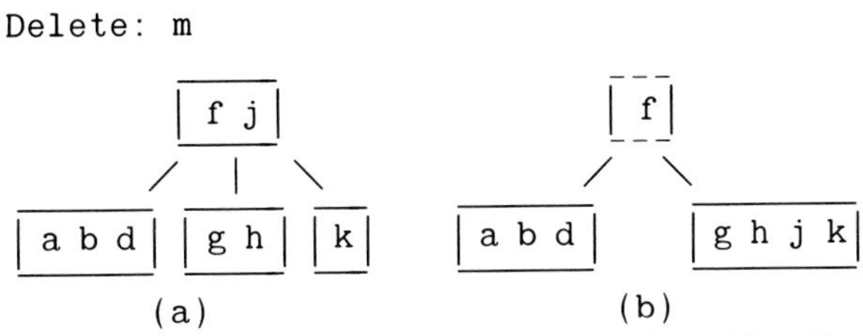

FIGURE 46

The B-tree shrinks on deletions. This is due to the coalescing of nodes. If f is deleted in Figure 44c, the tree will revert to a single node. This is shown in Figure 47.

The tree is maintained by "coalescing" the nodes when possible (on deletions, when the minimum number of keys is exceeded, downward).

There is a minimum number of keys (children) in a B-tree. This is 2 (keys), 3 (children) for the tree of Figure 38. When the minimum number of keys is exceeded, downward, nodes are coalesced, and, if possible, the tree "shrinks" (downward) (Fig. 47). If the f were deleted in Figure 46b, the g (immediate successor) would have been elevated.

The B-tree has a minimum and a maximum number of keys. This enables the tree to "explode" (grow a level at a time, at most) and "recede" (shrink upon deletion).

INVERTED FILES

Files organized on the secondary fields are so organized to permit access on these fields. An example is given in Figure 48.

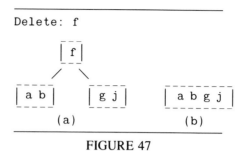

Delete: f

(a)   (b)

FIGURE 47

Characteristic

Age		Experience	Typing Ability
under 20	− 4	Poor − 4	Poor − 3
20–29	− 1	Good − 1	Good − 1,2
30–49	− 2,3	Exc − 2,3	Exc − 4

FIGURE 48

	Age	Experience	Typing ability	Dictation Ability
1	20	Good	Good	Poor
2	32	Exc	Good	Good
3	40	Exc	Poor	Good
4	18	Poor	Exc	Exc

FIGURE 49

The example is from Kent (23). The data are on job applicants for a clerical position. The data file is shown in Figure 49. Applicant 1 is age 20 and has good experience and typing ability, but is poor in dictation. Applicant 2 is 32, has excellent experience, good typing ability, and good dictation skills. These are the "secondary" fields (fields not the "id").

The file is organized for access on these fields by indexing on the fields ("characteristics") of interest. If dictation were included, the indices would appear as in Figure 50.

A typical query might be "I need someone with excellent typing and dictation skills" or "I need someone with excellent typing but fair dictation skills." The first query would result in applicant 4; the latter in applicant 4 as well. A query for good typing skills and good dictation would result in applicant 2 (or 2 and 4).

Inverted files organize (index) the data on the secondary fields. The intent is to query the data (database) on these fields.

MULTILINKED LISTS

Another method of pregrouping the data is by multilinked lists as shown in Figure 51. The example is from Bradley (24). The records are grouped on the State field (Texas, Alaska). In the full listing, there would be 50 linked lists.

Characteristic			
Age	Experience	Typing Ability	Dictation
Under 20 — 4	Poor — 4	Poor — 3	Poor — 1
20–29 — 1	Good — 1	Good — 1,2	Good — 2,3
30–49 — 2,3	Exc — 2,3	Exc — 4	Exc — 4

FIGURE 50

		Next Item on List
	1 T	3
Start of LL	2 A	4
T 1	3 T	5
A 2	4 A	—
	5 T	—

FIGURE 51

Student	Number	Major	Advisor	Year
Smith	1	Accounting	Zarter	Senior
Glover	2	Anthropology	Rattle	Freshman
Jones	3	Accounting	Smith	Junior
Black	4	Math	Smith	Junior

FIGURE 52

The start of the linked list is the first record in the file for that data value (T, A). There is one list for each data value in the field ("characteristic") (State). This is 2 in the example, 50 in the fuller example. The next item on the list is given in the data file (Next Item on the List) (1→3→5) (2→4) in the lists shown. The long dash indicates the "end of linked list" or simply "end of list."

The linked list groups the data in the data file. It does so by use of the "links" (pointers to the next data element).

DATABASE TECHNIQUES

The various file structures are combined in creating databases. This is shown in Figure 52.

The example is from Kroenke (25). The file is a file of students. The students (data) are identified by their name or student number. The file can be queried on this field (key) or on the secondary fields (Find Student with Major = Accounting). If the file is queried on the secondary fields, indices (inverted files or linked lists) can be created on these fields. This is shown in Figure 53, an index created on the "major" field. It indicates (groups) the records by major.

Files may also be related on the key. This is shown in Figure 54. The example is from Date (26). The data indicates the courses and the students in the school. They also indicate the registrations, which can be processed to obtain registration lists for a particular student or class lists for the classes. The files can be queried directly (Find Student

```
            ┌─────────────────────────┐
            │ Index                   │
            │ (Major)                 │
            │                         │
            │ Accounting     1        │
            │ Accounting     3        │
            │ Anthropology   2        │
            │ Math           4        │
            └─────────────────────────┘
```

FIGURE 53

Course			Student		
Course#	Title		Student#	Name	Year
M16	Trigonometry		001	Tallis	Freshman
M19	Calculus		002	Sharp	Senior
M23	Dynamics		003	Byrd	Junior
M24	Adv Dynamics				

Registrations

Stu#	Course#	Grade
001	M23	—
001	M19	—
002	M19	—

FIGURE 54

Name = ''Tallis'') or in conjunction (mapping from the registrations to the Student and Course files or vice versa).

A database is an integrated approach to file management. The basic file techniques are used in conjunction to make the data accessible.

SUMMARY

Files are accessed on the ''primary'' key (key field) or secondary fields. Some of the techniques for accessing files on the key are the use of sequential files, hashing, indices on the key, indexed sequential, and B-trees. Techniques for accessing the file on the secondary fields are indices (inverted files) and linked lists. The techniques are combined in database management systems. They are also used in operating systems, compiler design, and virtually every other field of computer science.

REFERENCES

1. Benjamin Bold and Alan Wayne, *Number Systems*, American Book Company, New York, 1972.
2. Carl H. Denbow and Victor Goedicke, *Foundations of Mathematics*, Harper & Brothers, New York, 1959.

3. May Risch Kinsolving, *Set Theory and The Number Systems*, International Textbook Company, Scranton, PA, 1967.
4. William J. Leveque, *Elementary Theory of Numbers*, Addison-Wesley, Reading, MA, 1962.
5. David A. Huffman, ''A Method for the Construction of Minimum-Redundancy Codes,'' IRE, *40*(9), 1098–1101 (1952).
6. John R. Pierce, *An Introduction to Information Theory: Symbols, Signals and Noise*, Dover, New York, 1980. (reprint of the 1961 edition, *Symbols, Signals and Noise*, Harper & Brothers).
7. Richard W. Hamming *Coding and Information Theory*, Prentice-Hall, Englewood Cliffs, NJ, 1980.
8. Claude E. Shannon and Warren Weaver, *The Mathematical Theory of Communication*, University of Illinois Press, Urbana, IL, 1972 (reprint of the 1949 edition).
9. Robert M. Fano, *Transmission of Information: A Statistical Theory of Communications*, MIT Press, New York, 1961.
10. C. C. Gotlieb and Leo R. Gotlieb, *Data Types and Structures*, Prentice-Hall, Englewood Cliffs, NJ, 1978.
11. Edward M. Reingold and Wilfred J. Hansen, *Data Structures*, Little, Brown and Company, Boston, 1983.
12. J. P. Tremblay and P. G. Sorenson, *An Introduction to Data Structures with Applications*, McGraw-Hill, New York, 1976.
13. William D. Haseman and Andrew B. Winston, *Introduction to Data Management*, Richard D. Irwin, Inc., Homewood, IL, 1977.
14. Donald E. Knuth, *The Art of Computer Programming, Vol. 3, Sorting and Searching*, Addison-Wesley, Reading, MA, 1973.
15. Robert Sedgewick, *Algorithms*, Addison-Wesley, Reading, MA, 1983.
16. Paul Helman, Robert Veroff, and Frank M. Carrano, *Intermediate Problem Solving and Data Structures: Walls and Mirrors*, Benjamin/Cummings, Redwood City, CA, 1991.
17. Niklaus Wirth, *Algorithms + Data Structures = Programs*, Prentice-Hall, Englewood Cliffs, NJ, 1976.
18. Robert L. Kruse, *Data Structures and Program Design*, Prentice-Hall, Englewood Cliffs, NJ, 1987.
19. T. G. Lewis and M. Z. Smith, *Applying Data Structures*, Houghton Miflin Company, Boston, 1976.
20. Jeffrey D. Smith, *Design and Analysis of Algorithms*, PWS-KENT Publishing Company, Boston, 1989.
21. George W. Cherry, *Pascal Programming Structures: An Introduction to Systematic Programming*, Reston Publishing Co., Reston, VA, 1980.
22. R. Bayer and E. McCreight, ''Organization and Maintenance of Large Ordered Indexes,'' *Acta Inform.*, *1*(3), 173–189 (1972).
23. Allen Kent, *Information Analysis and Retrieval*, John Wiley & Sons, New York, 1971.
24. James Bradley, *File and Data Base Techniques*, Holt, Rinehart and Winston, New York, 1982.
25. David Kroenke, *Database Processing*, Science Research Associates, Inc., Chicago, IL, 1977.
26. An Introduction to Database Systems, Third Edition, Addison-Wesley Publishing Company, Reading, MA, 1981.

ROGER R. FLYNN

SECURITY AND DISTRIBUTED SYSTEMS

INTRODUCTION

This article is an introduction to the subject of security in distributed systems. It is assumed that the reader is generally familiar with the concepts of computer and communications security, by which we mean protection against risks that can compromise data integrity, allow unauthorized disclosure of information, or lead to denial of service in systems. However, this article aims to be clear to the nonspecialist, and additional background information can be found in the Bibliography.

The term *distributed systems* has not yet acquired a completely firm meaning. In this article, we define it to be one in which several autonomous processors and data stores, supporting processes and/or databases interact in order to cooperate to achieve an overall goal. The processes coordinate their activities and exchange information by means of a communications network. See the Bibliography for additional information.

As an illustration, consider the distributed system for a hypothetical business shown in Figure 1. Here the financial department has its own network of clerical workstations with data storage and report printing facilities. This is linked to the production units, some of which may be on remote sites, that have specialist production control processing to perform. There are store systems to maintain inventories, sales departments that generate invoices, and so on. All these separate parts of the organization are in communication with the corporate center. Their information contributes to corporate planning, and their actions response to corporate policy. It is an illustration of a system which performs a vital part in the operation and management of a modern business. It, therefore, needs to be secured.

Security Risks of Distributed Systems

There are special factors of risk in distributed systems. Existing distributed systems offer significant opportunities for the introduction of insecure or malicious software. They also permit hacking and browsing. Even those distributed systems that are intended to support a low- or medium-risk area of business still have to be careful today not to leave themselves wholly unprotected. Vigilant management is required against attacks leading to denial of service. Even where these attacks do not compromise data integrity, they may be both inconvenient and expensive. The experience of people affected by the "Internet Worm" (1) illustrates this. A deliberately created program propagated itself across several networks, especially in the United States. Although it did not itself cause any damage, it reproduced itself continuously until it had absorbed all the resources of computers it had invaded and brought them to a halt. The cost of recovery was estimated at millions of dollars. Other risks of this kind are described in Ref. 2.

Similar effects can be caused accidentally. In particular, the incorrect handling of error reports in electronic mail systems can cause "mail storms" which swamp the net-

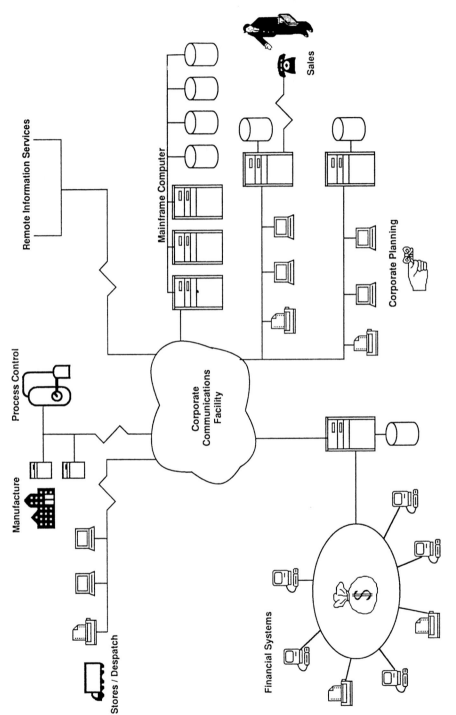

FIGURE 1   Distributed computer systems in a business.

work. This can be caused if a message containing errors is broadcast to multiple sites. If each receiver site reports the error back to the originator and separately triggers off a retry of the entire broadcast, the number of messages grows exponentially until the network halts.

Another risk is that unprotected systems may be used as an entry point into other inadequately protected but sensitive systems. The case of the German hackers who obtained access to many sensitive systems illustrated this risk (3). They used unprotected systems as bases from which to probe systematically for security weaknesses in other more-sensitive systems, with a surprisingly high degree of success. This resulted not only in the exposure of confidential information but also in extra costs for several sites who only discovered that they had been penetrated when their bills for communication were unexpectedly high.

There is a direct risk of exposure of confidential information in the uncontrolled, unprotected use of public networks between nodes of the system for information transfer. There are many opportunities for network staff to gain access to transmitted information but, in addition, any satellite or point-to point radio link may be intercepted with the appropriate equipment. If a secure network is required, encryption and access controls are essential.

Distribution not only introduces additional risks to computer systems but also adds complications to dealing with the risks. For example:

- Communication may introduce significant time lag into the system in respect of security-related information; this may make it difficult for the security management system to correlate information that, taken together, would indicate a security breach;
- Splitting the system into different geographical, political, technical, or administrative domains complicates the setting and management of a coherent security policy; it also adds to the difficulty of tracing security breaches that are initiated from a different domain.

Security Benefits of Distributed Systems

However, in addition to the downside of introducing risks, there are compensating factors in distributed systems that can be used to enhance system security.

Unauthorized access to corporate data can provide the intruder with valuable strategic information. The advantage of distribution in this case is that it allows sensitive data to be distributed throughout the system. Thus, only by knowing the way in which it is distributed and accessing it at all locations can an intruder obtain complete information.

The damage that can result when the processing capability of a system is disrupted can be very high, particularly when a high premium is placed on the ability to process information. Distribution can provide alternative locations from which to acquire processing resources. Accidental failures typically occur at one site at a time, and deliberate attempts to disrupt a service would require interference with a number of sites simultaneously.

There may be a variety of security requirements within a distributed system. One advantage of distribution is that it does not constrain all components of a system to accept the same security regime. If the environment is partitioned into separate security domains, each domain can reflect a different aspect of the organization's policy concerning security. Overall control is obtained either by negotiated security interaction policies between the managers of domains or by a hierarchical structuring of domains with one manager taking responsibility for coordinating the interactions of all.

SECURITY FRAMEWORK

The objectives of security within distributed systems can be defined at a number of different levels, from a high-level objective such as "to safeguard the organization's assets" to a low-level one such as "ensure that no dictionary words are used as passwords," with a hierarchy of objectives in between. Each level helps to achieve the objectives of a higher level. These objectives may be achieved by mechanisms at several different architectural levels within a distributed system. An example of this, mentioned (in the section Logical Access Control), is the protection of data in transmission. This can be achieved by link protection, by end-to-end protection, or at an intermediate level. The combination of security objectives and the architectural levels at which they may be supported together form a framework in which to describe security.

The International Standards Organisation (ISO) Open Systems Interconnection (OSI) Security Architecture (4) defines a set of security services based on generally agreed objectives and sets out the options for the architectural levels at which these may be provided. The objectives are described in more detail in the OSI Security Frameworks Overview (5). A summary of the OSI approach to security standards is given below.

Security Objectives

It is helpful to distinguish between the primary and secondary objectives of security. The primary objectives correspond to threats such as disclosure, corruption, loss, denial of service, impersonation, and repudiation. The secondary objectives lead to the specification of services to support the primary ones.

There are three primary security objectives which apply to both stored data and messages in transit:

- **Confidentiality**—maintaining confidentiality of information held within systems or communicated between them. This typically means the prevention of unauthorized access to stored data files and the prevention of eavesdropping on messages in transmission. However, in high-security applications, there may also be a requirement for protection against revealing information that may be inferred solely from the fact that data are being transmitted and not from its contents. This information can be derived from *traffic analysis*, analysis of the source, destination, and volume of communications. A classical case of traffic analysis is a military one in which preparation for troop movements could be revealed by the increased volume of communications between units.
- **Integrity**—maintaining the integrity of data held within systems or communicated between systems. This prevents loss or modification of the information due, for example, to unauthorized access, component failures, or communication errors. In data communications, it may also be important to prevent the repetition of a message. For example, a message in an Electronic Funds Transfer system authorizing the transfer of funds from one account to another must not be sent and acted on twice. Protection from this risk is known as prevention of *re-*

play. Integrity can be achieved in two different ways: either preventing the occurrence of failures at all or detecting the occurrence and recovering from it. Prevention may be achieved by a number of means: by physical protection, by access control against unauthorized actions, and by procedural measures to prevent mistakes. Detection and recovery require timely detection, combined with backup facilities that make it possible to start again from a situation of known integrity.

- **Availability**—maintaining the availability of information held within systems or communicated between systems, ensuring that the services which provide access to data are available and that data are not lost. Threats to availability may exist at a number of levels. A data file is unavailable to its user if the computer that provides the service is physically destroyed by fire, or if the file has been irretrievably deleted, or if the communication between user and computer has failed. As with integrity, two different modes of protection are available: prevention, and detection and recovery using backup facilities.

Two other primary security objectives apply specifically to communication between users and/or programs:

- **Authentication**—authenticating the identity of communicating partners and authenticating the origin and integrity of data that are communicated between them. It is important for several purposes. Authenticating the identity of the originator of a message gives confidence, in electronic mail systems, that messages are genuine. It also provides a basis for audit and accounting. It is a requirement for access control systems based on the identity of users of the system. Authentication of message contents enables the detection of integrity failures in messages.
- **Nonrepudiation**—the prevention of a user wrongly denying having sent or having received a message. The first of these is known as *proof of origin*, and the second as *proof of delivery*. Nonrepudiation is important in any situation in which the interests of the sending and receiving parties may be in conflict. For example, in a stock transfer system it would be in the financial interest of the sender to repudiate a selling order if the value of the stock subsequently rises, and in the interest of the receiver to repudiate it if it falls. It is a key issue for contractual systems based on EDI (Electronic Data Interchange), for example, purchase and supply systems.

The secondary security objectives identified by the Security Architecture are as follows:

- **Access Control**—providing access control to services or their components to ensure that users can only access services, and perform data accesses, for which they are authorized. Access control is one means that is used to achieve Confidentiality, Integrity, and Availability. It can be provided by physical and/or logical mechanisms. Unauthorized access to a personal computer may be prevented by a key lock disabling the keyboard. Access to a shared system may be controlled by a logical access control system using access rules based on the authenticated identity of users.
- **Audit Trail**—providing an audit trail of activities in the system to enable user accountability. An audit trail provides evidence of who did what, and when. The

important special case of audit of access control systems is discussed in the section Audit of access control systems.

- **Security Alarm**—the detection of occurrences indicating an actual or potential security failure should raise an alarm and cause the system to operate in a failsafe mode. Some security failures are not detected at the time and cannot be reported on, like the failure of the access control system to detect an unauthorized access because of its own weakness. Other activities may be indicative of possible security failures and need investigation; for example, a changed pattern of access by a user. The objective in this situation is to minimize, simultaneously, the risk of loss if there really is a security failure and the inconvenience to the user if there is a false alarm.

The security objectives outlined above are interdependent and should not be taken in isolation. Authentication is the basis for achieving many of the other objectives. Authenticated user identities are needed for identity-based Access Control, Nonrepudiation, and Audit Trail, but password-based Authentication requires both Access Control to protect the password file and encryption-based Confidentiality for further protection if the Access Control fails. Access Control, besides requiring and supporting Authentication, is a basis for Confidentiality, Integrity, and Availability. Audit Trails and Security Alarms both depend on and support the other objectives.

Architectural Levels of Security Services

The ISO Security Architecture identifies the possible communication protocol layers of the Open Systems Interconnection Basic Reference Model at which each security service could be provided. A security service, such as confidentiality, can be applied to communication at different layers in the model, but it is not sensible to apply the service at all of the layers. For instance, a user who is obtaining end-to-end confidentiality through encryption (see the section on Communication Security Mechanisms) at the Presentation Layer has no need of Data-link encryption as well (see Fig. 2). Further standards work will identify appropriate profiles of security services for particular applications.

SECURITY MECHANISMS

A number of different mechanisms are used to achieve security objectives. They include:

Physical and electronic security of components of the system
Authentication mechanisms

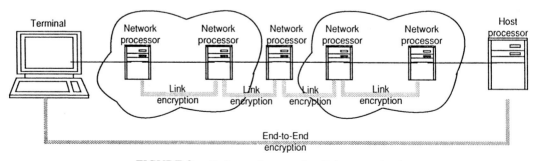

FIGURE 2   End-to-end versus data-link encryption.

Access control mechanisms

Communication security mechanisms

They are described briefly here. Interested readers are referred to the Bibliography for more detail.

Physical Security Mechanisms

Physical security mechanisms are used for protection of equipment and for access control outside the scope of logical access control or encryption. They are necessary for protection against risks such as fire, tempest, terrorist attacks, and accidental or malicious damage by users and technicians. Physical security requires a variety of mechanisms:

- **Preventive Security**—strong construction, locks on doors, fire resistance, and waterproofing
- **Detection and Deterrence**—movement detectors and door switches linked to alarms, security lighting, and closed circuit television;
- **Recovery**—the provision of a backup site, with alternative computing and communication arrangements.

A basic level of physical security is always necessary even in the presence of logical access control and encryption. In some situations, physical protection may be simpler and more secure than a logical solution; for example, by controlling physical access to terminals and personal computers and their data and by storing sensitive data on demountable media.

Figure 3 illustrates a situation in which encryption needs to be supplemented by physical line protection if complete end-to-end protection is to be achieved. It is necessary because the encryption unit is not an integral part of a secure terminal.

Electronic Security Mechanisms

Electronic security mechanisms may be needed for protection against interference from static electricity and RF (radio frequency) interference, both of which can cause computer and communication equipment to malfunction. They are also required for radiation security to avoid the passive eavesdropping of electromagnetic radiation from visual display units, printers, and processors. The modulated signals can be detected by nearby radio receivers and analyzed to reveal the data being displayed, printed, or processed.

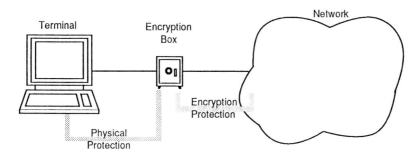

FIGURE 3   Encryption vs. physical protection.

Preventive devices are commercially available, and there are also military standards of protection (so-called "Tempest" proofing).

Authentication

Personal Authentication

The aim of personal authentication in computer systems is to verify the claimed identity of a human user. There are a number of different mechanisms for it, all based on one or more of the following principles:

- A personal characteristic of the user, (fingerprint, hand geometry, signature, etc.) that is unique to the individual
- A possession of the user, such as a magnetically or electronically coded card, that is unique to that person;
- Information known only to the user, for example, a secret password or encryption key.

Secret personal passwords are the simplest and cheapest method to implement, and they provide an adequate level of protection for medium- and low-security applications. They need a number of supportive measures if they are not to be undermined. The measures include regular change by the user, one-way encrypted storage, minimum length and controlled format (such as no dictionary words), limited number of permitted attempts, and logging and investigation of all failures. They can be reinforced by restricting users to logging in at specific physically protected terminals; for example, Payroll clerks may only log on in that capacity using one of the terminals sited within the Payroll Office.

The use of passwords across open communication channels in distributed systems is a particular problem because the password can be discovered by eavesdropping on the channel and then used to impersonate the user. One solution to this is the use of one-time passwords generated by smart cards (see below).

Magnetically coded cards have some advantages over passwords—they cannot be copied so easily and are less easy to forget. However, they also suffer from the potential exposure of their contents in open communication channels.

Smart cards offer increased security because they can be programmed to provide variable information. There are several modes in which they can be used for personal authentication. Two of these are the following:

- One-time password generators which generate a different password each time they are used. One commercial product changes the password every minute. In all cases the computing service must synchronize with the password generator.
- Challenge–response devices. The host sends a challenge number and the smart card has to calculate the correct response, including input from the user.

Smart cards are becoming cheaper and easier to use and they promise to provide a satisfactory way of overcoming the problems of personal authentication in distributed systems. However, any authentication system must cope with the problem of protecting the secure information on which it is based. This is an aspect of security management (see the section Security Management).

Message Authentication

The aim of message authentication in computer and communication systems is to verify that the message comes from its claimed originator and that it has not been altered in

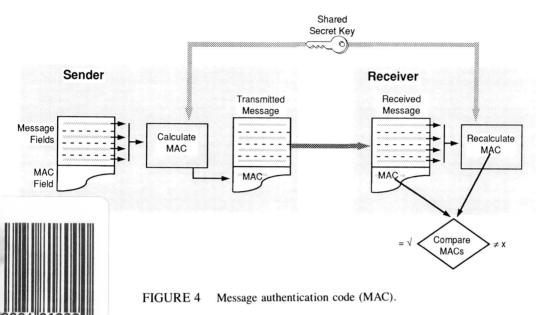

FIGURE 4   Message authentication code (MAC).

transmission. It is particularly needed for EFT (electronic funds transfer). The protection mechanism is generation of a Message Authentication Code (MAC), attached to the message, which can be recalculated by the receiver and will reveal any alteration in transit. See figure 4. One standard method is described in Ref 6. Message authentication mechanisms can also be used to achieve nonrepudiation of messages.

Logical Access Control

Logical access control has to be used when physical access control is impossible, as is the case in multiuser systems. A model for logical access control is provided by a Reference Monitor, which intercepts all access attempts and allows them only if the access is authorized. Otherwise the access is blocked, an error message is returned to the user, and appropriate logging and alarm actions are taken.

There are two main forms of logical access control: mandatory access control, based on fixed rules, and discretionary access control which permits users to share and control access (see the section on Computer Security Standards). The recommended discretionary access control approach is Identification/Authorization. The system ensures that the identities of users are authenticated when they log on, and the Reference Monitor makes a decision based on access rules that relate the user, the entity being accessed, and the operation the user is attempting to carry out.

There are two main implementations of access rules:

- An Access Control List (ACL) is attached to the target entities, defining the users who are authorized to access them and the operations that they can perform.
- Users obtain authenticated Capabilities which act as tickets authorizing them to access defined resources.

Many personal computing systems only provide access control based on file passwords. These provide a minimal, easy-to-use level of protection that is adequate for low-security systems.

Communication Security Mechanisms

There are two main mechanisms in ensuring communication security, in addition to physical protection of the lines and equipment: encryption and traffic padding.

Encryption is one of the most important techniques in computer and communications security. Cryptography means literally "secret writing." Encryption transforms (enciphers) plain text into ciphertext, which is impossible to read, and decryption transforms it back again into readable plain text (deciphers it). Cryptography has been practiced for thousands of years, but the advent of computer-based encipherment algorithms has changed it from a difficult and unreliable one to a simple and powerful one. Algorithms such as the Data Encryption Standard, described below, are easily available, simple to use, and provide a high degree of protection against threats to the confidentiality and integrity of communications.

Traffic padding will only be dealt with briefly here. Its purpose is to conceal the existence of messages on a communication line by inserting dummy messages on the line to ensure that there is a uniform level of traffic at all times. It is mainly of interest in a military level of security.

Encryption can be used for several purposes: the prevention of eavesdropping, the detection of message alteration, and, in conjunction with the use of unique message identities, the detection of message deletion and replay.

Link or End-to-End Encryption

Encryption may be used on individual links or on an end-to-end basis. These options were illustrated in Figure 2. Link encryption only covers the communication links, and the information is "in clear" at each communication processor. By contrast, end-to-end encryption is carried out directly between the initiating and target systems. An intermediate level is network encryption, where encryption spans an entire network, but not the gateways between networks. In all cases where encryption is carried out by a separate hardware unit, the link between the terminal and the unit is not covered by encryption, and physical protection is required in addition. See Figure 3.

Encryption Algorithms

There are two main types of encryption:

- Secret key encryption, which uses a single secret key shared between sender and receiver. See Figure 5.

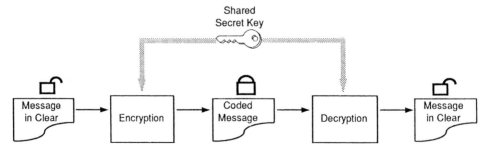

FIGURE 5   Secret key encryption.

- Public key encryption, which uses a related pair of keys. One key is publicly available and may be used to encrypt messages, whereas the other key is secret, known only to the receiver, and may be used to decrypt messages. See Figure 6.

Secret key encryption is available in a number of proprietary algorithms, and in the Data Encryption Standard (DES) which is an American, but not an international, standard. The DES is described in a number of text books (7). The DES algorithm is available in software and also in hardware as a semiconductor chip, providing higher performance. The chip is subject to export restrictions from the United States, and the hardware is, therefore, not suitable for multinational applications. Any secret key algorithm suffers from key management problems because of the need to transport secret encryption keys securely. There is a standard method of key management, described in Ref. 8, which covers key generation and distribution, protection of the key management facility, and protocols for the cryptographic service.

The most widely accepted method of public-key encryption is the Rivest, Shamir, Adleman (RSA) algorithm (9). Its performance is much poorer than the DES algorithm, but key management is easier because there is no need for secrecy of the key used by the sender. Some mixed-mode systems use RSA for key distribution and DES for message security, thus gaining many of the advantages of each method.

SECURITY POLICIES

Policies are the plans of an organization to meet its objectives. Within the context of security, a security policy defines the overall objectives of an organization with regard to security risks, and the plans for dealing with the risks in accordance with these objectives. Policies are usually hierarchical; the plans of a high-level policy are the objectives that a lower level policy must address.

All organizations should have a high-level security policy, defining the overall security goals of the organization and setting out a framework of plans to meet the goals. These high-level objectives vary substantially from organization to organization. Military organizations place a high value on secrecy, in contrast to academic institutions which value openness of information. Financial institutions are concerned above all with maintaining the integrity of data and messages that represent money. The default for simple social organizations is to have no security policy at all.

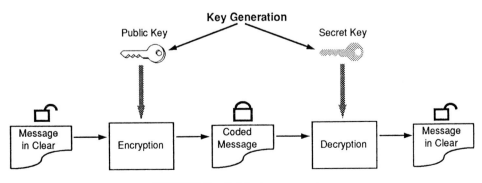

FIGURE 6   Public key encryption.

Security policies are not always precisely formulated or written down, but an effective computer security policy requires that the following questions are answered:

- What are the assets to be protected, and what is their value?
- What are the threats to these assets?
- Which threats should be eliminated and by what means?

The security policy for a distributed system should reflect the senior managers' expectations of the organization's security objectives. Often, just as an organization's security objectives may not be precisely formulated, those in a distributed processing environment are unstated and they must be extracted from other documents, or identified and agreed upon by persuasion and discussion with the staff of the organization in question.

A high-level security policy can make a general statement about the goals of the organization, but in order to be effective, it requires that a risk analysis to be carried out so as to understand the vulnerability of the organization and the consequences of security breaches. Risk management, discussed the section Risk assessment and management, is required because of the possible trade-offs between the anticipated cost of threats and the actual costs of security measures. The security measures taken to counter a threat should be commensurate with the threat itself. The results of a risk analysis may help to redefine or focus high-level policies, as well as define the lower-level policies for managing the system in a secure manner.

The choice of security services will have to reconcile a number of conflicting objectives that include the following:

- Security policy is often defined centrally but applied locally, or in each application, and at many intervening points in the communication between each user. There are, therefore, practical difficulties in ensuring that a security policy is met.
- Design of existing standard communication products and many operating systems has avoided or neglected considerations of security. Security requirements, therefore, have to be negotiated separately with system suppliers, requiring much greater effort in procurement than if they were defined as part of a standard or an intrinsic part of the operating system.

Security Interaction Policies

It is possible to create a distributed system in which all aspects of security are centrally managed to a common standard. Because a distributed system is more likely to evolve by the federation of a number of existing different (and heterogeneous) systems, they may have previously operated to a variety of security policies. It is always possible that these may be incompatible, either because the policies of the systems differ in the level of security they provide or tolerate, or because there is technical incompatibility, for example, because different encryption algorithms have been selected.

ISO have recognized this problem and have introduced the concept of a Security Interaction Policy as part of the Security Frameworks. This is a policy that is acceptable to all parties in an interaction. It has to be negotiated between them before they can communicate. The issues that have to be resolved between them are both the level of security and the technical compatibility of their security mechanisms. So far as the level of security is concerned, this is not limited to the security parameters relating to their communication. The security policy of one organization may insist that compatible standards of security are in force at the other organization's computing facilities before an interaction is permitted.

An interorganizational Security Interaction Policy, agreed upon and committed to by all parties, may be difficult to negotiate because of the need for more widespread compatibility than simply of communication security standards. For example, there may be incompatibilities in the levels of security of their operating systems. If a common security policy cannot be agreed upon it may be decided to decline to communicate, either because the risk is unacceptable or to avoid the imposition of unacceptable or uncongenial security practices. For example, most organizations that are running their installations to government military security standards do not allow electronic mail to run on any of their networked computers because of the known security exposures associated with it. They have to use a special free-standing electronic mail which is disconnected or buffered from the rest of their systems.

A Security Interaction Policy in a distributed system should lead to the generation of an agreed schedule of required security services and their supporting mechanisms.

The Practical Application of Information Technology Security Policies

To illustrate the practical application of information technology (IT) security policies in a distributed processing environment, some of the policies that could apply to a typical company are described. They are divided into the following areas:

- Security administration policies
- Security levels
- Communication security
- System access control
- Data access control
- Disaster planning
- System auditability
- Legal and regulatory policies relating to security

Note first of all the extent and limits of these policies. They include the areas needed to ensure the confidentiality, integrity, and availability of information, with two notable exceptions. First, they do not cover the backup and recovery procedures that are part of normal day-to-day IT operations. It is assumed that, in addition to a IT Security Policy, the organization has an IT Computer Operation Policy that covers day-to-day computer operating procedures, including recovery from incidents such as system failures and disk crashes, and also a IT Communication Management Policy covering procedures such as alternate routing in the event of line failures. The exclusion of these areas from security policies is to some extent arbitrary but is common to many organizations that prefer to regard them as aspects of system and communication operations. It is, of course, essential to ensure that these subjects are covered in one policy document or another.

Second, these security policies also exclude system change control. This, too, may be regarded as arbitrary, but the justification is, again, that it should be covered in other policies. Those aspects of change control relating to reconfiguration of the system by changing hardware components such as processing systems and networks should be covered by IT Computer Operations and Communication Management Policies. Software change control should be covered by policies for IT Computer Operations and Development.

In a typical commercial organization, security will make little or no direct contribution to each department's achievement of its immediate goals (until something goes wrong) while costing a substantial amount of effort and money. Therefore, if the security policies are to be effective, they need to be endorsed at the highest possible level of management, usually at Board level, and included in the targets that are set for each department. Only then will business managers regard them as an integral part of their goals.

Further, they must be communicated effectively. Many organizations have informal security policies that can be deduced from other policy documents and from management decisions that may be buried in internal memoranda and difficult to find. Effective security policies need to be separately and clearly documented, preferably as a Security Policy document or as a section in an IT Policy document. It is then possible for IT and user personnel to find out easily what the policies are; there is no possibility of effective implementation of a policy about which nobody knows.

The first recommendation for a company is, therefore, that the director responsible for IT obtains Board approval for the creation and enforcement of IT security policies, as set out in an IT Security Policy document.

Security Administration Policies

The foundation of the security policies of the organization will be an effective organizational structure. Although information processing is centralized, it is sufficient to put someone in charge of enforcement of IT security throughout the organization. However, as soon as it becomes distributed, it is necessary to have a two-tier organizational structure: a central Security Coordinator, and Security Administrators covering every department of the organization. To respect the autonomy of distributed systems, direct responsibility for security in each system should be held by its Security Administrator, but in order to ensure that the level of security is consistent throughout the organization, the Security Coordinator should have the goal of ensuring that each system is working to compatible standards and procedures. Typically, the Security Coordinator has two tasks: ensuring that each Security Administrator is aware of the standards and procedures and helping departmental business managers to ensure that they are followed.

The main concern of a company, apart from setting up its IT security organization, must be to ensure that the net is spread widely enough; every independent system that has eluded the control of communication or systems management is a potential security risk. The personal computers that have "gone independent" may or may not be operating to company standards of security. Each must be brought in under the umbrella of the appropriate Security Administrator.

Security Levels

Management policies should be made about groups of objects rather than individuals. Most organizations will need to apply this concept to security measures also. If just a few levels of security can be identified, and a package of security measures defined for each level, then detailed decisions about individual objects can be avoided.

Commercial organizations are likely to define two types of security level: for data and for users. Most aim to give the same level of protection to all their data, so that there will only be one security level defined for data. This is much easier to administer than multiple levels, and is in accordance with the usual requirement that sharing and mobility of data must be enabled but controlled. However, there may be a requirement to treat some data especially securely, either because its confidentiality is critical to the success of the business or, more commonly, because of the terms of a government contract.

On the other hand, it is quite common to wish to make distinctions between categories of users, especially when outsiders are given limited access to the system for special purposes or when insecure dial-in access is permitted. So there may be a policy to treat three categories of user differently: normal users, who have the least restricted access; the same users when they dial in, who are to be allowed access to specifically predefined data; and outsiders, with a similar restriction. Note that this concept of security levels has similarities to the military-type security levels of mandatory security but is must less formally defined.

Physical Security

Physical security is the basis of all other system security. There should be a policy that requires an appropriate level of physical protection for all physical assets within its control.

Communications Security

Communications security policies typically define the required levels of confidentiality, integrity, and availability. They are divided into two categories: the security of the corporate networks and the criteria for applications to provide a higher level of security on an end-to-end basis. Based on today's technology, the policy is likely to require assured integrity and a defined percentage of availability from the network but not to insist on assured network confidentiality. Within a few years, with increasing availability of cheap encryption products, the policy is likely to be upgraded to insist on network confidentiality also.

Assuming a relatively weak network security policy, an additional policy is required to ensure that applications requiring a higher level of security are provided with it by means of application-level security measures. Note that user authentication policies are dealt with in the section Authentication standards.

System Access Control

Perhaps the most important security measures to be taken in an organization with open distributed systems are to do with controlling the access of users to the system. There needs, therefore, to be a policy about system access control, with two main parts. The first part states the requirement for unique user identifiers and the need for users to respect them. The second defines the strength of authentication that must be applied to users who attempt to log on to the system. Typically there will be two levels of authentication:

- Normal users logging in from terminals and workstations within ABCs premises. The policy will state the standards for passwords, like the minimum length and required format, and the frequency of change.
- Users, whether company staff or external, who log in from outside ABCs premises. There will be a much higher level of authentication, probably using smart cards or other one-time password generators.

Data Access Control

The policy for data access control contains the following elements:

- Ownership of all elements of the organization's data should be defined, with the owner being responsible for decisions about the use of the data.
- All the data should be protected, and access should only be permitted when authorized by its owner.
- All systems should have access control systems that protect data to a defined standard. Typically the "Orange Book" C2 level of protection (see the section on Computer Security Standards) is suitable for a commercial organization.

Disaster Planning

Most organizations are now critically dependent on the working of many of their communications and computer systems. If any one of them fails, the business will have difficulty functioning at all. There needs, therefore, to be a disaster planning policy that requires each system to be considered for its criticality and defines how any critical system is to be recovered. It should define what is the maximum recovery time and how all data, communication, and processors are to be backed up to enable rapid recovery in the event of any conceivable disaster. For distributed systems, the problems of backup are eased by the existence of compatible systems at several sites.

System Auditability

There are several reasons for having a policy requiring the auditability of all systems, that is, the ability to trace any significant action which has taken place in the system. It gives a greater ability to control systems, it is usually a requirement of the auditors, and it enables the company to demonstrate that it is complying with legal requirements. It is normally impractical to log all actions all of the time, so there should be a policy dividing systems and applications into three categories: events, such as security administrators' actions and financial transactions, that should be logged all the time, events that can be logged whenever necessary, and events that are so trivial that they never need logging.

Legal and Regulatory Policies Relating to Security

A policy is needed which makes it clear to all staff that all legal and regulatory requirements are to be complied with; for example, data protection legislation.

Use of External Organizations

There are many applications in which external organizations are used for processing an organization's data; for example, EFT and EDI. The policy should require that an appropriate level of security should exist on the systems of any external organization that processes this organization's data.

Concluding Comment on the Security Policies

The security policies outlined above are a minimum set for a typical commercial organization. Most of them "state the obvious," but it is notable how often obvious security needs are ignored. A comprehensive set of policies, along the lines outlined above, at least ensures that the appropriate questions are asked and that no part of the organization can claim to be immune to the need for security.

SECURITY AND MANAGEMENT

Security Management

Security management is the activity of managing the functions and mechanisms that are used by the various services in a distributed system to implement security policies. The main security management functions include:

- The management of encryption keys (8) and other secret information such as passwords. This involves generation of keys as required and distribution of the keys to the relevant components in the system, storing keys and archiving keys. Keys should have a limited lifetime and so should be regenerated at regular intervals.
- Managing the registration of users and the information used to check their identity (public encryption key or password).
- Managing access control information relating to users and servers. This includes access control lists, capabilities, privileges, and multilevel security labels.
- Providing security audit trails. These record all exceptional events (attempts at unauthorized access, etc.) and selected normal events such as log-ons and file accesses. Their purposes is to enable investigation of security breaches and audit of a security administrator's actions.

Audit of Access Control Systems

Whatever the organization for security and wherever the perceived threat, one vital aspect of security management is the ability to maintain an audit trail of significant actions. In this way the system can not only carry out security management but also be seen to be carrying out security management. Indeed, maintaining a security audit trail where a system requires access through public communication services can help to meet legal requirements for demonstrating data protection.

It is virtually impossible to guarantee that unauthorized access or viewing of sensitive material will never occur. At best, it may only be possible to limit the potential size of an authorized access group and place its members under legal or contractual restraints over use or disclosure of the information. If the use of due legal process is seriously contemplated as an option, it is essential to maintain an effective audit trail of accesses. That in itself implies the need for a high level of security for the access control mechanism and its associated audit trail. There must be sustained at the expense of performance and in the event of multiple failures, if any real value is to be gained from them. However, securing the record is insufficient; a prompt and effective audit analysis mechanism must also be available.

Risk Assessment and Management

The term risk is frequently used in relation to information systems. Both the significance of risk and the relevance of risk management need to be clarified for distributed systems. Two quite different forms of risk need to be distinguished: *security* risk and *business* risk. Security risk is concerned with future events in which an occurrence leads only to loss. Examples are the risk of loss through fraud, breach of confidentiality, or equipment failure. This is the type of risk dealt with here. Business risk can result in either loss or gain and arises as a result of the normal management decisions of a business. It is not covered in this article.

Risk assessment and management is an activity that takes a rational view of the assets of an organization and the risks they face, and then makes decisions about the protection they are to be given. An essential element of the decisions is that the cost of protection should be commensurate with the expected costs arising from security losses. There are several computer-related security risk management methodologies available (11). They all have the following tasks in common:

- Identification and valuation of assets
- Construction of security risk scenarios
- Assessment of the probability of the scenarios and the losses that would ensue
- Identification and costing of possible security measures for each scenario
- Selection of a portfolio of security measures

Risk analysis is most effective when carried out during the specification and design phases of a distributed system development. In these phases, the risk implications of design decisions (identifying where the design shows its least robust characteristics) and the security requirements can be established and their consequences identified. However, this ideal policy is seldom practical for distributed systems because one of their characteristics is that they have often come into being by a process of evolution. For a system already in operation, risk analysis can help to identify where corrective action needs to be taken to remedy any vulnerabilities that had not previously been noted or had not been properly understood. The analysis, once made, provides a baseline from which subsequent analyses can be conducted as the distributed system continues to evolve over time.

SECURITY STANDARDS

There are three main categories of security standards which concern distributed systems. The first are standards related to the security of individual computers, which have been in existence for some time, and are quite mature. The second are standards for the protection of communication transmission and remote authentication. These too are quite mature. The third, still under development, are those that integrate computer and communication security standards to provide distributed systems security standards.

The standards do not generally prescribe physical or procedural mechanisms, nor do they prescribe risk management or risk assessment procedures or requirements for their use. These are all necessary elements to be considered and resolved for the resources that comprise the whole distributed system. Therefore, although security standards are an important support to distributed system security policies, they have to be viewed in the context of an overall security policy that uses other measures as well.

Computer Security Standards

The U.S. Department of Defense Trusted Computer System Evaluation Criteria (TCSEC—the Orange Book) (10), deals with access control to individual systems. It defines a number of possible levels of trust which may be placed in a system, ranging from the certified high security of the A1 level down to a low level of informally defined security at the C1 level. It is commonly used as a means of indicating the level of security required or supplied in computer systems.

Access control is divided by this standard into two categories: mandatory and discretionary access control. The former enforces policies that are built into the design of the system and cannot be altered except by installing a new version of the system. An example is the policy that in multilayer security systems data cannot be read by a user with a lower security classification than has been assigned to the data. Discretionary access control mechanisms are defined as those that allow users to specify and control sharing of resources with other users. For example, the C2 level discretionary access control policy is defined as requiring mechanisms that ensure that information and resources are protected from unauthorized access and that access permission is only assigned by authorized users.

The Trusted Network Interpretation of the Trusted Computer System Evaluation Criteria (12) (the Red Book) extends the criteria of the Red Book to networks. It is chiefly concerned with the security criteria to be met when accessing remote hosts.

The Red Book is now quite old, and it has always been more oriented to military-type security than to commercial security. A standards effort that is now under way is the Information Technology Security Evaluation Criteria (ITSEC) (13). This is a joint undertaking by the United Kingdom and Dutch, French, and German governments. Its aim is to take into account the needs of commercial users and to improve on the Red Book by separating concerns about security levels from the way in which the security is evaluated. In the United Kingdom, the Department of Trade and Industry and the Communications–Electronics Security Group have established the UK IT Security Evaluation and Certification Scheme (14) which evaluates and certifies products using the criteria of ITSEC. Similar efforts are under way in other countries.

Communication Security Standards and Encryption

Transmission Security

Transmission security standards are mainly concerned with encryption methods. One algorithm in particular has been the subject of standards efforts: the DES algorithm for secret key encryption which is an American, but not an international, standard. On the other hand, the RSA algorithm for public key encryption is the subject of U.S. patents. It has become a de facto standard for public key cryptography, but because of its patented status, it is not currently defined as a national or international standard. These two algorithms have been described briefly in the section Encryption algorithms.

For its strength, encryption depends on the security of the hardware that is used, and BSI 86/67937 (15) describes standards for the Physical Security of Cryptographic Equipment.

The basic standard for DES is NBS 46 (16) supplemented by ANSI, X3.92 (17). There are supplementary standards describing its Modes of Operation (18) and Guidelines for Installation and Use (19). The management of keys in banking applications is described in Ref. 8, but this standard is rather generally expressed and would apply to other applications also. A detailed discussion of DES standards is given in Ref. 7.

Authentication Standards

A number of standards have been developed for banking applications for peer-to-peer communication and message authentication. They, too, are quite general in format and could be used for other purposes. They include Ref. 20 for Message Authentication and Ref. 21 for personal authentication using a Personal Identification Number (PIN).

OSI Security Standards

Network security was not a primary concern when the Open Systems Interconnection (OSI) effort first got under way in the late 1970s. However, there is now a series of ISO standards under development that aim to add security to OSI. The standards define the security services that the partners in a communication could agree upon and the protocols to be used in setting up a secure interaction.

The security services which may be required for the communication facilities have been defined in the ISO 7498-2 Security Architecture (4). The protocols for their provision are still largely under development and are not yet available in OSI products.

The security services described in the Security Architecture are described in more detail in a series of Security Frameworks that are currently in production. They will eventually appear as International Standards 10181-1 to 10181-8. The planned framework parts are as follows:

1. Overview—a general introduction (5)
2. Authentication
3. Access Control
4. Nonrepudiation
5. Integrity
6. Data Confidentiality
7. Audit framework
8. Key management

Many other standardization efforts have security implications and, therefore, have security-related standards, e.g., in the areas of OSI Directory, OSI Systems Management, and Electronic Data Interchange (EDI). Several similar and related efforts are in progress, including profiles to describe the security characteristics of selected applications.

REFERENCES

1. Spafford, E. H., *"The Internet Worm Program: An Analysis,"* Report No. CSD-TR-823, Dept. of Computer Sciences, Purdue University, West Lafayette, IN (1988).
2. Denning, P. J. (ed.), *Computers Under Attack: Intruders, Worms and Viruses*, Addison-Wesley, Reading, MA, 1990.
3. Stoll, C., *The Cuckoo's Egg: Tracking a Spy Through a Maze of Compputer Espionage*, Doubleday, New York, 1989.
4. *Open Systems Interconnection—Basic Reference Model—Part 2: Security Architecture*, ISO 7498-2, ISO, 1988.
5. *Open Systems Interconnection—Security Frameworks—Part 1: Overview*, ISO 10181-1, ISO, 1991.
6. ANSI X9.9, *Financial Institution Message Authentication (Wholesale)*, American National Standards Institution, Washington, DC, 1986.
7. Davies, D. W., and W. L. Price, *Security for Computer Networks*, Wiley, New York, 1989.
8. ANSI X9.17, *Financial Institution Key Management (Wholesale)*, American National Standards Institution, Washington, DC, 1985.
9. Rivest, R., A. Shamir, and L. Adleman, *"*A Method for Obtaining Digital Signatures and, Public-Key Cryptosystems,*"* MIT Laboratory for Computer Science, Memo LCS/TM82, 1977.
10. Department of Defense (USA), *Department of Defense Trusted Computer System Evaluation Criteria* (Report No. DOD 5200.78 - STD), U.S. GPO, Washington, DC, 1985.

11. Gilbert, I. E., *Guide for Selecting Automated Risk Analysis Tools* (NIST Special Publication 500-174).

12. Department of Defense (USA), *Trusted Network Interpretation of the Trusted Computer System Evaluation Criteria* (Report No. NCSC-TG-005 version 1), Technical Guidelines Division, National Computer Security Center, U.S. GPO, Washington, DC, 1987.

13. CEC, *Information Technology Security Evaluation Criteria (ITSEC): Provisional Harmonised Criteria*; *Version, 1.2*, Office for Official Publications of the European Communities, Luxembourg, 1991.

14. CESG, *UK IT Security Evaluation and Certification Scheme. Description of the Scheme* (Report No. UKSP 01, Issue 1.0). Communications–Electronics Security Group, Cheltenham, England, 1991.

15. BSI 86/67937, *Physical Security of Cryptographic Equipment*, British Standards Institution, London, 1986.

16. NBS 46, *Data Encryption Standard*. National Bureau of Standards, U.S. Department of Commerce, Washington, DC, 1977.

17. ANSI X3.92, *Data Encryption Algorithm*, American National Standards Institution, Washington, DC, 1981.

18. NBS 81, *Data Encryption Standard Modes of Operation*, National Bureau of Standards, US Department of Commerce, Washington, DC, 1980.

19. NBS 74, *Guidelines for Installation and Use of the Data Encryption Standard*, National Bureau of Standards, U.S. Department of Commerce, Washington, DC, 1981.

20. ANSI X9.19, *Financial Institution Retail Message Authentication*, American National Standards Institution, Washington, DC, 1986.

21. ANSI X3.118, *Personal Identification Number—PIN Pad*, American National Standards Institution, Washington, DC, 1984.

BIBLIOGRAPHY

Information Security

Caelli, W., et al., *Information Security Handbook*, MacMillan, New York, 1991.
Denning, D. E., *Cryptography and Data Security*, Addison-Wesley, Reading, MA, 1982.

Distributed Systems

Sloman, M., and J. Kramer, *Distributed Systems and Computer Networks*, Prentice-Hall, Englewood Cliffs, NJ, 1987.
Tanenbaum, A. S., *Computer Networks*, 2nd ed., Prentice-Hall, Englewood Cliffs, NJ, 1988.

Distributed Systems Management

Langsford, A., and J. D. Moffett, *Distributed Systems Management*, Addison-Wesley, Reading, MA, 1992.

Computer Network Security

Davies, D. W., and W. L. Price, *Security for Computer Networks*, Wiley, New York, 1989.
Muftic, S., *Security Mechanisms for Computer Networks*, Wiley, New York, 1989.

JONATHAN D. MOFFETT

SEEK TIME EVALUATION

INTRODUCTION

The term *secondary storage* mainly implies disk devices, which may be *magnetic* or *optical*. Disks consist of several circular surfaces assembled with a common vertical rotating axis. On each surface, data are stored on concentric *tracks*, which are divided into a number of physical blocks called *sectors*. Sectors are the minimum quantity transferred from/to secondary memory to/from the primary memory. Reading and writing is performed by the *heads*, which are mounted on an *arm* so that they are aligned vertically with one another. The heads are kept very close to the disk surfaces, but they fly only microns from them, supported by a cushion of air. If the head crashes on the surface, then both are damaged, and data are lost. All the tracks that are under the heads at the same time constitute a *cylinder* (1).

Response time is the total time required to satisfy a user or system request. This quantity includes the *service time* as well as the *waiting time*, which is spent waiting in queues for a free drive or channel. Service time is characterized by three main cost factors. *Seek time* is the time required to move the arm from one cylinder to another. *Rotational* or *latency time* is the time required to position the heads on the correct sector of a given cylinder. Finally, *transfer time* is the actual time required to transfer the data from the disk to the main memory. The time consumed to select the appropriate head out of all the heads of the arm in order to service a request is considered to be negligible.

The two latter main costs of the service time depend on the rotation speed. For example, consider the IBM 3380 disk system which rotates at a speed of 3600 rpm. This means that the disk turns 60 revolutions per second, or, in other words, a full revolution takes 16.7 ms, whereas a half revolution takes 8.3 ms which is considered as the average latency time. The *data transfer rate* is performed at a speed of 3000 bytes/ms and a track of 48 kbytes is divided into 20 sectors; therefore, the transfer time is estimated to be 0.8 ms. Concluding, in general the following equation holds:

$$T_{ser} = T_{sk} + \frac{T_{rot}}{2} + \frac{T_{rot}}{m}, \tag{1}$$

where T_{ser} is the expected service time to satisfy a given request, T_{sk} is the expected seek time, T_{rot} is the disk rotation time, and m is the number of sectors per track. It is evident that these two costs could be decreased if the rotation speed was higher. However, a higher rotating speed (a) requires much more power, (b) generates more heat due to air friction which must be dissipated, and (c) results in higher transfer rate which would require a redesign of the channel to which the drive is attached. For these reasons, the industry has come to the conclusion to keep the rotating speed constant at this level (3600 rpm). Actually, this figure has not changed for the last 20 years (2).

Seek time is a much more heavy cost during disk operations. For example, the minimum seek time (i.e., the time to move from one cylinder to the next one) is approximately 3 ms, whereas the average seek time is approximately 16 ms, but it may reach much more greater values at the worst case. Although these figures are the actual parameters of the IBM 3380 disk device, they are typical for many magnetic disk drives (3). This is the reason why the minimization of the seek time is an issue well honored in studies concerning disk and file management.

It is noted that the previous presentation refers to *magnetic disks with movable heads*. There exist, also, *magnetic disks with fixed heads*, where there is a one-to-one correspondence between heads and cylinders. Therefore, in the latter case at the cost of the much more expensive hardware, no seeking is required during disk operations. Magnetic floppy disks have some basic differences when compared with the hard disks. In the latter devices, the service time includes another important cost factor, the *motor start time*, which is in the order of 1 s. In addition, the rotational speed is much lower, e.g., 300 rpm for a 5.25-in. disk, making the performance evaluation of floppy disk operations much different because the latency time is the dominant cost.

All types of optical disks (CD-ROM, WORM or erasable) have similar optical assemblies. The read/write mechanism is quite massive and for the sake of economical production of drives and disks, there is some degree of flexibility and imprecision in manufacturing. Thus, during rotation a certain track may take various positions in space. As a consequence, the objective lens may move to adjust its focus. This flexibility helps in accessing more than one track without moving the arm but by adjusting the lens position. The number of adjacent tracks that may be accessed this way is called *proximal window* or *span*. Typical values for the span lie in the range of 10–20 tracks to the right and left of the current head position. The time required to access a track not belonging to the current span takes considerably more time than for an access of a track in the current span. Therefore, seek time evaluation in optical disks is different than in the case of magnetic disks.

In the sequel, we will not examine disks with fixed heads, floppy disks or optical disks; however, the interested reader may find valuable material in Refs. 4–6, respectively. The rest of the present lemma is organized as follows. In the next section the scheduling policies are introduced. The third section presents in depth the conventional magnetic disk systems, whereas the fourth section presents the magnetic two-headed disk systems, which became commercially available a few years earlier. In the fifth section, the recent developments on parallel disk configurations are introduced, and results with regard to the seek time evaluation are mentioned. In all sections, technological, algorithmic, and analytical material are reported.

SCHEDULING POLICIES

The *disk controller* receives instructions from the CPU and orders the disk drive to execute them. In a multiprogrammed system, many concurrent disk access operations may be required. Therefore, disks are assigned a queue to store the requests waiting to be serviced. When a request has been satisfied, a new one from the queue must be selected for service. The request to be serviced next may be selected according to a number of algorithms, which are called *scheduling policies*. These policies have been studied extensively in the past. The basic knowledge about them occurred at the end of the 1960s (7,8), whereas the recent results have improved our understanding on the topic only marginally. For example, the textbooks of the seventies, such as Refs. 9 and 10, contain almost the same material as the textbooks of the nineties, such as Refs. 11 and 12.

The most simple scheduling policy is the *First-Come–First-Served* (FCFS) policy. This policy is fair as far as the order of the requests is concerned because it satisfies them according to the order of their arrival at the queue. For example, suppose that the disk consists of 100 cylinders and that initially the head lies on top of the 30th cylinder. Then eight requests referring to the cylinders numbered 70, 37, 20, 11, 60, 32, 17, and 93 arrive. It is evident that the head will move from the 30th cylinder to the 70th one, then to the 37th, and so on. Thus, in the worst case, the head may move back and forth from the inner to the outer cylinder to satisfy consecutive requests resulting in a high average service time.

The *Shortest-Seek-Time-First* (SSTF) policy decides to service next the request which refers to the cylinder closest to the one where the head currently lies. In other words, it selects to service the next request by minimizing the seek distance. If the figures of previous example are considered, then it may be easily verified that the order of cylinder visits according to the SSTF policy will be from the one numbered 30, to the 32, 37, 20, 17, 11, 60, 70, and 93 numbered cylinder. This algorithm results in a substantial improvement in terms of the seek distance traveled in comparison to the performance of the FCFS policy. The drawback of the SSTF policy is that it may cause the *starvation* of some requests which lie near the end points of the surface.

According to the *SCAN* or *elevator policy*, the heads move from the inner to the outer cylinder (and vice versa) and service every request that pends at each cylinder. Let us suppose that the head will move from the 30th cylinder to smaller disk addresses to reexamine the previous example. Thus, the next cylinders to be visit will be the ones numbered 20, 17, 11, 32, 37, 60, 70, and 93. SCAN is a very efficient policy resulting in a low average service time in comparison to the previous methods. As far as starvation is concerned, this drawback exists to some extent but not as much as in the case of the SSTF policy. The SCAN policy has drawn much research attention aimed at deriving variations with improved performance (13). A variation of the SCAN policy in the direction of behaving evenly with no discrimination to all the requests is the *N-step SCAN* policy. According to this scheme, the requests are divided in queues of length N. Every group of N requests is satisfied as if the SCAN policy was applied; therefore, for large (small) values of N, the performance tends to that of the SCAN (FCFS) policy.

A good summary of disk scheduling rules may be found in Ref. 14. Consideration has also been given in reducing the latency time (15). Other variations of SCAN, such as the *FSCAN*, the *Circular SCAN*, the *LOOK* policy, *Circular LOOK* policy, or the *Eschenbach* scheme [which tries to optimize both the seek and latency times (16)] are discussed in Ref. 13. More recently, a new scheduling policy has been proposed in Ref. 17, the *VSCAN* policy, or *V(R)* policy where $0 \leq R \leq 1$, which essentially is a continuum of disk scheduling algorithms between SSTF and SCAN. The latter ones are defined as special cases of VSCAN, i.e., $V(0) = $ SSTF and $V(1) = $ SCAN. Additional results on VSCAN are reported in Refs. 18–20. Another new scheme has been implemented in UNIX System V, the *System V Standard* (SVS) which groups successive requests in batches of size N (for example, $N = 16$ for UNIX System V Release 2 of AT&T, and $N = 8$ for Xelos R01 of Concurrent Computer Corporation). Thus, batches are served in an FCFS basis and requests of a single batch are satisfied via an SSTF policy (18).

CONVENTIONAL MAGNETIC DISK SYSTEMS

In this section, the performance of various types of magnetic disk systems is presented with respect the applied scheduling policy. The following material are extracted from Ref. 21, which collected and verified previous results on seek distances traveled by the disk heads. If it is accepted that every request is independent of the previous one and every cylinder is hit with equal probability, then a first estimate concerning the expected random seek distance, d, for a file residing in C cylinders is

$$E[d] = \frac{1}{c^2} \sum_{i=1}^{C} \sum_{j=1}^{C} |i - j| = \frac{C^2 - 1}{3C} \approx \frac{C}{3}. \tag{2}$$

Note, also, that this formula has been developed using different approaches in Refs. 5, 8, 22, and 23. (We will refer later to the proof which appears in Ref. 22).

However, in practice seeks are not independent of each other. It has been reported in Ref. 24 that almost two-thirds of all disk accesses do not require a seek; in other words, two consecutive requests want the same cylinder under probability equal to 2/3. This means that, in practice, seeks are not independent and that request distributions are non-uniform. This phenomenon is known as *disk locality referencing*, whereas *fragmentation* works in the opposite direction, e.g., it scatters file portions over many disk areas destroying the locality access (4). Often, the highly active records are stored in consecutive cylinders forming a "hit group." For example, suppose that the file is divided in three groups of C_1, C_2, C_3 cylinders accessed with probabilities p_1, p_2, p_3 respectively. The expected seek distance over the entire file approximately is

$$\frac{1}{3} (p_1^2 C_1 + p_2^2 C_2 + p_3^2 C_3) + p_1 p_2 (C_1 + C_2) + p_2 p_3 (C_2 + C_3)$$
$$+ p_1 p_3 (C_1 + C_3). \tag{3}$$

Note that this formula is consistent with the previous one for the limiting case where $C_2 = C$ and $p_2 = 1$. If, for example, the second group is the "hit" one, then $p_2 \geq C_2/C$, $p_1 = (1 - p_2)C_1/(C - C_2)$, and $p_3 = (1 - p_2)(C - C_1 - C_2)/(C - C_2)$. Thus, the previous formula may be rewritten as follows:

$$2 \frac{1 - p_2}{(C - C_2)^2} (p_2 C - C_2)C_1^2 - 2 \frac{1 - p_2}{C - C_2}(p_2 C - C_2)C_1$$
$$+ \frac{1}{3}[C + (p_2 C - C_2)(1 - 2p_2)]. \tag{4}$$

From this formula, after some algebra it is concluded that if the hit group of cylinders is placed at the center (end points) of the file, then the seek distance traveled is minimized (maximized).

Suppose, now, that the disk stores two files of C_1 and C_2 consecutive cylinders, each commencing at the addresses n_1 and n_2, respectively (evidently, $n_2 \geq n_1 + C_1$). Suppose, also, that the heads alternate from one file to the other. Then, the expected seek distance between the two files is the number of cylinders between their midpoints:

$$\frac{1}{C_1 C_2} \sum_{i=n_1}^{n_1 + C_1 + 1} \sum_{j=n_2}^{n_2 + C_2 - 1} |j - i| = \left(n_2 + \frac{C_2}{2}\right) - \left(n_1 + \frac{C_1}{2}\right). \tag{5}$$

Let us assume that a SCAN policy is applied to service a request of m random records satisfying a secondary-key-based query or a batch of m records satisfying m primary-key-based queries. Then it has been proved in Ref. 25 that the expected number of cylinders traveled is

$$\frac{(C - 1)m}{m + 1}, \tag{6}$$

$$\frac{C_m - 1}{m + 1} \tag{7}$$

if the m records reside in m nondistinct or distinct cylinders, respectively. These formulas generalize previous ones which appeared in Refs. 21 and 26. If the same scheduling policy is used to service a batch of m queries based on secondary key retrieval, each one accessing q_i nondistinct cylinders ($1 \leq i \leq m$), then the expected number of cylinders traveled (25) is

$$(C - 1)\left(m - 2 \sum_{i=2}^{m} \frac{1}{q_i + 1} - \frac{1}{q_m + 1}\right)$$

$$+ 2 \sum_{1=2}^{m} \sum_{j=0}^{C-2} \frac{\binom{C + q_{i-1} - j - 2}{q_{i-1} - 1} \binom{C + q_i - j - 1}{q_i + 1}}{\binom{C + q_{i-1} - 1}{q_{i-1}} \binom{C + q_i - 1}{q_i}}. \tag{8}$$

If each of the m queries accesses q_i distinct cylinders ($1 \leq i \leq m$), then the expected number of cylinders traveled (25) is

$$(C + 1)\left(m - 2 \sum_{i=2}^{m} \frac{1}{q_i + 1} - \frac{1}{q_m + 1}\right) - 1$$

$$+ 2 \sum_{1=2}^{m} \sum_{j=0}^{C-q_{i-1}} \frac{\binom{C + q_{i-1} - 1}{q_{i-1} - 1} \binom{C - j}{q_i + 1}}{\binom{C}{q_{i-1}} \binom{C}{q_i}}. \tag{9}$$

The latter two formulas replace a previous approximation which appeared in Ref. 27. These formulas represent only the expected distance traveled on the average, i.e., without trying to permute the requests in order to minimize this quantity. Reference 28 tackles this problem, deriving an algorithm which is based on the traveling salesperson problem and manipulates data of the requests (end-point cylinder addresses of each request) by means of an AVL tree.

In Ref. 29, disk searching is studied from the viewpoint of database queries which are identical or similar, and, thus, probability distributions functions based on the replacement models have to be assigned to them. It has been derived that under the latter assumption, the probability distribution functions, $P(k)$, of the number of cylinder hits are

$$P(k) = \binom{C}{k} \sum_{i=0}^{k-1} (-1)^i \left(\frac{k - i}{C}\right)^m \binom{k}{k - i}, \tag{10}$$

$$P(k) = \frac{\binom{C}{k}}{\binom{C + m - 1}{m}} \sum_{i=0}^{k-1} (-1)^i \binom{k - i + m - 1}{m} \binom{k}{k - i} \qquad (11)$$

which are based on the well-known Maxwell–Boltzmann and Bose–Einstein probability distributions functions, respectively. It is noted that $1 \leq k \leq C$, whereas m is the number of records satisfying the request. In addition, by assuming the Maxwell–Boltzmann probability distribution function, it has been derived that the expected number of cylinders traveled is

$$C - \frac{1}{C^m} \sum_{r=1}^{C} r^m \approx \frac{Cm}{m + 1} - \frac{1}{2}, \qquad (12)$$

whereas if the Bose–Einstein probability distribution function is adopted, then the expected number of cylinders traveled is given by relation (6).

A first approximate assumption, which was adopted in early works for the hardware of that time [such for the disk systems ICL 2802 (21), IBM 2314 (30), or IBM 3330 (31)], accepts that seek time is a linear function of the seek distance traveled, d:

$$T_{sk} = c_0 + c_1 d \qquad (13)$$

attributed by an initial constant factor representing the system inertia and a slope, c_0 and c_1, respectively. For example, for the Fujitsu 134 megabyte SMD drive, $c_0 = 5.94$ ms and $c_1 = 0.06$ ms (17), whereas for the IBM 3330 disk system, $c_0 = 10$ ms and $c_1 = 0.1$ ms; for the IBM 3380 disk system, $c_0 = 10$ ms and $c_1 = 0.05$ ms (23). Under this assumption, for each scheduling policy, the following conclusion holds: the time required to perform a seek from a specific cylinder to another is estimated (30) to be

$$\text{FCFS:} \quad T_{sk} = S_{min} + (S_{max} - S_{min}) \frac{(C + 1)(C - 1)}{3C^2}, \qquad (14)$$

$$\text{SSTF:} \quad T_{sk} = S_{min} + (S_{max} - S_{min}) \frac{(C - 1)\beta - 1}{2(C - 2)}, \qquad (15)$$

$$\text{where} \quad \beta = \frac{1}{L + 1} \left(1 + \frac{1}{L + 2}\left(\frac{C}{C - 1}\right)^{L+1}\right), \qquad (16)$$

$$\text{SCAN:} \ T_{sk} = S_{min} + \frac{S_{max} - S_{min}}{L' + 1}, \qquad (17)$$

$$\text{N-step:} \ T_{sk} = S_{min} + \frac{S_{max} - S_{min}}{L + 1}, \qquad (18)$$

where L is the mean queue length, L' is the mean number of requests serviced by SCAN in one sweep across the disk surface (given a mean queue length L), S_{min} is the seek time for the distance of one cylinder, and S_{max} is the seek time for the distance of the C - 1 disk cylinders.

At this point, it is emphasized that modern devices do not obey the above linear function. For example, recent high-performance disk systems with voice-coil actuators constantly accelerate and decelerate the access arms. This fact has been modeled by means of the following general relation:

$$T_{sk} = c_0 + c_1 \sqrt{d}. \qquad (19)$$

Various values have been plugged in place of the coefficients c_0 and c_1 in certain instances, e.g., $c_0 = 5$ and $c_1 = 0.5$ in Ref. 32, $c_1 = 0.6$ in Ref. 33, $c_0 = 8$ and $c_1 = 0.5$ in Ref. 34, $c_1 = 0.78$ in Ref. 35, $c_0 = 0.1$ and $c_1 = 0.9$ in Ref. 36, $c_0 = 7.8$ and $c_1 = 1.8$ to simulate the IBM 3350 machine or $c_0 = 2.1$ and $c_1 = 0.9$ to simulate the IBM 3380 machine (37). In Ref. 38 the following expression has been reported:

$$T_{sk} = c_0 + c_1 d^a, \tag{20}$$

where the range $0 \le a \le 1$ has been examined. Another approach uses the following expression:

$$T_{sk} = c_0 + c_1\sqrt{d} + c_2 d . \tag{21}$$

For example, in Ref. 22 the IBM 3380 model A machine was modeled by using the following values: $c_0 = 2.434$, $c_1 = 0.5555$, $c_2 = 0.01204$, and $d < C = 885$. In Ref. 39, the relevant values $c_0 = 2$, $c_1 = 0.4623$, and $c_2 = 0.0092$ were chosen to model the behavior of the IBM 0661 3.25-in. SCSI disk drive. Finally, a third approach uses a more complex expression to model these recent systems:

$$T_{sk} = c_0 + c_1\sqrt{d} \qquad \text{if } d < \text{cutoff}, \tag{22}$$

$$T_{sk} = c_2 + c_3 (d - \text{cutoff}) \quad \text{if } \ge \text{cutoff}. \tag{23}$$

For example, in Ref. 40, for the Tandem XL80 disk system the following figures have been used: $c_0 = 5$, $c_1 = 0.64$, $c_2 = 14$, $c_3 = 0.02$, and cutoff $= 0.2C$. The three previous expressions make mathematical analysis more complicated. Therefore, simulation results provide better insight into the topic. Nevertheless, it is noted that the hardware progress does not alter the qualitative conclusions of earlier works.

A new approach in algorithm evaluation in the notion of *amortization*, which considers the complexity of a sequence of operations. A recent study reconsiders the scheduling policies under the promising point of view (20). Their results appear in Table 1, where m is the number of requests considered. The length of the waiting queue is less than L after the $(N - L + 1)$th servicing. It is difficult to compare these disk scheduling

TABLE 1 Scheduling Policies

Method	Amortized complexity	Amortized complexity $(m \to \infty)$
FCFS	$\dfrac{m-1}{m}C + \dfrac{C}{m}$	C
SSTF	$(m + 1)\dfrac{C}{2m}$	$\dfrac{C}{2}$
SCAN	$\left(\dfrac{m-1}{m}\right)\dfrac{C}{L} + \dfrac{C}{m}$	$\dfrac{C}{L}$
N-step $(N < L)$	$\left(\dfrac{m-1}{m}\right)\dfrac{C}{N} + \dfrac{C}{m}$	$\dfrac{C}{N}$
N-step $(N \ge L)$	$\left(\dfrac{m-1}{m}\right)\dfrac{C}{L} + \dfrac{C}{m}$	$\dfrac{C}{L}$
Lower bound	$\dfrac{C}{L}$	$\dfrac{C}{L}$

policies for arbitrary m. However, the third column shows that SCAN and N-step SCAN with $N \geq L$ are optimal in the amortized sense. At the opposite site, FCFS is the worst among them. Additional results on the $V(R)$ scheduling policy may be found in Ref. 41.

As a first intuitive conclusion, it may be stated that all the policies are equivalent in the case of low workload, and, thus, the simple FCFS policy may be used. However, in the opposite extreme case that the workload is heavy, a selection between the SCAN or the C-SCAN policy has to be made, leaving the SSTF policy as a good choice for reasonable workloads. The above early approach does not take in consideration the system workload; in essence, queueing is an integral part of these algorithms. A thorough performance modeling and analysis has to be based on queueing theory (42) by using techniques such as Markov chains, random walks, queueing networks, etc. In this direction, the Refs. 4, 43, 44 adopt such an analytical approach and give mathematical tools for the quantitative evaluation of these issues. In addition, simulation should verify the analytical results. The literature is rich in such works which model the system by means of queues, mainly from the simulation point of view rather than the analytical one. The reader may found additional interesting analytical and simulation results in Refs. 45–52.

In the past, the effect of queueing has been overestimated. For example, in Ref. 7 it has been assumed that queues have a length of 10, whereas in Ref. 30, queues are considered to be in the range 100–140. More recent studies have reported that the disk utilization is quite low in general, e.g., in exceptionally overloaded systems queue lengths reach unity. Another interesting observation is that as much as 93% of successive requests are produced by the same job (53). This point is further evidence that the queues are most probably empty. Given this fact, it is reasonable to move the arm when the disk is idle, anticipating the future request so that the next seek cost paid will be smaller. In Ref. 22, this interesting topic has been investigated thoroughly. The profit of such an anticipatory disk arm movement will be shown by the next simple example. If the requests are assumed to (a) arrive independently of each other and uniformly distributed in the continuous interval $[0, 1]$ and (b) be processed by means of the FCFS policy, then given two successive requests at cylinders X and Y, the expected distance, d, between X and Y is

$$E[d] = C \int_0^1 \left(\int_0^x (x - y)dy + \int_x^1 (y - x)dy \right) dx$$

$$= C \int_0^1 \left(x^2 - x + \frac{1}{2} \right) dx = \frac{C}{3} . \tag{24}$$

This expected distance will be minimized if after every request the arm moves to the central cylinder. From the mathematical point of view, this result may be achieved by differentiating the second-degree polynomial of the above expression and solve the relevant equation. In this case the expected distance will be $E[d] = C/4$, which is 25% less than the previous result. Evidently, requests do not arrive uniformly distributed in the continuous interval $[0, 1]$. Suppose that there exist a "hot" cylinder numbered X (without loss of generality $X < 1/2$), which is visited with some probability p. The optimal location x to park the arm, if it is idle, is in the interval $[X, 1/2]$. Thus, the expected seek distance traveled from position x to the next requested position is

$$E[d] = p(x - X) + (1 - p)\left(x^2 - x + \frac{1}{2} \right). \tag{25}$$

Taking the derivative and solving the relevant equation results in a minimum for the position $x = (1 - 2p)/(2 - 2p)$. If the "hot" cylinders and the probabilities to be accessed are known in advance, then this kind of anticipatory arm movement improves the performance substantially. In high arrival rates, the effectiveness of this technique is reduced (22).

By placing data on the disk according to their access frequencies, the seek distances traveled and, consequently, the seek and service time are decreased (or even minimized) (54). The *organ-pipe arrangement* is a very popular technique from the theoretical and the practical points of view. According to this method, the most frequently accessed data are placed in the central disk cylinder, whereas the less frequently accessed data are ordered descendingly with respect to their access probabilities and placed alternatively to the left and to the right of the central cylinder. It has been proven in a classical mathematical work that this arrangement is optimal in terms of the distances traveled (55). For a given set of data, the number of these optimal arrangements is two, which are mirror images. The same conclusion has been reached via other proofs (56–58). In a few words, if p_i is the probability of visiting a specific cylinder, then the organ-pipe arrangement minimizes the expression

$$\sum_{i=1}^{C} \sum_{j=1}^{C} p_i \, p_j \, |i - j|. \tag{26}$$

Similar instances of this problems and related issues have been investigated broadly in Refs. 59–65; Refs. 58 and 66 develop these issues in depth. The topic has attracted the research efforts even until recently (19,67–70) due to its significance on the system's performance. Disk scheduling and data placement are complementary techniques in performance improvement: disk scheduling attempts to maximize the throughput during heavy workloads, whereas data placement techniques attempt to minimize the response time during the low workloads. This material is not only of a theoretical interest but has been implemented in many commercial products. For example, DEC's FILES-11 file system places directory information near the central cylinder.

TWO-HEADED DISK SYSTEMS

Three models of two-headed disk systems have been distinguished by whether there are two heads on the same arm or one on each of two arms. In the latter case, two further models arise, depending on whether the two arms are positioned by a single controller or by two independent controllers (44). Due to the additional physical constraints, a variety of problems has emerged and a limited number of publications exists in the literature, as the topic has not broadly been studied over these years.

Let us first consider the most flexible two-headed disk systems, i.e., systems having two arms, each one with one head on it; the two arms may move concurrently and independently of each other. This model is characterized by the facts that (a) the two arms may move past each other and (b) there is only one data path, therefore transfers take place one at a time. Suppose again that the cylinder address space is the range $[1, C]$ and that at some point in time the two heads lie on top of the cylinders numbered X and Y $(1 \leq X, Y \leq C)$. If the two heads are assumed to be randomly distributed and under a uniform probability distribution positioned on top of any cylinder and a request on the cylinder T arrives, then evidently it will be serviced by the head which is closer to T. It has been proved that the expected seek distance (71) is

$$E[d] = \frac{1}{C^2} \sum_{X=1}^{C} \sum_{Y=1}^{C} \sum_{T=1}^{C} \min(\ |\ T - X\ |\ ,\ |\ T - Y\ |\ ) \approx \frac{5C}{24}. \tag{27}$$

An alternative discrete-state modeling of this type of disk systems based on Markov chains has appeared in Ref. 72 by adopting similar assumptions. In Ref. 36, a more elaborated analytical work generalizes the previous material. A new feature of these systems is that while one head services a request, the other head may move, anticipating the cylinder address of the next request so that, in total, seeking is minimized. This sort of scheduling is termed *greedy method* or *nearer server rule* (73). Thus, if the requested cylinder is $T > 1/2$, then the idle head will jockey toward the $(T/3)$th cylinder, whereas if $T < 1/2$, then this head will jockey toward the $[1 - (1-T)/3]$th cylinder. It has been proved that if this scheduling policy is applied, then the expected seek distance covered (71) will be

$$\frac{1}{C^2} \Bigg| \sum_{X=1}^{\lfloor C/2 \rfloor} \Bigg[\sum_{T=1}^{X-1} (X - T) + \sum_{T=X+1}^{X+\lfloor (C-X)/3 \rfloor} (T - X)$$

$$+ \sum_{T=X+\lfloor (C-X)/3 \rfloor+1}^{X+\lfloor 2(C-X)/3 \rfloor\ -1} \left(\left\lfloor \frac{2(C - X)}{3} \right\rfloor + X - T \right)$$

$$+ \sum_{T=X+\lfloor 2(C-X)/3 \rfloor+1}^{C} \left(T - \left\lfloor \frac{2(C - X)}{3} \right\rfloor - X \right) \Bigg]$$

$$+ \sum_{X=\lfloor C/2 \rfloor+1}^{C} \Bigg[\sum_{T=1}^{\lfloor X/3 \rfloor-1} (\lfloor X/3 \rfloor - T) + \sum_{T=\lfloor X/3 \rfloor+1}^{\lfloor 2X/3 \rfloor} \left(T - \frac{X}{3} \right)$$

$$+ \sum_{T=\lfloor 2X/3 \rfloor+1}^{X-1} (X - T) + \sum_{T=X+1}^{C} (T - X) \Bigg] \Bigg| \approx \frac{5C}{36}. \tag{28}$$

If the workload is low, then it is possible to place both heads optimally so that future seeks are minimized. Suppose that the cylinder address space is the continuous interval $[0,1]$ and that the arms are placed at the x and y numbered cylinders (where without loss of generality $x \leq y$) while the request hits the t numbered cylinder. It has been proved that the expected seek distance (22) is

$$\int_0^{(x + y)/2} |\ x - t\ |\ dt + \int_{(x + y)/2}^1 |\ y - t\ |\ dt =$$

$$\frac{3x^2}{4} + \frac{3y^2}{4} - \frac{xy}{2} + \frac{1}{2} - y. \tag{29}$$

By taking the two partial derivatives with respect to x and y and solving the system of the two produced equations, it is derived that the optimal positions for x and y are $C/4$ and $3C/4$, respectively. In addition, it may be derived that under this condition, the expected seek distance is $C/8$. Evidently, if the workload is heavy, then no anticipatory arm movement may take place. However, if the above outcomes are compared to that of relation (2), then the advantage of this type of two-headed disk systems over the conventional disk systems is evident. If the successive requests are not independent and uniformly distributed, then this policy is also optimal, but the expression for the target cylinder is more complicated.

According to the second model, two-headed disk systems consist of arms which move independently but not concurrently. If each head is dedicated to service, a half-disk (the outer and inner cylinders, respectively), then the expected disk distance traveled to service a request is $C/6 = 0.1666$. This result is self-explained by reconsidering the relation. However, if the heads are not dedicated to a specific portion of the disk and may pass over the central cylinder, then it has been proved by some combination of analysis and numerical evaluation that the expected seek distance is $0.1598C$ (74). This result is optimal for the two-headed disk model considered.

If under low workloads, anticipatory movement is allowed, then the performance is improved. As in the previous model, the two arms should be placed on top of the cylinders numbered $C/4$ and $3C/4$. Each request should be serviced by the closer arm, which afterward should return to its starting position. Under these assumptions, the expected seek distance is again $C/8$ (22).

For the time being, only disk systems with two heads per surface separated by a fixed number of cylinders do exist commercially. Burroughs FD210, DEC RA81, and SA82, IBM 3380, and Sperry Univac 8450 and 8470 are a few examples of this type of machines. Although that these systems have less degrees of freedom in comparison to the previous two-headed disk models, they achieve better performance than systems with one head per surface. This is due to the fact that when the moving mechanism stops to service a request from a given cylinder, it may then service a request from the cylinder which lies under the other disk head without moving. We say that any two cylinders that may be visited in this way (i.e., one after the other at no extra seeking) form a *compound cylinder*.

A first problem, which has been investigated in the literature, concerns the optimum head separation distance with respect the minimization of the seek distances traveled. It has been found empirically with Monte Carlo simulations that the optimum head separation distance is $C/2$ under the SCAN policy (75). If the SSTF policy is used and the heads can move out of the recording area, then the optimum head separation reduces with the queue length, whereas if the heads must remain within the recording region then a head separation of $C/2$ is sufficiently close for all queue lengths (75). At this point, it is noted that for the sake of engineering purposes, the two heads must remain within the recording region and, in fact, the latter assumption has been accepted in the following references. It has been proved by using Markov chains that the optimum separation distance is $0.44657\,C$ if the FCFS scheduling policy is adopted (76). For this specific value, it has been proved that the expected seek distance to service a request is $0.16059C$ (76). In Ref. 38, the previous analysis has been extended by taking into account that the seek time is a nonlinear function of seek distance. More precisely, by adopting expression (20), it has been concluded that the head separation distance is very nearly independent of the value of parameter a of the relevant expression. If the SCAN scheduling policy is applied, then it has been proved by using combinatorial analysis that the optimum head separation distance equals $\lfloor C/2-1 \rfloor$ or $\lceil C/2-1 \rceil$ (77). In Ref. 78, it has been proved that for the specific environment the SCAN policy is optimal by using amortized analysis. As in the previous two cases, anticipatory movement of the arm so that the two heads lie on top of the cylinders numbered $C/4$ and $3C/4$ would minimize the expected future seek distance traveled to $C/8$.

Another problem that has been examined in this environment concerns the optimal data placement on two-headed disk systems. In Ref. 79, an extension of the organ-pipe arrangement is proposed, which is called the *camel arrangement* and may be viewed as two consecutive organ-pipe arrangements. In the same reference, it has been proved that if C is an even number, then the total number of these optimal camel arrangements is $2^{C/2+1}$. If it is assumed that each file access is executed after a directory access, then it is evident that the placement of the directory is a crucial factor with respect the disk performance. Ref. 80 examines this problem by means of a Markov chain analysis and under the assumption that requests fall independently in the continuous interval $[0, 1]$. The surprising conclusions are twofold. First, if in a two-headed disk system the directory is located at the $C/2$ ($C/4$) numbered cylinders, then the optimal head separation distance is $C/3$ ($C/2$). In addition, in both optimal cases the expected arm movement to service a request is $C/4$. Second, if in a conventional single-headed disk system two identical directories are maintained, then the optimal locations are at the $C/3$ and $2C/3$ numbered cylinders resulting in a expected seek distanced traveled equal to $5C/12$. If in the latter device three identical directories are maintained, then the optimal directory positions are at the $0.25986C$, $0.5C$, and $0.74014C$ numbered cylinders.

At this point, one should remember that for single-headed disk systems, the following relation gives the expected seek time cost to service m requests by using the SCAN scheduling policy:

$$T_{sk} = mS_{min} + \frac{d(S_{max} - S_{min})}{C - 1},$$

where the expected value of the distance traveled, d, may be calculated by using expressions (6), (7), and (12). However, the case of two headed-disk systems is different because the parameters m and d have to be recalculated. As far as the expected seek distance traveled is concerned, it has been proved (77) that under the optimum head separation, it is equal to

$$\frac{(C + 1)m}{m + 1} - \frac{C}{2} - 1 + \frac{1}{\binom{C}{m}} \sum_{i = 0}^{C/2 - 1} \left(C - \frac{1}{m} - 2i\right). \tag{30}$$

As far as the number of arm stops the relevant probability distribution function has been derived in Ref. 81.

$$P(m - i) = 2^{m - 2i} \frac{\left|\frac{C}{2} - i\right|\left|\frac{C}{2}\right|}{\binom{C}{m}} \quad \text{if } 0 \leq i \leq \left\lfloor \frac{m}{2} \right\rfloor, m \leq \frac{C}{2}, \tag{31}$$

$$P(m - i) = 2^{C - m - 2i} \frac{\binom{C/2 - i}{m - C/2 + i}\binom{C/2}{i}}{\binom{C}{m}}$$

$$\text{if } 0 \le i \le \frac{C}{2} - \lceil \frac{m}{2} \rceil, \, m > \frac{C}{2}. \tag{32}$$

Thus, the expected number of arm stops of a two-headed disk system (81) is

$$\sum_{i = 0}^{\lfloor m/2 \rfloor} (m - i) \, P(m - i) + \sum_{i = 0}^{C/2 - \lceil m/2 \rceil} \left(\frac{C}{2} - i \right) P(m - 1). \tag{33}$$

Numerically, it has been found that the expected number of arm stops is linear on the number of cylinder visits and may reach, on the average, 50% of the relevant figure for single-headed disk systems.

RECENT DEVELOPMENTS

When high disk reliability and/or data availability is desired, then a number of multidisk configurations may be applied. Thus, in case of a disk failure, the system may service the requests by using the other disk(s). Unless a case of global failure arises, such single disk failures remain transparent to the user.

These configurations may be divided in two basic categories. First, multiple copies (usually two) of the same data are stored on different disks accessible by different processors. Examples of this type of disk management are the techniques of *shadowed disks* (for two or more devices) or *mirrored disks* (for just two devices) (32,34,82–86), *interleaved declustering* (87,88), *inverted file strategy* (89), and *chained declustering* (90). The second category includes techniques that spread the data across an array of disks, such as the techniques of *synchronized disk interleaving* (91,92), *redundant array of inexpensive disks* (RAID) (39,93–97), *redundant array of distributed disks* (RADD) (98), and *parity stripping of disk arrays* (40,99). Whenever an error is detected, the data are restored by using the redundant information and, therefore, a minimal interruption is encountered.

Commercial products have already implemented some of the previous strategies; we mention among others the Tandem's NonStop SQL database machine which employs the shadowed disk technique, the Teradata's DBC 1012 database machine which uses the interleaved declustering technique, and IBM's AS400 system which adopts the RAID approach. The choice of the best approach is still an open problem, as each technique is attributed by advantages and disadvantages. However, it has been shown by simulation and experiments that all these aforementioned configurations improve both reliability and availability as well as performance. Performance improvement is achieved in part due to smaller seek distances traveled and, consequently, due to smaller seek times encountered. In the sequel, we outline the main analytical results on the seek distances traveled in the case of shadowed disks. At this point, it is noted that the shadowed disk technique is very efficient for database parallel operations and on-line transaction processing (40). Performance comparison to conventional magnetic disks is trivial.

In the environment of shadowed disks, where all disks are identical in terms of content, read operations are treated in a different way than write ones. In fact, a read is performed by the closest head to the specific cylinder, whereas a write is performed by all the heads in every disk. Therefore, different costs have to be paid as far as seek distances and seek times are concerned. For example, suppose that in a shadow set of k disks, the distances from the current cylinder to the next request may be viewed as k random variables $d_1, d_2, \ldots, d_k$ with identical distributions. Thus, the seek distance for a read operation is a random variable (32) which equals

$$d_r = \min(d_1, \ldots, d_k) \Rightarrow E[d_r] \approx \frac{C}{(2k + 1)}. \tag{34}$$

for $k = 1$, the previous formula reduces to Eq. (2), whereas for $k = 2$, it reduces to $(E)[d_r] = C/5$, which is a 40% performance increase. The seek distance for a write operation (32) is equal to

$$d_w = \max(d_1, \ldots, d_k) \Rightarrow E[d_w] \approx C(1 - I_k), \tag{35}$$

where $I_k = I_{k-1}(2k)/(2k + 1)$. Again, for $k = 1$, Eq. (2) is produced, whereas for $k = 2$, it becomes much higher: $E[d_w] = 0.46C$, which is a 38% performance decrease. However, this penalty converges with increasing k. For example, for $k = 10$, we have $E[d_w] = 0.73C$. If reads and writes occur with a probability $a\%$ and $(1-a)\%$, respectively, then the weighted seek distance traveled would be

$$E[d] = aE[d_r] + (1 - a)E[d_w].$$

It is evident that if reads are more than writes, then there is a substantial performance improvement.

The previous formulas may be used to derive the corresponding seek time estimates for reads and writes. By assuming that the disks have voice-coil actuators, relation (20) should be used. Thus, it has been derived that the expected seek times for a read or for a write operation in a mirrored disk set (32) is respectively

$$E[T_{sk, r}] = c_0 + c_1\sqrt{0.16\,C}, \tag{36}$$

$$E[T_{sk, w}] = c_0 + c_1\sqrt{0.43\,C}. \tag{37}$$

However, it has been observed that the previous approach is an approximate one because successive seeks distances should not be modeled as random variables because they are strongly dependent ones. In simple words, in the first few operations after a write one, a number of heads may lie on top of identical cylinders. The effect of this phenomenon is that the system behaves as if the number of disks is smaller than the real one. More specifically, the expression for $E[d_r]$ ($E[d_w]$) is optimistic (pessimistic). The exact formulas for the seek distances are produced by a Markov chain analysis (85):

$$E[d_r] = \frac{1}{\sum_{i=1}^{k} \prod_{j=1}^{i} \frac{(a_j - 1)}{(a_j + b_j)}} \sum_{i=1}^{k} \frac{C}{2i + 1} \prod_{j=1}^{i} \frac{a_j - 1}{a_j + b_j}, \tag{38}$$

$$E[d_w] = \frac{1}{\sum_{i=1}^{k} \prod_{j=1}^{i} \frac{(a_j - 1)}{(a_j + b_j)}} \sum_{i=1}^{k} C\,(1 - I_i) \prod_{j=1}^{i} \frac{a_j - 1}{a_j + b_j}, \tag{39}$$

where $b_j = 1/C, a_1 = C, a_k = 0$, and $a_j = j/C$ for $1 < j < C$. The interpretation of the previous complicated equations is that the system will behave as if it has only a few drives no matter how many physical drives exist in reality. For example, if reads occur with a probability of 60%, then five drives suffice to achieve almost optimal performance.

If anticipation policies are implemented, then the previous results may be improved. Assume that a future read request is anticipated in a mirrored disk set. In this case, the heads should be placed on top of the $C/4$ and $3C/4$ numbered cylinders, resulting in an expected seek distance $C/8$ on the average. If only write requests are considered, then if the heads were positioned on top of the $C/2$ numbered cylinders, the expected seek distance would be equal to $C/4$ cylinders. If both reads and writes should be taken into account, then it is concluded that heads should be placed on the central cylinder in both disks (22).

EPILOGUE

Seek time is the main cost for performing read/write operations from/to secondary storage devices such as magnetic disks. We gave short physical descriptions of these devices, with emphasis on conventional and two-headed magnetic disk systems. Analytical data for estimating the expected seek distances, seek times, and cylinder hits have been presented by taking into account the scheduling algorithms and the placement strategies used. Multidisk configurations tend to play a major role with time. Therefore, it is expected that more studies will appear in the future.

REFERENCES

1. S. H. Fuller, *Analysis of Drum and Disk Storage Units*, Lecture Notes in Computer Science No. 31, Springer-Verlag, New York, 1975.
2. S. W. Ng, "Improving Disk Performance via Latency Reduction," *IEEE Trans. Computers*, *C-40*(1), 22–30 (1991).
3. T. R. Harbron, *File Systems: Structures and Algorithms*, Prentice-Hall, Englewood Cliffs, NJ, 1988.
4. C. H. C. Leung, *Quantitative Analysis of Computer Systems*, Wiley, New York, 1988.
5. M. A. Pechura, and J. D. Schoeffler, "Estimating File Access Time of Floppy Disks," *Commun. ACM*, *26*(10), 754–763 (1983). Corrigendum: *27*(1), (1984).
6. D. A. Ford, "Performance Optimization for Optical Disk Architectures," TR-91-08, Computer Science Department, University of Waterloo.
7. P. J. Denning, "Effects of Scheduling on File Memory Operations," in *Proceedings of the AFIPS Spring Joint Computer Conference*, 1967, pp. 9–21.
8. H. Frank, "Analysis and Optimization of Disk Storage Devices for Time Shared Systems," *J. ACM*, *16*(4), 602–620 (1969).
9. E. G. Coffman, and P. J. Denning, *Operating System Theory*, Prentice-Hall, Englewood Cliffs, NJ, 1973.
10. A. M. Lister, *Fundamentals of Operating Systems*, McMillan, New York, 1979.
11. H. M. Deitel, *Operating Systems*, 2nd ed., Addison-Wesley, Reading, MA, 1990.
12. A. Silberschatz, J. L. Peterson, and P. Galvin, *Operating System Concepts*, 3rd ed., Addison-Wesley, Reading, MA, 1990.
13. G. Wiederhold, *File Organization for Database Design*, McGraw-Hill, New York, 1987.

14. T. J. Teorey, "Properties of Disk Scheduling Policies in Multiprogrammed Computer Systems," in *Proceedings of the AFIPS Fall Joint Computer Conference*, 1972, pp. 1–11.

15. S. H. Fuller, in "Minimal Total Processing Time Drum and Disk Scheduling Disciplines," *Commun. ACM*, *17*(7), 376–381 (1974).

16. A. Weingarten, "The Eschenbach Scheme," *Commun. ACM*, *9*(7), 509–512 (1966).

17. R. Geist and S. Daniel, "A Continuum of Disk Scheduling Algorithms," *ACM Trans. Computer Syst.* *5*(1), 77–92 (1987).

18. R. Geist, R. Reynolds, and E. Pittard, "Disk Scheduling in System V," in *Proceedings of the ACM SIGMETRICS 87 Conference*, 1987, pp. 59–68.

19. C. C. Wang, and B. P. Weems, "Some Considerations in using VSCAN Disk Scheduling with Optimal Page Arrangements," in *Proceedings of the ACM SIGMETRICS 88 Conference*, 1988, p. 273.

20. T. S. Chen, W. P. Yang, and R. T. C. Lee, "Amortized Analysis of some Disk Scheduling Algorithm: SSTF, SCAN and N-step-SCAN," *BIT*, *32* 546–558 (1992).

21. S. J. Waters, "Estimating Magnetic Disc Seeks," *Computer J.* *18*(1), 12–17 (1974).

22. R. P. King, "Disk Arm Movement in Anticipation of Future Requests," *ACM Trans. Computer Syst.* *8*(3), 214–229 (1990).

23. W. Kiessling, "Access Path Selection in Databases with Intelligent Disc Subsystems," *Computer J.* *31*(1), 41–50 (1988).

24. W. C. Lynch, "Do Disk Arms Move?" *ACM Perform. Eval. Rev.* *15*(12) 3–16 (1972).

25. Y. Manolopoulos, and J. G. Kollias, "Estimating Disk Head Movements in Batched Searching," *BIT*, *28*, 27–36 (1988).

26. J. G. Kollias, "An Estimate of Seek Time for Batched Searching of Random or Index Sequential Structured Files," *Computer J.* *21*(2) 132–133 (1977).

27. F. W. Burton, and J. G. Kollias, "Optimising Disc Head Movements in Secondary key Retrievals," *Computer J.* *22*(3), 206–208 (1978).

28. J. G. Kollias, Y. Manolopoulos, and C. Papadimitriou, "The Optimum Execution Order of Queries in Linear Storage, *Inform. Processing Lett.* *36*, 216–219 (1989).

29. Y. Manolopoulos, "Probability Distributions for Seek Time Evaluation," *Inform. Sci. 60* (1–2), 29–40 (1992).

30. T. J. Teorey, and T. B. Pinkerton, A Comparative Analysis of Disk Scheduling Policies, *Commun. ACM*, *15*(3), 177–184 (1972).

31. N. C. Wilhelm, "An Anomaly in Disk Scheduling: A Comparison of FCFS and SSTF Seek Scheduling using an Empirical Model for Disk Accesses," *Commun. ACM*, *19*(1), 13–17 (1976).

32. D. Bitton, and J. Gray, "Disk Shadowing," in *Proceedings of the 14th VLDB Conference*, 1988, pp. 331–338.

33. M. J. Carey, R. Jauhari, and M. Livny, "Priority in DBMS Resource Scheduling," in *Proceedings of the 15th VLDB Conference*, 1989, pp. 397–410.

34. S. Chen, and D. Towsley, "Performance of a Mirrored Disk in a Real-Time Transaction System, in *Proceedings of the ACM SIGMOD 91 Conference*, 1991, pp. 199–207.

35. H. I. Hsiao, and D. J. DeWitt, "A Performance Study of three Availability Data Replication Strategies," *Distributed and Parallel Databases*, *1*(1), 53–79 (1993).

36. C. H. Chien, "Seek Distances in Disks with Dual Arms and Mirrored Disks," *Perform. Eval.* 18, 175–188 (1993).

37. M. Y. Kim and A. N. Tantawi, "Asynchronus Disk Interleaving: Approximating Access Delays," *IEEE Trans. Computers*, *C-40*(7), 801–810 (1991).

38. A. R. Calderbank, E. G. Coffman, and L. Flatto, "A Note Extending the Analysis of Two-Headed Systems to More General Seek Time Characteristics," *IEEE Trans. Computers*, *C-38*(11), 1584–1586 (1989).

39. E. K. Lee, and R. H. Katz, "Performance Consequences of Parity Placement in Disk Arrays," in *Proceedings of the ACM SIGMOD 91 Conference*, 1991, pp. 190–198.

40. J. Gray, B. Horst, and M. Walker, "Parity Stripping of Disc Arrays: Low Cost Reliable Storage with Acceptable Throughput, in *Proceedings of the 16th VLDB Conference*, 1990, pp. 148–161.

41. T. S. Chen, and W. P. Yang, Amortized Analysis of Disk Scheduling Algorithm *V(R)*, *J. Inform. Sci. Eng.*, in press.

42. L. Kleinrock, *Queueing Systems*, Wiley, New York, 1975, Vols. 1 and 2.

43. C. H. Sauer, and K. M. Chandy, *Computer System Performance Modeling*, Prentice-Hall, Englewood Cliffs, NJ, 1981.

44. E. G. Coffman, and M. Hofri, "Queueing Models of Secondary Storage Devices," in *Stochastic Analysis of Computer and Communication Systems, H. Takagi (ed.), Elsevier Science, New York, 1990*.

45. E. G. Coffman, L. A. Klimko, and B. Ryan, "Analysis of Scanning Policies for Reducing Disc Seek Times," *SIAM J. Computing 1*, 269–279 (1972).

46. C. C. Gotlieb, and G. H. McEwen, "Performance of Movable-Head Disk Storage Devices," *J. ACM, 20*(4), 604–623 (1973).

47. W. C. Oney, "Queueing Analysis of the SCAN Policy for Moving Head Disks," *J. ACM, 22*,(3) 397–412 (1975).

48. V. Siskind, and J. Rosenhead, "Seek Time for Disc File Processing—Some Results from Probability Theory," *Computer J 19*, 301–305 (1976).

49. N. C. Wilhelm, "A General Model for the Performance of Disk Systems," *J. ACM, 24*(1), 14–31 (1977).

50. M. Hofri, "Disk Scheduling: FCFS vs. SSTF Revisited," *Commun. ACM, 23*(11), 645–772 (1980).

51. H. G. Perros, "A Regression Model for Predicting the Response Time of a Disc I/O System," *Computer J. 23*(1), 34–36 (1980).

52. E. G. Coffman, and M. Hofri, "On the Expected Performance of Scanning Disks," *SIAM J. Computing, 11*(1), 60–70 (1982).

53. B. McNutt, "A Case Study of Access to VM Disk Volumes," in *Proceedings of CMG*, 1984, pp. 175–180.

54. D. Gifford, and A. Spector, "The TWA Reservation System," *Commun. ACM, 27*(7), 650–665 (1984).

55. G. H. Hardy, J. E. Littlewood, and G. Polya, *Inequalities*, Cambridge University Press, Cambridge, 1952, Chap. 10.

56. J. McCabe, "On Serial Files with Relocatable Records," *Opera. Res. 13*, 609–618 (1965).

57. D. D. Grossman, and H. F. Silverman, "Placement of Records on a Secondary Storage Device to Minimize Access Time, *J. ACM*, 20, 429–438 (1973).

58. C. K. Wong, *Algorithmic Studies in Mass Storage Systems*, Computer Science Press, 1983.

59. P. P. Bergmans, "Maximizing Expected Travel Time on Geometrical Patterns by Optimal Probability Rearrangements," *Inform. Control, 20*, 331–350 (1972).

60. V. R. Prat, An *N* log*N* Algorithm to Distribute *N* Records Optimally in a Sequential Access File," in *Complexity of Computer Communications*, R. E. Miller and J. W. Thatcher (eds.), Plenum Press, New York, 1972.

61. P. C. Yue and C. K. Wong, "On the Optimality of the Probability Ranking Scheme in Storage Applications," *J. ACM, 20*, 624–633 (1973).

62. A. C. McKellar, and C. K. Wong, "Dynamic Placement of Records in Linear Storage," *J. ACM, 25*, 421–434 (1978).

63. J. R. Bitner and C. K. Wong, "Optimal and Near-optimal Scheduling Algorithms for Batched Processing in Linear Storage," *SIAM J. Computing, 8*(4), 479–498 (1979).

64. A. Vaquero and J. M. Troya, "Placement of Records on Linear Storage Devices," in *Proceedings of the 1980 IFIP Congress*, 1980, pp. 331–336.

65. U. I. Gupta, D. T. Lee, J. Y. T. Leung, J. W. Pruit, and C. K. Wong, "Record Allocation for Minimizing Seek Delay," *Theoret. Computer Sci. 16*, 307–319 (1981).

66. C. K. Wong, "Minimizing Expected Head Movement in One-Dimensional and Two-Dimensional Mass Storage Systems," *ACM Computing Surv.*, *12*(2), 167–178 (1980).

67. B. P. Weems, "A Study of Page Arrangements for Extendible Hashing," *Inform. Processing Lett.*, *27*, 245–248 (1988).

68. S. D. Carson, and P. Vongsathorn, "Error Bounds on Disk Arrangement using Frequency Information," *Inform. Processing Lett.*, *31*, 209–213 (1989).

69. S. D. Carson and P. F. Reynolds, Jr., "Adaptive Disk Reorganization," TR-2178, Computer Science Department, University of Maryland at College Park, 1989.

70. P. Vongsathorn and S. D. Carson, "A System for Adaptive Disk Rearrangement," *Software—Practice and Experience* to appear.

71. Y. Manolopoulos and A. Vakali, "Seek Distances in Disk Systems with Two Independent Heads," *Inform. Processing Lett.* *37*(1), 37–42 (1991).

72. S. D. Carson, V. Nirkhe, and P. Vongsathorn, "A Discrete-State Model of the Two-Headed Disk," *Inform. Processing Lett.*, *41*, 341–345 (1992).

73. M. Hofri, "Should the Two-headed Disk be Greedy?—Yes, It Should," *Inform. Processing Lett.*, *16*, 83–85 (1983).

74. A. R. Calderbank, E. G. Coffman, and L. Flatto, "Sequencing Problems in Two-Server Systems," *Math. Oper. Res.* *10*(4), 585–598 (1985).

75. I. P. Page and R. T. Wood, "Empirical Analysis of a Moving Headed Disk Model with Two Heads Separated by a Fixed Number of Tracks," *Computer J.* *24*(4), 339–342 (1981).

76. A. R. Calderbank, E. G. Coffman, and L. Flatto, "Optimum Head Separation in a Disk System with Two Read/Write Heads," *J. ACM*, *31*(4), 826–838 (1984).

77. Y. Manolopoulos, and J. G. Kollias, "Performance of a Two-Headed Disk System When Serving Database Queries Under the SCAN Policy," *ACM Trans. Database Syst.* *14*(3), 425–442 (1989).

78. T. S. Chen, "SIMPLE: An Optimal Disk System with Two Restricted Heads," *Inform. Processing Lett.*, to appear.

79. Y. Manolopoulos, and J. G. Kollias, "Optimal Data Placement in Two-Headed Disk Systems," *BIT*, *30*, 216–219 (1990).

80. A. R. Calderbank, E. G. Coffman, and L. Flatto, "Optimal Directory Placement on Disk Storage Devices," *J. ACM*, *35*(2), 433–436 (1988).

81. Y. Manolopoulos, "On the Arm Stops of a Two-headed Disk," Electrical Engineering Department, Aristotle University of Thessaloniki, 1992.

82. J. Gray, H. Sammer, and S. Whitford, "Shortest Seek vs. Shortest Service Time Scheduling of Mirrored Disc Reads," *Tandem Computers*, 1988.

83. D. Bitton, "Arm Scheduling in Shadowed Disks, in *Proceedings of the IEEE COMPCON 89 Conference*, 1989, pp. 132–136.

84. N. S. Matloff, and R. W. M. Lo, "A "Greedy" Approach to the Write Problem in Shadowed Disk Systems," in *Proceedings of the 6th IEEE Data Engineering Conference*, 1990, pp 553–558.

85. R. W. M. Lo, and N. S. Matloff, "A Probabilistic Limit on the Virtual Size of Replicated Disk Systems," *IEEE Trans. Knowledge Data Eng.*, *KDE-4*(1), 99–102 (1992).

86. J. A. Solworth and C. U. Orji, "Distorted Mapping Techniques to Achieve High Performance in Mirrored Disk Systems," *Distributed and Parallel Databases*, *1*(1), 81–102 (1993).

87. Teradata, *DBC/1012 Database Computer System Manual Release 2.0*, Document No. C10-0001-02, Teradata Corp., 1985.

88. G. Copeland and T. Keller, "A Comparison of High Availability Media Recovery Techniques," *Proceedings of the ACM SIGMOD 89 Conference*, 1989.

89. G. Copeland, W. Alexander, E. Boughter, and T. Keller, "Data Placement in Budda," in *Proceedings of the ACM SIGMOD 88 Conference*, 1988, pp. 99–108.

90. H. I. Hsiao, and D. J. DeWitt, "Chained Declustering: A New Availability Strategy for Multiprocessor Database Machines," in *Proceedings of the 6th IEEE Data Engineering Conference*, 1990, pp. 456–465.

91. M. Y. Kim, "Synchronized Disk Interleaving," *IEEE Trans. Computers*, C-35(11) 978–988 (1985).

92. M. Livny, S. Khoshafian, and H. Boral, "Multi-disk Management Algorithms, in *Proceedings of the ACM SIGMETRICS 87 Conference, 1987, pp. 69–77.*

93. D. Patterson, G. Gibson, and A. Katz, "A Case for Redundant Arrays of Inexpensive Disks (RAID)," in *Proceedings of the ACM SIGMOD 88 Conference*, 1988, pp. 112–117.

94. D. Patterson, P. Chen, G. Gibson, and A. Katz, "Introduction to Redundant Arrays of Inexpensive Disks (RAID)," in *Proceedings of the IEEE COMPCON 89 Conference*, 1989, pp. 112–117.

95. M. Schulze, G. Gibson, A. Katz, and D. A. Patterson, "How Reliable is RAID," in *Proceedings of the IEEE COMPCON 89 Conference*, 1989.

96. A. L. Chervenak and R. H. Katz, "Performance of a Disk Array Prototype," in *Proceedings of the ACM SIGMOD 91 Conference*, 1991, pp. 188–197.

97. J. Menon and D. Mattson, "Comparison of Sparing Alternatives for Disk Arrays," in *Proceedings of the ACM SIGARCH 92 Conference*, 1992, pp. 318–329.

98. M. Stonebraker and G. Schloss, "Distributed RAID - a New Multiple Copy Algorithm," in *Proceedings of the 6th IEEE Data Engineering Conference*, 1990, pp. 430–437.

99. K. Salem and H. Garcia-Molina, "Disk Stripping," *Proceedings of the 2nd IEEE Data Engineering Conference, 1986.*

YANNIS MANOLOPOULOS

SELECTING EXPERT SYSTEM DEVELOPMENT TECHNIQUES

INTRODUCTION

Expert systems (ES) are now widely accepted in business organizations. They have become critical components in many decision-making and problem-solving processes (1,2). Widespread adoption and dependence on ES has, however, resulted in rising user expectations. An important challenge facing ES developers and managers is to improve the development process and enable quick construction of systems that are sophisticated, economical, evolvable, and, above all, satisfy user's demands and expectations. Lu and Guimaraes (3) have addressed the selection of appropriate ES applications and development strategies in broader terms, using more detailed knowledge about the applications and how ES development techniques have performed in practice.

Expert systems using explicit decision rules extracted from domain experts are predominant today. However, the development process and resulting products suffer from serious limitations. First, the construction of a rule-based ES has proved to be difficult in many cases because it requires developers to determine the decision rules of human experts and to represent them in an ''if–then'' format. To extract the decision rules, developers, who are relative novices in the various domains, often fail to ask relevant questions and experience great difficulty in finding the domain knowledge. Due to the implicit nature of human knowledge (4), domain experts are often unable to articulate information requirements as well as they can use it (5). This results in a lengthy development process: the interviews and development process being a time- and labor-intensive task. Second, a sophisticated knowledge base must evolve from a simple one by adding new knowledge learned from experience; unfortunately, most conventional ES are incapable of learning through experience (6). Finally, rules in conventional expert systems can have relationships with many other rules; when a rule is modified or a new rule is added, one has to worry about its effect on existing related rules. Thus, a large conventional ES can become unwieldy and difficult to maintain (7).

To overcome these limitations, researchers have explored various ES development techniques. The most promising are inductive learning, artificial neural networks, case-based reasoning, and model-based reasoning (8–16). The applications of these methods have demonstrated their potential, not only for resolving the bottleneck of knowledge acquisition but also for enhancing the capabilities of an ES and broadening the scope. Due to their superior performance, it is important that developers and Information Systems managers become familiar with the basic concepts, strengths, and limitations of each ES method. No particular approach is consistently more effective. Each may be superior, depending on the characteristics of the application domain and the available systems development resources. Therefore, understanding the profile of applications best suited to each method becomes very important.

EXPERT SYSTEM APPLICATION DEVELOPMENT TECHNIQUES

Various ES techniques have been developed to cope with a broad range of domains. The four most promising techniques which have been demonstrated for effectively surmounting ES development problems are now discussed.

Inductive Learning

Machine learning involves acquiring new knowledge through instruction or practice and organizing it in general, effective representations that improve the system performance. One branch of machine learning is "inductive learning" or "learning by example"; it is concerned with the development of concept descriptions (or classification rules) from examples.

Unlike the development of a conventional ES, the developers of an inductive ES have to acquire a set of examples that human experts previously solved and then employ an inductive learning system to generate classification rules. The set of classification rules generated from the learning system is then used as the knowledge base of an inductive expert system. Therefore, the process of eliciting explicit classification rules from domain experts through interviews and observations becomes unnecessary. Various inductive learning algorithms exist, such as AQ (17), Version Space (18), ID3 (19), SPROUTER (20), and Thoth (21).

The most widely used inductive method is ID3. Its objective is to develop a decision tree that requires a minimum number of attribute tests for a set of examples [S]. Each example consists of a number of attributes and a predefined classification of the example. In order to minimize a decision tree, ID3 chooses the attribute whose discriminating power is largest among them and splits the examples into two sets (S_1 and S_2), according to the chosen attribute. A set (S_i) is then classified into two subsets by the attribute that has the largest discriminating power. The process is repeated until all examples are appropriately classified and/or no other attribute is available to be used for classification.

When calculating the discriminating power of each attribute, ID3 employs an information-theoretic approach adapted from communication and information theory which measures the expected information of a probability distribution P by

$$-\sum_x P(x) \log P(x).$$

Suppose a set S of training examples contain two classes, H and L. Let K denote the number of examples in class H in S, and G denote the number of examples in class L in S. An unseen example belongs to class H with probability $K/(K + G)$, and to class L with probability $G/(K + G)$. When classifying a new example, a decision tree is regarded as the source of a message indicating the class of the example, H or L. According to information theory, the expected information associated with the message is given by

$$M(S) = -\frac{K}{K + G} \log_2 \frac{K}{K + G} - \frac{G}{K + G} \log_2 \frac{G}{K + G}.$$

For an attribute with the alternative values of $A_1, A_2, \ldots, A_n$, the attribute test, T, produces a partition $\{S_1, S_2, \ldots S_n\}$ (Fig. 1). Suppose S_i contains K_i examples of class H and G_i examples of class L. The expected information of a branch A_i, $EI(A_i)$, is given by

Attribute Test

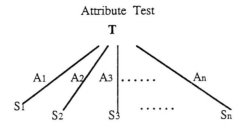

FIGURE 1   A decision tree structure for partitioning examples.

$$EI(A_i) = -\frac{K_i}{K_i + G_i} \log_2 \frac{K_i}{K_i + G_i} - \frac{G_i}{K_i + G_i} \log_2 \frac{G_i}{K_i + G_i}$$

The expected information of all branches with T at its root can then be defined as

$$E(T) = \sum_i \frac{(K_i + G_i)}{(K + G)} EI(A_i) \quad \text{for } i = 1 \text{ to } n.$$

The ratio $(K_i + G_i)/(K + G)$ represents the proportion of the examples in S that belongs to S_i. Thus, the information gained by performing the attribute test is given by

$$M(S) - E(T).$$

The next attribute to be tested is the one which gives the most information, i.e., the one for which $M(S) - E(T)$ is maximum.

To illustrate the inductive approach, consider the development of a risk classification system for capital project analysis. The risk of a project is determined by many factors: size, market, a project type, the national focus, the cost of the project, etc. A prototype ES classifies the risk of a project into one of two classes (High or Low), depending on the project type and the other risk factors. When using a conventional approach, the developer extracts classification rules from domain experts; whereas, in an inductive approach, the developer obtains a set of live examples (see Table 1) and applies an inductive algorithm like ID3 to those examples to generate classification rules. Consider the set of training examples that illustrate the process of generating a decision rule by ID3. The set S contains 11 examples in which 5 are in class H (High) and 6 are in class L (Low) in S; therefore,

$$M(S) = -\frac{5}{11} \log_2 \frac{5}{11} - \frac{6}{11} \log_2 \frac{6}{11} = 0.9940.$$

The information gained for the "Replacement" branch of an attribute test Project Type is as follows:

$$EI(\text{Replacement}) = -\frac{2}{5} \log_2 \frac{2}{5} - \frac{3}{5} \log_2 \frac{3}{5} = 0.970$$

and for the New branch

$$EI(\text{New}) = -\frac{3}{6} \log_2 \frac{3}{6} - \frac{3}{6} \log_2 \frac{3}{6} = 1.0.$$

TABLE 1   A Set of Training Examples Used to Illustrate the Concept of ID3

Project Type	Product	Market	Focus	Classes
Replacement	Existing	Existing	International	Low
Replacement	Existing	New	Domestic	Low
Replacement	New	Existing	Domestic	Low
Replacement	New	Existing	International	High
Replacement	New	New	International	High
New	Existing	Existing	Domestic	Low
New	Existing	New	Domestic	Low
New	New	Existing	Domestic	Low
New	New	Existing	International	High
New	New	New	Domestic	High
New	New	New	International	High

Thus, the expected information for all branches of the attribute test is

$$E(\text{Project Type}) = \frac{5}{11} (0.970) + \frac{6}{11} (1.0) = 0.986.$$

The information gained by testing the attribute Project Types is

$$0.9940 - 0.986 = 0.008,$$

which is negligible. Meanwhile, the information gained by testing the attributes Product, Market, and Focus is 0.4448, 0.0518, and 0.3113, respectively. Thus, the principle of maximizing the expected information gained from an attribute test leads us to select the "Product" as the first attribute to test and, thus, to form the root of the decision tree. Applying the same concept to the six examples which belong to the New branch of the attribute Product leads us to choose the Focus as the second test attribute and, finally, Market as the third; this yields the decision tree in Figure 2. The attribute Project Type is found unnecessary to classify the training examples. The decision tree is finally coded into a knowledge base in an "if–then" form to classify new examples.

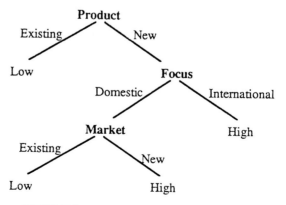

FIGURE 2   A decision tree developed by ID3.

Artificial Neural Network

Artificial neural network (ANN) research is based on the belief that human information processing takes place through the interaction of many billions of neurons, each sending excitatory or inhibitory signals to other neurons. A neuron in a human brain contains a nucleus, an axon, and one or more dendrites, as illustrated in Figure 3. The nucleus receives signals from other neurons through ramified dendrites, collects the input signal, and transforms the collected input signal. The single axon then transmits the transformed signal to other neurons, usually by the propagation of an "action potential" or "spike" (22). The signals that pass through the junction, known as synapses, are either weakened or strengthened depending on the strength of the synaptic connection. By modifying synaptic strengths, the human brain is able to store knowledge and, thus, allow certain inputs to result in specific output or behavior.

To implement such human information processing in an artificial system, the basic ANN model consists of computational units which emulate the functions of a nucleus in a human brain cell (23). Computational units in an ANN are connected by links with variable weights which represent synapses in the biological model. The unit receives a weighted sum of all its inputs via connections and computes its own output value using its own output function. The output value is then propagated to many other units via the connection between units, as shown in Figure 4. Receiving units repeat the process. In real-world problems, a computational unit represent a parameter, and a connection weight represents the association between parameters, as shown in Figure 5.

Some researchers have recently explored the use of an ANN to resolve the difficulty of generating a knowledge base, and thereby developed a new construct called a connectionist expert system (CES) — an ES developed with an ANN approach (24,25). Like an inductive approach, in lieu of decision rules elicited from a human expert, the CES approach obtains a set of training examples. This approach applies a learning algorithm to extract the functional relationships between input and output parameters and to encode them in the connection weights.

For example, supervised learning algorithms, like Back Propagation (26), require a set of attributes and a class identification for each training example. They use a gradient descent algorithm by which network connection weights are iteratively modified to reduce the difference between the system's classification and the expected classification over all examples. For the developmental process of a knowledge base, a set of weights is initially assigned at random. A collection of attributes then propagates forward to com-

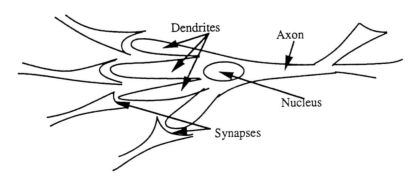

FIGURE 3   A classical neuron.

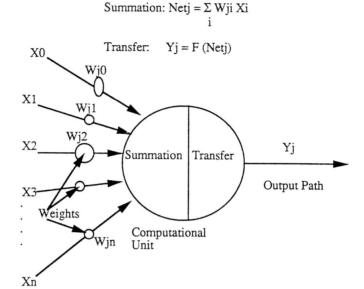

FIGURE 4   The basic components of an artificial neural network model.

pute the output values of the output units. These are then compared to measure the error according to

$$E = \frac{1}{2} \sum_{j=o}^{n} (D_j - O_j)^2$$

where D_j is the expected and O_j is the actual output value. Finally, the differences are propagated back to the weights in order to reduce the error.

This procedure is repeated for a number of epochs for all training examples; an epoch is completed after the network processes all of the input and output pairs for all examples. When the change in weights becomes negligible, the iterative learning process is terminated. The mapping (from input to output) of what the ANN has learned is encoded in the magnitudes of the weights of the connections. The network whose connection weights accurately represent the processing function becomes a knowledge base for the ES. Thus, the knowledge base of a CES is a multilayered network, and the pattern of weighted connections, produces implicitly what conventional ES developers must achieve by the specification of explicit decision rules.

The inductive approach and the ANN method are very similar in that both approaches use a set of examples to extract the decision rules. The major difference between these methods is that the final output of an inductive approach is an explicit decision tree in which a path can be traced, whereas the ANN approach produces an implicit network in which a decision path cannot be traced. Additionally, an inductive approach works with qualitative variables or quantitative variables whose values are categorized, whereas an ANN works with qualitative, discrete, or continuous quantitative variables.

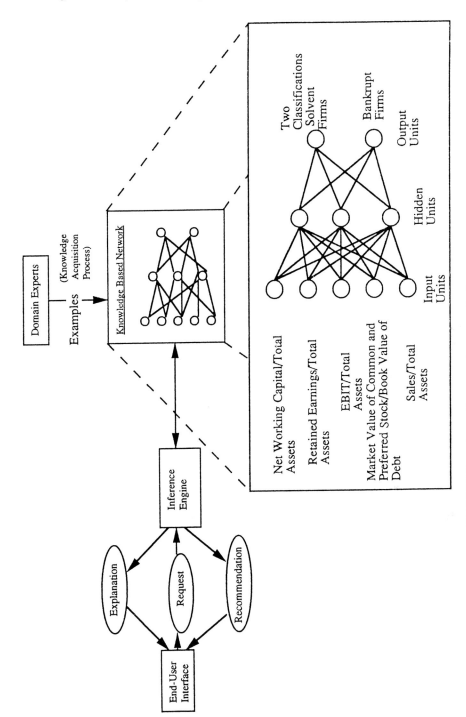

FIGURE 5 The architecture of a connectionist expert system.

Case-Based Reasoning

A case-based reasoning (CBR) technique is based on the human information processing model in some problem areas; human experts depend heavily on memory of past experiences when solving new problems, particularly in law, diagnosis, and strategic planning (27,28). CBR emulates this information processing model and maintains a historical case base. It retrieves cases relevant to the present problem situation from the case base and decides on the solution to the current problem on the basis of the outcomes from previous cases. To facilitate case-based reasoning, a case-based expert system (Fig. 6) consists of several components which perform the necessary activities: a case base, a retriever, an adapter, a refiner, an executer, and an evaluator (29).

A case base functions as a repository of prior cases. The cases are indexed so that they can be quickly recalled when necessary. The knowledge source for a case-based system are previous cases solved by human experts. A case contains the general descriptions of old problems and solutions; whereas, an example in inductive learning is defined in terms of its attributes and its class.

When a new problem is entered into a case-based system, a search is instituted to find the features similar to the stored cases; the search involves indices to aid in retrieval. When relevant prior cases are found, an adapter examines the differences between these cases and the current problem, and then applies rules to modify the old solution to fit the new problem; this adapter employs structural and derivational methods. *Structural adaptation* applies rules directly to the old solution. *Derivational adaptation* reapplies rules that generated the old solution, creating a solution for the new situation. The method of derivation adaptation is to store the planning sequence that constructed the original solution along with its solution. When a case is retrieved for analysis and adaptation the stored solution is, therefore, not changed directly, but reexecution of the original solution process is initiated with the variables of the new problem statement.

A refiner then critiques the adapted solution against prior outcomes. One way to do this is to compare it to similar solutions of prior cases. If a *solution* exists for a different

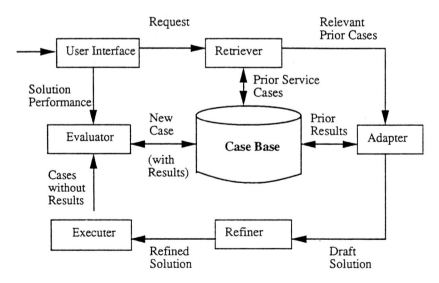

FIGURE 6   The architecture of a case-based reasoning system.

problem statement, then the system decides whether the solution is derived correctly. Alternatively, if a known *failure* exists for a derived solution, then the system must decide whether the similarities are sufficient to suspect that the new solution will fail.

Once a solution is critiqued, an executer applies the refined solution to the current problem, and an evaluator then analyzes the results. If they are as expected, no further analysis is made; the case and its solution are stored for use in future problem solving. However, if the results are not as expected, the case-based reasoner explains the failure and repairs it. In some situations, where the failure has been experienced before, the cause of the failure is explained and this guides the repair. In situations where the failure is unexpected, the repair occurs before the failure is formally explained. Repair and adaptation are similar in nature: A solution is modified to fit a problem statement. However, adaptation works with old solutions and new cases, whereas repair works with a solution, a failure report, possibly an explanation, and modifies the solution. Once a repair is made, a link is stored between the failed solutions and the one that finally worked. A case-based reasoning system can use such a link to determine whether there is anything in common with the original failed solution and the solution of a new problem.

Case-based systems must contain all components in order to solve the new problem. However, a developer may build a partial case-based system with only a case base and a retrieval subsystem if a domain is too complicated for development of all components. A partial system may not provide recommendations but can support decisions by providing relevant cases to the user. With a partial system, an end user must evaluate retrieved cases, determine their applicability to a current problem, and modify them to fit the problem.

Model-Based Reasoning

Manufacturing firms take measurements of processes in order to control product quality and prevent costly breakdowns. Similarly, fast, accurate fault diagnoses are needed for model-based reasoning techniques. A model-based system is a type of ES based on a model of the structure and behavior of the device that the system is designed to simulate (30). Figure 7 illustrates the fundamental idea: the comparison of observation and prediction.

In model-based reasoning, observed behavior (what the device is actually doing) is compared with predicted behavior (what the device is supposed to do). The difference between them is called a discrepancy, and this indicates that a defect exists in the device. Then a process is initiated to diagnose the nature and location of the defect. Such a technique can be implemented to develop a model-based expert system if a real-world me-

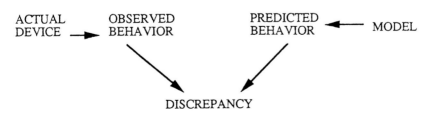

FIGURE 7   Fundamental idea of model-based reasoning.

chanical device exists whose behavior is observable, and a model can be built to simulate the structure and function of the mechanical device and, thus, to make predictions about its intended behavior.

To illustrate the concept of model-based reasoning, a device which contains three multipliers and two adders is used as an example (Fig. 8). The values at the five inputs are given. The predicted value at output F is 12, but the observed value is 10 (inside brackets). The value at output G is predicted to be 12, and the actual value is 12. The diagnostic task must use knowledge about the structure and behavior of the components to determine which one could have produced the discrepenacy at F. When diagnosing this, model-based reasoning techniques employ three steps: hypothesis generation, hypothesis testing, and hypothesis discrimination. The system first generates a set of suspended error points. These hypotheses can be generated in several ways. The simplest and most accurate way would be to suspect every component, but this is impracticable; another way is to consider only those components connected to the discrepancy. For example, only those components "upstream" from the discrepancy are suspect; i.e., MULTI-1, MULTI-2, and ADD-1.

After an hypothesis is generated, the system tests the suspected causes of error to determine which components could have failed, based on available observations of behavior. One of the approaches uses fault-model simulation. The fault model is created from a set of components that can malfunction. A simulation is run assuming that a component may malfunction as specified. If it malfunctions as specified, the hypothesis is retained; otherwise it is discarded. Another approach is based on the idea of fault corroboration, where only those components involved in the generation of incorrect prediction are considered for testing. For example, the correct output value at G is generated, indicating that the component, MULTI-2, functions properly; thus, it is eliminated from testing.

Almost always, more than one hypothesis remains after testing is completed. Therefore, hypothesis discrimination tests are conducted to distinguish between the remaining hypotheses. A probing technique is often used to accomplish this. The simplest form of probing involves starting the probe at the discrepancy and working upstream until a component is discovered producing the bad output from good input. For example, two components MULTI-1 and ADD-1 are probed in sequence to determine if one is a malfunctioning component. A disadvantage of this is the amount of time involved in the search: To improve search time, a binary search can be used. One possible alternative is

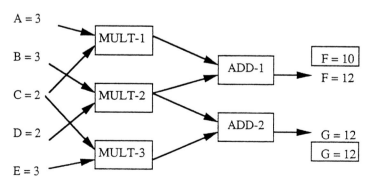

FIGURE 8   A multiplier example of model-based reasoning.

to consider the failure probabilities of the components, if available, and first consecutively test the components with the highest expected failure rates.

The development of a model-based system involves the analysis of a device and the creation of a model to simulate it. A developer also has to find methods for hypothesis generation, testing, and discrimination.

STRENGTHS AND LIMITATIONS OF EACH METHOD

Each of the ES development techniques have some advantages and disadvantages, as shown in Table 2. The inductive learning algorithm helps a knowledge engineer to develop a knowledge base from examples instead of eliciting decision rules from experts. The simplicity and efficiency of ID3 make it a desirable alternative in the case of ES applications characterized by particularly demanding knowledge elicitation. With inductive learning, it becomes unnecessary for a knowledge engineer to study the concepts in the domain before moving on to the specification of decision rules. The time that knowledge engineers and domain experts must spend is significantly reduced by the inductive learning development technique, with a favorable impact on the cost/time associated with the development process. Additionally, the generation of explanations for an inductive expert system is relatively trivial, as its knowledge base employs explicit decision rules extracted from examples, indicating that the decision path can be traced to disclose which variables and/or rules trigger a system's conclusion.

TABLE 2   Comparing ES Development Techniques Along Selected Variables

Variables	ID3	ANN	CBR	MBR
Input Data				
Required Data	Examples	Examples	Cases	Design specifications
Input Variables	Qualitative Quantitative (categorized only)	Qualitative Quantitative	Qualitative Quantitative (categorized only)	Qualitative Quantitative (categorized only)
Capabilities of a System				
Generalization	Poor	Good	Good	Poor
Explanation power	Good	Poor	Excellent	Good
Development				
Support of incremental development	No	No	Yes	Yes
Cost	Low	Medium	Medium	Medium
Difficulty	Low	Medium	Medium	Medium
Domain				
Problem structure	Well-defined	Ill-defined	Ill-defined	Very Well-defined
Appropriate domains	Diagnosis Instruction	Forecasting Interpretation Diagnosis	Planning Design Explanation	Fault Diagnosis Monitoring Control

However, ID3 is not an incremental approach: New examples cause a decision tree to be discarded and redeveloped to accommodate new information. The method also does not guarantee the *simplest* decision tree because the information-theoretic concept for choosing attribute tests is only a heuristic and cannot be optimized (31). Furthermore, the input variables of ID3 should be qualitative and have a small number of possible values because the efficiency and effectiveness of the algorithm can be significantly reduced when each possible value of the input variable represents a branch in a decision tree. Additionally, a continuous quantitative variable must be categorized to produce a finite number of branches, and a significant amount of information may be lost by classifying the variable.

Like an inductive learning approach, connectionist ES that use ANN learning algorithms are capable of generating a knowledge base from a set of examples. Regardless of the characteristics of input variables, ANN has been shown to be able to learn to generalize functional relationships between input and output, even though the relationships may be fuzzy, incomplete, or unclear (32): The "learned" function is encoded in the interconnection weights of a multilayered network, and knowledge is distributed over the network, with connection weights representing implicit decision rules. This provides a more direct and effective mechanism to represent knowledge, where the implicit knowledge remains in an implicit form. In a comparison with an inductive learning method, a Connectionist Expert System (CES) demonstrated slightly higher decision accuracy than ID3, regardless of knowledge domains (33).

A disadvantage of CES is that it cannot easily generate explanations (34): CES cannot explain decisions based on the underlying knowledge-based. CES in inductive systems employ explicit decision rules in an "if–then" format so that the system can be programmed to display the rules being used to reach a given conclusion. Connectionist ES use implicit decision rules which make such tracing very difficult. In addition, the CES technique does not support an incremental ES development approach, so new examples and new parameters result in redeveloping a completely new knowledge-based network.

The CBR development technique also facilitates the development of a knowledge base. Unlike a conventional ES, much of the knowledge needed for CBR is in the form of cases that are general descriptions of previous problems and solutions. Therefore, as long as historical cases are available, CBR may be useful for addressing ill-defined problems. A case-based system can easily incorporate new cases, thus facilitating the incremental development of an ES. A small number of cases can initiate a case-based system, and the system can be gradually expanded as more are incorporated.

Maintaining a case-based system is easier than maintaining conventional ES because case interactions are easier to understand. In a conventional ES, for any rule change the developer is forced to analyze the interactions among all rules with relationships to the changed rule. Another important advantage of CBR is higher system efficiency. It uses individual or generalized cases to provide an explanation; thus, they are relatively simple to generate and more satisfactory than a conventional ES. It can also propose solutions to problems quickly, requiring no time to derive answers from scratch (35). Remembering previous experiences (cases) is particularly useful in warning about potential problems; therefore, a case-based system can alert itself and users to avoid repeating past mistakes.

Although the CBR technique is found to have many advantages, its success depends largely on the quality of the indexing mechanism and consequent search technique. The match algorithm, including a way to deal with partial matches, is critical. Last, enforcing cross-case consistency is quite difficult in a case-based system because each case is defined separately and has no explicit relationship with others.

A major advantage of a model-based reasoning technique is its device independent. The process of knowledge acquisition starts from the ES design phase. The task of monitoring and diagnosing can, therefore, begin immediately, without waiting for human diagnostic expertise. Because its knowledge base is composed of a list of components and their functions, device modification poses no threat to diagnostic ability, and the knowledge base is simply modified to reflect the changes (36). With a conventional ES, device modification requires a major revision of the knowledge base. The development of a model-based ES is likely to be less expensive, as it is not necessary to acquire knowledge from human experts. Given a design description for a device, diagnostic work can begin right away, and given a new design description for a different device, one can start to work just as quickly.

Of even greater value is the model-based system's ability to detect uncommon failures. A rule-based system relies on expert experience, which is likely to be focused on common malfunctions; the rare failure is doomed to obscurity and may not be appropriately diagnosed. A model-based system can reason and diagnose even the nonintuitive anomalies because the system has extensive specifications used to build the device. A major limitation of the model-based reasoning approach is that it requires the complete specification of interaction between components.

PRESCRIBING THE APPLICATION OF EACH METHOD

Each of the four techniques is applicable to different kinds of problems. The inductive techniques work best for applications where problem-solving knowledge can be represented by explicit rules, but the acquisition of explicit decision rules from human experts is difficult. The technique is applicable when there are many examples that jointly determine which course of action is to be recommended and where an expert is available to verify the problem-solving process. An inductive technique would be a viable alternative to extract a set of rules from examples of problems. Each example should be defined in terms of attributes as well as its class identification; without a class identification, ID3 cannot create a decision tree.

The ANN approach is useful when the number of data points to be analyzed, or the range of values for each data point, is quite large or the reasoning about the data is fuzzy and ill-defined (37). A large set of examples must be available for the system to extract the mapping between input and output. CES is useful when examples are complete with no missing data and the class identifications of examples are consistent.

The ANN approach provides a group of learning algorithms able to fit a broad range of problems. Some algorithms require attributes as well as class identifications, whereas others require only attributes. Therefore, unlike inductive methods, the ANN approach is still applicable to a business problem where each available example does not have its class identification. Additionally, some ANN algorithms accept either continuous or discrete variables. In a business environment, CES is particularly useful in identifying the underlying pattern to be used for forecasting where the available data is so noisy, complex, or highly variable over time that rule-based ES are impractical. An example would be the analysis of financial statements using financial ratios whose values are continuous and difficult to categorize without losing important information.

A CBR technique is applicable to solve problems and make decisions when the knowledge needed to solve the problem is so obscure that formulating domain rules is infeasible, but cases are available. CBR can also be used when rules can be formulated but using them is expensive because the rule base is large or the average rule chain is long. A case-based system is an effective approach when cases with similar solutions have similar problem statements. Problems dealing with classification, evaluation by comparison, explanation of anomalies, dispute mediation, planning, design, and repair are all good candidate applications for ES development using a case-based reasoning technique. In a business environment, CBR can be quite useful in developing ES that assist managers in strategic planning. Extracting the complete decision specifications for strategic planning is very difficult; however, a case-based reasoning approach enables the ES developer to augment the memory of a planner by providing the outcomes of prior cases relevant to a current plan and by supporting the decision-making processes through suggestions based on prior cases.

Finally, the MBR approach can be most useful in diagnosing problems; however, model-based reasoning (MBR) is applicable only for problems that have a complete and accurate model. For example, a complete and accurate model for a human body cannot be built; thus, the MBR technique is not appropriate for developing ES to diagnose human diseases. In addition, if the problem constantly changes over time, it is impossible to construct a stable model for MBR. The use of the MBR technique for device-fault diagnosis has played a central role in broadening the scope of ES applications in engineering domains. However, any problem which is sufficiently well defined to enable the development of a causal model can benefit from this approach.

CONCLUSIONS AND RECOMMENDATIONS TO INFORMATION SYSTEMS MANAGERS

Given the widespread effort to develop ES in industry, the limitations of developing explicit decision-rule ES, the large number of development tools available, and the wide variety of problems being addressed, there is considerable risk that ES developers will use development techniques inappropriate to their task.

Information Systems (IS) managers must accept the need for development tools supporting all four major techniques. These are techniques whose strengths and weaknesses have been observed in practice. Only when experts are easily available and the decisions can be readily articulated is the conventional ES development preferred. The proper matching of development technique to specific applications is likely to produce cost reductions and system effectiveness well beyond the relatively small investment required for obtaining the tools. For a large organization, the cost of experimenting with these tools is insignificant and the potential benefits cannot be ignored. Smaller companies, unable to experiment concurrently with more than one shell, should select application areas most likely to benefit from ES development, and then select an ES shell that properly supports applications.

A number of ES shells are available to facilitate ES development. Depending on the maturity of the technique, the number of supporting commercial off-the-shelf (COTS) tools vary significantly. Inductive learning techniques have been used since the late 1970s and have enjoyed an abundance of supporting shells, whereas MBR techniques are relatively in their infancy and have a single commercially available shell. Table 3 presents a list of COTS tools for ES development.

The inductive method employed by 1st-Class, INDUCPRL, and Xi Plus is ID3; however, the underlying inductive algorithm employed in VP-Expert is not explicitly stated by the vendor. 1st-Class is one of the most popular inductive shells available. It allows users to create a table of examples and it generates rules from the table. INDUCPRL reads an ASCII table of examples and generates rules in the production-rule language for the LEVEL-5 and LEVEL-5 Object. Xi Plus provides a routine named Xi Rule that derives rules from examples. VP-Expert uses a command named INDUCE to construct rules from examples. Other COTS tools include Rule Master and TIMM which are large inductive tools to develop rules from a large number of examples. Small inductive tools, such as Super Expert, and KDS 2 & 3 are also available. All of these inductive tools are very easy to use and easy to learn; an end user, who has neither experience in

TABLE 3   A List of ES Shells That Support Inductive, CES, CBR, or MBR Techniques

ES Techniques and Shells	Platforms	Developers	Cost
Inductive learning			
1st-Class	PCs: OS/2, DOS	AI Corp.	$995
	VAX VMS		$2,500–$45,000
INDUCPRL	PC: DOS	OXKO	$95–$195
KDS 2 & 3	PC: DOS	KDS	$1,495
Rule Master	PCs: DOS, OS/2	Radian Corp.	$495–$2,495
	VAX: Unix, VMS		$7,500–$28,000
Super Expert	PC: DOS	Softsync Inc.	$199
TIMM	PC: DOS	General Research Corp.	$1,900–$19,000
VP-Expert	PC: DOS	Paperback Software	$249
Xi Plus	PC: DOS	Inference Corp.	$995
Xpert Rule	PC: DOS	ATTAR Software	$950–$28,000
Artificial Neural Network			
Neural Works	PC: DOS	Neural Ware, Inc.	$1,895
Professional II Plus	SUN WS		$3,995
NDS (Nestor	PC: DOS	Nestor, Inc.	$25,000
Development System)	SUN WS		$27,000
ExploreNet 3000	PC: DOS	HNC	$1,495
Brain Maker	PC: DOS	California Scientific	$795
Professional		Software	
Case-based Reasoning			
CABARET		U. of Massachusetts at Amherst	
RE: MIND	PC: DOS	Cognitive System	$3,000
	UNIX		$5,000
	Macintosh		$3,000
CBR Express	PC: DOS	Inference Corp.	$10,000
	SUN WS		$12,500–$15,000
Model-based Reasoning			
IDEA	PC: DOS	AI Square	$25,000

ES development nor an in-depth knowledge, can utilize the inductive tools to solve business problems if examples are available.

The CES tools are developed by a large number of software companies; only the four leading products are presented in this article. ExploreNet 300 supports 21 different learning algorithms and runs under Microsoft Windows. The Nestor Development System (NDS) utilizes the Nestor Learning System (NLS)—a patented ANN learning algorithm. Neural Works Professional II Plus and Brain Maker Professional support various learning algorithms and provide interfaces with ASCII files produced by Lotus 1-2-3, dBase III, Excel, and other products. Again, all of these software products require no programming to operate most applications and are easy to learn and to use. However, unlike inductive systems, the development of a CES requires the in-depth understanding of a chosen ANN learning technique, as the results from the system depend on several parameters, and those parameters should be well tuned in order to obtain an optimal solution. Another resource necessary for constructing a CES is a math coprocessor. Its development usually consumes relatively large amounts of CPU time due to the heavy computations. Math coprocessors are strongly recommended to speed up the development process and operation of a large CES.

Compared to the large number of tools available in inductive and ANN approaches, only a few COTS tools are available for implementing CBR techniques. Inference Corporation recently released Case-Based Reasoning Express which facilitates a case-based ES. The software allows a developer to construct knowledge bases by entering case histories. It then searches for prior similar cases and applies those solutions to new problems. Other systems, RE: MIND, developed by Cognitive Systems and CABARET from the University of Massachusetts at Amherst, perform similar functions. They are very sophisticated and their users will need extensive training. Last, MBR development techniques are still at an early stage, with only one supporting COTS shell. Most MBR applications have been developed jointly with universities, and LISP or Prolog have usually been used to implement the systems.

REFERENCES

J. Liebowitz, "Introducing Expert Systems into the Firm," *Expert Systems for Business and Management, J. Liebowitz (ed.), Yourdon Press, Englewood Cliffs, NJ, 1990, pp. 1–12.*

E. Feigenbaum, P. McCorduck, and P. Nii, *The Rise of the Expert Company*, Time Life, Alexandria, VA, 1988.

M. Lu and T. Guimaraes, "Expert Systems Project Selection and Development Strategies," *Systems Devel. Manag.* (December 1988). Reprinted in *J. Inform. Syst. Manag.* (Spring 1989) and *Expert Systems*, (Summer 1989).

M. Polanyi, *Personal Knowledge*, University of Chicago Press, Chicago, 1958

R. Michalski and R. Chilausky, "Knowledge Acquisition by Encoding Expert Rules Versus Computer Induction from Examples: A Case Study Involving Soybean Pathology," *Int. J. Man–Machine Studies, 12,* 63–87 (1980).

M. W. Firebaugh, *Artificial Intelligence: Knowledge-based Approach*, Boyd & Fraser Publishing Co, Boston, MA, 1988.

T. J. M. Bench-Capon, *Knowledge Representation: An Approach to Artificial Intelligence*, Academic Press, London, 1990.

J. Berger, "ROENTGEN: A Case-based Approach to Radiation Therapy Planning," in *Proceeding of the Second Workshop on Case-based Reasoning*, Pensacola Beach, Fl., 1989, pp. 218–222.

F. Daube and B. Hayes-Roth, "A Case-based Mechanical Redesign System," in *Proceedings of the International Joint Conference on Artificial Intelligence*, Detroit, 1989, pp. 1402–1407.

R. Davis, "Diagnostic Reasoning Based on Structure and Behavior," *Artificial Intelligence*, 24(3), 347–410 (1984).

J. de Kleer and B. C. Williams, "Diagnosing Multiple Faults," *Artifical Intelligence*, 32(1), 97–130 (1987).

S. I. Gallent, "Connectionist Expert System," *Commun. ACM, 31*, 152–169 (1988).

M. Goodman, "CBR in Battle Planning," in *Proceeding of the Second Workshop on Case-based Reasoning*, Pensacola Beach, FL, 1989, pp. 264–169.

T. R. Hinrichs, "Strategies for Adaptation and Recovery in a Design Problem Solver," in *Proceeding of the Second Workshop on Case-based Reasoning*, Pensacola Beach, FL, 1989, pp. 115–118.

W. Mark, "Case-based Reasoning for Autoclave Management," in *Proceeding of the Second Workshop on Case-based Reasoning*, Pensacola Beach, FL, 1989, pp. 176–180.

Y. Yoon, R. W. Brobst, P. R. Bergstresser, and L. Peterson, "A Connectionist Expert System for Dermatology Diagnosis," *Expert System, 1*(1), 22–31 (1990).

R. Michalski and J. B. Larson, "Selection of Most Representative Training Examples and incremental Generation of VL1 Hypotheses: The Underlying Methodology and the Description of Programs ESEL and AQ11," Technical Report 867, Computer Science Department, University of Illinois at Urbana-Champaign, 1978.

T. M. Mitchell, "Version Spaces: A Candidate Elimination Approach to Rule Learning," in *Proceedings of the Fifth International Joint Conference on Artificial Intelligence*, 1977, pp. 305–310.

J. R. Quinlan, "Learning Efficient Classification Procedures and Their Application to Chess End Games," in *Machine Learning: An Artificial Intelligence Approach*, R. S. Michaski, J. G. Carbonell, and T. M. Mitchell (eds.), Tioga Publishing Co., Palo Alto, CA, 1983, pp. 463–482.

F. Hayes-Roth and J. McDermott, "An Interference Matching Technique for Inducing Abstractions," *Commun. ACM, 21*(5), 401–410 (1978).

S. A. Vere, "Induction of Concepts in the Predicate Calculus," in *Proceedings of the Fourth International Joint Conference on Artificial Intelligence*, Tbilisi, USSR, 1975, pp. 281–287.

F. Crick and C. Asanuman, "Certain Aspects of the Anatomy and Physiology of the Cerebral Cortex," in *Parallel Distributed Processing: Exploration in the Microstructure of Cognition*, D. E. Rumelhart and J. L. McClelland (eds.), MIT Press, Cambridge, MA, 1986, pp. 333–371.

R. P. Lippmann, "Introduction to Neural Computing," *IEEE ASSP Mag., 4–22 (April 1987)*.

D. G. Bound, P. J. Lloyd, B. Mathew, and G. Waddell, "A Multi-layer Perceptron Network for the Diagnosis of Low Back Pain," in *Proceedings of the IEEE International Conference on Neural Networks*, June 1988, pp. II-481–489.

K. Saito and R. Nakano, "Medical Diagnostic Expert System based on PAP Model," in *Proceedings of the IEEE International Conference on Neural Networks*, June 1988, pp. I225–I262.

D. E. Rumelhart, G. E. Hinton, and R. J. Williams, "Learning Internal Representation by Error Propagation," in *Parallel Distributed Processing: Exploration in the Microstructure of Cognition*, D. E. Rumelhart and J. L. McClelland (eds.), MIT Press, Cambridge, MA, 1986, pp. 312–362.

B. H. Ross, "Remindings in Learning: Objects and Tools," in *Similarity and Analogical Reasoning* S. Vosniadou and A. Ortony (eds.), Cambridge University Press, Cambrdige, 1986, pp. 438–469.

B. H. Ross, "Some Psychological Results on Case-based Reasoning," in *Proceeding of the Second Workshop on Case-based Reasoning*, Pensacola Beach, FL, 1989, pp. 144–147.

J. L. Kolodner and C. Riesbeck, *Tutorial Book on Case-based Reasoning in the Eighth National Conference on Artificial Intelligence*, Boston, 1990.

R. Davis and W. Hamscher, "Model-based Reasoning: Troubleshooting," in *Exploring Artificial Intelligence: Surveying Talks from the National Conferences on Artificial Intelligence*, H. E. Schrobe (ed.), Morgan Kaufman, San Mateo, CA, 1988.

P. T. Jackson, *Introduction to Expert Systems*, Addison-Wesley, Reading, MA, 1990.

T. Kohonen, "An Introduction to Neural Computing," *Neural Networks*, *1*(1), 3–16 (1988).

D. H. Fisher and K. B. McKusick, "An Empirical Comparison of ID3 and Back-Propagation," in *Proceedings of the Eighth National Conference on Artificial Intelligence*, August 1989, pp. 788–793.

W. R. Hutchison and R. S. Kenneth, "Integration of Distributed and Symbolic Knowledge Representation," in *Proceedings of the First International Conference of Neural Networks*, June 1987, pp. II395–II398.

P. Koton, "Integrating Case-based and Causal Reasoning," in *Proceedings of the Tenth Annual Conference of the Cognitive Science Society*, Montreal, 1988, pp. 167–173.

S. L. Fulton and C. O. Pepe, "An Introduction to Model-based Reasoning," *AI Expert*, 48–55 (January 1990).

D. Hillman, "Integrating Neural Nets and Expert Systems," *AI Expert*, 54–59 (June 1990).

YOUNGOHC YOON
TOR GUIMARAES

SEMICONDUCTOR MEMORY TESTING

INTRODUCTION

In recent years, the density of semiconductor memory chips has increased dramatically. With the increasing complexity, it has been recognized that the efficient testing of large memories is very difficult. Small geometries has caused different kinds of faults in the memory circuits, which do not necessarily map into stuck-at faults. From a reliability point of view, it has been demonstrated that the conventional testing based on stuck-at faults does not cover a majority of realistic faults. The increasingly high density of memories has also posed a limitation that all bit locations cannot be exercised in a conventional way. Because the density of memories is quadrupling every 2–3 years, even a linear increase in test time becomes undesirable for large memories. A multimegabit random access memory requires an excessively large amount of time just to test all cell stuck-at faults. To overcome this problem, researchers have sought to develop innovative test generation algorithms and on-chip built-in test methods. Because of the large test time requirements, memory testing problem cannot be solved alone by clever test algorithms. The design for testability and built-in self-test methods become essential. In this article, first test generation algorithms are discussed to obtain a minimal number of test vectors while covering 100% faults under the specified fault model; second, built-in self-test and design for testability methods are given.

MEMORY FAULT MODELS

Many physical defects occur during the manufacturing of memory chips. In manufacturing, a physical defect may occur during numerous physical, chemical, and thermal processes. A defect may occur during the silicon crystal formation, as well as during oxidation, diffusion, photolithography, metalization, and packaging. Some of these defects occur in the area of the active circuit, whereas some occur in the inactive area. Not all defects which occur in the active area affect the operation of the circuit. The defects which do not affect the circuit behavior need to be examined only from the reliability point of view. From a circuit operation point of view, these defects can be assumed irrelevant. The discussion in this article is primarily limited to those defects that manifest themselves into a logical fault and, thus, affect the circuit operation. In recent years, research effort is directed to cover more realistic faults based on the analysis of physical defects (1,2).

ROM Fault Model

Generally, a read-only memory (ROM) fault model consists of line stuck-at faults, bridging faults, and missing or extra memory location faults. In EPROMs and EEPROMs, each memory location can be programmed and reprogrammed and, hence, programmability of a bit location needs to be considered instead of the extra/missing memory location fault. A ROM fault model includes the following faults:

1. Line Stuck-At Faults.   All single and multiple line stuck-at faults are considered under this category. This includes stuck-at fault at the input lines, at the address lines, at the bit lines, and at the output lines. All stuck-at faults in the input and output registers or in the sense amplifier and pull-up logic are also included here.

2. Bridging Faults.   All single and multiple bridging faults among the input lines, among the address and bit lines, and among the output lines are considered here. The bridging faults among the input lines and bit lines or among the bit lines and output lines are also included. The bridging faults among the input lines and the output lines are also possible. However, the possibility of such a fault is small. Unless very high fault coverage is required, these faults are not considered during testing.

3. Decoder Functionality.   In a ROM, a row or column decoder may not access the addressed cell, this fault is denoted as δ^-. Another possibility is that the decoder access a nonaddressed cell (δ^+ fault) or it may access multiple cells. It is also possible that the decoder does not access the specified cell but accesses some other cell; it is denoted as ($\delta^- + \delta^+$).

4. Missing or Extra Bit Faults.   An extra bit location may exist, or a bit location may be missing from an intended location in a ROM. These faults are known as extra and missing bit faults, respectively. In literature, these faults are also known as growth and shrinkage faults.

5. Bit-Pattern Faults.   In mask programmable ROMs, a fault may occur during programming causing a wrong bit pattern to be stored. The main reason for such a fault is an unblown or partially blown fuse at an intended location as well as a blown fuse at an unintended location. This results a "0" instead of a "1" and vice versa. These faults are generally referred as bit-pattern faults. In EPROMs and EEPROMs, a bit location can be programmed and reprogrammed. Because the state of a transistor switch defines whether or not a bit is present, testing for programmability covers all bit-pattern faults.

Multiple faults in a ROM may consist of more than one fault of one category or more than one fault of two or more categories. It should be noted that all the logical faults in a ROM can be categorized as above. It is worth mentioning that in ROMs the line open faults are equivalent to stuck-at-0 faults and transistor stuck-open faults are equivalent to missing bit faults. Hence, any open fault need not to be considered separately. In addition to these faults, a ROM also has parametric and/or timing faults.

RAM Fault Models

A widely used fault model for random access memory (RAM) devices is the fault model given by Nair, Thatte, and Abraham (3). In this model, a circuit is divided into three blocks, i.e., memory cell array, decoder circuit, and the sense amplifier or the read/write circuit.

In the decoder circuit, a decoder may not access the addressed cell, it may access a nonaddressed cell, it may access multiple cells, a particular address does not access any cell, or a cell is accessed by multiple addresses. The read/write circuit may have stuck-at-1/0 faults, which appear as memory stuck-at faults.

In the RAM array, a cell may have a stuck-at-1/0 fault or a cell may have a coupling fault with any other cell. In the recent years, the cell coupling faults are categorized as (a) inversion, (b) indempotent coupling, and (c) state coupling (4).

An inversion coupling fault implies that the data at location i will invert the data at location j. An indempotent coupling fault means that the data at location i will cause a fixed logic value at cell j. The state coupling fault implies that only specific data at location i will affect the data at location j.

Actual fault mechanisms based on physical defects in RAMs have been investigated in Ref. 5. It was found that all the faults in a RAM could be covered by the fault model given by Nair et al. with the addition of state transition faults and data retention faults. The state transition fault is recognized if a cell fails to undergo transition from 1 to 0 or 0 to 1, whereas the data retention fault implies that the content of a cell is lost with respect to time.

A more general fault model for RAMs would, thus, include the following (6):

1. Memory cell stuck-at-1/0 faults
2. Memory cell state transition 1-to-0 and 0-to-1 faults
3. Memory cell bridging faults with other cells (state coupling)
4. Stuck-at, multiple access, or wrong addressing faults in the decoder
5. Data retention faults

For RAMs, one more fault model has also been widely used, which is known as a pattern sensitive fault (PSF) model (7,8). According to this model, in the presence of some specific data in a part of memory (location i), the data in some other part (location j) may be affected. This affect may appear as a cell stuck-at-fault or a cell state transition fault for a small duration or as long as location i contains the specific data. For an n-bit memory, i and j may vary from 1 to n, where n is the number of bits, whereas $i \neq j$; thus, it is considered as a *global PSF*.

The global PSF model requires that an n-bit memory should be tested as an n-state finite state machine. Obviously, such testing is not feasible in practice when n is large. To overcome this difficulty, a simplified model is used, which is known as neighborhood cell pattern sensitive fault model. In this simplified model, data only in the neighborhood cell may affect the state of a cell. If the neighborhood pattern sensitive fault (NPSF) is based on a physical neighbor; it is referred as *physical neighborhood PSF*; if it is based on a logical neighbor according to the cell address, it is referred as *logical neighborhood PSF*.

Neighborhood cell pattern sensitivity can be considered with respect to all eight neighborhood cells (sometimes also referred as 9-cell PSF) or only with respect to four neighborhood cells (sometimes referred as 5-cell PSF). Schematically, these possibilities are shown in Figure 1. Some researchers have also considered the complete row and column of the base cell as the neighborhood. The reasoning behind the row/column neighborhood is that all the cells in one row share the same word line and the cells in one column share the same bit line.

It is worth noting that pattern sensitivity faults may be unidirectional, only such as if cell i is affected by the data in cell j, that does not mean that cell j will be affected by the data in cell i. The NPSF model has been further extended into *static* and *dynamic* NPSF. In the static NPSF model, a cell is affected by the presence of some specific data

n	n	n
n	B	n
n	n	n

(a) 8-cell neighborhood

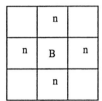
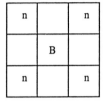

(b) 4-cell neighborhood

FIGURE 1   Illustration of PSF model.

in the neighborhood cell(s), whereas in the dynamic NPSF model a cell is affected by a change in content in the neighborhood cell(s).

The PSF is not a transient or intermittent fault. The cause of a pattern sensitive fault has been reported as a special case of state coupling and noise in the data bus. Although, it has been neglected in the literature, the testing for PSF is only sensible if the internal topological address mechanism is known and taken into account while generating the test patterns (9). The address scrambling, which is the relation between logical and topological addresses, is extremely important for the PSF model. Unfortunately, all test algorithms available for PSF fault neglected to include address scrambling. In many cases this information is not available.

In general, a RAM may also have a small number of faults that can only be modeled as transistor stuck-ON/stuck-open faults. Apart from these faults, a memory may also have parametric and timing or delay faults. It should be noted that the data retention faults are a subset of timing faults. The timing faults also include data access time, which is a very important parameter for memories.

TESTING OBJECTIVES AND METHODS

In recent years, the memory manufacturing process has matured to the extent that less than 1% of memories show early failure. The replacement cost of a defective or failed memory increases by about a factor of 10 at each integration level. A field or service call can easily cost a few thousand dollars. To check whether the purchased memories are fault-free, a continuity, DC and AC parametric tests are performed at the incoming inspection level. The objective of such testing is to detect all relevant faults and, thus, reduce the number of defective boards. Such testing also provides a protection against a

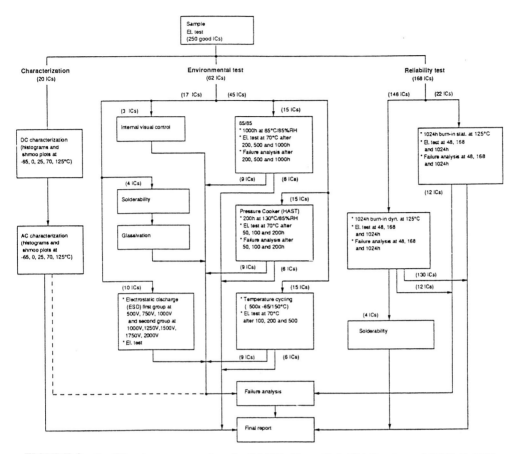

FIGURE 2   Qualification test procedure for RAMS. (From Ref. 10.) Courtesy of IEEE © 1989.

reduced incoming quality level. It should also be noted that such a test is performed by sampling and cannot guard against all possible faults in a shipment. For a development engineer, this testing is of limited use. Generally, a qualification test is needed that consists of a functional test, electrical static and dynamic characteristics, and a timing parametric test. Figures 2 and 3 give the detailed qualification test procedures for RAM and ROM, respectively (10). The data collected from these tests are entered into a database to perform various statistical operations. These operations include histograms, shmoo plots, line plots and scatterplots, and report files. These plots and report files help to determine faults and parametric drift. The prime objective is to reduce the overall cost while providing reliability. From this viewpoint, the test economy is extremely important, and, hence, test patterns should be chosen to reduce the overall cost. For example, the functional errors can be detected by a low-sensitive pattern, high-sensitive patterns can be used to detect dynamic parametric errors.

Static DC Electrical Characteristics and Testing

The DC testing ensures that the purchased memory meets the DC specifications given in the data sheet. The test consists of a continuity test to check that each pin is connected

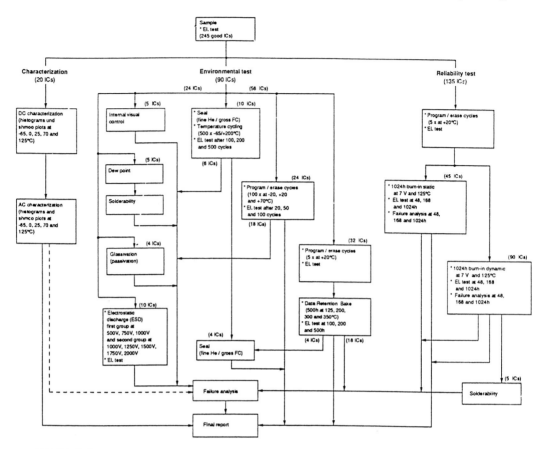

FIGURE 3   Qualification test procedure for EPROMs. (From Ref. 10.) Courtesy of IEEE © 1989.

properly. To perform a continuity test, a prescribed current (generally 100 μA) is forced into one pin while all other pins are grounded. The resulting voltage is measured. (The fault-free value is generally 0.1–1.5 V in a 5-V process.)

The second electrical test during incoming inspection is the verification of DC parameters. It is performed without restrictions according to the manufacturer's specifications. For this test, a precision measurement unit (PMU) is used to force a current, and high- and low-level voltages (VOH and VOL) are measured. Based on specifications, this test can be performed at different supply voltages and temperatures.

Besides the incoming inspection, electrical testing is also performed during the qualification test. It consists of characterization tests, environmental tests, and reliability tests. The characterization test investigates the parametric electrical performance and consists of different patterns. The detailed discussion on different patterns and test algorithms is given in the section Testing algorithms. Environmental tests examine the memory behavior during normal and stressed environments, whereas reliability tests determine the failure rate and wear-out.

Electrical AC Characteristics and Testing

Electrical AC testing ensures that a device meets the timing specifications given in the data sheet. One timing parameter is usually varied with respect to another by a search

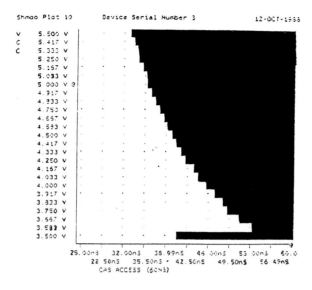

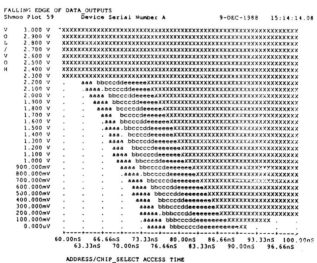

FIGURE 4   Composite shmoo plot of access time versus temperature (*a* for −65, *b* for 0, *c* for 25, *d* for 70, and *e* for 125°C), for fall time, 20 devices. (From Ref. 10.) Courtesy of IEEE © 1989.

routine, and the pass/fail threshold is measured. This information is generally provided by a shmoo plot. A sample shmoo plot for a 256K DRAM is given in Figure 4. All memories, in principle, should be exposed at several different patterns to detect any timing errors.

TESTING ALGORITHMS

Several innovative test algorithms for random access memories have been developed. These algorithms can be categorized into two classes. In one set of algorithms, whole memory is read after changing the value of one (or more) cell. In the second class of test algorithms, only that cell is read whose value is changed. In literature, test algorithms have also been classified according to the fault model, i.e., algorithms based on the memory cell stuck-at and state-transition fault model and algorithms based on the pattern sensitive fault model (11–13).

Memory Scan

Memory scan (called Mscan) is the simplest test. In this test, first "0" is written to each cell, the value is verified, and then a "1" is written and verified. For an n-bits memory, the whole procedure can be expressed as follows:

for i = 1 to n
write '0' to cell i
read cell i
write '1' to cell i
read cell i

This test procedure is very fast, but unfortunately its fault coverage is very poor. Except for the cell stuck-at fault, Mscan does not cover any other fault.

Algorithm GALPAT

This algorithm is also known as the Galloping 1 or Ping-Pong test. This algorithm first initializes all memory cells to "0." Then, for each cell, it writes "1," reads all the cells, and then writes back "0" to that cell. The procedure looks like that a "1" is shifting its position from cell to cell throughout the whole memory. The algorithm is given in Figure 5. It should be noted that a complementary pattern can also be used, i.e., instead of a "1," a "0" may be shifted through the memory.

In this algorithm each cell is read at least once, when it has a value "0" as well as when it has a value "1." Thus, all cell stuck-at-1/0 faults are detected. The switching of state 0-to-1 and 1-to-0, also detects state transition faults. As only one cell contains "1" at any time, and all cells are read, all address decoder faults are detected. Any two arbitrary cells under state 00, 10, and 01 are read; this covers a majority of state coupling faults. However, all state coupling faults are not covered. Because at any given time, only one cell contains a "1" and all other cells have "0," 50% of pattern sensitive faults are detected. By executing this algorithm twice, once with a "0" background and then with a "1" background, a majority of pattern sensitive faults can be covered. It should also be

```
/* Total address space is n bits
   For i = 0 to (n-1); Do
      write '0' in cell (i)
   End
   While i = 0 to (n-1); Do
      write '1' in cell (i)
      read all cells
      write '0' in cell (i)
   Continue
   End
```

FIGURE 5   GALPAT algorithm to test random access memories.

```
/* Total address space is n bits
While i = odd; j = even; Do
    write '0' in cell (i); write '1' in cell (j)
    read all cells
    complement all cells
    read all cells
Continue
End
```

FIGURE 6   Checker pattern test to detect RAM faults.

noted that to execute once, this algorithm requires $4n^2$ read/write operations, where n is the number of bits.

Checker Pattern Test

Checker pattern test writes a pattern of ''1'' and ''0'' in the alternative cells. After a pause, the whole memory is read. Then, all cells are complemented. Again, after a pause, the whole memory is read. The algorithm is given in Figure 6.

This algorithm detects all cell stuck-at-1/0 faults, data retention faults, and 50% of the state transition faults. The address decoder faults and all state coupling faults are not covered. The algorithm requires only $4n$ read/write operations. This is a fast algorithm; however, fault coverage is not extensive.

In a modified version, instead of two cycles of write/read operations, three cycles are performed. The obvious advantage of this version is the 100% coverage of state transition faults. It should also be noted that in this version each cell stores a ''0'' during the first cycle, a ''1'' during the second cycle, and a ''0'' during the third cycle, whereas all neighborhood cells have ''1,'' ''0,'' and ''1,'' respectively. This in-effect implicitly covers 4-cell neighborhood pattern sensitive faults.

Galloping Diagonal/Row/Column Test

This algorithm is based on the principle of GALPAT and is sometimes also called the Galloping Diagonal. In this algorithm, instead of shifting a ''1'' cell-by-cell through the memory, a complete diagonal of 1 is shifted. The whole memory is read after each shift.

The fault coverage of this algorithm is similar to GALPAT, except for some state coupling faults. However, it is faster than GALPAT and requires $4n^{3/2}$ read/write operations. The variations of this algorithm are Galloping row and Galloping column. In Galloping row, all the cells in a row contain ''1,'' and this row is shifted through the memory. In Galloping column (also known as GALCOL), all the cells in a column contain ''1,'' and this column is shifted through the memory.

In another variation, the whole memory is not read after each shift, but only those cells are read which are supposed to contain ''1.'' This procedure is called Shifting Diagonal/Row/Column. This reduces the number of read/write operations to $4n$. However, state coupling faults and 50% of the state transition faults are not covered. The procedure for shifting a row when the whole memory is not read is illustrated in Figure 7.

It should be noted that if the algorithm given in Figure 7 is executed twice, once with a ''0'' background and then when the background is ''1,'' the majority of state transition faults and majority of state coupling faults will be covered. The number of read/write operations will increase to $8n$, which is still practical.

```
/* Total address space is n bits arranged in k rows
For i = 0 to (n-1); Do
    write '0' in cell (i)
End
While i = 1 to k; Do
    write '1' in all cells belong to row
    read all cells belong to row
    write '0' in all cells belong to row
Continue
End
```

FIGURE 7   Shifting row algorithm to test RAMs.

Marching 1/0 Test Algorithm

The marching 1/0 algorithm is extensively used. In this test, a sequence of operations are performed on one cell before proceeding to the next cell. This sequence of operations is called the *march element*. A march element may constitute a simple sequence of Mscan, such as write "0," read (0), write "1," and read (1); or it may constitute a more complex sequence having many write/read operations. The simplest march test (also known as MATS) is given in Figure 8. It requires $5n$ read/write operations and detects all addressing faults, all cell stuck-at faults, and state transition faults.

A number of modifications to MATS have been reported by using different sequence of operations. In one variation, first the whole memory is initialized to either "0," or "1." Then, one cell is read, complemented, and read again. The procedure continues from first cell to the last cell. When all cells are completed, the whole memory is read. The algorithm is given in Figure 9. This version requires $6n$ read/write operations. A further modification of this version (requiring $7n$ operations) is shown in Figure 10 (it will be referred as $7n$-March). The algorithm of Figure 10 exploits parallelism in read/write operations. This algorithm covers all cell stuck-at-1/0 faults, 1-to-0 and 0-to-1 state transition faults, a majority of bridging faults between two cell (state coupling), data retention faults, and decoder faults (14).

In Figure 10, first the whole memory is initialized to "0" and the cell value is read. This detects any cell stuck-at-1 fault and also checks state 00 for any two arbitrary cells. During cycle one, two loops are initiated simultaneously, one addresses from the first cell

```
/* Total address space is n bits
For i = 0 to (n-1) Do
    write '0' in cell (i)
Continue
For i = 0 to (n-1) Do
    read cell (i)
    write '1' in cell (i)
Continue
For i = (n-1) to 0 Do
    read cell (i)
    write '0' in cell (i)
Continue
End
```

FIGURE 8   Algorithm MATS to test RAMs.

```
/* Total address space is n bits
For i = 0 to (n-1) Do
    write '0' in cell (i)
Continue
For i = 0 to (n-1) Do
    read cell (i)
    write '1' in cell (i)
    read cell (i)
    write '0' in cell (i)
    read cell (i)
Continue
End
```

FIGURE 9   A $6n$ version of the march test to test RAMs.

to the $(n/2)$th cell and other addresses from the last cell to the $(n/2 + 1)$th cell. During this cycle, read output is "1." Hence, any cell stuck-at-0 and transition 0-to-1 faults are detected. During the second cycle, again the read, output is "1." This cycle checks state 11 for any two arbitrary cells. Cycle three is similar to cycle one. Two loops are initiated simultaneously, one from the $(n/2 + 1)$th cell to the last cell and other from the $(n/2)$th cell to the first cell. In this cycle, the read output is "0," thus, transition 1-to-0 faults are detected. State 01 and 10 for two cells are tested during cycles one and three. Therefore, any bridging or state coupling faults between two cells are detected. Wait states are used in between initialization and the first cycle and between the first cycle and the second

```
/* Total address space is n bits
For i = 0 to (n-1); Do
    write '0' in cell (i)
    read cell (i)
End
/* Wait state detects retention of '0'. Typical time 100 msec.
PAUSE
    While i = 0 to (n/2 - 1); j = (n-1) to (n/2); Do
        write '1' in cell (i)
        read cell (i)
        write '1' in cell (j)
        read cell (j)
    Continue
/* Wait state detects retention of '1'. Typical time 100 msec.
PAUSE
    For i = 0 to (n-1); Do
        read cell (i)
    End
    While i = (n/2 - 1) to 0; j = (n/2) to (n-1); Do
        write '0' in cell (i)
        read cell (i)
        write '0' in cell (j)
        read cell (j)
    Continue
End
```

FIGURE 10   Modified marching 1/0 test. This algorithm has $7n$ read/write operations.

Address	Initialization	March Element 1	March Element 2	March Element 3	March Element 4	Wait	March Element 5	Wait	March Element 6
0	Wr(0)	Rd(0),Wr(1)	Rd(1),Wr(0)	Rd(0),Wr(1)	Rd(1),Wr(0)		Rd(0),Wr(1) Rd(0),Wr(1) Rd(0),Wr(1)		Rd(1) Rd(1) Rd(1)
1	Wr(0)	Rd(0),Wr(1)	Rd(1),Wr(0)	/	/	Disable RAM		Disable RAM	
2	Wr(0)	Rd(0),Wr(1)	Rd(1),Wr(0)	Rd(0),Wr(1) Rd(0),Wr(1)	Rd(1),Wr(0) Rd(1),Wr(0)				
⋮	\	\	\	Rd(0),Wr(1)	Rd(1),Wr(0)		\		\
N−1	Wr(0)	Rd(0),Wr(1)	Rd(1),Wr(0)	Rd(0),Wr(1)	Rd(1),Wr(0)		Rd(0),Wr(1)		Rd(1)

9n Test Algorithm   Data Retention Test

FIGURE 11   The 9*n* test algorithm for SRAMs with combinational read/write logic. A data retention test is added. Courtesy of IEEE © 1990.

cycle. These wait states detect data retention faults. It should be noted that similar wait states can also be used in other algorithms to detect data retention faults.

Dekker et al. (5,15) have presented 9*n* and 11*n* complexity algorithms based on March test. The 9*n* complexity algorithm is given in Figure 11 (5) in which an additional data retention test is added. In certain situations, the wait states are inserted between march elements 1 and 2, and between march elements 2 and 3. This algorithm covers all stuck-at, all multiple access, and all state coupling faults in neighborhood cells. To show the coverage of state coupling faults in a neighborhood cell, two arbitrary neighbor cells can be picked as cell 1 and cell 2. As shown in Figure 12, these cells go through all four possible binary states when this algorithm is executed (15).

This algorithm has been further extended to the memory, which has read/write logic with a data latch. In this situation, in the presence of a stuck-open fault, read/write logic is not transparent for all faults, e.g., read/write logic will not pass all memory faults to the output pins. This problem is solved by an extra read operation with every march element, such that the expected read value is alternating "1" and "0" (5). This ensures

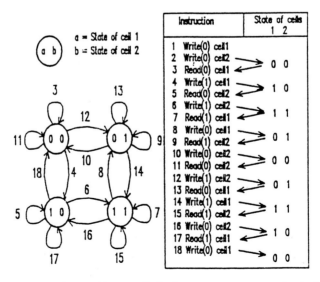

FIGURE 12   All states of two arbitrary cells in the memory array are checked with the 9*n* test algorithm. (From Ref. 15.) Courtesy of IEEE © 1988.

Address	Initialization	March Element 1	March Element 2	March Element 3	March Element 4	Wait	March Element 5	Wait	March Element 6
0	Wr(0)	Rd(0),Wr(1),Rd(1)	Rd(1),Wr(0),Rd(0)	Rd(0),Wr(1),Rd(1)	Rd(1),Wr(0),Rd(0)		Rd(0),Wr(1) Rd(0),Wr(1)		Rd(1)
1	Wr(0)	Rd(0),Wr(1),Rd(1)	Rd(1),Wr(0),Rd(0)	↗	↗	Disable RAM	Rd(0),Wr(1)	Disable RAM	Rd(1)
2	Wr(0)	Rd(0),Wr(1),Rd(1)	Rd(1),Wr(0),Rd(0)	Rd(0),Wr(1),Rd(1)	Rd(1),Wr(0),Rd(0)				Rd(1)
⋮				Rd(0),Wr(1),Rd(1)	Rd(1),Wr(0),Rd(0)		↘		↘
N–1	Wr(0)	Rd(0),Wr(1),Rd(1)	Rd(1),Wr(0),Rd(0)	Rd(0),Wr(1),Rd(1)	Rd(1),Wr(0),Rd(0)		Rd(0),Wr(1)		Rd(1)

13n Test Algorithm   Data Retention Test

FIGURE 13   The resulting $13n$ test algorithm for SRAMs with sequential read/write logic. A data retention test is added. (From Ref. 5.) Courtesy of IEEE © 1990.

that the expected read value is always different than the last read value. The algorithm is given in Figure 13. Again, in Figure 13, an additional data retention test is included.

The other variation of the march test is given in Figure 14 (4). The most general algorithm is March-G, Eq. (7) in Figure 14. It consists of seven march elements as shown in Figure 14. Two versions of March-G are shown in Figure 14, Eqs. (7) and (8). The total complexity in both version is $23n$ read/write operations. The two extra read operations in M_1 of Eq. (7) are distributed over M_2 and M_4 of Eq. (8) to make the test more symmetric. It has been reported that March-G covers all addressing faults, transitions faults, and coupling faults.

Testing Based on the PSF Model

A number of test algorithms have been proposed based on a concept called tiling of memory array. In this concept, the base cell is considered to be surrounded by four or eight characters (depending on 5-cell and 9-cell neighborhoods). A sample tiling with four characters is shown in Figure 15 (16). With first tiling arrangement keep the base cell at logic "0," all four tuples of tiling characters (16 patterns) are applied. The base cell is read after each pattern. The same procedure is repeated with the second tiling arrangement.

Recently, it has been observed that the PSF based test algorithms do not cover physical defects (9). The algorithms based on coupling faults are found best suited to cover physical defects. It has been shown that the march test given in either Eq. (7) or Eq. (8) in Figure 14, March-G, is sufficient to cover all coupling faults. While considering the physical and logical neighborhood and exploiting the parallelism in read/write operations, a $10n$ and a $12n$ algorithm have been developed for physical neighborhood coupling and logical neighborhood coupling faults, respectively. These algorithms are given in Figures 16 and 17, respectively.

Comparison and Modification for Word Oriented Memories

A study on the effectiveness of various algorithms to cover various faults was reported in Ref. 9. It was noted that some of the extensive test algorithms such as shifted diagonal, galloping column provide poor fault coverage and, hence, do not justify their lengthy test times. Further, the algorithms that detect coupling faults such as the march test provide excellent fault coverage. However, the extensive sequences in the march test do not provide significant improvement and, hence, are not justified. It was also noted that the decoder and read/write malfunction are translated to equivalent faults as has been assumed

x denotes that a cell or line is in logical state x; $x \in \{0,1\}$

L denotes that the faulty value is the value of the last read operation

$\uparrow$ denotes a write 1 'w1' operation to a cell containing a 0

$\downarrow$ denotes a 'w0' operation to a cell containing a 1

$\updownarrow$ denotes a 'w$\bar{x}$' operation to a cell containing an x

$\forall$ denotes any operation

$<....>$ denotes a particular fault

$<S/F>$ denotes a fault in a single cell

S describes the value/operation sensitizing the fault; $S \in \{0,1,\uparrow,\downarrow,\updownarrow\}$

S_T says that the sensitization effect appears after a time T

F describes the faulty value of the cell; $F \in \{0, 1\}$

$<S_1,S_2, ... ,S_{m-1};F>$ denotes a fault involving m cells. $S_1,S_2, ...$, S_{m-1} describes the conditions of the $m-1$ cells required to sensitize the fault in cell m (the faulty value is denoted by F); $S_i \in \{0,1,\uparrow,\downarrow,\updownarrow\}$ for $1 \le i \le m-1$.

(1) MATS+ algorithm; (2) March C– algorithm; (3) March B algorithm; (4) March test extended to detect DRFs; (5) March test extended to detect DRFs which behave as SOFs; (6) March C–test with inserted 'Del' elements; (7) March G algorithm; (8) Symmetric March G algorithm

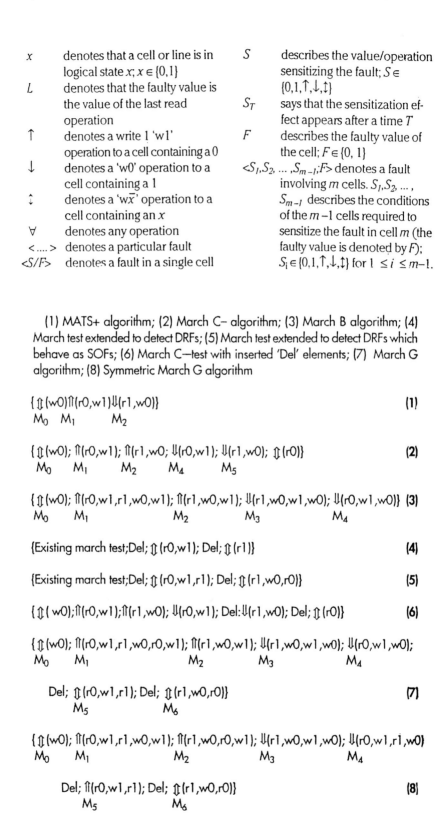

$\{\Updownarrow(w0)\Uparrow(r0,w1)\Downarrow(r1,w0)\}$ (1)
   M_0 M_1 M_2

$\{\Updownarrow(w0); \Uparrow(r0,w1); \Uparrow(r1,w0; \Downarrow(r0,w1); \Downarrow(r1,w0); \Updownarrow(r0)\}$ (2)
  M_0 M_1 M_2 M_4 M_5

$\{\Updownarrow(w0); \Uparrow(r0,w1,r1,w0,w1); \Uparrow(r1,w0,w1); \Downarrow(r1,w0,w1,w0); \Downarrow(r0,w1,w0)\}$ (3)
  M_0 M_1 M_2 M_3 M_4

$\{$Existing march test;Del; $\Updownarrow(r0,w1)$; Del; $\Updownarrow(r1)\}$ (4)

$\{$Existing march test;Del; $\Updownarrow(r0,w1,r1)$; Del; $\Updownarrow(r1,w0,r0)\}$ (5)

$\{\Updownarrow(w0);\Uparrow(r0,w1);\Uparrow(r1,w0); \Downarrow(r0,w1);$ Del:$\Downarrow(r1,w0)$; Del; $\Updownarrow(r0)\}$ (6)

$\{\Updownarrow(w0); \Uparrow(r0,w1,r1,w0,r0,w1); \Uparrow(r1,w0,w1); \Downarrow(r1,w0,w1,w0); \Downarrow(r0,w1,w0);$
  M_0 M_1 M_2 M_3 M_4

   Del; $\Updownarrow(r0,w1,r1)$; Del; $\Updownarrow(r1,w0,r0)\}$ (7)
    M_5 M_6

$\{\Updownarrow(w0); \Uparrow(r0,w1,r1,w0,w1); \Uparrow(r1,w0,r0,w1); \Downarrow(r1,w0,w1,w0); \Downarrow(r0,w1,r1,w0)\}$
  M_0 M_1 M_2 M_3 M_4

   Del; $\Uparrow(r0,w1,r1)$; Del; $\Updownarrow(r1,w0,r0)\}$ (8)
    M_5 M_6

FIGURE 14   Variations in the march test algorithm.(From Ref. 4.) Courtesy of IEEE © 1993.

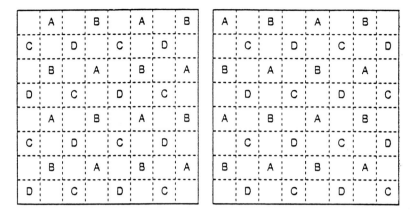

FIGURE 15 Illustration of the tiling concept from Ref. 16. Two possible arrangements are shown. (Courtesy of IEEE © 1990.)

in Ref. 3. A very interesting observation was made regarding the pattern sensitive fault model. It was noted that the algorithms based on the PSF model (surround disturb and API test) provide extremely poor fault coverage. The conclusion was drawn that the PSF model is not a good fault model, as it does not capture the realistic faults. On the other hand, coupling fault model was found the most effective for capturing the realistic faults. The results of this study are summarized in Figure 18 (9).

It should be noted that none of the algorithms given is restricted to a particular architecture. In addition, all algorithms are applicable to memory chips as well as memory boards. However, different algorithms are limited to different kinds of faults. A comparison among various algorithms is given in Table 1.

```
/* Test Start, cycle one
        write '0' in all cell      ; initialization in zero state

        For i = 1 to n Do
            write '1' in cell (i)
            read cell (i)
            write '0' in cell (i)
            read cell (i)
        continue

/* Cycle Two
        write '1' in all cell      ; initialization in one state

        For i = 1 to n Do
            write '0' in cell (i)
            read cell (i)
            write '1' in cell (i)
            read cell (i)
        continue
```

FIGURE 16 A 10n algorithm to detect neighborhood cell pattern sensitive faults based on physical neighborhood.

```
/* Test Start, cycle one
   write '0' in all cell        ; initialization in zero state

   For i = 1 to n Do
       write '1' in cell (i)
           If i=1, read cell (i) Then read cell (i+1)
           Else {for i > 1}  read cell (i-1)
                             read cell (i)
                             read cell (i+1)
       write '0' in cell (i)
       read cell (i)
   continue

/* Cycle Two
   write '1' in all cell        ; initialization in one state

   For i = 1 to n Do
       write '0' in cell (i)
           If i=1, read cell (i) Then read cell (i+1)
           Else {for i > 1}  read cell (i-1)
                             read cell (i)
                             read cell (i+1)
       write '1' in cell (i)
       read cell (i)
   continue
```

FIGURE 17   A $12n$ algorithm to detect neighborhood cell pattern sensitive faults based on logical neighborhood.

All the algorithms, in the form given above, are applicable to bit-oriented memory. However, these can be modified to m-bit-wide word-oriented memory. By using K different data background, where $K = \log_2 m$, any algorithm can be used for word-oriented memory. For example, for byte-oriented memory, we need three different data backgrounds, i.e.,

First data background   10101010
Second data background   11001100
Third data background   11110000

It should also be noted that a bit-oriented memory can also be designed such that it appears as byte oriented during the test mode. Thus, using different data backgrounds, total test time can be reduced by a factor of 8/3. In general, if a bit-oriented memory is tested as m-bit-wide word oriented memory, test time is reduced by a factor of $m/\log_2 m$, which is a significant savings.

As the memory size increases to multimegabits, the test time becomes extremely large. Even an $O(n)$ algorithm requires an excessive amount of time to be practically feasible. Assuming that a tester is running at 10 MHz, a 16-Mbit memory will require about 11.2 s if we use the $7n$ algorithm, but about 3.25 years if we use GALPAT. The estimated test time for various algorithms are given in Table 2.

From Table 2, it is clear that only linear time complexity algorithms can be used in production testing of large commercial memories. The algorithms with higher complexity

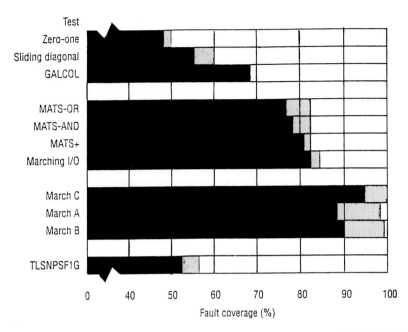

FIGURE 18   Fault coverage of some tests.(From Ref. 4.) Courtesy of IEEE © 1993.

TABLE 1   Comparison of Various Test Algorithms

Test method	Complexity	Stuck-at	State transition	Decoder	State coupling
GALPAT	$4n^2$	Yes	Yes	Yes	Yes
Checker pattern	$4n$	Yes	Yes	No	No
Galloping diagonal	$4n^{3/2}$	Yes	Yes	Yes	Yes
MATS	$5n$	Yes	Yes	Yes	No
7n-March	$7n$	Yes	Yes	Yes	Yes
March-G	$23n$	Yes	Yes	Yes	Yes

TABLE 2   Estimated Test Time for Different Sizes of Memories Using Various Algorithms

Test method	Complexity	1 Mbits	16 Mbits	64 Mbits
GALPAT	$4n^2$	111 h	1185 days	52 years
Checker pattern	$4n$	0.4 s	6.4 s	25.6 s
Galloping diagonal	$4n^{3/2}$	400 s	7.1 h	56.9 h
MATS	$6n$	0.5 s	8.0 s	25.6 s
7n-March	$7n$	0.7 s	11.2 s	44.8 s
March-G	$23n$	2.3 s	36.8 s	147.2 s

can be used only for small memories. For large memories, the test time with these algorithms become excessively large to be practical. To reduce the test time, testable designs and built-in self-test methods have been developed.

TESTABLE DESIGNS OF MASK PROGRAMMABLE ROMs

Due to difficulties in testing mask programmable ROMs with standard techniques, testable designs have been developed (17–23). These designs allow independent control of product lines, and input lines to check for corresponding bit faults. The original scheme as given in Refs. 18 and 19 provides a test independent of the function for all single bit faults and all single stuck-at faults. This scheme is modified by reducing additional hardware (17). However, the modified schemes have either increased the number of test patterns or made the test phase function dependent (17,20). The total test time, which depends on the number of test patterns, the delay per test, and the computational complexity, is same in all the schemes.

Testing with Parity Trees

The majority of easily testable designs use parity trees at the product lines and at the output lines to detect a fault. In this article, we will explain these designs with PLAs. The testable design can be obtained by adding extra hardware as follows:

1. Pass transistors at the inputs lines. A signal c_1 controls all pass transistors associated with the true inputs, whereas another signal, c_2, controls all the pass transistors associated with the complementary inputs. During normal operation $c_1 = c_2 = 1$, keep the pass transistors ON. During the test mode $c_1 = c_2$. This allows the activation of either the true inputs or the complementary inputs during testing.
2. An extra column of transistors in the AND plane of PLA. With this extra column if the number of columns is even, in each row in the AND plane, odd number of absence of crosspoints are made. Thus, in the absence of a fault, each input line will activate an odd number of product lines. If the number of columns is odd, then the number of absence of crosspoints on each row is made even. In this case, in the absence of a fault, even number of product lines are active.
3. An XOR tree at the product lines to check parity. The output of this tree is referred to AND parity.
4. An extra row in the OR plane of PLA. With this extra row if the number of rows in the OR plane is odd, in each column even number of absence of crosspoints are made. Thus, in the absence of a fault, even number of output lines are active. If the number of rows is even, odd number of absence of crosspoints are made on each column in the OR plane.
5. An XOR tree at the output lines to check parity. This is referred to OR parity.
6. A shift register connected to the product lines in the OR plane. This register is used to apply the test patterns to the OR plane.

The augmented design is given in Figure 19. In figure 19, XOR gates are shown in the cascade form. Alternatively, an XOR tree may be used. For this testable design a universal test set can be obtained which is independent of the bit pattern.

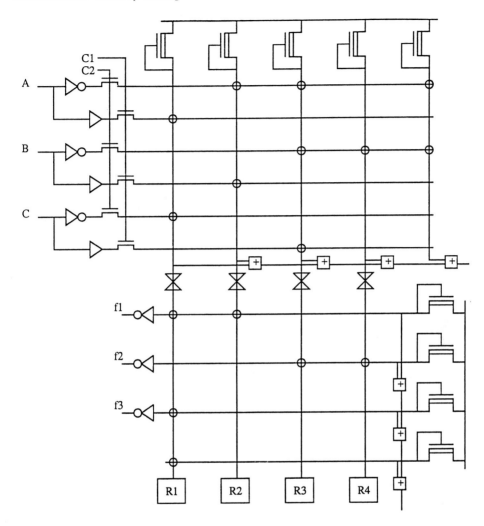

FIGURE 19 Augmented PLA with parity circuits for easy testing.

Universal Test Set

The test set for augmented design is divided into two parts. One set of vectors tests the AND plane and the second set tests the OR plane. To test the AND plane, first the true inputs are activated by making $c1 = 1$ and $c2 = 0$. One initialization vector is also required, which is the all '1' vector with $c1 = c2 = 1$. This vector ensures the absence of charge in the stray capacitances associated with the input lines. Test vectors follow this initialization vector. If the jth input is denoted by I_j, then the tests are given by the n-tuple: $T = \{T_1, T_2, \ldots T_i, \ldots T_n\}$ where n is the number of test vectors. The ith test vector T_i $(i = 1, \ldots n)$ is given by:

$$T_i = [I_1 \ldots I_j \ldots I_n];$$

where

$$I_j = 1 \text{ if } i = j;$$
$$= 0 \quad \text{if } i \neq j.$$

Each test vector basically sets one input to "1" and all other inputs to "0." As the number of absences of cross points is odd (even) on each input line, this, in effect, activates an odd (even) number of product lines in the AND plane. Thus, in the absence of a fault, AND parity is odd (even).

Similarly, the complementary inputs are activated, keeping the true inputs in the high-impedance state. In this case, initialization vector is $c1 = c2 = 1$, and all the inputs are "0's." The tests for the complementary inputs are given by

$$c1 = 0, \quad c2 = 1, \quad \text{and} \quad T = \{T_1, T_2, \ldots, T_i, \ldots, T_n\}.$$

The ith test vector is given by

$$T_i = [I_1, \ldots, I_j, \ldots, I_n],$$

where

$$I_j = 0 \quad \text{if } i = j,$$
$$ = 1 \quad \text{if } i \neq j.$$

The test set for the OR plane is found in a similar fashion. If the ith product line in the OR plane is denoted by R_i, then the test vectors for the OR plane are given by the p-tuple. $T = \{T_1, \ldots, T_j, \ldots, T_p\}$, where p is the number of product lines. The ith vector T_i ($i = 1, \ldots, p$) is given by

$$T_i = [R_1, \ldots, R_j, \ldots, R_p],$$

where

$$R_j = 1 \quad \text{if } i = j$$
$$ = 0 \quad \text{if } i \neq j.$$

Each such vector sets one product line to "1" and all the other product lines to "0" in the OR plane. This, in effect, activates an odd (even) number of output lines. Thus, in the absence of a fault, OR parity is odd (even).

The complete test set for the PLA given in Figure 19 is shown in Tables 3 and 4. This test set not only detects all single line stuck-at, bridging, and crosspoint faults, but it also detects majority of multiple faults.

TABLE 3   Test Vectors for the AND Plane

c2	c1	A	B	C
0	1	1	1	1
0	1	1	0	0
0	1	0	1	0
0	1	0	0	1
1	0	0	0	0
1	0	0	1	1
1	0	1	0	1
1	0	1	1	0

TABLE 4 Test Vectors for the OR Plane

R_1	R_2	R_3	R_4
1	0	0	0
0	1	0	0
0	0	1	0
0	0	0	1

The observations are summarized as follows:

1. In the testable design, all single bit faults, all single stuck-at faults, and all single bridging faults between product lines, associated with the AND array as well as in the OR array and the additional logic, are detectable.
2. In the testable design, all single crosspoint faults, all single stuck faults, and single bridging faults are detectable by a minimal universal test set of length $[2(n + 1) + p]$.
3. In the testable design, all odd number of bit faults and line stuck-at faults are detectable by a universal test set designed to detect all single faults.

An even number of faults on a row in the AND plane or on a column in the OR plane cannot be detected in the augmented design by a universal test set. Multiple bridging faults in the AND plane that involve more than one input line are also not detectable.

Variations of Parity-Based Testable Design

Many variations in the design given above are available. The PLA given in Figure 19 requires two parity trees, one register, two controls, one extra row, and one extra column. Instead of using two parity trees and one register, one can use two registers and one parity tree (20,21,24). One register is used at the input and the second register is used at the product lines. The parity tree is used at the output lines. The schematic design is shown in Figure 20. It should be noted that in such a variation in design, the test generation procedure also changes slightly. However, the test set can still be kept universal, independent of the bit pattern.

Another variation in this design is possible to reduce the total test time. By using a universal test set, minimum test generation time is obtained. The improvements are possible in test application time and response evaluation time. This improvement is obtained by testing the AND and the OR planes simultaneously in parallel.

A control signal c3 is added to the buffers at each product line in the PLA design given in Figure 19 (22). This control signal is controlled such that the buffers present a high impedance state when c3 = 0. In normal operation, c3 = 1 provides transparent buffers. During testing, the AND and the OR planes are isolated by making c3 = 0, and testing in parallel. This, in effect, reduces the total test time almost by a factor of 2, independently of the delay per test.

TESTABLE DESIGN OF EEROMs

In recent years, electrically erasable ROMs have been developed to overcome the problem of irreversible programming. In EEROMs, double polysilicon gate transistors are

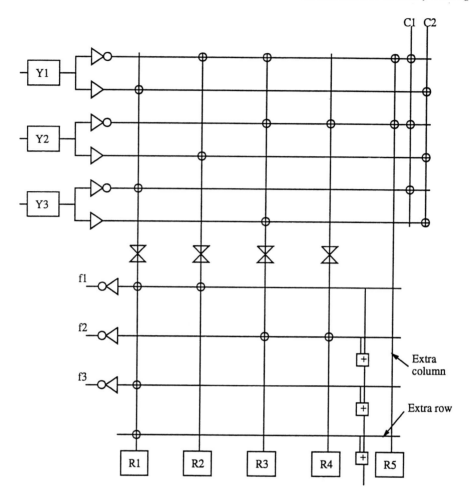

FIGURE 20   A different implementation of parity based PLA.

used instead of fuses and antifuses. These double polygate transistors work as reprogrammable switches at the memory bit location. Again, we will explain testable designs using
PLAs (known as EEPLAs).

The EEPLAs can be made testable by adding a single register to the product lines.
This register is referred to "product line register" (PL register). This register allows an
observer to check the response of the AND plane. Response of the OR plane is observed
through the output register. This design is given in Figure 21, in which all true and complementary signals are assumed to be independently controlled. This can be achieved by
a minor modification in the input decoder. It should be noted that the extra hardware used
in this design is only a *p*-bit-wide register (PL register). The test set for this EEPLA can
be obtained as follows (23).

During testing, only one input is activated at a time (set to "1"), all other inputs
are set to "0." The AND plane is programmed such that all the inputs that are set to "0"
have a crosspoint at every product line. The input, which is set to "1," has a crosspoint

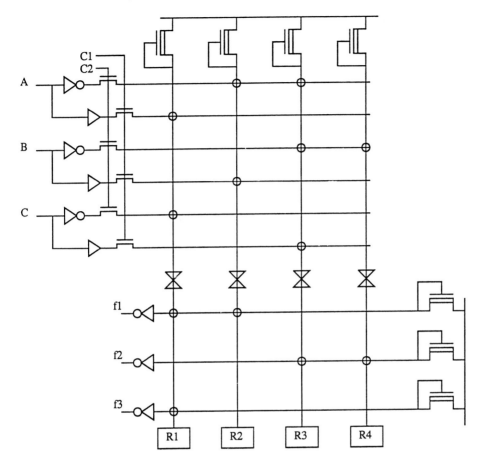

FIGURE 21   Augmented EEPLA for easy testing.

at all the product lines except one. Hence, under the fault-free condition, one product line is "1" and all others are "0." Consequently, only one bit in the PL register is "1" and all others are "0."

The OR plane is programmed similarly to the AND plane. It should be noted that the AND plane is programmed such that only one product line sets to "1." For the OR plane, product lines behave as inputs. Hence, the product line that will assume logic "1" has a crosspoint at every output line except one. All other product lines have a crosspoint at every output line. Thus, under the fault-free condition, one output line is "1" and all others are "0." Therefore, only one bit in the output register is "1" and all others are "0." This EEPLA programming procedure for testing is given in Figure 22.

The test set for the sample EEPLA of Figure 21 is shown in Figure 23. In Figure 23, of the AND plane and the OR plane is observed separately but simultaneously in two different registers. The observations regarding testing are summarized as follows:

1.   In the testable design, all single bit faults, all single product line stuck-at faults, and all single bridging faults between the product lines or between the output lines are detectable and diagnosable.

2. All single output line stuck-at faults and all single stuck-at faults in the output register are detectable but cannot be distinguished from each other.
3. To test an EEPLA for all single crosspoint faults, all single stuck-at faults, and all single bridging faults a test set of length np (if $n \leq m$) or mp (if $m \leq n$) is required. This is a minimal test set.

It should be noted that in the testable design as such, the output register stuck-at faults and output lines stuck-at faults are not distinguishable from each other. However, if the output register is designed using scan flip flops, this distinction can be obtained by additional testing of the output register.

In EEROMs, the program verification is also an important issue for the user. By using a bidirectional register instead of simple PL register, program verification can be done in $(n + p)$ vectors.

To verify the programming of the AND plane, one input (I_i, $i = 1$ to n) is set to "1," and all others are "0." In this condition, only those product lines go to "0" which have a crosspoint on input I_i. As the response is observed through the PL register, an observer is able to verify the crosspoints at input I_i.

After verification of the AND plane, the OR plane can be verified. For the OR plane, product lines behave as inputs, and the response is observed through the output register. To verify the OR plane, one bit (P_i, $i = 1$ to p) in the PL register is set to "1,"

```
/* Inputs are represented as I_i; i = 1 to n
/* Product lines are represented as P_j; j = 1 to p
/* Output lines are represented as O_l; l = 1 to m
/* Values at the inputs are defined as:
        For i = 1 to n Do
          Begin
            I_q = 1 if q=i
            I_q = 0 if q≠i
          end
/* Programming of the AND plane is defined as:
        For i= 1 to n Do
          Begin
            For j = 1 to p Do
              Begin
                no crosspoint at C_iw if w=j
                crosspoint at C_iw if w≠j
              end
            crosspoint at C_qj if q≠i
          end
/* Programming of the OR plane is defined as:
        For j = 1 to p Do
          Begin
            For l = 1 to m Do
              Begin
                no crosspoint at C_jr if r=l
                crosspoint at C_jr if r≠l
              end
            crosspoint at C_sl if s≠j
          end
```

FIGURE 22   Programming procedure of EEPLA for testing.

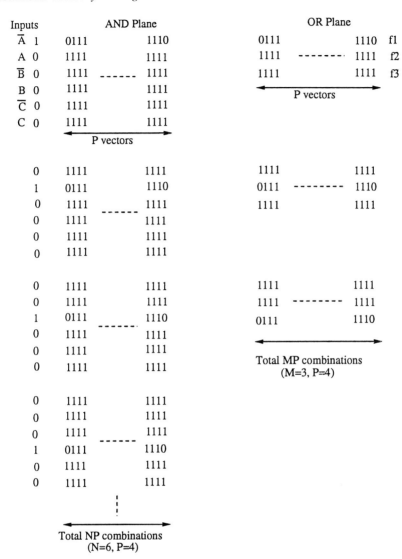

FIGURE 23 Test set for the EEPLA given in Figure 21. The length of the test set is *NP* as $N > M$.

and all others are "0." Due to the bidirectional PL register, all product lines become "0" except P_i. In this condition, only those output lines become "0," that have a crosspoint on P_i. As the functionality is known, an observer can verify the OR plane by looking at the response through the output register.

DESIGN FOR TESTABILITY IN RAMs

The basic philosophy behind design for testability and built-in self-test RAMs is to partition a memory into small blocks and test them in parallel. In the section Testing algorithms, it was mentioned that a test algorithm can be used for word-oriented memory using different data background. In a word-oriented memory (word size m bits), m bits are tested in parallel. Therefore, if a bit-oriented memory is designed such that it appears as a word-oriented memory during the test phase, test time can be reduced by a factor of $m/\log_2 m$. However, it should be noted that the implementation of such procedure at the chip level requires a modification in architecture. In general, memory address generation logic and data bus is designed with some extra control logic.

Built-in Self-Test RAMs

A generalized Built-in Self-Test (BIST) memory architecture is given in Figure 24 (25). You and Hayes (26), suggested a BIST design using an on-chip test generation and response evaluation scheme. In this design, the whole memory is divided into multiple blocks, whereas all memory cells in a block form a circular shift register during test mode. The on-chip logic scans all the blocks in parallel by shifting the same data concurrently in different blocks. The scanned-out data or responses from different blocks are compared using on-chip logic to detect a fault. The memory architecture for two blocks is shown in Figure 25. This architecture eliminates the need of external test generation. However, the hardware overhead in this design is high. It has been reported that for 1M-bits DRAM, the hardware overhead is about 5%. Another disadvantage is that due to the modification in sense amplifiers and refresh logic, this design causes a significant performance penalty.

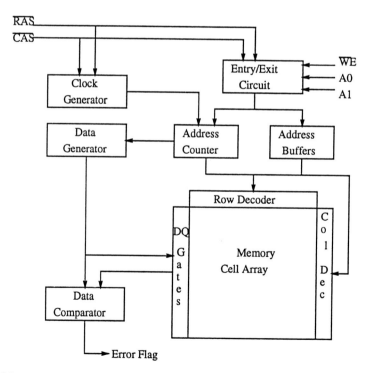

FIGURE 24   BIST memory architecture. RAS is Row Address Strobe and CAS is Column Address Strobe. (Courtesy of IEEE © 1987.)

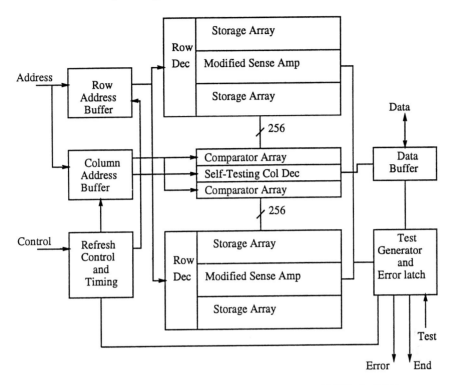

FIGURE 25   BIST DRAM architecture. (Courtesy of IEEE © 1986.)

Sridhar (27) has suggested partitioning a memory into small blocks and using an on-chip k-bit-wide parallel signature analyzer (PSA) to access k bits simultaneously. The overall design is shown in Figure 26a, and the PSA design is given in Figure 26b. The PSA is designed to operate in three different modes:

1. The scan mode.   During the scan mode, PSA works as a simple shift register. It is loaded serially with a seed pattern to generate test. At the end of test, the contents of PSA (k-bit signature) is scanned out.
2. The write mode.   During the write mode, the content of PSA is written to a number of memory cells (k bits) in parallel.
3. The signature/read mode.   During this mode, the contents of memory cells (k bits) are read and a new k-bit signature is generated. This signature is used to determine whether a memory has a fault.

The hardware overhead is reported about 2.2% to 3.1% in a 64Kbit SRAM using 64-bit PSA. Apart from the aliasing problem in PSA, the hardware overhead becomes significantly large in a multimegabit RAM.

RAM Partitioning Methods

Jarwala and Pradhan (28) have suggested partitioning a memory into small blocks and accessing them in parallel using a data bus. The memory is partitioned into small blocks making an H-tree using test comparators and switches in between the blocks. The design

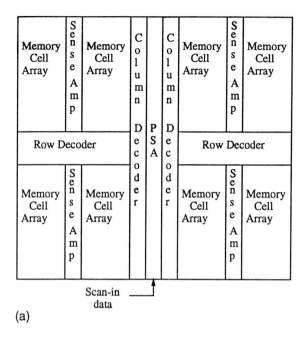

(a)

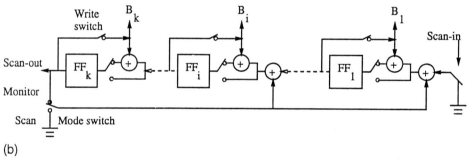

(b)

FIGURE 26   (a) Testable memory architecture using PSA. (Courtesy of IEEE © 1986.) (b) Block schematic of PSA used in (a). (Courtesy of IEEE © 1986.)

is shown in Figure 27. In this architecture, a memory can be partitioned into as many blocks as desired. However, the hardware overhead is significantly large due to the use of data bus for test application. It is reported that for 1Mbits RAM, the hardware overhead becomes 15% when memory is partitioned into eight blocks, each 128Kbits.

Recently, a new architecture has been developed, known as STD architecture (Structured Testable Design). The main idea behind STD architecture is to partition the memory address decoder into multilevels and design the memory accordingly (6,14). Thus, the whole memory is partitioned by itself without needing hardware overhead. The only requirement is a modified decoder for the most significant address lines.

Two examples are given to illustrate the STD architecture. These examples cover both 1-bit and m-bit word size memories and allow memory size to increase by a factor of 2^x. To express the memory size, the notation $n \times m$ is used, where n represents the number of words and m represents the word size. For example, 16K $\times$ 1 represents 16Kbits and 16K $\times$ 8 represents 16Kbytes.

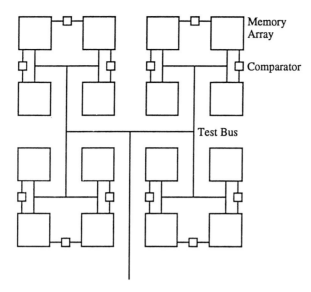

FIGURE 27 TRAM architecture when memory is partitioned into 16 blocks. (Courtesy of IEEE © 1988.)

EXAMPLE 1. 8K × 1 memory. This memory requires a 13-to-8K decoder which can be implemented at two levels, using a 10-to-1K decoder and a 3-to-8 decoder. Thus, the memory can be designed by eight blocks of 1Kbits (each associated with a 10-to-1K decoder) and a 3-to-8 decoder.

The design is made testable by modifying the 3-to-8 decoder, which contains the most significant address lines A10–A12. The modification is done by adding one extra control signal to the decoder. To illustrate the concept, the design of 2-to-4 decoder is given in Figure 28. In addition, a parity circuit is added at the outputs of the 1Kbit blocks. The testable design is given in Figure 29. The control signal added to the 3-to-8 decoder makes it possible to select all of the decoder output lines when control signal C = 1 (this is done during the test mode). When C = 0, the decoder is in its normal mode and selects only one of its output.

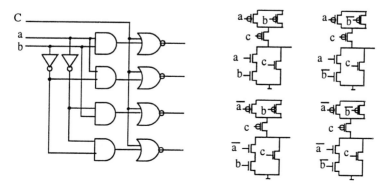

FIGURE 28 Circuit diagram of modified 2-to-4 decoder with an external control C.

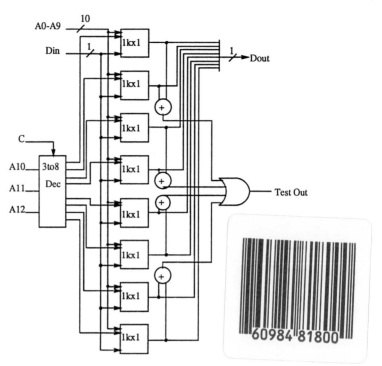

FIGURE 29   Testable design of 8K × 1 memory (Example 1).

To test this memory, the control signal C is kept to "1." Thus, the same data read/write operations can be done to all eight memory blocks using address lines A0–A9. During this mode, all eight block are tested in parallel. It should be noted that in the case of a fault in any block, the output of the parity circuit would be "1" and, hence, a fault is detected. Using the $7n$-March algorithm, all eight blocks can be tested by 7K read/write operations.

After the testing of memory blocks, the control signal C is switched to "0," converting the 3-to-8 decoder into normal mode. Under this situation, eight input combinations are needed to test the 3-to-8 decoder. It should be noted that if 1K × 1 blocks are tested by the $7n$-March algorithm, all cells contain "0" after the conclusion of the test. Hence, for each combination of address lines A10–A12, we can detect decoder faults by writing a "1" in a cell and reading it. However, to test the next combination, the cell should contain "0." Thus, 24 read/write operations are required (the last write is not necessary; thus, 23 operations are enough). These eight possible combinations are applied at the address lines A10–A12 while keeping A0–A9 to a fixed value (preferable, all 0's or all 1's). The response is observed at D_{out} line. Thus, the whole 8Kbit memory can be tested in a test time necessary to test 1Kbit memory, 7K + 24 read/write operations to be accurate. The hardware overhead in this design is one control signal, four XOR gates, and one OR gate. Because the control line is limited to the 3-to-8 decoder and does not extend to the memory blocks, the routing area is negligible for the control signal. The 10-to-1K decoders within the memory blocks can also be implemented in two levels or multilevels. However, these decoders need no modification because the partition size is 1Kbits.

EXAMPLE 2. 32K × 8 memory. This memory can be built by using four blocks of 8K × 8 memory and a 2-to-4 decoder. In this case, each block of 8K × 8 memory is equivalent to Figure 29. The additional 2-to-4 decoder, which contains the most significant address lines, is modified by adding a control signal. If we consider a separate control signal than used in 8K × 8 blocks, the memory can be tested by (7K + 48 + 12) vectors or read/write operations. The hardware overhead in this case is two control signals and [4 × (32 XOR + 8 OR) + 8 OR = 128 XOR + 40 OR] gates.

Another possibility is to design this memory by using eight blocks of 32K × 1 memory. This design will look similar to the design of Example 1, except for the size of partition block. In this case, a 32Kbyte memory can be tested by (7K + 96 + 12) vectors. The hardware overhead is one control signal and [8 × (16 XOR + 5 OR) = 80 XOR + 40 OR] gates.

In both approaches, the hardware overhead and test time are comparable. The amount of hardware overhead can be reduced significantly by using bigger blocks of memory arrays instead of 1K × 1 arrays. However with the larger blocks, memory test time will increase. For example, if 8K × 1 memory blocks are used, the whole memory can be tested by (56K + 12) vectors, whereas only (16 XOR + 8 OR) gates are required (see Fig. 30). It should be noted that, equivalently, 256K × 1 memory can be designed by four additional 3-to-8 decoders and can be tested by (56K + 48) read/write operations.

Pros and Cons of Design for Testability in RAMs

The main advantage of partitioning methods is that a very small test time can be achieved for any size of memory. Another advantage is that any fault model can be assumed and

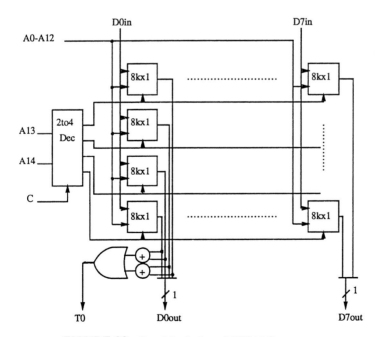

FIGURE 30 Testable design of 32K × 8 memory.

an appropriate test algorithm can be used. In general, the partitioning methods are highly structured and test vectors need not to be calculated for different memories having the same size partitions (except for a few additional vectors). With these architectures, large memories can be designed in significantly small time using existing memory blocks of small sizes. It should be noted that these architectures are not limited to the chip design. A memory board can be designed without any modification in the architecture.

The negative aspect of the BIST architectures or partitioning methods is the requirement of extra hardware. In BIST architecture, hardware overhead is significantly high to make these designs impractical. In partitioning methods, for large memories if the test time is kept extremely small (for example, a 4Mbit memory partitioned into 1Kbit blocks), the hardware overhead becomes significant. The hardware overhead is inversely proportional to the partition size and is minimal in STD architecture. The trade-off for STD architecture is shown in Figure 31. It should be noted that in Figure 31, the overhead is measured in terms of number of gates. Generally, overhead is expressed in terms of percentage, i.e., as a portion of memory size. However, the percentage overhead is an inadequate representation because it understates the actual situation. For example, 10% overhead for a 16Kbit memory might be acceptable, but for a 16Mbit memory it is highly undesirable.

Another disadvantage in BIST designs and partitioning methods is the penalty in performance. The extra hardware increases parasitic line capacitance, which causes a larger delay during normal operation. In some designs, sense amplifiers and address decoders are modified. This also increases the access time during the normal operation. The performance penalty is minimal in STD architecture. Partitioning of the decoder in multilevel, in fact, results in the decrease in signal propagation delay. Therefore, such partitioning is desirable for improving the performance.

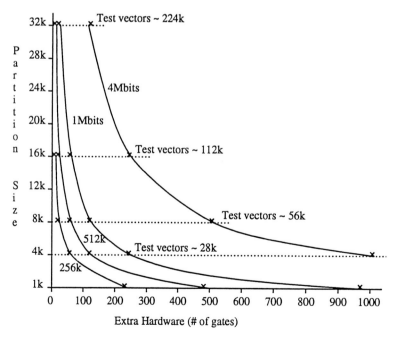

FIGURE 31 Trade-off in partition size versus extra hardware. Dotted lines represent constant test time.

SUMMARY

In this article, the different memory fault models are discussed. The validity of these fault models is examined with respect to the physical defects found in various memories. It is observed that the decoder and sense amplifier read/write faults do translate into cell faults in memory array. Although the cell coupling fault model is found most realistic, a little evidence is found for the pattern sensitive fault model. It is suggested that for a comprehensive fault coverage, the fault model of Ref. 3 should be used with the inclusion of data retention faults.

The most widely used test algorithm for memories are given. Different variations of most popular algorithms are discussed. Some of the algorithms are examined to find out their effectiveness. It is observed that the algorithms based on coupling fault model provide the best fault coverage, whereas the algorithms based on a PSF model provide the least fault coverage. The march test and its variations are found very efficient with respect to test time and fault coverage. A comparison among various algorithms is provided. In general, a user is adviced to choose the $O(n)$ algorithm, unless it is specified to use a higher-complexity algorithm. The another selection criteria is 100% fault coverage under specified fault model.

The testing of multimegabits memory is extremely time-consuming. For very large memories, test time becomes the critical factor in overall production cost. For multimegabit memories, even a linear time complexity algorithm may require too much time to be practical. Obviously, the memory testing problem cannot be solved alone by a clever test algorithm.

Easily testable ROM designs are described using PLAs. It is shown that the parity trees at the product lines and the output lines can effectively test a PLA. The variations in testable PLA designs are discussed. The testable design for EEROMs are illustrated using EEPLAs. The various trade-offs and penalty due to hardware overhead is discussed. The testable designs to help in RAM testing are given. The basic idea behind these testable architectures is to partition the whole memory into small blocks and test them in parallel. Each implementation has its own advantages/disadvantages. Based on hardware overhead, the use of STD architecture is recommended.

REFERENCES

1. G. R. Case, "Analysis of Actual Fault Mechanisms in CMOS Logic Gates," *Proc. Design Auto. Conf.*, 1976, pp. 265–270.
2. F. Fantini and C. Morandi, "Failure Modes and Mechanisms for VSLI ICs—A Review," *IEE Proc.*, *132*(3), 74–81 (1985).
3. R. Nair, S. M. Thatte, and J. A. Abraham, "Efficient Algorithms for Testing Semiconductor Random Access Memories," *IEEE Trans. Computers*, C-27(6), 572–576 (1978).
4. A. J. Van de Goor, "Using March Tests to Test SRAMs," *IEEE Design Test Computers*, 8–14 (March 1993).
5. R. Dekker, F. Beenker, and L. Thijssen, "A Realistic Fault Model and Test Algorithm for Static Random Access Memories," *IEEE Trans. CAD*, CAD-9(6), 567–572 (1990).
6. R. Rajsuman and K. Rajkanan, "An Architecture to Test Random Access Memories," *Proc. Int. Conf. on VLSI Design*, January 1992, pp. 144–147.
7. J. P. Hayes, "Detection of Pattern Sensitivity Faults in Random Access Memories," *IEEE Trans. Computers*, C-24(2), 150–157 (1975).
8. J. P. Hayes, "Testing Memories for Single Cell Pattern Sensitive Faults," *IEEE Trans. Computers*, C-29(3), 249–254 (1980).

9. P. K. Veenstra, F. P. M. Beenker, and J. J. M. Koomen, "Testing of Random Access Memories: Theory and Practice," *IEE Proc. 135*(1), 24–28 (1988).
10. A Birolini, W. Buchel, and D. Heavner, "Test and Screening Strategies for Large Memories," *Proc. European Test Conf.*, 1989, pp. 276–283.
11. A. J. Van de Goor, *Semiconductor Memory Testing*, John Wiley and Sons, New York, 1991.
12. R. Rajsuman, *Digital Hardware Testing*, Artech House Inc., 1992, Chap. 7.
13. A. Miczo, *Digital Logic Testing and Simulation*, Harper and Row, New York, 1986, Chap. 8.
14. R. Rajsuman, "An Algorithm and Design to Test Random Access Memories," *Proc. IEEE Int. Symp Circuits and Systems*, May 1992, pp. 439–442.
15. R. Dekker, F. Beenker, and L. Thijssen, "Fault Modeling and Test Algorithm Development for Static Random Access Memories," *Proc. Int. Test. Conf.*, 1988, pp. 343–352.
16. M. Franklin and K. K. Saluja, "Built-in Self-Testing of Random Access Memories," *IEEE Computers, C-23*(10), 45–56 (1990).
17. V. K. Agarwal, "Easily Testable PLA Design," in *VSLI Testing* T. W. Williams (ed.), North-Holland, Amsterdam, 1986.
18. H. Fujiwara and K. Kinoshita, "A Design of Programmable Logic Arrays with Universal Tests," *IEEE Trans. Computers, C-30*(11), 823–828 (1981).
19. S. J. Hong and D. L. Ostapko, "FITPLA: A Programmable Logic Array for Function Independent Testing," *Proc. 10th Int. Symp. Fault Tol. Comp.*, 1980, pp. 131–136.
20. R. Treuer, V. K. Agarwal, and H. Fujiwara, "A New Built-in Self Test Design for PLAs with High Fault Coverage and Low Overhead," *IEEE Trans. Computers, C-36*(3), 369–373 (1987).
21. XiAn Zhu and M. A. Breuer, "Analysis of Testable PLA Designs," *IEEE Design Test Computers*, 14–28 (August 1988).
22. R. Rajsuman, Y. K. Malaiya, and A. P. Jayasumana, "Reprogrammable FPLA with Universal Test Set," *IEE Proc. 137*(6), 437–441 (1990).
23. R. Rajsuman and P. K. Lala, "Fault Detection in EEPLAs," *Proc. Int. Symp. Circuits and Systems, ISCAS*, 1992, pp. 1109–1112.
24.
25. T. Ohsawa et al., "A 60-ns 4-Mbit CMOS DRAM with Built-in Self-Test Function," *IEEE J. Solid State Circuits, SSC-22*(5), 663–668 (1987).
26. Y. You and J. P. Hayes, "A Self Test Dynamic RAM Chip," *IEEE J. Solid State Circuits, SSC-20*(1), 428–435 (1985).
27. T. Sridhar, "A New Parallel Test Approach for Large Memories," *IEEE Design Test Computers*, 15–22 (August 1986).
28. N. Jarwala and D. K. Pradhan, "TRAM: A Design Methodology for High Performance, Easily Testable Multimegabit RAMs," *IEEE Trans. Computers, C-37*(10), 1235–1250 (1988).
29. M. Abramovici, M. A. Breuer, and A. D. Friedman, *Digital System Testing and Testable Design*, Computer Science Press, 1990.
30. E. Fujiwara and D. K. Pradhan, "Error Control Coding in Computers," *IEEE Computers, C-39*, 63–72 (1990).

ROCHIT RAJSUMAN

SEMIOTICS AND FORMAL ARTIFICIAL LANGUAGES

LANGUAGES WITH RESPECT TO OTHER SEMIOTIC SYSTEMS

A general semiotic system is a sign system endowed with a syntax (the relations among the various parts of the system, particularly among various elements of it), a semantics (the relations between the signs of the system and the world external to the system), and a pragmatics (the relations between the system and its users). A language is a particular case of a semiotic system, having the property of being sequential. So, more than any other semiotic system, languages are under the control of the left hemisphere of the brain, whose general orientation is toward controlling various processes of a sequential nature.

However, there are some intermediary situations when a semiotic system is apparently nonsequential, even nonlinear, but has a hidden sequentiality which requires an investigation to reveal it. The tool used to identify it is usually a generative grammar similar to those used to generate various parts of a natural language. So, sequentiality, in this case, is not an intrinsic property, but a property defined with respect to a considered class of generative grammars. For instance, the so-called picture grammars (where the elements of the terminal alphabet are various types of geometric polydimensional—usually bidimensional—figures, whereas concatenation of symbols is replaced by some geometric operations) are a way to introduce a linear order in an (apparently) polydimensional structure. Significant examples in this respect appear in the formal linguistic approach to molecular genetics; see (1).

In the above considerations, we accepted implicitly a semantic nonequivalence between linearity and sequentiality. The property of sequentiality is more restrictive than linearity because it adds the property of discreteness to linearity. Any language is formed by means of sequential combinations of elements selected from a finite nonempty set. Linearity is sometimes described by means of the concept of dimension and it means dimension equal to one. Sequentiality is modeled by means of the concept of a finite sequence. A language is a discrete semiotic system whose elements are of a sequential nature. There are, however, debates about the possible continuous (i.e., nondiscrete) character of the semantics of a language.

NATURAL AND ARTIFICIAL LANGUAGES

The distinction between natural and artificial is still controversial. The basic question in this respect is whether this distinction concerns only the history of these languages (very long in the case of natural languages, relatively short for the artificial ones) or is it also of a structural type. Most linguists support the second variant of the alternative and propose various features claimed to be characteristic for natural languages (such as English, French, German, etc.):

(a)   the fuzzy status of well-formed strings
(b)   the gap between the potentially infinite competence and the finiteness of performance
(c)   the dominance of integrative semantics (presence of idiomatic expressions) versus additive semantics (where the meaning of a string is to a large extent obtained by concatenation of the meanings of the components of the string)
(d)   quasi-universal, polyfunctional use beyond the initial purpose
(e)   presence of the phenomena of ambiguity
(f)   duality of patterning (2)
(g)   possibility of self-reference
(h)   impossibility to learn the language before using it
(i)   primordiality of the spoken form
(j)   tendency to develop rhetorical figures (mainly of metaphorical and of metonymical type)
(k)   tendency to develop connotative meanings

However, for each of these features a counterexample can be given. Condition (a) is fulfilled by any developed programming language because there is no necessary and sufficient condition for a sequence of instructions to be a computer program. The set of well-formed strings in a programming language is fuzzy (3). We could also observe that the meaning of an instruction in an advanced programming language is not always obtained by concatenation of the meanings of its components (see the case of DO 5 I = 1, M in Fortran), whereas the meaning of a program is not always obtained by concatenation of the meanings of its instructions (4), so condition (c) is fulfilled by Fortran. Programming languages are sometimes used beyond their initial purpose [for an opposite view, see (5)], for instance, Algol was used in logic and in the study of the semantics of English (6). Although the phenomena of contextual ambiguity are very reduced if not absent in third-generation programming languages (7), it should be observed that lexical homonymy cannot be completely avoided even in mathematical language (see terms like category, algebra, measure, etc.), whereas ambiguity in some formal grammars cannot be avoided [some strings are obligatory generated in several ways; see, for instance, (8)]; so, feature (e) is present in some artificial languages. The formal language simulating the heredity (1) develops a duality of patterning, where the units of the first articulation are the codons (the morphemes of the genetic language, in correspondence with the amino acids), whereas the units of the second articulation are the nucleotid bases (the phonemes of the genetic language), so feature (f) also is not specific to natural languages. The possibility of self-reference [condition (g)] in formal artificial languages was discussed and confirmed by Smullyan (9) and Bar-Hillel (10). The language LINCOS proposed by Freudenthal (11) for communication with potential intelligent beings other than the human ones has the capacity to function as its own metalanguage, so its self-referential capacity is deliberate and systematic. Condition (h) was asserted by Moreau (5) as a specific feature of natural languages, but it is fulfilled to a large extent by programming languages too. Primordiality of the spoken form for natural languages is contrasted by Naur (12) with the fact that programming is done mostly in writing, but primordiality of the written form is a general feature of any scientific language and, in particular, it is essential for mathematics. However, if we consider artificial languages, like Esperanto, Volapûk, and Ido [for a general description of them and their history, see (13)], we may observe that they are often made by pieces of natural languages, and their spoken form is of the same importance as their written form. The presence of features (j) and (k) in some artificial languages is manifest in both the natural and the artificial component of the mathematical language (14).

A provisional conclusion on this point is that artificial languages, as soon as they develop their pragmatic dimension, share more and more features with the natural languages. It is difficult to find a characteristic structural feature of natural languages, but it may be that the totality of their features succeeds to approximate better their status. It also remains the psychological difference between the spontaneous way in which we acquire our mother tongue and the deliberate way in which artificial languages are acquired.

FORMAL LANGUAGES AS PARTICULAR ARTIFICIAL LANGUAGES

Although formal languages can model some aspects of natural languages, it is questionable whether they could be sometimes direct parts of the latter. Montague (15) answers this question in the affirmative sense because he does not see an important difference between natural and formal languages and claims the possibility of building a syntax and a semantics valid for both. This idea is shared by Chomsky (16), who, instead of natural and formal languages, uses the generic term of human language. However, although for Montague large portions of English are formal languages, it can be observed that implicitly the latter are only logical models for the former in the Chomsky approach. So, we may accept that human languages are of two types: formal and nonformal. Volapûk, Esperanto, and Ido are nonformal artificial languages; the language of propositional calculus is a formal artificial language; the language of mathematics is a combination of two components, a natural and an artificial one, between which a balance should be kept (17). Some intermediate situations have to be accepted; as it was shown, programming languages share features of both natural and artificial languages and of both formal and nonformal languages.

Being human, formal languages, to the extent to which they are developed in the right direction, have a strong interaction with natural languages; the latter are the intuitive base for the former, the former have a modeling capacity with respect to the latter. Moreover, because all types of human languages share the property of being sequential, they are under the control of the left hemisphere of the brain and so biologically and psychologically related. However, some philosophers like Steiner (18) and Henry (19) reduce human language to natural languages only. This attitude leads to a dramatic conflict between science and humanity. Indeed, beginning with Galileo, Descartes, and Leibniz, scientific language has developed more and more of its artificial component. In our century, this component became dominant, so the distance between the common language and scientific language has increased tremendously. But, to a large extent, the artificial component of the scientific language is a formal one because one of the main reasons to develop the artificial component is to face the increasing requirements of precision and rigor, requirements that are beyond the capacities of the everyday language. Obviously, the degree of formalization depends on the field under consideration; for instance, low when dealing with formulas in organic chemistry, increasing in mathematics, and reaching perhaps its maximum in texts of mathematical logic and foundations of mathematics, where the natural component almost disappears.

THE RIGOROUS CONCEPT OF A FORMAL LANGUAGE AND THE RELATED MAIN PROBLEM

If we take formal languages as used in computer science, they appear as having only syntactic aspects. Given a finite nonempty set A called an alphabet, a mapping f from the set $\{1,2, \ldots, n\}$ of the first n natural numbers into the set A is said to be a word of length n over A and it is written $a_1 a_2 \ldots a_n$, where $f(i) = a_i$, for i from 1 to n. Any set of words over A is called a formal language over A. The universal language A^* over A is the set of all possible words over A. We also accept the word of length zero, called the empty word. Because A is not empty, A^* is always infinite (but countable). Obviously, any language over A is either finite or infinite, but countable. The set of all possible languages over A is infinite and uncountable.

Beginning in the 1970s, the formal language theory became a part of theoretical computer science. The main problem in this respect is to characterize a language from a generative point of view, i.e., to find a generative device—called a grammar—which generates the given language. The generative device we are looking for has to be of a finite nature, whereas its generative activity, so as not to be trivial, should lead to an infinite language. So, what makes this problem interesting is the contrast between the finiteness of the grammar and the possible infinity of the language generated by the grammar. A technical form to this idea is given below.

THE GENERATIVE TYPOLOGY OF FORMAL LANGUAGES

A generative grammar is an ordered quadruple $G = \langle T, N, S, R \rangle$, where T and N are disjoint finite nonempty sets called the terminal and, respectively, the nonterminal (or auxiliary) alphabet, S is an element in N called the starting (or initial) symbol, whereas R is a finite set of rules $f \rightarrow g$, where f and g are words over the total alphabet $A = T \cup N$ and $\rightarrow$ is not an element of A. The word v over A is directly derivable from the word u over A, by means of G, if there exist the words x, y, f, and g such that $u = xfy$, $v = xgy$ and $f \rightarrow g$ is a rule in R. (Given two words $p = a_1 a_2 \ldots a_n$, and $q = b_1 b_2 \ldots b_n$, their concatenation pq is the word $r = c_1 c_2 \ldots c_{m+n}$ of length $m + n$, where $c_i = a_i$ for i smaller than $m + 1$ and $c_i = b_j$ for $i = m + j$, where j is between 1 and n.) The word v is derivable from u in G if there exists a finite sequence of words $s_1, s_2 \ldots, s_n$ such that $s_1 = u$, $s_n = v$, and for each i between 1 and $n-1$, s_{i+1} is directly derivable from s_i in G. Any word over T is said to be a terminal word. The set of all terminal words which can be derived, in G, from the starting symbol S is called the language $L(G)$ generated by G.

It was proved that the class of languages L over a given alphabet T for which a generative grammar G exists such that $L(G) = L$ coincides with the class of recursively enumerable languages over T. This class is an infinite, but countable set; so, taking into account that the class of all possible languages over T is not countable, it follows that, from the point of view of the cardinality, most languages cannot be generated by generative grammars.

A rule $f \rightarrow g$ in R is said to be context sensitive if there exist three words x, y, z over A, z not empty, and a nonterminal symbol B such that $f = xBy$, $g = xzy$. If all rules in R are context sensitive, then G is said to be context sensitive, whereas $L(G)$ is said to be a context-sensitive language. The class of context-sensitive languages is contained in the class of primitive recursive sets and coincides with the class of languages recognized by the so-called linearly bounded Turing machines with one tape and one head [for these concepts, see (8, 20)].

A rule in R is regular if it is either of the form $B \rightarrow aC$ or of the form $B \rightarrow a$, where B and C are nonterminal symbols and a is a terminal one. If all rules in R are regular, then G is said to be a regular grammar, and $L(G)$ is a regular language. Another possibility for obtaining a regular grammar is to require to any rule in R to be either of the form $B \rightarrow Ca$ or of the form $B \rightarrow a$. Regular languages coincide with languages recognized by finite automata and are a particular case of context-free languages (8), generated by rules of the form $B \rightarrow x$, where B is in N and x is a non-empty word over A. Simple examples are $\{a^n\}$ is regular, $\{a^n b^n\}$ is nonregular, but context free; $\{a^n b^n c^n\}$ is not context free, but it is context sensitive.

FORMAL LANGUAGES AND FORMAL SYSTEMS

This generative hierarchy of languages is known under the name of the Chomsky hierarchy because it was introduced by Chomsky (21), with motivations related to natural languages and with reference to Post combinatorial systems (22,23). As a matter of fact, Chomsky grammars are strongly related to Hilbert formal systems, where the set of axioms is a language contained in the set of theorems, which is a language contained in the more comprehensive language whose elements are relations. A set of (deductive) rules gives the possibility to start from axioms and, by successive applications of deductive rules, to reach various theorems. It is easily seen that Chomsky's generative grammar is essentially a formal system where axioms are replaced by nonterminal symbols, deductive rules are replaced by rules of derivation, proofs are replaced by derivations, and theorems are replaced by well-formed strings (i.e., the words generated by the grammar).

The analogy between Chomsky's formal grammars and Hilbert's formal systems shows how a semantics of a formal grammar can be introduced as one of its possible interpretations. Most applications of Chomsky grammars to linguistics use such particular interpretations, among which the most frequent is obtained by taking the Sentence as a starting symbol and the noun group NG and the verbal group VG as further nonterminal symbols, continuing with other (usually syntactic) categories of traditional grammars as nonterminal symbols. But in other situations, the interpretation of the categorial meaning of nonterminal symbols has to be discovered by means of the derivational context of the generative process. This categorial meaning may correspond to no traditional morphological or syntactic category; in this way, new categories, having an explanatory capacity leading to a deeper understanding of the language, are discovered.

As formal systems, the formal grammars are faced with all the difficulties pointed out by Kurt Godel and leading to a genuine gap between syntax and semantics: The syntactic level of correctness is always inferior to the semantic level of truth.

THE ANALYTIC TYPOLOGY OF FORMAL LANGUAGES

The analytic strategy is complementary to the generative one. Instead of using generative devices external to the language under investigation, we look for intrinsic features characterizing linguistic structures. Because languages which can be generated by Chomskian grammars form a countable set, most languages (on a given alphabet) are, as we have seen, beyond the Chomskian hierarchy, so the only strategy available for them is the analytic one; but even for languages which can be generated by Chomsky grammars, it is important to have available alternative strategies.

Mathematical analytic tools in the study of natural languages started in the 1960s, mainly in eastern Europe but also in some western European countries such as Belgium and France, stimulated by the first researches in the field of automatic translation. Their systematic presentation was done by Marcus (24,25).

The basic concept in the analytic approach is the domination relation $\dashv$. Given a language L over the alphabet A and two words x and y over A, we have $x \dashv y(L)$ if for any two words u and v such that uxv is in L the word uyv is also in L. When L approximates one of the levels of grammaticality of a natural language, the relation $x \dashv y$ can be interpreted in the sense that the contextual ambiguity of x is not larger than that of y. When x and y are flexional forms, contextual ambiguity becomes what is called in traditional grammar a morphological homonymy. For each word x, we define the distributional class $G(x)$ consisting of all words dominated by x and dominating x with respect to L. A language L is regular if and only if the number of distributional classes with respect to L is finite. The set $G(x) = \{y; x \dashv y\}$ is the elementary grammatical category (EGC) generated by x. Any union of EGC-s is a grammatical category which covers various types of morphological categories analyzed in linguistics, such as the case, the number, and the gender. On the other hand, with respect to a finite partition P of the alphabet A we can define the alphabet $\{P(x); x$ in $A\}$, where $P(x)$ is that term of the partition P which contains x. A sequence $P_1 P_2 \ldots P_s$ of terms of P is L-accepted if there is a word $a_1 a_2 \ldots a_s$ in L such that $P_i = P(a_i)$ and $a_i \in A$ for i from 1 to s. The set of all L-accepted words over the alphabet $\{P(x); x$ in $A\}$ is a new language, with respect to which the distributional classes define a new partition P^1 of A, called the derivative partition of P. Starting from the partition P of flexional paradigms, we get the partition in parts of speech as a derivative. A rich typology of languages follows from various possible configurations of distributional classes and derivative partitions.

Other analytical models are related to syntactic relations of dependency (by means of binary relations) and subordination (defined as the reflexive and transitive closure of the dependency relation). The mathematical model of a sentence is obtained by means of what is called in graph theory a rooted tree. Important in this respect is the property of syntactic projectivity: If the term a is subordinated to the term b in a given word, then any intermediate term is also subordinated to b. This property seems to belong to most words in any human language, be it natural or artificial.

SHORT HISTORY OF FORMAL LANGUAGES

The systematic study of formal languages begins in the 1960s with explicit motivations coming from automata studies (26), machine translation (27), switching circuit theory and logical design (Shannon), descriptive linguistics (28), modeling of biological systems (29,30), but, before all, from logic and recursive function theory (20,22), with the prolongation in the study of natural languages (31). Later, it was found that some particular problems of formal language theory were implicitly considered at the beginning of this century (32), whereas some older combinatorial problems that are potential sources of interesting formal linguistic approaches (33,34) were discovered only recently (35,36).

An extensive presentation of the history of formal languages is given by Greibach (37). To this presentation, we have to add the characteristic line of development started in the 1960s and followed by researchers in eastern Europe, concerned with the mathematical modeling of languages with rich morphology, such as the Slavic languages, German and Romanian (in contrast with the poor morphology of English, a reason for which morphology is marginalized in the Chomskian approach). The basic tools in this respect come from binary relations, set theory, graph theory, closure operators, Galois connections, and some particular aspects of the theory of free semigroups (for a survey of this approach, see (24,25)).

FORMAL GENERATIVE GRAMMARS AND PROGRAMMING LANGUAGES

A turning point in the evolution of Chomsky generative grammars is the year 1960, when a report on the algorithmic language Algol was published (38,39). In this report, the syntax of Algol is defined by means of some metalinguistic formula known under the name of Backus Normal Form (BNF). As Ginsburg and Rice (40) have shown, the BNF is equivalent to the context-free grammar. Moreover, various operations during compiling can be done by various automata. So, Chomsky's formal grammars, introduced by considerations related to natural languages (the need to replace the traditional descriptive approach by a generative one), became a natural tool in modeling the syntax of programming languages. Because context-free grammars play a special role in this respect, they became immediately an object of major concern from a mathematical point of view (41). But as soon as syntactic definitions are supplemented with semantic conditions, the required generative rules have to transgress context-free grammars; these rules are sometimes no longer context free, but context sensitive. Among Algol programs written by means of BNF only some of them fulfill the required semantic conditions, so only some of them are correct. We can no longer assert that Algol is context free; as a matter of fact, it is not (42).

Various classes of context-sensitive grammars were introduced to find a better approximation of the structure of programming languages. The strategy was to look for generative devices stronger than context-free grammars, but admitting derivation trees, to associate meanings to the nonterminal symbols used in derivation (this is not possible in a context-sensitive grammar). A basic idea here is to introduce various types of restrictions in derivation to increase the generative power of context-free rules. For instance, the matrix grammars are defined by means of context-free rules arranged in ordered sets of rules (matrices), the order in arrangement being just the order in which the rules are applied. However, no theorem of the type ⟨⟨Algol is not a matrix language⟩⟩ exists so far. It was shown (43) that Algol is neither a simple matrix language nor a finite index matrix language. A similar theorem is valid for Fortran and Cobol.

However, it should be pointed out that some parts of Algol (Fortran, Cobol) such as those considered by Floyd (42) and Aho and Ullman (44), parts which are not context-free, can be generated by means of what is called a regular simple matrix grammar. For the corresponding concepts and for related results, see (43,45–47).

Semantics of programming languages has been developed in four directions: operational, denotational, axiomatic, and algebraic. The distinction between the syntactic and the semantic aspects of programming languages is to a large extent conventional.

Moreover, syntax and semantics have to be supplemented by the study of pragmatic aspects, such as how to introduce the program in the computer, how to translate the program into the machine language (compiling), and how to perform the program.

Logic programming such as in Prolog deserves specific semiotic investigations. Connections with semiotics, with linguistics, and with mathematics are discussed by Zemanek (48), Naur (12), and Marcus (49).

Sgall observes (50) that the features of natural languages have made it possible to abandon the difference between a program and an algorithm in some domains. The possibility of programming in a natural language is discussed more and more, together with the possibility of enabling the programmer to use a part of a natural language to be translated automatically into a language that is immediately processed by the computer.

FORMAL LINGUISTIC MODELS IN NATURAL SCIENCES

The most important researches in this respect were done in organic chemistry and mainly in cellular and molecular biology. Applications of generative grammars in chemistry were considered in various papers published in the journal *MATCH* (*Mathematical Chemistry*) and sometimes in the journal *Chemical Documentation*; they are a direct continuation of the use of graph theory in chemistry.

More spectacular are the results in the field of biology. The pioneer in the field of cellular biology is Aristid Lindenmayer (51,52), who introduced a new type of generative device, contrasting with Chomskian grammars in two respects: the absence of nonterminal symbols and the property of parallelism (the possibility to process simultaneously all terms of a sequence of symbols). The generative rules in a Lindenmayer grammar simulate the development of cells in a living organism.

Lindenmayer grammars were, for a period, one of the most important research topics in the field of formal language theory.

Less known is another line of research, related to molecular biology (1). DNA and RNA are long, but finite strings over the alphabet of four elements represented by different types of nucleotides. Some words—always of length 3—in this alphabet are called codons; they are in correspondence, through the genetic code, with 20 types of amino acids. In this way, ARN are converted in other strings (called proteins) over the alphabet of amino acids and so the metabolism is established. To simulate the syntax of amino acids, a context-free grammar of 50 rules was defined (53), following a recursive procedure of representing the formation of proteins (54). The language of derivations in Vauquois' grammar is context sensitive, but no longer context free.

FORMAL LINGUISTIC MODELS IN HUMANITIES AND SOCIAL SCIENCES

Let us first discuss the approach to learning processes. The traditional mathematical models in this field are of a stochastic nature and start with an empirical view on learning processes, viewed as a stimulus–response interaction. To take into consideration the interaction between innate and acquired, a topological model is built in the following way (55). An object to be learned is represented by a mapping $f : N \rightarrow N$, which leads to an infinite sequence of ordered pairs $(i, f(i))$ of natural numbers, where $f(i)$ is the response given to the stimulus i. Empirical learning is limited to a finite number of such pairs, i.e., to a finite section d of f: $(1, f(1))$, $(2, f(2))$, . . . , $(p, f(p))$. We say that f is compatible with d. Let us denote by $s(d)$ the set of all objects f compatible with d. The family $\{s(d);$ d in $D\}$, where D is the set of all finite sequences of ordered pairs of natural numbers, is the base of a topology t over the set F of objects to be learned. If S and T are parts of F, then we say that the object f in F can be learned by means of the knowledge $\langle\langle f$ in $T\rangle\rangle$ under the innate information $\langle\langle f$ in $S\rangle\rangle$ when there exists a finite section d of f such that f is in $S\cap s(d)$, and $S\cap s(d)$ is contained in T; in other words, when $T\cap S$ is a neighborhood of f in the topology obtained from t by relativization with respect to S. One can prove that the topological learning space (F, t) is homeomorphic to a part of the metric space of all languages over some finite alphabet A. The distance between two languages is induced by a norm, in the following way: The norm of the language L is obtained as a power of 2, the exponent being equal to $-l(L)$, where $l(L)$ is the length of the shortest word in L. If L is empty, then its norm is equal to zero. The sum of two languages is interpreted as their symmetric difference.

In the field of praxiology, Nowakowska (56) considers the alphabet A of elementary actions occurring in a given field F of human practice, whereas any other action in F is represented as a word over A. Pragmatic aspects, such as the duration of an elementary action, are also considered in this respect. A lot of human and social activities, from the simplest possible (such as a telephone call, the driver, or the kitchen competence) to the most complex (such as a tennis game or the various types of economic processes) (57), can be approached in this way. Fields like ethnology, folklore, narrativity, theater, enigmistic games, music, visual arts, and international relations have already profited from this approach, looking for the hidden generative mechanisms of the corresponding processes [for a synthesis of these works, see (58,59)].

FORMAL GRAMMARS AND UNIVERSAL GRAMMARS

In strong connection with the above-considered learning processes is the problem of universal grammars.

The problem of universals was raised earlier in the scholastic philosophy. The $\langle\langle$quarrel of universals$\rangle\rangle$ was concerned with various modalities to interpret the relations between individual and general, between perception and concept. This quarrel continues to today and perhaps it will never stop.

Initially, linguistics was involved in detecting those directly perceived features that are common to all languages. In a second step, researchers like Greenberg (60), Roman Jakobson, and Eugenio Coseriu introduced a higher level of abstraction, looking, for instance, for linguistic universals as specific structural oppositions between the categories *marked* and *unmarked*, in phonology and in grammar. In a third step, the problem of universals is considered under the form of identification of some generative mechanisms common to all (natural) languages (16), whereas Montague (15) gives an extension of this view to all human (i.e., both natural and artificial) languages. A further step is considered in the field of formal grammars, where the universal grammar is a metatheoretic mechanism, a metagrammar depending on a parameter whose particular values give all possible individual grammars in a given class of grammars. For instance, Kasai (61) has shown that for any alphabet A there exists a (universal) context-free grammar G such that for any context-free language L over A we can find a regular control C (i.e., a set of finite sequences of rules in G which, in the alphabet formed by the rules of G, is a regular language) with the following property: G generates exactly L as soon as the only accepted sequences of rules in the derivational process are those of C. Greibach (62) has shown the existence of a context-free grammar universal (in the sense of the Kasai's theorem) for the class of recursively enumerable languages, as soon as the control set in the generative process is a linear context-free language (any regular language is linear context free, but the converse is not true). Rozenberg (63) has proved the existence of a grammar of type zero, universal (with respect to a regular control set) for the class of recursively enumerable languages.

All these results show that the possibility of finding a universal grammar as particular as possible for a class of languages as large as possible is dependent on the choice of a control set that is general enough. The more particular the desired control set is, the more general the selected universal grammar has to be. In both the results of Greibach and Rozenberg, the universality is valid with respect to a class of languages, be they natural, computational, logical, or of another type. Moreover, it is interesting to note the nonexistence of a context-sensitive universal grammar for the class of context-sensitive languages (62).

The above-discussed results are strongly connected with the learning process. It was shown that the universal grammar works like a hypothetical brain, explaining how a particular intellectual activity is actualized at some time through the corresponding particular grammar, whereas at another time, another particular grammar is actualized. The metagrammar in charge of this management operation is just a universal grammar, which could be one of the types considered in the above theorems (64).

CONCLUSION

Proliferation of sequentiality, due to computer information processing, leads to the proliferation of formal languages and of their combinatorial syntactic dimension. But this is both a danger [see, for instance, the traps of the existing programming languages in (65) and the loss of meaning in so many activities] and a chance. Are we able to exploit the latter and to keep the former under control?

REFERENCES

1. S. Marcus, Linguistic Structures and Generative Devices in Molecular Genetics, *Cahiers Ling. Theor. Appl. 11*, 77–104 (1974).
2. A. Martinet, (ed.), *Le langage*, Gallimard, Paris, 1968.
3. S. Marcus, Semiotics of Scientific Languages in *A Semiotic Landscape. Proceedings of the First Congress of IASS*, Milano, June 1974, S. Chatman, U. Eco, and J. M. Klinkenberg (eds.), Mouton, The Hague, 1979, pp. 29–40.
4. C. Calude, Quelques arguments pour le caractère non-formel des langages de programmation *Cahiers Ling. Theor. Appl., 13*, 257–264 (1976).
5. R. Moreau, in Natural Languages and Programming Languages, *Linguaggi nella societa e nella tecnica*, Edizioni di Comunita, Milano, 1968, pp. 303–324.
6. A. Van Wijngaarden, On the Boundary Between Natural and Artificial Languages in *Linguaggi nella societa e nella tecnica*, Edizioni di Comunita, Milano, 1968, pp. 165–176.
7. S. Marcus (ed.), *Contextual ambiguities in natural and in artificial languages, II, Communication and Cognition*, Ghent, Belgium, 1983.
8. A. Salomaa, *Formal Languages*, Academic Press, New York, 1973.

9. R. M. Smullyan, Languages in Which Self-Reference is Possible, *J. Symbol. Logic*, *22*, 55–67 (1957).
10. Y. Bar-Hillel, Do Natural Languages Contain Paradoxes? *Studium Generale*, *19*, 391–397 (1966).
11. H. Freudenthal, Cosmic Languages, in *Current Trends in Linguistics*, Vol. 12, Th. A. Sebeok (ed.), Mouton, The Hague, 1974, pp. 1019–1042.
12. P. Naur, *Commun. ACM*, *18*, 676–682 (1975).
13. M. Pei, Artificial Languages: International (Auxiliary) in *Current Trends in Linguistics*, Vol. 12, Th. A. Sebeok (ed.), Mouton, The Hague 1974, pp. 999–1017.
14. S. Marcus, Syntactics, *Rev. Roum. Ling.– Cahiers Ling. Theor. Appl.*, *27*, 25–42 (1990).
15. R. Montague, *Theoria*, *36*, 373–398 (1970).
16. N. Chomsky, *Semiotica*, 1–2 (1979).
17. P. Halmos, *I Want to Be a Mathematician*, Springer-Verlag, New York, 1985.
18. G. Steiner, *Language and Silence*, Atheneum, New York, 1967.
19. M. Henry, *La barbarie*, Grasset, Paris, 1987.
20. A. M. Turing, On Computable Numbers, With an Application to the Entscheidungs problem, *Proc. London Math. Soc.*, Ser. 2, *42*, 230–265 (1936–37); Correction: *43*, 544–546 (1937).
21. N. Chomsky, *IRE Trans. Inform. Theory IT-2*, 113–124 (1956).
22. E. L. Post, Finite Combinatory Processes, *J. Symbol. Logic*, *1*, 103–105 (1936).
23. E. L. Post, Formal Reductions of The General Combinatorial Decision Problem, *Amer. J. Math.*, *65*, 197–215 (1943).
24. S. Marcus, *Algebraic Linguistics; Analytical Models*, Academic Press, New York, 1967.
25. S. Marcus, *Introduction mathematique a la linguistique structurale*, Dunod, Paris, 1967.
26. A. W. Burks, D. W. Waren, and J. Wright, *Mathematical Tables and Other Aids to Computation*, 8, 53–57 (1954).
27. W. N. Locke, and A. D. Booth, *Machine Translation of Languages*, MIT Technology Press, Cambridge, MA, 1955.
28. Z. S. Harris, *Methods in Structural Linguistics*, University of Chicago Press, Chicago, 1951.
29. W. S. McCulloch and E. Pitts, A Logical Calculus of the Ideas Immanent in Nervous Activity, *Bull. Math. Biophys. 5*, 115–133 (1943).
30. S. C. Kleene, Representation of Events in Nerve Nets and Finite Automata, in *Automata Studies*, C. D. Shannon and J. McCarthy (ed.), Princeton University Press, Princeton, NJ, 1956, pp. 3–42.
31. Y. Bar-Hillel, A Quasi-Arithmetical Notation for Syntactic Description, *Language*, *29*, 47–58 (1953).
32. A. Thue, *Videns, selskapets Skrifter*, Kristiania, 1–22 (1906).
33. K. F. Gauss, *Werke. Teubner, Leipzig*, 272, 282–286 (1900).
34. B. Netto, *Lehrbuch der Combinatorik*, Teubner, Leipzig, 1901.
35. S. Marcus and G. Paun, Langford Strings, Formal Languages and Contextual Ambiguity, *Int. J. Computer Math.*, *26*, 179–191 (1989).
36. L. Kari, S. Marcus, G. Paun, A. Salomaa, *Bull. European Assoc. Theoret. Computer Sci* (EATCS), 46, 124–139 (1992).
37. S. Greibach, Formal Languages: Origins and Directions, *Ann. History Comput.* 3(1), 14–41 (1981).
38. P. Naur (ed.), Report on the Algorithmic Language ALGOL 60, *Commun. ACM*, *3*, 299–314 (1960).
39. P. Naur (ed.), Revised Report on the Algorithmic Languag ALGOL 60, *Commun. ACM*, *6*, 1–17 (1963).
40. S. Ginsburg and H. G. Rice, Two Families of Languages Related to ALGOL, *J. ACM*, *9*, 350–371 (1962).
41. S. Ginsburg, *The Mathematical Theory of Context-free Languages*, McGraw-Hill, New York, 1966.

42. R. W. Floyd, On the Non-Existence of a Phrase-Structur Grammar for ALGOL 60, *Commun. ACM*, *5*, 483–484 (1962).
43. G. Paun, On the Place of Programming Languages in the Chomsky Hierarchy (in Romanian), *Studii Cercet. Matematice*, *33*, 455–466 (1981).
44. A. Aho and J. D. Ullman, *The Theory of Parsing, Translation and Compiling*, Prentice-Hall, Englewood Cliffs, NJ, 1972.
45. B. Brainerd, An Analog of a Theorem About Context-Free Languages, *Inform. Control*, *11*, 561–568 (1968).
46. O. Ibarra, Simple Matrix Languages, *Inform. Control*, *17*, 359–394 (1970).
47. G. Paun, *J. Computer Syst. Sci*, *18*, 267–280 (1979).
48. H. Zemanek, Semiotics and Programming Languages, *Commun. ACM*, *9*, 139–143 (1966).
49. S. Marcus, Linguistics For Programming Languages, *Rev. Roum. Ling.– Cahiers Ling. Theor. Appl.*, *16*, 29–38 (1979).
50. P. Sgall, The Role of Linguistics in the Development of Computers, *Prague Studies Math. Ling. 9*, 125–132 (1986).
51. A. Lindenmayer, *J. Theoret. Biol.*, *30*, 455–484 (1971).
52. A. Lindenmayer, *Proceedings of the IV Intern. Congress Logic, Method, Philosophy Sci, Bucharest, Romania, 1971* P. Suppes, et al. (eds.), North-Holland, Amsterdam, 1973.
53. B. Vauquois, *Oral Commun.*, July 1971.
54. Z. Pawlak, *Gramatyka i matematyka*, Panstwowe Zakady Wydawnictw Szkolnych, Warszawa, 1965.
55. Y. Uesaka, T. Aizawa, T. Ebara, and K. Ozeki, A Theory of Learnability, *Kybernetik*, *3*, 123–131 (1973).
56. M. Nowakowska, *Language of Action and Language of Motivation*, Mouton, The Hague, 1973.
57. G. Paun, *Generative Mechanisms of Economic Processes* (in Romanian), Editura Tehnica, Bucuresti, 1980.
58. S. Marcus, Mathematical And Computational Linguistics And Poetics, *Rev. Roum. Ling. 23*, 559–588 (1978).
59. S. Marcus, "The Romanian School of Mathematical Linguistics," in *Actas del IV Congreso de Lenguajes Naturales y Lenguajes Formales*, *1*, Carlos Martin Vide (ed.), University of Barcelona, 1989, pp. 397–411.
60. J. H. Greenberg, "Language Universals," in *Current Trends in Linguistics*, Vol. 3, Th. A. Sebeok, (ed.), Mouton, The Hague, 1966, pp. 61–112.
61. T. Kasai, A Universal Context-Free Grammar, *Inform. Control*, *28*, 30–34 (1975).
62. S. Greibach, Comments on Universal and Left Universal Grammars, *Inform. Control*, *17*, 359–394 (1978).
63. G. Rozenberg, A Note on Universal Grammar, *Inform. Control*, *34*, 172–175 (1977).
64. C. Calude, S. Marcus, and G. Paun, The Universal Grammar As A Hypothetical Brain, *Rev. Roum. Ling. 24*, 479–489 (1979).
65. E. W. Dijkstra, How do We Tell Truths That Might Hurt? *ACM Sigplan Notices*, *17*(5), 13–15 (1982).

Note added in proof. The bibliography should be supplemented with: Benson, D. B., *Formal Languages vis-à-vis 'Natural' Languages*. In "Computers in Language Research" (eds. W. A. Sedelow Jr., S. Y. Sedelow), Trends in Linguistics, Studies and Monographs 5. Mouton, The Hague, Paris, New York, 1979 and Edmundson, H. P., *Mathematical Models in Linguistics and Language Processing*. In "Automated Language Processing (ed. H. Borko), Wiley, New York, 1967.

BIBLIOGRAPHY

Allan, K. *Linguistic Meaning*, Routledge & Kegan Paul, London, 1986.

Bach, E., and R. T. Harms, *Universals in Linguistic Theory*, Holt Rinehart & Winston, New York, 1968.

Barr, A., P. R. Cohen, and E. A. Feigenbaum, *The Handbook of Artificial Intelligence*, William Kaufmann, Los Altos, CA, Vol. 1, 1981; Vol. 2, 1982; Vol. 3, 1982.

Barrett, E. (ed.), *Text, Context and Hyper Text: Writing with and for the Computer*, MIT Press, Cambridge, MA, 1988.

Barton, G. E., Jr., R. C. Berwick, and E. S. Ristad, *Computational Complexity and Natural Language*, MIT Press, Cambridge, MA, 1987.

Bellert, J., *Feature System for Quantification Structure in Natural Language*, Foris, Dordrecht, 1989.

Bunge, M., *Treatise of Basic Philosophy*, D. Reidel, Dordrecht, 1974.

Burghardt, W., and K. Holker, *Test Processing*, De Gruyter, Hamburg, 1979.

Charmiak, E., and D. V. McDermott, *Introduction to Artificial Intelligence*, Addison-Wesley, Reading, MA, 1985.

Cole, P., and J. Sadock, (eds.), *Syntax and Semantics*, Vol. 8, Academic Press, New York, 1977.

Comrie, B., *Language Universals and Linguistic Typology*, University of Chicago Press, Chicago, 1981.

Cooper, W. S. *Foundations of Logico-Linguistics. A Unified Theory of Information, Language and Logic*, D. Reidel, Dordrecht, 1978.

De Beaugrande R., *Text, Discourse and Process*, Ablex, Norwood, NJ, 1980.

Desclés, J. L., and S. K. Shaumyan, *Langages applicatifs, langues naturelles et cognition*, Hermès, Paris, 1989.

Fauconnier, G., *Mental Spaces*, MIT Press, Cambridge, MA, 1985.

Fodor, J. D., "Semantics," in *Theories of Meaning in Generative Grammar*, Harvard University Press, Cambridge, MA, 1980.

Granger, G. G., *Langages et Épistémologie*, Klincksieck, Paris, 1979.

Janta-Polczynski, M., *Texte en langage naturel, vu comme une specification de haut niveau*, École des Hautes Études en Sciences Sociales, Paris, 1991.

Katz, J. J., *Language and Other Abstract Objects*, Rowman & Littlefield, Totowa, NJ, 1981.

Knuth, D. E., *The Textbook*, Addison-Wesley, Reading, MA, 1984.

Marciszewski, W. (ed.), *Dictionary of Logic as Applied in the Study of Language*, Martinus Nijhoff, The Hague, 1981.

Melčuk, I. A., *Dependency Syntax: Theory and Practice*, State University of New York, Albany, 1988.

Minsky, M., *The Society of Mind*, Simon & Schuster, New York, 1986.

Moulin, B., and G. Simian (ed.), *Informatique Cognitive des Organisations: ICO '89*. L'Interdisciplinaire, Limonest, France, 1989.

Norrick, N. R., *Semiotic Principles in Semantic Theory*, John Benjamins, Amsterdam, 1987.

Peirce, Ch. S., *Collected Papers* A. W. Burks (ed.), Harvard University Press, Cambridge, MA, 1960.

Petitot-Cocorda, J., *Morphogenese du sens*, Presses Universitaires de France, Paris, 1985.

Petöfi, J., *Logic and the Formal Theory of Natural Language*, Zunke, Hamburg, 1978.

Sabah, G., *L'intelligence artificielle et le langage*, Hermès, Paris, 1989.

Salkoff, M., *Une grammaire en chaîne du francais*, Dunod, Paris, 1973.

Schank, R. C., and P. G. Childers, *The Cognitive Computer. On Language Learning and Artificial Intelligence*, Addison-Wesley, Reading, MA, 1984.

Sebesta, R. W., *Concepts of Programming Languages*, Benjamin/Cummings, Redwood City, CA, 1989.

Sethi, R., *Programming Languages. Concepts and Constructs*, Addison-Wesley, Reading, MA, 1989.

Vanderveken, D., *Meaning and Speech Acts*, Cambridge University Press, Cambridge UK, 1990.

Winograd, T., *Language as a Cognitive Process*, *Vol. 1*, *Syntax*, Addison-Wesley, Reading, MA, 1983.

SOLOMON MARCUS

SIMILARITY SEARCHING IN DATABASES OF THREE-DIMENSIONAL MOLECULES AND MACROMOLECULES

INTRODUCTION

There is intense interest in the development of techniques for searching databases that contain the machine-readable representations of chemical of biological substances. The traditional representation of a molecule in a chemical database is the two-dimensional (2-D) chemical structure diagram (1), whereas a substance (e.g., a carbohydrate, a protein, or a nucleic acid) in a macromolecular database is typically represented by its primary sequence (2,3).

As Rouvray has noted (4), the measurement of similarity between pairs of substances has long played an important part in scientific research. This may be effected by means of *similarity searching*, which involves scanning a database for those molecules that are most similar to a user's *target* structure. In such a search, the similarity between the target and each database molecule is defined by some quantitative measure of resemblance that is based on the structural representations stored in the database. Thus, molecular biologists make very extensive use of *homology* searching in sequence databases, where the similarities are calculated using dynamic-programming algorithms (5,6), whereas a chemist might want to search a database to find those molecules that are most similar to a target compound that has been shown to exhibit potential pharmaceutical activity in a biological test system (7). Two other types of search that may be provided in a database system are a *structure* search, which involves scanning a database to retrieve information associated with a particular substance (e.g., a biologist might wish to retrieve the literature reference for the first sequencing of a specific gene), and a *substructure* search, which involves scanning a database to retrieve all of those records that contain a user-defined partial structure (e.g., a chemist might be interested in retrieving all molecules that contained a cephalosporin ring) (8). Over the last few years, an increasing amount of three-dimensional (3-D) structural data has become available, and this has resulted in the development of structure and substructure searching methods that can be used to access databases of 3-D molecules and macromolecules: in this article, we provide an overview of current research into the development of techniques for similarity searching in such databases.

There are very many ways in which the similarity between a pair of objects may be calculated, as is evident from even a cursory inspection of standard cluster-analysis texts [see, e.g., (9–11),] and this holds true even if we restrict ourselves to the measurement of intermolecular structural similarity. Thus, Johnson (12) has reviewed mathematical definitions that may be used for the measurement of structural similarity, and Willett (7) discusses measures that are appropriate for the calculation of the structural similarity between pairs of chemical compounds represented by 2-D connection tables. Perhaps the most important single factor that must be taken into account when seeking to measure structural similarity is the structural representation that is used to characterize a substance, as this will constrain the similarity and feature-selection algorithms that may be applied to it; for example, we might wish to characterize the geometry of a 3-D protein structure by the positions of the Cα atoms, of the side chains, or of the secondary structure elements, *inter alia*. Once an appropriate representation and the associated features have been identified, we may then need to weight or standardize the data in some way; for example, the characterization of a molecule by a set of real-valued physical or chemical properties will normally require the use of a standardization procedure to ensure that the resulting similarities are not dominated by one, or by some small number, of the properties. Finally, there are many different types of similarity coefficient that can be used to quantify the degree of resemblance between a pair of objects, these including both simple association coefficients and distance metrics, as well as probabilistic and correlation measures of various sorts.

Most similarity measures are *global* in character such that they return a single number that describes the overall degree of similarity between a pair of objects. This is nearly always the case with nonchemical applications of similarity and also applies to the fragment-based measures that are used in 2-D similarity-searching systems (as discussed further in the subsection below), where the calculated similarities do not provide any information as to which particular parts of the molecules that are being compared are responsible for the observed degree of similarity. Such measures may be less appropriate in the context of 3-D similarity searching, as the biological activity of a ligand molecule at a receptor site is determined by the presence of a particular set of atoms in a particular geometrical arrangement, that is, the pharmacophore (13); they are still less appropriate when dealing with 3-D macromolecules, the biological activity of which is often determined by only a very few of the constituent residues. This suggests the use of a *local* similarity measure, which not only quantifies the degree of resemblance between a pair of structures but also identifies the structural equivalences that have contributed to the overall global similarity.

The final point to be noted when selecting a measure of structural resemblance is that there is often a trade-off between the *effectiveness* of a similarity-searching technique, that is, the extent to which the technique is able to identify structures that the user also perceives as resembling an input target structure, and its *efficiency*, that is, the associated computational requirements. Accordingly, it may not be possible to use the most effective measure if a very large database is to be searched, which is often the case with databases of small molecules, where a pharmaceutical or agrochemical company may wish to search a corporate database that contains several hundreds of thousands of 3-D structures. It is currently less of a problem with 3-D macromolecular similarity searching owing to the relatively small number of structures that have been solved to date; indeed, much of the work on macromolecular similarity has considered the matching of individual pairs of structures rather than the matching of a target structure against a complete database (as discussed further in the section Similarity searching in databases of 3-D macromolecules). However, the development of improved experimental techniques is resulting in a very rapid growth in the number of macromolecules for which à 3-D structure is available, and this will increase the need for effective and efficient methods for database searching.

The techniques that are currently available for searching molecular and macromolecular databases have evolved from very different disciplinary backgrounds, and we have thus treated these subjects separately. In the section Similarity searching in databases of 3-D molecules, we provide a detailed review of the techniques that are currently being developed for similarity searching in databases of 3-D small molecules; and the third section provides a comparable review for 3-D macromolecules. The latter section focuses on the 3-D protein structures in the Protein Data Bank (14,15) because there are currently insufficient 3-D structures available for the other main classes of biological macromolecules, for example, complex carbohydrates or nucleic acids, to necessitate the use of sophisticated database-searching methods. Then, in the section Integration of techniques, we discuss two areas where there has been some degree of overlap between the two areas of research, specifically in studies of ligand docking and of the use of graph-theoretic approaches for protein similarity searching. The article concludes with a brief summary of the current state of the art and a note of areas where further research is needed.

SIMILARITY SEARCHING IN DATABASES OF 3-D MOLECULES

Introduction

Techniques for the representation and searching of 2-D chemical compounds have been available in chemical information systems for some two decades (1). However, these systems are being rapidly enhanced by the development of techniques for the representation and searching of three-dimensional (3-D) representations of molecular structure (16–18).

Similarity searching is widely used for searching databases of 2-D chemical structures (1). The primary rationale for its use is the *similar property principle* of Johnson and Maggiora (19), which states that structurally similar molecules are expected to exhibit similar properties; thus, if a biologically active molecule is used as the target in a similarity search, then the top-ranked molecules are expected to have a greater probability of exhibiting the same activity than would be the case if they were selected at random. Accordingly, given a single compound that has been shown to be active in a biological test system, similarity searching provides an excellent way of exploring a database to identify additional active compounds.

Similarity searching is normally effected using an approach first suggested by Adamson and Bush (20). Here, the degree of structural similarity between a pair of compounds is expressed in terms of a simple association coefficient (the Tanimoto coefficient (7) is normally used) based on the substructural fragments that are common and that are not common to the two molecules being compared. This approach was chosen in the first instance because it makes use of the fragment-occurrence data that is encoded in the bit strings that are used for the screening stage of a substructure search. It proved to be an excellent choice, as subsequent work has amply demonstrated that the use of such data results in similarity and clustering methods that are effective in operation and that can be used to make reasonably accurate predictions of molecular properties (7,21). In addition, such similarities can be calculated very efficiently using an inverted-file, nearest-neighbor algorithm that permits interactive searching of databases containing hundreds of thousands of structures (22).

Fragment-based similarities can also be used as the input to a clustering method to produce groups, or clusters, of structurally related molecules. These clusters can then be used to assist in the selection of compounds for random biological screening, which is an important method for the identification of potential lead compounds in drug-discovery programs (23–25). The use of cluster analysis in 2-D chemical information systems is reviewed in a recent article by Barnard and Downs (26).

Nearly all systems for 2-D similarity searching involve fragment-based similarity measures: There is much less consensus as to what should form the basis for similarity searching in databases of 3-D structures. We have noted previously the conflict that may exist between the effectiveness and the efficiency of a similarity-searching procedure. This trade-off is of particular importance here because many of the quantum-mechanical and molecular-modeling procedures that have been used for measuring structural similarities in the molecular-graphics and structure-activity literatures are far too time-consuming to be considered for use in a database-searching environment, where a target molecule must be matched against many thousands of database structures.

Methods Based on Alignments

Steric similarities between pairs of molecules can be estimated using procedures based on the matching of atoms or of superimposed volumes. For example, Dean and co-workers have discussed the matching of pairs of atoms, one from a target structure and one from a database structure, so as to minimize the sum of the squared distance errors; both deterministic (27) and nondeterministic (28) algorithms have been reported. Meyer and Richards (29) measure the similarity of a pair of molecules by the extent to which their volumes overlap, and describe an efficient algorithm to obtain good, but not necessarily optimal, overlaps for pairs of structurally related molecules.

The molecular volume provides one direct and readily calculable description of molecular shape. More sophisticated approaches to the quantification of molecular shape, and hence to the measurement of resemblance between pairs of structures, have been reported in a series of articles by Mezey and his co-workers, who have developed a range of topological similarity measures; an overview of this work is presented by Mezey (30). Such approaches provide detailed insights into the similarity relationships that exist between pairs of structures, but their computational requirements may be too great for searching large numbers of structures unless some alternative procedure is used to identify a subset of the database. A much simpler approach involves characterizing molecular shape by a single number or ratio; examples of this have been described by Cano and Martinez-Ripoll (31) and by Petitjean (32), but there have not been any evaluations, to date, of their search effectiveness.

Carbo et al. (33) suggested that the similarity between a pair of molecules could be estimated by a similarity coefficient based on the overlap of the molecules' electron-charge clouds. This idea has been taken up by several workers, using both electron densities and molecular electrostatic potentials (34–38). A molecule is positioned at the centre of a 3-D grid and the electrostatic potential is calculated at each point in the grid. The similarity between a pair of molecules is then estimated by comparing the potentials at each grid point and summing over the entire grid, with a suitable normalizing factor to bring the resulting similarities into the range -1.0 to $+1.0$. This numerical approach necessarily involves the matching of very large numbers of grid points, unless very coarse grids are to be used; Good et al. (39) have recently reported an alternative approach in which the potential distribution is approximated by a series of Gaussian functions that can be processed analytically, with a substantial increase in the speed of the similarity calculation and with only a minimal effect on its accuracy. Good and Richards have subsequently reported the use of an analogous approach for the rapid evaluation of a measure of shape similarity (40). This elegant idea removes one of the main limitations of field-based approaches to 3-D similarity searching but still requires searching for the best possible alignments of the two molecules that are being compared so as to ensure that analogous grid points are matched.

Field-based similarity searching in large databases will be feasible only with the identification of an appropriate alignment procedure. Exhaustive searching for alignments is completely infeasible unless extremely coarse grids are used, in which case the calculated similarities are unlikely to reflect accurately the true degree of resemblance of the molecules that are being compared, and even stochastic searching procedures can run for extended periods if one wishes to conduct a detailed examination of the alignment space. For example, Kearsley and Smith (41) have described a method, called SEAL (Steric and Electrostatic ALignment), which uses a Monte Carlo procedure to optimize the alignment of two rigid 3-D molecules and which bases the matching on atomic partial charges and steric volumes. The method generates high-quality alignments, but the comparison of a pair of molecules requires tens of minutes of CPU time on an IBM 3090 with a vector-processing unit.

The procedures discussed above are all far too slow for database-searching applications, unless coupled with an initial screening procedure that can eliminate the bulk of the database from this extremely time-consuming calculation; an example of such a two-stage approach is provided by the SPERM program of van Geerestein et al. (42,43), which is discussed in detail in the next section. Future developments in computer hardware may enable similarity procedures such as these to be used for database searching; meanwhile, more efficient similarity algorithms are starting to be developed that use interatomic distance information. This provides a simple and obvious way of exploring the steric similarities between pairs of molecules, and several distance-based, similarity-searching techniques have been reported that seem to be sufficiently fast in execution to be used on databases of nontrivial size and that seem to provide effective measures of structural resemblance. These approaches are discussed further below.

Methods Based on Distance Information

Pepperrell and Willett (44) carried out a detailed comparison of four different ways of calculating the similarity between pairs of molecules that were characterized by their interatomic distance matrices. The comparison involved structures for which both 3-D coordinate and biological activity data were available, these data being used in simulated property-prediction experiments that allowed a quantitative evaluation of the effectiveness of the various similarity measures that were tested. The best results were obtained using the *atom-mapping* method, which is calculated in two stages. In the first stage, the geometric environment of each atom in the target structure is compared with the corresponding environment of each atom in a database structure to determine the similarity between each possible pair of atoms. The geometric environment of an atom is represented by the set of interatomic distances in which it is involved, and thus the calculated interatomic similarities reflect the extent to which a pair of atoms lie at the center of similar patterns of atoms and the extent to which they can be mapped to each other (i.e., to be regarded as being geometrically equivalent). In the second stage, the similarity values associated with these atomic equivalences are used for the calculation of the overall intermolecular similarity. Pepperrell et al. have described a range of experiments that demonstrate the robustness and general effectiveness of this approach to the measurement of 3-D similarities (45).

The atom-mapping algorithm has a time complexity of order $O(N^3)$ for the matching of a pair of structures each containing N atoms. The run-time requirements can be reduced by means of upperbound calculations that permit the elimination of many of the structures in a database from the full atom-mapping search (46); alternatively, parallel hardware can be used to enable a target structure to be matched against large numbers of database structures at the same time (47). A prototype search system has been implemented at Zeneca Agrochemicals, using the upperbound procedures on a file of 4500 structures. A typical search of this file for the 50 nearest neighbors of an input target structure requires about 60 s on a Unix workstation. Thus, similarity searches on a corporate database containing a quarter of a million structures would be expected to take about 1 h using comparable equipment, the precise time depending on the target structure and the search parameters that are used. Pepperrell et al. discuss the results of searches using this system and demonstrate the substantial differences that exist between the outputs of 2-D and 3-D similarity searches that are based on the same target molecules (48).

An alternative use of interatomic distance information has been reported by Bemis and Kuntz (49). Here, a structure is decomposed into all possible three-atom substructures (so that a molecule containing N heavy atoms will produce $N(N - 1) (N - 2)/6$ such substructures). The procedure represents a molecule by a frequency distribution, the 64 elements of which are initially set to zero. A three-atom substructure is selected, and the sum of the squared interatomic distances calculated over all of the pairs of atoms in the chosen substructure; this sum is then used to increment one of the elements of the frequency distribution. The procedure is repeated for all of the possible three-atom substructures, and the resulting frequency distribution is then used to provide a simple characterization of the shape of the chosen molecule. The similarity between a pair of molecules is obtained either by comparing hash values that are derived from the elements of the corresponding frequency distributions or by comparing the distributions directly. The latter procedure is analogous to one of the similarity measures (which they called the *distance–distribution* method) that was tested by Pepperrell and Willett (44) in their evaluation of 3-D similarity-searching methods; they found the approach to be less effective than atom mapping but considered only pairs of atoms rather than the more discriminating three-atom substructures studied here. As described, the Bemis–Kuntz procedure is limited to the comparison of pairs of molecules that differ in size by one heavy atom, at most. However, the methodology would seem to be extendible to more disparate sets of structures and to be sufficiently fast in operation for searching large files (even if use is made of the full frequency distributions rather than the hash codes that were used in Bemis and Kuntz's experiments). That this is, indeed, the case is demonstrated by the work of Nilakantan et al., who have used a similar atom-triplet representation for shape-based similarity searching in the corporate database of Lederle Laboratories (50).

The distance-based measures discussed thus far are all global in nature (although the atom-mapping method also provides some local similarity information in that it identifies pairs of atoms that are geometrically equivalent). The remaining procedures are all local similarity measures that consider the precise alignment of the target structure in the calculation of similarity and are, thus, much slower in operation. Similar comments apply to the docking procedures that are discussed in the section Integration of techniques.

The SPERM (Superpositioning by PERMutations) program has been developed by van Geerestein et al. (42,43) to provide a computationally efficient means of quantifying the degree of shape similarity between pairs of 3-D molecules. Following previous work by Dean and co-workers (51–53), the shape of a molecule in SPERM is described by mapping a specified property onto each of 32 points on a sphere surrounding the molecule, these points being the 12 vertices of an icosahedron and the 20 vertices of a dodecahedron oriented such that its vertices lie on the vectors from the center of the sphere through the midpoints of the icosahedral faces. In fact, not one but two properties are used to characterise a molecule, these being the distances from each hedral point to the nearest surface of the molecule and to the surface of the molecule along the vector linking that point to the center of the sphere. A database molecule is matched with an input target molecule by orienting the sphere representing the former molecule so as to give the greatest degree of agreement between the two sets of property values, this orientation being obtained using an algorithm due to Bladon (54). The molecules in a database are ranked in decreasing order of the resulting similarities, and some number of the top-ranked molecules are then input to the electrostatic similarity measure described by Hodgkin and Richards (36). This is based on the superposition of a pair of electron-density grids and is about three orders of magnitude slower than the sphere-matching procedure; it is, thus, typically applied to just the top 250 structures in the ranking resulting from the distance-based search. The orientation with the best Hodgkin–Richards score for a particular molecule is then taken to be the shape similarity for that molecule with the target structure.

Van Geerestein et al. discuss the use of SPERM to search a 30,000-structure subset of the Cambridge Structural Database for molecules that are similar to the antitumor antibiotics netropsin and daunomycin, which bind to DNA. The best-matching molecules represented a wide range of structural types, included some known active compounds, and also suggested novel DNA-binding molecules. This search took about 24 h on a VAXstation 3100; van Geerestein et al. suggest that this could be reduced substantially by the use of screening methods that could eliminate 80–90% of the file prior to the SPERM search (although this initial search might result in a reduction in the quality of the final output).

A *subgraph-isomorphism* algorithm is a computational procedure that is used to determine whether a query graph is completely contained within another, larger graph. Such algorithms have been used for many years in 2-D substructure searching systems, where the nodes and edges of a labeled graph are used to represent the atoms and the bonds of a 2-D molecule (or of a query substructure) (1) and are now being used in 3-D substructure searching systems, where the nodes and edges of a labeled graph can be used to represent the atoms and the interatomic distances of a 3-D molecule (or of a query pharmacophoric pattern) (16,18). Similarity (rather than substructure) searching can also be effected by graph-theoretic means if a *maximal-common-subgraph-isomorphism* (rather than a subgraph-isomorphism) algorithm is used to match a target structure against each of the structures in a database, where a maximal common subgraph (MCS) algorithm identifies the largest subgraph that is common to a pair of graphs. Such algorithms have been used for many years to determine the overlap between the reactant and product molecules in reaction-indexing systems (55) and, more recently, for 3-D similarity searching, where the MCS measures the extent to which two molecules' atoms and corresponding interatomic distances overlap in 3-D space. Ho and Marshall have described a program, called FOUNDATION, that retrieves all structures from a database that contain any combination of a user-specified minimum number of matching atoms, for example, all structures that contain at least seven atoms in the same geometric arrangement (to within any allowed distance tolerances) (56). Alternatively, Brint and Willett have discussed the ranking of a database in order of decreasing structural overlap, with the top-ranked structures being those with the greatest degree of overlap with the target (57). The latter approach has also been taken by Moon and Howe (58) in their program MOSAIC, which provides facilities for MCS-based similarity searching and for both substructure and superstructure searching, with all three being implemented by means of a clique-detection algorithm.

A range of different clique-detection algorithms may be used for MCS-based similarity searching. Ho and Marshall use an exhaustive enumeration procedure that derives from an early 3-D substructure searching algorithm described by Jakes et al. (59), Brint and Willett (57) use a much more efficient algorithm due to Bron and Kerbosch (60,61), whereas Moon and Howe use the routines developed by Kuntz for the DOCK program (which is discussed in the subsection Docking studies).

The Bron–Kerbosch algorithm has also been used in ligand-binding studies by Kuhl et al. (62) and by Smellie et al. (63), and, most recently, by Martin et al. in the program DISCO (64). This is designed to find the maximum overlap (to within allowed interatomic distance tolerances) between a set of structures, which can either be a set of different molecules or a set of different conformations for the same molecule. If the structures are all active in a biological test, then this provides an effective way of identifying a putative pharmacophoric pattern that can be searched for using a conventional 3-D substructure searching system.

Methods Based on Property Information

Some of the distance-based similarity procedures discussed in the previous section can also be used to allow property-based similarity searching.

The description of the atom-mapping procedure assumes that some atom in the target structure is considered for mapping to some atom in a database structure if, and only if, they are both of the same elemental type. However, there is no a priori reason why this should be so, and it is thus possible, if the user so wishes, for the program to match molecules on the basis of the arrangement of some specific atomic property (or properties) in 3-D space (46). Specifically, methods have been developed that allow an atom to be characterized by its hydrogen-bonding characteristics, its partial charge, its atomic radius, or a combination of these three types of property (rather than the elemental type as in the basic form of the method). It is also possible to specify weights when the elemental, hydrogen-bonding or partial-charge classes are used, which allows the user to designate certain atoms as being of greater importance than others. If very high weights are assigned to some atoms, it is possible to obtain an output in which the top-ranked structures will contain all (or most) of the highly weighted atoms, so that one can execute a form of ranked 3-D substructure search.

The SPERM program can also be used with property information, as the matching algorithm can be used with any property for which values can be calculated at the 32 vertices, for example, electrostatic or hydrophobic factors; indeed, searching using electrostatic potential is a standard option of the program that can be used instead of the distance criteria described in the previous section. The most recent version of the DOCK similarity program that is described in the section Integration of techniques augments the steric matching scores with electrostatic and molecular–mechanics interaction energies for the ligand–receptor complex. The inclusion of the additional information provides more accurate dockings, but this is at the expense of considerably enlarged run times, which might be too great to allow rapid searching of a large database.

An alternative use of property-based searching has been reported recently by Fisanick et al. (65), who describe experiments using a set of 6000, 3-D structures for which molecular-property data are available. Each structure is represented by a total of 29 computed properties (these including molar refractivity; van der Waals' surface area, dipole moment, and the heat of formation, *inter alia*). The standard deviation across the whole database is calculated for each such property. The overall similarity between the target structure and a database structure is incremented by 1, 2, 3, or 4 if the property value for the target structure is within 1.0, 0.75, 0.5, or 0.25 standard deviations, respectively, of the corresponding value for the database structure; this simple matching procedure is repeated for some or all of the properties. Initial experiments suggest that the most-similar structures resulting from a database search do, indeed, closely resemble the target molecule in structural terms.

SIMILARITY SEARCHING IN DATABASES OF 3-D MACROMOLECULES

Introduction

The molecules discussed in the previous section typically contain a few tens of nonhydrogen atoms, and they are, thus, in marked contrast to macromolecules, such as proteins, nucleic acids, polysaccharides, and lipids, which can contain thousands of such atoms. To date, most work on the computational analysis of macromolecular structural data has involved the 3-D protein structures in the Brookhaven Protein Data Bank (hereafter PDB) (14,15), and the review is, hence, restricted to this type of macromolecular structure. For those seeking an introduction to the studies that have been carried out on other types of database, Artymiuk and Rice provide an overview of biological database systems (66), Fuchs and Cameron (67) review the analysis of nucleic-acid data, Berman et al. (68) describe a comprehensive relational database of 3-D structures of nucleic acids, and van Kuik and Vliegenthart outline the work that has been carried out to date on the analysis of carbohydrate structures (69).

We now give a brief introduction to the structure of 3-D proteins; a more detailed account is provided by Branden and Toote (70). This provides the necessary background, for those unfamiliar with the subject, to the database-searching mechanisms that are discussed in the remainder of this section of the article. The structures of proteins can be analyzed at several levels. The sequence order of the amino-acid residues in the main chain of a protein defines its *primary structure*. This chain folds up into a specific 3-D shape, with regions of the chain forming regular repeating structures of two main types: the α-helix and the β-strand. These *secondary structures* are formed by hydrogen bonds linking nonconsecutive amino-acid residues in the chain. A higher level of structural organization, called the *supersecondary structure*, arises because the secondary structures form *structural motifs*, in which numbers of helices and strands are held in characteristic 3-D substructures via disulphide bonds or noncovalent interactions. Several of these motifs occur sufficiently frequently among the known proteins to have been given names, for example, the three strands in a sheet flanked by two helices that comprise a Rossmann Fold, and the five strands in a sheet that comprise a Greek Key. Both of these motifs are *sequence dependent*, in that their constituent strands and helices always occur in the same order along the main chain of the protein. The detailed arrangement of the amino acids in 3-D forms the *tertiary structure* of a protein and it is this level of description that is of importance in what follows.

It is very straightforward to determine the primary structure of a protein, and there are now several large sequence databases, for example, the NBRF-PIR and SWISS-

PROT databases both contain in excess of 25,000 sequences. A large amount of software has been developed to carry out *homology searching* of such databases (3,66), that is, to identify proteins that have a sequence that is similar to that of a query sequence, as the extent of the homology between a pair of sequences can provide valuable evidence as to the functional and evolutionary relationships between the corresponding proteins. It is far more difficult to obtain the tertiary structure of a protein, and database-searching software is, thus, still at a much earlier stage of development. The first structures to be elucidated, those of myoglobin and of lysozyme, were obtained in the late fifties and early sixties by means of X-ray crystallography, and this remains the main source of structural data to this day (71,72). X-ray studies provide detailed information about the overall spatial arrangement of the atoms in the amino-acid residues along the main chain and can also show where regions of secondary structure are located. However, despite considerable methodological development, X-ray crystallography is time-consuming and extremely labor-intensive. A more recent approach to the determination of protein structures comes from the use of NMR spectroscopy (73–75). This is far more rapid and requires just a liquid solution of the protein, rather than a crystalline sample; it is, however, currently restricted to proteins containing relatively small numbers of amino acids.

Protein structures that have been solved are made available via the PDB, which has been maintained by the Brookhaven National Laboratory in the United States since the establishment of the PDB in 1977 (14,15). The April 1993 release of the PDB contained coordinate data for a total of 982 protein structures. It is interesting to note that the PDB is comparable in terms of its computer storage requirements to the Cambridge Structural Database (15,76), which is the primary source of X-ray crystallographic data for 3-D small molecules and which currently contains approximately 90,000 such structures, that is, about 100 times as many as there are in the PDB. There is no doubt that the limited amount of data that is available has restricted the rate at which database-searching techniques have been developed for searching 3-D proteins; instead, it has focused attention on the development of methods for identifying similarities between individual pairs of proteins to assist in the generation of new 3-D structures, as discussed below. However, the last couple of years has seen a marked growth in the rate at which new sets of protein coordinates are being deposited in the PDB, with the result that it is expected to contain several thousands of structures within the next 5 years.

Atomic coordinate data, and the distance and angular information derived from such data, are now widely used to provide insights into problems such as protein structure prediction, conformational analysis, receptor–ligand docking, and the design of novel proteins (77). The work in these areas has progressed to such an extent that there are now a few database systems that have been developed specifically for the analysis of different aspects of protein structure (see, e.g., Refs. 78–81). In this review, we shall focus just upon those algorithms and methods that are based on the measurement of 3-D structural similarity.

Homology Modeling

There is much evidence to suggest that there is only a limited number of ways in which the secondary-structure elements in proteins can pack together. This is exemplified by the fact that there are well-known examples of distinct groups of proteins that show core regions of similar secondary and tertiary structure, though there may be no detectable sequence homology. If, on the other hand, different proteins do show sequence homology, with respect to one another, then this implies that they will have similar 3-D structures. As a consequence, protein *homology modeling* has become widely used as a way of obtaining a model structure for a protein of unknown 3-D geometry, using information derived from related or homologous proteins for which a 3-D structure does exist. Similarity is, thus, being used here to make predictions about the structure of an unknown macromolecule, as against the activity of molecules in a database in much of the work on similarity searching that has been described in the section Similarity searching in databases of 3-D molecules.

The sequence of the model protein is first aligned with the sequence(s) of related protein(s) of known 3-D structure to define the core region for the protein family. This is done using a conventional dynamic-programming algorithm, such as that due to Needleman and Wunsch (5,6), and the resulting alignment(s) are then optimised via 3-D superposition (as discussed in the following subsection). The core structure of the model protein is constructed by combining appropriate 3-D fragments from the homologous proteins. These fragments are identified by taking a set of consensus 3-D fragments from a Cα distance–matrix analysis of the structurally conserved regions in the homologous proteins that are being used for the prediction of the model structure (82). The variable regions, such as loop connections and turns linking α-helices and β-strands, are next built up from 3-D substructure libraries (83). Assignments of the orientations of the side chains is then attempted, based on protein homologs if at all possible, and the resulting crude model is then refined by means of energy-minimization and molecular-dynamics procedures. The strengths and weaknesses of this approach are now well established, and it is widely used.

An alternative to this general approach has been described by Srinivasan et al. (84). Their homology-modeling approach uses distance geometry techniques (85) in the final stages to smooth an ensemble of structures. Specifically, the methods described are employed to obtain model-structure coordinate assignments for the regions of core structure and tentative coordinate assignments for the more flexible structural areas. Distance-range constraints are then used to ensure that the atoms in these parts of the model structure are in standard geometries.

Superposition Methods

Superposition techniques were born out of the realizations that the best sequence alignments did not necessarily coincide with the best structural alignments and that structures could be similar even in the absence of sequence similarity. Superposition involves calculating a rotation matrix and translation vector that optimally superimposes a set of atomic coordinates from one protein onto a second set of atomic coordinates from a comparison protein. The best rotation matrix and translation vector are calculated by an iterative least-squares method, using algorithms such as those described by McLachlan (86,87), Kabsch (88), Liu and van Rapenbusch (89), and Zuker and Somorjai (90). The similarity of the two proteins is then estimated by the overall root mean square (RMS) deviation between the two sets of superimposed atoms. The main drawback of this approach to the calculation of interprotein similarity is that it is necessary to identify the equivalent amino-acid residues (and hence the equivalent constituent atoms) in the two proteins before any superposition can take place.

Examples of superpositioning procedures are described by Rossmann and co-workers (91,92) and by Remington and Matthews (93), using a range of techniques to identify the initial atom mappings that form the input to the least-squares minimization. The procedure due to Remington and Matthews involves taking a segment probe of a set length from the first protein, which is then matched systematically against similar-sized segments in the comparison protein. Rossmann's method can be used on proteins that do not possess immediately recognizable equivalences and involves the calculation of probabilities of equivalences between atoms calculated from interatomic distance vectors.

Thus far, we have considered the superposition of proteins at the atomic level. Superposition at the secondary-structural level has been described by Murthy (94) and Abagyan and Maiorov (95). The latter workers define the secondary-structural elements as vectors, using a representation technique that is not dissimilar to those described by Richards and Kundrot (96) and Mitchell et al. (97) (as discussed later in this section). The similarity of two protein-structure fragments, a strand-helix-strand unit in the example quoted by Abagyan and Maiorov, is determined by a penalty function that includes terms relating to the vector lengths and planar and dihedral angles. Fragments that possess penalty functions below a certain threshold are superposed using the least-squares algorithm of McLachlan (87).

Distance-Matrix Methods

Another major approach to comparing 3-D structures of protein molecules is provided by the *distance matrix*, or DM. This was first mooted by Phillips (98) and subsequently developed by Nishikawa and Ooi (99) as a distance map (or diagonal plot) for locating secondary-structural elements and tertiary-structural domains within a single protein. An $N \times N$ matrix is formed, where N is the number of amino-acid residues in the protein and where the IJth element of the matrix represents the distance between the Cα atoms of the Ith and the Jth of the residues. The structural organization of the protein is then identified by selective contouring of the DM elements.

The similarity between two protein structures may be investigated by comparing their distance matrices, specifically by the construction of the *difference distance matrix* (DDM) (99). Here, the IJth element in the DDM contains the difference between the Cα interatomic distances in each of the two proteins that are being compared. The total difference between the two proteins is calculated and then averaged over every pair of residues to give a value, ΔD, that is, thus, a measure of the similarity between the two proteins. It is possible to use the Cα atomic coordinates themselves, rather than the Cα–Cα interatomic distances, in the matching procedure. However, use of the latter is generally preferred because the comparison procedure is then independent of any coordinate frame.

Other types of 3-D geometric information have been used in the DDM approach. Thus, Levine et al. (100) use the differences between dihedral angles along the amino-acid chains of two proteins in the matrix to provide a ranking of the probability that pairs of proteins possess some structural similarity. An analogous idea is discussed by Karpen et al. (101), who use the calculated RMS differences of the torsion angles along fragments of 3-5 amino-acid residues in pairs of protein structures to locate similar substructures. Finally, Factor and Mehler (102) have used the distances between hydrogen-bonding groups in the DDM.

It is simple to apply the DDM method to the comparison of chains of equal length. However, it is more difficult to identify the regions of structural commonality if this is not so, that is, if the DDM is of size $N \times M$ (where N and M are the numbers of amino-acid residues in the two proteins that are being compared and where $N \neq M$). Such occurrences are common and result from insertions and/or deletions of stretches of the amino-acid chain in one of the two proteins that are being compared. Taylor and Orengo note that solutions can be found in such cases if the larger protein contains a domain that corresponds well to the smaller protein, that is, if the latter is, or is almost, a substructure of the former, or if the smaller protein represents a protein fragment in which insertions and/or deletions are not expected (103). Solutions can also be found by the superposition or alignment of the two sequences prior to the DDM analysis, to pinpoint initial areas of equivalence in the two structures; this, however, is not always possible.

Taylor and Orengo (103,104) describe an approach to structure matching that removes deletion and insertion problems by combining the DDM method with the dynamic-programming technique of Needleman and Wunsch (5). Residue environments in proteins are defined by sets of vectors (rather than by just the simple interatomic distances as in the conventional DDM method). The proteins are aligned by comparing vector sets in lower-level matrices, using dynamic programming to find the optimal path through the matrices. An upper-level matrix is scored by accumulating all the lower-level paths and a consensus alignment path is found in the upper-level matrix by a second application of the dynamic-programming procedure.

Comparison of Nonhomologous Proteins

It will have been realized from what has been said thus far that much, but not all, of the research on the comparison of protein structures has focused on the comparison of homologous proteins. We now consider additional techniques that can provide quantitative measures of similarity between proteins whose global architecture and sequences are not, apparently, similar or related. These sequence-independent techniques have been used to classify large numbers of proteins into structural classes and to identify stable folding motifs or areas of common functionality (either of which might otherwise have remained unnoticed).

Richards and Kundrot (96) use the distance-matrix approach to define regions of secondary structure. Helix-rich parts of a protein give filled areas along the main diagonal of the distance matrix, whereas strand-rich parts give filled areas parallel to, or perpendicular to, the main diagonal. Searches for substructures composed of two secondary structures, for example, the helix-turn-helix motif found in some DNA-binding proteins, are made by systematically comparing a "mask" representing such a motif against all filled off-diagonal "boxes" of the distance matrix. The presence and the location of the required secondary-structural motif is given if the overall RMS difference between the mask and any box is less than a threshold value. Richards and Kundrot's work involved only Cα interatomic distances, but they noted that secondary-structure elements could be represented by vectors and that proteins could then be compared by matching their constituent vectors, using the intervector distances and angles. They also suggested that searches for motifs containing more than two secondary-structure elements could be effected by carrying out a series of two-element comparisons. However, they do not seem to have put these ideas into practice on a large scale.

Vriend and Sander (105) identify substructure matches between proteins by comparing all fragments of a specified length (10–15 residues in their work) from one protein against all fragments of the same length from another protein, which can be totally unrelated. Fragment mappings are rejected if the compared Cα interatomic distances between the start and end of the fragments do not fall within a defined threshold. Pairs of retained fragments are superposed using the least-squares algorithm due to Kabsch (88) and accepted if the observed distance deviations are within user-defined tolerances. Accepted fragments are then elongated, by one residue at a time, and superposed again until the threshold limits are violated. The final sets of matching fragment pairs are clustered to identify the largest possible regions of matching substructure in the two proteins, and these regions are then superposed to yield the final structural equivalences. Alexandrov et al. (106) have described a similar approach that also utilizes superposition and clustering techniques to locate similar spatial arrangements of backbone fragments. Sali and Blundell (107) use a variety of information from all of the hierarchy of levels of protein structure to compare structures, combining 3-D structural information with physicochemical properties and sequence information. Each structural level has a number of properties defined, including 3-D information, and this information is stored in a series of similarity matrices. These matrices are compared using simulated annealing and the best alignments obtained via a dynamic-programming algorithm.

Finally, Rackovsky (108) uses both distance and angular information in a quantitative approach to the production of a structural classification of 123 proteins. The procedure involves the calculation of the virtual bond lengths, angles, and dihedral angles for all 4-$C\alpha$ units along a protein's main chain. A structural fragment distribution, or *fingerprint*, for a particular protein is constructed based on the frequencies of occurrence of the lengths and angles within specified ranges (a procedure that is not completely dissimilar to that of Bemis and Kuntz (49), which has been described in the subsection Methods based on distance information). The similarity of two protein structures, I and J, is calculated by comparing the corresponding fingerprints, and the resulting similarity measure then forms the IJth element of a global, 123×123 interprotein similarity matrix. This matrix acts as the input to a cluster-analysis routine, which successfully groups together proteins with similar architectures, for example, all helical proteins or all extended-sheet proteins.

INTEGRATION OF TECHNIQUES

In this section, we describe two areas of current research that, in very different ways, provide a link between the two types of similarity searching that we have discussed thus far.

Use of Graph-Theoretic Methods

We have noted in the subsection Methods based on distance information the importance of graph-theoretic approaches to the representation and searching of small molecules and of chemical reactions, and such approaches are also used in several other applications of chemical structure handling, such as the identification of rings in molecules (109). There is now increasing interest in the application of such methods to the representation and searching of 3-D proteins, and the work that has been carried out to date suggests that graph-theoretic methods are as applicable here as they are to the processing of small molecules. Of particular importance is the fact that they can process homologous and nonhomologous proteins with equal ease and are, thus, far less restricted than methods that need to take account of the primary sequences when matching two protein structures.

If a graph-matching algorithm is to be used to identify structural resemblances, ways must be found to represent a protein structure by a graph, and there are several levels at which this could be done. In the case of a small-molecule graph (whether in 2-D or in 3-D), the nodes are the individual atoms (typically the nonhydrogen ones) and it is clearly possible to represent a protein in an analogous way. However, small molecules typically contain only a few tens of nonhydrogen atoms, whereas a protein may contain several thousands of such atoms, and the inherently combinatorial nature of isomorphism algorithms means that it is completely infeasible to process graphs of this size. Accordingly, it is normal to consider reduced representations, in which proteins are described by graphs that contain small numbers of nodes.

The Cα atoms provide an obvious level of description, and these were used by Lesk (110) in what was probably the first reported use of a graph-matching algorithm for the analysis of 3-D proteins. Lesk sought to locate regions of α-helix in polyalanine using a five-atom pattern. Interatomic distances and atom-type and bond-type information were used to extract pairs of atoms separated by less than a threshold distance; these atom pairs were then incorporated into larger sets based on matching distances in neighboring atoms. Brint et al. (111) describe a two-stage technique to locate patterns of Cα atoms in protein molecules using primarily interatomic distance information. Their program used the Lesk algorithm as a precursor to a more precise search based on Ullmann's subgraph-isomorphism algorithm (112) and achieved further reductions in the numbers of nodes that needed to be matched by introducing residue-type and secondary-structural-type information in the matching process. More recently, a similar approach to locating equivalences in proteins at the Cα level using interatomic distances has been taken by Haneef et al. (113,114), who use both the Ullmann algorithm and another isomorphism algorithm due to Bersohn et al. (115).

The comparison of 3-D protein structures at the secondary-structure level has been studied in detail in a long series of articles by Artymiuk and his co-workers (see, e.g., (97,116–118)). Thus, Mitchell et al. (97) describe a program that allows searches for structural motifs to be carried out using Ullmann's subgraph-isomorphism algorithm. The α-helix and β-strand secondary-structure elements are represented by vectors drawn along the major axes of the elements: These comprise the nodes of the graphs that are searched and the intervector distances and angles comprise the edges. A similar representation has been used by Grindley et al. (118) for the identification of 3-D structural resemblance between pairs of proteins using a maximal common subgraph algorithm, specifically the Bron–Kerbosch clique-detection procedure that has been discussed in the subsection Methods based on distance information. This program, called PROTEP, takes either a partial structural motif or an entire protein as the target structure, and then matches it against each of the proteins in the Protein Data Bank. The matching operation identifies all sets of secondary-structure elements in a database protein that are geometrically equivalent to a comparable set in the target structure, subject to the user-defined search tolerances (118).

The great complexity of protein structures means that it is often difficult to identify areas of structural commonality by eye. The exhaustive nature of an isomorphism procedure means that all such areas can be detected, and graph-theoretic methods thus provide a mechanism for the identification of previously unrecognised structural resemblances. Examples of this characteristic include the identification of close relationships between the families of bacterial signal-transduction proteins and of G proteins

(116) and between leucine aminopeptidase and carboxypeptidase A (117), and the identification of several previously unknown ψ-loops (119), *inter alia.*

Further work on graph-theoretic representations of protein structure has been reported by Koch et al., who describe methods for the characterization of the topological (rather than the geometric) arrangement of β-sheets (120), and by Artymiuk et al. (119), who have described the extension of their methods to the representation and searching of amino acid side chains, using graphs in which the nodes are vectorial representations of side-chain orientations and in which the edges are the intervector distances.

Docking Studies

"Docking" is the name given to the fitting of a ligand into a biological receptor site and, thus, involves the simultaneous manipulation of both molecular and macromolecular structures. Docking is most obviously effected by means of an interactive molecular graphics system, but there is also interest in the development of automated methods for docking. The earliest such program, the DOCK program of Kuntz et al. (121), is designed to retrieve those molecules from a database that are geometrically most complementary in shape to a protein binding site and that might, thus, be putative ligands for this site. The approach assumes that the geometry of the binding site is known, typically from crystallographic or NMR analysis, so that it can be described by a set of spheres that are complementary to the grooves and ridges in the receptor's surface and that fill the available binding site. The atoms comprising a putative ligand are represented by a similar set of spheres, and the shape similarity of the ligand to the site is then determined by the extent to which it is possible to overlap, or to dock, the two sets of spheres. The output from the program is a list of the best-matching equivalences, these being assumed to correspond with the preferred orientations of the ligand in the site; these orientations can then be checked by using crystallographic studies of the bound ligand. Further developments of DOCK are discussed by Shoichet et al. (122) and by Meng et al. (123).

Kuntz et al. (121) considered only the docking of a single ligand into a site, but the procedure was soon generalized to permit the searching of a whole database of 3-D structures, with the structures being ranked in decreasing order of their likelihood of fitting the receptor site on steric grounds (124,125). A detailed evaluation of the use of DOCK for this purpose is described by Stewart et al. (126), who docked 103 ligands that had been previously tested as inhibitors of α-chymotrypsin catalysis into the active site of the enzyme. A statistically significant relationship was found between the DOCK goodness-of-fit scores of the docked ligands and the observed inhibition strengths, with 8 of the 10 most active inhibitors appearing at the top of the DOCK ranking. More recently, Shoichet et al. (127) have reported an analogous study in which they have used DOCK to identify putative inhibitors for another important chemotherapeutic target, thymidylate synthase. This type of application is in marked contrast to a conventional similarity search of a database of small molecules, where the ranking is in decreasing order of similarity to a target structure that, typically, has previously been shown to be active in some biological test.

Lawrence and Davis (128) have reported a program, called CLIX, that performs a similar function to DOCK but that uses information from the GRID program of Goodford (129), which identifies interaction sites, that is, regions of high affinity for chemical probes on the molecular surface of a bonding site. CLIX takes a 3-D structure from the Cambridge Structural Database (the main database of experimentally determined 3-D structures) and then exhaustively tests whether it is possible to superimpose a pair of the candidate's substituent chemical groups with a pair of corresponding favorable interaction sites proposed by GRID (only nonhydrogen atoms are considered). All possible combinations of ligand pairs and GRID binding-site pairs are tested; if a match is obtained, then the candidate ligand is rotated about the two pairs of groups and checked for steric hindrance and coincidence of other candidate atomic groups with appropriate GRID sites. Lawrence and Davis demonstrate that the program is capable of predicting the correct binding geometry of sialic acid to a mutant influenza-virus hemagglutin and also report the best-matching potential ligands resulting from a search of 29,720 3-D structures from the Cambridge Structural Database; this search took 33 CPU hours on a Silicon Graphics 4D/240 workstation.

A further docking program has been reported recently by Bacon and Moult (130), who describe the use of an iterative least-squares fitting program (86) to match patterns of points on the surface of protein molecules and respective ligand molecules. Once the sets of matched points have been identified for a given docking, the residual RMS distances are taken as inverse measures of the surface complementarity for that docking. There is increasing interest in this whole area (see (131) for a recent overview), and it is thus likely that the next few years will see substantial developments. For example, Wang considers the problem of docking two proteins together (132), rather than docking a ligand into a protein active site, and Goodsell et al. discuss the use of simulated annealing in docking (133,134). However, extensive operational use of docking techniques for the design of novel ligands is likely only once it has become possible to extend the current rigid-ligand algorithms to take full account of conformational flexibility.

CONCLUSIONS

Structural chemistry provides an extremely fruitful area of application for similarity and clustering methods (7). Similarity searching is carried out on a routine basis on databases that contain hundreds of thousands of 2-D structures, and the recent development of databases of 3-D structures has already resulted in substantial interest in the development of comparable methods for 3-D similarity searching. Several of the methods that have been discussed in the second section are already in use in pharmaceutical and agrochemical organizations, but are currently used much less than 2-D similarity searching owing to the associated computational costs: it is difficult to carry out highly interactive, browsing-type searches if even a small database requires a CPU-day or more to identify the nearest neighbors for a user's target structure. It is, hence, to be expected that the next few years will see the development of new software techniques that can increase the speed of 3-D similarity searching (either by improvements to currently available similarity methods or by the development of new methods), and developments in computer hardware will bring about further increases in search performance. Such improvements are particularly needed if full use is to be made of the highly effective, but very inefficient, overlap-based similarity methods that have been discussed in the subsection Methods based on alignments and if full account is to be taken of the inherent flexibility of most 3-D molecules. Although the latter problem is starting to be addressed at the substructure-searching level (135), there have been no attempts thus far to develop comparable algorithms for flexible similarity searching. Given these limitations of current similarity-searching algorithms, it seems unlikely that operational systems for the effective clustering of databases of 3-D structures will become available for some considerable amount of time (whereas clustering of 2-D structures followed extremely rapidly after the development of the first rapid similarity-searching systems (7)).

The extension of similarity searching to databases of 3-D macromolecular structures is at a much earlier stage of development than in the case of 3-D small molecules. There are at least two reasons why this is so. First, the small number of substances for which accurate structure determinations are available has meant that most interest has been devoted to the comparison of small numbers of proteins, rather than to the development of fast algorithms that can carry out very large numbers of similarity matches in a short amount of time. Second, the huge numbers of sequences and sequence-searching algorithms that have been developed over the last two decades has meant that many (but not all) of the similarity-searching techniques that have been developed are based on primarily the sequence of a macromolecule, rather than on its structure. There are, of course, exceptions to these sweeping generalizations (e.g., the techniques described by Vriend and Sander (105) and by Grindley et al. (118) are examples of sequence-independent matching procedures that can be used to search the entire PDB), but the general problem remains. We believe that this situation will change dramatically over the next few years given the current rapid growth in the size of the PDB and the introduction of novel matching algorithms from disciplines such as graph theory, computer vision, and information science.

Finally, we wish to emphasize the range of applications for which similarity searching is used. In the case of 3-D small molecules, even the crude, first-generation database systems that have been developed to date are already being used to find molecules that are geometrically similar to a known active lead compound and to identify ligands that may act as inhibitors of macromolecules of biological interest. In the case of 3-D macromolecules, structural similarity is widely used for protein homology modeling, for the identification of substructures common to two or more proteins (at both the atomic and the secondary-structural levels), and for the generation of classifications of protein structures. With the development of faster algorithms and with the extension of current techniques to encompass the fields around (macro)molecules that are the main determinants of activity or function and to encompass the torsional flexibility that characterizes most (macro)molecules, it is clear that 3-D similarity searching will play a significant role in the future development of structural chemistry and molecular biology.

ACKNOWLEDGMENTS

We acknowledge the contributions of our colleagues Frank Allen, Peter Artymiuk, Peter Bath, Andrew Brint, Jonathan Davies, Trevor Heritage, Catherine Pepperrell, Andrew Poirrette, David Rice, Robin Taylor, David Thorner, David Turner, David Turner, David Wild, and Matt Wright to the work reported here. We thank Yvonne Martin of Abbott Laboratories for helpful discussions of much of the work discussed in the second section, and Peter Artymiuk and Andrew Poirrette for a careful reading of an initial draft of this manuscript. Funding for the research on three-dimensional chemical similarity searching in Sheffield is currently provided by the Cambridge Crystallographic Data Centre, the James Black Foundation, the Science and Engineering Research Council, Shell Research Centre, Tripos Associates, and Zeneca Agrochemicals. The Krebs Institute for Biomolecular Research at Sheffield University is a designated center for Biomolecular Sciences of the Science and Engineering Research Council.

REFERENCES

1. J. E. Ash, W. A. Warr, and P. Willett, (eds.), *Chemical Structure Systems*, Ellis Horwood, Chichester, 1991.
2. M. Sillince and J. A. A. Sillince, *J. Docum.*, *49*, 1–28 (1993).
3. A. M. Lesk (ed.), *Computational Molecular Biology*, Oxford University Press, Oxford, 1988.
4. D. H. Rouvray, *J. Chem. Inform. Comput. Sci.*, *32*, 580–586 (1992).
5. S. B. Needleman and C. D. Wunsch, *J. Mol. Biol.*, *48*, 443–453 (1970).
6. D. Sankoff and J. B. Kruskal (eds.), *Time Warps, String Edits and Macromolecules: The Theory and Practice of Sequence Comparison*, Addison-Wesley, Reading MA, 1983.
7. P. Willett, *Similarity and Clustering in Chemical Information Systems*, Research Studies Press, Letchworth, U.K., 1987.
8. J. M. Barnard, *J. Chem. Inform. Comput. Sci.*, *33*, 532–538 (1993).
9. A. D. Gordon, *Classification*, Chapman and Hall, London, 1980.
10. B. S. Everitt, *Cluster Analysis*, 3rd ed., Edward Arnold, London, 1993.
11. P. H. A. Sneath and R. R. Sokal, *Numerical Taxonomy*, W. H. Freeman, San Francisco, 1973.
12. M. A. Johnson, *J. Math. Chem.*, *3*, 117–45 (1989).
13. P. M. Dean, *Molecular Foundations of Drug-Receptor Interaction*, Cambridge University Press, Cambridge, 1987.
14. F. C. Bernstein, T. F. Koetzle, G. J. B. Williams, E. F. Meyer, M. D. Brice, J. R. Rodgers, O. Kennard, T. Shimanouchi, and M. Tasumi, *J. Mol. Biol.*, *112*, 535–542 (1977).
15. E. E. Abola, F. C. Bernstein, S. H. Bryant, T. F. Koetzle, and J. Weng, "Protein Data Bank," in *Crystallographic Databases: Information Content, Software Systems, Scientific Applications*, F. H. Allen, G. Bergerhoff, and R. Sievers (eds.), Data Commission of the International Union of Crystallography, Chester, 1987, pp. 107–132.
16. P. Willett, *Three-Dimensional Chemical Structure Handling*, Research Studies Press, Taunton, 1991.
17. P. Willett, *J. Chemomet.*, *6*, 289–305 (1992).
18. Y. C. Martin, *J. Med. Chem.*, *35*, 2145–2154 (1992).
19. M. A. Johnson and G. M. Maggiora (eds.), *Concepts and Applications of Molecular Similarity*, Wiley, New York, 1990.
20. G. W. Adamson and J. A. Bush, *Inform. Stor. Ret.*, *9*, 561–568 (1973).
21. M. A. Johnson, "Similarity-based Methods for Predicting Chemical and Biological Properties: A Brief Overview from a Statistical Perspective, in *Chemical Information Systems. Beyond the Structure Diagram*, D. Bawden and E. M. Mitchell (eds.), Ellis Horwood, Chichester, 1990, pp. 149–159.
22. P. Willett, "Algorithms for the Calculation of Similarity in Chemical Structure Databases, in *Concepts and Applications of Molecular Similarity*, M. A. Johnson and G. M. Maggiora (eds.), Wiley, New York, 1990, pp. 43–63.
23. P. Willett, V. Winterman, and D. Bawden, *J. Chem. Inform. Comput. Sci.*, *26*, 109–118 (1986).
24. L. Hodes, *J. Chem. Inform. Comput. Sci.*, *29*, 66–71 (1989).
25. M. A. Johnson, M. Lajiness, and G. Maggiora, *Prog. Clin. Biol. Res. Ser.*, *291*, 167–171 (1989).

26. J. M. Barnard and G. M. Downs, *J. Chem. Inform. Comput. Sci.*, *32*, 644–649 (1992).

27. D. J. Danziger and P. M. Dean, *J. Theoret. Biol.*, *116*, 215–224 (1985).

28. M. C. Papadopoulos and P. M. Dean, *J. Comput. Aid. Mol. Des.*, *5*, 119–133 (1991).

29. A. M. Meyer and W. G. Richards *J. Comput. Aid. Mol. Des.*, *5*, 427–439 (1991).

30. P. G. Mezey, *J. Chem. Inform. Comput. Sci.*, *32*, 650–656 (1992).

31. F. H. Cano and M. Martinez-Ripoll, *J. Mol. Struct. (Theochem.)*, *258*, 139–158 (1992).

32. M. Pettitjean, *J. Chem. Inform. Comput. Sci.*, *32*, 331–337 (1992).

33. R. Carbo, L. Leyda, and M. Arnau, *Int. J. Quant. Chem.*, *17*, 1185–1189 (1980).

34. C. Burt, W. G. Richards, P. Huxley, *J. Comput. Chem.*, *11*, 1139–1146 (1990).

35. R. B. Hermann and D. K. Herronn, *J. Comput. Aid. Mol. Des.*, *5*, 511–524 (1991).

36. E. E. Hodgkin and W. G. Richards, *Int. J. Quant. Chem.: Quant. Biol. Sympos.*, *14*, 105–110 (1987).

37. F. Manaut, F. Sanz, J. Jose, and M. Milesi, *J. Comput. Aid. Mol. Des.*, *5*, 371–380 (1991).

38. A. M. Richard, *J. Comput. Chem.*, *12*, 959–969 (1991).

39. A. C. Good, E. E. Hodgkin, and W. G. Richards, *J. Chem. Inform. Comput. Sci.*, *32*, 188–191 (1992).

40. A. C. Good and W. G. Richards, *J. Chem. Inform. Comput. Sci.*, *33*, 112–116 (1993).

41. S. K. Kearsley and G. M. Smith, *Tetrahed. Comput. Methodol.*, *3*, 615–633 (1990).

42. V. van Geerestein, N. C. Perry, P. D. J. Grootenhuis, and C. A. G. Haasnoot, *Tetrahed. Comput. Methodol.*, *3*, 595–613 (1990).

43. N. C. Perry and V. van Geerestein, *J. Chem. Inform. Comput. Sci.*, *32*, 607–616 (1992).

44. C. A. Pepperrell and P. Willett, *J. Comput. Aid. Mol. Des.*, *5*, 455–474 (1991).

45. C. A. Pepperrell, A. R. Poirrette, P. Willett, and R. Taylor, *Pest. Sci.*, *33*, 97–111 (1991).

46. C. A. Pepperrell, R. Taylor, and P. Willett, *Tetrahed. Comput. Methodol.*, *3*, 575–593 (1990).

47. D. J. Wild and P. Willett, *J. Chem. Inform. Comput. Sci.*, *34*, 224–231 (1994).

48. P. J. Artymiuk, P. A. Bath, H. M. Grindley, C. A. Pepperrell, A. R. Poirrette, D. W. Rice, D. A. Thorner, D. J. Wild, and P. Willett, *J. Chem. Inform. Comput. Sci.*, *32*, 617–630 (1992).

49. G. W. Bemis and I. D. Kuntz, *J. Comput. Aid. Mol. Des.*, *6*, 607–628 (1992).

50. R. Nilakantan, N. Bauman, and R. Venkataraghavan, *J. Chem. Inform. Comput. Sci.*, *33*, 79–85 (1993).

51. P.-L. Chau and P. M. Dean, *J. Mol. Graph.*, *5*, 97–100 (1987).

52. P. M. Dean and P.-L. Chau, *J. Mol. Graph.*, *5*, 152–158 (1987).

53. P. M. Dean, P. Callow, and P.-L. Chau, *J. Mol. Graph.*, *6*, 28–34 (1988).

54. P. Bladon, *J. Mol. Graph.*, *7*, 130–137 (1989).

55. P. Willett (ed.), *Modern Approaches to Chemical Reaction Searching*, Gower, Aldershot, 1986.

56. C. M. W. Ho and G. R. Marshall, *J. Comput. Aid. Mol. Des.*, *7*, 3–22 (1993).

57. A. T Brint and P. Willett, *J. Comput. Aid. Mol. Des.*, *2*, 311–320 (1988).

58. J. B. Moon and W. J. Howe, *Tetrahed. Comput. Methodol.*, *3*, 697–711 (1990).

59. S. E. Jakes, N. J. Watts, P. Willett, D. Bawden, and J. D. Fisher, *J. Mol. Graph.*, *5*, 41–48 (1987).

60. C. Bron and J. Kerbosch, *Commun. ACM*, *16*, 575–577 (1973).

61. A. T. Brint and P. Willett, *J. Chem. Inform. Comput. Sci.*, *27*, 152–158 (1987).

62. F. S. Kuhl, G. M. Crippen, and D. K. Friesen, *J. Comput. Chem.*, *5*, 24–34 (1984).

63. A. S. Smellie, G. M. Crippen, and W. G. Richards, *J. Chem. Inform. Comput. Sci.*, *31*, 386–392 (1991).

64. Y. C. Martin, M. G. Bures, E. A. Danaher, J. DeLazzer, I. Lico, and P. A. Pavlik, *J. Comput. Aid. Mol. Des.*, *7*, 83–102 (1993).

65. W. Fisanick, K. P. Cross, and A. Rusinko, *J. Chem. Inform. Comput. Sci.*, *32*, 664–674 (1992).

66. P. J. Artymiuk and D. W. Rice, "Database Systems in Molecular Biology," in *Chemical Structure Systems*, J. E. Ash, W. A. Warr, and P. Willett (eds.), *Ellis Horwood*, Chichester, 1991, pp. 299–328.

67. R. Fuchs and G. N. Cameron, *Prog. Biophys. Mol. Biol.*, *56*, 215–246 (1991).

68. H. M. Berman, W. K. Olson, D. L. Beveridge, K. J. Westbrook, A. Gelbin, T. Demeny, S-H. Hsieh, A. R. Srinivasan, and B. Schneider, *Biophys. J.*, *63*, 751–759 (1992).

69. J. A. Van Kuik and F. G. Vliegenthart, *TIBTECH*, *10*, 182–185 (1992).

70. C. Branden and J. Toote, *Introduction to Protein Structure*, Garland Publishing, New York, 1991.

71. J. P. Glusker and K. N. Trueblood, *Crystal Structure Analysis: A Primer*, Oxford University Press, Oxford, 1972.

72. T. L. Blundell and L. N. Johnson, *Protein Crystallography*, Academic Press, London, 1976.

73. A. M. Gronenborn and G. M. Clore, *Prot. Seq. Data Anal.*, *2*, 1–8 (1989).

74. T. F. Havel, *Prog. Biophys. Mol. Biol.*, *56*, 43–78 (1991).

75. K. Wuthrich, *NMR of Proteins and Nucleic Acids*, Wiley-Interscience, New York, 1986.

76. F. H. Allen, J. E. Davies, J. J. Galloy, O. Johnson, O. Kennard, C. F. Macrae, E. M. Mitchell, G. F. Mitchell, J. M. Smith, and D. G. Watson, *J. Chem. Inform. Comput. Sci.*, *31*, 187–203 (1991).

77. A. M. Lesk, *Protein Architecture*, IRL Press, Oxford, 1991.

78. M. Huysmans, J. Richelle, and S. J. Wodak, *Proteins: Struct. Funct. Genet.*, *11*, 59–76 (1991).

79. S. A. Islam and M. J. E. Sternberg, *Prot. Eng.*, *2*, 431–442 (1989).

80. J. M. Thornton, S. P. Gardner, and E. G. Hutchinson, "Protein Structure Databases: Design and Applications," in *Computer Modelling of Biomolecular Processes*, J. M. Goodfellow and D. S. Moss (eds.), Ellis Horwood, Chichester, 1992, pp. 211–230.

81. L. Holm, C. Ouzounis, and C. Sander, *Prot. Sci.*, *1*, 1691–1698 (1992).

82. R. H. Lee, *Nature*, *356*, 543–544 (1992).

83. T. A. Jones and S. Thirup, *EMBO J.*, *5*, 819–822 (1986).

84. S. Srinivasan, C. J. March, and S. Sudarsanam, *Prot. Sci.*, *2*, 277–289 (1993).

85. G. M. Crippen and T. F. Havel, *Distance Geometry and Molecular Conformation*, Research Studies Press, Letchworth, 1988.

86. A. D. McLachlan, *Acta Crystallogr.*, *A28*, 656–657 (1972).

87. A. D. McLachlan, *J. Mol. Biol.*, *128*, 49–79 (1979).

88. W. Kabsch, *Acta Crystallogr.*, *A32*, 922–923 (1976).

89. Z. J. Liu and R. van Rapenbusch, *Comp. Chem.*, *13*, 5–23 (1989).

90. M. Zuker and R. L. Somorjai, *Bull. Math. Biol.*, *51*, 55–78 (1989).

91. S. T. Rao and M. G. Rossmann, *J. Mol. Biol.*, *76*, 241–256 (1973).

92. M. G. Rossmann and P. Argos, *Annu. Rev. Biochem.*, *50*, 497–532 (1981).

93. S. J. Remington and B. W. Matthews, *Proc. Nat. Acad. Sci., USA*, *75*, 2180–2184 (1978).

94. M. R. N. Murthy, *FEBS Lett.*, *168*, 97–102 (1984).

95. R. Abagyan and V. N. Maiorov, *J. Biomol. Struct. Dynam.*, *5*, 1267–1279 (1989).

96. F. M. Richards and C. E. Kundrot, *Proteins: Struct. Funct. Genet.*, *3*, 71–84 (1988).

97. E. M. Mitchell, P. J. Artymiuk, D. W. Rice, and P. Willett, *J. Mol. Biol.*, *212*, 151–166 (1990).

98. D. C. Phillips, "British Biochemistry Past and Present," in *Biochemistry Society Symposium No. 31*, T. W. Goodwin (ed.), Academic Press, New York, 1970, pp. 11–28.

99. K. Nishikawa and T. Ooi, *J. Theor. Biol.*, *43*, 351–374 (1974).

100. M. Levine, D. Stuart, and J. Williams, *Acta Crystallogr.*, *A40*, 600–610 (1984).

101. M. E. Karpen, P. L. de Haseth, and K. E. Neet, *Proteins: Struct. Funct. Genet.*, *6*, 155–167 (1989).

102. A. D. Factor and E. L Mehler, *Prot. Eng.*, *4*, 421–425 (1991).

103. W. R. Taylor and C. A. Orengo, *J. Mol. Biol.*, *208*, 1–22 (1989).

104. C. A. Orengo and W. R. Taylor, *J. Mol. Biol.*, *233*, 488–497 (1993).

105. G. Vriend and C. Sander, *Proteins: Struct. Funct. Genet.*, *11*, 52–58 (1991).

106. N. N. Alexandrov, K. Takahashi, and N. Go, *J. Mol. Biol.*, *225*, 5–9 (1992).

107. A. Sali and T. L. Blundell, *J. Mol. Biol.*, *212*, 403–428 (1990).

108. S. Rackovsky, *Proteins: Struct. Funct. Genet.*, *7*, 378–402 (1990).

109. D. H. Rouvray (ed.), *Computational Chemical Graph Theory*, Nova Science Publishers, New York, 1990.

110. A. M. Lesk, *Commun. ACM*, *22*, 219–224 (1979).

111. A. T. Brint, H. M. Davies, E. M. Mitchell, and P. Willett, *J. Mol. Graph.*, *7*, 48–53 (1989).

112. J. R. Ullmann, *J. ACM*, *16*, 31–42 (1976).

113. N. Subbarao and I. Haneef, *Prot. Eng.*, *4*, 877–884 (1991).

114. N. Kasinos, G. A. Lilley, N. Subbarao, and I. Haneef, *Prot. Eng.*, *5*, 69–75 (1992).

115. M. Bersohn, S. Fujiwara, and Y. Fujiwara, *J. Comput. Chem.*, *7*, 129–139 (1986).

116. P. J. Artymiuk, D. W. Rice, E. M. Mitchell, and P. Willett, *Prot. Eng.*, *4*, 39–43 (1990).

117. P. J. Artymiuk, H. M. Grindley, J. E. Park, D. W. Rice, and P. Willett, *FEBS Lett.*, *303*, 48–52 (1992).

118. H. M. Grindley, P. J. Artymiuk, D. W. Rice, and P. Willett, *J. Mol. Biol.*, *229*, 707–721 (1993).

119. P. J. Artymiuk, H. M. Grindley, A. R. Poirrette, D. W. Rice, E. C. Ujah, and P. Willett, *J. Chem. Inform. Comput. Sci.*, *34*, 54–62 (1994).

120. I. Koch, F. Kaden, and J. Selbig, *Proteins: Struct. Funct. Genet.*, *12*, 314–323 (1992).

121. I. D. Kuntz, J. M. Blaney, S. J. Oatley, R. Langridge, and T. E. Ferrin, *J. Mol. Biol.*, *161*, 269–288 (1982).

122. B. K. Shoichet, D. L. Bodian, and I. D. Kuntz, *J. Comput. Chem.*, *13*, 380–397 (1992).

123. E. C. Meng, B. K. Shoichet, and I. D. Kuntz, *J. Comput. Chem.*, *13*, 505–524 (1992).

124. R. L. DesJarlais, R. P. Sheridan, G. L. Seibel, J. S. Dixon, I. D. Kuntz, and R. Venkataraghavan, *J. Med. Chem.*, *31*, 722–729 (1988).

125. R. L. DesJarlais, G. L. Seibel, I. D. Kuntz, P. S. Furth, J. C. Alvarez, P. R. Ortiz de Montellano, D. L. Decamp, L. M. Babe, and C. S. Craik, *Proc. Nat. Acad. Sci. USA*, *87*, 6644–6648 (1990).

126. K. D. Stewart, J. A. Bentley, and M. Cory, *Tetrahed. Comput. Methodol.*, *3*, 713–722 (1990).

127. B. K. Shoichet, R. M. Stroud, D. V. Santi, I. D. Kuntz, and K. M. Perry, *Science*, *259*, 1445–1450 (1993).

128. M. C. Lawrence and P. C. Davis, *Proteins: Struct., Funct. Genet.*, *12*, 31–41 (1992).

129. P. J. Goodford, *J. Med. Chem.*, *28*, 849–857 (1985).

130. D. J. Bacon and J. Moult, *J. Mol. Biol.*, *225*, 849–858 (1992).

131. T. Slater and D. Timms, *J. Mol. Graph.*, *11*, 248–251 (1993).

132. H. Wang, *J. Comput. Chem.*, *12*, 746–750 (1991).

133. D. S. Goodsell and A. J. Olson, *Proteins: Struct. Funct. Genet.*, *8*, 195–202 (1990).

134. D. S. Goodsell, H. Lauble, D. C. Stout, and A. J. Olson, *Proteins: Struct. Funct. Genet.*, *17*, 1–10 (1993).

135. D. E. Clark, P. Willett, and P. W. Kenny, *J. Mol. Graph.*, *10*, 194–204 (1992).

RECOMMENDED BASIC READINGS

The following items will provide an introduction to the main areas of research that have been discussed in this review.

Abola, E. E., F. C. Bernstein, S. H. Bryant, T. F. Koetzle, and J. Weng, "Protein Data Bank," in *Crystallographic Databases: Information Content, Software Systems, Scientific Applica-*

tions, F. H. Allen, G. Bergerhoff, and R. Sievers (eds.), Data Commission of the International Union of Crystallography, Chester, 1987, pp. 107–132.

Ash, J. E., W. A. Warr, and P. Willett (eds.), *Chemical Structure Systems*, Ellis Horwood, Chichester, 1991.

Barnard, J. M. and G. M. Downs, *J. Chem. Inform. Comput. Sci.*, *32*, 644–649 (1992).

Branden, C. and J. Toote, *Introduction to Protein Structure*, Garland Publishing, New York, 1991.

Johnson, M. A. and G. M. Maggiora (eds.), *Concepts and Applications of Molecular Similarity*, Wiley, New York, 1990.

Lesk, A. M. (ed.), *Computational Molecular Biology*, Oxford University Press, Oxford, 1988.

Lesk, A. M., *Protein Architecture*, IRL Press, Oxford, 1991.

Martin, Y. C., *J. Med. Chem.*, *35*, 2145–2154 (1992).

Sillince, M. and J. A. A. Sillince, *J. Docum.*, *49*, 1–28 (1993).

Thornton, J. M., S. P. Gardner, and E. G. Hutchinson, "Protein Structure Databases: Design and Applications," in *Computer Modelling of Biomolecular Processes*, J. M. Goodfellow and D. S. Moss (eds.), Ellis Horwood, London, 1992, pp. 211–230.

Willett, P., *Similarity and Clustering in Chemical Information Systems*, Research Studies Press, Letchworth, 1987.

Willett, P., *Three-Dimensional Chemical Structure Handling*, Research Studies Press, Taunton, 1991.

HELEN M. GRINDLEY
PETER WILLETT

SIMULATION AND MODELING

INTRODUCTION

Simulation and modeling have long been used as a numeric technique for the study of the behavior of actual or postulated dynamic systems. Simulation techniques are used in business, industry, and government for conducting preliminary studies of large-scale complex projects and plans to assess their suitability before they are actually implemented. This technique which yields results quickly and at relatively low cost involves modeling of the system under study and experimenting with the model to study the behavior of the system. With the introduction of modern digital computer, simulation has taken on a vastly increased importance as a technique employed to study the behavior of actual or postulated systems. Historically, the concept of modern digital simulation was proposed by John Von Newman, who visualized the automation of gathering repetitive statistical data on a modeled phenomena. This was termed the "Monte Carlo" process, described in detail later, because it imposed randomly generated parametric changes on the model (1).

Simulation has been one of the most consistently useful and productive applications in computer sciences. Simulation, in essence, is a multidisciplinary technology, comprised of elements of mathematics, engineering, and management science. Many academic institutions, responding to the rapidly increasing demand for this useful technology, give courses in simulation that are sponsored mainly in multidisciplinary curricula: computer science, operations research, information science, or industrial management. Due to its versatility, simulation is in use in hundreds of application areas (2).

DEFINITION OF SIMULATION

Simulation has many meanings depending on the area in which it is used. According to the dictionary, to simulate means to assume the appearance or characteristics of reality. Reider (3) defines "simulation as the act of presenting an appearance of something without the reality." In Roth (2, p. 1265), "simulation is the representation of certain features of the behaviour of another system." Bobillier et al. (4) consider simulation as the technique of constructing and running a model of a real system in order to study the behavior of that system, without disrupting the environment of the real system. Newell and Simon (5) define "simulation as a method for analyzing the behaviour of a system by computing its time path for given initial conditions and given parameter values." According to Gordon (6) the term "simulation now commonly refers to the use of any procedure of establishing a model and deriving a solution numerically."

From the foregoing review on the definitions of simulation, it is not surprising to find differences of opinion on what constitutes a simulation and how it should be used and interpreted. However, simulation traditionally involves modeling and experimenting with the model of the system under study. The noun model means the representation or fascimile of something, and simulation, on the other hand, has come to mean the act of presenting an appearance of something without the reality (3, p. 660).

MAJOR CHARACTERISTICS OF SIMULATION

A description of the major characteristics of simulation will help in a deeper understanding. Turban (7) outlines the following characteristics of simulation:

First, simulations is not strictly a type of model; models in general represent reality, whereas simulation imitates it. In practical terms, this means that there are fewer simplifications of reality in simulation models than in other models.

Second, simulation is a technique for conducting experiments. Therefore, simulation involves the testing of specific values of the decision or uncontrollable variables in the model and observing the impact on the output variables.

Finally, simulation is a descriptive rather than normative (prescriptive) tool; that is, there is no automatic search for an optimal solution. Instead, a simulation describes and/or predicts the characteristics of a given system under different circumstances. Once these characteristics are known, the best among several alternatives can be selected. The simulation process often consists of the repetition of an experiment many, many times to obtain an estimate of the overall effect of certain actions. It can be executed manually in some cases, but a computer is usually needed.

Simulation is usually described as an art, or a soft science, because the useful results of the study depend on the skill of the modeling team. At the present state of the art, there is no scientific theory to guarantee the validity of the simulation process before the experiment is performed. Instead, the suitability of a model is judged by the correspondence of results from the model with known results obtained by observations of systems comparable with the system under examination. However, simulation provides a means of generating artificial history that can be used to identify problem areas (4, p. 6).

A common interpretation of simulation is the use of a computer to study the behavior of a complex system that otherwise could not be possible by classical means, including traditional mathematics. When we are engaged in simulation we are concerned with three major elements: system, model, and computer (8). A brief description of each of these elements is presented here for the sake of elicitation of relationships among them.

System

The term "system" is used in a variety of ways (see Chorafas (9), Klir (10), and Churchman et al. (11); therefore, it is difficult to provide a definition broad enough to cover many uses and at the same time concise enough to serve a useful purpose. Gordon (6, p. 4) defines a system as an aggregation or assemblage of objects joined in some regular interaction or interdependence." Although this definition is broad enough to include static systems, the principal interest in the context of simulation will be in dynamic systems where the interactions cause change over time. Bobillier et al. (4, p. 7) remark that the term "system" is applied to the whole situation being studied for the duration of such studies. Thus, systems generally change dynamically with time. The behavior of the total system depends on the internal relationships among the subsystems and also on the external relationships that connect the system to the environment, that is, the universe outside the system.

Thus, a system is affected by both endogenous and exogenous factors. Endogenous factors affect activities occurring within the system, and the exogenous factors affect activities in the environment that affect the system. The former state of the system is said to the static and the later is known to the dynamic (6, p. 4).

Systems are also analyzed from the perspective of the activities involved. The distinction can be drawn between deterministic and stochastic activities. When the outcome of an activity can be described completely in terms of its input, the activity is said to be deterministic. When the effects of the activity vary randomly over various possible outcomes, the activity is said to be stochastic. Representing a system with stochastic processes implies that there are random events that change the state of the system by discrete steps at specific points in time. For stochastic activities, there is no known explanation for its randomness. Sometimes, however, when it requires too much detail or is just too much trouble to describe an activity fully, it is considered to be stochastic (12).

Systems are continuous or discrete. Systems in which changes are predominantly smooth are continuous. The flight of an airplane is a continuous system because the flight is not modeled in a series of discrete steps but rather a continuous flow of movement. Systems like a factory in which changes are predominantly discontinuous are discrete systems. Few systems are wholly continuous or discrete. For example, the aircraft may make discrete adjustments to its trim as altitude changes, whereas in the factory, machining proceeds continuously, even though, the start and finish of a job are discrete changes. However, in most systems one type of change predominates, so that the systems can usually be classified as being continuous or discrete (6, p. 5).

Modeling

Studying the salient features of the system involves a measure of abstraction, known as modeling. The goals of modeling in the first place are to facilitate an understanding of how a system works, like a scientist studying phenomena in nature (8, p. 5). In this process, models are used to embody hypotheses about the underlying and inaccessible structure of the system. The term "modeling" includes both the construction of models and their manipulation (simulation) (3, p. 660).

Systems and Their Models

Systems studies are generally conducted with a model of the system. For the purpose of most studies, it is not necessary to consider all the details of a system; so a model is not only a substitute for a system, it is also a simplification of the system (13).

According to Gordon (6, p. 6) a model is the body of information about "a system gathered for the purpose of studying the system." Because the purpose of the study will determine the nature of the information gathered, there is no unique model of a system. Different models of the same system will be produced by different analysts interested in different aspects of the system or by the same analyst as his understanding of the system changes.

TYPES OF SIMULATION MODELS

Models can be typified in many ways, as proposed by Emshroff and Roger (14). Highland (15), and Rivett (16), but most can be broadly classified into two types, namely, physical and mathematical, according to their degree of abstraction (3, p. 660). Physical models are representative of actual physical objects. They are of three types: iconic models, scale models, and analog models. Iconic models represent systems through a visual form. An example is a land-based replica of an aircraft flight deck with devices to change altitude and orientation. Another example is a model employed to replicate the complicated form of a-to-be-manufactured item, usually at a reduced size, in such a manner that the interaction of parts can be seen before the actual item is built. Scale models are employed for quantifying the behavior of an engineering system with its scaled reproduction and the use of the similarity principle. The similarity principle assumes the models to be geometrically and dynamically similar to the systems they represent. The empirical procedures used for this approach to simulation has the reputation of being able to predict the action of extremely complex systems even where good mathematical models and solutions are not available (3, p. 66).

Analog models are used as aids in computations and, thus, in simulation. An analog model means a physical entity bearing a resemblance in behavior, in some type of ratio sense, to an entirely different physical entity. Some examples are organizational charts, maps, blueprints of a machine or house, a speedometer, and a thermometer. This type of models, considered as highly specialized, is more prevalent among scientists and engineers (6, p. 10).

MATHEMATICAL MODELS

Mathematical models use symbolic notation and mathematical equations to represent a system. The system attributes are represented by variables and the activities are represented by mathematical functions that interrelate the variables (6, p. 9).

Oren (17) provides a classification of mathematical models applicable to simulations. The classification that identifies 80 types of models is based on the following:

1. Descriptive variables (i.e., to their existence, the values of their ranges, their time dependence, and the number of their trajectories)
2. Nature of the functional relationships of variables (e.g., determination, anticipation of the future, linearity and stiffness)
3. Formalism used to describe the model
4. Intended use
5. Deposition of submodels
6. Goals to be pursued
7. Organization of submodels

The mathematical models, however, are most broadly classified into two types: static and dynamic. Static models represent the values that system attributes take when the system is in balance. Dynamic models, on the other hand, follow changes over time that result from the system's activities (6, p. 9).

Mathematical models can be further classified by the technique used for the study of the system. Thus, a distinction is made between analytical and numerical methods. Analytical methods involve the use of the deductive reasoning of mathematical theory to solve a model. However, use of an analytical solution may, in fact, require a considerable amount of computation. For example, the solution may be derived in the form of a complicated integral that then needs to be expanded as a power series for evaluation. However, mathematical theory for making such expansion exists, and, in principle, any degree of accuracy in the solution is obtainable if sufficient effort is expended (6, p. 10).

In systems in which it is not possible to derive information by analytical means, it becomes necessary to use the numerical computation method. The procedures involved in the method allow solutions in steps: Each step gives the solution for one set of conditions, and the calculation must be repeated to expand the range of solutions. This procedure is "simulation." To make it more explicit, "simulation" is used to describe any procedure of establishing a model and deriving a solution numerically. System simulation is considered to be a numerical computation technique used in conjunction with dynamic mathematical models (6, p. 10). Simulation as a numerical computation technique is usually invoked when it proves impossible to formulate a problem in terms of a mathematical model of a problem that cannot be solved by other methods developed within the field of operations research (12, p. 567).

Another category is comprised of deterministic and stochastic simulation models. According to Bobillier et al. (8, p. 8), a process is defined as deterministic if for every value of the input, the output can be determined in some reproducible fashion. For example, if the equation $Y = x + 4$ is considered as a process, then whenever the input x is equal to 3, the output Y equals 7. The formulas is true for all values of x.

There are many activities where the output is random. Activities or processes of this nature are said to be stochastic. The terms "stochastic" and "random" are used interchangeably. More formally, a stochastic process is defined as being an ordered set of random variables; the ordering of the set usually being with respect to time. In particular, stochastic activities used in system simulation give rise to a stochastic variable represented by a sequence of random numbers over time (6, p. 112).

Stochastic activity can be discrete or continuous. In the discrete activity model the dynamic state changes in discrete steps, e.g., changes are abrupt, steplike. Interstate transients are not considered. Such systems behavior usually results from disruption of system status caused by the allocation and disallocation of resources within the system. In this model situation, no smooth mathematical functions can be solved to obtain system behavior.

Discrete event models, although possibly differing in "world view" (organization of model logic and structure), may be considered to have a common basic purpose and, therefore, a common basic set of elements. Discrete event models are basically focused on system users, who consume systems resources and expend time. Where resources are unavailable queueing and queue—serving may occur. Models may differ in the generation of events in the method of accumulation of time and queueing statistics. However, all discrete event models possess the basic element set: users, resources, queues, and demand. Elements may be described as entities having referenced attributes that enable classification and accumulation (2, p. 1261).

Thus, discrete event models follow a certain probability distribution function. As stated by Gordon (6, p. 112), this means that if a stochastic variable can take I different values, x_i ($i = 1, 2, \ldots, I$) and the probability of the value x_i being taken is $p(x_i)$, the set of numbers $p(x_i)$ is said to be a probability mass function. Because the variable must take one of the values, it follows that

$$\sum_i^I = 1, \quad p(x_i) = 1.$$

Examples of a discrete variable that can occur in a simulation study are the number of items a customer buys in a store, or the origin of a message in a communication system where the terminals creating messages have been numbered from 1 to n.

If the continuous event model variable being observed is continuous and not limited to discrete values, an infinite number of possible values can be assumed by the variable. Gordon (6, p. 115) provides that the probability of any one specific value occurring must logically be considered to be zero. To describe the variable, a probability density function, $f(x)$, is defined. The probability that x falls in the range x_i to x_2 is given by

$$\int_{x_i}^{x_2} f(x) \quad dx, \qquad f(x) \geq 0.$$

Intrinsic in the definition of a probability density function is the property that the integral of the probability density function taken over all possible values is 1; that is

$$\int_{-\infty}^{\infty} f(x) \quad dx = 1.$$

The lower limit of the integral is shown as $-\infty$. In practice, most variables in a simulation study have a finite lower limit, generally zero. The probability density function at and below this limit is then identically zero, and the lower limit of the integral can be replaced by the finite value. The same effect may occur at the upper limit (6, p. 114).

The cumulative distribution function, which defines the probability that the random variable is less than or equal to x, is denoted by $F(x)$ in the case of a continuous variable. It is related to the probability density function as follows:

$$F(x) = \int_{-\infty}^{x} f(x) \quad dx.$$

From its definition, $F(x)$ is a positive number ranging from 0 to 1, and the probability of x falling in the range x_1 to x_2 is $F(x_2)$.

PROBABILISTIC SIMULATION

Discrete and continuous event models follow certain probabilistic distribution. The process of simulation of discrete and continuous models involving probabilistic distribution follow the following steps as outlines by Turbon (7, p. 88):

1. Describe the system and obtain the probability distributions of the relevant probabilistic elements of the system.
2. Define the appropriate measure(s) of system performance. If necessary, write in the form of an equation(s).
3. Construct cumulative probability distributions for each of the stochastic elements.
4. Assign representative numbers in correspondence with the cumulative probability distribution.
5. For each probabilistic element, take a random or pick one from a table of random numbers.
6. Derive the measures of performance and their variances.

7. If stable results are desired, repeat steps 5 and 6 until the measures of system performance "stabilize."
8. Repeat steps 5–7 for various alternatives. Give the values of the performance measures and their confidence intervals, and decide on the appropriate alternative.

THE MONTE CARLO METHOD

The Monte Carlo method is not a simulation model perse, although it has become almost synonymous with probabilistic simulation (7, p. 88). The principle behind the method is the replacement of an actual statistical universe by a universe described by some assumed probabilistic distribution and then sampling from this theoretical population by means of pseudo-random numbers. However, when it is not possible to describe a process in terms of a standard probability distribution such as normal. Poisson, gamma, exponential, etc., an empirical probability distribution can be constructed. Essentially, the process is the generation of simulated statistics (random variables) that can be explained in simple terms as picking up a random number and substituting this value in a standard probability density function to obtain random variable or simulated statistics. When a probability density function is not standard for a given process, empirical probability density functions are built along with the likely values or process parameters. The random number is generated either on a computer or is selected from a table, the value is compared with a cumulative probability distribution, and the likely value of the process parameters is obtained.

Monte Carlo simulation requires the generation of a sequence of random numbers that constitute an integral part of the model and that help in obtaining random observations from the probability distribution. In random numbers, probability of occurrence is same as that of any other number. Any variable of a model can be represented as a random variable and assumed to follow some theoretical probability distribution (i.e., normal, Poisson, exponential, etc.) or an empirical distribution. Random numbers are assigned in such a manner that their proportion is exactly equal to the probability distribution. Random numbers may be obtained manually, by computer, or by tables. Manual methods are generally not practical for generating random numbers because they are highly labor intensive. These methods usually involve such devices as roulette wheels, card shuffling, dice rolling, etc.

The most common process for obtaining random numbers is to generate them through a computer program. These numbers are between 0 and 1 (0 and 100%) in conjunction with the cumulative probability distribution of a random variable, including 0 but not 1.

Tables of random numbers have been published. The random numbers were generated using some random physical process and are considered to be truly random numbers. When taking random numbers from a random-number table, the starting point in the table is immaterial (i.e., we can start with any number in any column or row, and proceed in the same column or row to the next number), but a consistent, unvaried (i.e., we should not jump from one number to another indiscriminately) pattern should be followed in drawing random numbers. If random numbers are to be taken for more than one variable, then different numbers for each variable should be used, because the same random numbers would imply dependence among different variables.

The general procedure of Monte Carlo simulation comprises the following steps:

1. Define the problem. This involves defining clearly the objective of the system and identifying the variables (constraints) that have maximum effect on the problem objective.
2. Construct an appropriate model. The model should represent the real situation.
3. Specify values of variables to be tested. Supply values for input parameters and measure the output values.
4. Collect information required and determine the functional relationships and the types of probability distribution to apply.
5. Define coding system that will correlate the factors identified in step 1 with the random numbers that will be generated for the simulation.
6. Select a random-number generator and the random numbers to be used in the simulation.
7. Correlate the generated random numbers with the factors identified in steps 1 and 5.
8. Summarize and examine the results in an appropriate table.
9. Evaluate the results of the simulation and select the best course of action.
10. Formulate proposals for advice to management on the course of action to be adopted and modify the model, if necessary.

The application of the Monte Carlo technique for computation has been illustrated with the following example (18).

An engineering organization plans to manufacture shafts and rings of definite sizes and specifications. Quality control data reveals that shaft diameters are normally distributed with a mean average of 0.980 in. and a standard deviation of 0.010 in. Similarly, rings have a mean average of 1.000 in. and a standard deviation of 0.010 in. The rings have a mean average of 1.000 in. and a standard deviation of 0.020 in. If it is required to locate the number of misfits, i.e., shaft diameter exceeding the ring diameter through the Monte Carlo method, the following simulation procedure will be followed.

In order to locate the number of misfits, it is necessary to simulate the size of shafts and rings through a random deviate (z) from Table 1 which gives the area under the normal curve with mean equal to 0 and standard deviation equal to 1. The calculations are given in the table 1.

The Monte Carlo simulation follows the following path:

1. In finding a random normal deviate from Table 1 showing the area under the normal curve, four-digit random numbers are generally used.
2. The following procedure is used for finding z corresponding to a random number:
   (a) If the random number varies between 0 and 5000, z can be found from the table column; suppose the random number is 2952, then z (against area 0.2952) is 0.82.
   (b) If the random number exceeds 5000, then 5000 is substracted from the random number and z corresponding to the remaining figure is found. But a negative ($-$) sign is given to the z so found. Suppose the random number is 6641, then z for 1641 (6641−5000) is 0.42 but this will be read as -0.42, as the original number was more than 5000.

TABLE 1 Simulating Sizes to Locate the Number of Misfits

Assembly No.	Shafts			Rings		
	Random numbers	Random normal deviate (z)	Simulating size $x = u + z(0)$	Random numbers	Random normal deviate (z)	Simulating size $X = u + z(0)$
1	2952	0.82	$0.980 + 0.82(0.01) = 0.9882$	3992	1.28	$1.0 + 1.28(0.02) = 1.0256$
2	3170	0.91	$0.980 + 0.91(0.01) = 0.9891$	4167	1.38	$1.0 + 1.38(0.02) = 1.0276$
3	7203	-0.59	$0.980 - 0.59(0.01) = 0.9741$	1300	0.33	$1.0 + 0.33(0.02) = 1.0066$
4	3408	1.00	$0.980 + 1.0(0.01)\ \ = 0.9900$	3563	1.06	$1.0 + 1.06(0.02) = 1.0212$
5	0560	0.14	$0.980 + 0.14(0.01) = 0.9814$	1112	0.28	$1.0 + 0.28(0.02) = 1.0056$
6	6641	-0.42	$0.980 - 0.42(0.01) = 0.9758$	9792	-2.04	$1.0 - 2.04(0.02) = 0.9592$
7	5624	-0.16	$0.980 - 0.16(0.01) = 0.9784$	9525	-1.67	$1.0 - 1.67(0.02) = 0.9666$
8	5356	-0.09	$0.980 - 0.09(0.01) = 0.9791$	2693	0.74	$1.0 + 0.74(0.02) = 1.0148$
9	2769	0.76	$0.980 + 0.76(0.01) = 0.9876$	6107	-0.28	$1.0 - 0.28(0.02) = 0.9944$
10	5246	-0.06	$0.980 - 0.06(0.01) = 0.9794$	9025	-1.29	$1.0 - 1.29(0.02) = 0.9742$

In Assembly Nos. 6, 7, and 10 the shaft size turns out to be longer in diameter than that of the ring and, therefore, these are the cases of misfit out of the 10 assemblies simulated here.
Source: Ref. 18.

3. Because $z = X - \mu/\theta$, $X = \mu + z(\theta)$ and the same can be used to find the simulating size concerning the variable.

According to Shreider (19), the Monte Carlo method is often used on integrals of many variables by using a random number for each of the variables. Although random numbers are used, the problems to be solved are essentially of a deterministic nature. There are many other applications of the Monte Carlo method, including those where the problem being solved is of a statistical nature, such as the calculations concerned with reliability of nuclear reactors (20).

The Monte Carlo method is sometimes classified as being simulation. In addition, simulation is some times described as being an application of the Monte Carlo method, presumably because so many simulations involve the use of random numbers. Simulation and Monte Carlo methods are both numerical computational techniques. The Monte Carlo method is a computational technique applied to static models, whereas simulation applies to dynamic models (6, p. 41).

COMPUTER AND SIMULATION PROCESS

The relationship between computers and simulation is based on the fact that computers are used for generating behavioral data when supplied with suitably encoded model instructions of the significant features of a dynamic system. Experimenting with a dynamic system in some situations may be impractical without the use of a computer. Therefore, computers are employed in the simulation process with the object of providing an experimental model for observing the way in which all variables of the dynamic system change with time. Many simulation runs have to be made to understand the relationships involved among variables of the systems so that the use of simulation in a study must be planned as a series of experiments. Turban (7, p. 85–86) provides the following methodology for conducting repetitive experiments on a model of dynamic systems:

- Problem Definition. The real-world problem is examined and classified. Here it should be specified why simulation is necessary. The system boundaries and other such aspects of problem clarification are attended to here.
- Construction of the Simulation Model. This step involves gathering the necessary data. In many cases, a flowchart is used to described the process. Then a computer program is written.
- Testing and Validating the Model. The simulation model must properly imitate the system under study. This involves the process of validation.
- Design of the Experiments. Once the model has been proven valid, the experiment is designed. Included in this step is determining how long to run the simulation and which data to include. This step deals with two important and contradictory objectives: accuracy and cost.
- Conducting the Experiments. Conducting the experiment may involve issues such as random-number generation, stopping rules, and derivation of the results.
- Evaluating the Results. The final step is the evaluation of the results. Here, we deal with issues such as a what the results mean. In addition to statistical tools, we may use a sensitivity analysis (in the form of a ''what-if'' questions).

- Implementation. The implementation of simulation results involves the same issues as any other implementation. However, the changes of implementation are better, as the manager is usually more involved in the simulation process.

The experimental nature of the simulation technique makes it essential that the study be planned by deciding on the major parameters to be verified, the number of cases to be conducted, and the order in which runs are to be made. This procedure will help gauge the magnitude of the simulation effort and may cause a reappraisal of the model. As the simulation experiment is to be carried out on a digital computer, a program must be written. Actually, this step is likely to be carried out in parallel with the study planning, once the model structure has been decided. The steps involved in the simulation process are illustrated by Figure 1 (7, p. 85).

The activities in the simulation process are normally performed in the order presented. Others, such as Naylor et al. (1, p. 64) and Gaver (21), have expressed the steps in nearly the same way.

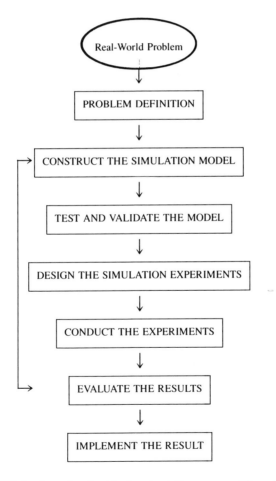

FIGURE 1   Steps involved in the simulation process. (From Ref. 7.)

ADVANTAGES AND LIMITATIONS OF SIMULATION

The increased acceptance of simulation is probably due to a number of factors as identified by Turban (7, pp. 84–85), Bobillier et al. (3, pp. 14–15), and Law and Kleton (22):

1. Simulation theory is relatively straightforward.
2. A simulation model is simply the aggregate of many elementary relationships and the interdependencies, much of which is introduced slowly by request and in a patchwork manner.
3. Simulation is descriptive rather than normative. This allows the decision maker to ask ''what-if'' type questions. Thus, managers who employ a trial-and-error approach to problem solving can do it faster and cheaper with less risk, using the aid of simulation and computers.
4. Computer simulation experiments are completely repeatable and nondestructive.
5. Experimenting with the real system may be costly and time-consuming, or even impossible in some situation. Substituting the real system with a model and experimenting with it is under no such constraints.
6. A simulation model is built for one particular problem and, typically, will not solve any other problem. Thus, no generalized understanding is required of the manager; every component in the model corresponds one-to-one with a part of the real-life model.
7. Simulation can handle extremely wide variation in problem types such as inventory and staffing, as well as higher managerial level functions like long-range planning. Thus, it is ''always there'' when the manager needs it.
8. The manager can experiment with different variables to determine which are important, and with different alternatives to determine which is the best.
9. Simulation, in general, allows for inclusion of the real-life complexities of problems; simplifications are not necessary. For example, simulation utilizes the real-life probability distributions rather than approximate theoretical distributions.
10. Simulation is an iterative process. A simulation experiment gives the value of the parameters during and at the end of simulation. Analysis of the output will suggest modifications to the strategy, such as changes in priority or sequencing rules. Thus, step by step, the decision maker gains more knowledge about the system and its performance until three is sufficient information to make final recommendations about the system to be implemented.
11. Simulation allows a great amount of time compression, giving the manager some feel as to the long-term (1–10 years) effects of various policies, in a matter of minutes.
12. There is no limit to the complexity of simulation models. When a complicated system defies mathematical analysis or when the inclusion of random variables with nonstandard distributions makes a statistical formula difficult to find, a simulation model may still be constructed.
13. The structure of a simulation model gives access to all the variables within the model. Therefore, during model building, some relations may be discovered among internal variables. Such relations should always be validated, and any extension beyond the domain studied during simulation must be justified. Such discoveries increase the analyst's understanding of the problem and aid in the development of more realistic models.

LIMITATIONS OF SIMULATION

The following are some of the limitations of simulation:

1. Simulation may not give the optimum solution of a problem.
2. The accuracy of simulation results is somewhat unpredictable, even for well-defined models.
3. In simulation, the experiment is conducted only with limited samples and random variables. The results depend on the input data's accuracy, which is also limited for practical reasons. Increasing the accuracy (or reducing the confidence intervals of the results) usually requires more machine time and increases costs.
4. The validation of complicated models, especially of systems in planning stage, can be very defficult. If the programming is consistent with the rules of the simulation language, then errors, due to invalid data or incorrect logic, unfortunately do not usually prevent the model from working, thereby producing spurious results.
5. Simulation can be very expensive in terms of computer time. Whenever was an attempt was to reduce computer time by using a variance-reduction technique, the result was an increase in the complexity of the model.
6. An inexperienced manager when faced with a complex problem may try simulation to define the model by reproducing the structure of the system on the basis of one-to-one correspondence rather than its form, resulting in extrapolating properties of the model found outside the cases studied, leading, finally, to answering questions relating to cases not covered by the model.
7. Simulation and inferences from a simulation study are usually not transferable to other problems. This is due to the incorporation into the model of the unique factors of the problem.
8. Simulation is sometimes so easy to sell to managers that analytical solutions that can yield optimal results are often overlooked.

SIMULATION MODELING AND THE COMPUTER

The simulation process of real systems, especially of discrete event models, can be accomplished more quickly and efficiently through computerization. There are two distinct stages in any computerized simulation study: first, systems analysis—to define the simulation model; second, computer programming to code the model for data processing (4, p. 16). Through systems analysis, fundamental components or entities common to many models are explored. Then characteristics or attributes of each entity are identified to be used to describe details of functions of each entity in the simulation model. To facilitate the communication of simulation models to the computer so that execution may occur, computer coding of models, known as computer programming, is carried out. In order to reduce the coding efforts, simulation programming languages have been developed.

SIMULATION LANGUAGES

Simulation languages, as distinguished from general purpose languages, are problem oriented. Such languages are usually written in a largely computer-independent notation for a particular problem area and contain statements or constructs appropriate for formulating solutions to specific types of problems. Simulation languages contain, to varying extents, constructs or structures that facilitate communication of a model to the computer: Control features such as data aggregation, event-timing routines, entity generation and destruction, data collection, and presentation of random variable generation are contained as subroutines or procedural operations in simulation languages. General purpose programming languages, such as FORTRAN, require that these operations be programmed ad hoc (2, p. 1265).

Because simulation models do not follow any formal structure, it is not surprising that there is a wide variety of approaches used in simulation programming languages, making it impractical to review them (12, p. 578). Nevertheless, Kiviat (23), Kleine (24), Palme (25), and Teichroew et al. (26) have reviewed the simulation languages in existence, identifying their basic features. Table 2, abstracted from Kay's articles (27), provides an overview of the simulation languages in existence.

Simulation languages can be broadly classified into two types: process oriented and event oriented. According to Gordon (12, p. 574), a process-oriented language is concerned with programming a process-interaction control. A process is considered to be a set of time-oriented events through which an entity must pass. A process-interaction control method will move each entity through as many events as it can at the current time. To be effective, it must be able to detect when an entity that has become blocked is able to move again, and immediately restart its advance through the process. Of the several process-oriented languages, more common are GPSS, SIMULA, BOSS, FLOW Simulator, Gesim, GPDS, QUIKSIM, and SIMON.

In contrast, event-oriented languages are concerned with event scheduling. Using this form of control, the machining would be considered one event, and a single routine would be responsible for executing all the changes that might occur as a result of that event. The routine must decide whether the event is just the simple event of ending a machining or whether it is a complex event, requiring another part be taken from the waiting line and committed to machining (12, p. 575). Some common event-oriented simulation languages are SIMSCRIPT, SIMSCRIPT II, and GASP.

DESCRIPTION OF SIMULATION LANGUAGES

The following material presents a brief description of important simulation languages of each type: process oriented and event oriented (2, pp. 1265–1278).

General-Purpose Systems Simulator (GPSS)

The General-Purpose Systems Simulator (GPSS) language has been developed over many years, principally by Gordon (28) at IBM Corporation. Originally published in 1961, it has evolved through several versions, to the latest versions—GPSS-360 and GPSS V. All but GPSS/360 and GPSS V are obsolete. Of the two current versions, GPSS/360 models can operate with GPSS V, with some minor exceptions and modifications. GPSS V is more powerful and has more language statements and facilities.

The system to be simulated in GPSS is described as a block diagram in which the blocks represent the activities, and the lines joining the blocks indicate the sequence in which the activities can be executed. Where there is a choice of activities, more than one line leaves a block and the condition for the choice is stated at the block. Each block is, in effect, a macroinstruction, representative of a system activity. Transactions moving through the block diagram represent temporary activities. Permanent activities are presented by program elements such as storages and queues, and their attributes such as utilization or current length, are made available. It also provides a large variety of automatically generated measurements about the simulated model. The current versions provide limited capability for using FORTRAN and assembly language subroutines. GPSS-360 version provides conversational features, user-interactive input, and control through a CRT display unit.

However, there are major snags with GPSS as a ''language.'' The first is that it is difficult to model many types of systems, as they are not easily squashed into the transaction flow mould without overdistortion. The second is that GPSS provides no sampling routines; thus, generating accurate stochastic variates is impossible within GPSS (29). Similar, is an extension of Algol developed by Dahl and Nygaard (30) of the Norwegian Computing Center, is process oriented. A process (user) continues until it is prevented from execution. An operative process is considered ''active''; a queued or suspended process is considered ''passive.'' Simula contains recursiveness, list-processing capability, and allows complete user access to Algol. An advanced version, also called SIMULA, is a general purpose scientific language containing simulation capability.

Boss (Burroughs Operational System Simulator):

Boss as a process-oriented simulation language was developed at the Burroughs Corporation by A. J. Meyerhoff, P. F. Roth, P. Shafer, and J. P. Troy. Although this language does not follow GPSS block format, it is similar in that it allows the use of its own flowchartlike blocks for coding processes. Boss blocks, however, contain multiple functions; for instance, it has implicitly invoked queueing when a process task cannot obtain a resource. This imparts to Boss an extremely compact notation that is sufficiently powerful for most modeling applications (2, p. 1268).

SIMSCRIPT

SIMSCRIPT is a very widely used event-oriented language for simulating discrete systems, developed by H. Markowitz, G. Hausner, and H. Karr at the Rand Corporation. Beginning with two early versions, it has progressed through two major, intermediate versions: SIMSCRIPT I.5 and SIMSCRIPT II, to the current and most powerful version SIMSCRIPT II.5. It has been implemented on several different manufacturer's computers. SIMSCRIPT II is generally compatible with SIMSCRIPT II.5. However, there are some important differences, some of which are dependent on the particular machine implementation.

In contrast to GPSS, a SIMSCRIPT program has very little prearranged structure. The program uses the terms ''entities'' and ''attributes.'' Entities having attributes interact with activities. Activities are represented by event routines, which are separately compiled subroutines describing the events that occur, or could occur, as a result of the activity. Data structures for representing the system entities are defined in a preamble section of the coding. Permanent entities are represented by individual words, arrays, or multi-indexed tables to record attributes or gather statistics. Temporary entities are represented by records that can be organized in sets. Instructions create and destroy the

TABLE 2 General Information About Digital Discrete Simulation Languages

Language name	Type	Developing organization	Authors	Computer implementation	Documentation of reference
Boss	Process	Burroughs	Meyerhoff, Roth, Shafer	B5000, B6000 series	Boss Mark II Reference Manual, Report 66099A; Burroughs Corp., Paoli, Pa., 1972
Flow simulator	Process	RCA CSD	Unknown	RCA 3301 Spectra 70 series	Flow simulator Reference Manual 70-00-617, April 1969
Gasp	Event	U.S. Steel, Arizona State	Kiviat and Pritsker	With appropriate modification, any computer with FORTRAN IV compiler	*Simulation with GASP II*, Kiviat and Pritsker, Prentice-Hall, 1969; *The GASP IV Simulation Language*, Pritsker, Wiley, 1974
Gesim	Process	GE	Unknown	HIS Sys. 600 and 6000 Series	GESIM User's Manual GES-1022
GPDS	Process	Xerox	Unknown	Sigma 5–9	Xerox General Purpose Discrete Simulator, Sigma 5–9 Computers, Xerox Data Systems, April 1971
GPSS	Process	IBM	Gordon et al.	IBM 7090 7094, 7040 7044, System 360/370; UIVAC 1107/1108/1110; CDC 6000 series; Honeywell 600 and 6000 series.	General Purpose Simulation System/360 CS Version 2 Users Manual, SH20-0694-0, IBM Corp.
GPSS/360 Norden	Process	Norden Div., United Aircraft	Katzke and Reitman	IBM System 360w/2250 Display unit	Norden Report 4269R 0003, Users Guide to Conversational GPSS, December 1969
Quiksim	Process	National Cash Register	Weamer	NCR 315 RMC	Proc. Third Conference on the Application of simulation, Dec. 1969.

Name	Type	Organization	Author(s)	Machines	Reference
Simon	Process	Bristol College of Science and Technology and ICL	Unknown	Elliott 503, 803; ICL 1900 series	ICL Reference Manual Simulation Language SIMON, January 1969.
Simscript	Event	RAND	Markowitz, Hausner, and Karr	IBM 7090, 7094, 7040 7044, 360/370; CDC3600, 3800, 6400, 6600, 7600; UNIVAC 494, 1107, 1108, 1110; RCA Spectra 70 series; NCR 200 series; PHILCO 2000 series; HIS 615, 625, 635, 655, 6030, 6040, 6060, 6080; STANDARD IC-6000	*SIMSCRIPT. A Simulation Programming Language*, Markowitz, Hausner, and Karr. Printice-Hall, 1963
Simscript-II	Event	RAND	Kiviat, Markowitz, Hausner, and Villaneueva	IBM System 360/370; RCA Spectra 70	*SIMSCRIPT II-A Programming Language* Kiviat, Villaneueva, and Markowitz, Prentice-Hall, 1969
Simpl/1	Event	IBM	Unknown	IBM 360/370	Simpl/1 General Information Manual (GH19-5053), IBM, 1972
Simula	Process	Norwegian Computer Center	Dahl and Nygaard	UNIVAC 1107; 1108, 1110; CDC 6400, 6600, 6700, 7600; Burroughs B5000, B6000, B7000 series.	Simula-A language for programming and description of discrete event system; Users Manual, Dahl, and Nygaard, Norwegian Computer Center, 1965
Sol	Process	Burroughs, Case Inst. of Tech.	Knuth and McNeley	Burroughs B5000/B5500; UNIVAC 1107/2208	Sol-A symbolic language for general-purpose systems simulation, Knuth and McNeley, 1963

Source: I. M. Kay. "Digital Discrete Simulation Languages. Discussion and Inventory." *Progress in Simulation.* I. M. Kay and J. McLeod (eds.), Gordon and Breach Science, New York, 1972. Vol. 2.

temporary entities at different points of the model. Other instructions will file, locate, and extract them from the sets under a variety of queueing or logical conditions (12, p. 578).

SIMSCRIPT distinguishes between temporary and permanent entities and attributes. The former type represents entities that are created and destroyed during the execution of a simulation, whereas the latter represents those that remain during the run. The purpose of a temporary entity, which is called an event notice, is to control the progress of the simulation. However, an event notice does not necessarily pass through the complete process of an entity. Event notices are usually destroyed upon execution of an event, and a new event notice is created for the following event. Each event notice carries the name of the event it is to schedule. When an event notice has been created, a special instruction schedules the notice to implement an event routine, either at the current time or at some time in the future. The simulation control algorithm files the event notices in chronological order and proceeds by advancing the clock to the time of the next most imminent event notice (12, p. 579).

The event routines are responsible for making all the changes of the state implied by the event. This implies making tests to see what conditions prevail and deciding on the type of change to be made. The event routines must also incorporate the processing needed to gather statistics, such as incrementing counters or marking times from which to calculate transit times. An event notice, having initiated an event routine, is usually destroyed. It may, however, be rescheduled, as might be done, for example, to generate a stream of arriving entities from the interarrival time statistics. If the execution of the event implies some other event, the routine must create the appropriate event notices and schedule them for execution, either immediately or at some future time (12, p. 580).

The SIMSCRIPT program includes an extensive report generator that allows the user to describe how the report will appear, naming the items for data to be inserted, and giving instructions on the manner of printing repetitive information.

SIMSCRIPT also provides aids which ought to ease the task of debugging simulation programs. Although the programmer must learn a new language in order to use SIMSCRIPT, these aids can make the programming task much quicker and easier for substantial programs.

SIMSCRIPT II

SIMSCRIPT II, initially designed by Markowitz and Karr, was further refined by P. Kiviat and R. Villaneueva at RAND Corporation. This is a scientific programming language that enables discrete event simulation. Although, it was a descendant the original Simscript, but not compatible with it, SIMSCRIPT II contains five "levels" that provide a wide range of capabilities for use as a scientific and/or data processing language, as well as providing event-oriented simulation capability (2, p. 1268).

GASP

GASP (General Activity Simulation Program) is a simulation language that essentially augments FORTRAN with a set of event-oriented simulation structures such as event timing, set manipulation, and statistical data collection and reporting; GASP II was developed by Kiviat and Pritsker. The GASP user must be familier with FORTRAN. Lately, Pritsker and associates have developed a PL/I version, Gasp1-I, and a new scientific language version Gasp IV (2, p. 1260).

Microcomputers and Simulation

Although, fast mainframe computers are required for the simulation study of most of the dynamic systems involving huge data sets or lengthy iterative analysis, many of the simulation analyses can be done on microscomputers that now offer the capabilities of mainframes in use only a few years ago. Microcomputers are now being used routinely to build models of phenomena with so many variables. In intricacy, methodological sophistication, and effectiveness, these microcomputer-generated models are stunning advances over what was possible just a few years ago. The success of applying microcomputers to the simulation study of one phenomenon after another has spawned the development of new applications of simulation techniques, and improved technologies extend the substantive range of sumulation application.

The refinement and sophistication of simulation languages that can be applicable on microcomputers are opening up new possibilities of the application of simulation techniques for a number of promising areas. One of these areas is the automatic evaluation of the various tactics possible within a selected strategy for solution of a complex problem. Furthermore, microcomputers are offering the opportunity for use of simulation as a technique for finding the detailed implications of a complex theory or model requiring too burdensome logical operations to conduct mentally because of the mathematical complexity of the model or because deductions have to be obtained with continual reference to a large database that provides the context for analysis.

Simulation study is a costly affair and time-consuming. It is now possible to use low-cost microcomputers to develop initial models, perform data analysis for distribution, fitting and sampling, programming the simulation, and creating output displays and analysis. The low cost and widespread accessibility of microcomputers are fostering movement toward simulation applications to solve complex problems in a variety of diversified areas.

REFERENCES

1. T. H. Naylor, J. L. Balintby, D. S. Burdick, Computer Simulation Techniques. John Wiley, New York, 1966.
2. P. F. Roth, "Simulation," in *Encyclopedia of Computer Science*, A. Ralston (ed.) Petrocelli/ Charter, New York, 1976, p. 1265.
3. W. G. Rieder, "Simulation and Modeling," in *Encyclopedia of Physical Science and Technology*, Academic Press, New York, 1987, Vol. 12, p. 660.
4. P. A. Bobillier et al., *Simulation with GPSS and GPSS V*, Prentice-Hall, Englewood Cliffs, NJ, 1976, p. 6.
5. A. Newell and H. A. Simon, "Simulation," in *International Encyclopedia of Social Sciences*, D. L. Sills, (ed.) Mcmillan, New York, 1968, Vol. 14, pp. 262–263.
6. G. Gordon, *System Simulation*, Prentice-Hall, Englewood Cliffs, NJ, 1978, p. 38.
7. E. Turban, *Decision Support and Expert Systems: Management Support Systems*, 2nd ed. Mcmillan, New York, 1990, pp. 84–85.
8. B. P. Zeigler, *Theory of Modelling and Simulation*. Robert E. Krieger Publishing, Malabar, FL. 1976, p. 3.
9. D. N. Chorafas, *Systems and Simulation*, Academic Press, New York, 1965.
10. G. J. Klir, *An Approach to General Systems Theory*, Van Nostrand Reinhold, New York, 1969.
11. C. W. Churchman et al., *Introduction to Operations Research*. John Wiley, New York, 1957, Chap. 7.

12. G. Gordon, "Simulation Computation," in *Handbook of Operations Research: Foundations and Fundamentals*, J. J. Moder and S. E. Elmaghraby (eds.), Van Nostrand Reinhold, New York, 1978, p. 566.

13. D. Mishram and G. A. Mishram, "Human Knowledge: The Role of Models, Metaphors and Analogy," *Int. J. General Syst.*, *1*(1), 41–60 (1974).

14. J. R. Emshroff and L. S. Roger, *Design and Use of Computer Simulation Models*, Mcmillan, New York, 1970.

15. H. J. Highland, "A Taxonomy of Models," *Simulation*, 4(2), 10–17 (1973).

16. B. H. Rivett, *Principles of Model Building: The Construction of Models for Decision Making*, John Wiley, New York, 1972.

17. T. I. Oren, "Concepts for Advanced Computer Assisted Modeling," in *Methodology of Systems Modelling and Simulation*, B. P. Zeigler et al. (eds.), North-Holland, New York, 1979, pp. 29–55.

18. B. C. Gupta, *Contemporary Management*, Ashish Publishing, New Delhi, 1992, pp. 171–172.

19. Y. A. Shreider, *The Monte Carlo Method: The Method of Statistical Trials*, Pergamon, London, 1966, Chap. 2.

20. W. Good, and R. Johnston, "Monte Carlo Method for Criticality Problems," *Nucl. Sci. Eng.*, 5(5), 371–375 (1959).

21. D. P. Gaver, "Simulation Theory," in *Handbook of Operations Research: Foundations and Fundamentals*, J. J. Moder and S. E. Elmaghraby (eds.), Van Nostrand Reinhold, New York, 1978, pp. 545–546.

22. A. M. Law and W. D. Kelton, *Simulation Modeling and Analysis*, McGraw-Hill, New York, 1982.

23. P. J. Kiviat, "Digital Computer Simulation: Computer Programming Languages," RM-5883-PR, Rand Corporation, Santa Monica, CA, 1969.

24. H. Kleine, "A Survey of User's Views of Discrete Simulation Languages," *Simulation*, *14*(5), 225–229 (1970).

25. J. Palme, "Comparison Between SIMULA and FORTRAN," *BIT*, 8(3), 203–209 (1968).

26. D. Teichroew, J. F. Lubin, and T. D. Truitt, "Discussion of Computer Simulation Techniques and Comparison of Languages," *Simulation*, 9, 181–190 (1967).

27. I. M. Kay, "Digital Discrete Simulation Language, Discussion and Inventory," in *Progress in Simulation*, I. M. Kay and J. McLeod (eds.), Gordon and Beach, New York, 1972, Vol. 2.

28. G. Gordon, "A General Purpose Systems Simulation Program," in *Proceedings of the EJCC, Washington, D.C.*, Mcmillan, New York, 1961, pp. 87–104.

29. M. Pidd, "Computer Software for Simulation," in *Managing with Operational Research*, J. Kidd (ed.), Philip Allan, Oxford, 1985, p. 274.

30. O. J. Dahl and K. Nygaard, *SIMULA—A Language for Programming and Description of Discrete Event Systems: Introduction and User's Manual*, Norwegian Computing Center, Oslo, 1967.

YOGENDRA P. DUBEY

SIMULATION TECHNOLOGY

Simulation, using computers to implement models of systems and experiment with them, has long been among the most popular and fascinating applications of computer technology. With roots and connections in gaming, operations research, management science, robotics, artificial intelligence, neural networks, and other fields, it seems to be an obvious candidate for continuing growth and development. Yet, in practice, it has remained a small discipline, involving only a few percent of the overall computer community. Why? In part, surely because solving meaningful problems has turned out to be far more difficult than anyone expected. In this, simulation has shared the fate of artificial intelligence, voice and speech processing, and robotics. Another problem is that simulation's results are seldom useful immediately. They generally require extensive analysis and interpretation.

What about the future? Will simulation become a major field? Many recent developments surely favor its continuing emergence. Wider availability of increased amounts of computing power, faster and larger storage devices, greatly improved graphics capabilities at lower cost, better methodologies for developing large, complex programs, and multimedia all will surely make simulation less expensive, easier to use, and easier to relate to underlying systems. But the promise has been obvious for some time with meager results.

TYPES OF SIMULATION

We generally divide simulation into two areas:

- Continuous simulation (1,2), involving the solution of differential equations to model weapons systems, vehicles, power plants, refineries, communications systems, electrical circuits, chemical and physical processes, and biological systems. Perhaps the best known application is the flight simulator, covering everything from trainers for advanced airplanes and space vehicles to the popular games for personal computers. Another famous (and quite different) application is Jay Forrester's world model (3), which the Club of Rome (4) used to predict a dismal future for human society unless drastic policy changes occurred.
- Discrete simulation (5,6), involving the use of event-driven programs to model manufacturing systems, hospitals, government agencies, industrial processes, and social systems. Many utilization, capacity planning, and performance studies have analyzed waiting rooms, assembly lines, and government offices.

A typical simple continuous system (7) uses a damped harmonic oscillator as a model. Its equations are

$$\frac{dx}{dt} = x,$$

$$\frac{dx}{dt} = -wx - rx.$$

One can then examine the step response in time for various values of the damping coefficient r and determine the best one to use in a practical system. The solution requires numerical integration of the equations by means of Euler's method, Simpson's rule, or a more advanced Runge–Kutta approach.

A popular simple discrete application is the problem of determining how may tellers are needed to handle customers at a bank. Common terminology is to refer to the customers as "clients," the tellers as "servers," and the process of reaching the window and performing the transactions as "seizing a server." (This sounds particularly strange in discussions of surgical suites, when one talks about patients seizing doctors for the purpose of having an operation performed.) Typical outputs are average utilization of servers, average and maximum waiting line lengths, and average and maximum waiting times. Other, perhaps more practical, applications include hospital waiting rooms, airports and seaports, toll plazas, truck or emergency vehicle dispatching stations, telephone and other communications systems, and assembly lines. For example, an airport authority would surely want to run a simulation to determine the expected value of an additional runway or terminal. The high costs, extensive public hearings, and long lead times for such construction make simulated results invaluable.

SIMULATION LANGUAGES

Many special simulation languages exist. CSSL (Continuous Systems Simulation Language), CSMP (Continuous Systems Modeling Program), and ACSL (Advanced Continuous Simulation Language; see Fig. 1) simplify the development of continuous applications. GPSS (General-Purpose Systems Simulator) (8) and Simscript (see Fig. 2) do likewise for discrete applications. GASP (General Activity Simulation Program) and SLAM (Simulation Language for Alternative Modeling; see Fig. 3) combine discrete, continuous, and other capabilities (9,10).

The key aspects of simulation languages, as dictated by their applications, include:

- High-level approach that allows programmers to think in terms of complex objects rather than simple numbers or characters
- Ability to handle very large problems requiring long run times
- Support for huge amounts of data and results
- Ability to accept meaningful inputs and provide interpretation of complex outputs

Simulation obviously fits well with current trends toward graphical input and output, structured program development methods, computer-aided software engineering, and object-oriented programming. In fact, the Simula language (11, 12), developed in Norway for simulation applications, is an important precursor of languages such as Ada and C++.

```
PROGRAM Lunar Landing Maneuver
  INITIAL
    constant . . .
      r = 1738.0E3, c2 = 4.925E12, f1 = 36350.0,  . . .
      f2 = 1308.0, c11 = 0.000277, c12 = 0.000277,  . . .
      h0 = 59404.0, v0 = -2003.0, m0 = 1038.358,  . . .
      tmx = 230.0, tdec = 43.2, tend = 210.0
    cinterval cint = 0.2
  END $ ''of INITIAL''
  DYNAMIC
    DERIVATIVE
      thrust = (1.0 - step(tend))* (f1 - (f1 - f2) * step(tdec))
      cl = (1.0 - step(tend)) * (c11 - (c11 - c12) * step(tdec))
      h = integ(v, h0)
      v = integ(a, 90)
      a = (1.0/m) * (thrust - m * g)
      m = integ(mdot, m0)
      mdot = -cl*abs(thrust)
      g = c2/(h + r)**2
    END $ ''of DERIVATIVE''
    termt(t.ge.tmx .or. h.le.0.0. .or. v.gt.0.0)
  END $ ''of DYNAMIC''
END $ ''of PROGRAM''
```

FIGURE 1   Example ACSL program. (Courtesy of Mitchell and Gauthier Associates.)

```
1    Event AIRPLANE.GENERATOR
2       saving the event notice
3
4       Define .TIME.TO.QUIT as a real variable
5       Let .TIME.TO.QUIT = RUN.LENGTH / hours.v
6       If time.v <= .TIME.TO.QUIT
7          Schedule a NEW.AIRPLANE now
8          Reschedule this AIRPLANE.GENERATOR
9            in uniform.f (MINIMUM.INTER.DEPARTURE.TIME,
10                         MAXIMUM.INTER.DEPARTURE.TIME,
11                         1) minutes
12      Endif ''time.v <=   .TIME.TO.QUIT
13   End ''AIRPLANE.GENERATOR

1    Event FINAL.REPORT
2
3       Print 4 lines with time.v * hours.v,
4                    MAX.WAITING.TIME * hours.v * minutes.v;
5                    MAX.NO.OF.WAITING.AIRPLANES thus
6    The simulation ended at **.* hours
7       The maximum waiting time was **.** minutes
8       The maximum number of aircraft waiting at any one
9          time was **.
10
11      Stop
12
13   End ''FINAL.REPORT
```

FIGURE 2   Example SIMSCRIPT II.5 program. (Courtesy of CACI Products Co., Arlington, VA.)

```
 1    GEN,OREILLY,INGOT PROBLEM, 7/1/83,1;
 2    LIMITS,1,4,40;
 3    STAT,1,HEATING TEMP,20/2000/10;
 4    STAT,2,WAITING TIME;
 5    CONT,11,1,.1,10,10;
 6    TIMST,SS(11),FURNACE TEMP.;
 7    SEVNT,2,SS(12),XP,2200,50.;
 8    NETWORK;
 9    ;
10         RESOURCE/PIT(10),1;
11         CREAT,EXPON(2,25),,1;           CREATE INGOT ARRIVALS
12         ASSIGN,ATRIB(2)=UNFRM(400.,500.);   CREATE INGOT TEMP
13         AWAIT,PIT;                       AWAIT A PIT
14  LOAD EVENT,1;                           LOAD INGOT INTO PIT
15         ACT/1,STOPA(ATRIB(3));           SOAKING ACTIVITY
16         COLCT,INT(1),HEATING TIME;       COLLECT STATISTICS
17         FREE,PIT;                        FREE THE PIT
18         TERM;                            EXIT THE SYSTEM
19         ENDNETWORK;
20  INIT,0,500;
21  FIN;
```

FIGURE 3   Part of a SLAM program. (Courtesy of Pritsker Corp., Indianapolis, IN.)

WHERE IS SIMULATION USED?

Simulation has been used in virtually every aspect of business, government, engineering, education, the sciences, and the professions. Applications range literally from accounting to zoology. Particularly important areas include:

- Vehicles.   Simulators have been built for almost every major vehicle (airplane, missile, rocket, ship, submarine, spacecraft, etc.) developed since 1950. They help guide design, predict performance, train operators and pilots, perform safety analyses, and direct emergency planning. They have even become popular as sophisticated amusement rides and computer games. Simulators also help with the development of related applications such as air traffic control systems, automated transportation systems, and collision avoidance systems.
- Power plants.   Here simulators are a standard part of system development, capacity planning, operator training, and safety analysis.
- Industrial assembly lines.   Discrete models help in design, performance analysis, troubleshooting, and reconfiguration. The emergence of flexible manufacturing systems has made simulation particularly important.

In recent years, as development of new military systems has slowed, military use of simulation has decreased (although it is gaining interest as a cost-saving method to avoid expensive tests and training manuevers) (13). Among the new, rising areas are:

- Modeling of computer networks (14,15).   These systems usually involve many levels of complex hardware and software. Designing them is difficult, and evaluating their performance is usually far beyond the capabilities of analytic tools.

Simulation models can help with design, planning, testing, troubleshooting, expansion, and reconfiguration.

- Educational applications.   Why not use simulation to allow students to manage a hospital or city, run an international business, change the governmental system, respond to international crises (16), or even devise an ideal society? Popular games such as SimCity have shown the way. Certainly, the range of applications appears limitless, particularly considering the emergence of low-cost multimedia. One can see, hear, and perhaps eventually smell the results of one's actions. The widely used business and management games (and war games) (17–19) are only the beginning. Simulations can even help teach ethics and social behavior as in the well-known BLUE EYES–BROWN EYES (20) activity for spotlighting prejudice and discrimination.
- Virtual reality (21,22).   Developers of flight simulators have long worked on making every aspect seem and feel real. Now these same techniques can apply to a wide variety of systems.
- Electronic circuits and devices.   The ability to put millions of gates or devices on a VLSI chip has made breadboarding totally unrealistic as a design and test method. Simulation is an essential part of today's CAD/CAE systems and silicon factories.

WHY IS SIMULATION USED?

Computer simulation serves many purposes (23). It allows users to test systems that have not yet been built, evaluate performance, compress or expand time, make changes at will, consider uncommon or extraordinary conditions, and provide training. Note, in particular, that simulation lets users do the following:

- Consider alternative designs of complex systems that may take years to build and involve great expense.   It also provides opportunities to begin software development, training, and systems and safety analysis early in the design cycle.
- Provide training for pilots, navigators, and operators of complex power plants and refineries.   Actual training is expensive, difficult to obtain, and rarely available for more than a limited time and set of conditions. Simulator pilots, for example, can easily fly in and out of airports around the world in a single session, without doing any damage to billion dollar aircraft, expensive airport facilities, or the frazzled nerves of air traffic controllers.
- Evaluate performance and determine the effects of changes.   Often the actual system, such as a power plant controller or a large computer or communications network, cannot be taken off-line or used for experimentation.
- Compress or expand time.   Users can examine electronic systems where events occur in nanoseconds, social or ecological systems where changes take years, and even geological or astronomical systems where transitions require millions or billions of years.
- Determine the effects of rare events, such as power failures, floods, hurricanes, earthquakes, or nuclear accidents.   Airplane pilots can experience a range of conditions in a day that they probably would not encounter in a lifetime of flying. Training instructors can introduce problems or failures as desired. Similarly, emergency planners can consider a variety of situations and see where live

drills might be warranted. Note also that everyone walks away from a simulation unscathed and without having to explain anything to the media or legislative investigating committees!

• Offer real-life experience to students, the handicapped, people in remote locations, and the merely curious.

• Debug, test, troubleshoot, and document complex systems that are expensive to run and difficult to understand or evaluate.

• Suppress disturbances (such as mechanical failures, outside influences, and load variations) that are unavoidable in real systems. You can also focus attention on particular social problems, such as racial prejudice or drug addiction, in isolation from the overall environment.

INPUT AND OUTPUT MODELS

A major issue in simulation is finding adequate models for producing inputs and interpreting outputs. One may, for example, assume a normal distribution of outputs and not consider time dependence at all. This approach, called *static* or *Monte Carlo* simulation, produces adequate results when the intermediate details are difficult to calculate and of little interest anyway. For example, one may want to know what percentage of bombs or artillery shells will destroy their targets without delving into the details of individual paths or trajectories.

Most problems require some consideration of probability distributions (24,25). Commonly used ones are:

• A uniform distribution that is equally likely to take on any value, such as an honest pair of dice.

• An exponential distribution that models random interarrival or service times with a known rate. This distribution is memoryless (it can be started at any time).

• A normal distribution that provides values symmetric about a specific mean and characterized by a known variance.

Other popular distributions include truncated normal (where values cannot go beyond a physical limit such as the speed of light or below zero), gamma (generalization of the factorial function), Erlang (used to describe multistage processes), and Weibull (often used to establish failure rates). The more versatile distributions have adjustable parameters that modelers can calibrate to fit experimental data.

Any input distribution is likely to produce unrealistic results during an initial or start up period. After all, the real system, such as an airport or telephone switch, may actually operate continuously; or, as with an industrial assembly line, start up may be highly variable and irregular, dependent on exactly when workers arrive and how long machines take to warm up. The common solution is to run the simulation until a steady state occurs, discarding the initial results (26).

PROBLEMS WITH SIMULATION

As one might expect, simulation presents problems as well as opportunities. Surely the most important issue is validation (27). How do we know that the model is correct and its results are reasonable? Unfortunately, no certifying agency exists.

Among the common validation methods are:

- Trying to recreate the past. If the simulation cannot accurately reproduce the past, how can we expect it to predict the future? Unfortunately, as investors know, past performance does not guarantee future results.
- Getting the opinions of subject matter experts. This can range from seeing whether scientists or administrators think the results are realistic, to having experienced operators or pilots take turns in simulators. Of course, expert opinions are subjective and vary greatly. Statistical methods can help summarize or evaluate the data.
- Checking simple cases for which results are well known or can be obtained analytically. Here again, if the simulation cannot reproduce trivial situations, how can we trust it in more complex cases? Unfortunately, the extension from doing the simple to doing the complex is less obvious. One's ability to climb a local hill does not guarantee that one can conquer Mount Everest.

Some simulation specialists even claim validation is a waste of time. If the results are interesting and point to areas for exploration or analysis, who cares if the model is valid? Of course, in practice, everyone knows that models, like legal expert witnesses, tend to support the aims and objectives of their sponsors. Ethical issues occur in simulation, as in all other fields.

However, validation surely increases users' confidence in modeling, modelers, and simulation results. The U.S. Department of Defense has been a leader in developing standard measures of validity (28).

Other problem areas in simulation are:

- Difficulty in preparing inputs and interpreting outputs. Here the advent of better, less expensive graphical methods is a major advance. Charts and pictures are far more meaningful than endless tables of numbers.
- Need to determine the range of validity of a model. Surely no model applies everywhere.
- Inability to consider behavioral changes resulting from new policies or events. This is an obvious difficulty for social or economic models that depend on historical patterns for their parameters. Thus, for example, actual receipts from new taxes are often quite disappointing despite model predictions. The reason is that people change their behavior quickly to match the new circumstances.
- Inability to include social, cultural, or political factors that are difficult to quantify. The practitioners of system dynamics (29), first developed by Forrester at MIT, have been leaders in trying to assign numerical values to abstractions.

MICROCOMPUTERS AND SIMULATION

Microcomputers and personal computers have yet to play a major role in simulation. In theory, they should:

- Extend its range, particularly in education and business. Computers have become commonplace in small businesses and in elementary and secondary schools, but simulation applications are still quite rare (30,31).

- Make simulators cheaper, easier to build, more powerful, and more flexible. Unfortunately, a counterbalance here has been recent downturns in industries that have been major users of simulators. There are simply fewer large military systems, aircraft, ships, refineries, and power plants being built.

The future still seems bright. Powerful desktop computers with multimedia capabilities could surely run a variety of complex models effectively. Whether such uses will, in fact, become commonplace is a speculative matter.

FINAL NOTE

An obvious advantage of simulation is the blame factor. One can always shift responsibility for incorrect predictions and erroneous results to the unsuspecting computer model. Fortunately, despite the advent of multimedia and artificial intelligence, no model (and no computer) has yet tried to make excuses or even respond to criticism. As Churchill wrote, "Everyone threw the blame on me. I have noticed that they nearly always do. I suppose it is because they think I shall be able to bear it best."

SOURCES OF INFORMATION

The leading source of information about computer simulation is the Society for Computer Simulation (SCS, P. O. Box 17900, San Diego, CA 92177). It sponsors and sells proceedings for such conferences as the Summer Computer Simulation Conference (emphasizing continuous simulation), the Winter Simulation Conference (emphasizing discrete simulation), and the Annual Simulation Symposium. SCS also sponsors an annual conference on Modeling and Simulation on Microcomputers. Another good source of information is the Association for Computing Machinery's Special Interest Group on Computer Simulation (ACM SIGSIM, 1515 Broadway, New York, NY 10036).

Trademarks

ACSL	Mitchell and Gauthier Associates
GASP	Pritsker Corp.
GPSS	IBM
SimCity	Maxis Corp.
Simscript	CACI Products
SLAM	Pritsker Corp.

DEDICATION

This article is dedicated, with my deepest personal respect, to John McLeod, a founder of the Society for Computer Simulation and a leader in the field for over 40 years. "Genius . . . is the capacity to see ten things where the ordinary man sees one, and where the man of talent sees two or three. . ." (Ezra Pound).

REFERENCES

1. F. E. Cellier, *Continuous System Simulation*, Springer-Verlag, New York, 1992.
2. F. E. Cellier, *Continuous System Modeling*, Springer-Verlag, New York, 1991.
3. J. W. Forrester, *World Dynamics*, Wright-Allen Press, Cambridge, MA, 1971.
4. D. L. Meadows et al., *Dynamics of Growth in a Finite World*, MIT Press, Cambridge, MA, 1974.
5. A. M. Law and W. D. Kelton, *Simulation Modeling and Analysis*, 2nd ed., McGraw-Hill, New York, 1991.
6. J. Banks and J. S. Carson, *Discrete-Event System Simulation*, Prentice-Hall, Englewood Cliffs, NJ, 1984.
7. G. A. Korn, *Interactive Dynamic System Simulation*, McGraw-Hill, New York, 1989.
8. T. J. Schriber, *An Introduction to Simulation Using GPSS/H*, Wiley, New York, 1991.
9. A. A. B. Pritsker, *Introduction to Simulation and SLAM-II*, 3rd ed., Halsted Press, New York, 1985.
10. A. A. B. Pritsker, *Papers, Experiences, Perspectives*, Systems Publishing, West Lafayette, IN, 1990.
11. O. J. Dahl and K. Nygaard, "SIMULA—An Algol-Based Simulation Language," *Commun. ACM*, 9(9), 671–678 (1966).
12. B. Kirkerud, *Object-Oriented Programming with Simula*, Addison-Wesley, Reading, MA, 1990.
13. I. Oswalt, "Current Applications, Trends, and Organizations in U.S. Military Simulation and Gaming," *Simulation and Gaming*, 24(2) 153–189 (1993).
14. A. Chai and S. Ghosh, "Modeling and Distributed Simulation of a Broadband-ISDN Network," *IEEE Computer*, 26(9) 37–51 (1993).
15. A. M. Law and M. G. McComas, "Simulation of Communications Networks," in *Proceedings of the 1992 Winter Simulation Conference*, pp. 170–173.
16. S. Kraus et al., "The Hostage Crisis Simulation," *Simulation and Gaming*, 223(4) 398–416 (1992).
17. R. V. Colter and D. J. Fritzsche, *The Business Policy Game*, 3rd ed., Prentice-Hall, Englewood Cliffs, NJ, 1991.
18. M. B. Aronson et al., *Strategic Management Game*, Strategic Management Group, Inc., Philadelphia, PA, 1987.
19. D. Crookall and R. L. Oxford (eds.), *Simulation, Gaming, and Language Learning*, Newbury House, New York, 1990.
20. W. Peters, *A Class Divided: Then and Now*, New Haven, CT, Yale University Press, 1987.
21. M. W. Krueger, *Artificial Reality II*, Addison-Wesley, Reading, MA, 1991.
22. K. Pimentel and K. Teixeira, *Virtual Reality: Through the New Looking Glass*, Intel Books, Mount Prospect, IL, 1993.
23. A. A. B. Pritsker, "Why Simulation Works," in *Proceedings of the 1989 Winter Simulation Conference*, pp. 1–6.
24. R. C. H. Cheng, "Distribution Fitting and Random Number and Variate Generation," in *Proceedings of the 1992 Winter Simulation Conference*, pp. 74–81.
25. L. Devroye, *Non-Uniform Random Variate Generation*, Springer-Verlag, New York, 1986.
26. L. Schruben, "Detecting Initialization Bias in Simulation Output," *Oper. Res.*, 30 569–590 (1980).
27. R. G. Sargent, "Validation and Verification of Simulation Models," in *Proceedings of the 1992 Winter Simulation Conference*, pp. 104–114.
28. D. K. Pace, "Simulation, the Defense Community, and DMSO," *Simulation*, 59(1), 62–64 (1992).
29. G. P. Richardson and A. L. Pugh, *Introduction to System Dynamics Modeling with DYNAMO*, MIT Press, Cambridge, MA, 1981.

30. J. Richards et al., ''Computer Simulations in the Science Classroom,'' *J. Sci. Educ. Technol.*, *1*(1), 1992.
31. N. Roberts and T. Barclay, ''Teaching Model Building to High School Students: Theory and Reality,'' *J. Computers Math. Sci. Teaching* (Fall 1988).

LANCE A. LEVENTHAL

SIMULATIONS AND SIMULATORS—THEIR ROLE IN SCIENCE AND SOCIETY

The field of simulation is one of the broadest in all of modern science. It includes the analysis and modeling of all kinds of engineered systems, medical and life sciences, all of the pure sciences, such as physics and chemistry, economics, operational analysis, and, of course, computer science to name just a few. Almost ever tool in simulators and simulation is found somewhere in science. For centuries before the technological breakthroughs that have brought a computer to every desktop, man has used the techniques of approximation and simplifications of complex system as a method to better understand nature. The use of simulation and simulators in modern times evolved from the basic idea that man can learn from interaction with copies (simulations) of what really is. Before the development of digital computers, analog simulations were widely used in the design and analysis of complex systems. With the availability of inexpensive digital computers in the late 1970's, simulation is now almost entirely based in the use of these machines.

The most basic aim of simulation is the enlargement of human understanding of something. What that something is, how humans interact with it, and how well we need to understand its behavior, determines what the properties the simulation or simulator will have. There is a great deal of different kinds of simulation and simulators. These can be broken down into several sets of classes. The first set of classes of simulations or simulators as real time simulations versus non real time simulation. Another set of classes deals with the amount of continuing human interaction the simulations or simulators are required to provide. The scope of simulation depends upon functional, psychological or physiological equivalence that can perceive, discern, ascertain or infer (1). Simulators are simulations that include some amount of continuous interaction with the simulation, usually human interaction. The most complicated simulators are full scope real time simulators. Real time refers to the requirement for these simulators to simulate the system that they are modeling in exactly the same time frame (not slower or faster) as the system actual functions in its real environment. This requirement is very important in full scope simulators. Full scope simulators are simulators that are designed to include *all* important characteristics of the systems to be modeled. What characteristics need to be included depend on the uses the simulator is designed for. For aircraft simulators, the physical movement of the simulator as well as the visual displays, and all of the instruments and controls in the cockpit of the aircraft must mimic reality as it happens. Real time simulators were first developed for training of operators of highly complex systems, (military and civilian aircraft, nuclear power plants etc.) In this application of simulators the human interaction is the primary concern (2). The Federal Aviation Administration and the Nuclear Regulatory Commission require that pilots and nuclear power plant operators be trained and tested on real time simulators. These agencies also require that the simulators be certified as to their ability to simulate the real system that they are modeling.

There are many applications for which a full scope simulator is not needed. For many of these applications part task real time simulators can be used. A part task real time simulators is a simulator that operates in real time but is only concerned with one aspect of the system being simulated. Part task simulators are often used to train an operator on a single sub task. For example, in operating a power plant an operator needs to perform many tasks. One of these tasks is control of the turbine generator. If the primary design goals is to build a simulator to improve the skill of the operators in controlling the turbine generator, then a simulator that only models the turbine generator may be a good choice. In addition to simulators that only model one subsystem of the whole system of interest, simulators that model the whole system but have a simplified interface with the operators are also considered part task simulators. These simulators are also some times known as non replica simulators, to distinguish them from full scope simulators, which are some times referred to as replica simulators. This classification refers to the fact that most full scope simulator include a nearly exact replica of the human machine interface that the simulated system has. These non replica simulators have become increasingly common as human factors studies have shown that many simulation applications do not require full scope replica simulators. These non replica simulators use other human interface systems, usually computers, (microcomputers in almost all cases) to mimic the real human interfaces that are on the real system. One example of this would be a flight simulator that used a computer screen and keyboard as an interface as opposed to a cockpit. This would not be a good choice of simulator design if the goal was to test a pilot on his or her capability to perform complicated actions, however it might be a excellent choice if the goal was to teach a pilot basic aerodynamics. The simulation interfaces for these simulators can be made to enhance the particular task that the operator is studying. In the case of the pilot learning aerodynamics, the interfaces could include information on lift and drag on the airfoil as well as computer graphics of the actual cockpit displays.

The next class of simulation is non real time simulators. The class includes all simulation that have continuous human interaction, but do not function in real time. In most cases these simulators operate slower than real time. The vast majority of simulation done today is classified as general simulation. This category includes the simulations that do not have continuous human interaction. Before the power of computers increased, the use of simulations was mostly restricted to special purpose application, such as full scope simulators. As the power of computers increased the field of simulation expanded into almost every field of human endeavor. A short list of the major areas that use general simulation would include: Aerospace Systems, Automatic Control, Biological Modeling, Biomedical System, Chemical, Computer Networks, Computer Vision, Computer-aided design, Economics, Electrical Engineering, Energy Systems, Environmental Systems, Financial Decision Support Systems, Geophysical Systems, Health Care Systems, Industrial Processes, Information Systems, Life Sciences, Manufacturing Systems, Marine applications, Mechanical Systems, Medical Imaging, Neural Networks, Parallel and Distributed Computing, Production and Inventory Control, Robotics and Manipulators, Software, System Reliability, Management Sciences, Telecommunications, Undersea Systems and VLSI and Circuit Design (3).

Simulation and Simulators have had many significant contributions. For new military aircraft and for spacecraft, a simulator for training and performance evaluation is virtually assumed, their value having been proven many times over. For commercial aircraft, safety is the overwhelming justification for simulators and simulation design studies. For nuclear power plants and commercial aircraft, government regulations require operators to be licensed by examination on a certified simulator. The accidents at Three Mile Island and Chernobyl could very possibly been prevented had the operators been properly trained, including simulator training. For other applications, including air traffic control, biomedical communications, electrical power transmission and distribution, emergency engineering and management, fossil power plants, gaming, land vehicles, process plant, weapons, etc., the past accomplishments is not as apparent. The use of simulators for training is far less than the cost of operating the simulated equipment (this is one of the primary reasons simulators are used in the military). Based on fuel (energy) savings alone, simulators in the land vehicle and process plant industry have reported direct saving as a result of the use of simulator and simulation training from 0.5% to 3.0% of total energy costs. In many industries the cost of set up for production is a large part of the total cost to a product. In these areas the use of simulation as a design tool has had great success. Simulation has been used to explore the dynamic behavior of systems prior to manufacture and improve all aspects of the design, including such things as operating instructions, emergency systems, reliability of the produce and optimization of production.

One of the greatest advantages of simulation or simulator is in the area of emergency management. Simulators are used to test procedures for emergencies that we do not wish the subject the real system to, or in some cases can not subject the real system to. During the Apollo 13 mission, when the liquid oxygen tank exploded on the way to the moon, simulators were used to devise procedures to successfully manage the emergency (2). The use of simulation in environmental analysis and restoration has been increasing. Simulation and modeling of the environment allows us to examine alternative technologies and procedures. Almost every major decontamination and restoration effort in the country is using simulation to test their strategies without the cost and time of testing each technique.

The power of microcomputers now allows for very sophisticated simulations to be performed on relatively inexpensive computers. Many simulations are now done on micro-computers and engineering workstations. The tools are now available to develop simulations for micro-computers. The future of simulations and simulators, especially on microcomputer based simulation will include the use of the multimedia capabilities that are now becoming available. With these capabilities very sophisticated part task simulators can be designed. The use of large groups of micro-computers to perform integrated simulations will also be a major part of the future developments on this area. As the capabilities of micro-computers and networks increase the use of simulation to understand our environment, and control it for the betterment of mankind.

REFERENCES

(1) J. H. Bradley, Principles of Simulation in Simulators. Proceedings of the Simulators Multiconference XI, SCS, pp 255–257, La Jolla, CA (1994).

(2) B. T. Fairchild, and A. B. Chymer, Simulator Justifications. Proceedings of the Simulators Multiconference VII, SCS, pp 284–292, Nashville, TN (1990).

(3) J. H. Bradley, Characterizations and Classifications of Civilian Continuous Simulators, Proceedings of the Simulators Multiconference IV, SCS, pp 194–199, Orlando, FL (1987).

BIBLIOGRAPHY

(1) John M. Rolfe, and Ken J. Staples, Flight Simulation, Cambridge University Press, London, 1986.

(2) Donald C. Glaser, The PC Simulator, Chemical Engineering Progress, pp 45–48, September, 1986.

(3) Earl S. Stein, Roles For Simulation in Air Traffic Control Systems' Development, Proceedings of Simulators Multiconference V, SCS, pp 15–20, San Diego, CA, 1988.

(4) G. V. Amico, and A. B. Clymer, Simulator Technology—Forty Years of Progress, Proceedings of Simulators Conference, SCS, pp 315, La Jolla, CA, 1984.

STEVEN A. ARNDT

SNOBOL

INTRODUCTION

SNOBOL is a string processing language. It was developed at Bell Telephone Laboratories, Incorporated (1–5). It is an interpreted language. The version of SNOBOL described here is SNOBOL4 (v. 3) (5).

SNOBOL was developed to enable programs for manipulating symbolic formulas (6). This would include not only factoring polynomials but also applications in natural language processing, compilation techniques, and symbolic mathematics. The original SNOBOL operated only on the STRING. The first system consisted of a translator, an interpreter, and an allocator. The allocator was to handle the space for strings. The coding was done in assembly language for the IBM 7090. It included a package of string-manipulation macros. Every construction was valid syntactically, although very few were valid semantically. A new implementation with the addition of built-in functions led to SNOBOL2. Programmer-defined functions (recursive) led to SNOBOL3. Independent applications were undertaken for other machines, leading to language dialects. It was distributed through Bell Laboratories and SHARE (6). An interest in standardization and extensions to the language and faster third-generation machines with virtual memories offering essentially unlimited space led to SNOBOL4. SNOBOL4 has an extensive set of data types as well as built-in functions and the ability to define user functions and data types.

A SNOBOL4 program consists of a series of statements. However, there is a distinction between SNOBOL and ordinary programming languages in that the statements are assignment statements, pattern matching statements, replacement statements, and the end statement. The assignment statement can be used to assign values of various data types to a variable. The data type of the variable depends on the last assignment. Transformations are performed among data types readily; for example, strings representing numerals may be included in arithmetic statements, and numerals may be concatenated to strings. The pattern matching statement is of the form "subject pattern" where the subject is searched for the pattern. The replacement statement has the form "subject pattern = object" where the subject is searched for the pattern and, if found, replaced by the object. The end statement marks the physical end of the program. Labels and gotos are provided for flow of control. There are implicit IFs in the conditional transfer of control statements [Goto on true (S for success) and failure (F)]. There is also indirect referencing, which is akin to indirect addressing. The operations may be combined in ways not familiar to "normal" programming languages. There are several primitive functions to implement common operations and a facility to define user functions. Predicates are included, which return null for true (due to the use of concatenation), nothing (not the null string) on false. Omitted arguments to functions are taken to be the null string. Arrays may be defined with dimensions and initial values, the dimensions being explicit or set by data (dynamic). Tables are sets of pairs of objects. There are also programmer-defined data types. Comments are indicated by an asterisk (at the beginning of the line). A program is a set of SNOBOL statements followed by END (the END statement). There are no declared data types. A program is run by entering the program through the input stream; this varies from system to system (operating system). SNOBOL is not a standardized language (in its implementation).

PATTERN MATCHING

Pattern matching is one of the fundamental operations (and statements) of the SNOBOL language. All statements have the form "label statement goto," where the pattern matching and replacement statements have the forms

```
"label subject pattern goto"
"label subject pattern = object goto"
```

where the first searches the subject for the pattern, and the second searches the subject for the pattern and replaces it (by object) if found. Patterns may also be built with concatenation, and alternation and concatenation, as well as primitive pattern structures built into the system and primitive functions that return patterns. Patterns are matched by the scanner, which uses a cursor to mark the position in the subject and a "needle" to traverse the pattern. The programmer can control the method in which patterns are matched by sequencing the patterns (in alternatives). He or she can then ensure that certain patterns are "matched first." The programmer can also indicate whether a pattern can be matched anywhere ("unanchored") or only at the beginning of the "string" (subject) ("anchored"). LEN is a function that matches a string (any string) of a specified length. It can be used to extract fixed length fields from a record structure. Variable length fields can be matched (and extracted) by matching the separating character (delimeter). SPAN and BREAK are functions that span over characters (e.g., to crunch out blanks) or find the next occurrence of a character (BREAK at ' '). SPAN matches the longest string of the character or set of characters [enclosed in quotes, SPAN('ABC . . . Z')]. Fixed length fields can be transformed into variable length fields by these functions and concatenation. ANY and NOTANY match the first occurrence of a character (ANY, ANY('AEIOU')) or the first occurrence of a character not in the set (NOTANY('AEIOU')). A program to recognize SNOBOL statements is less than three pages long, four with the pattern definitions. Fail can be used to force failure and search for all alternatives (PROLOG FAIL). The pattern STR PAT $ OUTPUT FAIL can be used to "watch" the scanner in action, with $ OUTPUT assigning the matches to the output ($ is immediate assignment). FENCE can cause a break in the back up of the cursor (in the subject string) (PROLOG CUT). FENCE can be used to temporarily anchor a program that otherwise operates in unanchored mode (by "breaking" at a match so that the cursor does not needlessly back up over a known set of characters). PAIR is a function that matches pairs of identical characters. ARB is a function that matches arbitrary substrings ('*' in pattern matching languages). BAL matches balanced parentheses.

QUICKSCAN MODE

Quickscan mode is a mode in which the scanner does not try to match patterns that cannot succeed. It facilitates scanning by using information on the context of the string. One possible context is the number of characters remaining. Patterns larger than the number of characters remaining (in the subject) are not tried. A count is kept with the patterns of the subsequent number of characters (including this portion of the pattern) that must be matched. If this exceeds the number of characters left in the string (subject), the pattern is not "searched."

In the fullscan mode all heuristics to improve the pattern matching efficiency are turned off. The two modes recognize strings of a different patterns.

PRIMITIVE FUNCTIONS, PREDICATES, AND OPERATIONS

Primitive functions are functions built into the system (language). Several primitive functions are the predicate functions (LE, LT, EQ, NE, GE, GT). These act as expected, with the exception that the null string is returned for "true." IDENT and DIFFER are functions that test data objects (of any type) for identity or nonequivalence. IDENT means the identical data object. Data objects are stored once, so that two variables with the same data object as "value" point to the same data object. This is not true of expressions, which are evaluated as they are encountered. EQ tests data objects for equality. EQ will succeed where IDENT does not (e.g., in testing an integer 2 against the string '2', two different data objects, but "equal" when evaluated). Similarly, for X = 3.0, Y = 3, IDENT will fail (real, integer).

LGT

LGT compares strings lexically. As might be expected, the lexical ordering is implementation (code) dependent.

Other Functions

SIZE is a function that determines the length of a string (LEN in other languages). REPLACE replaces single occurrences of a character by a "substitute" character (in all occurrences). Several characters can be replaced at once. For example, REPLACE('01','10') replaces all 0's by 1 (the first string is the character to be replaced) and ones by 0. The result of the replacement must be assigned (the original remains unchanged). TRIM trims trailing blanks (in a string). DUPL duplicates a string a given number (N) of times. It takes the string and the duplicate count as arguments, DUPL(' ', MAX − SIZE(S)). REMDR is the mod function (with the sign being the sign of the dividend, on the mod). DATE and TIME give the date (of the year) and TIME since program execution began (compilation time is not included). TIME is approximate within the timing constraints (interval between updates) of the system ("clock" or program).

EVAL is a function that evaluates expressions (LISP EVAL). Syntactic errors (in the expression) cause EVAL to fail. APPLY executes a function call (LISP APPLY). It applies the function to the argument list (APPLY(F,a1, . . . ,an)). The correct number of arguments must be sent to the function (F). It applies the function to the entire argument list (rather than individually, as in LISP APPLY, rather than MAPCAR). It can be used to apply various functions (through a variable holding the function name) to an argument list.

NEGATION (¬) is the function NOT. It complements the argument [null if true, not null if false, NOT to either reverses ("complements") the value]. INTERROGA-TION asks if its operand succeeds (it returns the value of the interrogation). INTERRO-GATION is used to convert a function that returns a non-null value into a null (Yes) or nothing (No) value, i.e., an ordinary function into a Predicate Function.

External functions, written in FORTRAN or assembly language, are provided in a library. External functions can be used to calculate arithmetic expressions or perform i/o or create and operate on data types not supplied in the language (extend the language). SNOBOL provides a function to LOAD the user-defined external functions into the library, but the functions themselves are implementation dependent. Functions may be deleted ("unloaded") with the UNLOAD function. This applies to library functions (external) or primitive (system defined) functions. In the case of external (library) functions, the space occupied by the function (definition) is reclaimed.

Functions can be renamed (have synonyms created for them) by using OPSYN. For example, OPSYN('SAME','INDENT') creates the name SAME for the function IDENT. This can be extended to synonyms for operators (e.g., & for * in boolean multiplication). Synonym functions must have the correct number of arguments (trailing arguments may not be omitted). For example, OPSYN('&','*',2) would rename '*' as '&' ('*' is still operative). Both are binary operators. Symbols (such as '+') may also be used for (made synonymous with) function names; e.g., OPSYS('+',F,2) replaces the function F(arg1, arg2) with the binary operator '+'. The "call" N+M would generate the call F(N,M). (The arguments are represented positionally.)

ARITHMETIC OPERATORS

SNOBOL offers the usual complement of operators. These are binary (*,+) and unary [¬, ?, $ (indirect reference))] with the standard precedences and the precedences listed by SNOBOL, with the exception that multiplication has higher precedence than division. The unary operators are not separated from their operands. The binary operators are separated by a space, a + b. The primitive functions can be changed (in name) by OPSYN. The precedence and associativity remains unchanged.

User-defined Functions

The programmer may define functions using the function DEFINE. The DEFINE function takes the name of the function, its "formal" arguments, any local variables, and the entry point of the function as arguments. The execution of DEFINE('F(X,Y)V1, V2','ENTRYF') defines the function F with arguments X, Y, local variables V1, V2, and entry point ENTRYF. If there are no local variables, they may be omitted, as in DEFINE('G(X,Y)','ENTRYG'). It is also possible to omit the second argument, in which case the entry point is the same as the name of the function (the entry point appears in the function as a label). If there are no formal arguments, these are omitted: DEFINE('F( )').

The body of the function is defined with the label indicated in the entry point. For example,

```
ENTRYF_____
```

followed by a set of SNOBOL statements would constitute the function body. It is terminated by a RETURN (in the goto field).

The DEFINE statement is the function prototype. The function definition (body) may occur anywhere in the program (outside of the program flow). The result of the function is returned in the function name (the name should appear on the left of an assignment statement or otherwise receive a value in the function).

RETURN, FRETURN, AND NRETURN

RETURN indicates that the function was successful. The value of the function (reference) is the value of the function name (at that point).

FRETURN indicates failure on the function "call" (reference). No value is returned on failure (the statement fails). NRETURN can be used to return a computed name as the value (computed as in a concatenation statement). The call (in the computed name) may occur on the left of an assignment statement in the calling program (procedure), e.g.,

```
F(X,Y) = X
```

The value of F(X,Y) will be the computed value.

Functions are called by value. When a procedure (user-defined function) is called, the arguments are evaluated first. The values of the formal arguments and local variables as well as the (current value of) the function name are saved and assigned null values (function name, local variables) or the values of the actual arguments (or expressions). Then control passes to the statement labeled with the entry point (entry point or function name). Upon return, the value of the function name (current value) is assigned (returned) as the value of the reference, and the values of the saved variables (formal arguments, local variables, original value of the function name) are restored. They are restored in the reverse order of which they were saved.

On FRETURN, the values saved are restored, but the function fails (no return value to the reference). When NRETURN is used, the value of the reference ("call") is a variable constructed in the function name. Hence, in the call

```
F(X,Y) = X
```

the value of F(X,Y) is the value (name) returned (F's value). The values of the saved variables are restored.

If a function is called with two few arguments, the value of the omitted (trailing) arguments is set to null (the null string). If there are too many arguments, they are evaluated, but ignored. Functions may also be redefined (with OPSYN).

RECURSIVE FUNCTIONS

Functions may be defined recursively. For example,

```
        DEFINE('F(N)')
F   F   =   EQ(N) 1    :S(RETURN)
    F   =   EQ(N,1) 1  :S(RETURN)
    F   =   N * F(N - 1)   :S(RETURN)
```

defines the factorial (function) with F the name of the function and also the entry point (leftmost F on the first line of the function).

ARRAYS, TABLES, AND DEFINED DATA TYPES

An array is an indexed aggregate of variables. The variables are the elements of the array. Each element of the array may have any type (a different type) of data object as value.

Arrays are defined with the ARRAY function. The form of the function is $A(p,e)$ where p is the string (or value) representing the size of the array (dimension) and e is the initial value of each element (in this case uniform).

Arrays are referenced through the index value. Hence,

    V<8> = X

sets V<8> to the value of X, and

    OUTPUT = BOARD<2,3>

outputs the value of the second row, third column (cell) of BOARD. Each element of the array may have any type of data object for its value.

An array may be processed without knowing its size. This is because a reference outside the range of the array results in a failure, which can be used to terminate processing of the array.

If the second element of the array definition [e in $A(p,e)$] is omitted, all elements are initialized to the null string. Because this argument is optional, care must be taken when defining an array. For example, A = ARRAY('3,3') creates a 3 × 3 array, all elements of which are initialized to the null string. A = ARRAY(3,3) creates a one-dimensional array (1..3) of elements with initial value 3.

Arrays are assumed to be 1-based (the lower index), but other bounds can be specified, e.g., A = ARRAY('-5:5'). There is no intrinsic limit on the size (or number of dimensions) of arrays.

Tables are aggregates of variables, but they may be referenced by values (variables) other than index values. A table is created with the TABLE function, T = TABLE( ):

    T<'A'> = 3

assigns the value 3 to the Ath element (element 'A') of T. The referencing argument can be any value of any data type. By using the same value in a subsequent reference, the same element is "referenced." If no such element exists, one is created and given the null string as its initial value. References such as T<1> and T<'1'> are to distinct elements. As in arrays, the elements, too, may be of any data type.

If the table is defined without arguments, as in T = TABLE( ), the table is of unspecified size. However, the table may be defined as T = TABLE(N, M), where N is the initial size (number of elements) of the table and M is its "extension" size. If N is exceeded, elements (room for elements) are (is) added in increments of M. Hence, the definition T = TABLE(20, 15) starts with 20 elements (objects) and increases these (the space) in increments of 15 (35, 50, . . . , in the total number of elements).

The default values of N and M are 10. Either may be omitted.

Arrays may be assigned to one another. They point to the same data object. If two distinct arrays are desired, the COPY function may be used. Hence, the statements

```
A = ARRAY(p,e)
B = A
```

produce a single copy of the array, with two pointers (A,B) to it, whereas

```
A = ARRAY(p,e)
B = COPY(A)
```

produce two distinct arrays.

The function PROTOTYPE can be used to obtain the dimensions of an array. Tables and arrays can be converted into one another with the CONVERT function:

```
A = CONVERT(T,'ARRAY')
```

converts a table, T, into an array A, and

```
T = CONVERT(A,'TABLE')
```

converts an array, A, into a table T. Both consist of pointers to the data elements.

Programmer-defined data types can be defined with the function DATA, DATA(p), where p is the ''prototype'' (description) of the data type. For example,

```
DATA('COMPLEX(R,I)')
```

defines a data type COMPLEX with two fields, R and I. The fields are identified after the type is assigned to a variable

```
C = COMPLEX(1.5,2.0)
```

which assigns 1.5 to C.R (in dot notation), 2.0 to C.I. The fields are accessed by a distinct notation

```
X = R(C)
Y = I(C)
```

where C is the variable, and R(C) and I(C) are the ''field operators'' (the dot notation). A primitive function VALUE is also available for accessing fields, as well as other data types.

KEYWORDS

SNOBOL provides several keywords that control the operation of the system. For example, &ANCHOR = 1 turns ''anchoring'' mode on, &ANCHOR = 0 turns it off. Some of the keywords are &ALPHABET, which produces a string of all the characters on the machine on which SNOBOL4 is implemented, &DUMP, which DUMPS the values of the variables and unprotected keywords, &TRACE and &FTRACE (for functions), and &TRIM (to trim blanks on input). Some keywords such as &ALPHABET and &ABORT are protected; i.e., they cannot have their value changed by the program, whereas others, such as &ANCHOR, are ''unprotected'' (can have their value changed during execution).

NAMES

SNOBOL distinguishes between ''natural'' variables (names) and ''created'' variables, e.g., an array created with A = ARRAY(10). The distinction is of interest with respect to the passing of data values to functions. If one passes a value, such as BUMP(N), to a function, the variable N will not be "bumped" (incremented by one). This is due to pass by value. However, one can pass the name of the variable

```
BUMP('N')
```

and access the variable indirectly, through the name, in the routine. The function would be defined as

```
DEFINE('BUMP(VAR)')
         .
         .
         .
BUMP  $VAR = $VAR + 1    :(RETURN)
```

where $VAR references the item "at" 'N' (or other argument "name"), the value of the variable N (i.e., $'N' dereferences the string).

GOTOS, LABELS, AND CODE

Flow of control is governed by unconditional and conditional, success and failure, gotos. In the goto fields, variables indicate the statement to be executed next. These are labels. For example, the code

```
DELETE  STRING CHAR =     :F(FRETURN)
D2      STRING CHAR =     :S(D2)
        DELETE = STRING   :(RETURN)
```

deletes the character CHAR (value of CHAR) from the string STRING [after pattern matching, CHAR is matched in STRING, and CHAR = performs the deletion (= "nothing")] in all occurrences. If the CHAR is not found in the string, DELETE fails (line 1); if it is found, control passes ("naturally," i.e., sequentially) to D2. A success (on "match") deletes the character (CHAR =) and transfers control to D2 [:S(D2)]. When there are no more matches ("fail"), control passes to the statement

```
DELETE = STRING
```

which returns [unconditionally, :(RETURN)].

Success and failure branches can be indicated in the same statement. For example,

```
        COLOR = 'RED' | 'GREEN' | 'BLUE'   (| = "or")
BRIGHT  TEXT COLOR =      :S(BRIGHT)F(BLAND)
BLAND
```

returns control to BRIGHT on success [after matching (and deleting) 'RED', 'GREEN,' or 'BLUE'] and to BLAND on failure [after all deletions are made (or none occur originally)].

The DELETE function would be defined as

```
DEFINE('DELETE(STRING,CHAR)')
```

indicating the string, STRING, and the character (value), CHAR, to be deleted. Labels are created by including them in column 1. If a statement has no label, it must begin with at least one blank character. The END statement is a label (END in column 1).

Code may be generated "on the fly" in SNOBOL with the CODE function. An example is the program

```
    GET = '       &TRIM = 1;'
  +        '       N = 10;'
  +        '       LINE = ;'
  +        'LOOP   N = GT(N,0)   N - 1   :F(OUT);'
  +        '       LINE = LINE INPUT    :(LOOP);'
```

followed by the assignment

```
    NUCODE = CODE(GET)
```

The CODE for GET is "compiled" (processed) and assigned to NUCODE. The code is executed by

```
    :<NUCODE>
```

in the goto field, or by generating a goto to a label in NUCODE, e.g.,

```
    :<LOOP>
```

which precedes any prior definition of LOOP (or placing a label on the first line).

Statements using CODE may have the same label as statements in the (original) source program. The label attribute (in the symbol table) for the label (name) is updated (the first label is superceded).

DATA TYPES

SNOBOL offers the standard data types, integer, real, string, array and table (somewhat unique), as well as some unique data types, PATTERN, ARRAY, TABLE (the operators create the types), EXPRESSION, and CODE, among others.

The call DATATYPE(object) returns the data type of an object. For example, DATATYPE(37) returns INTEGER, and DATATYPE(LEN(1)) returns PATTERN [LEN(1) is a PATTERN]. The DATA function can be used to define data types. These may redefine "standard" [built-in or program (language) defined] data types, e.g.,

```
    DATA('STRING(FIRST,LAST)')
```

defines a "new" STRING data type.

The two data types are distinguished correctly by the SNOBOL4 system, but they cannot be differentiated during program execution by their name (STRING).

Data types may be converted (explicitly) by CONVERT, CONVERT(object, data-type) (CONVERT object to datatype). Any data type can be converted to STRING. However, this is most meaningful for integer, real, ARRAY, and TABLE. Not all conversions are allowed.

A number of conversions are performed by SNOBOL automatically. This includes the standard conversions, integer to real, real to integer, as well as integer to STRING and STRING to integer (and real).

Data Types of Functions and Operations

Functions usually require a specific data type (of its arguments). However, arguments of incorrect data type, e.g., SIZE(1234), where 1234 is an integer, are automatically converted by SNOBOL (1234 to '1234', the STRING) where possible. In most cases, the problem of data type conversion can be ignored because the common ("expected") conversions are performed. However, in using IDENT and DIFFER, no conversions are performed. In some conversions, e.g., SIZE(+00732), the result (3, LEN 3) is surprising because of transformations performed in the conversion (omission of the sign and the leading zeroes). A list of the primitive functions and their expected data types (and returns, return values) is given.

Unary Operators

A unary operator is like a function with one argument, with a more compact representation. For example, ¬A and -A indicate not-A and negative A, respectively. Unary operators are not separated from their operands by a space.

Binary Operators

Binary operators are essentially the same as a function with two arguments. Automatic conversion is performed as necessary. Conversion to STRING is the most common. Conversion to PATTERN from integer, real, string, and expression is also provided. An EXPRESSION is a data type, e.g., for arithmetic expressions. STRING to integer conversion is provided in arithmetic contexts, as in STRING to real.

TRACING

Tracing is provided for diagnostic information (DEBUG). It is turned on by assigning a positive integer to &TRACE (0 = "off," nonzero (positive) = "on"). The TRACE indicates changes in the values of a variable, calls and returns from functions, transfers to a label, and changes in the value of certain keywords.

The trace includes the statement number in which the action occurs, the result of the action, and the time, in milliseconds, from the beginning of the program (execution). The value of &TRACE is decremented every time an action is traced. Hence, the positive number can limit the amount of tracing.

Value Tracing

```
TRACE(name, 'VALUE', tag)
```

causes VALUE tracing. The printout, of the values, is made each time the name (value) is changed. Only the result of the assignment is printed.

VALUE tracing is the default type of tracing and is assumed if the 'type' (second argument) is omitted. Hence, TRACE('CH') or TRACE('STRING') would trace the variables CH and STRING (values). Value tracing does not occur on input.

The tag is used for created (not "natural") variables; e.g., the statement TRACE(.SUM<3>,'VALUE','SUM<3>') traces the third element of an array. The dot (.SUM<3>) indicates a name.

Function Tracing

Function tracing traces the call, return or both, to and from a function. The 'types' CALL, RETURN and FUNCTION (both) are provided to indicate each.

CALL tracing gives the level of the call and the current value of the arguments. RETURN tracing gives the level to which the return is made. FUNCTION gives both.

&FTRACE can be used to trace all function calls and returns (&FTRACE = a positive number). &FTRACE, like &TRACE, is decremented on each "action" (call,return). When the value of &FTRACE reaches zero, tracing stops.

Label Tracing

```
TRACE(name, 'LABEL')
```

causes LABEL tracing. The label is traced when it is the object of a goto. It is not traced if the program flows into it.

Keyword Tracing

Keyword tracing traces the values (changes) of the keywords ERRTYPE, FNCLEVEL, STCOUNT, and STFCOUNT. STCOUNT is the statement count, STFCOUNT counts the number of failed statements, FNCLEVEL is the level of a function call, and ERRTYPE is an integer code identifying the error. Keyword tracing is turned on by

```
TRACE(name, 'KEYWORD')
```

where name is one of the four types (of keywords that can be traced).

Tracing can be discontinued for a particular trace by

```
STOPTR(name, type)
```

For example,

```
STOPTR('CH', 'VALUE')
```

would stop the tracing of the variable CH. The type VALUE can be omitted.

The programmer can supply functions for tracing. The statement

```
TRACE(name, type, tag, function)
```

uses the programmer-defined function 'function' to do the tracing.

Primitive functions and operators can be traced using programmer-defined functions and OPSYN. OPSYN is primitive function that provides a synonym for a function or an operator.

A dump of all natural variables can be obtained with DUMP. DUMP is a primitive function, DUMP(N), where N is a nonzero integer if dumping is wanted, zero if not. It can be turned on and off during program execution (by various calls to DUMP).

INPUT AND OUTPUT

Input and output go on during the execution of a program without any explicit i/o statements. The variable OUTPUT is associated with the system printer. OUTPUT is printed whenever OUTPUT is assigned a value. Hence,

```
    OUTPUT = 'HELLO'
```

prints the value of 'HELLO' and

```
    OUTPUT = X
```

prints the value of X. PUNCH output is also available in the original SNOBOL.

INPUT is associated with the standard input. This is the keyboard (or card) for the most part. OUTPUT = INPUT echoes the input. Failure can be used to indicate the end of file. For example,

```
    READ  DATA<I> = INPUT   :F(OUT)
```

detects the end of file and transfers control to the statement labeled OUT.

The i/o system is handled by FORTRAN subroutines in the original SNOBOL. It is system dependent in implementation.

Programmer-defined i/o associations can be made using the INPUT and OUTPUT functions. Other functions such as ENDFILE (write an end of file marker on the output device/medium), REWIND, BACKSPACE, and DETACH (detach the association) are available.

INPUT and OUTPUT can be turned off by setting the variables &INPUT and &OUTPUT to zero. This suppresses printing and reading of data values. Normal (automatic) input and output can be restored (by a nonzero value).

RUNNING A SNOBOL PROGRAM

Running a SNOBOL program is system dependent. However, the compiler produces intermediate code (polish-prefix notation for the program) and interprets it. The program is entered via the normal (standard) input stream. This was device 5 (FORTRAN) in the original SNOBOL.

Several options are available to control the listing. LIST turns on the listing of the program. It also indicates whether the statement numbers are placed on the left or the right:

```
    -LIST LEFT
```

or

```
    -LIST RIGHT
```

The dash indicates a ''control'' (listing control) directive. UNLIST turns off the listing and EJECT causes a page eject.

OPERATOR PRECEDENCE AND ASSOCIATIVITY

Binary operators, other than exponentiation, are left associative. Exponentiation is right associative. Unary operators, except NOT ($\neg$), are left associative. NOT is right associative. The precedence is normal, parentheses, exponentiation, multiplication and division, and addition and subtraction, with the exception that multiplication and division have different precedences. Addition and subtraction have the same precedence (5).

Multiplication has higher precedence than division. This would result in a statement like

    A/B*C

being right associative rather than left if the precedences are implemented. Various error messages are given. Normal termination occurs when control is transferred to the END statement (label).

Error termination occurs if an unconditionally fatal error occurs or an error occurs and &ERRLIMIT is zero. Another form of error termination occurs when an i/o error occurs. In this case, the message CUT BY SYSTEM appears.

A program may also be canceled. However, SNOBOL loses control in this situation (dumps are lost, as are statistics). A program may be canceled by the operating system (timeout in an infinite loop).

PROGRAMMING DETAILS AND STORAGE MANAGEMENT

The key to efficient use of SNOBOL is understanding of its implementation. The implementation is complex.

The SNOBOL (SNOBOL4) system consists of three parts: the compiler (translator to intermediate code), interpreter, and storage allocator.

The compiler translates the program into polish-prefix notation. During the execution phase, this is interpreted. Storage allocation occurs frequently during both compilation and interpretation. Strings are stored in the storage area. During execution, new strings, patterns, arrays and other data objects are created and stored. Allocation of new data objects usually occurs throughout execution. As a result of continued allocation, storage may be exhausted. Storage regeneration (garbage collection) is an important part of the system.

Strings of any (unspecified) length are supported. This is true of string constants and variable names. Hence, the string storage allocation mechanism (as in BASIC) is important.

Any string may also be used as a variable (through indirect referencing, &'HELLO'). Hence, all strings are stored as variables. Each string occurs exactly once in storage. When a new string is created, storage is searched for an occurrence of that string. Special techniques (including hashing and linked allocation) are used (7,8). The value of a (natural) variable is accessed by referencing its pointer. Values are assigned (strings) by returning the pointer to the variable referenced. If a string is created, it is looked up, and if it exists, that pointer is returned; otherwise, storage is allocated for it and the new pointer returned. Obtaining and assigning values is relatively simple. Creating strings is time-consuming.

Indirect referencing is relatively easy, due to the use of the pointers. Patterns are relatively complex to construct. Hence, they should be created outside the pattern matching statement (in an assignment statement). Anchored mode also prevents extensive string searching. When searching for a known delimiter, BREAK should be used (BREAK at ','). ARB is more time-consuming, matching each character individually. If one of a number of characters is sought, ANY should be used. Alternation requires a number of patterns (or subpatterns) to be matched. SPAN is also efficient. (ARBNO should be used only when necessary, i.e., when the characters are truly arbitrary.) Quickscan mode can also improve efficiency by eliminating testing of "impossible" patterns (too few characters left). Output can be eliminated when possible. [It avoids a table lookup of output associated variables) (&OUTPUT = 0).] Using &TRIM = 1 causes shorter strings (no trailing blanks, 80 in the case of INPUT).

STORAGE MANAGEMENT

Storage is allocated dynamically. All data objects and code compete for space. When storage is exhausted, the storage allocator regenerates storage. Storage regeneration takes 20 to 100 times as long as a typical statement. (This is dependent on the system and the typical statement.) A programmer can force storage regeneration (garbage collection) by the function COLLECT. COLLECT forces storage regeneration and returns the amount of storage available (in bytes). COLLECT(N) fails if less than *N* bytes remain.

The function CLEAR( ) clears variables (sets them to the null string). This saves space when the variables are no longer needed (like an overlay). CLEAR does not affect the values of keywords and created variables. It also does not affect function definitions (or i/o associations). If values are saved by a function call, they are restored when the function returns. This can be used to selectively save and CLEAR values. Values are cleared only at the level of the function (CLEAR) call.

SYNTAX

Digits are $0|1|2|3|4|5|6|7|8|9$. Letters are $A|B|C|D|E|F|G|H|I|J|K|L|M|N|O|P|Q|R|S|T|U|V|W|X|Y|Z$ (upper case in the original SNOBOL). Alphanumerics are letter $|$ digit $(| = $"or" or alternation). These are standard definitions. An identifier is a letter followed by alphanumeric (unspecified number).

The number of statements is small, assignment, matching, replacement, degenerate, and end. A degenerate statement is a statement consisting of a label (optional), subject field (optional), goto field (optional), and an eos (end of string, carriage return). These reduce to the two forms

```
label subject goto
label goto
```

or a blank line. Degenerative statements contain the subject field without an assignment (=), pattern (pattern match), or pattern = (match and replace). Degenerative statements are evaluated as the replacement statement, omitting the missing pieces. A SNOBOL (SNOBOL4) program consists of a sequence of statements followed by the END statement (label). Statements may be separated by semicolons (eos).

Data type conversions require syntactic analysis of the string to be converted (conversions from STRING). This may be an integer, real, expression, or code (statement [; statement] . . .). The character codes for various machines are machine dependent. They may be found with &ALPHABET (the characters, not the codes).

VERSIONS 2 AND 3

Versions 2 (4) and 3 (5) of SNOBOL are significantly different, but the differences that require changes in programs are minor. For example, in version 2, the values of &TRACE

and &FTRACE can be negative to turn on the tracing mode; in Version 3 they must be positive (and are decremented). The CONVERT function is more extensive (permissive and converting STRING to INTEGER and vice versa) and several constructions that are erroneous in version 2, e.g., mixed mode, are acceptable (the conversions are performed) in version 3. Program listing formats and messages are somewhat different in the two versions.

Certain functions and keywords not available in version 2 are available in version 3. For example, DUMP, &CODE, and &ERRLIMIT are not available in version 2. There are many differences in regard to type conversions.

A SAMPLE PROGRAM

A sample program is

```
          DATA('COMPLEX(R,I)')
          DEFINE('MUL(X,Y)')
          OPSYN('%','*',2)
          OPSYN('*','MUL',2)
                              :(END)
   MUL  MUL     = DIFFER(DATATYPE(X),'COMPLEX')
   +              DIFFER(DATATYPE(Y),'COMPLEX')
   +              X % Y          :S(RETURN)
        MUL     = DIFFER(DATATYPE(X),'COMPLEX')
   +              COMPLEX(X % R(Y),X % I(Y))        :S(OUT)
        MUL     = DIFFER(DATATYPE(Y),'COMPLEX')
   +              COMPLEX(Y % R(X),Y % I(X))        :S(OUT)
        MUL     = COMPLEX(R(X) % R(Y) - I(X) % I(Y),
   +              R(X) % I(Y) + R(Y) % I(X))
   OUT  MUL = EQ(I(MUL))  R(MUL)       :(RETURN)
```

The program (fragment) multiplies complex variables or ordinary integers or reals. It can be tested with the statements

```
   A = COMPLEX(5,3)
   B = COMPLEX(6,2)
   PR = A * B
   PR = 4 * A
   PR = B * 5
   PR = 5 * 4
```

The program is from Ref. 5.

A complete program is

```
        K = 0
   LOOP  FRIEND = TRIM(INPUT)
         FRIEND POS(0) ' ' :S(LOOP)
         K = K + 1
         FRIEND POS(0) 'END' :F(LOOP)
         OUTPUT = ' ' K
   END
```

The program is from Ref. 9. The program counts the number of labeled statements in a program. It can be used as its own input. POS indicates that a match should begin in a certain position.

Another example is

```
        &ANCHOR = 0
MORE    LINE = INPUT           :F(PRINT)
AGAIN   LINE 'WILLIAM' =       :F(MORE)
        COUNT = COUNT + 1      :(AGAIN)
PRINT   OUTPUT = 'NUMBER OF OCCURRENCES OF "WILLIAM" IS ' COUNT
END
```

The program is from Ref. 10. It counts the number of occurrences of 'WILLIAM' in a text (set of lines). The statement (fragment) 'WILLIAM' = deletes the occurrence of 'WILLIAM' matched and the branch :(AGAIN) looks for more occurrences.

SNOBOL is case sensitive when referring to names. Hence, the convention of using uppercase letters has been retained.

The maximum length of a string in SNOBOL varies but is in excess of 10,000 in the usual case. Lowercase or uppercase letters may be used in current versions of SNOBOL.

Variables are created as they are named. Hence, a mistyped variable creates a new variable (as in FORTRAN). The null string is the initial contents of a variable.

Spaces are part of the syntax in SNOBOL. Operators must be separated from their operands by a space, A + B. Statements begin with a space. Labels are placed in column 1. Statements are executed sequentially, except for the goto branches.

Because of its close ties to FORTRAN, statements should not extend beyond column 72 in SNOBOL. Other traces of FORTRAN are the treatment of mixed mode in version 2; formats in the OUTPUT statements and the use of columns 73–80 to sequentially number the lines.

Numbers are input as strings. This is facilitated by the automatic conversion of STRINGS to numbers (REAL or INTEGER) in arithmetic contexts. The arithmetic functions GE, GT, LE, LT, EQ, can be used to control loops. For example,

```
MORE    OUTPUT = INPUT       :F(END)
        LT(COUNT,4)          :F(END)
        COUNT = COUNT + 1    :(MORE)
```

inputs at most five lines.

In converting tables to arrays, an array $n \times 2$, where n is the number of elements in the table, is created. The two dimensions are the initial subscript to the table (which may be any data object, but is usually a STRING) and the entries (value) of that data cell. This is useful for counting words or characters in a program. For example, the table

```
'THE'  | 4 |
       -----
'CAT'  | 1 |
       -----
'SAT'  | 2 |
       -----
```

would be converted to the array

```
| THE | 4 |
-----------
| CAT | 1 |
-----------
| SAT | 2 |
-----------
```

The array can then be printed out sequentially.

The counts are usually obtained from the input text. For example, the program

```
        &ANCHOR = 1
        LETTERS = 'ABCDEFGHIJKLMNOPQRSTUVWXYZ'
        WORDPAT = BREAK(LETTERS) SPAN(LETTERS) . WORD
        T = TABLE()
        LINE = 'THE CAT SAT ON THE MAT AND THE DOG SAT ON THE
        RUG'
AGAIN   LINE WORDPAT =              :F(PRINT)
        T<WORD> = T<WORD> + 1   :(AGAIN)
PRINT
```

would break out the words for the line and assign them to WORD (.WORD in the WORD pattern), storing each in the table (T<WORD> = T<WORD> + 1), with its count. The table, T, can then be converted to an array

```
    A = CONVERT(T, 'ARRAY')
```

and printed, sequentially. The example is from Ref. 10.

STRING AND LIST PROCESSING

SNOBOL stands for StriNg Oriented and symBOlic Language. It is, however, used for both string and list processing. String processing is the processing of characters or text. List processing is the processing of data structures called lists (linked lists). Both are extensive in SNOBOL4.

Pattern matching is the most powerful and most extensive major feature of the SNOBOL4 language (11). One example of pattern matching is to break items out of a list. For example,

```
        LIST = 'LEFT,RIGHT,HALT,CANCEL,RIGHT,'
        NEXTI = BREAK(',') . ITEM LEN(1)
          .
          .
          .
GETI    LIST NEXTI =              :F(DONE)
          .
          .
          .
```

breaks items (words) out of a list. The pattern, NEXTI, indicates the BREAK character (',') and assigns the pattern (string) matched before the break character to ITEM, then matches the character [LEN(1)].

Pattern matching is often used to implement grammars. A grammar describes the structure of strings ("sentences") in the language. An example is given in Figure 1, which indicates the BNF (Backus Naur form or Backus normal form) notation for integers (a string of digits) and identifiers (consisting only of letters). They can be implemented by

---

```
<digit>  ::= 0|1|2|3|4|5|6|7|8|9
<integer> ::= <digit> | <digit> <integer>
<letter>  ::= A|B|C|D|E|F|G|H|I|J|K|L|M|N|O|P|Q|R|S|T|U|V|W|X|Y|Z
<identifier> ::= <letter> | <identifier> <letter>
```

FIGURE 1

```
INT = SPAN('0123456789')
```

and

```
IDENTIFIER = SPAN('ABCDEFGHIJKLMNOPQRSTUVWXYZ')
```

The program for listing Fibonacci numbers illustrates the style of SNOBOL:

```
DEFINE('F(N)')
        .
        .
        .

F   LT(N,1)                      :S(FRETURN)
    F = LE(N,2) 1                :S(RETURN)
    F = F(N - 1) + F(N - 2)    :(RETURN)
```

The function tests $N < 1$. In this case, the function fails (0 or a negative number). It then tests LE(N,2), and if it succeeds, it returns the null string followed by 1. Otherwise, it returns $F(N - 1) + F(N - 2)$.

The function is a recursive function. It implements the definition

```
f(n) = 1                     for n = 1,2
f(n) = f(n-1) + f(n-2)       for n > 2
f(n) is undefined otherwise
```

The example is from Ref. 11.

SNOBOL is more powerful in its analytic ability than in its synthetic facility. It is relatively easy to generate a pattern to recognize algebraic expressions; it is difficult to generate them (in all possibilities).

THE REPRESENTATION OF DATA TYPES

All data can be visualized as occupying a cell with two parts: the data type and the value. For example, an integer might be represented as

```
 _____
| I | 734|
 ---------
```

and a real as

```
 _____
| R | 2.0|
 ---------
```

The values of other data types in SNOBOL are pointers to the objects.

An array is a pointer from the name of the array to the array

```
     _____              _____
X | A | *-- | ----->| I | 10|
     ---------              ---------
                            | I |  5|
                             ---------
                                .
                                .
                                .
                             _____
                            | I | 19|
                             ---------
```

A indicates the data type ('ARRAY'). The data types of the elements need not be the same.

Two variables with the same value, say Y = X, have the same pointer

```
    _____              _____
X | A | *-- | ----->| I | 10|
    _____   ->   _____
    _____    |   | I | 5|
Y | A | *-- | ---|    _____
    _____

                      .
                      .
                      .

                    _____
                   | I | 19|
                    _____
```

If an element of X is changed, X<2> = 5, this is reflected in Y(Y<2> = 5). Common data structures, e.g., stacks, may be implemented using arrays or tables (or user-defined data types). Other structures, e.g., binary trees, are implemented using user-defined data structures (data types).

Mathematical Applications

Although SNOBOL is a string (and list) processing language, it can be used to implement mathematical applications. One example is the use of complex numbers. Another is the use of linked lists to process integers (11,12).

Symbolic mathematics, e.g., theorem proving and formula manipulation, such as algebraic transformations, show the more powerful string processing capabilities of the language. Typical examples are operations on arithmetic expressions. However, an example from standard mathematics is differentiation (11). Another is cryptography, although this is not strictly mathematical. The functions REPLACE (characters) and REVERSE (STRINGS) can be used to encode and decode messages. The REVERSE function is a user-defined function (11). The TABLE function can also be used to do cryptanalysis (collect the statistics).

Document Preparation

Although document processing has recently become a major topic, it was an initial concern of SNOBOL programming. Editors, text formatters, and other document processors could be implemented using SNOBOL (as well as other specialized languages, such as AWK). The generation of indices, tables of contents, and other supplementary listings are other applications. Automatic numbering of pages can also be provided.

Grammars

A grammar for arithmetic expressions is given in Figure 2. It can be implemented by defining patterns for the nonterminals and then defining patterns for the grammar.

```
<ADDOP>  : : =  -|+
<MULOP>  : : =  *|/
<VARIABLE>  : : =  A|B|C
<TERM>  : : =  <VARIABLE>  |  (<EXP>)  |  <TERM><MULOP><VARIABLE>
<EXP>  : : =  <TERM>  |  <EXP><ADDOP><TERM>
```

FIGURE 2

IMPLEMENTATION

SNOBOL4 is implemented by a set of macros (assembly language, macros, in SNOBOL4). FORTRAN subroutines perform the i/o. The idea for the first SNOBOL arose out of the need to manipulate symbolic strings, e.g., factor polynomials $(x**2+2xy+y**2 = (x+y)**2)$ (1). In retrospect, the tools (SNOBOL) have turned out to be more interesting than the original problem (6). The original SNOBOL was designed to be a simple, high-level language for manipulating strings. Strings were the only data type. Even arithmetic operations were performed on strings.

The first system consisted of a translator, interpreter, and allocator (storage allocator). Implementation was complicated by the extensive use of strings. Strings could hold values (through indirect referencing) as well as be the value of data objects (of type STRING). The translator converted the source-language program into an internal table of flags and pointers. The interpreter was driven from this table. The allocator allocated space for strings and performed "garbage collection." The coding of the SNOBOL system was in assembly language for the IBM 7090 (13,14). The implementation of the system was facilitated by the use of a package of string manipulation macros (15). Every construction was valid syntactically. The SNOBOL translator would readily accept a CO-MIT program, but the interpreter would not (6).

The main defect was the lack of built-in functions. Determining the length of a string, for example, was difficult (6). A new implementation, with the addition of built-in functions, produced SNOBOL2. SNOBOL2 existed for only a few weeks. Programmer-defined recursive functions produced SNOBOL3 (2). SNOBOL3, like SNOBOL, was coded in macro-assembly language for the IBM 7090/94. More of the code was written in macro calls. Independent implementations were undertaken for other machines. One unpleasant result of this was the development of language dialects (LISP). The languages were supported by the authors, and sometimes not at all. This was the motivation for SNOBOL4.

The built-in data types of SNOBOL4 are STRING, INTEGER, REAL, PATTERN, ARRAY, TABLE, NAME, EXPRESSION, and CODE. Arrays are created during program execution [by A = ARRAY('30')]. Tables are created similarly. Tables can, however, have only one dimension. Keywords are provided for communicating between the program and the system. Protected keywords cannot be changed by the program; unprotected keywords can. Examples of a protected keyword are STCOUNT (the statement count) and STNO (the current statement number). Indirect referencing, represented by the unary operator &, is a result of the extensive use of pointers (to point to data objects). Indirect referencing permits the use of associative references. For example, if

```
BLUE    = 'WALL'
RED     = 'FLOOR'
WHITE   = 'CEILING'
```

and COLOR = 'BLUE', then the value of &COLOR is 'WALL'. This can be used to implement query systems.

The name pointer (., adjacent to the variable) returns a variable's address. Assignment to the variable can then occur through indirect referencing (&V).

The simplest pattern is the string (identity). Other patterns are composed of alternation and function operators and variables. Patterns that match can be assigned using the conditional assignment (. WORD, with a space between . and WORD, a binary operator) and immediate value assignment ($, a binary operator). Immediate value assignment succeeds even if the entire statement fails.

Built-in patterns are provided to expand the facility of the language, e.g., ARB, which matches an arbitrary string of characters (including the null string).

Pattern-valued functions are built-in functions that construct patterns. For example,

```
VOWEL = ANY('AEIOU')
```

constructs a pattern that matches any string of vowels, and

```
NOTVOWEL = NOTANY('AEIOU')
```

does the reverse (inverse).

Unevaluated expressions (*N) are used to allow the variable (N) to take on different values at execution time, even if the pattern is created in an assignment statement (outside a loop). For example,

```
NGRAM = LEN(*N) . GRAM
```

would be evaluated for N each time it is referenced,

```
LOOP TEXT NGRAM =
```

even though it was constructed in an assignment statement (NGRAM = LEN(*N) . GRAM). If it had been written

```
NGRAM = LEN(N) . GRAM
```

only the value of N at compilation would be used.

Patterns such as

```
WPAT = BREAK(LETTERS) SPAN(LETTERS) . WORD
```

and

```
LETTERS = 'ABCDEFGHIJKLMNOPQRSTUVWXYZ'
```

can be used to find words.

DECLARATIONS

SNOBOL4 does not have declarations. Arrays, tables, programmer-defined data types, and recursive procedures (functions) are implemented without predefined declarations. SNOBOL also does not fix the data type of variables. This may change with each assignment. Even arrays may have elements of different data types. Finally, variables may be created during execution. Every non-null string is a variable and may be assigned a value.

Portability and machine independence were major considerations. This was a direct result of the experience with SNOBOL3.

STRUCTURE OF THE SNOBOL4 SYSTEM

The most basic decision with respect to the system was that it be an interpretive language. An interpreter (as opposed to a compiler) has the ability to be easily modified and extended.

The translator generates polish-prefix code. The prefix code is not machine dependent. All procedures (of the translator, interpreter, and storage allocator) have the same structure and are autonomous. Some of the procedures are ANALYZ, BLOCK (to allocate storage), CNVRT, and BINOP. Data consists of resident data (the SNOBOL data area) and allocated (to the source program) data.

DATA REPRESENTATION

Data objects are represented by a descriptor that has three fields:

```
 _____
| T | F | V |
 _____
```

T is the type of the data. This is an integer code for each data type (built-in or programmer-defined) and is illustrated by a letter (I, R, A) for the built-in types. V is the data value or a pointer to the data value. F is a set of flags, e.g., allocated data or static (resident) data, of interest to the compiler (interpreter).

STRINGS

Strings are handled differently from other data objects. They have the three basic fields (T, F, V) and two additional fields, the offset (O) and length (L) of the string. For example, the strings 'OR' and 'ALGORITHM' would be stored as

0 is the offset to the pointer for ALGORITHM, 3 for OR. The length of ALGORITHM is 9 and the length of OR is 2. The general representation is

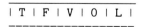

```
 _____
| T | F | V | O | L |
 _____
```

where V is a pointer to the base of the first (or basic) string stored. The descriptor for a string is called a Qualifier (QUAL).

```
 _____
| 2 | F | * |  --> =2
 _____
| S | A | * |  --> {X}
 _____
| 2 | F | * |  --> *2
 _____
| S | A | * |  --> {Y}
 _____
| 1 | F | * |  --> -1
 _____
| 1 | F | * |  --> SIZE1
 _____
| S | A | * |  --> {Z}
 _____
```

FIGURE 3

Blocks of descriptors are used for patterns, arrays, tables, and natural variables. The translator translates the source program into internal form. The interpreter interprets this. There are two kinds of code descriptors: function and operand. Function descriptors have an F flag to distinguish them, and the V field points to the code. Operand descriptors are those for source language data. The internal code for the string

    X = Y * -SIZE(Z)

is shown in Figure 3. This corresponds to the internal notation for the prefix

    = 2 × *2 Y -1 SIZE1 Z

The numbers indicate the number of operands for an operator (or function). = is binary, as is *; - (negation) and SIZE are unary. The variables, X, Y, and Z are represented by their descriptor $(S,A,\rightarrow\{X\})$.

NATURAL VARIABLES

Natural variables are represented as shown in Figure 4. The title descriptor indicates that it is a natural variable (N) and the title descriptor (T). Natural variables are structures containing strings. The 6 is the length of the string (HUNTER). The asterisk represents a pointer to itself, which is used in storage regeneration. The data value is an Integer (I) of value 5. If the variable (HUNTER) had the value 'WOLF' (HUNTER = 'WOLF'), the descriptor would be as in Figure 5. The S in the initial descriptor (S,A,-->) indicates a string, the A an allocated variable (String). The null string is represented as

```
 _____
| S | 0 | 0 |
 _____
```

The operations, =2, *2, -1, and SIZE1, are carried out by procedures. Each function or operator has a procedure associated with it. The procedures for -1 and -2 are distinct. In functions, the arguments are evaluated by the function procedure.

```
| S | A | * |   -->   | 6 | NT | * |      title descriptor
-------------         --------------
                      | I | 0  | 5 |      value descriptor
                      --------------
                      |   |    |   |      label descriptor
                      --------------
                      |   |    |   |      chain descriptor
                      --------------
                      |HUNTER     |       string
                      --------------
```

FIGURE 4

Several operators are polymorphous and perform different operations, depending on the data types of the operands. The operands are checked and converted as necessary. If an operator is polymorphous, the data type checking selects the appropriate procedure.

If a function or operation fails, the statement fails and further evaluation ceases.

Functions may create variables or values. If a variable, the return is by name; if a value, the return is by value. Functions that return a variable (name) may appear on the left of assignment statements [F(N) = 2]. There are three return signals from functions: failure, name, and value.

PROGRAM CONTROL OF FLOW

Statements are executed by following the pointer to the code. There is a code base value (pointer) and an offset. Gotos change the sequence of evaluation. These are unconditional [:(DEST)] and conditional [:S(DEST), :F(DEST)]. The label descriptor of the destination has a CODE data type. This is illustrated in Figure 6.

The pointer in the label descriptor is a pointer to the Code (location of HEAD). Conditional gotos select the routine by setting offsets to the failure or success codes.

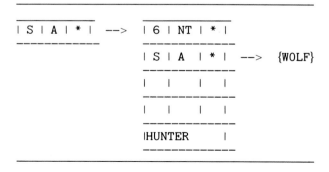

FIGURE 5

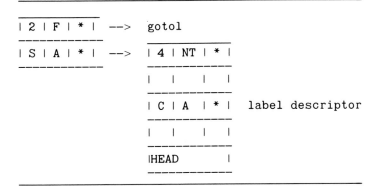

FIGURE 6

The translator converts the source code into the prefix code implemented by the tables and pointers. A statement has the general form

```
label rule goto
```

where the rule is

```
subject = object   (assignment)
subject pattern    (pattern matching)
subject pattern = object  (replacement)
```

The first two types are special cases of the third.

The word element is used to describe self-delimiting components such as literals, identifiers, and parenthesized expressions. These are called "primaries" in other language descriptions. The word expression is used to describe binary operations and "elements." These rules can be summarized as follows:

1. An identifier is an element.
2. A unary operator applied to an element is an element.
3. An element is an expression.
4. An expression enclosed in parentheses is an element.
5. A binary operation on an expression is an expression.

Examples of elements are

```
A
'A'
-32
F(A + B)
(SIZE(X) + 2)
```

All elements are expressions. Other expressions (not elements) are

```
A + B
SIZE(X) * 2
A | B | C
'A' | 'B' | 'C'
```

All components of a rule can be expressions except the subject. The subject must be an element. Two procedures, ELEM and EXPR, analyze elements and expressions.

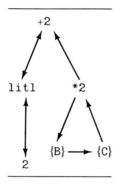

FIGURE 7

Tokens

Tokens are names for classes of characters (or codes). DIGIT, LETTER, SQUOTE, INTCOD, and LITCOD are examples. INTGER, IDENTF, and others are tables used in the analysis.

Token analysis involves applying STREAM to the input text. STREAM is a procedure to consume (and analyze, into tokens) text.

Source language input to the translator consists of line images. Usually, each line is a statement. The continuation (+ in column 1) allows a statement to span over several lines, and the semicolon (after the statement) allows several statements per line. The translator operates on a continuous STREAM of text.

THE TRANSLATION PROCESS

Code trees are transient representations of expressions and elements, built up as the relationship between operators and operands is determined. For example, the expression

    2 + B * C

has the code tree shown in Figure 7.

The code tree is built up in pieces. This is shown in Figure 8. Each operand is accessed individually. This is 2 (Fig. 8a), litl 2; +2 litl (2), {B} (Fig. 8b); and +2 litl (2) *2 {B} {C} (Fig. 8c). The tree is modified as the precedences (* "over" +) occur. The arrow downward (from the root) points to the leftmost son (child); an arrow upward points to the father (parent); arrows sideways (to the right) point to siblings.

Nodes of code trees are implemented by blocks of descriptors. Elements may be unary operators applied to elements, identifiers, integers, and reals, parenthesized expressions, function calls, and others (e.g., array and table references, quoted literals, or STRINGS). Elements are defined (found) by STREAM. They are incorporated into the trees as trees.

EXPRESSIONS

Expressions consist of elements separated by binary operators. EXPR obtains elements, by calling ELEM, and operators, by calling STREAM. The binary operators are ranked

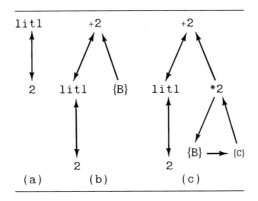

FIGURE 8

according to their precedence. This is used in building the tree. In the implementation of SNOBOL4, addition and subtraction have the same precedence, although multiplication is higher than division (if this is implemented).

STATEMENTS

Statements are processed by processing the label, statement initialization, rule processing, and goto processing. ELEM is called to analyze the subject, and EXPR is called to analyze the pattern, if there is one. EXPR is also called to analyze the object. By the time rule analysis is completed, the type of statement and the appropriate code descriptor, =2, match2, replace3, has been determined and placed into the prefix tree.

Code trees are an intermediate representation in the translation. The prefix code is obtained by "left listing" the tree (preorder traversal, NLR). The order is given by the rules

    1.   Start with the root.
    2.   Copy the code descriptor of the current node.
    3.   If the current node has a left son, move to the left son and go to rule 2.
    4.   Otherwise, if the node has a right sibling, move to the right sibling and go to rule 2.

followed by

    5.   Otherwise, if the node has a father, move to the father and go to rule 4.
    6.   Otherwise, the listing is complete.

ERRORS

Syntactic errors may occur in various contexts. Most are reported by STREAM. An incomplete expression is determined by context. ELEM and EXPR call each other recursively, and when an error occurs, it is identified by that routine and signaled appropriately (missing operand, missing operator). ANALYZ receives the failure signal.

A considerable portion of the statement may already have been analyzed. ANALYZ resets the code offset to the beginning of the statement and writes a code descriptor for error1 over the init1 field. If that statement is subsequently executed, error1 transfers control to an error routine. If it is not executed, no harm is done, although an error indicator will appear in the listing.

THE TABLE OF NATURAL VARIABLES

In a sense, the natural variables (strings) are the symbols of SNOBOL4. These are contained in the symbol table. The symbol table is maintained with hash coding (7,8,16). The natural variables are included in categories. The categories are hashed to, and, within a category, the entries are linked.

EXECUTION OF FUNCTIONS

Functions are executed by evaluating the arguments, saving the current values of the formal arguments and local variables, and transferring control to the code (label). When the function returns, values are restored.

KEYWORDS

Keywords are kept in two tables: one for the protected keywords, one for the unprotected keywords. They are consulted by the relevant code.

PATTERNS AND PATTERN MATCHING

Pattern matching is the most extensive feature of SNOBOL4. The way it is implemented is not always obvious. It constitutes a language of its own within SNOBOL4.

Patterns are data objects. Some, such as ARB, are built-in to the SNOBOL system. Others are constructed during execution. For example, in the statement

```
     BIT = '0' | '1'
```

the alternation operator creates a pattern which is assigned to the variable BIT (the value of BIT). Patterns can be constructed in the pattern field. Thus,

```
     TEXT '0' | '1'
```

matches the pattern "0 or 1," as does

```
     TEXT BIT
```

with the above assignment.

Pattern matching is performed interpretively and patterns are constructed in a manner similar to the prefix code.

```
'B'     'E'     'D'
___    ____    ____
'R'     'EA'    'DS'
```

FIGURE 9

Alternation and concatenation produce structural relationships between pattern components. These relationships give the order in which components are matched. These are indicated in a 'BEAD' diagram. This is shown in Figure 9.

The pattern

BR = ('B' | 'R') ('E' | 'EA') ('D' | 'DS')

is matched by the diagram in Figure 9. It is from Ref. 5. The vertical (alternation) matches are tried first, before the concatenation (movement to the next portion of the pattern). This is illustrated with the matching of 'READS' in Figure 10. The B is tried first and it fails. The R is tried next and it succeeds. This causes the movement of the cursor, as in Figure 11, and the movement to the next portion of the pattern ['E', in ('E' | 'EA')]. The 'E' succeeds, but the 'D' and 'DS' fail (on 'A'). This causes a backup to ('E' | 'EA') and the trial of 'EA'. 'EA' succeeds and the pattern ("matcher") tries 'D'. This fails, but 'DS' succeeds. This is shown in Figure 12.

The arrow is like a thread through the pattern. For example, 'BEADS' would be as in Figure 13. The initial arrow shows where to begin.

Using the bead diagrams (or concept), the programmer can arrange to have the patterns evaluated in the order he or she wishes. Matching procedures perform the actual matching and advance the cursor. The arrow is referred to as the "needle." The needle points at the bead the scanner is currently trying to match. The trace of the needle leaves the "match."

HEURISTICS

The heuristics used in pattern matching rest on the observation that length can often be used to optimize pattern matching. This is the basis of discarding certain matches (attempts) in quickscan mode. Pattern matching is inherently subject to combinatorial explosion. These length checks combat this.

When patterns are constructed, length information is placed in the heuristic descriptors. These consist of the number of characters necessary to match the pattern, if this pattern and the following are to be matched. This is illustrated in Figure 14.

The minimum length to match 'BE' and its possible "followers" (concatenation) is 4 ('BE' and 'A', 'D'). The minimum for the final 'D' is 1. The length includes the pattern being matched (needle) itself.

```
READS  -->    'B'     'E'     'D'
   ^         ___    ____    ____
   |          'R'     'EA'    'DS'
```

FIGURE 10

```
R  EADS     'B'  —→     'E'     'D'
    ^         ---       ----    ----
    |         'R'       'EA'    'DS'
```

FIGURE 11

```
READS       'B'         'E'        'D'
     ^      ---         ----       ----
     |      'R'  —→     'EA'  —→   'DS'
```

FIGURE 12

```
BEADS  —→   'B'  —→    'E'         'D'
     ^      ---        ----        ----
     |      'R'        'EA'  —→    'DS'
```

FIGURE 13

```
BEAD  —→    'BE'  4    'AR'  3    'DS'  2
   ^        ----       ----       ----
   |        'B'   3    'A'   2    'D'   1
```

FIGURE 14

Failure to match because there are not enough characters left is different from failure to match because the characters are not found. The two are distinguished because length failure can often be transmitted backward to avoid futile matches of other (previous) patterns (in alternation).

OTHER OPERATIONS

Four unary operations, which are important, but simple to implement, are indirect referencing, the unary name operator, the unevaluated expression operator, and negation.

Indirect addressing (referencing) is facilitated by the pointers. The value of any variable is in the V field. The reference returns a STRING, a NAME, or an INTEGER converted to a string.

The unary name operator is the inverse of the indirect referencing operator and is semantically equivalent to a literal. Unevaluated expressions are used in conjunction with pattern matching. Negation (NOT, ¬) evaluates its argument, and if this returns by name or value (success), it signals failure. Otherwise (if the evaluation of the argument fails) it signals success (the null string).

STORAGE MANAGEMENT

Storage management is, to an extent, largely independent of the rest of the SNOBOL system. Storage management is called to allocate space (blocks of descriptors), look up strings in the table of natural variables (symbol table), and provide space for strings. It also performs storage regeneration.

ALLOCATION

The allocated region is a large block of descriptors. The descriptors are allocated in order and a free (space) pointer is moved to the next descriptor. Hence, the region is divided into the "used" descriptors (space) (low area of memory) and the "free." Two types of object are allocated: blocks and natural variables. The pointer returned is the title descriptor (value of the free pointer at the call). Blocks and natural variables are physically mixed in the allocated region. The allocation of a natural variable allocates the block of descriptors associated with that variable. A pointer to the title field is returned.

STORAGE REGENERATION

Storage regeneration is the reclamation of space that is no longer needed. This is accomplished by marking the objects that must be kept. These are moved to the low end of memory and the free pointer adjusted.

MARKING

Superficially, the problem is simple: Any object that may be referenced must be saved. Objects are pointed to from the basic blocks in the resident (SNOBOL) data area. Any block pointed to from one of these blocks is marked. Any block pointed to by a marked block is marked. This allows for indirect references. The marking process occurs recursively, following the marked blocks.

RELOCATION

After the marking process is complete, the unmarked blocks are deleted by writing over them. A marker of the next available location in the storage area is kept. The V fields of title descriptors are usually self-pointers. During the movement process, however, they are pointers to their destination. After they are moved, the self-pointer is restored.

Natural variables require additional processing. The chain descriptors, in the chain of natural variables in a category, must be followed and adjusted. Some elements on the chain may no longer be necessary. These are deleted from the chain (by adjusting pointers) and overwriting data areas.

THE SNOBOL IMPLEMENTATION LANGUAGE

The SNOBOL Implementation Language (SIL) is a macro language (taking advantage of the macro assemblers) to implement SNOBOL. Implementing SIL for a particular machine reduces to the problem of writing the appropriate macros in that machine's assembly language. This facilitates the portability of the language.

SIL consists of about 130 different macros. The macros reference data in the resident data area. There is no concept of a machine register as such. Storage is assumed to consist of descriptor-sized units. Most SIL macros are simple. A few are troublesome or involve i/o.

SIL macros have the assembler format

```
label  operator  operand list  comment
```

where the operator is the macro and label (loc) is optional. The names of the macros are mnemonic, e.g., ADD, MOV, CVT, with the data types incorporated into the suffix, e.g., CVTIR for ConVerT Integer to Real, and MOVTC for MOV a constant into the T field of a descriptor (type).

Descriptors are used to describe data. For example, the null string is described as

```
NULSTR DESCR S,0,0
```

The format of the descriptor is

```
DESCR  T,F,V
```

The format for a qualifier (string) is

```
QUAL  T,F,V,O,L
```

These follow the descriptions described above (or vice versa).

The macro MOVDD moves descriptors from one place to another. GETD is used to get descriptors. PUTD is used to put a descriptor in a computed target location.

Arithmetic operations are performed for both real and integer arithmetic. An example is INCVC, where the V field is incremented by the constant C, and DECVC, as well as ADDVV, which adds two V fields and puts the result in a third.

Data comparison macros, like EQLDD, compare data values. The form is

```
EQLDD  D1,D2,NE,EQ
```

If D1 and D2 are EQUAL, control is passed to the label in EQ; if not, then NE. For example,

```
       EQLDD  X,Y,,BYPASS
       MOVDD  X,Z
BYPASS MOVDD  Y,W
```

causes a transfer of control to BYPASS if X and Y are EQUAL; no transfer (the null field) if not.

CMPVC compares the V field to a constant. Flag macros allow operations on the flag fields (F, function, A, allocated, etc.). Operations on blocks of descriptors are facilitated by macros such as CLRBLK ("clear BLOCK," which indicates how much space is to be cleared and points to the first descriptor of the block). Type conversion macros, like CVTIS, are plentiful. String manipulation and Syntax Table macros operate on qualifiers and their associated strings. A copy of a string pointed to by Q2 is appended (concatenated) to a string pointed to by Q1 by

```
APDQQ  Q1,Q2
```

TRIMQQ deletes trailing blanks.

```
INVOKE  PROC     ,                         Invocation Procedure
        POPD     INCL                      Get function descriptor
        GETDC    XPTR,INCL,0               Get link descriptor
        EQLTT    INCL,XPTR,INVK2           Check argument counts
INVK1   BRANIN   INCL,0                    If equal, branch indirect
INVK2   TESTF    XPTR,VFLG,ARGNER,INVK1
*                                          Check for variable number
```

FIGURE 15

String analysis is performed by STREAM. STREAM is used mainly by the translator in analyzing arguments of ARRAY, DATA, DEFINE, and LOAD (which loads an external function). Stack management is provided by SYSSTK. All function calls are recursive. PUSHD and POPD push and pop descriptors (to save and restore values). RCALL calls the procedure. P, the procedure, is identified by

```
P       PROC  [primary name]
```

where primary name is optional and indicates an enclosing procedure. RRTURN returns from the procedure.

Flow of control is handled by RCALL and RRTURN, and by BRANCHLV, a "computed" goto, BRANCH L (unconditional), BRANCHIN (branch indirectly), and other Branches. Pattern building and matching macros, like MAKPAT, CPYPAT, and COMMML (compute minimum match length), are plentiful.

Storage management macros are used to construct natural variables and other data objects. System interface macros provide i/o and other system-dependent functions. An example is the INVOKE macro shown in Figure 15.

INVOKE is the entrance to all function procedures. It pops its argument (obtained from the prefix code) and checks it against the argument count in the procedure descriptor. In most cases, these are the same; if not, there are missing [omitted, default (null string)] arguments. If the arguments (number) agree or defaults are permitted, the function succeeds; otherwise, it fails.

SIL has been used to implement SNOBOL (SNOBOL4) on several computers. Examples of IBM 360 macros are found in Ref. 6. The CDC 6000 series is also described.

HISTORY

SNOBOL3 was completed in mid-1964. SNOBOL4 evolved over the following years, with the initial decision being made in 1966, and most features available and released in 1967. Language development continued, and in 1968 unevaluated expressions and the cursor position operator were introduced. Among the last features added were tables (in mid-1969) and error control and operator definition in 1969. The many data types evolved slowly, from the single data type STRING in SNOBOL3, to the number of data types available in 1968 and 1969. Interestingly, INTEGERS were not added until late in the project. This had its origin in SNOBOL3, in which integers were handled as STRINGS.

NONSTANDARD SNOBOL

Although SNOBOL is not a standardized language, SNOBOL4 (v.3) is usually taken to be the standard. Other versions, usually optimizing efficiency, exist. One of these is SPITBOL (17).

SPITBOL is a compiled SNOBOL. It is downward compatible with SNOBOL4; that is, programs in SNOBOL4 will generally (almost always) run on SPITBOL, but the reverse is not true. Both standard and nonstandard SNOBOL are available, or have been available, for microcomputers (10).

SPITBOL stands for SPeedy Implementation of snoBOL4. It was designed by Dewar and Belcher at the Illinois Institute of Technology (17). It is an in-core compiler in the spirit of WATFOR (18). SPITBOL is a true compiler. Hence, it is not necessary to implement SNOBOL interpretively. SNOBOL4 machines have been investigated but have not achieved the success of LISP machines. Other SNOBOL translators are FAS-BOL (a compiler) (19), which does not implement all of SNOBOL4, and SITBOL (20–24). SITBOL is an interpreter for the PDP-10.

SUMMARY

SNOBOL is a string processing language. It can be used for system and compiler (language) programming. Its primary functions (statements) are pattern matching and replacement. This facilitates the implementation of grammars.

SNOBOL was developed over a several year (decade) period. It is available on both mainframe and microcomputers.

REFERENCES

1. D. J. Farber, R. E. Griswold, and I. P. Polonsky. "SNOBOL, A String Manipulation Language," J. Assoc. Comput. Mach., 11(1), 21–30 (1964).
2. D. J. Farber, R. E. Griswold, and I. P. Polonsky, "The SNOBOL3 Programming Language," Bell System Tech. J. 45(6), 895–944 (1966).
3. Allen Forte, *SNOBOL3 Primer*, The MIT Press, Cambridge, MA, 1967.
4. R. E. Griswold, J. F. Poage, and I. P. Polonsky, *The SNOBOL4 Programming Language*, Prentice-Hall, Englewood Cliffs, NJ, 1968.
5. R. E. Griswold, J. F. Poage, and I. P. Polonsky, *The SNOBOL4 Programming Language*, Prentice-Hall, Englewood Cliffs, NJ, 1971.
6. Ralph E. Griswold, *The Macro Implementation of SNOBOL4: A Case Study of Machine-Independent Software Development*, W. H. Freeman and Company, San Francisco, 1972.
7. W. W. Peterson, "Addressing for Random Access Storage," IBM J. Res. Develop., 1(2), 130–146 (1957).
8. Robert Morris, "Scatter Storage Techniques," Commun. ACM, 11(1), 38–44 (1968).
9. Douglas W. Maurer, *The Programmer's Introduction to SNOBOL*, North-Holland, New York, 1976.
10. Susan Hockey, *SNOBOL Programming for the Humanities*, Clarendon Press, Oxford, 1985 (© Susan Hockey).
11. Ralph E. Griswold, *String and List Processing in SNOBOL4: Techniques and Applications*, Prentice-Hall, Englewood Cliffs, NJ, 1975.

12. Aaron M. Tenenbaum and Moshe J. Augenstein, *Data Structures Using Pascal*, Prentice-Hall, Englewood Cliffs, NJ, 1981.

13. Philip M. Sherman, *Programming and Coding the IBM 709–7090–7094 Computers*, John Wiley and Sons, New York, 1963.

14. James A. Saxon, *Programming the IBM 7090: A Self-Instructional Programmed Manual*, Prentice-Hall, Englewood Cliffs, NJ, 1963.

15. M. D. McIlroy, "A String Manipulation Program for FAP Programs," Bell Telephone Laboratories, Murray Hill, NJ (1962).

16. Frederick P. Brooks, Jr. and Kenneth E. Iverson, *Automatic Data Processing, System 360 Edition*, John Wiley & Sons, New York, 1969.

17. Robert B. K. Dewar, "SPITBOL version 2.0," SNOBOL4 Project Document S4D23, Illinois Institute of Technology, Chicago (February 12, 1971).

18. Peter W. Shantz, R. A. German, J. G. Mitchell, R. S. K. Shirley, and C. R. Zarnke, "WATFOR—The University of Waterloo FORTRAN IV Compiler," Commun. ACM, 10(1) 41–44 (1967).

19. Paul Joseph Santos, Jr., "FASBOL, A SNOBOL4 Compiler," Memorandum No. ERL-M314, Electronics Research Laboratory, University of California, Berkeley (December 1971).

20. J. F. Gimpel, "A Guide to the Implementation of SNOBOL4B," SNOBOL4 Project Document S4D13, Bell Telephone Laboratories, Holmdel, NJ (August 11, 1969).

21. J. F. Gimpel, "A User Manual for BLOCKS Version 1.4," SNOBOL4 Project Document S4D11c, Bell Telephone Laboratories, Holmdel, NJ (August 15, 1970).

22. J. F. Gimpel, "A Theory of Discrete Patterns and Their Implementation in SNOBOL4" *Commun. ACM*, *16*(2), 91–100 (1973).

23. J. F. Gimpel, "SITBOL Version 3.0," SNOBOL4 Project Document S4D30b, Bell Laboratories, Holmdel, NJ (June 1, 1973).

24. James F. Gimpel, *Algorithms in SNOBOL4*, John Wiley & Sons, New York, 1976 (© Bell Telephone Labs, Inc.).

ROGER R. FLYNN